Those Who Have Vanished
An Introduction to Prehistory

Those Who Have Vanished

An Introduction to Prehistory

RONALD L. WALLACE
University of Central Florida

 1983

THE DORSEY PRESS Homewood, Illinois 60430

ISBN 0-256-02448-0

Library of Congress Catalog Card No. 82–72763

Printed in the United States of America

1 2 3 4 5 6 7 8 9 0 D 0 9 8 7 6 5 4 3

To my mother and the memory of my father,
and to Susan
in gratitude and love.

R.W.

There was a time, long, long ago, when the world seemed to man to be so charged with meanings that he didn't have time to ask himself questions, the manifestation was so spectacular. The whole world was like a theater in which the elements, the forests, the oceans and the rivers, the mountains and the plains, the bushes and each plant played a role that man tried to understand, tried to explain to himself, and give an explanation of. But the explanations were less important: what was essential, what was satisfying, was the evidence of the presence of the gods, it was plenitude, everything was a series of glorious epiphanies. The world was full of meaning. The Apparition was nourished by the spirit of the gods, of what can be called gods; the world was dense. Exactly when did the gods retire from the world, exactly when did the images lose their color? Exactly when was the world emptied of substance, exactly when were the signs no longer signs, exactly when did the tragic break take place, exactly when were we abandoned to ourselves, that is to say, exactly when did the gods no longer want us as spectators, as participants? We were abandoned to ourselves, to our solitude, to our fear, and the problem was born. What is the world? Who are we?

FROM THE MEMOIRS OF EUGENE IONESCO

Preface

The pace of archeological discovery, especially within this century, has generated a strong curiosity about our own past. Through a wide range of popular writings, films, lectures, and museum displays, a modern society is encountering earlier times. And increasingly, many Americans are placed directly in touch with prehistory. The growth of public archeology has made it possible for a great many people to share in the process of researching ancient society.

Those Who Have Vanished was written with the objective of explaining the past to those who are encountering prehistory for the very first time. It almost goes without saying that such a treatment is never really complete. I have attempted, to my own best ability, to make the book as up-to-date as I could. Even so, archeologists are working in every part of the inhabited world. A developing science can never be "captured"; some discovery is always left out. But this problem is a symptom of growth—and so I hope it endures.

The scope of the book is global; the time span, nearly 3 million years. It begins with the ancient humanity that foraged on the African plains, and it ends with the emergence of the earliest cities and states. That narrative itself is of interest, but there is another fascination as well: the attempt to understand why societies behaved as they did. Most people are incurably curious about the causes of behavioral change. Why is it that certain societies endured for many thousands of years while other societies emerged and collapsed "overnight"?

Examining questions like these is the excitement of researching the past. At almost every turn of the story, I have considered alternative theories of why an ancient people behaved a particular way. I have presented my own thoughts on these questions and evaluated differing views. This is not—and, indeed, never can be—an attempt to resolve the debates. No ultimate viewpoint awaits us. There is no Truth that will someday be found. Here, as in every science, we deal with tentative views of our world. Such a strategy has long been a part of our approach to the past. I am hopeful that such a presentation will spark many classroom debates. But more than that, I have tried to suggest here something of scientific argumentation—of how theories are compared to determine their problems and strengths.

The result is a world prehistory that deals extensively with human behavior as well as the relation of behavior to rites and belief. Arrowheads, pottery, and harpoon points are all part of this text as well. But I have tried to keep a constant awareness that prehistory is a study of people. When I have examined the material record—the debris that is dug from the ground—I have sought out its connection with the way people lived in the past.

On occasion, I have drawn comparisons between societies in the past and today. I have done so out of the conviction that modern people are not really that different: there are meaningful parallelisms with earlier times. Such comparisons, I think, will intensify as archeology continues to grow. By excavating the past, in a sense, we discover ourselves.

During five years of research and writing, I have become grateful to several individuals. Joseph W. Michels, Penn State University; William L. Rathje, University of Arizona, Tucson; and Richard B. Woodbury, University of Massachusetts, Amherst, were valuable critics. Their observations have strongly contributed to whatever qualities the book may possess. Responsibility for any of its shortcomings, of course, is my own. The chapters examining domestication and its impact on human society resulted from a grant from the University of Central Florida Division of Sponsored Research. I am grateful to Dr. Frank E. Juge and the members of the Division for freeing me from the pressures of teaching while the research was done. Sheila Call turned spaghetti-like scribbles into elegantly typewritten pages. She provided candid and valuable assessments of the writing as well. Some of the illustrations were prepared by Gail Delicio.

I am additionally grateful to Kathryn Hallenstein, photo researcher; Nina Cummings, Field Museum of Natural History; Leo Johnson, Milwaukee Public Museum; John Larson, The Oriental Institute of the University of Chicago; Ellen Gantner, Center for American Archeology at Northwestern University; and Ann Merritt and Kathy Shaw of the Art Institute of Chicago. Richard Priske and his family provided valuable and gracious support.

My parents encouraged my archeological interest, and one of them will read this book. I am hopeful that she will like it, although in no fashion can it repay her support. And I like to think that my father would have found it enjoyable to read.

To my wife Susan I am strongly indebted for her encouragement and remarkable patience. She was there when an upstart book moved into the house and took over our lives. Amidst all, she has supported my work every step of the way.

Ronald L. Wallace

Contents

The origins of domestication: The beginnings of theory. Arnold J. Toynbee: A prehistoric challenge. V. Gordon Childe: An adaptive explanation. Robert Braidwood and the Mediterranean foothills. Foraging in the eastern Mediterranean. The concept of population pressure. Exchange and sedentism. Social complexity, political power, and ritual.

The millet growers of northern China. Adaptations in the Asian tropics. Domestication in Africa. Domestication in the Americas: The Mexican Mesa Central. Maize and its origins. Richard MacNeish and the Tehuacan Valley. Domestication in the Andes.

The changing European woodlands. The technology of the European farmers. Theories of global migrations. Archeology's darkest hour. The nature of human invention. V. Gordon Childe and a scientific crisis. Migrations into Anatolia. Mediterranean farmers. First farmers in Central Europe. The megaliths of Europe. Megaliths, power, and trade.

Domestication south of the Sahara. Archaeology and the African kingdoms. East Africa: Kush and Axum. The West African grassland kingdoms: Ghana, Mali, and Songhay. Environment, iron, and kings.

Leonard Woolley and the emergence of method. The early settlement of Mesopotamia. The marshlands and irrigation. Southern Mesopotamia: Systems of exchange. The Southwest Asian highlands: A passage to the Indus. Tepe Sialk and the making of metals. Djeitun: The land in-between. Mundigak and Shahr-I Sokhta: The subtleties of exchange. The environment of the Indus Valley. Early settlements in the Indus Valley.

Agricultural society in Southeast Asia: The two kinds of forest. The silent millenia. Rice paddies and exchange adaptations. Village life on the rivers of China. Humanity goes to sea. Early pressures and the settlement of Melanesia. The paradise that never was found. The end of prehistoric Polynesia.

Mythology along the Ohio. Adena: Early transformations. Hopewell and the Hopewell debate. Hopewell as exchange adaptation. Collapse of Hopewell exchange. The emergence of social complexity in the American Southeast. The Mississippi chiefdoms. Moundville, information, and chiefs. The end of the Mississippian.

The southwestern mosaic. A. V. Kidder and the discovery at Pecos. Networks of technological change. The Mogollon people. Irrigation and the Hohokam. Anasazi of the Colorado Plateau. Natural cycles and the end of complexity. Village life in Mesa Central. Networks and ritual in the Andes.

The costs of urbanization. In praise of the city. Urbanization and the problem of power. City and state: The development of theory. A general theory of the urbanized state.

The land between the rivers. Ideology and the rise of the state. Mesopotamia at the beginning of history.

Indus Valley urbanization. The Indus collapse. Egypt: The desert and the river. Power in Egyptian society. The earliest cities of China. China in the presence of enemies.

Olmec beginnings. Networks in Veracruz. Olmec decline. Monte Alban and Teotihuacan. Peten networks. The Maya: Commerce and conflict. The classic Maya collapse.

The Aztec. The problem of Aztec sacrifice. Nutrition, sacrifice, and conquest. The Andean kingdoms. The Inca. Inheritance, civil war, and the end.

For further exploration.

Part One / The Emergence of Hunting

1 / The Science of Archeology

It was very cold at daybreak, and Ukwane had huddled close to the dying fire. A little later in the day, the women would go to search for wood, but at the moment they were shivering together in the frosty morning. There were murmurs and quiet talking as the sun began to rise, and Ukwane began to talk of the parents of Gai. In that time long ago when Gai's mother had first conceived, her husband Gwena had suddenly died, and she found that she was pregnant and without a man. She had gone, Ukwane said, to the villagers at Chukudu, and before she gave birth, she had managed to find herself another husband. All the while, as he told the story, Gai had been listening at the edge of the fire. Embarrassed and a little angry, he raised himself up on one elbow in the sand and told Ukwane before the others that the story was wrong. He knew very well, certainly better than Ukwane, that the man who had brought him up was his actual father. The argument dragged on as the day grew brighter and warmer; most of the older people seemed to be on the side of Ukwane.

Eventually all of the women left the fireside to search for wood. When they returned a short time later, they had more than enough for the night. Tsetchewe had found not only wood but had gathered up 20 melons and, with her infant, this was a load of 100 pounds. The quiet talk resumed as they gathered again by the fire. When the night came back, a jackal cried in the distance.[1]

The study of ancient society: Method and theory

The San that gathered around the campfire in Africa's Kalahari Desert are reminders of the earliest structure of human society. For many thousands of years, humanity followed a hunter-and-gatherer pattern: living from the plant and the animal foods of the natural world. In more recent times, there were big-game hunters, with a highly specialized strategy of life. They preyed on the caribou, the horse, and the bison of tundra and steppe. More recently still were the first of the villages: mud-walled houses at the edge of a spring. The settlements grew, and in time the first cities were born.

---

[1] Elizabeth Marshall Thomas, *The Harmless People* (New York: Penguin Books, 1969), pp. 93–94.

Because the written word is so recent—it is approximately 5,000 years old—there are not any histories to tell us of these ancient societies. For that reason, if we wish to understand the evolution of human behavior, we must proceed a bit differently than analysts of more recent times. The science of *archeology* is the *study of ancient societies.* It examines how our behavior has changed over thousands of years. It seeks to reconstruct the activities of people who long ago vanished. When possible, it seeks to discover their views of the world. More than that, archeological science attempts to determine the causes of change: how behavior and belief are transformed in the passage of time.

Traditionally, archeologists have made use of controlled excavation as a means of discovering what people were like in the past.[2] The litter of ancient societies—bone fragments, the flakes of their tools—are often all that is left of a people who lived long ago. Buried inside the earth's layers, they are the record of an earlier time. Often very meager, such remains must be treated with care.

A collection of exotic specialties has necessarily become part of the science.[3] We might smile at the archeologist peering through a magnifying lens at the edge of a tool or observing a porcupine gnawing on bones. But a knowledge of porcupine tooth marks can help distinguish a bone that was carved from another that was simply an item in an animal's lair. The recognition of telltale fractures in the flint that was struck to make tools can distinguish it from flint that was fractured by rocks in the ground. To describe every one of these specialties would require a separate book. Regardless of how esoteric some of these curious analyses seem, they all have in common the objective of knowing the past.

Dating techniques

Out of all archeological strategies, those that perhaps have the greatest importance are the ones that enable us to measure the passing of time. There are actually two ways to do this—and both are important for reconstructing the past. One is a relative variety of measurement; it does not give us a date for a find. It places the find in a sequence with other discoveries. The technique is especially useful in sites that have visible layers—the strata of earth that pile up over hundreds of years. The garbage of an ancient society becomes covered by layers of soil. A later group of people will litter new things on the ground. These, too, will in time become buried—and then the process will happen again. This layering of the earth is a critical key to the past.

The deepest layers, of course, are the oldest. Those near the surface

---

[2]This is by no means the only strategy used. Other techniques of archeology will be briefly presented in subsequent parts of the text.

[3]There are many available introductions to archeological method and theory. A good one is David Hurst Thomas, *Archaeology* (New York: Holt, Rinehart & Winston, 1979).

Milwaukee Public Museum

Controlled excavation. The spatial relationships of buried materials provide information about humanity's past. Excavation is systematic, and must always be carefully done.

are younger in time. This means that the layers' materials have been placed in an orderly sequence. We can now notice changes in pottery, types of houses, resources, and tools. The discoveries trapped in the layers can be related in a meaningful way. Like parts of a book, they are ordered from beginning to end.

Often, this is not straightforward; there are problems with every technique. Animals can burrow through layers with little regard for their damage to science. Tree roots play havoc with the strata. Tools and fragments of pottery drop down the holes or they follow the root lines. There is not any foolproof approach for understanding the past.

This is true of the other strategy that is used for the measure of time:

Center for American Archeology, Northwestern University

Experimental archeology. Anthropologist John White lecturing students inside a longhouse. The structure was built by archeologists using stone tools and natural materials. The modern attempt to duplicate ancient behavioral strategies is a valuable technique for reconstructing the past.

the chronometric means that provide the numerical dates. Two of these are widely used: carbon-14 and potassium-argon. They have yielded the majority of the dates that are used in this book. Shellfish, charcoal, wood, and bone—any carbon-containing substance—can frequently provide us with a date through carbon-14. This unstable form of carbon decays at a regular rate. By measuring the amount of it, the age of the sample is found. Potassium-argon, however, uses the potassium present in rocks. Infinitesimally throughout time, it is changed into argon gas, which is trapped inside the crystal of the rock itself. By measuring the amount of argon contained within the crystal lattice, the date of the rock and its layers of earth can be found. If it happens that ancient materials are sandwiched between two rock-bearing layers, we have an upper and a lower date for the relics' existence.

In the best of all possible worlds, these two could validate one another, but nature has been very obstinate on this issue. Carbon-14 is only useful for the last 50,000 years; beyond that point it yields unreliable dates. Potassium-argon, by contrast, is a technique that is not useful at all unless the materials are at least 400,000 years old. Between 50,000 and 400,000

Center for American Archeology, Northwestern University

The study of weaving techniques. Experimental archeology as well as observation of living people can provide understandings of ancient human societies.

lies a span which is hard to date. Archeologists all over the world have abhorred that vacuum.

Yet, a collection of new dating techniques—and a refinement of the ones that we have—are making possible a more accurate timing of ancient events. "Amino-acid dating," and a variety of other approaches, are closing the gap and enriching our view of the past.

These strategies of archeology can tell us of events that occurred long ago: the huts that were built or the beasts that were hunted for food. This in itself is a worthy objective: the description of an earlier time. Archeologists who seek culture history wish to know how our ancestors lived. They hope to reconstruct the behavior of an ancient society.

More recently, another objective has become part of archeological re- **Behavioral change**
search: the attempt to determine the causes of behavioral change. No society has ever been "frozen"—remaining the same throughout all of its existence. Societies everywhere in the world become different through

Center for American Archeology, Northwestern University

Laboratory analyses of excavated materials have long been a method of archeological research. Nutrition, disease, climate, and even prehistoric patterns of trade are among the dimensions of the past explored in this way.

time. Why is this so? Why have human societies changed, at times, with an infinite slowness while, at other times, they have undergone change with incredible speed?

Questions like these have long been of interest to those archeologists hoping to find the forces that have changed our behaviors and beliefs in the past. There are subtleties involved in this outlook that we should try to understand from the start. The discovery of why the past changes is something that cannot be dug out of the ground. It is not like a fragment of flint or a sliver of bone. It begins with the archeologist—with a theory of why things have changed. The archeological record is used as a test of that view.

We should notice that this is not speculation—it is a special way of approaching the world. A *theory* is a *causal statement which is susceptible to falsification*. It should always be possible to prove that a theory is wrong.[4] More than that, it should be *parsimonious: it should explain a large number of facts*. It should never give rise to more problems than it is attempting to

---

[4]A valuable discussion of theory appears in Patti Jo Watson, Steven A. LeBlanc, and Charles A. Redman, *Explanation in Archeology* (New York: Columbia University Press, 1971).

solve. Above all, we should note that while a theory is something that can be proven wrong, it is, technically, something that can never be proven correct. This is not philosophical double-talk; it is a critical feature of science. It means that no theory ever developed can be viewed as unchallengeable truth. In principle, there is some possibility that later scientific investigations will cause the theory to be changed or, perhaps, altogether abandoned. At one time, it was thought by zoologists that experience, in a sense, was inherited. If you built up your muscles through exercise, your children would be well-muscled too. This theory was "the inheritance of acquired characteristics." It has since been endlessly falsified by experiments in animal breeding. Bobbing the tails of dogs does not lead to bobtailed puppies. The theory collapsed and, most likely, will not be revived.[5] Other theories have had longer standing. The view that infectious diseases can be caused by microscopic life is not likely to collapse as the theory of inheritance did. Still, we must view this as possible: any theory is open to change. Certainly this is true of the theories we form of our past.

Cultural evolutionism is the theoretical approach used in this book. It is a general theory for explaining humanity's past.[6] More specifically, it seeks to explain transformation in *cultural systems*. These are the *patterns of technological behavior, social relations, and religious beliefs that are humanity's means of adapting to the natural world.* Like many systems, they are highly cohesive. A change in a behavioral pattern, or in an aspect of social belief, can set off a chain reaction of changes throughout the whole system.

The theory of cultural evolutionism

Many anthropologists, impressed by that process, have called theory to a halt at that point. They suggest that a change in a culture can begin at any part of the system. A new myth, a new kind of marriage, a new tool, or a new grouping of kin: any one of these could well be the cause of a cultural change. Perhaps the greatest problem involved here is that nothing is ever really explained. We are left with very little idea of why cultures have changed in the past, or for that matter, of why cultural systems are changing today.

---

[5]Except, perhaps, in a minor form. Recent studies in immunology suggest a possible inheritance of acquired characteristics, but the experimental results are still being widely debated. A good discussion of this is in Susan West, "Fighting Lamarck's Shadow," *Science News*, March 14, 1981, pp. 174–75.

[6]The term *cultural evolutionism* has been most widely used by Elman Service, Marshall Sahlins, and Leslie A. White. The specific form of it developed in this chapter derives from a number of sources. Two very different anthropological theorists, Marvin Harris and Kent Flannery, have probably been the strongest influences on my own thinking. Harris, in *Cultural Materialism: The Struggle for a Science of Culture* (New York: Random House, 1979), defends the primacy of technology and environment in cultural change. Flannery, in "The Cultural Evolution of Civilization," *Annual Review of Ecology and Systematics* 3 (1972), discusses the significance of information in adapting to the natural world.

An approach that seems much more rewarding is to assume that all parts are not equal, that certain features of culture play a more critical role in its change. The viewpoint expressed in this book is that *technology and the natural environment have placed constraints, or limitations, on the variety of human behaviors and social beliefs.* Expressed in such general terms, the theory can be easily misunderstood. It is perhaps worth our while to examine this view at some length.

Technology, as I understand it, is much more than a collection of tools. It is the *material culture, the behavioral strategies, and the adaptive information that exist as a system and modify the natural world.*

Material culture

The material culture of a human society is the most obvious of all of these features. Stone axes, bone harpoons, dugout canoes, fiber baskets, and nets are the tools that humanity has used to survive in the past. Material culture is not always simple; it often becomes more complicated through time. The bone harpoon of the big-game hunter was a forerunner of technological patterns that endure to our day. An invention of greater complexity, it was a compound tool made out of more than one substance. It used bone for the point, wood for the shaft, and strips of leather attached to the point. Without each of these resources, the weapon could not have been made. More than that, the strips of leather were knotted around a variety of ancient balloons—the inflated stomach or bladder taken from an animal's body. When the harpoon was thrown into a fish—likely a salmon moving upstream—the balloons would float on the water, slow the fish, and prevent its escape. It could be speared again, perhaps netted, and then butchered and carried to camp. Bones of salmon are thick in the sites where the hunters once lived.

But even more is involved in this weapon than the substances from which it was made. There is the fact that these materials were fashioned by separate tools. Carving tools of flint or obsidian were needed to whittle the point; a shaft-straightener of bone put the finishing touch on the wood. Knives were needed to butcher a carcass for leather strips and the crucial balloons. And these implements themselves had, of course, been created by tools. We have discovered a kind of regression: the use of tools to make tools to make tools. The process is one that has continued until our own time.

The point that I am striving to make here is not the complexity of ancient harpoons but of parallel trends in the evolution of material culture. Increasingly, in many societies, tools have been made from many different materials, requiring many other types of tools and many different techniques. These trends are especially evident in the most recent industrial societies, in which combinations of materials and tools are involved and complex. This spiral of increasing intricacy was not accomplished for its own sake. Human beings, whenever possible, prefer less effort to meet

Field Museum of Natural History

Travois of the Crow Indians, used for transporting people and goods. As an artifact of material culture, it existed in a behavioral context. Its usefulness also depended upon a system of information. Travellers needed to know the strength of both the travois and the horse, the distance to be covered, and nature of the terrain.

their own needs. A more intricate material culture has, in many (not all!) circumstances, made possible more efficient control of the natural world.

Because tools, or more often, their fragments are directly recovered in archeological research, there has been a tendency to emphasize these more than anything else. The result has been a misunderstanding of technology in ancient societies. That behavior played a critical role is often overlooked. Without a system of *behavioral strategies*, material culture has no meaning at all. William S. Laughlin has described how a hunter must scan the environment for traces of prey; how he stalks, kills, and butchers the animal, and how he carries it home.[7] The elaborate description that

Behavioral strategies

[7]William S. Laughlin, "Hunting: An Integrated Biobehavioral System and Its Evolutionary Importance," in *Man the Hunter*, ed. Richard B. Lee and Irven de Vore (Hawthorne, N.Y.: Aldine Publishing, 1968).

Laughlin provides us of an isolated Eskimo hunter is less intricate than the behavioral patterns of hunters in groups. Killing large numbers of animals is more than one person can handle alone. There must be planning in advance of the hunt and preparation of tools to be used. It is important to determine the job that each hunter must do. The kill is itself a collection of strategies, and every one must be perfectly timed. In Colorado—as we will see in this story—a team of hunters surrounded a herd. Nearly 200 bison were driven over the edge of a gorge. There was a team that killed the survivors and a team that dragged carcasses out of the ditch. There were butchering teams that sliced off sinew and meat. The Colorado kill is a striking example of patterns of behavior at work in the past: an intricate matrix that is part of technological life. Like elaborations in material culture, these patterns have often become more complex. This has not made our lives more leisurely; on the contrary, it has led to more work. An irrigation farmer will labor more hours than a rainfall farmer who works with a plow. The plowman will labor more hours than a man with a hoe. But the digging-stick farmer will work even less; the hunter and gatherer will work least of all. More intricate behavioral strategies have meant more to do; but as the tasks have become more numerous, humanity has often become more secure. An increase in critical resources—including, especially, that of food—has made survival less chancy in many different parts of the world.

Adaptive
information

Generations of social evolution have witnessed these tools and behavioral strategies transforming the features of the surrounding natural environment. Because humanity, for most of its lifetime, has been equipped with an intricate brain, the transformations, in a critical sense, were a learning experience. Berries that nearly killed a person with poison were not eaten again; but they were useful for poison arrows or even for killing fish. Laughlin's hunter, when stalking an animal, needed to know what its behavior was like: if it was wounded, would it fight or take flight? How fast could it run? Without a tradition of such *information*, human society could have never evolved. Behavior and tools have no meaning without an intricate "map" of the natural world: of its resources, seasonal changes, and patterns of life.

A crucial dimension of such information is the development of scheduling systems—the placing of behavioral strategies in a framework of time. "To everything," said The Preacher, "is a season"; this is true of our technological lives. Indians in the Ohio River Valley planted their corn late enough in the spring so that rivers were receding and there was not any danger of floods. And yet, if it were planted *too* late, there was not enough time for the corn to mature; unripened ears would be killed by the frost in the fall. Through such sensitive systems of knowledge, behavioral strategies were appropriately timed. Because they were mental, they were seldom considered when reconstructing the life of the past. But archeologists are now turning their attention to the study of living societies as a means of reconstructing the patterns of earlier times.[8] This makes possible a more accurate idea of both our ancient behavioral strategies and of the information systems that were a critical part of our past.

The natural world that was changed by humanity would have changed   Environment
if we had never existed. Of exquisite complexity, it had been evolving for millions of years. Our species came into a world of animal and plant populations, topography, soils, and waters that were our *environment*. More than that, we inherited climates, as well as the cycles of seasonal change. Above all, it is crucial to recognize that human beings have always had neighbors: the environment of a society includes other peoples as well. This has made it possible for many societies to have access to other resources. The flint for an axe could be gained through a network of trade. But if hell is, in fact, "other people," then this has also been true in the past. In a period of regional scarcity, neighboring peoples were often a threat. Raiding activities were part of our earlier days.

But perhaps the most critical feature of the environment in which we evolved is that its own evolutionary process never came to an end. Tundra has turned into forest, and there were times when our deserts have bloomed. Waters, plants, animals, and climates have experienced change. Many of these transformations have had their origin in the natural world—in changes of sunlight and atmosphere and shifts in the earth. Yet, others were affected by humans, and in turn, have had effects upon us. Migratory patterns of reindeer have changed when they were constantly hunted. Hunters have adapted to shifts in the routes of their prey. Clearing forests for planting attracted the pests that eat crops, led to bushes and grass, and often depleted the soil. Humanity, in turn, adapted through its systems of trading and war and through attempts to grow food using the hoe and the plow. Technology and the natural environment have often been caught in a circuit of change. This pattern is especially true of our culture today.

Because environment and human technology are so closely bound up   Choice and
with survival, transformations within them will lead to a cultural change.   change
The process involved is more subtle than anthropologists earlier thought. Many critics have rejected the notion of strong controls on our beliefs and behavior. Human beings, they feel, have always had a wide spectrum of choices. Such a view is, perhaps, a reflection of the freedom that exists in

---

[8]This is known as *ethnoarcheology*. A number of examples will be presented in later parts of the story.

our lives. I find it highly doubtful that this always was true of the past. In Europe, some 4,000 years ago, farming peoples had depleted the soil.[9] They fought one another in an effort to capture more food. Like villagers of more recent periods, they adjusted their social behavior as a means of adapting to the pressure of ongoing raids. Adult males remained in the household, even after they had taken a wife. They did not leave their parents to start a new home of their own. This meant that, within the household, adult males were on hand at all times— a warrior force to be used in the event of a raid. When warfare is virtually constant, there is very little choice in such matters. The new pattern is developed, or the household is not apt to survive.

But pressures on human society have not consistently been this severe.

Villagers chat in the community house at Aduru, Fly River, New Guinea. The behavioral patterns of human society are its social organization. These patterns are everywhere limited by technology and the natural world.

Field Museum of Natural History

---

[9]Archeological examples presented here will be discussed and referenced in detail in later parts of the story.

A spectrum of choices has existed at times in the past. Irrigation farmers in Southwestern Asia grew cereals, and they raised goats and sheep. Technology again was the basis of cultural change. Irrigation required the farmers to spend their time in constructing canals, in repairing the system, and also in harvesting grain. But their animals, in the spring of the year, had to be taken to outlying pastures. Not all of the household could be in two places at once. What would happen would depend on the kin group—on what they thought was best for themselves. Some people left farming entirely; they spent all their time with their herds. Others herded their animals and occasionally planted some grain. A great many became full-time farmers and created a system of trade. Their grain was exchanged to the herders for meat, milk, and hides. These examples might serve to remind us that the pressures on human societies will vary remarkably in the ranges of choice they provide. It is fruitless to ask if society has freedom or if it does not. It is more rewarding to relate human choice to conditions of life.

I believe there are two implications of this view of our cultural past. Both of them are shared with any science of human society. First of all, because humans are characterized by a varying range of behaviors, their behavior cannot be predicted in the manner of a nonliving thing. Unlike chemicals or large-scale objects or simpler forms of plant and animal life, the behavior of humans can follow a number of paths. This does not mean that human behavior can never be predicted at all. It means that we can state what a people are most likely to do. Sodium hydroxide and hydrochloric acid, if combined under certain conditions, will result in salt water 100 percent of the time. But in the study of human society, we assert what will *probably* happen. The problem is greatest when the spectrum of choices is wide.

Beyond that, it is important to realize that the choices do not always work out. This second implication has occasionally been overlooked. The cultural evolutionist theory does not mean that our social behavior is carefully adapted to technology and the natural world. An option may be open to humans which, in fact, is a very bad choice. As we will see in the story, this has often occurred in the past. An unusual political system was developed by the Peruvian Inca which required each ruler to capture his treasure in war. It grew out of the problem of scarcity, and it worked for a limited time. But when conquest was no longer possible, taxation became more severe. The ruler would acquire his treasure from people at home. That, in turn, led to widespread rebellion, and the empire was shattered by war. Clearly, entire societies have followed pathways that led to the worst. What was possible was not necessarily the best thing to do.

A society's behavioral options are reinforced by the realm of belief: the ideas and rituals that make up its philosophical world. Every living human society has some notion as to how it began, of the "right" way to

American Museum of Natural History

Snake dance of the Hopi Indians. In every human society, behavioral strategies are reinforced by the realm of belief.

live, and where people will go when they die. Such ideas are not as old as our species, but they do extend far back in time. They play a significant role in the process of cultural change. Ideas reinforce our behaviors—legitimatize them—make them seem right. What is just as important, they make deviation seem wrong. In this way, philosophical systems serve the function of social control. This was especially so in the time of the earliest states. Conceivably, a change in philosophy could initiate behavioral change. Although this is possible, the reverse has more often been true. Humans attempt to reduce uncertainty. We are more comfortable when seeking to rationalize a pattern of behavior that already exists than we are in acting out an idea that has never been tried. Revolutions create revolutionaries, in the present as well as the past. But revolutionaries strengthen a change through the use of belief.

Cultural evolutionist theory is the approach I take to the past. I believe it is additionally useful for understanding our time. Here and there, at appropriate moments, I will suggest parallels between present and past. I will mention them more often as the story draws close to our day. But it is proper to begin with beginnings—and that is exactly what this story will do. We will see how the African grasslands were the earliest homes of our kind; how a scattering of small, fledgling humans appeared in the world.

2 / The Search for the Earliest Humans

In the beginning, there was the forest, unlike any woodland we have seen. It extended across Western Europe and the entirety of Africa. From the Cape to the English beaches there was a world of trees. Some 70 million years before humanity first appeared, the climate had shifted and given rise to forests and flowers. Exactly why this happened is a point much debated. There was possibly a slight change in our orbit around the sun, or the earth could have wobbled slightly on its axis. For whatever reason, the planet's temperature became cooler throughout time; an earlier world of swamps and marshes was disappearing. The forest had dominated all of Africa until some 12 million years ago, when the climate began to dramatically change again.

The African homeland

It was a time of foul weather, a turbulent season. In the polar regions and the higher mountains were massive sheets of ice that expanded and receded across the land. When the glaciers expanded, much of the water that would normally have been in the sea became frozen and formed part of the block of ice. Sea levels naturally fell, and massive beaches were created. When the glaciers retreated, water was freed, and the beaches flooded. Shorelines around all of Africa were constantly changing because of the ice, and in the interior was a complex cycle of drought and rainfall.

These periods of heavy rainfall (*pluvials*, they are usually called) were once thought to be directly related to the movements of glaciers. It seemed reasonable to suppose that, in a time of heavy precipitation, colder places would have ice and snow while warmer regions would have rains. It seemed reasonable—but there were difficulties with the theory. Problems in dating techniques and in comparing the strata of different regions have made the correlation of glacials and pluvials a nettlesome matter. It is probably wisest to say that the African continent became a shifting mosaic: a patchwork of forest and grassland with stretches of steppe.[1]

---

[1] The mosaic interpretation of the African environment is discussed in Glynn L. Isaac, "East Africa as a Source of Fossil Evidence for Human Evolution," in *Human Origins: Louis Leakey and the East African Evidence,* ed. Glynn L. Isaac and Elizabeth R. McCown (Menlo Park, Calif.: Benjamin-Cummings, 1976), p. 131.

Field Museum of Natural History

The African mosaic environment.

Seasonal changes in rainfall created shifts in the water table. Swampy forests eventually developed in the wetter parts of the African plains; drier regions had an abundance of year-round grasses. Grazing animals equipped with hooves, *ungulates* as zoologists call them, naturally flourished along the miles of savannah pastures. There were waterbuck, oryx, zebralike horses (and three-toed forms), okapi, various antelopes, and wild cattle.[2] A curious animal similar to an elephant, the dinothere, was around as well, but it was different from the elephants we know today. This remarkable beast was totally lacking in the familiar tusks of the upper jaw. It had instead two down-curving tusks attached to its lower jaw, which made it look like it was born with a built-in hoe.

Within the wetter, swampier regions were hippopotami and various pigs. The latter animal in particular seemed to thrive within the muck: 11 genera of early pigs have been identified by the bones; L. S. B. Leakey believed there were as many as 23 species. Lurking also within these thickets were animals that lived on meat—including, possibly from time to time, the meat of a human. Leopards and lions were prowling the country, as was the cat called the *Dinofelis*. This genus of early predator was as large as the African lions and came equipped with canine teeth that were even larger.

But we can drift too far in this picture of shadowy thickets and carnivorous beasts. Early humans, or hominids, through lack of fire, were active by day; the family of cats, in all probability, hunted at night. If the earliest hominids stayed clear of the woodlands and did their hunting

---

[2]Sonia Cole, *The Prehistory of East Africa* (New York: Mentor, 1963), pp. 88–95.

and gathering by daylight, and if they promptly took shelter at dusk in the branches of trees, then the problem of predator pressure was not so severe.

In addition to the animal populations, there were also abundant plants. Wild grasses that came into being with the shifts in the water table provided quantities of vegetable proteins in their edible seeds. There were bushes laden with berries, edible roots, and fruit-bearing trees. While meat was undoubtedly present among the foods of the hominid bands, there is little evidence that we were a totally carnivorous society.[3]

This reconstruction of early Africa can explain many facets of our cultural emergence, but it is a portrait of surprisingly recent creation. Well into the present century, the majority of scholars were prone to believe that the African continent had little to do with our own evolution. Its fossil deposits were seldom explored by generations of early researchers. There was ready acceptance of European candidates for the earliest humans. The fossils in question had been ferreted out of a gravel deposit along the Thames. They were poetically christened *Eoanthropus*, which means "the people of dawn," and they ultimately entered the textbooks as Piltdown man. There was something vaguely comforting about the demeanor of these people of dawn: their jaws were apelike, but their cranial vaults were as large as our own. The *cranial vault*, it should be noted, is the *part of the skull that encases the brain*. It was therefore reasoned that the human species had not only started in Europe but that the earliest hominids were almost as intelligent as people today. But the flattery turned out to be fraud—the fossil materials were the results of a hoax. A skillful prankster had taken advantage of archeology's simpler beginnings. The jawbone of a fossil orangutan had been modified to fit the cranial vault of a Roman soldier.

With the discovery of the Piltdown fraud, the continent of Africa was no longer neglected. Prehistorians who had worked there for years found a refreshing change in the climate of opinion. The world was beginning to discover what Charles Darwin had suspected before: that Africa, and not Western Europe, was our earliest home.

Dart and Broom: The earliest finds

A deserving beneficiary of this belated change in attitude was a South African anatomist named Raymond Dart. Thirty years before Piltdown was demonstrated to be a hoax, he had discovered a hominid fossil in Southern Africa. As it happened, a student of Dart's was enjoying dinner one quiet evening at the home of a Mr. Izod, who directed a limeworks.[4]

---

[3]In any event, at the very beginning. Increasing human carnivorousness will be extensively discussed in subsequent chapters.

[4]The discussion of Dart and Broom is taken largely from William Howells, *Mankind in the Making: The Story of Human Evolution* (New York: Penquin Books, 1967), pp. 132–48.

Her interest was suddenly taken by an object perched on the mantle, which turned out to be the skull of a fossil baboon. The skull had come from the area of Taung, just northwest of the town of Kimberley, where limestone cliffs were being blasted to supply the kilns. When Dart was told of the fossil baboon, he was thrown into great excitement and anxiously asked to see any other bones found at the site. Not long after, he was granted his wish. A box was delivered to Dart containing bones embedded in limestone. Among these chunks of encrusted fossils he was startled to find an unusual relic. Limestone and sand had filled up the cavity of what was either an ape or a human skull and had created a natural cast of an ancient brain. His curiosity aroused, he searched further among the rocks and found a mysterious lump of limestone with a cavity exposed. He dropped the cast of the brain into the cavity. It fitted exactly.

What, then, was inside the rock in which the telltale cavity was found? That was something Dart would not know until a tedious 10 weeks had gone by, during which he was carefully picking at the difficult stone. All

Sites of early humans in Africa.

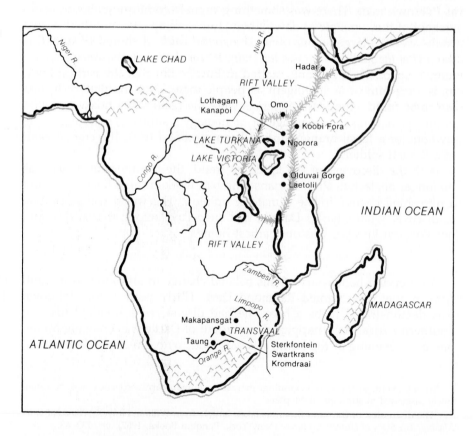

at once, a few days before Christmas, the last part of the rock fell away: prehistory was suddenly confronted with the face of a child.

The bone structure was light and delicate. The lower part of the face was less protruding than is usual in fossil apes; there was not even the slightest evidence of a ridge of bone just above the eyes, which is typical of the members of the ape family, ancient and modern. Milk teeth were fully intact, suggesting an age of between four and six, and four of the permanent molars had already erupted. From the cusps on these molars—which were relatively rounded, not pointed and sharp—it was evident that the skull was a juvenile human. The final deciding factors were the *foramen magnum* and the size of the brain. The *foramen magnum* refers to the *opening through which the spinal cord passes to connect with the brain.* In nonhuman primates, the opening is toward the back of the skull; in humans, it is directly underneath. This is because human beings normally walk on their own two feet: the trunk of the body is vertical, and the skull is balanced on top. The center of gravity for the human skull is thus directly underneath, which is where we consistently find the *foramen magnum.* By contrast, among the apes, there is typically a four-footed gait, or numerous variations upon that theme. The trunk is thus more horizontal with reference to the ground; the *foramen magnum* is noticeably shifted toward the rear. In the little skull from Taung, the opening was directly underneath, additional evidence for Raymond Dart that the skull was human. His final exhibit was brain size: 500 cubic centimeters, the size that we find today among chimpanzees. Admittedly, the volume was small— our modern brains are three times that size—so the Taung skull was widely dismissed as the skull of an ape.

The Taung skull.

Was it human after all? Looking at the evidence today, it appears that it was. In fairness to Dart's detractors, it was a juvenile skull. This suggests a role for *neoteny*, the *preservation into adulthood of infantile characteristics*, which is found today among juvenile chimpanzees. Before adulthood, a chimpanzee will be very hominid in its appearance: the snout is considerably reduced; the forehead is high, with the tiniest of brow ridges; even the *foramen magnum* is beneath the skull. But upon maturity, all of this changes. Dormant genes now go into action; body and skull are vastly transformed; yesterday's furry hominid is a full-blown ape. It seemed possible, then, that the Taung skull was simply a neotonous chimpanzee and that it was rash for Dart to describe it as a human being. But this overlooks the permanent molars, four of which had already erupted, and which were different from those of an ape, whether fossil or modern. This leaves us with the matter of brain size, the most peculiar debate of them all, for it seems to contain the seeds of the Garden of Eden. Unless, indeed, we are willing to believe that our modern-size brains appeared out of nothing, the only alternative would seem to be that they were smaller in the past. This is a general evolutionary feature: systems usually start out small and are energetically less complex; increases in size and complexity happen gradually through time. Evolution is rarely "saltatory"; it seldom makes jumps.[5] Dart was eventually widely supported in his view that the skull was human. He classified it *Australopithecus africanus*.

Isolated and controversial for 12 long years, the Taung skull held the stage as the oldest human fossil discovered in Africa. But the situation changed abruptly in the summer of 1936. If the search for our earliest ancestors had momentarily suffered a lapse, the South African tourism business was starting to prosper. At a limeworks close to Taung known as Sterkfontein, fragments of early baboon skulls were being sold to the local tourists, who were urged to come and look for the missing link. Word of this burgeoning enterprise was ultimately brought to Robert Broom, a paleontologist at Pretoria's Transvaal Museum. Several visits were paid by Broom to the director of the site, and within a mere nine days, he had a hominid fossil.

Plesianthropus transvaalensis, as he originally called the skull, was strikingly similar in its form to the child from Taung. But this time it was an adult with light bones and diminutive brow ridges. Delicate skeletal features, then, were not confined to young children alone. They were possibly characteristic of a whole population. The brain size was 560 cc—additional evidence that our brains were once small—and the *foramen magnum* was a clear indication of an upright posture. Robert Broom was

---

[5] For an alternative view of saltatory evolution, the reader should consult "Bushes and Ladders in Human Evolution" by Stephen Jay Gould in his highly readable *Ever since Darwin: Reflections in Natural History* (New York: W. W. Norton, 1977), pp. 56–62.

understandably dazzled by such a discovery within so short a time. The African fossils, after long years of slumber, had been roused with a bang.

Literally enough with a bang, since Broom was dynamiting the limestone cliffs. This volatile approach caused a good deal of stir in the Historical Monuments Commission, but strange as it seems, his technique was successful because it was careful. In excavation, a charge of dynamite is periodically a useful tool: it creates vectors, or lines of force, that can be precisely controled. Robert Broom, with his geological background, was very familiar with dynamite's use; he understood that, in the South African hills, it was a necessity. We must remember that the limestone cliffs were, for all practical purposes, as hard as cement. A dental pick and a camel-hair brush were virtually useless. His fossils were recovered intact, and the limestone matrix was blasted to pieces; such selectivity would not have been possible without close control.

One site after another yelded up a wealth of fossils. The vigorous Scot was controversial but he got results. At a limestone bluff called Kromdraai, on the outskirts of Sterkfontein, he found an assortment of skeletal fragments that were surprisingly different. Parts of a skull had been found by a schoolboy, a juvenile jawbone had been detonated by Broom; the scattered fragments created a portrait of a different people. The bones were thicker than Plesianthropus from neighboring Sterkfontein, the brow

Skull of *Australopithecus boisei* (left) and *Australopithecus africanus.* The differences indicated have been used as evidence for the existence of different species of early humans.

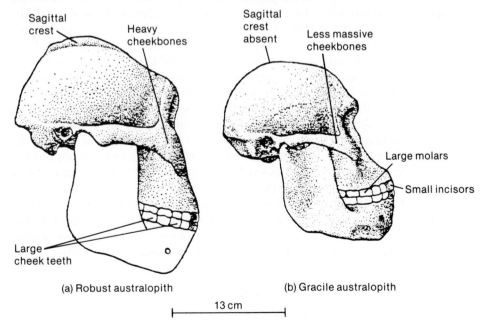

(a) Robust australopith   (b) Gracile australopith

13 cm

ridges were larger, and the entire skull appeared more rugged. The *zygomatic arch*, or cheekbone, to which a set of jaw muscles is attached, was similarly greater and thicker, and there were large molar teeth. The size of the brain was 650 cc, which was noticeably different than the earlier find. Robert Broom had encountered the first of his robust fossils.

It might appear at this point that our story has gotten sidetracked in a jungle of bones. In fact, as I hope to explain, this is far from the case. The endless debates in prehistory over jawbones, brow ridges, and crania are seldom merely to satisfy an affection for bones. Above all, we are concerned with the adaptations of groups of humans and the reconstruction of their relationships with one another.

An example from the study of primates should make this clear. If you visited the Ethiopian highlands, you would find a picture of true desolation: not a tree or bush, but a stony desert for endless miles. But if you were lucky, you would spot a rather persistent group of animals that managed somehow to survive on these open plains. Hamadryas baboons, as these particular animals are called, look different than the baboons found in the forest.[6] Their fur is lighter in color; their faces are a bright reddish-pink. They have also become highly unique in their social behavior. The adult males are generally larger, which is convenient for troop defense, but a larger animal consumes a greater amount of food. As a consequence, natural selection has given rise to a troop called a harem: one dominant male presides uneasily over infants and females. This odd little arrangement is not without friction. Bachelor males within the troop begin to notice the maturing females. Competition ultimately develops between the bachelors and the ruling male. Eventually the troop will divide and new harems will form.

Such an arrangement is uniquely adapted to an environment where food is scarce. It differs markedly from the social structure of the common savanna baboon. Here we discover not one but several of the larger, dominant males and a distinctly less-monopolized mating behavior. We recognize these differences by placing the animals in separate species, a crucial category for understanding human evolution. As the majority of biologists understand the term today, a *species* is a *reproductively isolated population*. More exactly, it is sometimes said that a species is "a population or group of populations of actually or potentially interbreeding animals that are reproductively isolated from other such groups." In the case of the hamadryas and the common savanna baboons, this means that a splitting of a group of animals has occurred. One population became adapted to desert conditions; the other became adapted to open grasslands. In the course of time, the two have diverged in both their biology

---

[6] These animals were described by Hans Kummer, "Two Variations in the Social Organization of Baboons," in *Primates: Studies in Adaptation and Variability*, ed. P. Jay (New York: Holt, Rinehart & Winston, 1958), pp. 293–312.

and their behavior so that, even if they were brought together within the same physical environment, it is unlikely that any breeding would occur between them. This is *branching speciation;* it can often give rise to many new species. The other variety of species creation is known as *linear speciation.* This means, as you might suppose, that a single lineage of evolving animals has become biologically very different from their ancestors in the course of time. As a consequence, if the descendants, through the aid of a time machine, could somehow be reunited with their distant, direct ancestors, there would be little or no exchanging of genes between them. The best example of this is later hominid evolution. *Homo erectus* people changed so greatly in the course of time that they eventually became *Homo sapiens,* our modern species.

What about the bones, then? Clearly, they exist as the only biological remains of an earlier living and breeding population. So, *the similarities and differences in the structure of fossil bones become the basic evidence for the discovery of earlier species.* If three African sites produce human fossil fragments very different from one another, the anthropologist might conclude that the disparity between the bones is so great that it is evidence of three separate species. We should pause for just a moment and reflect on what this might mean. If the earliest human beings were three separate evolving lines, then why is there only a single species today? What happened to the other two? Did they fail to get enough to eat? Were they living in the woodland areas in which predators mostly lived? Or did our own ancestors aggressively wipe them out? Such questions may have implications for the nature of humans today, for the biological roots of our own behavior. It is not the crania, the jawbones, and the collections of fossil teeth themselves that are of anthropological interest. The interest lies, rather, in what they suggest of our early behavior—and in the possibilities and the constraints of behavioral change.

It was beginning to appear to much of the scientific world that early humanity had started out as two separate species. The smaller, more delicate bones of the Taung site and Sterkfontein became labeled *Australopithecus africanus.* The larger, heavier-boned fossil discoveries at the Kromdraai site were descriptively labeled *Australopithecus robustus.*

But Kromdraai was not alone as a plentiful site for these raw-boned humans. At another farm on the outskirts of Johannesburg, there was a limestone cavern called the Swartkrans Cave. A deep natural shaft ran vertically downward and connected the underground cave with the surface. Stones and fossils, dirt and debris tumbled into the gaping shaft and were slowly cemented in limestone within the cave. An earlier expedition had explored the site with little to show, but Broom, the Midas of fossils, had instant success. A nearly complete lower jaw was found, and over 100 isolated teeth; but more sensational than either of these was the Swartkrans skull. Its bones were thick and heavy, reminiscent of the Kromdraai find, and on its cranium were the broken remains of a *sagittal crest.* This is a *vertical ridge of bone to which a set of jaw muscles attaches.* The other set is anchored to the zygomatic arch. The early fossils were beginning to fall into a pattern. The oversized molar teeth found throughout the Swartkrans site, the remnants of a sagittal crest on the nearly complete skull, and the rugged cheekbones present on both the Swartkrans and the Kromdraai skulls seemed to be the skeletal evidence of a plant-eating creature.

A vegetarian diet of wild plants, nuts, and seeds places demands on our musculature and bones. Large molars are beneficial; they have a greater surface area for grinding. Vegetable matter is tough, requiring bigger jaw-bones and bigger jaw muscles. One set of these attaches to the cheekbones, requiring that they be more massive, while another set is attached to the top of the skull. Ordinarily there is not enough bone there to anchor a large set of muscles, so the sagittal crest has evolved and fulfills this function.[7] Vegetarian primates, such as the gorilla, are characterized by such features today, which suggest that the robust humans had a plant-eating diet.

What of the lighter-boned humans? Apparently their diet was different. It was reasoned that a menu with meat does not require such heavy chewing equipment. Perhaps then, there was a plant-eating species, *Australopithecus robustus,* and a meat-and-plant-eating species, *Australopithecus africanus.* This immediately sparked many questions (and continues to provoke them today) about the environments and fates of the two different species. The picture of our own evolution was becoming more complex than scientists had dreamed. But greater challenges were still to come from a bleak northern valley.

Olduvai Gorge: A fossil canyon

A giant, spreading rupture along the surface of the earth is known to fossil hunters as the Great Rift Valley.[8] Four thousand miles long, it is a deepening, spreading trench creating a future ocean and tearing the continent in two. It extends from the Zambezi River in the region of Mozambique far northward to the Red Sea, where it veers to the Middle East and then slices into the present-day countries of Israel and Lebanon. Persistently through the ages, at about a millimeter per year, the steep walls of this African valley are moving apart. Bodies of magma, or molten lava, move upward from within the earth and riddle with punctures the delicate crust left behind. This has meant that the African valley during the days of the earliest humans was a chain of exploding volcanoes and buck-

---

[7]It should be noted that this does not happen because of a purpose or deliberate design. The dietary pattern, a feature of the environment, selected genes that would produce an attachment area for larger muscles.

[8]John E. Pfeiffer, *The Emergence of Man,* 2d ed. (New York: Harper & Row, 1972), pp. 84–86; and Uwe George, "Africa—An Ocean Is Born," *Geo* 1, no. 1, pp. 44–72.

Photos courtesy of Dr. William R. Maples, Florida State Museum, University of Florida

Olduvai Gorge in East Africa. The "fossil canyon" was once a lake. Early humans lived on its shores. The strata of lake sediments and lava (bottom) have provided extensive information about early humanity.

ling earth. On the shores of lakes Rudolf, Baringo, Magadi, and Natron, human bones have been covered with sediments as the lake waters rose and fell and then sealed by a stream of lava flowing over the land. This has happened over and over, a flood of sediments and a flood of lava, so that fossils have been sandwiched between the volcanic deposits. Researchers have had the good fortune to be able to date these layers of lava and revolutionize our own understanding of human antiquity.

Much of this region today is a wretched and empty land, but a group of determined scientists have called it home. In the country of Tanzania, they have labored in a dusty canyon known to the world today as Olduvai Gorge. It is a mile wide and 25 miles long, with a depth of 300 feet—and some 2 million years. It is a part of the Great Rift Valley and shared fully in the violent forces that were transforming the entire region of Eastern Africa. Some 2 million years before the present, Olduvai Gorge was a stream-fed lake; australopithecines and grassland animals lived on its shores. Then suddenly a nearby mountain, which was probably just to the south, fired a giant cloud of fragments over 1,000 feet in the air. They fell back to the sides of the mountain and rolled to the lake in an avalanche, covering like a red-hot river everything in their path. Then, curiously, the world became quiet. But the interlude was short-lived: a fresh burst of volcanic explosions spilled lava into the hapless lake, and the ground began to buckle with the blistering heat. There was finally a succession of droughts that turned the region into a desert; what had once been a stream-fed lake was now windblown sand. Had they remained underneath this desert, the fossils would probably never have been found, but 50 millenia before the present, the earth moved again. A cascading river appeared and cut its way through the ancient deposits. Eventually, a gorge was created, and the river was gone. A setting with such a turbulent history deserved an appropriate pair of explorers. The indefatigable Leakey family had found their home.

He was the offspring of missionary parents, born in a mud-walled bungalow in Kenya.[9] She was the daughter of a landscape painter and spent her summers in southern France. Louis Seymour Bazett Leakey and Mary Leakey, born Mary Nicol, brought a mixture of backgrounds and cultures to the African gorge.

Louis Leakey spent his boyhood in the wilderness of Kenya, but how African he was is open to debate. At his birth, a group of Kikuyu gathered somberly around his cradle, and as a gesture of acceptance, they spat upon him. What seems repulsive to Western eyes was done out of

---

[9]The biographical sketch of the Leakeys is taken from Melvin M. Payne, "The Leakeys of Africa: Family in search of Prehistoric Man," *National Geographic*, February 1965, pp. 194–231; and J. Desmond Clark, "Louis Seymour Bazett Leakey, 1903–1973," in *Human Origins*, pp. 521–41. I also profited from the reminiscences of William Maples of the University of Florida of a visit to the Leakeys at Olduvai Gorge.

trust and contagious magic. The Kikuyu believe, like many societies, that to possess a part of one's body makes it possible to work a malevolent magic against him. Symbolically, through that gesture, they had put their lives into his hands; his socialization into Kikuyu had begun. The years that followed were largely a period of growing up among their society. He was taught to throw a spear through a rolling hoop made of twigs, to fashion snares, to stalk an antelope, and to submerge himself up to his mouth in the waters of a rain-filled lake—green moss on his head, camouflaged as a stump—until he could manage to grab the feet of a careless duck. In due time, he was initiated into adulthood within the group. He was given a Kikuyu name: "Son of the Sparrow Hawk."

But he was never completely Kikuyu; it was a cultural impossiblity. Born into a British family, he learned English and French as an infant. An early interest in ornithology was encouraged by both of his parents; he cut his teeth on the voluminous and exquisitely detailed *Origin of Species*. At the age of 16, he was in public school in England; a short while later, he was on the rugby fields of Cambridge. It seems wisest, in view of this background, to see Louis Leakey as a cultural hybrid: a special synthesis of Kikuyu villager and upper-class Briton. But throughout his life, he paid

Louis Leakey. Dramatic, controversial, and vigorous, he proposed a multiple-species viewpoint of humanity's African past.

Field Museum of Natural History

regular homage to his boyhood days in the bush; the patience and attention to detail so crucial in his search for fossils he attributed to his early years with the Kenya people.

For Mary Nicol Leakey, archeology was born of art. On the travels with her father to the fields of southern France, the paintings of an earlier epoch had intrigued them both. At a cave site called Cabrerets, where Upper Stone Age paintings were found, the paleontologist Abbe Lemozi noted the interest she had in his work and allowed her to assist him in the excavation. Her fascination with archeology had been sparked on that pleasant summer, as was her introduction to field techniques. From that beginning, her course was fixed: there were studies in geology and prehistory at the University of London, an elegant excavation of a hill-fort site in Devon, and a thorough training in the craftsmanship of European excavation that would prove an invaluable skill at the African gorge.

But dividends were long in coming. For 20 years they explored the canyon and found not a splinter of human fossil material. Funding agencies that supported their research were, perhaps understandably, becoming impatient. Eventually the money ran out. The Leakeys decided to continue their work, without any funding, for as long as they could. They continued to dig on through the heat of the early summer until Louis, exhausted, was taken ill with a fever. Reluctantly, he decided that he would have to stay in bed. So on July 17, 1959, Mary Leakey made the trip to the gorge alone.

That morning she was walking near a slope of eroded rubble where a rockslide had exposed a buried deposit. Unexpectedly, she noticed an unusual bone within the cliff. It was a fragment of a skull which appeared different than that of an ape; close by she found the remains of two human teeth. When she brought the news to Louis Leakey, his fever was magically cured. For 19 days they delicately brushed and picked at the rocks that encrusted the skull. In early August, they uncovered the face of an Olduvai human.

The face that stared back at them was remarkably complete.[10] The jawbone was missing, but much of the cranial vault was intact. The bones were massive and thick, the heaviest found so far, including the robust hominids that were found by Broom. On the top of the braincase was a definite sagittal crest, implying jaws that customarily did a lot of chewing. The probability was strengthened by the appearance of the teeth, for the molars of the upper jaw were very large. They were, as it developed, some 40 percent larger than the average size of *Australopithecus robustus'* teeth. The premolars, too, were much wider than usual, and the palate of the upper jaw was deeply arched. This last feature makes possible a freer movement of the tongue, which is also necessary for extensive

---

[10]L. S. B. Leakey, "A New Fossil Skull from Olduvai," *Nature*, August 15, 1959, p. 491.

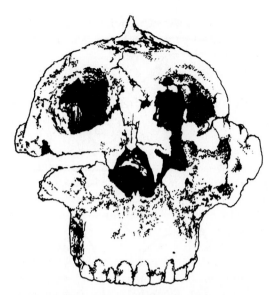

Australopithecus boisei. Note the presence of a
sagittal crest.

chewing. It seemed likely that the skull had come from a plant-eating
population which flourished along the shores of the Olduvai lake.

Zinjanthropus boisei was what the Leakeys named their find. Today it is
sometimes classified as *Australopithecus robustus;* others prefer to label it
as a third evolving species, referring to it as *Australopithecus boisei.* Were
there two species, then, or three? What were the relationships between
them? The simplicity of our own evolution seemed to diminish with every
discovery. The world was wondering what the Leakeys would turn up
next.

The answer was quick in coming, this time within the space of a year.[11]
Within the same geological deposit in which *Zinjanthropus* had been found,
the Leakeys' son Jonathan found most of a jawbone and the sides of a
skull. The teeth were small and the bone structure was light, reminiscent
of *Australopithecus africanus.* But the sides of the skull made it possible to
roughly estimate the size of the brain. It was 650 cc, the largest anyone
had seen so far. The Leakeys debated then made their announcement:
the skull had belonged to a hominid population so similar to modern
humans that it could properly be considered in the genus *Homo.* Capable
people—*Homo habilis*—became a part of a baffling debate. Prehistorians
were growing uneasy over the clutter of hominid species. There was *Aus-*

---

[11]L. S. B. Leakey, "A New Species of the Genus *Homo* from Olduvai Gorge," *Nature,*
April 4, 1964, pp. 7–9.

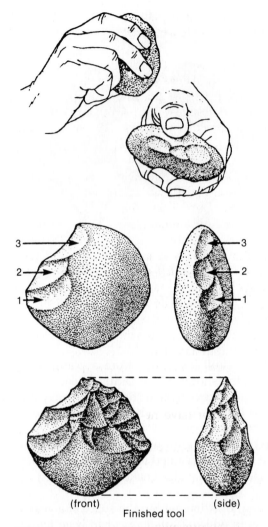

(front)   (side)

Finished tool

Pebble tools were manufactured by stone-on-stone percussion. The result was an irregular cutting edge.

tralopithecus africanus and *Australopithecus robustus*. For those anthropologists who agreed with the Leakeys, there was also *Australopithecus boisei*. Now, with the discovery of the cranial fragments and the jaw, there was also the mysterious *Homo habilis*. Two genera and, perhaps, four species: was our evolution that complex? Were the Leakeys inventing species that had never existed?

The Leakeys were strongly convinced that they were not. In their opinion, the cultural debris that littered the layer where the fossils were found was ample evidence of the work of their capable people. Pebble tools were found in abundance and were evidence for the Leakeys' case. A *pebble tool* is a *large, rounded rock that has been smashed against another, resulting in flakes and an irregular cutting edge.* Not only were these found, but they were of several different kinds. There were engraving and gouging tools, scrapers of different sizes, primitive chisels and hammerstones, and tools made of lava and quartz. These last are particularly difficult to shape into a useable tool. Early toolmakers were aquiring both patience and skill.

Then, too, there was the living area.[12] It was 3,400 square feet in extent and was littered with the debris of the Olduvai humans. Bones of lizards, pigs, antelope, birds, amphibians, and various snakes were preserved within the sediments of the ancient camp. There was also a dense concentration of pebble tools and smashed animal bones. It is within the boundary of the camp itself and is roughly 15 feet in diameter. Mary Leakey's interpretation is that the cluster was an "activity area": early humans were smashing the bones to extract the marrow.[13]

Beyond the margin of this ancient camp, there is a separate pile of animal bones noticeably different from the heap in the living area. None of these bones have been smashed; they have simply been thrown together. Intriguingly, they are also the bones, such as the jaws and various parts of the skull, which do not contain any marrow. Between this accumulation and the living area itself, there is a crude semicircle of rocks that seems deliberately placed.

What could the assemblage mean? The Leakeys have suggested a tentative answer. The clutter of bones that have never been smashed was simply a pile of early hominid garbage. Animals were skinned there and the carcasses butchered, a feat that was possible with the rough pebble tools. Louis Leakey once took a flint flake that was virtually identical to the Olduvai types and skinned and disjointed a sheep in about 20 minutes. Between the butchering-and-skinning area and the site of the camp itself, there was the rough semicircle of stones that was possibly a windbreak. It lies directly in the path of the prevailing winds today and could have provided the simplest of shelters for the open-air camp. Branches pushed into the ground and braced by the rocks against the wind might have been one of the earliest shelters in humanity's history.

The author of these cultural creations was the *Homo habilis* line; at any rate, this was the Leakey's interpretation. "While it is possible," they cautiously wrote, "that *Zinjanthropus*[14] and *Homo habilis* both made stone tools,

---

[12]Pfeiffer, *Emergence of Man,* p. 97.

[13]An *"activity area"* is a spatial location in which, on the basis of archeological evidence, a particular set of behaviors is believed to have occurred. The concept is encountering controversy, and in time, it may be refined by archeological studies of living societies.

[14]Today frequently classified as *Australopithecus boisei.*

it is probable that the latter was the more advanced tool maker and that the *Zinjanthropus* skull represents an intruder (or a victim) of a *Homo habilis* living site."[15] This view, at that time and later, was fuel for the imagination. Did our earliest direct ancestors outcompete their rivals for food, or did they annihilate the smaller-brained humans on the open savanna? The discussion was becoming more heated, for it was obvious to anthropologists now that the issue was not stones and bones, but our ancient behavior.

It was in this volatile climate that Richard Leakey and a group of associates resolved to continue the investigation that his parents had begun. In a region to the north of Olduvai, he began to make aerial searches. The storm over *Homo habilis* had just begun.

Turkana and Afar: The recent discoveries

It was on the grayish-brown wasteland of Kenya's Lake Turkana where the fossil hunters met their first encouragment.[16] In a steep and barren gully, one of the workers noticed a bone that was projecting out slightly from the sandy sediments. For the remainder of that day in August 1972, they sifted the layer and found over 30 of the tiny fragments. Putting the pieces together took a month and a half of labor, but they were rewarded with a magnificent reconstruction. It was a nearly complete human cranium—reminiscent of *Homo habilis*. On the basis of its number in the National Museum of Kenya, the find today is simply known as "1470".

The 1470 skull. Richard Leakey has placed it within species *Homo habilis*, and believes it is on the direct line of human descent.

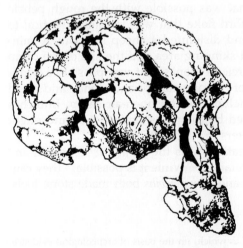

---

[15]L. S. B. Leakey, "A New Species of the Genus *Homo*," pp. 7–9.

[16]R. E. F. Leakey, "Skull 1470—New Clue to Earliest Man?" *National Geographic* 143.

Inspired to look for additional fossils, they excavated the entire hill-side.[17] A vertical stretch of over 100 feet was dug and screened through the last of the summer. Then they halted to try to make sense of their fossil discoveries. In the first place, there was 1470. Its bones were light and more modern in appearance; the brow ridges were small, and the cranium was shaped like a dome. Its capacity was 810 cc, surprisingly larger than the brain of *Australopithecus*. But there was more: some 70 feet directly above where 1470 had first been found was the completely preserved left thighbone of a human being. To the anatomist, there is nothing at all unusual about this thighbone, which is, of course, exactly what Richard Leakey had hoped for. The neck of the thighbone projected from the shaft at the exact same angle that it does today, and the shaft was rounded in comparison to *Australopithecus*. The bone, in short, was indistinguishable from the thighbone of a human today, but it, and the skull below it, were assuredly old. How old were the fossils? There is part of an answer provided by a layer of lava which was encountered some 40 feet above the thighbone. This layer, the KBS Tuff, was dated at 2.6 million years, and all the fossils found at the lake were discovered below it.[18] Turkana fossils appeared to be over 2.6 million years old, yet they bore a considerable resemblance to modern-day humans. Richard Leakey had no hesitation in announcing his verdict on east Lake Turkana: he thought the materials were clear-cut evidence of *Homo habilis'* existence.

At this point, there was probably a goodly number of anthropologists longing for the innocent days of Dart at Taung. It had all been so simple then, a single skull and a single species, but now it was Byzantine in its complexity. Yet, like the mysteries of any science, the growing problem of multiple species had only served as an enticement to exploration. Thus, Donald Carl Johanson of the Cleveland Museum of Natural History became intrigued by the complex problems of understanding our own beginnings, and he ultimately journeyed to the burning wastelands of Ethiopia.

It is a stretch of eroding canyons along the margins of the Awash River.[19] Like Lake Turkana, it is also part of the Great Rift Valley. Here, too, were stream-borne sediments that flooded across the lightly forested plains to seal the bones of Pleistocene fauna and ancient humans. Volcanoes erupted frequently and covered the sediments with a bath of lava. The fossil remains can therefore be dated with considerable accuracy. By a charming linguistic coincidence, this desolate region is known as Afar. Johanson began combing its gullies on the lookout for fossils.

---

[17] R. E. F. Leakey, "Evidence for an Advanced Plio-pleistocene Hominid from East Rudolf, Kenya," *Nature* April 13, 1973, pp. 447–450.

[18] This date may not be correct. Problems with the KBS Tuff will be discussed a bit later.

[19] Donald C. Johanson, "Ethiopia Yields First 'Family' of Early Man," *National Geographic*, December 1976, pp. 791–811.

On a boiling day in late November 1974, he spotted an arm bone protruding from an eroding hillside. As he and his associates brushed away the surrounding dirt, it was evident that they had discovered a hominid skeleton. "As mad as any Englishmen," as Johanson recalled it later, they hugged each other and danced in the midday sun. When the various bones were finally collected, they were some 40 percent of a human skeleton—the most complete Lower Pleistocene human ever found. There was a nearly complete lower jaw, fragments of arm bones, vertebra and ribs, a large part of the left side of the pelvis, the left thighbone, and portions of the hand. The celebration of the find was a tribute to surrealism: beer-drinking anthropologists and their Ethiopian field assistants ceremonially roasted a goat on the banks of the Awash River, while a tape recorder played "Lucy in the Sky with Diamonds." Inspired by this tableau, Johanson referred to his find as "Lucy"—but there remains the problem of her scientific classification.

Johanson's verdict was slow in coming. He continued his excavations at another locality in Afar—a dried-up, stony ridge that was simply designated "333"—and discovered the remains of what might well have been an early hominid family. Fragments of lower and upper jaws, isolated bones of hands, feet, and legs, the partial skull of an adult, and the lower jaw and palate of a baby were dug out of the ridge in a race against time and the season of rainstorms. Sudden rains that rise in the highlands and swell the waters of the Awash River were possibly true of the region of Afar in the past. In fact, the geological analysis of the layers of 333 suggests a lakeshore that was suddenly covered with river-borne sediments. This is the telltale sort of stratigraphy left behind in the wake of a flood. Site geologist Maurice Taieb has suggested a scenario of an ancient disaster: "They could only have been buried together. Some natural catastrophe. I think maybe a flash flood, perhaps while they were resting or sleeping." Perhaps we shall never know. However they got there, they were additional fossils, a substantial enlargement of Johanson's sample. He ultimately compared the complete collection with the hominid discoveries at the East African sites. Years later, in early January 1979, he announced his decision that the Afar materials were a new hominid species.[20] His conclusion was based primarily upon his analysis of the teeth: they seemed more apelike than any of the primitive humans discovered in Africa so far. This feature, in combination with a two-legged posture and a small-size brain, suggested a separate species for the Northeastern african region. It became *Australopithecus afarensis.*

The continent of Africa was now an embarrassment of riches. Like Pandora's box, her fossil caches had been pried open by anthropologists, and a welter of confusing debates had bedeviled the world. There is hardly a more striking example in the history of any science of the fallacy of the

[20]Donald C. Johanson and T. D. White, "A Systematic Assessment of Early African Hominids," *Science,* January 1979, pp. 321–30.

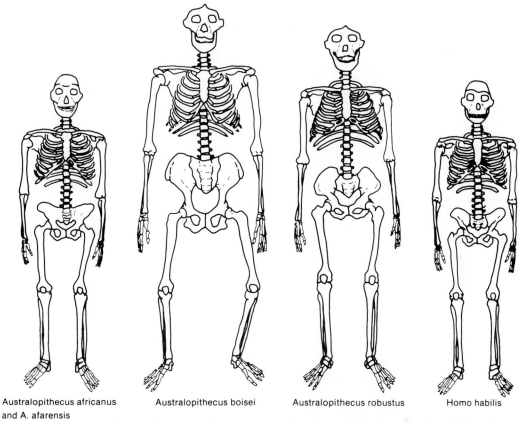

Australopithecus africanus   Australopithecus boisei   Australopithecus robustus   Homo habilis
and A. afarensis

Adapted from Bernard Campbell, *Humankind Emerging*, 3d ed. Copyright © 1982 by Bernard G. Campbell. Reprinted by permission of the publisher, Little, Brown and Company.

The African fossil species described in this chapter. What was the cause of such variation among the earliest humans?

shopworn notion that "the facts will speak for themselves." Here was a body of fossil material and a collection of devoted scientists who were examining in many instances identical scraps of bones and yet arriving at widely varying interpretations. But far from being an illustration of the futility of fossil research, the debates afforded considerable insight into its strengths. Any serious interpretation of the discoveries of prehistory should provide a causal explanation for all of the differences under study and should illustrate the limitations of alternative theories. Such rigor was not as apparent in the earlier decades of fossil research, but it is increasingly characteristic of the present time. In a sense, the various theories that we will consider in a moment reflect the historical development of prehistory as a science: emerging from an antiquarianism that was preoccupied with stones and bones to a collection of independent, but conceptually related, minor sciences, in which the possibility of cross-verification is greatly enhanced.

3 / Interpretations of the Fossil Evidence

The earliest interpretations of our African beginnings were based largely upon the fossil remains themselves. The Leakeys were sufficiently impressed by the contrasts in fossil materials to suggest that several human species had become extinct. Their *Australopithecus boisei, Australopithecus robustus,* even the lighter-boned *Australopithecus africanus* were failures of evolution: they did not survive. The greater physical similarity of *Homo habilis* to ourselves—including a brain which is the largest of any hominid of that time—implies that they were directly ancestral to modern-day humans.

For Richard Leakey, the Turkana discoveries would seem to offer support for this view. Besides the appearance and the early date of the 1470 skull, there is the fossil context of materials at other locations. As he has recently pointed out, the parallel trends in human evolution are an increase in the size of the brain and a reduction of jaws.[1] Among the australopithecines, we discover small brains and large jaws. This would seem to disqualify them as ancestral to us. Robust australopithecine fossils have been discovered at Lake Turkana in deposits as recent as those containing *Homo erectus*. This is the name of a later species in hominid evolution. If australopithecines were the ancestors of later human populations, then how could the two possibly have overlapped in time? Why, then, did *Australopithecus* eventually become extinct? Leakey supplies no single answer. He is inclined toward the view that *Homo habilis* developed a culture. In the lineage of *Australopithecus,* this never occurred. "We would nominate *Australopithecus* for the role of hominid without culture." Why did our own ancestral lineage develop a complex cultural system? Leakey is unsure. The answer remains to be found.

The Leakeys and Human Evolution: Were there extinctions along the way?

---

[1]Alan Walker and Richard E. F. Leakey, "The Hominids of East Turkana," *Scientific American,* August 1978, pp. 61–62.

John Robinson and ancient environments

Agreeing with Richard Leakey that there were early human extinctions, John Robinson has approached the problem in a different way.[2] Like Leakey, he derives much of his view from the examination of fossil materials. He has suggested that it is possible, when examining ancient bones, to discover discontinuities in physical structures. These result, in his opinion, from genetic isolation. They serve as evidence of the existence of separate species. Unlike Leakey, Robinson has devised a tentative explanation of species' extinctions. By comparing the teeth of the African fossils, he has found evidence of different environments. The finer-boned human beings with a set of smaller grinding teeth were members of the genus *Australopithecus*. They were toolmakers, he believes, who had a diet of meat and plants. Other African hominids with massive bones and large grinding teeth made few, if any, tools, and they lived in a forest environment.[3] Their diet likely consisted of nuts, seeds, and vegetable fibers. Large back teeth had been selected by chewing such food. But their habitat was slowly disappearing. Vast forests were shrinking in size. Incapable of locating food, these early plant eaters became extinct.

Dentition of *Australopithecus boisei*. John Robinson suggested that the large back teeth were adapted to a diet of plants. Susan Cachel has recently challenged this view.

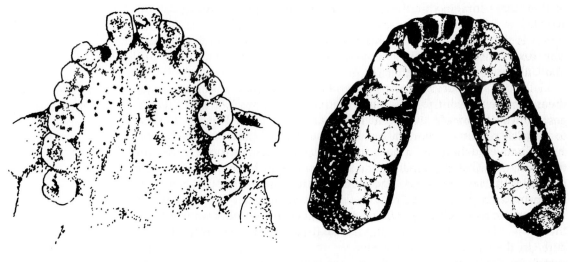

Homo sapiens

Australopithecus

[2]John Robinson, "Variation and the Taxonomy of the Early Hominids," in *Evolutionary Biology*, vol. 1, ed. T. Dobzhansky, M. K. Hecht, and Wm. C. Steere (New York: Appleton-Century-Crofts, 1967), pp. 69–100.

[3]Robinson has labeled these hominids *Paranthropus*.

Robinson's view is especially valuable in calling attention to the human environment. He has emphasized that fossil materials once belonged to living humanity subjected to the pressures of a particular part of the world. One difficulty with his approach is the nettlesome question of size. Even if Robinson's theory successfully accounts for variations in teeth, there still remains the question of difference in stature and weight. Robust humans, on the average, were taller and heavier than lighter-boned forms. We need to understand why this difference was true of the past.

The question is a critical feature in the interpretation by C. Loring Brace.[4] In a simple but intriguing explanation, he suggested that the difference in size was actually a sexual difference within the same species. *Sexual dimorphism*, as it is called, is the *occurrence of male and female differences apart from their primary sexual characteristics.* The monkeys and apes of Africa provide us with striking examples. Male adult baboons are almost twice the size of the females. Among the African gorillas, there is a similar average difference in size. But among gibbons and forest-dwelling chimps, such striking distinctions do not occur. Chimp females are only slightly smaller and lighter in weight than males. Among tree-dwelling gibbons there is scarcely any difference at all. For C. L. Brace, the earliest hominids were highly dimorphic animals. Unlike chimps that spend most of their lives foraging closely around the trees, primitive humans were adapted to life on the open savanna. Males were larger because greater size was very useful in group defense. With the gradual development of complex culture, such differences were of lesser importance; in later hominid times, they were greatly reduced.

The sexual dimorphism theories

Biologist R. D. Alexander has elaborated on this theme by proposing a theory for the evolution of sexual behavior.[5] Greater size, he has suggested, was extremely significant for early males. Competition for access to females places a premium on aggreassion and size. The outcome of such a pattern, when practiced over thousands of years, would have been the elimination of the smaller-sized males. Females and dependent infants would thus be defended by a larger male, and the entire band could be protected against predation. The earliest males were aggressive; they were competitive with one another. Females were more passive; they were the sex that bore children; they did not play a significant role in the group's defense. Such a scenario has some affinity to male power in the industrial world. How ancient is the familiar pattern of male aggressive behavior? Are competitive, aggressive males responding to potentials wired in their

---

[4]C. L. Brace, "Sexual Dimorphism in Human Evolution," *Yearbook of Physical Anthropology*, vol. 16 (American Association of Physical Anthropologists, 1973).
[5]R. D. Alexander, "The Search for an Evolutionary Philosophy of Man," *Proceedings of the Royal Society of Victoria* 84 (1971), pp. 99–120.

genes? It should be obvious that such questions are enormously complex, and that we probably will not be satisfied by immediate answers.[6] In that spirit, I am offering a highly tentative scenario of the causes that led to the earliest human societies.

Environment and the earliest humans

An event that was likely decisive in the emergence of the earliest humans was the gradual retreat of the African tropical forest. More than likely, this never resulted in a savanna with islands of forested streams. Grass was in patches, and the country was dotted with swamps.[7]

Game was abundant in such an environment, and this affected our earliest life. The celebrated "descent from the trees" and the two-footed walking of primitive humans have often been explained as the outcome of climatic change. Droughts and irregular bursts of rainfall that troubled the land were believed to have resulted in forests that were smaller in size. Populations of tree-dwelling apes were eventually forced from the trees. Necessarily, they had to adapt to an open terrain.

But the process was possibly different. The descent may have never been forced. Even if there were large populations of apes in the tropical trees, this does not necessarily imply there was a shortage of food. Indeed, because forest and grassland were both so inextricably mixed, savanna resources were only a short distance away. Seeds and edible roots were abundant on these patches of grass. The climatic change may have led to no pressure at all.

It may have been sheer opportunity that gave rise to our earliest culture. The African mosaic environment likely brought about an increase in game. Grass-eating cattle, antelope, waterbuck, and zebralike horses now flourished on the pastures that grew at the edge of the trees. Wild pigs were also abundant; they foraged for roots in the grass. A rich source of food was now part of the African world.

Meat eating may have been a decision and not the result of genetic mutations. Studies of Japanese monkeys—more distant from us than the apes—have revealed the existence of deliberate behavioral change.[8] A troop

---

[6]One problem involved is the need for a greater precision of terms. *Aggression* (or agonistic behavior) is defined as "threatening and fighting" and includes "defensive responses. . .such as submitting and fleeing." The term, although meaningful, perhaps requires a more exact definition. Agonistic behavior is defined by David P. Barash in *Sociobiology and Behavior* (New York: Elsevier, 1977), p. 325.

[7]The African environment is described by Glynn L. Isaac "East Africa as a Source of Fossil Evidence for Human Evolution," *Human Origins: Louis Leakey and the East African Evidence,* ed. Glynn L. Isaac and Elizabeth R. McCown (Menlo Park, Calif.: Benjamin-Cummings, 1976), p. 131.

[8]The observations of macaque innovative behavior were first reported by J. Itani, "On the Acquisition and Propagation of a New Food Habit in the Troop of Japanese Monkeys at Takasakiyama," *Primates* 1 (1958), pp. 84–98. They have been summarized by Jane B. Lancaster, *Primate Behavior and the Emergence of Human Culture* (New York: Holt, Rinehart & Winston, 1975), pp. 45–46.

Photo courtesy of Dr. William R. Maples, Florida State Museum, University of Florida

Baboons raiding a farmer's field by a roadside in Kenya. Crop thievery is an innovation, like potato washing among Japanese macaques.

of macaque on Koshima Island was foraging on a sandy beach. Sweet potatoes had been dropped on the ground and were covered with sand. Monkeys avoid gritty food, and this is likely biologically based: the grit will wear down the teeth to the gumline, which will cause a monkey to starve. Millenia of natural selection created an aversion to sand-covered food. But the solution to the problem was, here, a deliberate choice.

A one-and-a-half-year-old female picked up a sand-covered potato, washed it in water, and contentedly sat down to eat. The simple and effective invention was adopted by her playmates at first, then by their mothers and, at last, by the rest of the group. Perhaps here, the researchers suggested, was a model for behavioral change—for the kinds of innovations that likely occurred in the past. It began among younger animals who had not mastered all of the rules. This is not because the young are adventurous and the elderly are set in their ways. That explains very little; in fact, it tells us nothing at all. I suspect that innovative behavior most often begins with the young because results are uncertain, and survival itself is at stake. Suppose there was a less happy ending—that the water was a poisonous pool. When the potato was washed and consumed, the innovator would die. Such misfired creativity almost certainly occurred in the past. If the inventors were those who were older, then the risk would be greater for all. Reproduction, defense, and food capture are performed by the adults in the group, as are the critical behaviors of nurturant care. It is adults who are less expendable, from the standpoint of natural selection. This would explain why, in primate societies, innovations begin with the young and why they spread very slowly to adults that are part of the group.

I believe it is a reasonable premise that such a process occurred in the past. Young apes, on the fringes of forest, soon discovered a new source of food. They may have scavenged an animal carcass and then sought security back in the trees. The single innovation was a crucial behavioral change.[9] From it, came a network of changes affecting body, behavior, and brain. The tapestry of life on this planet was never to be the same.

Hunting and biological evolution

The new strategy had quick repercussions on the appearance of early humanity. Our skeletons changed, and we moved through the world on two feet. I suspect that this process was rapid and grew out of our hunting existence. More than anything else, it developed from sharing our food.

There is no reason to assume the first humans had been generous right from the start. Very possibly, like modern orangutans—and chimpanzees, to a certain extent—they rarely shared food; they consumed every bit by themselves.[10] But such strategy is a poor adaptation when scavenging and hunting is the basis of life. This technology is a social behavior, unlike foraging for insects or seeds.

The solitary hunter, in all likelihood, seldom survived. He[11] would have scanned a much smaller area than hunters operating in groups and been less successful in trying to kill larger prey. Most important, he was totally dependent on the sum of his technical skills. He did not have available the variety of skills in a group. Through the pressure of natural selection, group hunting evolved. Reinforcing this social technology was a tradition of sharing one's food. It was the daily reward for involvement in a hunting society.

Consequences for our social behavior have reverberated down to the present. At the moment, we should notice the effect on our body and gait. Sharing most often meant carrying meat back from a kill.[12] Armloads were shared with the others who were part of the group. Killing was most effective from a two-footed (bipedal) stance. A club could be used

---

[9]Scavenging was a likely prelude to the earliest hunting. Reasons for this are explored in the following section.

[10]Orangutans and chimpanzees, both highly omnivorous, routinely share only the meat of occasional small vertebrate prey. Their adaptive patterns are summarized by Birute M. F. Galdikas and Geza Teleki, "Variations in Subsistence Activities of Female and Male Pongids: New Perspectives on the Origins of Hominid Labor Division," *Current Anthropology*, June 1981, pp. 241–47.

[11]I am using this pronoun advisedly. Evidence of hunting as a male activity will be discussed in a later part of this chapter.

[12]This includes the kills made by humans themselves as well as carnivore kills that were scavenged.

Illustration by Gail Delicio

Food sharing among early humans.

or a stone could be hurled at the prey. These behaviors selected in favor
of a series of genetic mutations for a body that was perfectly balanced on
the soles of its feet.

This is why, as Glynn Isaac has argued, the early sites in the Rift Valley
region contain evidence of carrying activities as well as butchered re-

mains. Deeper layers of Koobi Fora in Kenya—about 2.5 million years old—contain tiny stone flakes and a litter of broken bones.[13] The flakes were remarkably similar to the fragments of stone used today by hunters and herders when they butcher a carcass for food. When Isaac was living in Kenya, he encountered a Shangilla herdsman butchering an antelope killed earlier by a lion. Metal tools are used by the Shangilla, but the herdsman had forgotten his knife. He picked up a cobble of lava and broke off a thumbnail-size flake. Watching him, Isaac remembered the flakes at his site. The herdsman split open the carcass and trimmed off the usable meat. It seems almost certain that this often was done in the past.

Tools used in the butchering process were often not found locally. At times, they were carried from sources for over a mile. Humans, capable of transporting tools and of hunting and butchering prey, were conceivably transporting meat and sharing their kill.

The new strategy was quickly adopted; it offered an abundance of food. It may also have been accelerated for biological reasons. Apes that evolved into humans likely hung from the branches of trees. They *moved hand-over-hand* in a pattern called *brachiation.* The structure of a shoulder blade fragment excavated at Sterkfontein suggests our possible evolution from animals that moved in this way.[14] This would have meant a rapid transition to an animal that could walk on two feet. In brachiation, as in two-footed movement, the body is held in a more vertical stance. Massive skeletal change was not needed to walk as we do.

More than that, early scavenging and hunting may have directly affected our size. I believe it was a critical factor in species formation. As Susan Cachel has suggested, the size of a predator species is often directly related to the size of its prey.[15] In early Africa, primitive humans had at the most a club or a stone. The material culture of hunting was not yet complex. This would have meant that size was important—a crucial element in making the kill. The animals of Africa selected for hominid species.

Wild pigs, waterbuck, and antelope were medium-size prey. They were successfully hunted by humans who were smaller in size. Elephant, giraffe, hippopotami, and zebralike horses also selected for a hunter that was taller and heavier.[16] Lighter-boned and robust lineages consequently

---

[13]The Koobi Fora stone tools are described by G. L. Isaac, "The Activities of Early African Hominids: A Review of Archaeological Evidence from the Time Span Two and a Half to One Million Years Ago," in Isaac and McCown, *Human Origins,* pp. 496–500.

[14]C. E. Oxnard, "A Note on the Fragmentary Sterkfontein Scapula," *American Journal of Physical Anthropology* 28 (1968), pp. 213–17.

[15]Susan Cachel, "A New View of Speciation in *Australopithecus,*" in *Paleoanthropology: Morphology and Paleoecology,* ed. Russell H. Tuttle (The Hague: Mouton, 1975), pp. 183–201. The "new view" is a valuable and elegant approach to early human evolution.

[16]An older view that the earliest hominids preferred to hunt immature prey has not been sustained by more recent archeological research. Isaac's Koobi Fora article mentions this point.

H. Armstrong Roberts

Apes may have required relatively few changes to become adapted to upright posture.

came into existence. Both likely resulted from the prey that they chose to pursue.

This scenario is not in agreement with, for example, John Robinson's view. For Robinson, the large molar teeth in the heavy-boned hominid fossils were evidence of a lineage of humans that feasted on plants. But tooth size may have had little relation to the diets of the earliest humans.

It might, instead, have been related to the quantity of food that they ate. Their larger bodies required more nourishment, which affected the shape of the skull. Molar teeth, over time, became larger; this made it possible to process more food. The increase in their size led to growth in the size of the jaw. One set of jaw muscles attaches to an area at the top of the skull. Gowth in these muscles selected for a sagittal crest. Large molars are questionable evidence of a prehistoric diet of plants. They may have been a simple adaptation to the animal's size. Beyond that, they are improperly structured for a fruit-, root- and nut-eating life. Crowns are lower and roots are much deeper than the ones in a plant eater's teeth. Their ancient teeth were like those of an omnivore—an animal that eats plants and meat. More than likely, *all* ancient humanity, about 3 million years before the present, followed a pattern of gathering and hunting in their African home.

If humanity was "prey-selected," as Susan Cachel has suggested, coexistence was probably peaceful—at least at the start. Smaller humans pursued smaller animals; the larger hunters killed larger prey. Although they lived in the same environment—the vast mosaic of grassland and wood—their strategies were different; they rarely competed for food.

But likely from the very beginning, small humans faced a different competitor: a hunter nearly as social and brainy as they. Four-footed, carnivorous, clever—wild dogs had arrived in their world, after long evolution in America, Asia, and Europe. Skeletal remains of these predators have been found near the South African Cape. The layers that preserved them were possibly 4 million years old. To the north, near Lake Rudolf in Kenya, is the massive Shungura Formation: layer after layer of silt, clay, and volcanic ash. Close to the bottom of the strata—which is nearly 4 million years old—were the bones of *Lycaon,* an ancestor of African dogs.[17]

Inhabiting the mosaic environment, the dogs likely caught middle-size prey. Perhaps, like their modern descendants, they hunted in groups and shared their food. Communicating by barking and yelping, they may have coordinated kill after kill. But there were curious, two-legged beings afoot in the land.

Strategy competed with strategy; brain was in a race against brain. Wild dogs were carnivorous animals with a specialized pattern of life. They had evolved no alternative system for getting their food. All early humans were omnivores—they hunted and also ate plants. But humanity was faced with the problem of seasonal change. Rains in the forests and grasslands would slacken as dry days began. In the season of minimal rainfall, plant food was harder to find. Nutritonal stress was very likely a part of our past. Anthropologist Milford H. Wolpoff has examined aus-

---

[17]The estimated date of the Lower Shungura is taken from W. W. Bishop, "Pliocene Problems Relating to Human Evolution," Isaac and McCown, *Human Origins,* pp. 144–45. The date of the South African material is taken from Cachel, "A New View," pp. 183–201.

tralopithecine teeth. Often the growth of enamel had stopped and then started again.[18] The pattern is typical of childhood nutritional stress. It is conceivable that, during these periods, hunting provided most of the food. Competition with dogs was severe in the season of drought.

Anatomy was—partially—destiny; at least, it played a significant role. It is true that a two-legged hunter was not as fast as the four-footed kind, but speed was not a necessary factor in hunting success. George Schaller once cornered a wildebeest and then quickly got out of its way.[19] He was not part of a group and did not have a club or a stone. Early humans, if armed and together, could likely have taken such prey. Our two-footed stance meant that weapons were easily used. Beyond that, it would seem very likely that humans met dogs at the kill. Meat-eating species competed for a freshly killed prey. In such encounters, weapons were useful for preventing a pirated kill. Stones could be thrown at the dogs and the meat butchered and carried away. The canines, skulking back later, would nibble at bones. Even when the dogs were successful, only limited food could be shared. The animals dined on a carcass, then returned to the rest of the pack. They regurgitated food, and the hungry ones ate it again. This picture—not especially pleasant—is important for understanding our past. Wild dogs were severely limited in the quantity of meat they brought back; and part of *that* was digested and lost on the journey back home. Early humans, with armloads of meat, clearly had an adaptive advantage: a few successful hunters could provide enough food for the group.

For these reasons, the odds of the contest were weighted heavily for the humans. Early humans were capturing food at the expense of the dogs. This would explain why the African canines today are crepuscular hunters: they chase prey at the first morning light and at the last part of the day. These few hours were all that was left to them by the humans who were active by day and the various species of cats that hunted at night.

The contest, before it was ended, may have lasted for millions of years. It had selected for larger-brained humans, capable of designing new skills for the hunt. Conceivably, if dogs could communicate, it selected for the emergence of hominid speech. Human vocalizations were useful in taking prey. Techniques that came out of this process provided unexpected rewards. As hunting became more efficient, it became the best way to survive.[20] Smaller humans had now become a match for the larger-sized prey.

The lineage of larger humanity had been spared this competition for

---

[18]Milford H. Wolpoff, *Paleoanthropology* (New York: Alfred A. Knopf, 1980), p. 151.

[19]Experiments in prey capture are discussed by George B. Schaller and Gordon R. Lowther, "The Relevance of Carnivore Behavior to the Study of Early Hominids," *Southwestern Journal of Anthropology*, Winter 1969. A highly readable summary is offered by John E. Pfeiffer, *The Emergence of Man* (New York: Harper & Row, 1972), pp. 130–32.

[20]This concept, which here is simply stated, will be elaborated in the next chapter.

prey. It had continued to pursue larger animals for millions of years. In the absence of competitive pressure, its brain grew at a much slower rate. Its methods of hunting very likely changed little at all. Ultimately, smaller-size humans probably forced the line into extinction, but exactly how the event might have happened remains to be found. There may have been aggressive encounters, or it might have been more subtle than that. A group of communicating people, armed and intelligent, dismembering prey would perhaps not be threatened at all by a smaller-brained group. The elephant, giraffe, and the hippo became the food for the more adept hunters. Robust humanity dwindled; in time they were gone.

I believe that the fossil materials lend support to this view of the past; but I believe it is necessary to evaluate a problem of time.[21] Richard Leakey's Turkana discoveries—especially the 1470 skull—are evidence that *Homo habilis* is ancient in date. The KBS Tuff that lies over it may be 2.6 million years old. Specimens below it might be even older in time. But the potassium-argon method, which provided the date for the Tuff, like all such techniques, can result in erroneous dates. Animal bones in that layer were very similar to those found at Omo, a fossil bed near Lake Turkana, not far to the north. But the animal assemblage at Omo was 1.8 million years old! Is *Homo habilis* a million years younger than Leakey believes? I suspect that this might be the case; certainly there is evidence for reasonable doubt. The troublesome KBS bone scrap was also similar to Olduvai fos-

The author's interpretation of human biological evolution. It should be viewed very tentatively. Many alternative theories exist.

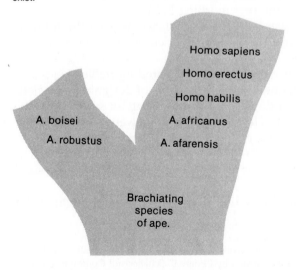

Homo sapiens

Homo erectus

Homo habilis

A. boisei   A. africanus

A. robustus   A. afarensis

Brachiating
species
of ape.

[21]My view of the KBS Tuff chronology was influenced by Wolpoff's arguments in *Paleoanthropology*, p. 15.

sils. This comparison suggested they were less than 2 million years old; and when a totally different physical method was applied to the KBS Tuff, the date that resulted was about 2.2 million years. The dovetailing of all these discoveries suggests that these hominids were younger in date. The *Homo habilis* materials are probably 2 million years old.

The question is much more than a quibble about layers, bone scraps, and dates. If we accept the younger date as the right one, we see a sequence begin to unfold. *Australopithecus afarensis*—"Lucy" and the bones from Hadar—were conceivably the earliest of humans anywhere in the world. If we separate the rest of the fossils into light-boned and robust remains, it is possible to see how their appearance was changing through time. Among the smaller, more delicate humans, *Australopithecus africanus* was next. Its fossils are approximately 2.5 million years old.[22] We may follow them by *Homo habilis*, if we accept that the date has been changed. *Homo erectus* humanity was the next to appear. The heavy-boned, larger human beings would begin with *Australopithecus robustus*. They likely first appeared about 2 million years ago. Some 300,000 years later, *Australopithecus boisei* evolved. They survived for 200 millenia and then were gone from the world.

These dated and labeled discoveries have been approached in a much different way. Anthropologist David Pilbeam has calculated the weight of each species, using skeletal materials and the findings of primate anatomy. When the weights and brain sizes together are recorded as points on a graph, the points for the species result in two separate lines. The lines are in total agreement with the sequences I mentioned above.[23] More than that, in the lighter-boned lineage, the brain was rapidly increasing in size. In fact, it was increasing much faster than the size of the body. In the lineage of robust humans, that trend was exactly reversed. They grew larger in size but were never very "brainy" at all.

These discoveries are closely in keeping with the theory of Susan Cachel. Competition with social carnivores selected for a larger-sized brain—among smaller human beings who were hunters of middle-size prey. This agrees with the dates for the fossils and with what we know of the African past, especially its seasons and the animal groups that lived there.[24] It links a

---

[22]Based on the dating of Sterkfontein and Makapansgat in Wolpoff, *Paleoanthropology*, p 139.

[23]The only difference is my early placement of *Australopithecus afarensis*. Inadequate cranial materials prevents the brain size from being known. It therefore cannot be recorded on Pilbeam's graph. This investigation, which also involved paleontologist Stephen Jay Gould, was described in "Size and Scaling in Human Evolution," *Science* 186 (1974), pp. 892–901. A good discussion of it is provided by Gould in his very enjoyable *Ever since Darwin: Reflections in Natural History* (New York W. W. Norton, 1977), pp. 179–85.

[24]The sexual dimorphism theory could be part of this view of our past, but at the moment there is little fossil evidence to lend it support. R. B. Eckhardt has noted that none of these African fossils present sufficient evidence for (or against) such a theory. See the discussion in Tuttle, *Paleoanthropology*, p. 288.

lineage to *Homo erectus*, the species that was later in time, and it generates a pattern of smooth technological change. As we will see in the chapter that follows, the strategy of hunting increased. It became more complex and spread to many parts of the world. But the tradition had roots that went deeper—back to the African grassland and trees—where ancient humans and four-footed hunters competed and killed.

Hunting and human society

What we know of our ancient biology, and of the vast out-of-doors that we shared, can tell us something about how our early behavior might well have been. Biologically, our brain was increasing, growing in size and complexity. The growth of the cerebral cortex—the outer layer of brain cells—made it possible to learn a more complicated manner of life. Information about the environment could be stored in those outermost cells. Imitation (and speech?) could transmit the information through time.

The growth of the brain's information is a subtle behavioral fact. Something curious was happening to the groups on the African plains. Much more than their tree-dwelling ancestors did, they *thought* about the external world. Necessarily, this thinking was different than thinking today. Certainly I am not using the word in the modern philosophical sense. I mean, for example, that an edible grass stem would be seen and remembered. A pool of posion water was viewed and remembered with fear. The intricate cerebral cortex is the classifying part of our brain. It screens out a million sensations; it concentrates on particular ones. It helps us to notice whatever is important to us. An array of ideas was growing and separating us from the world. Our behavior was increasingly guided by thoughts in our heads.

Our environment also was changing, at least partly because of the brain. The possibility of conscious invention was rapidly growing through time. This could lead to new forms of behavior—this is part of our external world—which in turn would select for a brain that could learn even more. More than that, this made life problematic for other brains that were sharing the land. Social carnivores, too, were evolving; their brains were increasing in size. Very possibly, their methods of hunting were growing complex. This meant that the earliest people had to polish their hunting techniques. The process affected the structure of human society.

The very earliest groups of humanity, perhaps 3 million years in the past, were scavenging carcasses and gathering fruits, roots, and seeds. They were small, about four feet in height, and could not capture even middle-size prey. Even if they *had* managed to do so—such instances must have been rare—one wonders how they cut up the meat to transport it away. Not until about 2 million years ago was humanity making stone tools. Wherever we find them, they seldom are very well worked. At Omo, they were mere broken pebbles, showing hardly any pattern at all. The same is true of the earliest tools at the Olduvai site. In the KBS Tuff at Turkana was a scattering of broken stones. Nearly patternless, they are among the most primitive tools ever made.[25]

And earlier? We are lacking the evidence, but conceivably they used sticks and bones. Stones, if they were useful at all, were for throwing at dogs. Sticks and bones were for grubbing up insects and digging roots from the African grass. The limitations of material culture led to a highly omnivorous life. Plant foods, roots, insects, bird eggs, and pirated game were probably the earliest diet in human prehistory.

It seems likely that, even this early, ancient humanity was sharing its food. Wild dogs in the forest and grassland were hunters active by day. Because mouthfuls—and gutfuls—of food were all that these animals could carry back home, carcasses of meat were abandoned on the African plains. The prey was already cut open; fresh meat could be carried back home. Two-legged African scavengers were equipped for protecting their food. Stones could be thrown at the vultures that often competed for a kill. They could be hurled at the straggling dogs who would not go away.

Sharing of meat was a critical feature of survival in the African world. Primatologist Katherine Milton has argued that the protein obtained in this way was particularly suited to the needs of the earliest humans.[26] Our species depends upon proteins for the amino acids of which they are made. Chains of protein brought into the body are broken down into thousands of parts. These are put back together to manufacture the proteins we need. The proteins in meat come assembled in ways that are useful to us: there is less rearrangement required to put them to use. Then too, it is generously packaged: wild pigs have more protein than seeds. Meateating is often more efficient than gathering plants. More than that, during the African droughts meat protein was especially needed. Infants and their lactating mothers require protein on a regular basis. If they fail to obtain it, there is a good chance the infant will die. During a drought, when plant food was scanty, meat was more necessary than at any other time. Food sharing was especially prevalent when the weather was dry.

These novel, two-footed behaviors selected for changes in our skeletal frame, and those changes quickly had an effect upon human society. The pelvis became somewhat smaller, which permitted a more balanced gait. But it profoundly affected the complexity of hominid life. Among females, a narrower pelvis meant facility in walking about; but it also might have meant greater problems in child-birth. Through a powerful adaptive arrangement, in time the dilemma became solved. Our brains—unlike those of all other primates—developed *after* the time of our birth. Inquisitive and helpless, young humans came into the world.

---

[25]Wolpoff, *Paleoanthropology*, p. 166.

[26]Katherine Milton, "Distribution Patterns of Tropical Plant Foods as an Evolutionary Stimulus to Primate Mental Development," *American Anthropologist* 83 (1981), pp. 543–45.

Born with brains that had just begun growing, infants were dependent on nurturant care. Dependency is true of all infants, but usually for a very short time. A colt shakily stands; very soon it will graze on its own. Human infants, born totally helpless, were dependent for a much longer time. This meant that a human could learn a great deal as a child. Beyond that, over thousands of years, our brains would double—even triple—in size. Our brains grew *after* birth, and so the pelvic limitation was gone. In a world of competitive carnivores, the change had particular value. New strategies were created and learned by a larger-size brain.

Dependency brought a new transformation to the rhythms of hominid life. A mother, with a new born infant, needed food for herself and her child. Protein, especially, was required for nurturant care. If a female hunted or scavenged, she endangered herself and her child. Food sharing in our earliest culture was beginning to change. Scavenging and hunting was done by the males; hominid females gathered plants. A division of labor was created in human society.

The new pattern, I think, was a tendency; it was not an invariable rule. If it *had* been invariable, we likely would not have survived. Changes in the plants and seasons, predator pressure, and the threat of disease: any one of these could easily alter the needs of the group. Then too, there were subtler questions. How many women were nursing their children? How many were about to give birth? How many had children beginning to live on their own? The arrangement was flexibly altered; there was a blurring of sexual roles. The strategy was probably never an unchangeable rule.

Out of these social arrangements, came a remarkable human invention. Recognition of *kinship* developed in ancient society. The discovery was, in fact, an idea developed in the cortical part of our brain. It was a classification of the members that lived in a group. It was a *concept of organic relatedness; the recognition of a biological link.* It has affected humanity's behavior for millions of years.

For the first generations of humans, mating could well have been a random affair. Sexual activity had few limitations at all. This is likely because the first peoples followed a highly omnivorous life. There were insects, fruits, roots, berries, and, occasionally, pirated meat. Collecting available plant foods was a task that could be done alone. It was only the capture of meat that required a group. If conflicts occurred over mating, these did not pose a serious threat. Technological patterns would hardly have been altered at all. This is probably why omnivorous primates, such as forest-dwelling chimpanzees, have very few restrictions on mating within their society.[27]

The nurturant mothers with children brought a change to productive

---

[27]Behavioral patterns of forest chimpanzees are described by Vernon Reynolds, *The Biology of Human Action* (New York Oxford University Press, 1976).

arrangements. Females remained longer with their offspring as the period of dependency grew. This increased the requirement for captured and shared protein. Males were hunting more often and competing with dogs for a kill. Their behavior was becoming cohesive—they learned the habits of those in the group. Conflict would have presented a threat to technological life.[28]

At least two strategies were possible at this juncture of human existence. We might have developed a dominance structure akin to that of savanna baboons. Who mates with whom, and how often, would have caused little conflict at all. Conceivably, more-powerful males might have had the first pick of a mate, and less-powerful males would have had a more limited choice. An alternative behavioral pathway was to mate with an external group. A pattern would exist: you would not choose your mate from "at home."

In all likelihood, both of these games were attempted by early societies.[29] But the second, I think, was a much better game than the first. Mating with another society reduced conflict that could happen at home—and it also introduced a new system of social relations. Adults in these early societies almost certainly cared for their children, in both an emotional and nurturant sense of the word. Caring, itself, was an outgrowth of the helplessness of hominid infants. As helplessness lengthened, our caring grew stronger as well. This meant that a young adult human, leaving home for another society, was part of a matrix of caring that lasted for years. By joining the other society, a new set of relations was born. If you harmed the other society, you might easily harm one of your own people. If you often could help them, your own would become more secure. This was true for the other society when they sent a young human to you. The new system created a bundle of social behaviors. As Claude Levi-Strauss has suggested, mate exchange was a "total exchange"; it bound separate cultures together in intricate ways.[30]

---

[28]This reconstruction closely parallels that of R. L. Holloway, "Early Hominid Endocasts: Volumes, Morphology and Significance for Hominid Evolution," in *Primate Functional Morphology and Evolution*, ed. R. H. Tuttle (The Hague: Mouton, 1975), p. 409. The origin of such intra-group conflict was very probably the hunting technology which selected for preferential and monogamous mating. Females required those males most capable of providing them with food. Males required the healthiest females, due to the lengthy period of nurturant care. Monogamy "closed" such pair-bonds to genetic exchange with less-adapted individuals. This also limited the number of available mates. Not surprisingly, monogamous mating systems of mammals are frequent among social carnivores. See David P. Barash, *Sociobiology and Behavior* (New York; 1977 Elsevier), 160-162.

[29]A game, here, is an evolutionary strategy in which survival could well be at stake. This particular approach to the past is discussed by John Maynard Smith, "The Evolution of Behavior," *Scientific American*, September 1978, pp. 176–94. A well-written discussion of evolutionary games appears in Nigel Calder, *The Life Game: Evolution and the New Biology* (New York: Dell Publishing, 1973), pp. 34–69.

[30]Claude Levi-Strauss, *The Elementary Structures of Kinship* (Boston: Beacon Press, 1969), pp. 60–61.

From the beginning, it probably made possible the earliest webs of *exchange*: the *trade of services, goods, and information between human societies.* Plant and animal resources, tools, stones, and help with a hunt—all of these could be given from one human group to the next. A gift might include information about predators, plant food, or game. A fabric of adaptive relations was quickly evolved.

It seems to me very likely that women were the persons exchanged. The African environment selected for humans with more information. Because of this, the period of infant dependency grew. This escalated protein requirements and scavenging and hunting activities. The technology was practiced by males and performed as a group. Competitors were social carnivores; they had cohesively organized packs. To survive, it was necessary to be as cohesive as they were. If a male left his society and a new male was gained in exchange, the new arrival would require adjustments to the meat-getting group. The practice, done over and over, would have damaged their technical skills. The meat would be lost to the dogs, and the humans would die.[31].

To reinforce the adaptive behavior, this became a psychological rule: the people among whom you were born were now thought of as being your kin. Other people on the African plains were not kinfolk at all. Very likely, the earliest kin groups included a cadre of males, females without mates, elder people, and a scattering of children. Out of these simple beginnings came intricate systems of rules stating who was related and who was an eligible mate. It was not a sheer love of complexity that gave rise to these elaborate thoughts. Humanity, as Robin Fox has suggested, would inhabit many parts of the world. We would experience diversity in he material conditions of life. Warfare and changes in technology would require new "permanent groups." Our rules would adjust; we would develop new systems of kin.[32]

The pattern already established was the atom of an elaborate structure that would slowly unfold with the growth of our hunting existence. Permanent groupings of males, already allied through mates and exchange, would combine their strategic behaviors in hunting large prey. Possibly, these larger alliances would conceive of one another as kin. A flexible idea would adapt to the natural world.

It is difficult, at least at the moment, to say which early hominid species experienced these changes in social and technological life. *Australopithecus afarensis* and *Australopithecus africanus* perhaps had a culture adapted

---

[31]A similar reconstruction is presented by Pierre L. van den Berghe, *Man in Society: A Biosocial View* (New York: Elsevier, 1975), pp. 36–40.

[32]Robin Fox, "Kinship Categories as Natural Categories," in *Evolutionary Biology and Social Behavior: An Anthropological Perspective*, ed. Napoleon A. Chagnon and William Irons (North Scituate, Mass.: Duxbury Press, 1979), pp. 134–35.

to demands of the hunt. But there was a time in that lineage of hunters when a novel transformation occurred. In all human evolution, the event never happened again. We know from the fossilized skeletons, and from the patterns of their bodies and brains, that a lineage of larger humanity came into existence. Brains were smaller in relation to bodies in this new human line. They diverged and survived for millenia—and then they were gone.

I suspect that this distant divergence grew out of our hunting behavior. Indeed, without hunting, I doubt it could have happened at all. As the pursuit and killing of animals became polished in ancient society, it became possible for humans to hunt larger species of game. The pattern was especially possible because no competition existed. Wild dogs almost never hunted larger-size prey. This meant that the larger-size animals—elephant, hippo, and giraffe—evolved no avoidance behaviors to help them survive.

The new strategy, in the beginning, likely made little difference at all. Pioneering clusters of hunters killed elephants on the African plains. Old methods of hunting were used with the larger-size game. But, invisible to a living observer, a process had been set into motion. Over thousands of years, a new species of human was born.

The immediate cause of that process might not have been our bodies at all (though the two types of hunters *were* starting to differ in size). The brain, more than anything else, might have triggered this ancient divergence. Different systems of "wiring" were driving early humans apart. Hunters of middle-size animals faced competitors in getting their food. The hunters that lived were the ones with more intricate brains. Charles Laughlin and Eugene G. d'Aquili have argued that, out of this difference, came critical differences in the complexity of cultural life.[33] Child-rearing and food-sharing patterns, play, hunting, and systems of speech: these probably were made very different by two kinds of brains. Through the remarkable system of culture, an avoidance came into existence. The two lineages of humans evolved in their separate ways.

The others were living in Africa when *Homo erectus* was there. But their numbers were dwindling; they would never inherit the world. Skillful and larger-brained hunters, the descendants of competitive times, *Homo erectus* was killing the larger-size prey. The death of the robust lineage was a shadowy, distant event; but in a way it reminds us of something we choose to ignore. Humanity has no special privilege—no immunity to extinction at all. A human lineage vanished. Perhaps it will happen again.

Everywhere on the forested grasslands, there were carcasses left from the kill. A new kind of animal was leaving its mark in the world. The

---

[33]Charles D. Laughlin, Jr., and Eugene G. d'Aquili, *Biogenetic Structuralism* (New York: Columbia University Press, 1974), pp. 18–36.

hunters created new strategies, and they discovered uninhabited lands. There were vast herds of prey that had never seen humans at all. Slowly—and almost inevitably—hunters moved closer to Europe and Asia. Our lineage was exploring a tapestry of forest and steppe. Out of this would come new adaptations, generating a more intricate brain. New inheritors—African hunters—were leaving their homes.

4 / *Homo Erectus:* The Evolution of Hunting

In Heidelberg, not far from the University, there is a building that barely blends in with the Renaissance facades and mazes of winding brick streets. The anomaly is the city museum. It is a somber, mausoleumlike structure unnoticed by crowds on the sidewalks, rarely glimpsed by shoppers in streetcars that race down the alleys. For the occasional visitor who does wander in, an official awaits in the foyer. He asks if you wish something special and leads the way through a network of halls. He stops at the resting place of Heidelberg's earliest citizen.

For many, it is probably a disappointment.[1] It is a single glass case which contains a human jaw, nothing more. The jaw is complete, with nearly all of its teeth. It has a comparatively wide ramus (the vertical blade that attaches to the skull); it has no projecting chin, which is very different from our jawbones today. The remainder of Heidelberg man— the jaw was found in Mauer, seven miles from the city—has never been discovered, nor were there any traces of tools.

Why has this morsel attracted attention? Not because of what little was found, but because it is far to the north of the African plains. It belongs to a species of human that traveled to many parts of the world. *Australopithecus* and *Homo habilis* fossils have not been discovered in Europe or Asia. But *Homo erectus* remains have been found in that northerly world. In a valley of the Spanish Pyrenees, in Germany, Hungary, and France, bones and tools of the hunters were sealed by the earth. Europe was not their only new province. The earliest discoveries of *Homo erectus* were on a jungle-rimmed river in Java. The richest site of all is in China at Dragon Bone Hill.

In their appearance, they were somewhat more modern. Two million years of bipedal movement selected for leg bones that are much like our own. The entire skeleton, except for the skull, is strongly similar to ours. The skull, which is strikingly different, was probably adapted to a hunt-

The jaw in the cabinet

---

[1]The description of the jaw found in Mauer on the outskirts of Heidelberg is taken from William Howells, *Mankind in the Making: The Story of Human Evolution* (New York: Doubleday, 1967).

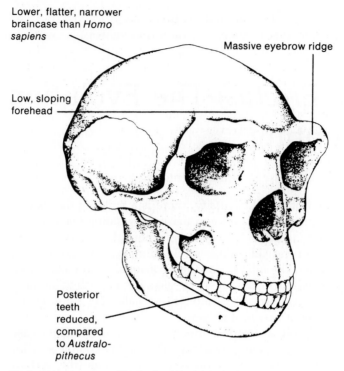

Lower, flatter, narrower braincase than *Homo sapiens*

Massive eyebrow ridge

Low, sloping forehead

Posterior teeth reduced, compared to *Australopithecus*

Skull of *Homo erectus*. The brain size of this species averaged two-thirds that of our own. Hunting probably selected for larger and more complex brains.

ing existence. Projecting, heavy-boned jaws were suitable for the chewing of meat. This required a back-sloping cranium to balance the skull on the spine. But more important than the skull was the brain that was protected inside.

Its mean size had approximately doubled, compared with humans of earlier times. Skull capacity of *Australopithecus,* on the average, was 450 cc.[2] Brain sizes of *Homo erectus* averaged out at 1000 cc. The smallest skulls of this wide-ranging species were close in size to those of *Homo habilis.* The largest of their brains are well within the modern-day range. The "braininess" that started in Africa now was reaching other parts of the world. Herds of animals in Europe and Asia that had never seen humans before were easy prey for the hunters that came to the northerly lands. But the animals learned to be cautious—or aggressive, if trapped in a hunt. In the north, as in Africa, brain was competing with brain.

---

[2]"CC" represents cubic centimeters (1 cm × 1 cm × 1 cm). The figure is often derived by filling a skull with shot then measuring the quantity required to fill it.

There are today, in the world's remote regions, societies that survive by hunting. They use strategies and information that evolved in humanity's past.[3] Caribou Eskimo and Siberian Tungus are not replicas of *Homo erectus*. With their fully modern brains, their societies are far more complex. Yet they do inhabit environments somewhat similar to ancient Eurasia: a world of marshes and cold-weather plants, where there are herds of big game. Anthropologist William S. Laughlin has studied living hunting societies in the hope of discovering what hunters were like in the past. He has encountered an elaborate complex of information, behavior, and tools that grew out of an intricate contest of hunter and prey. Almost as soon as a hunter is born, he is socialized into this complex. He begins to be schooled in the skills that will help him survive. Exercises to strengthen the tendons, competitive throwing of miniature darts: both are in the repertory required to live in that world. Beyond that is ethological knowledge—the understanding of animal prey: when and where do they feed: How often? are they likely to fight?

Several days before pursuing an animal, a hunter begins searching for signs. Relying upon his knowledge of local animals, their plant foods, their tracks, and their feces, he is led to an area where the species is apt to be found.

If he is fortunate, he will actually see them. Even then, he will rarely kill an animal, but will stalk for hours, and sometimes for days, to get as close to the animal as possible before making the kill. Now he is concerned with the freshness of the tracks and the behavioral patterns of his quarry. He will need to know the flight distance—the space at which the prey will attempt to escape. If the animal is aggressive, he needs to know the signs of a fight.

The kill is usually made at a distance of around 30 feet. the animal is butchered, and the parts are carried back to the camp. For the butchering, the hunter is reliant upon his anatomical knowledge. Is the hide of the animal to be used for clothing, or will it be cut into strips for a line? Depending on the purpose, different butchering patterns are used. Information is also required for the butchering of internal organs. Some structures are edible—a cultural decision—but others are not eaten at all. Long bones can be split to make awls; tendons and ligaments are useful as twine. An animal carcass is useful in multiple ways. Living hunters are thus highly knowledgeable in what we usually call gross anatomy, a fact that was known when this century had hardly begun. Skirokogorov, a Soviet anthropologist, lived among the Siberian Tungus. He discovered that the Tungus hunter is interested, as Laughlin said, ". . . in the comparative study of bones and soft parts of the body and he comes to form

---

[3]William Laughlin, "Hunting: An Integrating Biobehavior System and Its Evolutionary Importance," in *Man The Hunter*, ed. Richard B. Lee and Irven Devore (Hawthorne, N.Y.: Aldine Publishing, 1968).

a good idea as to the anatomical similarities and dissimilarities in animals and even man."

This maze of behavior and knowledge was required for the solitary hunter. Such lone expeditions have probably always occurred. In a season of drought, or in winter, game animals are harder to find. Hunters must scatter and look for food on their own. But hunters that sought larger animals—mammoth, rhino, and giant baboon—had to hunt as a group, or they probably would not have survived. The systems of scattering and hunting in groups were closely related. Social hunting is more than technology; it is also a form of exchange. Strategies of tracking and killing, butchering methods, and ways to make tools were created and shared among the members of a hunting society. The sharing itself made possible new techniques for the hunting of prey. Three different methods of stalking could be blended into a different approach. On the next expedition, the strategy could be tested. In lean times, when hunters were scattered, each one would very likely survive. He had developed his own skills and had learned from his life in the group.

Other learning was also required, if a group was to be successful at all. Animals were adapting to hunters; this often made them more dangerous prey. It was necessary to know the behaviors of people around you. The hunters who were more (or less !) skillful, the younger, the experienced, the ones not as strong: these quirky, individual traits had to be understood. A notion of human personality was beginning to emerge—growing out of the spiraling contest of hunter and prey.

Tools and hunting: The mind's evolution

The knowledge of another's behavior, ideas, emotions, and moods was useful for the prevention of conflict in the hunting society. On the surface, this seems fairly obvious, yet the process was highly complex. It involved both symbolic behaviors and ways to respond. A *symbol,* in any society, is a *thing which represents something else.*[4] A smile or a frown carry meaning everywhere in the world. In a sense, the understanding of symbols was required in the world of the hunt. If an animal snorts through its nostrils, does this indicate anger or fear? For a wrong interpretation, a hunter could forfeit his life. Very likely this schooling in symbols was transferred to human society. You learned about smiles and grimaces, about pushing and baring of teeth. You learned what was friendly or threatening and what to ignore. But beyond the decoding of symbols, we must understand ways to respond. If a frown does not mean you are threatened, then violence would not be correct. Indeed, such reactions would jeopardize any society. So, each symbol is matched with a for-

---

[4]Symbolic behavior, here only mentioned, will be discussed in more detail in Chapters on Neanderthal times.

Chimpanzees and an orangutan at play. Widespread
among species of mammals, play seems genetically
influenced. It has probably always been characteristic
of humans.

mula—a highly workable way to respond. Coding, decoding, and customs were growing complex.

These critical symbolic behaviors were also part of the nurturant world:
the subtle interactional system of mother and child. The bearing and nursing
of children, and release from demands of the hunt, meant that females

were especially concerned with the care of the young. That care involved socialization—teaching the meanings that are shared by the group. Almost certainly it involved supervision of the meanings in play.

We all play. Every human society has its games that are shared by the young. More complicated patterns of playing persist through our lives. In these harmless, theatrical movements such as chasing, wrestling, and hide-and-go-seek, there is casual preparation for the games of a serious world. More than that, human play is symbolic: there is a message that "this is just play." Our stances and facial expressions communicate that we are just having fun.[5] In fact, we can only have fun when we master the code. Adult females, perhaps more than males, watched over this make-believe time. Separating the inevitable bullies, interfering when play was too rough, they introduced children to the richness of symbolized life.[6]

This network of social relations created a group called a *band:* the simplest and most ancient structure of human existence. *Numbering perhaps about 25 people, believing themselves to be kin, they lived from the animals and plants of the natural world.* Whatever power was in such societies was probably shifting and fluid through time. A good hunter was likely a leader among a group that embarked on a hunt. A person with trading "connections" was useful in times of exchange. Old people were important for memory—knowing the events that occurred in the past. Such a system was *egalitarian.* It had *no permanent center of power.* It was the earliest political system to exist in the world.

In the marginal parts of our planet, there are bands that are living today. From them, we can reckon what bands may have been like in the past. Beyond that, there is more direct evidence: the materials dug out of the ground. In a moment, we will look at the postholes, the charred bones and deposits of skulls that are the evidence of hunting and ritual in Asia and Europe. But first we might glance at the "lithics"—stone tools that the hunters once used. Imperishable and patterned, they are clues to behavioral change.

The toolkit of *Homo erectus*—"Acheulean," as it is formally known—was more efficient than the choppers and flakes of an earlier time.[7] Yet it grew from that ancient tradition, which is the pattern of cultural change.

---

[5]The symbolic "vocabulary" of children's play is described by N. G. Blurton-Jones, "An Ethological Study of some Aspects of Social Behavior of Children in Nursery School," *Primate Ethology* (Hawthorne, N.Y.: Aldine Publishing, 1967). A review of evolutionary aspects of child behavior studies is provided by John E. Pfeiffer, *The Emergence of Man* (New York: Harper & Row, 1972), pp. 474–83.

[6]We should guard against the easy temptation to view this process in terms of ourselves. The play patterns of *Homo erectus* were very likely as different from ours as our "recess" is different from the games of the Amazon Basin. Attitudes toward bullying behavior and definitions of what is too rough are remarkably varied in the play groups of different societies.

[7]A description of *Homo erectus* toolmaking techniques appears in Francois Bordes, *The Old Stone Age* (London: World University Library, 1968), p. 51.

Photo by Billy E. Barnes

Young humans at play. The activities are socialization into the intricate world of symbols. The situation was likely also true of our past.

Innovations are built from behaviors that worked in the past. As early as 2 million years ago, human beings struck flakes from a core. The flakes themselves were useful for butchering, and the core could be used as a tool. A pair of side-by-side scallops left in the core—the scars from removing the flake—would produce a very crude cutting edge.

As a minimal change in this pattern, more pairings were struck from the core. The wavy edge lengthened; the core was becoming less round. This hand axe was held in the palm; perhaps it was used as a butchering tool.

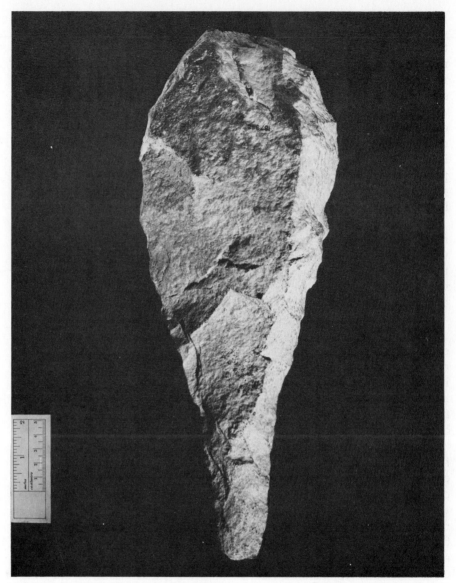

Field Museum of Natural History

A handaxe. The straighter edge was achieved by using a hammer of bone or antler.

However, a problem persisted, and the method of toolmaking changed. A wavy edge is not as sharp as a straight one, and this fact was discovered in time. An improvement was made by a new kind of tool used to make tools. Instead of striking one stone with another—which is what left the irregular scars—a soft hammer was used for removing the flakes from the core. This, perhaps, was a bone or antler; it made greater control possible. Regular flakes were removed from the axes; the round core became a flattened tool. Both faces of an axe were prepared in very much the same way. A tool known as a "cleaver" was fashioned through the novel technique. Looking something like a modern-day axe head, its edge was remarkably straight. It may have been used for dismembering larger-size prey.

There might be more to these tools than their functions and the procedures through which they were made. They are possibly a record of change in humanity's mind. "Mind," it has been noted, is "minding"; it is a process, not really a "thing."[8] More exactly, it amounts to the logic performed by our brains. For Thomas Wynn, the stone axes and cleavers are a reflection of logic at work.[9] Without certain kinds of thinking, the lithics could not have been made.

Consider an early toolmaker about to fashion a cleaver from stone. The flattened core is in his hand; he will flake it from left to right. Hopefully, when he is finished, his flaking will have left a straight line. But what if the series of flake scars is in line from the left to the right, but crooked when we follow the scars from the right to the left? It cannot happen—and that is the point here. Our logic tells us that this can never be so. If A, B, and C are in line, so are C, B, and A.

We might take a closer look at alignment—view it, in fact, in a number of ways. A straight line can appear very different, depending upon how it is seen. If a pencil is turned slowly toward you, it seems to shrink until it appears as a point. A line appears different whenever the perspective is changed. This means that an ancient toolmaker, removing each flake from the edge, had to keep his perspective—conserve it—or the tool would be ruined.

These matters seem obvious to us, but that is because we are no longer five years old. Reversibility and conservation, as these logical patterns are called, develop in children along with the growth of the brain. They make possible elaborate systems of social relations. The systems—and the logic—very likely were true of our past. If A is kin to B, then it follows that B must be related to A. Children grasp this—and straight lines—at about the same time. Then too, the male child of a male is a relative; we would call it "his son." The same relation exists when the son has a son of his own. The discovery that a certain relationship can be repeated again and

---

[8]A lucid, perhaps classic, discussion of this is by Leslie A. White, "Mind Is Minding," *The Science of Culture: A Study of Man and Civilization* (New York: Grove Press, 1949), pp. 49–54. More recently, Steven Rose, biochemist and neurobiologist, presents a similar argument in his well-written book *The Conscious Brain* (New York: Alfred A. Knopf, 1973), pp. 13–35.

[9]Thomas Wynn, "The Intelligence of Later Acheulean Hominids," *Man* 14 pp. 371–91. This significant, and difficult, article derives from the theories of Jean Piaget. This strategy provides a linkage between material culture and patterns of thought; it may prove very useful in reconstructing the "mind" of the past. I know of no easy introduction to Piaget's psychological theories. His discussion of "rational operations," describing conservative and reversible thought in our early development, appears in "The Mental Development of the Child," *Six Psychological Studies,* ed. David Elkind (New York: Vintage Books, 1967).

again is the conservative logic involved in our kinship and tools. New patterns in cleavers and axes may reflect more than technological change. They may well be the trace of a mind that was much like our own.

Homo erectus in Southeast Asia

An anatomy student in Holland had steeped himself in evolutionary theory and grew curious over fossilized bones turning up in the East.[10] Eugene Dubois, amid considerable discouragement, left Amsterdam for Sumatra. When he was there, he spent three lonely years fruitlessly searching its vine-covered caves, hoping to discover some evidence of ancient humanity.

Homo erectus sites.

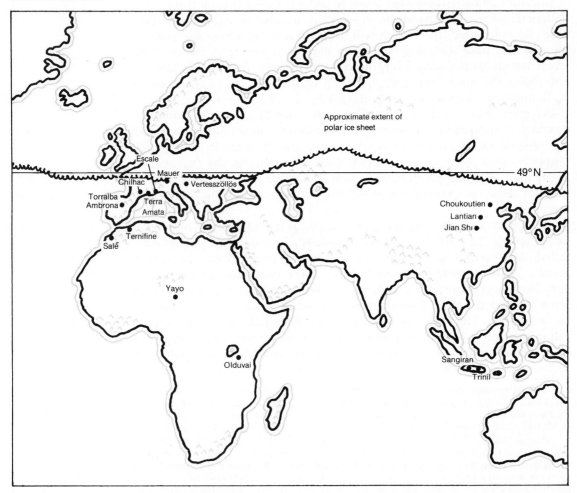

[10]Howells, *Mankind*.

His perseverance was finally rewarded, but not in the caves of Suma-tra. On the neighboring island of Java, near a small village that was known as Trinl, he found a fossilized bone in a deposit near the banks of a river. At first blush, it looked more like a turtle shell, but Dubois knew it was the top of a skull. Then, 35 feet from the fragment, he discovered a human thighbone as well. It appeared to be exactly like thighbones of humans today.

The news of Dubois' discovery soon brought others to this part of the world. Gustav Heinrich Ralph von Koenigswald spent three years in the forests of Java, unearthing fossilized animal bones from limestone deposits. Koenigswald was slowly discovering what kinds of animal life had been there and how these became different as climate and environment changed. *Homo erectus* had inhabited Java 1.5 million years before the present—the approximate date of the earliest deposits of all. What became of that first population is something we still do not know. Above these earliest fossils; lie 800,000 years of deposits; within them, there are no traces of humans. Then, suddenly there are human skulls, flaked stone tools, and animal bones. Rhinocerous, deer, tapir, and elephant reveal a warm and highly forested world that persisted in Java for over 500,000 years. Finally, 100,000 years ago, the climate cooled, and the forests diminished. The animals then became different: there were giant buffalo with a wide span of horns, and a species of cold-loving crane. *Homo erectus* in Southeastern Asia was adapted to a changing environment. But there was evidence of possible ritual behavior as well.

Gustav von Koenigswald and his assistants excavated the back of a skull from the limestone deposits that were 1.5 million years old. As the pieces were put back together, it was evident that the cranium was smashed. This perhaps had been done as a method of extracting the brain. Cannibalism was a local tradition: succeeding strata yielded four partial crania and a number of limb bones as well. All bore the markings of possible cannibalistic behavior. The fossils provoked troubled questions about the meanings of this ancient behavior. The questions echoed again at a site that was far to the north.

The cave site of Choukoutien is 27 miles southwest of Peking. It has been investigated longer than any other site from this time.[11] It is every archeologist's fantasy. A rounded hill composed mostly of limestone, its soils have a high alkalinity. This has acted as a natural preservative for fossilized bone. The cave has traces of human activities; it was occupied by animals other than humans. It provides evidence of the environment and the strategies used to survive.

The hill is called Lungkushan, or more commonly, Dragon Bone Hill. Human teeth were dug out of its soils and sold as dragon's teeth in downtown Peking. One tooth, said to have magic powers, found its way

---

[11]Chia Lan-Po, *The Cave Home of Peking Man* (San Francisco: China Books, 1975).

into a paleontologist's hands. The tooth was ultimately traced to its quarry, and a preliminary survey was made. A 70-year probe of the past was about to begin.

The object of archeological interest has always been the mouth of the cave. On the northern slope of Dragon Bone Hill, looking out over pine and cedar forests, the mouth was a cathedral-like chamber a hundred feet wide. For a period of 300 millennia, people and animals lived in the cave. Floods and occasional cave-ins have covered up the ancient debris. Thirteen separate layers reached over 100 feet high. In the opinion of Chinese officials, the site is not even one-half explored. A wealth of undiscovered information may remain in the ground.

Cannibalism at Choukoutien

The skulls that were discovered in Java strongly hinted that brains had been eaten. Shortly afterward occurred the discoveries at Choukoutien. Fourteen human skulls were encountered; the *foramen magnum* in each was enlarged. Human long bones were split down the center; they were charred from being burned in a fire. There is little doubt that cannibalism was practiced at Choukoutien. Psychologists for many decades have been concerned with this form of behavior. What were the beliefs and emotions that made this practice a part of our past? Were they the same as the psychology of cannibals living today? Although we can never be certain of what *Homo erectus* believed, we can nonetheless speculate why this behavior occurred. Richard Leakey provides a distinction that is valuable in approaching this act.[12]

There are two major types of cannibalism that exist in the world today. The most common is endocannibalism. It occurs *within* a human society and is an act of reverence for one of their dead. The Chiribichi Indians of Latin America have long practiced this form of behavior. A dead relative is roasted in a fire; the melting fat is collected in a cup. Survivors drink it in the belief that the spirit of the dead is preserved. Contrasting with this act of reverence is exocannibalistic behavior. It occurs in a *context of warfare*. Most often, it is an act of revenge. The Jale of the New Guinea highlands celebrate a victorious raid by cannibalizing the flesh of the enemy's body.[13] Shortly after, the enemy village will raid them as an act of revenge. This cycle might well have existed for thousands of years.

It is possible that *Homo erectus* was behaving in similar ways: designing beliefs adapted to a difficult world. Perhaps hunters in the forests of China had created a ritual act that insured the preservation of patterns that worked in the past. In consuming an ancestor's body, that person, in a sense,

---

[12]Richard Leakey, *Origins* (New York: E. P. Dutton, 1977).

[13]Jale cannibalism is described by Klaus-Friedrich Koch, "Cannibalistic Revenge in Jale Warface," *Natural History*, February 1970. He relates the behavior not to technology and environment but to socialization practices and personality theory.

becomes you. Not only the flesh but behavior—and ideas—were being consumed.[14] Patterns of the past, in the ritual, were being reborn. It is perhaps our most vivid example of Wynn's conservative logic at work. A complex of thought and behavior was being transferred by people through time. Because of this, the past and the present were somehow the same.

And perhaps, in Southeast Asia, a very different tradition emerged. It may have grown out of regional scarcity of plant food and game. Here the crania had been broken open; very often, they were mashed in the face. The *foramen magnum* had not been enlarged, unlike the crania of Choukoutien. This hints more of violence than of funereal rites. Today, exocannibalism creates distance between rival peoples. It is obviously safer to be far from the enemy's home. Seen in an adaptive perspective, this reduces the pressure on food. The space-in-between is a preserve for available game.

Of course, for this pattern to function, it had to continue through time. This means that it likely was recognized that revenge is a reciprocal thing: band B raiding band A is the reverse of when A raided B. In Java, as on the woodlands of China, human logic was growing complex. Very likely, that logic was mirrored in ritual life.

Excavators at Choukoutien encountered more than a collection of skulls. Evidence of the use of fire was discovered as well. More than most other inventions, this has inspired imaginative flights. There is much speculation on exactly how fire began. A storm gathers over a forest. Lightning fires the trees and the grass. The flames gather wind in the branches; the cedars explode. Days later, a small group of hunters moves cautiously across smoking ash. They find the carcass of a deer, and they taste it. They carry it home.

How fire transformed the world

Accidental Prometheans using fires they could not have made: such opportunism was possibly true of our past. Accidental usage, however, is not suggested by Choukoutien. Four layers of ash and charcoal were discovered in the mouth of the cave. One of the layers was approximately 20 feet deep. Such deposits are not left by accident, but through a tradition of deliberate use. Even if the very first fires had resulted from nature and chance, these hunting societies had learned to manufacture their own. In a sense, the creation of fire was almost an inevitable act, catalyzed by the making of tools and the growth of the brain. Striking one stone with another gives rise to an occasional spark. The incidental event had been happening for over 1 million years. A larger, more complicated brain and greater control in the making of tools made fire-manufacture a tradition of hunting society.

---

[14]The notion that behavior and ideas are carried in an individual's "blood," though naive, has persisted unbroken until our own time.

Here for the very first time was energy outside of the body. The fire's heat could accomplish in minutes tasks that muscle power never could do. Food could be cooked in the fire; at Choukoutien this was done. The layers of ash and charcoal contain the burned bones of a spectrum of species. Wild pig, bear, sika deer, and thick-jawed deer were unearthed in the layers. There were also hedgehogs, hamsters, frogs, rats, bats, hares, and harvest mice. Ostrich eggs were broken open and heated; ham and eggs were consumed at the site.

The innovative style of cuisine had an impact on human biology. Large molars were no longer as necessary for crushing the softer, cooked meat. The back teeth and the jaw became relatively smaller in size.

More significant than change in dentition is the effect that fire has had on our lives. In addition to the cooking of food, greater warmth was provided as well. Pollen and animal bones that were discovered at Choukoutien provide a picture of a temperate climate with four distinct seasons. Beyond warmth, it is also protection. The dark cedar forests of the region were home for many predator species. *Homo erectus,* to them, was no more than a meal. Hyenas, leopards, and tigers have left their skeletons in the cave's lower strata. Within these deposits, there is no trace of humans at all. Upper layers which contain ash and charcoal have no traces of the predator species. *Homo erectus* had acquired control of the cave.

In addition to warmth and protection, fire was a good source of light. Since our earliest emergence in Africa, we were active only during the day. The heritage lingers in biological rhythms closely adapted to light from the sun. Blood pressure, body temperature, and heartbeat move in cycles regulated by light. The sun is a *Zeitgeber:* a star that has given us time.

A burning log, for *Homo erectus,* was a shift from that star-given time. It was an extension beyond the hours of daylight. Long hours after the sun had gone down, there was visiting and playing with infants. There was a moment for the telling of stories, the planning of hunts. Through such innocent early beginnings, our own time had become out of sync. In a sense, social time was the stepchild of *Homo erectus'* invention of fire. Playtime, worktime, and resttime: they are dimensions of our cultural lives. Often, they are totally at odds with the natural world.

A final critical value of fire was the use it had in the hunt. Archeologist Kenneth Oakley suggested that when fire was used for protection, its value as a weapon in hunting would have quickly been seen. A burning hearth will discourage a predator, but only to lurk within shadows nearby. Frustrated and sufficiently hungry, hyenas and leopards will jump through the flames. Such accidents, in all probability, occurred many times in the past. Burning branches waved in the air or cinders flung against the animals' hides would scatter the predators to a much safer distance away. From that discovery, it was only a step to the deliberate setting of fires. Animals were made to stampede before a curtain of flames. An entire herd could be driven to the marshes, where they bogged down and were more easily killed. Choukoutien has yielded no evidence that such a tactic was used at the site. But at Torralba and Ambrona in Spain, *Homo erectus* hunted mammoths with fire. It seems possible that the strategy was known in many parts of the world.

A lighted cave in a forest in China is not our only *Homo erectus* encampment. Traces of their huts were discovered not far from the sea. Evidently, at least one group of hunters spent their summers on the French Riviera. The site in question is believed to be 300,000 years old.[15] It is designated Terra Amata and is on a street in the city of Nice. The site was once a sandy beach near the Mediterranean Sea. At that time, the Mindel glacier was melting; the Mediterranean's waters grew high. Eighty-five feet above their present-day level, they crested and began to recede. The old floor of the sea was now changed into forested dunes.

Early hunters in Western Europe

The pine and oak forests were home to many species of life. Stag, boar, ibex, elephant, Merk's rhinocerous, ox, rabbit, and birds—all of these were not far from the huts at the edge of the sea. Oysters, mussels, and lim-

Homo erectus in Europe.

Field Museum of Natural History

---

[15]Henry de Lumley, "A Paleolithic Camp at Nice," *Scientific American*, May 1969.

pets were gathered, and a small amount of fishing was done. The wide variety of animal species is reminiscent of Choukoutien. Humanity was becoming more efficient in the capture of prey.

Twenty-one separate living floors were encountered at Terra Amata. They were measured and mapped as the cautious excavation was done. The early houses were oval, brush huts, from 26 to 49 feet in length. To construct them, bunches of branches had been cut from the forested dunes, stuck in the ground, and lashed together not far from their tops. The framework was surrounded with stones, so the branches would not slip in the soil. Such houses are often built by the foragers of forested lands.

In the floor of each hut, there were scooped-out depressions filled with charcoal and animal bones. Around one hearth was a small pile of stones which probably screened the fire from the wind off the sea. There were scattered flint flakes on the living floors, where stone tools were very possibly made. In one hut was the imprint of where the toolmaker actually sat.

Fossilized fragments of excrement were found at Terra Amata as well. This is not a romantic discovery, but it can often tell us much of the past.[16] The content of human feces can reveal to us what foods were consumed; it can suggest the state of health and the methods of food preparation. Sometimes it has even been possible to tell the season when the site was in use. Insect-transported and windborne pollens were in the excrement at Terra Amata. Identification of plants from that pollen pro-

Artist's reconstruction of a dwelling at Terra Amata.

Adapted by Gail Delicio from "A Paleolithic Camp at Nice," by Henri de Lumley. Copyright © 1969 by *Scientific American, Inc.* All rights reserved.

---

[16]Vaughn M. Bryant, Jr., and Glenna Williams-Dean, "The Coprolites of Man," *Scientific American,* January 1975.

vided evidence of a warm-weather site. Charcoal was also encountered—evidence of food cooked in a hearth—and occasional fragments of dietary shellfish as well.

Hunters at Terra Amata arrived in the warm days of late spring. Here and there along the strand they found traces of their earlier huts. Cutting branches from the woods near the seashore, they reconstructed their fallen homes. Once settled, they moved through the forests. They hunted stag, and they trapped smaller game. Shellfish were gathered from the sand at the edge of a cave. In idle moments, which were probably many, they chatted, and they worked on their tools. They butchered game and cooked meat at the fireside. They took shelter with the coming of night. Fires flickered in the huts, as the wind began to blow from the sea.

To the west, beyond Terra Amata, lie Torralba and Ambrona in Spain. Hunters in this region were bringing down dangerous prey.[17] The Spanish sites are in a steep-walled valley that, in the past, was a seasonal swamp. Since the valley was so poorly drained, the water table very often was high. Sometimes it was close to the surface; a large animal could sink into the ground.

The early hunters of Torralba-Ambrona, like hunters living today, were intimately aware of changes in the natural world. They likely kept regular vigil on the plateau overlooking the valley. They saw lumbering elephants coming to the water to drink. Stealing down into the valley, edging ever closer to the herd, they came as close as they could—and set fire to dry leaves of grass. Flames crackled through the floor of the valley; the elephants broke into a run. The hunters watched them draw closer to the marsh and saw the ground buckle under their weight. In moments, the elephants were up to their bellies in muck. The small band of hunters moved forward. They clubbed and speared the immobilized prey. They trimmed away the meat, and they piled it at the edge of the swamp.

Discoveries at Torralba suggest that something much like this occurred. Strewn bones of at least 30 elephants, 25 horses, 25 deer, 10 oxen, and 6 rhinoceroses were recovered from the site. Flake tools used for the butchering were scattered throughout the debris. The left side of a fallen elephant was found undisturbed at the site. In the nearby butchering areas were three piles of bones. Throughout the surrounding soil were the pollen spores left by a swamp. A thin scattering of charcoal fragments remained from the fire. Their pattern revealed to Clark Howell, the archeologist who excavated the site, that fire had been deliberately used to provoke a stampede.

Ambrona is strongly similar, and it is only one mile away. It might even be the debris of the same hunting group. Here too, was the scattering of charcoal and the pollen remains of a swamp. Bones of 40 to 50 elephants, horses, red deer, and wild oxen were unearthed. Flint scrapers

[17]The sites are described by John Pfeiffer, *The Emergence of Man* (New York: Harper & Row, 1972), pp. 127–40.

Olorgessalie.

Photos by Glynn Isaac, Anthropology Department, University of California, Berkeley. Copyright © G. Isaac.

were littered among them, and the bones bore their butchering marks. Two thighbones and the tusk of an elephant were arranged end-to-end in a line. Perhaps hunters moving armloads of meat arranged the bones into a path through the muck. Hunting strategies were now being rewarded as never before.

Traces of big-game hunting have been encountered on the African grass. Olorgessalie is in the Great Rift Valley, an hour's drive from Nairobi in Kenya.[18] In the time of *Homo erectus,* it was a region of open terrain, blanketed by a long roll of swampgrass and dotted with lakes.

Hunting on the African plains

At one campsite in Olorgessalie, there was a jumble of butchered animal bones. The majority were from giant baboon, a good match for any human today. The adult males were five feet tall, with dangerously sharp canine teeth. The animal was possibly hunted over an extensive period of time, or a troop of baboons were conceivably killed at one time.

If, in fact, a whole troop had been hunted, baboon gluttony was likely involved. On the streams of this African grassland, baboons drink in the heat of the day. They gorge themselves by gulping water until their bellies seem ready to pop. Then, peacefully they lapse into sleep at the edge of the stream. Hunters who knew of this habit could have hidden close by in the grass and safely attacked the baboons after they had dropped off to sleep.

In the intricate matrix of hunting, our brains and behavior evolved. *Homo erectus* was increasingly coming to resemble ourselves. A brain that could fashion a ritual could very likely design a belief. A new kind of thinking had slowly emerged in the world. The unseen—what was never experienced—became woven into everyday life. Where were we before we existed? What will happen to us when we die? From the tentative thinking and rituals of ancient Java and Choukoutien, came beliefs that, along with our brains, were evolving through time.

---

[18]Olorgessalie is described by Frank E. Poirier, *Fossil Evidence: The Human Evolutionary Journey,* 2d ed. (St. Louis: C. V. Mosby, 1977), pp. 224–25.

5 / Neanderthal: The Emergence of Ritual

A schoolteacher on the outskirts of Dusseldorf, a city on the banks of the Rhine, once thought of himself as being so spiritually akin to the classic Greeks that he decided to change his name out of homage to the ancients. "Joachim Neumann," he felt, had a distinctively un-Greek sound, so his last name instead became "Neander." This was the ancient Greek word for "new man"—a translation of his former German surname. Nineteenth-century Europeans were very tolerant of eccentric teachers, so the change of name was accepted within the community. They even went so far as to name a valley in his honor: a thickly wooded limestone gorge along the edge of the Dussel River that in time became Neander's Valley—or Neander Tal.

This sleepy bit of history would have probably been totally forgotten, were it not for a curiosity—a "freak," as many would call it—that eventually was dug out of the limestone that formed most of the valley. In August 1856, three years before *The Origin of Species,* a group of workmen were quarrying limestone at Feldhofer Grotto in Neander's Valley when they happened upon a skeleton that struck them as strange. Whatever it was, it didn't seem to be human, so they tossed away many of the bones. Stopped at the last minute by the owner of Feldhofer Grotto, they surrendered the remaining bones—arms, thighs, the pelvis, and the uppermost part of the skull—to the local Natural Science Society for a detailed analysis.

It was then that the peaceful valley disturbed the world. The cautious verdict of the earliest analysts was that the skeleton was an ancient human being, but this view was nearly forgotten in the furor that followed. Rudolf Virchow, the German pathologist, said that Neanderthal was a victim of rickets. It was a view to which he would stubbornly cling for well over 30 years, and he would apply it to a number of different Neanderthal finds. Actually, this was modest when seen in contrast with many alternative explanations. "It may have been one of those wild men," as a British critic expressed it, "half-crazed, idiotic, cruel and strong. . .who now and then appear in civilized communities to be consigned perhaps to the penitentiary or the gallows."

The monster from Feldhofer Grotto

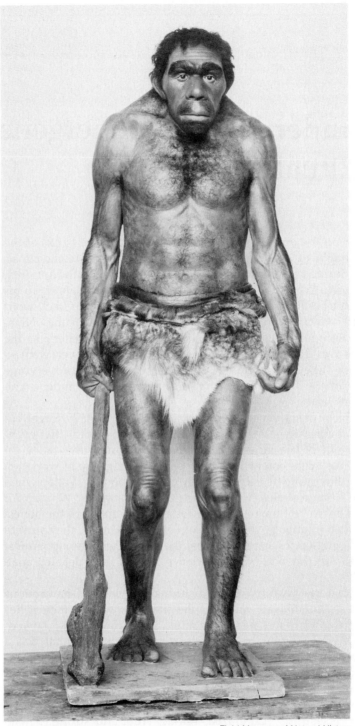

Neanderthal as ancient oaf. The slow-witted look of this reconstruction is
entirely imaginary. It does not have any basis in what we know of their
past.

Other scholars were not in agreement. Some felt that the skeleton was the remains of an early Celt, while others believed it was possibly a Russian cossack. The latter opinion was arrived at by the appearance of the skull, thought to be very similar to that of a Mongol. This, in combination with the bowed thighbones of the discovery (indicating that the deceased had ridden a horse) and the massive brow ridges that were present on the front of the skullcap (suggesting a bony growth resulting from puckering the face when in pain), completed the evidence for a victim of the days of Napoleon. When the Russians were invading Europe during the days of 1814, one of their cossacks had presumably strayed into the depths of the Neander Valley where, overcome by disease and freezing from the cold, he had ultimately waddled into the gorge to die.[1]

Neanderthal sites.

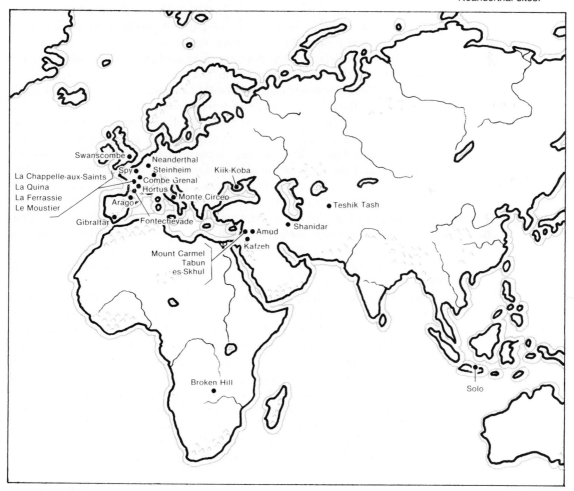

<hr />

[1]William Howells, *Mankind in the Making: The Story of Human Evolution.* Middlesex, England: Pelican, 1967.

It is easy enough today for us to smile at these early notions, but we should attempt to understand what caused them. For one thing, the Neanderthal discoveries occurred in something of a fossil vacuum. The excavations in the Dordogne region of southern France that would uncover Cro-Magnon (early *Homo sapiens sapiens*) were still a decade in the future, and the discovery of *Homo erectus* was over 30 years to come. The australopithecines were unknown; chemical dating did not exist. As a consequence, it was impossible for these troubled Victorians to have any way of knowing the sequence of transformations in humanity's physical appearance, or of the time required for these to occur. Beyond this, there was Darwin's evidence. In *The Origin of Species*, published in 1859, there was not only no discussion of human fossil materials, but there was scarcely any treatment of humans at all. The book was largely a compendium of natural history observations, with implications for the evolution of the human species. Just as scholars today are very hesitant to draw conclusions about much of our human behavior from the study of nonhuman species, the biologists of Darwin's time were cautious about analogies taken at any length between beast and man.

But what did Neanderthal look like that created such a stir? You might suppose that they looked quite different from the Victorians who dug them up, and in that regard you would certainly be correct. The Neanderthals of Western Europe were a rugged-looking population: their skulls were long and low—the forehead sloping back from directly above the eyebrows—and the back of the skull projected like a bun. The brow ridges were large and continuous—beetle-browed, this is sometimes called—so that they formed a projecting shelf on the lower forehead. The jaw was also large, and it sloped to the rear in the region of the chin, while throughout the entire skeleton, the bones were heavy. Nonetheless, the average size of their brains was the same as that of humans today (1,500 cubic centimeters); they were a cerebral—albeit a coarse-looking—lot of humanity.

So there is some substance after all to the cave man caricature. Neanderthal people, amid the snows and evergreen forests of Western Europe, really were short and muscular with flattened brain cases and thrusting jaws. Probably, too, they were clothed in skins in that glaciated climate, and there is ample evidence to suggest that they lived in caves. Aside from that, there are emotional biases and early blunders. There is nothing in the archeological record that suggests a Pleistocene courtship pattern of bashing women in the head and then dragging them by their hair to a nearby cave. In a similar vein, the descriptions of these admittedly rugged people which spoke of slumping shoulders, bowed legs and opposable toes were the result (in some instances) of faulty skeletal reconstructions and, in many others, of the ravages of arthritis. And finally, there is the matter of Neaderthal's facial expression. There is no way to know, with nothing left except the bones, whether Neanderthals characteristi-

Field Museum of Natural History

A reconstruction of Neanderthal that is, perhaps, more accurate than many. The woman is cleaning a reindeer skin with a scraper.

cally looked intelligent, foolish, or bored. The reconstructions scattered throughout museums and early textbooks usually show a somewhat bewildered and, very possibly, dangerous oaf who had more in common with Quasimodo than evolution.

A related point is worth mentioning and revisiting later on: the Neanderthal populations were extremely variable. From caves in the Middle East have come Neanderthal remains, some of which are strikingly different than many found in Europe. While their cranial capacity is approximately the same, the configuration of their skulls is noticeably modern.

There exists here the beginnings of a rising, vertical forehead; brow ridges are present, although substantially reduced; the lower face is less-thrusting than in the European finds; and there is the development of a projecting chin. These Neanderthals, in other words, looked considerably like ourselves; but this, at least for the moment, is not the point. The fact is simply that Neanderthal has been the victim of much abuse: understandable, generally, in the context of the times, but nonetheless deleterious in its effects. There is no stage in our evolution that more strongly illustrates the complexity of biological and cultural adaptation ignored because of oversimplification. The past is not an enigma; there is much we can understand. But for any of prehistory to have significance for ourselves, we must distinguish at every step our experimental observations from views that are purely derived from imagination.

A world of symbols

Perhaps the greatest irony in the rejection of the Neanderthal discoveries is the similarity in psychological and emotional behavior of these hunting-and-gathering populations to ourselves. For the first time in prehistory, we are encountering material evidence of pondering, self-conscious, and compassionate human beings—of minds that are aware of the human condition. The details of that awareness we shall probably never know. Neanderthal archeology is tantalizingly incomplete: an isolated human skull in the interior of a cave, an earthen tomb sealed over with a slab and containing the skulls of 20 bears. These artifacts of ancient rituals are all that is left behind; much of their meaning is almost certainly lost forever. Imagine a rosary bead, a star of David, a stained-glass fragment, and a communion cup. Bury them for a thousand centuries then unearth them to a candid world. Could we reconstruct from these our religious tradition?[2]

Yet we can say something about the significance of such remains: they amount to our earliest evidence of the use of symbols. A *symbol* can be understood as a *thing which stands for something else*; it is the basis for much of the complexity of human existence. The crucial feature of the use of symbols is their purely arbitrary nature. There is no connection between the symbol and the actual thing. In language, one of the most elegant symbolic systems, different collections of acoustic vibrations are the symbols of things. If I say "knife" and you are a speaker of English, an image comes into your mind; or I might even mention the word while I point to the object. However, there is no inherent connection between these particular sounds and that sharp, metallic thing in the outside world. If we were French, then "couteau" would serve our purposes just as well, and "nosh" would be appropriate for Czechoslovakians. None of these,

---

[2]The example was suggested by reading James Deetz, *Invitation to Archaeology* (Garden City, N.Y.: Natural History Press, 1967).

United Press International Photo

The Rolls-Royce. More than an automobile, it is a symbol of human affluence. Our species, in a certain sense, is immersed in an ocean of symbols. This condition became pronounced in Neanderthal times.

of course, bears any resemblance to the thing; they are sets of acoustic vibrations that label the word.

It is also important to realize that the things themselves have symbolic dimensions. They stand for ideas, feelings, and values within the surrounding cultural system; for modern humanity, things are never "just what they seem." Black is our color for mourning, but the traditional Chinese prefer white. A suntanned face, in an earlier America, was a symbol of the low-class worker; it was prestigious to have the palest skin possible. Today, despite all warnings concerning the dangers of overexposure, suntanned skin is a coveted symbol of a leisurely life. Thinking about it, one quickly realizes that we are immersed in an ocean of symbols—a condition that had its beginnings in Neanderthal times.

The discovery of death

The greater complexity of a symbolizing brain has brought us sorrow as well as joy. Part of the intrinsic humanness of Neanderthal society is the growing awareness of mortality—the fact of death. If earlier human beings were aware of the end of life, there is little evidence of it in the archeological record. The bones of australopithecines are strewn over the beaches of lakes; *Homo erectus* bones are found on the floor of a cave. The impressions that one gains from these stages of evolution is that human beings were simply abandoned wherever they happened to fall; that no special notice was given to death and dying.

With the emergence of Neanderthal, this indifference was lost forever. Humanity was now beginning to bury its dead in the earth and furnishing the shallow graves with food and flowers.[3] At the site of Le Moustier on the Vezere River in southern France, a group of Neanderthals mourned the death of an adolescent. They placed the body on his right side, face turned toward the ground, and a pillow of small flint stones beneath his head. A hand axe was near his right hand, and burned bones were beside the body. Apparently either a bison or an ox had been killed and roasted, and some of the meat had been placed in the grave as a ceremonial offering.

While we will probably never discover what the ritual of that burial was like, there are at least two intriguing possibilities derived from the site. The tools and roasted meat placed as offerings inside the grave are evidence of a possible belief in an afterlife. We can imagine that sorrowing Neanderthals provided weapons and food for the dead to help them in their journey to another existence. And while it is only speculation, the Neanderthal offerings suggest as well that the afterlife was a projection of their present society. In the forests of Pleistocene Europe, stone tools were a part of survival; they were probably needed as well in the world beyond death.

Even more tantalizing than the site of Le Moustier is a Neanderthal group burial at La Ferrassie. It is a rock shelter in the Dordogne region of France, where two adult Neanderthals and four children were buried; very possibly they were the members of a family. The adult male and female were buried side-by-side in separate graves and flexed in a fetal position. This particular form of burial was common in Neanderthal sites and has invited nearly a century of speculation. Perhaps the corpses were bound with thongs to keep the spirit from escaping the grave, or possibly it was some sort of symbolic identification with the security of a child in its mother's womb. To unromantic archeologists, it is economy of effort and nothing more—a flexed burial requires less grave digging than does an extended one.

The burials of the children are mysterious as well; their graves seem rich in symbolic associations. Two of the older children—about five years of age—were placed in graves at the feet of the elder male. Was this deliberate or accidental? Is it symbolic of a kinship system? The answers to this we shall probably never know. Just beyond the childrens' graves were nine small mounds that looked like burials; one mound contained an infant, and the other eight were empty. Possibly they were reburied,

---

[3]Bernard G. Campbell, *Humankind Emerging* (Boston: Little, Brown, 1976); N. J. Sauer, *Hominid Fossils* (Dubuque, Iowa: Wm. C. Brown, 1969).

or a scavenging animal could have found them; all we have are the empty graves and mounds of soil. Finally, in a small grave at the innermost part of the shelter, a six-year-old child was buried beneath a triangular stone. The underside of the slab showed a number of cup-shaped impressions. (Had symbolic notation begun in Neanderthal times?) When the curious slab was removed, a more perplexing discovery was made: the child's skull was three feet away from the rest of the body. The French prehistorian Bouyssonnie believed this was due to the manner of death. An animal had attacked and decapitated the child; the unfortunate was then buried with its head upslope from the body so that the spirit could later descend and unite the parts. For Capitan and Peyroney, it was possibly cannibalism: the skull had been mutilated to extract the brains.

The skull cult and cannibalism

This final, grisly suggestion has some archeological substance behind it. It appears as though cannibalism or, possibly, a "cult of the skull" was part of the ritual behavior of Neanderthal times. Bodiless Neanderthal skulls have been found in both Europe and Asia, sometimes with marks of violence and sometimes without. At a cave in the Rock of Gibraltar, was the skull of a five- or six-year-old child; Neanderthal tools were encountered, but the body was gone. And at a quarry on the north face of the rock, there was the isolated skull of an adult; in this instance, there were not even any tools found in the grave. Then, there is Ehringsdorf, Germany, on the banks of the river Ilm. Here, the jawbone of an adult, the skeleton of a 10-year-old child, and the cranial bones of a young woman were found in a quarry. The jaw and the skeleton of the child had nothing unusual about them, but five separate wounds were found in the young woman's forehead. When the distinguished anthropologist Sir Arthur Keith examined the bones, he felt that the wounds were inflicted when the bone was still fresh. Reminiscent of Choukoutien, the *foramen magnum* was somewhat enlarged. Cannibalism was possibly a part of Neanderthal times.

The site of Ganovce, in Czechoslovakia, suggests as well that a skull cult was there. With the bones of a horse, wild pig, and rhinocerous, as well as birds and a scattering of shellfish, was the top of a Neanderthal skull missing its body. At a gravel pit in Saccopastore, on the outskirts of present-day Rome, the skulls of an adult male and female were found in the same grave. But it was the site of Monte Circeo, 55 miles south of Saccopastore, where the most dramatic evidence of the ritual was found. At a Mediterranean seaside resort, a cave was discovered in a limestone hill. Sealed off for some 60 millenia, the entrance had been found by Italian workmen who crawled on their hands and knees through the shadowy chamber. At the deepest part of the cave, their lanterns flickered on a shallow trench that contained the battered remains of a Neanderthal skull.

The skull was face down in the earth, surrounded by an oval of stones. Like the skull discovered at Ehringsdorf, the *foramen magnum* had been somewhat enlarged. The right temple had been smashed by a blow, and no evidence of a cave-in was found. It seems likely that the owner of the skull had been murdered. On the outside of the oval ring were the charred remains of cooked animal bone. Deer, hyena, rhino, and elephant had apparently been cooked in the cave, possibly in connection with a Neanderthal feast. Cannibalism, then, was a part of religious tradition; the severed head had become the focus of ceremonial rites.

Why were they cannibalistic? The answers are pure speculation. Possibly a skull had to be taken as proof of one's manhood. Perhaps a known enemy was slain so that a father could give a name to a child—a belief that is practiced today in the New Guinea jungles. Nutritional possibilities are weaker, for humans are very poor food. Anthropologist Stanley Garn has approached cannibalism from a dietary standpoint and found that, except in huge quantities, it is not worth the effort.[4] A human weighing 110 pounds will yield some 10 pounds of edible protein (providing, Garn adds somewhat wryly, that he has been very well cooked). Since Neanderthals were a hunting society, dietary cannibalism does not make much sense. Perhaps, as in earlier times, there was cannibalistic revenge. It may have "spaced" the populations and created hunting preserves. Then too, the more peaceful variety—cannibalizing one's kin after death—may have stabilized adaptive traditions in ancient society.

The cave bear cult and the function of ritual

No less intriguing than the puzzle of Neanderthal cannibalism is the symbolic attention that they devoted to the animal world. In sites throughout Europe and Asia, are the bones of Pleistocene animals—not, apparently, as the remains of a feast, but as the focus of ritual. At Teschik Tasch, in the Soviet Union, wild goats became part of a burial. It was a small grave in which a young child had been placed, and it was slightly disturbed. Apparently a wild animal—very possibly a cave hyena—had dug through the fresh earth at the center of the grave, but fortunately had left the edge of the burial intact. Along the edges was a well-preserved circle of ibex horns from a mountain goat that is found today in the highland regions of Central Asia. They could have been placed there as a marker or for decoration. But seen in the context of other Neanderthal remains, there were possibly religious motives involved as well.

There are sites, for example, in which the bear is a central figure—suggesting a religious link with the animal world.[5] In fact, the presence

---

[4]Stanley Garn and W. Block, "The Limited Nutritional Value of Cannibalism," *American Anthropologist*, vol. 72, 1970, p. 106.

[5]Johannes Maringer, *The Gods of Prehistoric Man* (New York: Alfred A. Knopf, 1960), pp. 53–54.

The cave bear.

Field Museum of Natural History

of bears is such a strongly recurrent motif that archeologists have long suspected a "cave bear cult." In the densely forested regions of Western and Central Europe, there was a thriving population of giant bears. With few significant enemies—other than the human species—and a shaggy coat to protect them from the severe European winters, these animals naturally flourished from the lowland approaches to the Alps to caves over 8,000 feet up into the mountains. From Drachenhohle, a cave in Austria, it is possible to gain some notion of the sheer abundance of these animals in Neanderthal times. Within this cave, archeologists found multiple deposits of giant bear bones, saturating the entire length of the ancient floor. Modern technology has destroyed a significant part of the Austrian cave, smashing the bones in order to extract industrial phosphate. Nonetheless, prehistorians have estimated the total number of bears: probably in the vicinity of 50,000. Given an animal that was this abundant and (like Neanderthal) lived in caves, it was virtually inevitable that the two would meet. At Drachenloch in eastern Switzerland, nearly 1.5 miles above sea level, one such meeting took place regularly between cave bears and humans.

Drachenloch is a mountain cave with a spacious, high-ceilinged entrance. The antechamber, however, although it was roomy and open to daylight, held scarcely any bear or human remains. But in a deeper, narrower chamber, some 60 feet away from that entrance, lay a deliberately stored treasure of cave bear bones. There was a barrier of limestone slabs nearly three feet high and parallel to the wall. In the narrow space that separated these two, was a pile of cave bear skulls, most of which had been battered. In one instance, a skull was smashed open at the rear; two had a pair of holes bored in their sides; and almost all were buried with their upper vertebrae. Apart from this, there were bones from extremities—only two or three of which belonged to the same bear—and a few of these had been split (to extract the marrow?). A second stone "chest" was close by, sealed with a slab nearly five inches thick. This contained seven cave bear skulls, all facing the entrance. Even deeper inside the mountain were bear skulls in niches within the cave wall. And, in one remarkable instance, the skull of a three-year-old bear had the thighbone of a younger animal thrust into its cheekbone.

Drachenloch is an embarrassment of riches, but it is still not unique. From one end of Europe to the other, the bear sites are found. In southern France, there is the Regourdou cave and its buried stone chest. In a hole scooped out of the floor and walled with stone slabs, were the skulls, and no other remains, of at least 20 large bears. A rock weighing over a ton sealed the animals' tomb. Lying on the floor close beside it, was the postcranial skeleton of a bear missing its skull. At Wildenmannlisloch in Switzerland, a cave nearly 500 feet long, a bear skull—missing its jaw—was wedged into a wall fissure with three long bones. Still deeper inside the cave, five additional jawless skulls were discovered, all of which were buried together with bones of extremities. Even as far as Yugoslavia, the bear cult was practiced. At Mornova, both a cave and a hunting camp, there was the traditional skull minus the jaw, with limb bones in a niche just above it and others lying across it.

What could the ritual have meant? Prehistorians for over a century have searched for an answer. The bear cult, in one school of thought, is a total misnomer. It had nothing to do with religion and was not even a cult. The Drachenloch assemblage was an ancient supply depot, a place where Neanderthal hunters stored their meat. Closely akin to this view is the suggestion of trophies. Like the deer head, trout, or tarpon stuffed and mounted on a living room wall, the cult was merely a display of the hunters' successes.

The problems with these explanations were pointed out nearly 40 years ago. It seems unlikely that hunters would display their trophies in the most inaccessible portions of their caves or, for that matter, cover them with rocks weighing a ton. The storage view is equally unlikely, for a number of reasons. In some instances, there are only the skulls, implying that Neanderthal hunters were preserving the brains. It could reasonably be asked why other portions were not preserved—particularly since a brain will spoil quickly. Also, the bones were often placed together in an extremely close arrangement, only possible if the flesh had first been removed.

The view that it was a ritual has always been more convincing—largely because of the behavior of contemporary hunters. On the Siberian coast in the 18th century, hunting societies often sacrificed bears. They acknowledged a powerful god who could grant hunting success. Heads of bears were mounted on bark to gain favor from the god. This variety of ritual behavior is extremely widespread. In Lapland, Finland, Northern Europe, and the steppes of Asia, religious ceremonies involving the bear have been thoroughly described. For one group—the Siberian Koryak—the description of the bear ceremony seems like an eyewitness account of a Neanderthal rite:

> An elaborate ritual has been developed to honor the slain bear. As soon as it is trapped, but especially after it has been killed, the hunters offer it their profound apologies. (They) welcome the dead bear to their camp with dancing and by swinging torches. One of the women puts the bear's head on her own head, wraps herself in its skin, and dances in this attire, at the same time exhorting the bear not to be angry or sad. Afterward, the skin, with head attached, is displayed in the place of honor. The bear is a guest at the feast where its own flesh is eaten. The banqueters shower it with fine phrases and offer it their choicest dishes. . . . The hunters make offerings to it, address speeches to it, and become increasingly boisterous. Finally, they carve the bear up, drink its blood and share its flesh. But the high point is always eating

Artist's reconstruction of cave bear hunt.

Field Museum of Natural History

the flesh of the head, which, as a rule, includes the brain. The last act of the ceremony is the deposition of the skull in a hallowed place, or its solemn interment, usually along with the rest of the bones.[6]

The bear is a ceremonial offering, among many of these hunting groups, to the supernatural powers that grant hunting success. But why is it not some other animal? A deer could more easily be sacrificed. Why for 200 millenia have we sacrificed bears? A possible factor in the preference is the nature of the animal itself. Bears can stand upright; they hold objects with their paws; much of their skeleton is astonishingly similar to that of a human. Possibly through the centuries, this similarity has been perceived. There may have been a sense of kinship with these humanlike creatures. Such a belief is *totemism:* the *recognition of a kinship link with the animal world.* But the killing of a totem is a rarity and even then is apologetically done. Were there possibly deeper meanings to the ancient ritual?

It is useful, in such a speculation, to remember what rituals are all about. For cultural anthropologist Roy A. Rappaport, they are the "more or less standard actions" that are undertaken with respect to religious beliefs.[7] For the believers, ritual behavior need not be defended or justified. It is bound up with religious beliefs never seriously questioned. It is also communication. The Maring of the New Guinea highlands perform dances in the villages of friends as a means of pledging their support if their friends are at war. Political influence in Melanesia is symbolized through competitive feasting. Whoever gives away the most food is a powerful person. Ritual, then, is a complex matter. It is justified by religious beliefs; yet it often communicates messages that are very mundane.

As to Neanderthal ritual "messages," we can hazard a guess. A bear is a dangerous animal, not easily killed. It was probably the most difficult challenge for a Neanderthal hunter. The bear skulls at the Drachenloch site had wounds that had healed; very possibly, in earlier hunts, they had been the winners. The killing of such an animal was the ultimate test of both courage and skill and a means of insuring that these were passed on in the hunting tradition. For this reason too it was sacred. The human brain was now exquisitely developed; critical thinking was a new possibility. If hunters seriously questioned the legitimacy of endangering themselves, then the Neanderthal way of life would itself be endangered. So, ultimately the notion of the sacred has had a function in our own evolution. Rebellion was defined as sacrilege. Tradition survived.

Hunting and everyday life

Technology sanctified by religion is a powerful force. The Neanderthals hunted successfully; they took a large toll. At Salzgitter-Lebenstedt, a campsite in a north German wilderness, traces of Pleistocene hunting have

---

[6]Maringer, *The Gods of Prehistoric Man,* pp. 53–54.

[7]Roy A. Rappaport, "The Sacred in Human Evolution," *Annual Review of Ecology and Systematics* 2 (1971), pp. 23–42.

been minutely described.[8] The site was an open-air campground—some Neanderthals did not live in caves—and apparently was occupied regularly during the summer. Pollen spores collected from the soil revealed a world on the fringes of the Arctic. There was the grassy monotony of the tundra, with patches of pine, birch, willow, and spruce trees. Some six miles west of the site was a freshwater stream.

It was a world that was rich in resources—and Neanderthals knew it. Reindeer bones were abundant—some 72 percent of the total—and there were mammoth, bison, horse, and the woolly rhinocerous. Archeologists discovered single-specimen animals as well, killed occasionally but never favored within the diet. Wolf, muskrat, perch, pike, crab, insects, a duck, and a vulture were scattered throughout the refuse of the Lebenstedt site.

The large proportion of reindeer bones suggests a developing skill in hunting—a trend that was set into motion in earlier times. Neanderthals were persevering in a technology that offered rewards, but the limits of the hunting tradition were soon to be reached.

Greater insight into the complexities of the big-game hunting way of life, and into some of the difficulties of archeological interpretation, is provided by the analyses of Combe Grenal. The site is a hillside cave along the banks of the Dordogne River, a region in France where Neanderthals lived for some 50 millenia.[9]

Combe Grenal was a cache of surprises from the very beginning. It appeared to Francois Bordes—the French prehistorian who excavated the site—that the dig would probably last little more than a summer. Intermittently, the cave had been sampled since as early as 1916; a few layers seemed to be all that remained and then nothing but bedrock. But Combe Grenal required more than a summer. It took, in fact, 11 long years, and the arguments over its findings are still going on.

The appearance of the site was misleading. The bedrock, thought to be level, sloped sharply downhill. To reach the bottom, Bordes had to remove 64 different layers. There were spores of pollen, animal bones, ash, charcoal, and Neanderthal tools: Bordes recovered them all and described each separate layer. When he had finished, he presented his findings and a picture of Later Pleistocene times. But that picture is now being clouded by a heated debate.

There are 19,000 stone tools at the heart of the matter—the total number that Bordes excavated at the Combe Grenal site. In his opinion, the entire collection can be classified into four different tool kits; the stones are material evidence of different cultural traditions. When the strata are viewed from this perspective, the result is intriguing. The top four layers belong to the same tradition; the six succeeding layers represent a second tradition; the six following after that contain yet a third tradition—the

[8]D. K. Bhattacharya, *Paleolithic Europe* (Atlantic Highlands, N.J.: Humanities Press, 1977).
[9]Ibid.

changes continue apace for some 55 layers. The implication would seem to be that different cultures inhabited the site; it is, in fact, the very conclusion that Bordes has drawn. "Our point of view," he concluded, "is that during Mousterian (Neanderthal) times different cultures, with different traditions of toolmaking and toolusing, coexisted on the same territory but influenced each other very little."[10]

A recent challenge to Bordes' understanding of the results of his Combe Grenal dig has emerged from the work of Lewis and Sally Binford.[11] Their argument has provoked much debate, for there is more than a site involved. The controversy is about stone tools and human behavior. The Binfords gathered together a large collection of Neanderthal tools from sites in Israel, France, and Syria for statistical analysis. All of the tools had been classified by Bordes into a total of 40 different categories. The Binfords took each of the categories and compared it with the others for every layer in every one of the sites in the sample. Suppose, for example, that the categories were a retouched blade and a side scraper. In collection A, these two categories might be 25 percent of the tools; in collection B, the two categories rise to 30 percent of the tools; and they parallel one another through the rest of the entire tool sample. In such a case, these two types of tools would be varying exactly together. In the Binford analysis, they would receive a rating of 1. On the other hand, it might be the case that there is an inverse relation between them: where retouched blades are abundant, there are few side scrapers (and vice-versa) for every collection of tools within he whole sample. Relationships such as these received a rating of − 1, while no predictable relationship at all was given a zero. These are, of course, extreme, perfect cases. There were types that mostly varied together and some that were mostly inverse. These were given intermediate values on the +1 to − 1 scale. The calculations were obviously enormous and were done by computer.

The point of this factor analysis was to discover what varied together and then to explain the discovery in behavioral terms. The Binfords found five such clusters—*factors* they are commonly called—of tool types that varied together in the different collections. When these five different factors of tools were seen in the context of the sites where they were found, their relationship to behavior was clear—at least to the Binfords.

In one instance, for example, a toolkit consisted of three types of spear points, as well as several different varieties of scrapers. This suggested to the investigators that the tools were used for killing and butchering. Because this particular factor was dominant at a temporary campsite in Syria, it seemed plausible that hunters had stopped there to dismember their prey.

---

[10]Francois Bordes, *A Tale of Two Caves* (New York: Harper & Row, 1972).

[11]Sally R. Binford and Lewis R. Binford, "Stone Tools and Human Behavior," *Scientific American*, April 1967.

Field Museum of Natural History

Neanderthal stone tools. Implements similar to these were analyzed by Lewis and Sally Binford. Francois Bordes suggested that many Neanderthal tools were used to make other tools from wood or bone.

The Middle East findings were promising—and the next task was Combe Grenal. Not only did the Binfords analyze every one of the thousands of tools, but pollen spores and animal bones were included as well. Again, the objective was factors—items in a sample that vary together. Were particular groupings of tools found with particular groupings of pollen? Or, for that matter, with particular animal species? If so, what does that tell us of human behavior at Combe Grenal? These were the kinds of questions that the Binfords were asking.

The result is a developing picture of Neanderthal daily life. In all, there were 14 toolkits, conceivably related to different tasks. There were food-processing kits, for example, made up of denticulates—saw-toothed flakes which could have been used for cutting meat into strips. Bones of wild horses and reindeer have been found with this particular kit, adding archeological evidence to the Binfords' ideas. If meat was cut into strips, then this was a possible step in preserving. Like other hunter-and-gatherer groups, the Neanderthals of the Dordogne Valley could have preserved their meat by drying it on racks in the sun. Did the Combe Grenal people really do this? In the 15th layer from the surface, which contained mostly saw-toothed flakes, there was a sharp soil discoloration where a post was driven into the ground. Lewis Binford has recently suggested that this is the evidence of a meat-drying rack, but more extensive tests of his view will have to be made. The same can be said of the theory that women were responsible for drying the meat. Usually among hunters and gatherers, women are involved in the processing of food as well as in caring for children around a base camp. From this, the Binfords suggested that the denticulate food-processing tools were made from flints in the immediate environment of the Neanderthal site. This turned out, in fact, to be the case, but a good deal more evidence is needed before we can describe the division of labor at the Combe Grenal site.

The emergence of human compassion

If Combe Grenal is a striking example of modern methods of understanding our past, then Shanidar Cave is a reminder that this past was, after all, very human.[12] Periodically, we might tend to forget that a scattered jumble of anonymous bones was at one time a thinking, acting, and emotional being. But occasionally we are reminded, through discovery and chance preservation, that the often ridiculed "cavemen" (and women) were much like ourselves.

In the Zagros Mountains of northern Iraq, there is a limestone mountain overlooking a valley. The tidal action of ancient seas eroded a cavity in the southern face of the peak, a triangular opening that was later known as Shanidar Cave. From 75,000 years ago until 20th-century times, the cave has served as a home for a succession of cultures. Even at the time it was dug, Kurdish nomads were living inside. Brush huts, animal dung, communal campfires, and corrals of goats were surrounding the archeologists as they dug through the floor. Protected from the winds by bluffs, exposed to sunlight during most of the day, overlooking the Zab River valley, a source of water and, probably, game, Shanidar Cave has been a favored location for many thousands of years.

It was during the second season of the Shanidar excavations that the first of nine human skeletons was discovered. It was the badly crushed burial of an infant Neanderthal. It was flexed, and there were no apparent grave goods. Ralph Solecki, the archeologist who directed the excavation, had shoveled through 25 feet of cave floor deposition when he encountered a few milk teeth that were part of the burial. Very probably,

---

[12]Ralph Solecki, *Shanidar: The First Flower People* (New York: Alfred A. Knopf, 1971).

the enormous weight of deposits above the infant had crushed the bones until they were almost beyond analysis.

The excavators shoveled inside the cave for two more seasons. Ultimately, they were rewarded with eight additional Neanderthal burials and a glimpse of emotional life in preliterate times. Three of the eight were so fragmentary that little could be learned from the bones, and three others were crushed by cave-ins, a persistent problem at the Shanidar site. But the two remaining skeletons—a man in his 40s and an adolescent—provided unexpected details of everyday life. The man, nicknamed "Nandy," was crushed by stones that fell from the roof, but fortunately the soil beneath him absorbed some of the blow. Life for Nandy had been difficult; his bones revealed much of his story. He had been crippled by extensive arthritis, which probably had grown worse as he aged. There was massive bone scar tissue along the left side of his face; examination of the area suggested that he was blind in one eye. Beyond this, T. Dale Stewart the physical anthropologist who assisted Solecki, determined that part of the body was underdeveloped. The right shoulder blade, the right collarbone, and the upper bone of the right arm were so small that, for all practical purposes, they were probably useless. At some point during his life, the smaller arm had been amputated: the bone was completely cut through just above the elbow. Here was obviously a human being not fully equipped to provide for himself, who nonetheless survived to old age in a Neanderthal band. A dimension of symbolic complexity is the understanding of pain; compassion was now fully a part of the human condition.

Emotion is evident, too, in the burial of the adolescent. The youth was found in a niche of the cave with provisions of flint and animal bones. Soil samples taken from the grave contained the pollen of pine boughs and mountain flowers. Very possibly, these had been gathered and then placed with the body.

Shanidar is thus an eloquent testimony to the emergence of psychological complexity. Recognition of human mortality, compassion, and altruistic behavior: these are traits that seem fully developed in Neanderthal times. If we add the concept of ritual, very evident at many other sites, and the possibility of a belief in an afterlife, then we are presented with much of the evidence for a developing language.

The growth of language

Here is a powerful symbolic system, called "a burning fire" by Swinburne, that has strongly affected the course of our own evolution. For thousands of years, humanity has speculated about how such a system began, and the question continues to tantalize; we still do not know. A mimicry of natural sounds, grunting and groaning with heavy muscular work, babbling with sheer delight, and crying out with pain or surprise— each one was proposed in the past as a possible answer.

Languages, of course, never fossilize, so archeology is of little help here. But the study of nonhuman primates, in the laboratory as well as in the wild, is contributing valuable insights concerning the problem. The essential idea of such studies is to describe the communication process as it exists among our closest biological relatives. In this way, we are given an idea of what communication was possibly like before language and indications of how such a system could have undergone change.

In approaching such a question, it is useful to be aware that language is only one form of communication. The communication process is the transmission of information, a transmission that can occur in a number of ways. There are movements, for example—particular kinds of motor behavior—that can convey particular messages within a species. A stickleback fish swims on its head and flutters its fins; this is recognized, by another stickleback, as a mating gesture. Honeybees perform a dance to indicate the direction of honey; the raised hair of an angry dog needs no explanation.

Nonverbal communication can be surprisingly complex, especially among our closest biological relatives. Fifty-three expressive movements were once discovered among chimpanzees and were connected with five separate social contexts.[13] Given 53 movements for only 5 situations, either redundancy or subtlety is at work. The detailed studies of chimpanzee communication suggest that it is a remarkably subtle system. There is the

Nonverbal communication in chimpanzees. Among species that are highly social, these systems are complex and graded.

Courtesy of Chicago Park District

Courtesy of NASA

[13]Robert A. Hinde, *Biological Bases of Human Social Behavior* (New York: McGraw-Hill, 1974).

silent bared-teeth display, for example: lips are drawn back and the mouth is partially opened; this means (roughly) "I am friendly," when one chimp is meeting another, and, when playing, "Don't hurt me; it's all in fun." This particular chimp display, possibly related to the human smile, can be given in at least three different ways. This means that chimpanzees are perfectly capable of graded messages, expressing differences in intensity and shades of meaning. If we add to this the fact that there are other expressive movements—eyebrow flashing, bowing and crouching, bobbing the head, embracing, and touching—that also can be finely graded and can frequently occur together, we are made aware of an exquisitely complex system.

For primatologist Jane Lancaster, this is crucial to social behavior. Species that experience a high level of interaction—grooming, foraging, playing, banding together for defense—must develop such a system to coordinate their daily behavior and to minimize the amount of friction inside their groups.[14]

Among the living monkeys and apes, nonverbal communication is a system that seems crowded to its very limits.[15] In some instances, the repertoire of physical movements is so complex that new messages can be unusual or even cumbersome. A striking example of such bizarre communication is found among the Japanese macaques. To express the idea that "it is safe to feed here," a dominant male macaque will climb to the

Nonverbal communication in *Homo sapiens*. The subtleties of this system developed before the first use of language. When combined with our verbal abilities, the result is communication behavior that is highly complex.

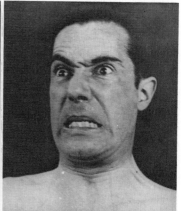

Frois-Whittman series, courtesy Brown University

[14]Jane B. Lancaster, *Primate Behavior and the Emergence of Human Culture* (New York: Holt, Rinehart & Winston, 1975).

[15]Jane H. Hill, "On the Evolutionary Foundations of Language," *American Anthropologist*, 74, no. 3, (1972) pp. 308–317.

upper branches of a tree and shake them back and forth in a sweeping arc. Aside from the obvious clumsiness of this type of communication, it makes it possible for the male in charge of troop defense to be perched in the top of a tree if his troop is threatened. This, of course, is the very behavior that can endanger a primate troop, so the message can on occasion be totally wrong.

Such forms of communication, says primatologist Jane H. Hill, are making use of "everything but the kitchen sink."[16] Yet, monkey and ape vocalizations—barks, grunts, and assorted sounds—are surprisingly underdeveloped by comparison. So here indeed is a curious problem in communication evolution: why didn't the nonhuman primates resort to speech?

The answer to the question is not to be found in the animals' brains. They can master, after all, their own nonverbal communication, and they can manipulate a variety of different symbols. In a series of famous experiments, primatologists have repeatedly shown how chimpanzees can communicate with sign language and plastic shapes and even through the keyboard of a computer console.

A possible answer to the question takes us back 3 million years to the emergence of human beings and cultural systems. As we have seen, the earliest humans adapted to life on the forested grasslands by, among other

The vocal tract of modern humans was more "bent" than in earlier times. This may have made possible a wider acoustical range.

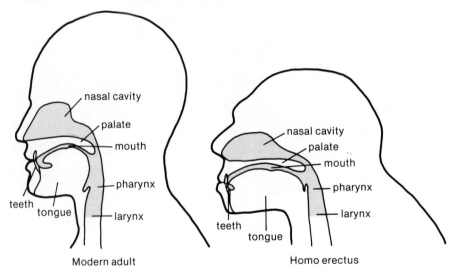

Modern adult   Homo erectus

---

[16]Ibid.

things, developing upright posture. The spinal column was shifted to underneath the human skull; the organs we use for speech were thereby changed. Our vocal tract became more bent—in the vicinity of 90 degrees—which created an enormous range of possible sounds. The other African primates never developed upright posture, which literally blocked them from evolving a language system.

Considering the earliest cultures, the number of utterances was probably small but then multiplied as our way of life became more complex. As the number of sounds increased, the differences between them became less pronounced. This selected, along with hunting, for an increasingly complex brain which could recognize delicate differences of various sounds.

The evolution of human language, then, was almost certainly a gradual thing, but it was probably highly developed in Neanderthal times. It made possible ritual behavior and magico-religious beliefs. It facilitated the teaching and learning of more complex cultural systems. In its impact on human life, it was a major transition.

Displacement and human evolution

The evolution of complex language made displacement a possibility: *communication concerning different locations and times.* Nonverbal communication is almost totally here-and-now. Baboons have a danger call for a leopard that is visibly present, but they cannot refer to a leopard in the past or the future. Nor, for that matter, can they make reference to a leopard in a different location or to the double remove of a different place and time. Even honeybees, the famous exception, can only displace concerning honey; they have nothing at all to say about the rest of the world. This is an everyday feature of language; we understandably take it for granted. But "It was lovely yesterday down the river" is a truly extraordinary notion. There is no other living thing on this planet that can get that idea across.[17]

Displacement created new possibilities for both cultural complexity and change.[18] It became possible to remember the past—as we are doing right now. Humanity could fashion mythologies to account for the origins of things; the idea of kinship—organic relatedness—could be extended farther into the past; acts of kindness and generosity, as well as selfishness and breaches of rules, could be remembered and shared by the people of a cultural system. Past behavior that had proven successful, such as hunting at a special location or at particular times of the year, could be stored

---

[17]At least under natural conditions. Chimpanzees in laboratory settings are capable of occasional displacement, but only humans can recurrently displace in their own social systems.

[18]Charles Hockett, "The Origins of Speech," *Scientific American,* September 1960.

in the language and brains of a Neanderthal band. Very possibly, the prestige of elders intensified during this time. Accumulation of human experience could now be imparted to a new generation. Old Nandy might well have been spared as a result of displacement.

The future also was opened up; there was the concept of purpose. Should the band leave the valley in spring? Would there still be more snow? The calculation of future behavior, which also involves what we recall of the past, was now a significant dimension of human survival. Displacement is also involved when we refer to a life beyond death. It is central to much of our thought about human existence.

But displacement has drawbacks as well. The ability to converse about a separate place or time is a unique and powerful means of human deceit. If we are together on a wintry day and I tell you that the weather is warm here, understandably you will treat my remark as not seriously meant. But if I tell you that it is warm at some place remote from ourselves, then perhaps I can manage to convince you that my message is true. The example may seem trivial (although it would not be for an Eskimo hunter!) but much more is involved in displacement than simply the weather. Consider just the following statements: "The neighboring village is plotting against us"; "Our ruler was descended from God"; "The future will be very prosperous"; "The government will wither away." Are all of these statements deceitful? Some undoubtedly are; others, not. But a feature they all have in common is their removal from immediate surroundings. Displacement, then, has been a mixed blessing; a two-edged sword of our own evolution. Lying, manipulation, suspicion, and the clashes among alternative beliefs: such developments would scarcely have been possible had we referred only to the immediate present. Displacement has made our lives richer, but we have paid a considerable price. The dilemma has not been resolved with the passing of time.

Genocide in the stone age?

A major theme of this chapter has been that Neanderthals were much like ourselves. Complex in their beliefs and behavior, close to us in evolutionary time—it seems only logical to think that they were our precursors. Yet, in an intriguing parallel to the old days of the Feldhofer Grotto, contemporary prehistorians have suggested a quite different fate. Impressed by the obvious differences between the European Neanderthals and ourselves, these evolutionists were led to propose a "catastrophist" theory.[19] For anthropologist W. E. LeGros Clark—and somewhat earlier, Teilhard de Chardin—there was an invasion of modern-looking Cro-Magnon—probably from the Eastern Mediterranean—which wiped out the Neanderthal people of Pleistocene Europe.

[19]C.L. Brace, "The Fate of the Classic Neanderthals: A Consideration of Hominid Catastrophism," *Current Anthropology*, vol. 5, no. 3 (1964).

This is genocide, of course, pure and simple—but there seems little to support such a theory.[20] At an earlier time, it appeared that there were indeed significant differences between the Neanderthal remains found in Europe and those found in the Eastern Mediterranean. From the Israeli site of Tabun, came a Neanderthal jaw and female skeleton. Both were similar in their appearance to the more robust Neanderthal materials discovered in Europe. A neighboring site known as Skhul produced 10 Neanderthal skeletons that were more gracile in appearance, very much like ourselves. When these finds were originally dated by the radiocarbon method, it appeared that they were the same age—some 40,000 years old. This became a key piece of evidence in the Cro-Magnon invasion hypothesis. But refinements in carbon-14 led to a reexamination of the bones. In conflict with the invasion hypothesis, the original dates were 10,000 years off! The skeletal remains at Tabun are indeed 39,000 years old. But the bones from Skhul are not at all contemporaneous; in fact, they are 10,000 years younger. If one group had invaded another, they would of course have to be the same age. The Cro-Magnon invasion hypothesis was seriously weakened.

Other difficulties came from two quarters: the more accurate placement in time of the Cro-Magnon and Neanderthal peoples, and the reexamination of the tools that they both left behind. In the first case, there was not a single instance of physically modern human beings existing earlier than the Neanderthal did, or even at the same time. When the tool types were closely examined, another piece of evidence collapsed. Traditionally, anthropologists had thought that there were typical Cro-Magnon assemblages which had suddenly replaced the Neanderthal tools. But a detailed comparative analysis by David Brose and Milford H. Wolpoff demonstrated that a sudden interruption had not taken place. The use of bone tools, for example, or long, parallel-sided flint blades was not unique to the Cro-Magnon people but was true of Neanderthal as well. Both artifacts increased in their frequency from Neanderthal to Cro-Magnon times. There was no sudden replacement of tools that suggests an invasion.

The fate of the Neanderthal people, then, was not to succumb to invasion. Through slow biological changes, they turned into Cro-Magnon. Better tools for shredding and slicing allowed the teeth and jaws to be smaller. To balance the skull, the cranial vault became higher. Ridges of bone in the front and back became reduced as a part of this process. By 30,000 years before the present, the change was complete.[21]

---

[20]David Brose and Milford H. Wolpoff, "Early Upper Paleolithic Man and Late Paleolithic Tools," *American Anthropologist* 73 (1971).

[21]Adaptation of the human body to different kinds of climatic conditions may explain the post-cranial variations in Neanderthal finds. Massive bodies (with heavier bones) are adapted to colder climates. The warming of Western Europe may have slenderized the Neanderthals there. This likely occurred parallel to the changes in tools.

More than our species was changing; the world around us was evolving as well. Massive glaciers were slowly retreating; their melting waters were flooding the shores. The seas and oceans climbed higher; the swollen rivers were teeming with fish. Northern regions of Europe and Asia were now freed from the tonnage of ice. The sunlight could now touch the ground, and the soil was changed. Green shoots burst out from the earth; grasses rapidly conquered the land. Gigantic herds of animals were moving in waves through the open terrain. A wide-ranging, tragic adventure was about to begin.

6 / Cro-Magnon: The Great Exploration

It was the end of our longest winter. For 5 million years of humanity's existence, great ice sheets had blanketed the northern reaches of the world. They had retreated and advanced: an interminable ebb and flow. A wall of ice had marched through Canada and across much of northern Europe; Scandinavia had been buried, and so had much of the Russian plains. But between 30,000 and 40,000 years before the present, the last of these frozen giants began to die.

The thaw was slow in coming: it lasted 20,000 years. But seen in the

The age of the Cro-Magnon hunter

Glaciers at one time covered much of the northern Eurasian land-mass. The retreat of the ice 30,000 years ago transformed the natural environment, creating a world of abundant resources for Cro-Magnon people.

Milwaukee Public Museum

105

perspective of our species' total existence, it was a climatological flash, a burst of spring. The ice was often a mile deep, but it slowly began to melt and change the lives of human beings across the world. There was a vast inhabited plain called the continental shelf that slowly began to flood as the oceans rose. In some regions of western Europe, it stretched for nearly a thousand miles, but the waters grew ever higher and covered it over. Rivers that had once plunged over the edge of the massive shelf now flowed down a gentle slope to the open sea. Within these quieter waters, barrier islands and lagoons were born. Plankton multiplied and became the food of the small fish. They, in turn, provided food for increasing numbers of salmon and sturgeon which easily invaded the calmer rivers for the springtime spawn.

The land itself was changed, and a curious world was born—a bleak but delicate region that was called the *tundra*. It is a *plant and animal community of the northern subarctic regions, in which the soil is frozen a few feet beneath the ground*. It had been buried under the glacier, but now its soils were touched by the sun. Mosses and lichens covered the ground for as far as the eye could see. Trees could not take root in the shallow layer of thawed soil, so the forest never invaded the tundra world.

The tundra was poorly drained—there was no place for the water to go. Lakes and marshes by the thousands were dotting the land. On oc-

Tundra. The low vegetation supported large herds of big game, both in Eurasia and in much of the Americas.

Milwaukee Public Museum

casion, a lake would freeze and then be covered by windblown sand. Frozen subsoil would push against it and explode it out of the ground. The tundra seemed to belong to another world.

And yet, harsh as it might have seemed, it was a delicate region as well. If temperatures were slightly warmer, the frozen subsoil would have thawed. Lakes and marshes would have drained away; coniferous forest would have covered the land; mosses and cold-weather grasses would have been harder to find. Or, if the average temperature had dropped, then lakes and marshes would have turned into ice; vegetation would have quickly dried up in a permafrost desert.

But as the last of the glaciers retreated, the tundra region was carefully balanced. Grasses and flowering plants were adapted to its seasons and soils. For nine months out of the year, the tundra was locked in an ocean of ice. But suddenly, from June to August, there was 24-hour-a-day sunshine. Flowering plants grew and pollinated quickly, for slow development was selected against. Their roots spread out horizontally, since the thaw might be only inches deep. Dwarf willow, flowering catkin, monkshood, bunchberry, and mountain cranberry—all these managed to flourish in this bleak northern land.

This was literally a pasture of plenty for the animals that came to the region. There were large herbivorous animals that lived off the plants and the lichens, a thriving population of rodents that fed upon grass stems and insects, and a number of carnivorous species that preyed on the herds. Caribou, mammoth, and horses were probably dominant among the grasseating mammals. During the winter months of the year, they took refuge in southerly forests, and then with the coming of spring, moved onto the tundra. But there were also bison and ground sloth (the latter could stand twice as high as a human), beaver (with eight-inch incisors), mastodon, camel, antelope, and a predator population of foxes and wolves.

There was never such an environment for the Pleistocene hunter as this. During the Cro-Magnon period, a hunting technology that developed in close relation with the human brain attained a complexity that was never surpassed. Hunting came to mean more than simply a means to get food; it was glorified to the point of apotheosis. The tools for hunting went beyond the familiar materials of stone and bone; they were fashioned of antler and ivory and were more elaborate than ever before. Blade tools had first appeared with Neanderthal but were present now in abundance.[1] They were struck off from a large block of flint, either directly through the use of a bone hammer, or indirectly through the use of a hammerstone and a bone punch. By peeling away strips of flint in this fashion, stone technology was remarkably improved. A pound of flint in a pebble-tool technology would produce about two inches of cutting edge.

---

[1] Frank E. Poirier, *Fossil Evidence: The Human Evolutionary Journey* (St. Louis: C. V. Mosby, 1977).

Field Museum of Natural History

Blades of flint were struck from a core and fashioned into tools. The burin (left), the borer (center), and the end-scraper (right) resulted from minor modifications in the stone blade.

The same pound of flint with the peeling technique could yield 40 feet of razor-sharp edges. Economic use of materials was obviously a value in the use of blades, besides the fact that they could be so quickly produced.

Once struck off, they were easily refashioned into a wealth of functional tools. There was the *burin,* a *chisel-shaped blade* used for working in bone, wood, and antler. Borers, with their narrow, sharp points, were used for making holes in bones, shells, and hides, while notched blades were probably used for scraping the shafts of arrows and spears. Tools had become highly varied and now included more tools-to-make-tools. Humanity was equipping itself for a hunting adventure.

By some 17,000 years ago, the hunting kit was more elaborate still. At the site of Cueva de Ambrosio, in the mountains of southeastern Spain, small projectile points were discovered with a stem for attachment to a shaft. This suggests that Upper Pleistocene hunters had developed the bow and arrow. And yet, the first direct evidence of this—the preserved remains of over 100 wooden arrows—comes from Stellmoor in northern Germany, dating from 7,000 years later. The bow and arrow's beginnings

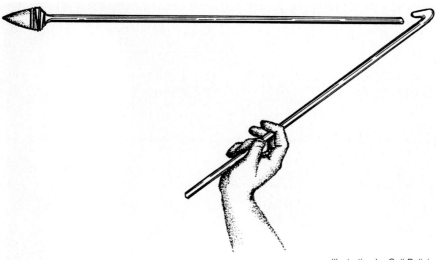

Illustration by Gail Delicio

The spear thrower (atl-atl). By artificially extending the arm, it added velocity to the spear.

are uncertain, but this is not the case with other complex tools. Both the barbed harpoon and the spear thrower are striking examples of the tool-maker's skill; both make their appearance in Cro-Magnon times. Harpoons were economically significant along the rivers that were filled with spawning salmon. The spear thrower—a hooked rod of wood or bone— was an artificial extension of the arm. This increased the killing force of the spear, at the possible expense of a certain amount of accuracy, and became a valuable weapon in hunting large game.

Much of the hunting technology, of course, was behavioral strategy as well, derived from the now-distant days of Torralba-Ambrona. The tundra region was dotted with thousands of shallow lakes and boggy marshes. Mammoth on the Soviet wastes were probably driven into the bogs, killed, and butchered as in the days of *Homo erectus*. In the river valleys of Western Europe, caribou and horses were major staples and were stampeded into blind canyons or over a cliff. The supply of game was more dependable than it ever had been before; in some regions, there might have been a surplus of food.

A knowledge of animal behavior was more elaborate than it ever had been, especially as it applied to the movements of herds. Hunters needed to know when the caribou would arrive in the spring and when they would migrate to southerly forests in the last part of autumn. But the seasons were no more important than a knowledge of the routes of migration. Upper Pleistocene hunters were closely familiar with the animals' routes and probably lived a short distance away from the trails of game. Such campsites would have made it possible to gain a living from "un-

Field Museum of Natural History

Herd of mammoth. The species was especially abundant on the Asian tundra.

earned resources."[2] Instead of scanning, tracking, and stalking across an extensive region for game, hunters could wait at the edge of the trails for the herds to arrive. This technique was probably known in the time of *Homo erectus*, but the changed climatic conditions and the flourishing animal populations made it more rewarding than ever before.

Closely bound up with the hunt was the need for migration. Not since *Homo erectus* and the emergence of specialized hunting had so vast a region been glimpsed by human explorers. Outside Africa, Europe, and Asia, the Cro-Magnon hunters discovered new lands. They traveled by boat and on foot to Sumatra and beyond to Asutralia; they migrated across a stretch of tundra that later flooded and became the Bering Strait. From that point, the migration moved southward, across the Canadian wilderness, and came down to the game-rich grasslands of early America. Eventually, the waves of migration reached the hills of Tierra del Fuego. The human species had suddenly traversed the inhabitable world.

What led to this great exploration? Was Cro-Magnon beginning to grow curious about the world beyond the tundra's horizon? Or was it big-game technology itself, and an incessant pursuit of the herds, the animals leading the trailing hunters to the world's distant reaches? Most probably it was neither of these—although this might seem surprising. Curiosity does not really tell us why the migration took place when it did. For at least 200 millenia, human beings have had modern brains. Neanderthal had the capacity to be curious about existence itself, but these earlier intellec-

---

[2]Bernard G. Campbell, *Humankind Emerging,* (Boston: Little, Brown, 1979).

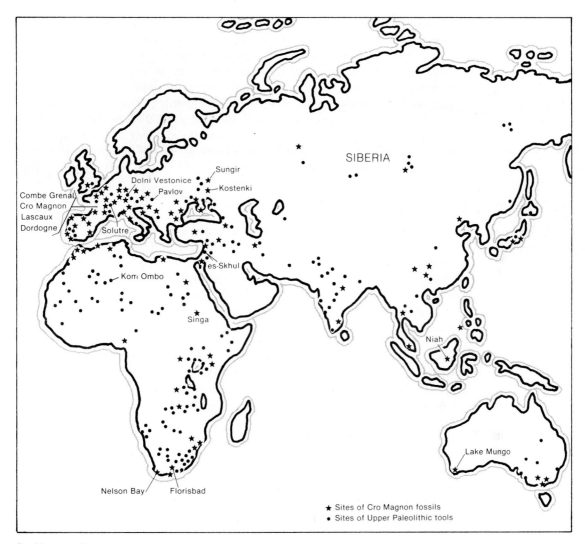

Cro-Magnon sites.

tual adventures did not lead to migration. Nor could it have been simply the result of following the animals wherever they went. The big-game hunters that are living today—such as the Caribou Eskimo of Canada—stay within a defined territory in which they wait for the herds to arrive.[3] Their unearned resources strategy is an ancient survival.

Rather than curiosity and pursuit, we might consider the game herds themselves. They had been increasingly hunted by humans for thousands

[3]J. B. Birdsell, *Human Evolution* (Skokie, Ill.: Rand McNally, 1972).

of years. Nothing ever evolves in a vacuum, but rather in relation to all parts of its world. Very likely, as humans grew skillful in the killing of larger-size prey, the animals learned to be wary of two-footed life. Conceivably, an encampment of hunters could prey on a herd many years, as they followed their usual route to the tundra in spring. But the animals learned from predation; in time, there was a shift in their route. Hunters sought out new encampments, very likely in unsettled lands. There, the herds had not learned to avoid them—and the process began once again. Through such waves of settling and probing, the planet became dotted with humans. The strategies of hunters and animals were peopling the world.

The hunters of Western Europe

Wherever the hunters journeyed, a record was left behind. Human settlements were becoming more permanent; the middens grew deep. This clutter of daily existence—ash and charcoal, outlines of shelters, ornaments, tools, statuettes, human burials, and butchered bones—has afforded a great deal of insight into Cro-Magnon life.

A rich cluster of such sites has been excavated in the southwestern portion of France in a region of forested valleys that is called Les Eyzies. Today it is a network of streams flowing through steep limestone valleys. Deciduous and coniferous forests now blanket the land. The sheer cliffs that lead down to the rivers are pocketed with caves and rock shelters which served for some 20 millenia as the dwellings of hunters.

One such shelter, Laugerie-Haute, is found today in the village of Les Eyzies.[4] The Vezere River is a short distance away, flowing south to where it meets the Dordogne. It is a protective overhang of rock, some 12 feet deep and nearly 60 feet long. Here the litter of a hunting encampment has created deposits close to 18 feet thick. Archeologists for over a century have probed through its layers.

There were 42 of those layers to dig through, going back to 19,000 years before the present. Southern France was bitingly cold then, and Les Eyzies was a nearly treeless tundra. The lowest levels have frost-shattered rocks—éboulis, as French geologists call them—and contain only the faintest traces of the pollen from trees. But the hunters endured on the tundra. Fires were built on the floor of the shelter; animals were hunted along the Vezere. The bones of caribou, wild horse, ibex, mammoth, bear, and wild cattle are found in the earliest layers on the floor of the shelter.

By 17,000 years ago, the climate had grown much warmer. The final 16 layers of the shelter contain a rich diversity of tools and some evidence that the Laugerie hunters were dabbling in art. There are burins, scrapers, awls, borers, bone points, and needles; excavators found the possible

---

[4]D. K. Bhattacharya, *Palaeolithic Europe: A Summary of Some Important Finds with Special Reference to Central Europe* (Atlantic Highlands, N.J.: Humanities Press, 1977).

remains of a composite bow. Just above these uppermost layers, there are lines along the roof of the shelter. They vaguely suggest two animals—and the emergence of artistic creation. The hunters at Laugerie-Haute had done more than survive.

Some insight into their artistry is afforded through other discoveries: engravings in bone and antler that were found in the shelter. From the layers of 20,000 years ago, a flat fragment of bone was recovered with 33 separate lines carved into its surface. Microscopic examination of the fragment revealed subtle distinctions among the lines. Some had been deeply gouged out, and others were scratched on the surface. Most of the lines were vertical, but a few of them were canted at an angle. There were noticeable differences, too, in the length of the lines. Alexander Marshack has long investigated such curious markings. He believes they were used to keep track of the moon's changing phases.[5] The number of marks corresponds exactly with the number of nights that the moon can be seen. (In a bone recovered from Blanchard, France, the marks are carefully shaped into crescents.) Very possibly, the Laugerie people kept a tally of the moon and the seasons. When would the game herds depart? Was there time for a hunt before winter? Some 20,000 years in the past, we were living by schedules.

There was another engraving as well, found just above the flat bone with the markings. On a fragment of caribou antler, a hunter had sketched out the heads of two mammoths. The elephants are facing each other; their heads are in contact. For Marshack the antler engraving is a depiction of sexual behavior: bull elephants are butting their heads in a struggle for mates. But why was this carved on the antler? What meanings could it possibly have? Questions about such creations amount to a searching of the Cro-Magnon mind—a provocative investigation that we will explore. But for the moment at least, it is evident that the artist has come into being, along with abundant resources and a more secure life.

All across the European tundra, humanity was settling down. There was greater control over the environment than ever before. About a hundred miles southeast of Paris, along the banks of the river Cure, is a cave that humans have lived in since Neanderthal times. Inside the cave of Arcy-sur-Cure, the cultural deposits are 12 feet thick and date back to the very beginning of Cro-Magnon times. Some 32,000 years ago, Cro-Magnon moved into the cave and, like the hunters at Laugerie-Haute, had to fight off the winter.

Pollen that was found in the lowest layers revealed a tundra barely free of the ice. The region was probably cold nearly all of the year. Temperatures along the tundra can drop to 70 degrees below zero and even lower when the open country is lashed by the wind. Inside the cave, the hunters built shelters to shield their fires, and themselves, from the cold. Tusks

---

[5]Alexander Marshack, *The Roots of Civilization* (New York: McGraw-Hill, 1972).

of mammoth were pushed into the ground—one of these was discovered in place—and hides were probably stretched over them to serve as a windbreak. But caribou bones were abundant; they were discovered throughout the deposit. Through the strategy of specialized hunting, people were surviving in a difficult land.

But that strategy was growing spectacular, and perhaps it was dangerously so. At a campsite in eastern France that is locally called Solutré, there are jutting, steep-sided cliffs that overlook the Rhone valley.[6] At the foot of these towering cliffs, some 20,000 years before the present, groups of Cro-Magnon hunters lay in wait for their herds. Wild horses once thundered through this region, perilously close to the edge of the cliff. The hunters apparently stampeded the animals and drove them over the edge to their deaths. The floor of the peaceful valley is strewn with their bones.

Over 10,000 horses were killed there, although this took perhaps 3,000 years; among their butchered skeletal remains are the tools of the hunters. Even these are mildly spectacular; perhaps some of them were not tools at all. They were certainly virtuoso examples of blade-making art. Flaked on both sides with precision, some very thin and with continuous edges, these strikingly different blade artifacts have a very brief span. They are abundant throughout Solutré and in the upper layers of Laugerie-Haute. They appear 20,000 years before the present; 3,000 years later they are suddenly gone. What could this flash of uniqueness have possibly meant?

One explanation is an immigrant culture that had hunted its way into Europe through the process of settling and budding from some distant region. Similar blades have been discovered in North Africa, Hungary, and Spain.[7] Did the Solutrean big-game hunters come from one of these three? Prehistorian Philip Smith believes that their origins were in southern France; the other possibilities just do not seem to fit. The finely chipped blades that have been unearthed in North Africa, Hungary, and Spain are part of a more elaborate toolkit than Solutrean blades found at Laugerie-Haute. The best examples of an early Solutrean are in France itself.

More vexing has been the question of why humans would fashion such blades. What function could they possibly have in a hunting society? The celebrated laurel-leaf points have a sharp, continuous edge. Dangerous to hold in the naked hand, impossible to bind to a shaft, they appear to be totally lacking in an obvious function. For this reason, Smith has suggested that they were "showpieces and luxury items"; for John Pfeiffer, they might have been trade items, a primitive money. It is difficult to think of experiments that would help us to resolve such a question, but always useful to remember the context in which something is found. At

[6]Philip Van Dorn Stern, *Prehistoric Europe* (New York: W. W. Norton, 1969).
[7]Philip E. L. Smith, "The Solutrean Culture," *Scientific American*, August 1964.

Volgu, to the west of the Dordogne, laurel-leaf blades had been buried together, the type of treatment that might have been reserved for luxury items. But at the type site of Solutré, the laurel-leaf blades had been dropped on the ground. They were found among the bones of the horses at the foot of the cliff.

Perhaps the curious objects are the relics of ancient beliefs. It seems possible that Solutré hunters, after butchering the horses' remains, may have left ceremonial blades among the jumble of bones. It might have been a variety of magic to insure the return of the game. The blades may have blended religion with hunting and art.

Striking evidence of magical behavior has been found in a bleak coastal land. Eleven miles north of the city of Hamburg, in the flatlands of northern Germany, the dramatic evidence of a hunting ritual was still in the ground.[8] This region was desolate tundra then, some 12,000 years before the present, a wind-blasted naked shingle at the edge of the world. Only recently freed of the glacier, the land was covered with marshes and lakes; violent blizzards would howl through the country almost all of the year. But during the brief months of summer, the caribou would come up to the lowlands; Cro-Magnon hunters would establish their camp at the Meiendorf site.

Archeologist Alfred Rust discovered a litter of reindeer bones scattered across the ground of the north German camp. From the stage of their antler growth, as well as the pollen and wood in the soil, Rust determined that the campsite was used in the summer months. Caribou were obviously crucial to the hunters at the Meiendorf site; they supplied almost all of the food and the bone tools as well. Antlers were worked into needles and points; some were curiously grooved on the sides. One—a thong cutter perhaps—had been fitted with a fragment of flint. Throughout the debris of bones were the hunters' stone tools. Most of these were smaller-size blades—*microliths,* they are generally called—including scrapers of various kinds and many bone-working tools. (There was one type of blade in particular that caught the attention of Alfred Rust. He called it a *Papageienschnabelklingenendhohlkratzerbohrerschraber,* evidently because it looked like one to him. Other archeologists—people of fewer syllables than Rust—quickly suggested that the little burin be called a *Zinke.*)

At the edge of the Meiendorf camp, where there was once a silt-bottomed lake, Rust encountered the buried remains of a Cro-Magnon rite. The complete skeleton of a two-year-old reindeer was discovered in the lake-bottom silts with a rock weighing 18 pounds behind the animal's rib cage. The bones were not cracked or split; the skeleton was perfectly intact. There seems to be only one way that this could have been done. When the hunters had killed the animal—perhaps it was the first of the season—they slashed it open and forced the rock up behind its ribs. Then,

---

[8]Johannes Maringer, *The Gods of Prehistoric Man* (New York: Alfred A. Knopf, 1960).

H. Armstrong Roberts

Herd of caribou. The mutual adaptations of hunters and prey were probably a significant factor in the migrations of Cro-Magnon into the Americas.

possibly after sewing it back up, they tossed the body into the waters of the lake. The carcass sank to the bottom; the ritual was done.

Like Neanderthal cave bear behavior, the reindeer sacrifice is not well understood. It was conceivably related to fertility or to a spirit believed to live in the lake; such details will almost certainly remain unknown. But in a larger sense, we can see such rituals as religious adaptation, as a strategy reaching back to Neanderthal times. Magical and religious behavior is reinforcing the role of the hunter. In some regions of Europe and Asia, it involved the creation of visual art. But this is to venture somewhat ahead of our story.

The hunters of the Asian tundra and early Australia

Thousands of miles from the Meiendorf site, in Central Europe and the wilds of Asia, the strategy of big-game hunting was intensely pursued. Here the mammoth was the dominant prey—other animals were not as abundant—and the sites along the eastern tundra are thick with their bones. At Dolni Vestonice, a Czechoslovakian dwelling site, a pile of mammoth bones nearly 40 feet wide and 135 feet long had accumulated right in the middle of a hunting encampment.[9]

Dwellings were close to the edge of the pile and were solidly built. The first one to be discovered was some 15 feet wide and nearly 30 feet long, with limestone blocks and stones along its perimenter. Deposits inside

[9]J. Jelinek, *The Pictorial Encyclopedia of the Evolution of Man.* (Hamlyn, N.Y., 1975).

the dwelling contained over 30,000 stone tools, more than a thousand of which were clustered near a central fire. There were five fireplaces in all—two at each end and one in the center—suggesting that resident groups were becoming larger. Beyond this house, there were tentative traces of three additional dwellings and, at the farthest end of the settlement, a separate hut.

The hut was smaller—about 15 feet wide—and well removed from the rest of the dwellings; a single, oval fireplace was found in the center. When Czechoslovakian archeologists began removing the ashes from the

Cro-Magnon figurine from Dolni Vestonice. Exaggerated sexual characteristics suggest a fertility symbol.

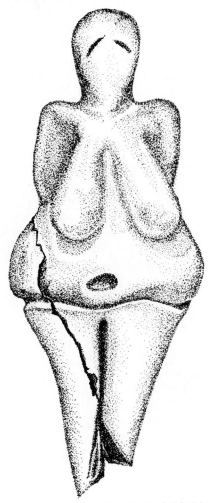

Illustration by Gail Delicio

hearth, they found molded pieces of clay that had been left in the fire. There was a statuette of a bear, a horse's head, a catlike animal, and a lioness with a gash just above its left ear. Conceivably, this was deliberate: a possible symbol of wounding. Also within the ashes was a Venus figurine—a tiny, fired-clay sculpture of a human female. Similar figurines have been discovered at Cro-Magnon sites in both Europe and Asia. The body is nude, breasts and buttocks are large, the stomach is swollen, and the extremities small. The figurine is almost certainly a fertility symbol.

More abstract representations of the human female were discovered as well. There were incisings that possibly illustrated the buttocks and sexual organs, drilled ivory pendants carved into the shape of breasts, and a highly stylized pendant of a female figure. This is all very powerful evidence for the existence of a fertility ritual. But whether hunters were recognizing the specific fertility of human females or more generically celebrating the fertility of the herds or of nature is an aspect of Cro-Magnon life of which little is known.

But throughout Asia, the hunters were moving. Human settlements conquered the tundra. At Kostienki, in the Soviet Ukraine, longhouses and half-sunken huts were built out of mammoth skeletons and covered with hides.[10] One such house was nearly a 100 feet long with 10 fireplaces

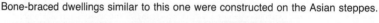

Bone-braced dwellings similar to this one were constructed on the Asian steppes.

Field Museum of Natural History

---

[10]Ibid.

aligned down the center and divided by molded steps into three different sections. There was also a three-section longhouse at Pushkari on the banks of the Don, a settlement built in the middle of mammoth debris. And at Mezhiritch, the jawbones of mammoths were used to reinforce circular huts, while entire skulls were used at Mezin in the Ukraine. Moving deeply into Siberia, the hunters continued to set up encampments. At Malta, dwellings were built from molded-clay blocks and the bones of the mammoth, reinforced by a line of flat stones on the inside of the wall.

The migration moved southward as well, toward the islands of Southeast Asia. The route that was taken is uncertain—through Java or perhaps Borneo—but eventually the Pleistocene hunters set foot in Australia. This must have involved a boating technology, since there was no land bridge that reached to that continent, but simple boats would have presented no problem to a Cro-Magnon craftsman. Long familiar with hides and wood frameworks—they had used them for dwellings at Moldovia in the Ukraine—the hunters could have easily put together small vessels perfectly suited for crossing 40 or 50 miles to the Australian mainland.

The appearance of the island continent then was little different than it is today.[11] Some 30,000 years before the present, the core of Australia was already a vast desert with a northern border of tropical monsoons and a cooler coastal fringe along the south. At Lake Mungo, in Southeastern Australia, five campsites on the edges of lakes provide evidence that humans were adapting to local conditions in distant reaches of the world. It was a lake chain in a scrub forest area, very different from the tundra of Asia. There were perch and cod in the lakes, which were netted or speared and then brought back to camp; there were rabbit-size kangaroos that were hunted in the brush of the scrub; there was the bandicoot, a rat-size marsupial with a long tail but ears like a rabbit. The eggs of the emu, an ostrichlike bird, were collected as well in the scrub, while shellfish were scooped from the mud of the lakewater shallows.

Their dead were ceremonially cremated; the remains of this practice were at Lake Mungo as well. The body of a young woman was burned; her bones were smashed and then buried in the ground. This identical burial procedure was practiced by Southeastern Australian aborigines as recently as a 100 years ago. Their culture in many respects has been remarkably stable.

At the approximate time that the Lake Mungo woman was buried, big-game hunters were expanding far east into the depths of Siberia. By gradual shifts in their campsites, they were moving through a desolate terrain. Winter came, and they gathered at their fires. Meat was dug from deep caches in the ice. Spring came, and there were great herds of mammoths. There were mastodon, musk-ox, and deer. The settlement grew. Some

---

[11]M. Barbetti and H. Allen, "Prehistoric Man at Lake Mungo, Australia, by 32,000 Years BC," *Nature* 240 (November 3, 1972), p. 46.

hunters moved onward. Autumn came, and the skies were like metal. Flurries of snow whisked and danced in the air. The hunters gathered again at their fires. What had happened to the ones that moved on? Their trails had quickly been covered with the winter's first snow. And many miles distant, along the same tundra and in the chill of the fog-shrouded coast, the migrants were also gathering by the warmth of their fires.

Season flowed on into season. The morning and sunset were day. The winter darkness was blazing with colors. Curious fires pinpointed the night. Yet the restless movement continued. The hunters broke camp and pushed on.

And discovered a world.

The earliest migrations into the Americas

"Beginnings are apt to be shadowy," as Rachel Carson once said. This is especially true of the original discovery of America. Three fundamental questions are, as always: how? when? and where? For all three, the existing answers are still controversial.

The question of where the migrations occurred is the best understood of the three, although even here there are a number of still unsolved problems. At the outset, we can dismiss the fantastic. Sunken civilizations and the seven "Lost Tribes of Israel" are explanations that sound like an echo out of Feldhofer Grotto. Indeed, many of them were voiced at that time and for similar reasons. Archeology, until the present century, was only sparsely done in North America, and often what little had been done was not well understood. Besides, Darwin's ideas were feared and distorted. American Indians were viewed as heathens. Except for the use of one's fantasy (widely exercised in these early speculations), there was scarcely any other route open for exploring the past.

But 50 years of scientific archeology have cleared away at least part of this darkness. Tools found in Siberia and Alaska are noticeably similar. The geology of both regions reveals that they shared a tundra environment; there was pasturage in Asia and America for migrating game. And significantly, the continents were connected. The expansion of the Wisconsin glacier (called the Wurm or the Weichsel in Eurasia) caused sea levels to drop in what is now the Bering Strait region. This exposed a shelf of land, known as Beringia, between Siberia and western Alaska, covered with tundra, and sometimes as much as a 1000 miles wide.

Yet difficult questions remain. It is not enough to say that the migration occurred between Siberia and western Alaska; we need a more specific idea of where the entry took place. The problem is made more complicated by the presence of two huge sheets of ice that covered Canada almost as far south as the U.S. border. One of these, the Cordilleran, extended from close to the Pacific coast to somewhere on the eastern fringe of the Rocky Mountains. The other, the Laurentide, ranged from east of the Rocky Mountains, across Hudson Bay and Quebec, and as far south as the present-day Great Lakes area. Between the two sheets of ice, there may have been an ice-free corridor, through which hunters and game moved southward into the New World. But this view has been recently challenged by archeologist K. R. Fladmark. "A wide range of data suggests," he wrote in 1979, "that a mid-continental corridor was not an encouraging area for human occupation."[12] The massive Laurentide ice sheet may have blocked an easterly flow of soil drainage. Instead of a belt of verdant tundra, the corridor might have been a region of ice and floods. Soil samples, taken from the area where the corridor is thought to have been, suggest a territory almost barren of plant and animal life from 27,000 to 11,000 years ago. Beyond this, the only recognizable archeological complex discovered in the corridor area dates from around 11,000 years before the present. This is a late date when seen in the context of other sites and is a major piece of evidence for Fladmark's view.

So, which route did the hunters take? At this moment, no one is certain, but K. R. Fladmark favors the coast of the northern Pacific. Its waters were warmed by the Japanese current; there is no evidence that it was covered with ice. Cold air from the glaciated mainland, blowing over the warm ocean waters, in all likelihood created a coastland with much fog and rain. As in this region today, there was probably heavy vegetation, an environment that was very well suited to hunters and herds.

If Fladmark is correct, this brings to mind new questions of how the hunters migrated into America. The presence of Cro-Magnon people on the island of Australia indicates that boats were now probably a part of human technology. A gradual southerly movement in boats made of hides: this might well have been the way the migration was done. But the archeological evidence—if, in fact, it exists at all—would have been lost in the flooding shoreline as the Wisconsin glacier melted and then strewn across the floor of the northern Pacific.

The last essential question, of when the migration occurred, involves difficulties with the methods of archeology. Radiocarbon (carbon-14) is used for a time span that makes it appropriate for dating the majority of sites in both the Americas. But carbon-14 is only useful for some 50,000 years into the past; close to that limit, the dates are generally not as reliable. But the resolution of this difficulty is hopefully not far away. A new array of techniques is extending the range of carbon-14, and an independent method is being developed. Amino-acid racemization, as the new technique is called, involves aspartic acid which is found in the protein of bone. This molecule changes slowly, perhaps at a stable rate, from an optically active substance—which will rotate a plane of light—into a racemic substance—one that is optically inactive. By determining the amount

---

[12]K. R. Fladmark, "Routes: Alternate Migration Corridors for Early Man in North America," *American Antiquity* 44, no. 1, (1979), pp. 55–70.

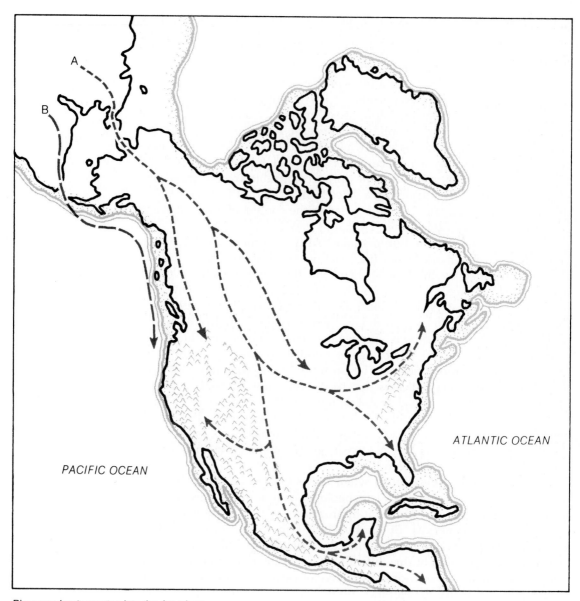

Big-game hunter routes into the Americas.

of converted amino acid within the bone, it is ultimately possible to arrive at a date for the sample.

Some recently dated materials have sent a mild tremor through New World prehistory. They seem older than many archeologists would have ever suspected. A human skull fragment unearthed near San Diego may be 44,000 years old; a skull and jawbone from the same general region may be 48,000 years old. If this dating proves to be accurate, it could obviously alter our view of the antiquity of the earliest societies that found the New World.

That world was an unspoiled wilderness some 40,000 years before the present, from the tundra of central Alaska to Tierra del Fuego. Virtually all of present-day Canada was under Cordilleran and Laurentide ice. Possibly there were isolated areas—*refugia*, they are usually called—where the tundra survived near the edges of these massive ice sheets. The continental corridor and the Pacific coastland may have been refugia tundra, and so might have been the region of present-day Nova Scotia. Below the ice, but just above the forest and near the United States-Canada border, there was a meandering stretch of tundra from Washington State to just south of Massachusetts. South of that, there extended an almost unimaginable forest.

Early Paleo-Indian adaptations

Across the northern United States, it was a tract of *boreal forest: a subarctic woodland that is dominated by coniferous trees.* Towering pine trees, spruce, larch, and fir extended west to what is now the Great Plains, while southeastern United States was deciduous forest. In the northeast region of the country, there was tundra and cold-weather grassland; scattered throughout this southerly tundra were patches of ice. Below the tundra, the American southwest was not the desert that it is today but an expanse of open grassland with stretches of forest. Mexico and Central America were also a wooded terrain, where evergreen forests blended into savanna grasslands. The Amazon Basin of Latin America, a tropical forest today, was a 9-million-square-mile region of woodland-savanna. An arid Pacific coastal desert followed the spine of the Andes Mountains, and in southernmost Latin America, there was subarctic forest.

Gigantic grazing and browsing animals lumbered across the Americas then, the chosen prey of the Upper Pleistocene hunting tradition. Horses and mammoths grazed on the tundra; the mastodons browsed on the leaves of the woodlands. The American West was the home of the camel, and there were great herds of bison as well. Like the wilderness of Europe and Asia, the Americas was a land for the hunter. The stage had been set for the climax of an ancient tradition.

The hunting societies that migrated across Beringia into the Americas are known in archeology as the *Paleo-Indians.* The earliest sites that we have for this period of American prehistory are the subjects of an extensive controversy. Much of the controversy is concerned with routes and methods of travel and much with the special problems of dating techniques. But added to these difficulties is another theme of debate: the ability of scientists to recognize a primitive tool. The movements of glaciers and frozen lakes can splinter rocks in the surrounding soil. The resulting fragments can be mistaken for human tools.

It was exactly such a difficulty that was presented by the Calico site in the Mojave Desert of southern California.[13] The ubiquitous L. S. B. Leakey and Ruth Simpson excavated the site and found 170 stones within undisturbed soil. They had dug down 13 feet into the silt of an ancient stream, a cone-shaped deposit that is known as an *alluvial fan.* There they found large stone flakes that bore the marks of having been struck. Some of the stones appeared to be scrapers; others seemed to have been chipped on both sides. Louis Leakey and Ruth Simpson considered these finds to have been "unquestionably the result of human activity."

Other archeologists were not as convinced. C. Vance Haynes has pointed out that the Calico flints were discovered within a matrix of gravel and cobblestones that conceivably could have flaked them through natural pressure.[14] Were Leakey and Simpson in error? We still do not know. But if distinctive cultural materials (the remains of a hearth, for example) were ever unearthed from the layer where the fragments were found, it could significantly revise our views of the American past. The weathered gravels in question are more than 70,000 years old and "an age of 500,000 cannot be precluded." An age of 500,000, of course, is *Homo erectus* times. Clearly, the Calico finds are to be treated with caution.

The controversy over the earliest Americans continues to gather momentum. New excavations generate materials for the natural versus cultural debate; excavations of decades ago are evaluated again as contemporary dating techniques are applied to the finds.[15] From Santa Rosa Island, off the southern California coast, four samples of dwarf mammoth bones may be 29,000 years old; the reddened earth in which they were found was possibly a hearth. Two sites on the outskirts of La Jolla were dug in the late 1920s, and the materials could very well be of considerable age. There is no question in this case about natural versus cultural remains; both of the sites produced human skeletal material. From one individual, there was one complete rib and a number of rib fragments surviving, with a cluster of beads adhering to some of the bones. Amino-acid dating yielded an age of 28,000 years, but this was modest in comparison with other results. At a deeper level than the ribs and beads, the front of a human cranium was found and dated to 44,000 years before the present. Ultimately, a skull and a jawbone, long bones, and a shoulder-blade fragment have been amino-acid dated to 48,000 years.

Far to the north of La Jolla, along the Yukon's Old Crow River, are additional traces of early Paleo-Indians.[16] This is a valley of subarctic forest with small lakes and a meandering river: a 3,000-square-mile basin

---

[13]L. S. B. Leakey, Ruth De Ette Simpson, and Thomas Clements, "Archeological Excavations in the Calico Mountains, California: Preliminary Report," *Science,* May 31, 1968.

[14]C. Vance Haynes, Jr., "The Earliest Americans," *Science,* November 7, 1969.

[15]J. Bada, R. Schroeder, and G. Carter, "New Evidence for the Antiquity of Man in North America Deduced from Aspartic Acid Racemization," *Science* 184 (1974), p. 791.

[16]W. N. Irving and C. R. Harrington, "Upper Pleistocene Radiocarbon-Dated Artifacts from the Northern Yukon," *Science,* January 26, 1973.

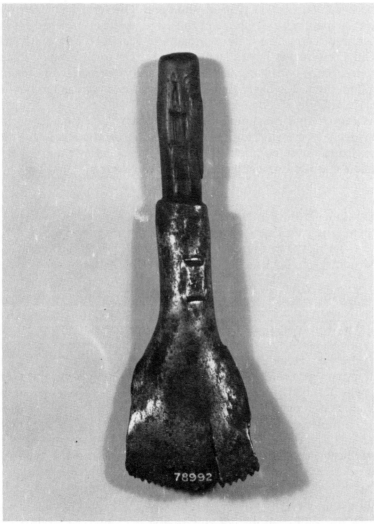

Field Museum of Natural History

Bone flesher similar to the one discovered at Old Crow River. Note the serrated edge of the tool.

that was teeming with game. Every spring the melting snow replenishes the water of the Old Crow River, which gouges out fossilized bones from the silt of its banks. Strewn along the edges of the river are the bones of mammoths and horses, as well as the jawbones of what were possibly domesticated dogs. Archeologists have excavated more than 20 sites in this basin where the river continues to churn fossils out of the ground.

In one instance, excavators found on the surface of an eroding bank a dark-stained caribou tibia or shinbone. One end had been whittled flat into a spatulalike device, and the edge had been notched into a series of serrated teeth. The Ojibwa Indians of Manitoba and the Kutchin of the Old Crow region have used such bones for defleshing or scraping down hides. Since bones are most easily carved when they are fresh, the excavators think it is likely that the notches are as old as the bone itself. The caribou bone was dated to about 27,000 years before the present, as old as the charred mammoth bones on Santa Rosa Island. Site by site the evidence is growing for an early presence of humans in the Americas. It may turn out to be true that by 40,000 years before the present, humanity had set foot into most of the inhabitable world.

The later Paleo-Indians

Wherever the hunters traveled, they adapted to the wilderness around them. The later Paleo-Indian sites—30,000 to 11,000 years before the present—are rich with animal bones and stone tools, and the strata are deeper. Meadowcroft Rockshelter in Pennsylvania—an overhanging sandstone ledge—has been lived in by hunters and gatherers for nearly 18,000 years, reminiscent of the rock-ledge homes in the Dordogne Valley. James M. Adovasio and the students at the Meadowcroft site have removed over 200 tons of livingfloor soil.[17] The digging was done with trowels and occasionally with razor blades. Nearly 3.5 million artifacts have been found at the site. Stone projectile points and knives, scattered flakes from the chipping of tools, the blackened soils of cooking fires, and the butchered bones of rabbit and deer: these and other materials reveal an almost continuous occupation from Paleo-Indian to recent Colonial times.

A similar depth of tradition is found in regions as far removed as the Kobuk River of northern Alaska and the mountain-ringed valleys of southern Peru. At the Onion Portage site, just to the south of Alaska's Brooks Range, hunters had camped for thousands of years along the Kobuk River.[18] A patchy forest of spruce and willow lay directly south of the camp, and the tundra—with wild onions—stretched out to the north. Like the hunters at the Meiendorf site, the people of Onion Portage probably camped and awaited the arrival of the spring herds. Through more than 70 campsite surfaces in a deposit that is 20 feet thick, archeologists have traced a tradition of seasonal occupation that endured for nearly 17,000 years. The earliest layers—around 15,000 years before the present—suggest the litter at the Meiendorf site. There were microlith burins and scrapers, and caribou antler projectile points. From northern Germany to northern Alaska, wherever the forest disappeared into tundra, hunters were camping year after year in the path of the herds.

[17]Thomas Y. Canby, "The Search for the First Americans," *National Geographic*, September 1979.

[18]Douglas D. Anderson, "A Stone Age Campsite at the Gateway to America," *Scientific American*, (June 1968).

Far to the south, in the Andean highlands 200 miles southeast of Lima, Peru, there is evidence of such long-term traditions in Latin America.[19] Nine thousand feet above sea level, on the eastern slope of a volcanic rock, Richard MacNeish excavated Pikimachay (in English, Flea Cave). The cavern is 40 feet high in some places and runs 80 feet deep into the mountain. There is a basinlike hollow in the lava that makes up the floor of the cave, and it was here that MacNeish excavated the earliest strata. In a 1.5 feet thick layer nearly 15,000 years old, there were scattered stone flakes and the bones of a sloth and a horse. Just below this, MacNeish encountered a shoulder blade fragment of a sloth some 1,000 years older than the animals buried above it. At the very bottom of the fossil-rich basin, were the ribs and vertebra of a sloth and the leg bone of what might have been a horse or a camel. This deepest layer of all is nearly 20,000 years old. At that time, the surrounding countryside was probably a temperate forest. Here too, there was a stable existence in a plentiful world.

Throughout the Americas, as in Europe and Asia, the deeply stratified hunters' sites are the archeological remnants of a successful tradition. In Meadowcroft and Pikimachay, Onion Portage and Meiendorf, Pushkari and Kostienki, and the shelters along the Vezere, hunters revisited their hearths and homes season after season. But the way of life of the big-game hunters was slowly nearing its end. The world in which humanity lived was about to be changed.

Diorama exhibit entitled "Ventana Cave, Arizona, 10,000 years ago." Overview of Paleo-Indian environment in Arizona.

The Arizona State Museum, The University of Arizona, Helga Teiwes, Photographer

[19]Richard S. MacNeish, "Early Man in the Andes," *Scientific American*, April 1971.

The final 3,000 years of the Paleo-Indian adaptation saw a climax in the efficiency of the big-game hunters. Sites are far more numerous; tools are similar to each other. The implication would seem to be that human populations were increasing and maintaining cultural contact throughout North America. The tools that date from this period have a distinctive style of manufacture. The Americas were moving away from their Old World traditions.

It was at about this time—12,000 years before the present—that the distinctive "Clovis points" made their first appearance. They were about four inches long, with concave bases and bifacial chipping. A flake was removed just above the base on each side of the projectile point, leaving behind a groove or a channel that is called a flute. These unique projectile points had deadly effectiveness in killing big game. They have been discovered at kill sites across the North American continent.

One such site was Blackwater Draw, on the outskirts of Clovis, New Mexico. Twelve thousand years ago, it was marshland and bogs. Here, hunters surrounded a mammoth (probably as it came to the marsh to get water), drove it into the mire, killed it, and butchered the meat. A similar strategy was probably used to kill a mammoth at Silver Springs, Florida, and a mastodon along the banks of the Sewanee River. By 11,000 years ago, the mammoth was extinct in North America, along with horses, camels, dwarf elephants, and saber-toothed cats.

The world was unquestionably changing; the strategies of the hunters were evolving as well. A drama was being played out to its very last act. The fluted points were shortened to a length of around two inches, conceivably to produce more weapons from an outcropping of flint. These Folsom points, as they are called, are often found with the bones of bison, a species that was now existing on borrowed time. The first Folsom point ever discovered was embedded in clay near the ribs of a bison, on a tributary of the Cimarron River near Folsom, New Mexico. The same type of point has been found in Texas and Colorado as well, in most cases with the skeletal remains of the Pleistocene bison.

But it was along a branch of the Big Sandy Creek, on the bunchgrass plains of east Colorado, where archeologists were afforded a glimpse of the end of an era. Sixteen miles southeast of Kit Carson and just north of the Arkansas River valley, there is a dried-out gully (or arroyo) that is called Olsen-Chubbuck. It was here, some 9,000 years ago, that Paleo-Indians surrounded a herd of bison, drove nearly 200 of them into the gully, and then slaughtered them all. In this instance, unlike Solutré, there is little question as to how many animals were killed at one time. The skeletal remains of the bison—there were 193 animals in all—were found in "butchering groups" through the entire length of the gully. Almost all of the bison had apparently been pulled out of the ditch. They were butchered by teams and their bones were piled into groups.

Archeologist Joe Ben Wheat used meat-to-bone ratios of modern bison

Field Museum of Natural History

Fluted projectile points of the American big-game hunters. In time, these points were shortened as an economizing measure. A greater number of tools could be made from an outcropping of flint.

The Arizona State Museum, The University of Arizona, Helga Teiwes, Photographer

Diorama exhibit entitled "Ventana Cave, Arizona, 10,000 years ago." Mammoth hunting scene.

to estimate the amount of meat that was hauled from the site. The final calculation is somewhat staggering: 56,640 pounds! Wheat wrote of this figure,

> A Plains Indian could completely butcher a bison in about an hour. If we allow one-and-a-half hours for the dissection of the larger species, the butchering at the Olsen-Chubbuck site would have occupied about 210 man-hours. In other words, 100 people could have done the job in half a day.[20]

One hundred Indians butchering buffalo on the Colorado plains is a picture of human society in transformation. Hunters were gathering together into larger social groups; human existence was now becoming more complex. The scale of the butchering activities at the Olsen-Chubbuck site, the size of the dwellings at Kostienki and at Dolni Vestonice, are the archeological traces of larger gatherings. In fact, "crowds," according to John Pfeiffer, were "invented" by the hunters themselves in order to more

---

[20]Joe Ben Wheat, "A Paleo-Indian Bison Kill," in *New World Archaeology: Theoretical and Cultural Transformations*, ed. E. B. W. Zubrow, M. C. Fritz, and J. M. Fritz (San Francisco: W. H. Freeman, 1974), p. 221.

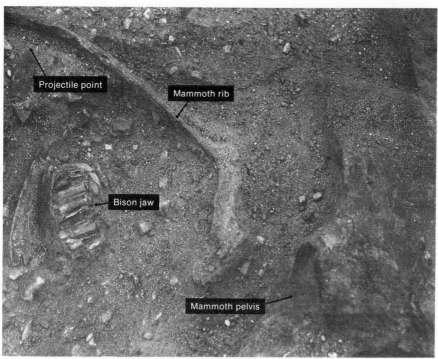

Courtesy of the Arizona State Museum, The University of Arizona, E. W. Haury, Photographer

Close-up of 1955 excavation showing bison jaw, Mammoth pelvis and rib, and Clovis points in site.

effectively prey on the herds.[21] "Crowd" is not a good word for describing organized human groups, but Pfeiffer has made a point that is worth exploring.

From studies of modern-day caribou hunters, we have learned not only of unearned resources, but something of the size and structure of hunting societies. Modern groups of caribou hunters can number about 500 people, a level of society often known as a *tribe*.[22] It is a *group that is usually*

The emergence of the earliest tribes

---

[21]John E. Pfeiffer, *The Emergence of Man* (New York: Harper & Row, 1972).

[22]The concept of tribe has been strongly criticized by anthropologists in recent years. It has been defined in several different ways, which contributed to much confusion, and its very existence in prehistoric times has been challenged as well. Social anthropologist Morton H. Fried in *The Evolution of Political Society* (New York: Random House, 1967) suggested that tribes are historic, a social reaction to the expansion of states. I agree that this pattern existed, but I believe these were not the first tribes. In short, I find the term valuable for designating leaderless, cooperating bands—both within the prehistoric record and in more recent times.

lacking in permanent political authority. It is made up of neighboring bands that maintain contact with one another and share a common language and cultural tradition.

Something similar to the modern-day tribe could well have evolved during the Upper Paleolithic. The steppe and tundra regions that had been freed of arctic ice had caused the game herds to increase to prodigious numbers. By concentrating their technology increasingly on the herds, Cro-Magnon hunters could capture greater amounts of energy (see Chapter 3). Plant foods became less favored within the human diet; the hunters were consuming increasing amounts of meat. Thus the Upper Paleolithic sites of Western Europe usually contain the bones of a limited number of species, and these frequently occur in massive concentrations. Caribou is certainly the most striking example of this. At many sites, it was almost the only animal hunted. In a similar way, the mammoth became the dominant prey of Asia, and bison was intensely hunted on the American plains.

The remnant hunting societies of the American tundra and grasslands are a reflection of this "golden age" of the hunter. Said Nicholas David,

> Gathering, for which we have no direct evidence, is likely to have been at least as important to (hunters in southern France) as to recent hunters of the North American arctic and the northern plains. Amongst land mammal hunters in these areas, dependence upon the gathering of wild plants and small land fauna is in the range of 6–25 per cent, and tends to increase from north to south.[23]

Combined with the animal bones from the archeological sites themselves, this suggests a widespread pattern of increasing dependence upon the hunt that was probably most intense in the northerly regions.

Gigantic herds and unearned resources: it was indeed a time of abundance. Yet, lurking within the system, there was a flaw—in fact, a danger: dramatic shifts in the populations of the animal world. There is probably nowhere else on earth where such changes are more pronounced than in the special, delicate region of the subarctic tundra. Disease, erratic seasons, forest fires in the boreal south, sudden and sweeping glaze storms that cover the moss and the lichens with ice: it is all of these that make the tundra a difficult land. The numbers of bird and mammal species—"from mice to moose," as David has said—are susceptible to sudden and dangerous changes. For a meat-dependent society, it was obviously necessary to be able to cope with the occasionally unstable nature of their plentiful world.

It was perhaps out of this necessity that the earliest tribes were born.

---

[23]Nicholas David, "On Upper Paleolithic Society, Ecology, and Technological Change: The Noaillian Case," in *The Explanation of Culture Change: Models in Prehistory,* ed. Colin Renfrew (London: Duckworth, 1973).

Cooperating bands could plan and execute larger hunts; more meat could be stored to prepare for a shortage. In lean times, a neighboring band could provide a necessary supply of meat. Hunters were not strictly dependent, then, on the herds that came through their own territories. There was meat that could come from more fortunate regions as well.

Out of this more secure existence, human expressive behavior emerged: music, dance, and the beginnings of painting and sculpture. There is a good possibility, of course, that such behavior goes back a very long time. It is fruitless to search for the original artistic expressions. It is not impossible, for example, that the first human beings could whistle or sing, but this behavior would have left no traces in the African record.

The emergence of expressive behavior

Not until the Upper Paleolithic do we discover any evidence of art, and most of this has been found at sites in Europe and Asia. At Moldovia in the Soviet Union, archeologists found the remains of a circular, bone-braced dwelling on the Ukranian plains.[24] At the same site, the excavators retrieved a flute that was made from an antler. Four holes were on one side of the antler, and two were bored through the other. The instrument could possibly be 15,000 years old. And at the Ukranian house site of Mezin, Pidoplichko and Shovkoplyas discovered bones that might well have been used as a source of percussion. There was a mallet fashioned out of an antler and a rattle that was made from ivory. Five pieces of mammoth bone were arranged in a bracelet. It was the bracelet in particular that was of interest to the archeologists, given the possible musical context in which it was found. The bracelet would certainly have rattled, much like a modern-day castanet. It is the closest we have come so far to any evidence of dance.

More familiar than the Paleolithic orchestra is the evidence of sculpture and painting, especially the dramatic illustrations on the walls of the caves. Altamira in northern Spain was the first of these caves to be found—a vaulting polychrome gallery of Cro-Magnon art.[25] At least 25 big-game animals—the majority of which were bison—were painted across the walls and roof of the cave. Using clays and minerals of reddish-brown hue, with black strokes for outlines of the animals, the artists captured the color and movement of the Pleistocene herds. At one time, it was thought that these paintings were simply a collection of isolated pictures and that the artists were not attempting a grander design. But a detailed drawing of the cave by the French prehistorian Abbe Breuil suggests that the paintings were probably meant to be viewed as a whole. Interpretation is risky (as it is with contemporary art), but Altamira would seem to represent a scene from a hunt. Four bison were wounded or dead, and the

[24]Sergei N. Bibikov, "A Stone Age Orchestra," UNESCO Courier, June 1975.
[25]T. G. E. Powell, *Prehistoric Art* (London: Thames and Hudson, 1966).

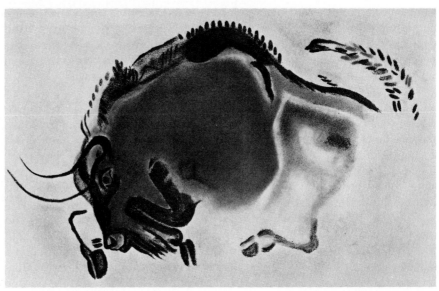

American Museum of Natural History

Bison painting at Lascaux cave. It is possible that these paintings were involved in rituals of hunting magic.

rest of them have turned toward the danger. Two boar, a deer, and a young horse were also startled by approaching hunters, and have begun to move in close to the jittery herd.[26]

Altamira is a magnificent example of the emphasis of Cro-Magnon cave art: the big-game animals that provided the basis of their stable existence. Human beings were rarely depicted on the walls of the shelters and caves. The exceptions, more often than not, are very sketchily done. Nowhere is this trend more evident than on the walls of the Lascaux cave, located in the Dordogne region of southwestern France. Here wild horses, aurochs, and cattle flow in a frieze over the roof of the cave. Foals and yearlings are grouped together, the shapes of cattle horns are accurately drawn, and different colors are used for the seasonal changes of coat. But humans are barely depicted: they are little more than simple stick figures. The animal herds are clearly the focus of the art of the caves.

The opposite is true of the sculpture that was created in Cro-Magnon times. Almost always it is a human being that is shaped in the round. From the Ukranian plains to Belgium and France, these figurines have been discovered. They are usually about four inches tall and around 25,000 years old, but they reflect the existence of multiple artistic traditions. Some,

[26]This is an interpretation offered by T. G. E. Powell. Others have suggested that Altamira is a pastoral scene.

like the one from Savignano in the northern Italian plain, are nothing more than breasts, belly, and buttocks, with the body tapered to a point at each end. Others, like the Venus of Willendorf, Austria, are fairly complete, although enormously fat and even include such surprising details as braids in the hair.

This explosion of human creativity in the midst of a hunting technology came as an unsettling shock to the industrialized world. The paintings were denounced as forgeries made by contemporary artists. The excavators—at the very best—were seen as victims of fraud.[27] At the heart of this early criticism, was a bias that lingers today: the view that real art is exclusively produced by the urbanized world. Thus, Praxiteles or Michelangelo, da Vinci or Pablo Picasso are artists who create masterpieces of human expression. But technologically simpler societies create folk art or ethnic art; masterpieces are not likely to be found in a hunting society. This view is absurd on the face of it, since *all* art is, of course, ethnic art: a reflection of the cultural tradition from which it emerged. But it was largely this point of view that was more responsible than any other factor for the early rejection of the art of the Paleolithic.

Closely bound to this idea is another that dies equally hard: the notion that art is uniquely produced by a leisured society. Indeed, as recently as 1976, a cultural anthropologist wrote that,

> Later in the Paleolithic. . .tools and weapons were improving in number, variety and complexity. The increased availability of food allowed more people *to take more time off from foraging to engage in other activities— in political and ritual specialization and in the arts* (emphasis mine).[28]

But if leisure is the basis of art, there should be more art found in bands than in cities. Hunters and gatherers are the most leisured societies on the face of the earth.[29] Clearly, something else is involved here besides the hours of idle time in a day. That something is perhaps the emergence of a settled existence.

Very possibly, artistic expression before the Upper Paleolithic was closely adapted to a nomadic society. Body painting, singing, dance, perhaps the carving of small amulets—these forms of expression are easily carried around. But with the stability of big-game resources, new varieties of art could emerge. Permanent homes made art possible on a much grander scale.

And yet there was almost certainly much more involved than just this. Johannes Maringer suggested that the art of the caves was hunting magic— part of a ritual to gain control over the herds of game.[30] For Andrë Leroi- Gourhan, it was sexual symbolism. Through a detailed statistical analysis

[27]Herbert Wendt, *In Search of Adam* (Boston: Houghton Mifflin, 1956).

[28]Peter B. Hammond, *Physical Anthropology and Archaeology* (New York: Macmillan, 1976).

[29]This point will be explored in some detail in the following chapter.

[30]Maringer, *The Gods*.

Field Museum of Natural History

Reconstruction of a Cro-Magnon artist. Causes of artistic variations among societies past and present appear related to technology, but still are not well understood.

of the placement of different paintings, he decided that certain animals, such as horses, represented males, while other species, such as bison, were females. He wrote,

> In the last (though still provisional) analysis, we arrive at the idea that
> Paleolithic people represented in the caves the two great categories of

living creatures, the corresponding male and female symbols, and the symbols of death on which the hunters fed. In the central area of the cave, the system is expressed by groups of male symbols placed around the main female figures, whereas in other parts of the sanctuary we find exclusively male representations, the complements, it seems, to the underground cavity itself.[31]

The emergence of art is obviously far from being well understood. A good theory of the origins of large-scale art in Western Europe should explain its comparative absence in the Americas. Why are there such elaborate paintings at Altamira, but not at Meadowcroft Shelter or Pikimachay? Perhaps when we learn more about art in different cultures today, we will better understand its early development. For the moment, it seems clear enough that settled existence was likely involved, but it is equally clear there is much we do not understand.

The end—and a new beginning

Since the time of *Homo erectus* and the Torralba-Ambrona valley, specialized hunters had slowly been changing the face of the world. It was the technology of *intensification—concentrating on particular responses*—which can often mean a technology of borrowed time. In the short run, intensification will generate immediate rewards. If people are given a natural resource that is abundant and close at hand, they can capture that resource and lead a more stable existence.

But in the long run of human evolution, the strategy is a dangerous one. *Intensification can ultimately lead to depletion.* It is evident that the human species was confronted with precisely this danger and that it ultimately transformed the structure of human existence. Sometime between 15,000 and 8,000 years before the present, 31 genera of plant-eating mammals disappeared from the earth. The mastodon, Columbian mammoth, woolly mammoth, imperial mammoth, dwarf elephant, giant ground sloth, two species of bison, and American horses—all these animals and more could no longer be found.

What happened? There have been many answers, and the debate still continues today. But a general picture of the extinctions is now taking form. The natural environment was changing, that much at least is certain, but how strongly this contributed to the extinctions we still cannot say. Loren Eiseley believed it was crucial.[32] The final retreat of the Wurm glacier produced generally warmer temperatures. Steppe and tundra vegetation retreated to more northerly regions. Changes in the natural environment could have caused many species to die out and not simply the herbivorous animals that were food for the hunters. Hunting practices

[31] Andrë Leroi-Gourhan, *Treasures of Prehistoric Art* (New York: Harry N Abrams, 1967).

[32] Kenneth MacGowan and Joseph A. Hester Jr., *Early Man in the New World* (Garden City, N.Y.: Anchor Press, 1962).

can conceivably explain the disappearance of, say, bison or horses—but what of those animals never significantly a part of our diet? There were mollusks, a variety of toad, the dire wolf, and the saber-toothed tiger which were never much a part of our menu, but they suddenly vanished.

Perhaps there were changes in breeding patterns that victimized some of the species. An early variation of this theory was suggested by Sewall Wright. As the animal populations declined and their natural habitat shrank, they became more vulnerable to the harmful effects of inbreeding. Others have emphasized not genetics but animal behavior. The change to more temperate conditions meant that the climate for a time was erratic. This, in turn, could have severely disrupted the large herbivores' mating patterns, which were closely adapted to a regular changing of seasons.

But for archeologist Paul S. Martin, the culprits were the hunters themselves.[33] It was "Pleistocene overkill" that created the massive extinctions. The migrations of the Cro-Magnon hunters coincided with waves of extinctions; wherever the hunters appeared, the great animals died. Humanity discovered Australia, and a giant marsupial became extinct. Hunters moved into Central Asia; the woolly mammoth and the woolly rhino died. They crossed Beringia into the Americas, and the long-horned bison disappeared. It strains the imagination to call this a coincidence. For Martin, this is clear-cut evidence of the hunters as "super-predators." The technology of massive killing, whether at Solutré or at Olsen-Chubbuck, amounted to nothing short of an extermination.

Predator-prey relationships are obviously very complex, especially if the predator species is equipped with a culture. Paul Martin's evidence of a sequence for a great many of the Pleistocene extinctions strongly suggests that the big-game hunters were likely involved. Yet, as Eiseley and others have noted, natural conditions were changing as well; how else can we account for the extinction of toads and mollusca?[34] In my own view, *both* of these factors were largely responsible for the "Great Death." The generalized warming of temperatures between 15,000 and 8,000 years before the present was probably a factor in the extinction of the nonfood species. As for the giant herbivorous animals, survival was now very difficult. It is true that most of these animals had lived through earlier climatic changes. Warmer interglacial periods had happened before. But the combination of higher temperatures and a very sophisticated hunting technology was a double threat that the animal species had never experienced.

As the climate became more temperate, some species migrated north. But the majority gathered closer and closer to sources of water. And this

---

[33]Paul S. Martin, "Pleistocene Overkill," Natural History, December 1967.

[34]It is conceivable that these species could have been "emergency food," but if this were the case, we should find their remains in the hunters' encampments.

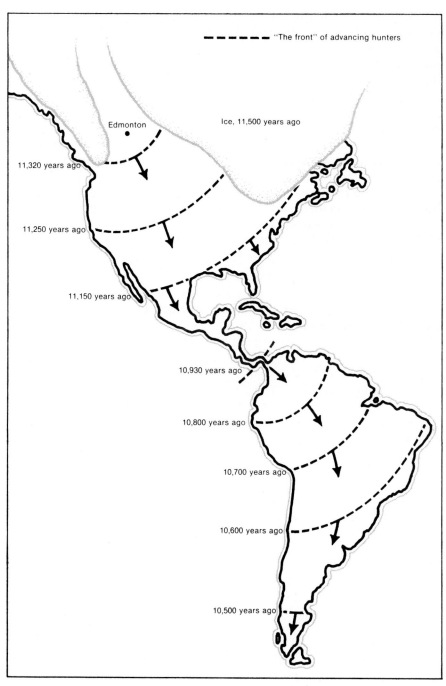

"Waves" of extinction of big-game animals. They correspond closely with the chronology of hunters' migrations.

is where we find their bones—at the edges of lakes and streams—where they were easily surrounded and killed by Pleistocene hunters. W. J. Judge and J. Dawson have found that the Paleo-Indian camps were usually set up close to a source of water.[35] Also, most of these camps were no more than a thousand yards away from a natural trap like an arroyo, a cliff, or a canyon. The Great Death, in the final analysis, was probably a cultural and natural disaster, with repercussions that affected the structure of prehistoric society.

And yet the human species survived. There are few events in prehistory that demonstrate human resiliency better than the subsequent emergence of the foraging traditions. In every part of the inhabited world, technology and resources changed. A broad spectrum of animals and plants became part of the diet. This might seem to be a retrograde movement—a rediscovery of our earliest subsistence—but, as we shall see in the chapter that follows, this is far from the case. Equipped with a modern brain and the inheritors of improved technology, these latter-day foragers would establish the basis for far-reaching change.

---

[35]W. J. Judge and J. Dawson, "Paleo-Indian Settlement Technology in New Mexico," *Science* 176, June 16, 1972, pp. 1210–16.

7 / The Foraging Traditions

The stagecoach rattled across the desert, 250 miles from Salt Lake City. It **Lazy people?** was the dead heat of August, and the driver shouted at the mules, but they could travel no more than 8 or 10 miles an hour. One of the passengers, a young writer traveling to Nevada, began to notice groups of Indians outside the window. He really had not expected to see any signs of human life. He looked closer—and then his interest turned to disgust. In his eyes, they were

> a silent, sneaking, treacherous-looking race; taking note of everything, covertly, like all the other "Noble Red Men" that we . . . read about, and betraying no sign in their countenances; indolent, everlastingly patient and tireless, like all other Indians; prideless beggars—for if the beggar instinct were left out of an Indian he would not "go," any more than a clock without a pendulum; hungry, always hungry, and yet never refusing anything that a hog would eat, though often eating what a hog would decline; hunters, but having no higher ambition than to kill and eat jackass rabbits, crickets and grasshoppers, and embezzle carrion from the buzzards and coyotes; savages who, when asked if they have the common Indian belief in a Great Spirit show a something which almost amounts to emotion, thinking whisky is referred to; a thin, scattering race of almost naked black children . . . who produce nothing at all, and have no villages, and no gatherings together into strictly defined tribal communities—a people whose only shelter is a rag cast on a bush to keep off a portion of the snow, and yet who inhabit one of the most rocky, wintry, repulsive wastes that our country or any other can exhibit.[1]

Upset and a little bewildered by all that he had seen, the passenger made an attempt to compose his thoughts. He settled back for the rest of the journey. The stagecoach clattered along. Mark Twain had had his first sight of the Great Basin Shoshone.

A number of years before, it was an equally young Charles Darwin who had had a similar experience on the island of Tierra del Fuego. There he saw naked Indians with only a scattering of personal possessions and

---

[1]Samuel L. Clemens, *Roughing It* (New York: Harper & Row, 1899). This particularly vehement expression of older attitudes toward foraging groups was also quoted by Peter Farb, *Man's Rise to Civilization* (New York: Avon Books, 1968), p. 36. His discussion of forager leisure is similar in many respects to the one offered here.

Field Museum of Natural History

Great Basin foragers. Contact with such peoples prompted critics in the industrial world to form incorrect motions of leisure in human society.

a nomadic life that he found difficult to imagine. The characteristic objectivity of the great scientist all but vanished. To him, the Ona were an utterly wretched form of existence.

What was it that provoked such incredulous, angry reactions from two reasonably educated men of the 19th century? It was not, I think, simply a matter of that century's preoccupation with a horde of personal possessions and "modest" clothing. More than likely, it was a reflection of a deeper misunderstanding—a misunderstanding of the nature of leisure in human society.

Here is a concept that has often been seriously misunderstood, for both present-day and prehistoric humanity. Why is it that certain cultures, like the Ona or the Shoshone, seem to do practically nothing for almost 24 hours a day, while industrial societies are hard at work almost all of the time? The average Kalahari "Bushman" collects food for 12 hours a week.[2] The remaining time is usually devoted to sleeping, visiting, dancing, gossiping, caring for infants, eating, drinking, and making love. It is important to understand why such leisure has long existed. It is also important to understand what leisure is not.

A part of the misunderstanding has grown from our industrialized view of the world. Our complicated system of highways, factories, businesses, cities, and trade requires us to labor by explicitly timed schedules. Our activities have to be synchronized, or the system begins to fall apart. Steelworkers cannot labor one week and assembly-line workers the next. Our labor—and leisure—are usually timed by a clock.

This has led to considerable problems in understanding the foraging world. Very often, we have understood *labor* as the activity of bringing back food. Preparation of meals is occasionally included as well. All else we have thought of as leisure; after all, it is time spent at home. But foragers, during these periods, make plans for the tracking of game. They tend to their sick and to their children; they work with their tools. Without many of these domestic behaviors, their society could never survive. Leisure among foragers is not always what it has seemed.

Yet, even if this is allowed for, they are idle much more than ourselves. The time spent in those activities that have no connection with survival at all is undoubtedly greater in the life of a foraging band. Perhaps, as is often suggested, this is due to the natural world. The !Kung San inhabit a desert, and might conceivably labor each day in a nine-to-five pattern, amassing a great store of food. But the pattern would quickly destroy them; their society would never survive. Plants and game would be quickly exhausted; there is no way of preserving the food.[3] Leisure plays a critical role in their marginal land.

Beyond that, there are also the seasons—and the special changes each one brings. Different plant foods—fruits, roots, and berries—are found at different times of the year. There are seasonal changes in migratory patterns of game. A scheduling system is crucial—though not as rigidly timed as our own. Foragers along the Ohio built their dwellings in the hills in the fall. It was the season when the hickory forests had plentiful deer. Spring and summer were spent on the floodplain, where there was

---

[2]The typical range recorded by Richard B. Lee was 12 to 19 hours a week. !Kung San "Bushman" labor requirements are discussed in his "What Hunters Do for a Living, or How to Make Out on Scarce Resources," in *Man The Hunter,* ed. Richard B. Lee and Irven de Vore (Hawthorne, N.Y.: Aldine Publishing, 1968), pp.30–48.

[3]Problems of hunter-and-gatherer storage are discussed by Jean T. Peterson and Warren Peterson, "Implications of Contemporary and Prehistoric Exchange Systems," in *Sunda and Sahul: Prehistoric Studies in Southeast Asia, Melanesia, and Australia,* ed. J. Allen, J. Golson and R. Jones (New York: Academic Press, 1977), pp. 533–64.

edible plant food and game. Many foraging societies followed a "seasonal round."[4]

This meant they were usually mobile; they might move several times in a year. Personal possessions simply had to be carried along. If foragers had labored intensely and been able to store away food, it would all be abandoned; they traveled as light as they could. Contemporary urban societies can move houses for thousands of miles. But we were limited to what our muscles could carry throughout most of our past.

The constraints of limited resources and of seasonal changes as well imposed leisurely patterns on the hunting-and-gathering life. Even so, it was not all that simple. Perhaps more than this was involved. Foraging in the past was much different that we find it today. There is a "tyranny," as Martin Wobst put it, that the living have over the dead; surviving hunters and gatherers are the models for what "must have been."[5] We have watched their behavior and projected it into the past.

The problem that lurks in this method is that the past was a much different world. Nature was rich in resources, more so than on our planet today.[6] Abundance was often a part of the foraging life. More than that, modern hunters and gatherers have been pushed into marginal lands. Such societies imperfectly mirror much earlier times.

Middens of hunters and gatherers, and the remains of the dwellings they built, are the evidence of settled existence that was often secure. There were regions in Europe and Asia, in Africa and the Americas, too, where food was abundant throughout every month of the year. Here, there was very little danger of foragers exhausting the resource supply. There was not any need for them to follow a seasonal round. What, exactly, was the function of leisure in a world as "affluent" as this? The answers from the Kalahari !Kung do not seem to apply.

It is valuable here to remember that humans work when they have little choice. When given the chance, we are attracted to a leisurely life. Perhaps more than limited foodstuffs, or the demands of a seasonal round, it is *scarcity* that leads to more labor in the human society. The distinction is important but subtle; it does not mean simply "limited food." Scarcity, for the Kalahari !Kung, is not a problem at all. It means that *some critical resource is not present in sufficient supply. Because of this, the culture begins to*

---

[4]Forager seasonality in the riverine Midwest is described by Stuart Streuver, "Woodland Subsistence—Settlement Systems in the Lower Illinois Valley," in *Perspectives in Archeology*, ed. Sally R. Binford and Lewis R. Binford (Hawthorne, N.Y.: Aldine Publishing, 1968).

[5]H. Martin Wobst, "The Archaeo-ethnology of Hunter-Gatherers, or the Tyranny of the Ethnographic Record in Archaeology," *American Antiquity* 43, no. 2 (1978).

[6]For this reason, Marshall Sahlins has described the foragers of post-Pleistocene times as the "original affluent society"; *Stone Age Economics* (Hawthorne, N.Y.: Aldine Publishing, 1972). But this concept has limitations, too. Forager scarcity is discussed in the present chapter and in the chapter that follows.

United Press International Photo

A computer plant assembly line. How much of this sort of work would we do if we did not have to?

experience stress. Medicinal herbs, food, water, and special stones for the making of tools: any one could be a critical item in ancient society. As long as the item is present, there is no stress—thus a leisurely life. When supplies are diminished, the labor requirements change.

Food is sought out more intensely during seasons of blizzards or droughts. Scarce minerals and medicines can trigger a long-distance trade. Gardens are seeded and tended in a summer when plant food is scarce. Through lack of essentials, our leisure is eroded away.

As we will see in the chapters that follow, such stresses very likely occurred among foraging peoples in several different parts of the world. Leisure shortened; the pace of life quickened. We worked longer than ever before. Perhaps too, as Peter Just has suggested, we then took greater notice of time.[7] Our hours of leisure were shrinking; they were more precious than ever. Like the wheat that was stored in a granary, time suddenly was measured and saved. Our leisure—hardly noticed before—was a valuable thing.

---

[7]Peter Just, "Time and Leisure in the Elaboration of Culture," *Journal of Anthropological Research* 36 (1980), pp. 105–15.

The world of the hunters and gatherers

Around 12,000 years before the present, on every continent where humans were found, a generalized food-collecting technology was the basis of life.[8] Such technology is a *foraging tradition*: a *mobile, unspecialized collecting of animals and plants*. While it is true that *Australopithecus* was an unspecialized collector of food, it is also true that the new foraging tradition was significantly different.

Part of this difference is technology—a wide array of strategies and tools, many of which were derived out of Cro-Magnon traditions. Microlith tools, for example, had been used in big-game hunting times, but now they were a dominant artifact of the foraging life. The small blades have the obvious advantage of more economic use of materials. A single pound of flint could now produce 150 feet of cutting edge; this amounted to some 4,000 tools that were thumbnail-size. This is roughly 3.75 times as economical as the blade tools of the Upper Paleolithic; it is about 900 times as economical as the pebble tools of *Australopithecus*. Thus, the same resource could be stretched a lot farther. Microlithic tools were very abundant and highly diverse.[9]

Necessarily they had to be attached to bone, antler, or wood. They were generally between one half inch and two inches in length, too small to be efficiently used in the hand. For this reason, the *composite tool—a useful implement that is made of different kinds of raw materials*—dominates the foraging technologies of many parts of the world. Scrapers, borers, saws, burins, axes, and adzes—most of these were essentially microliths socketed into some kind of handle. Most likely, they were secured with the pitch that came from pine trees or, in some regions of the world, with asphalt that bubbled from springs. Axes and adzes in particular were important among woodworking tools; they were a crucial part of technology in forested lands. The *adze*, a *woodworking tool with a blade at right angles to the shaft* was, like the axe, very possibly made of three different materials. The flint blade, triangularly shaped, had its cutting edge at the widest end. The tapering butt was mounted in a section of antler with a socket for inserting a wooden handle.

With the increased use of these tools, the forest provided a wealth of raw material. Saplings could be easily cut to make the framework of temporary dwellings; larger trees could be hollowed out into dugout canoes. Axes and adzes helped make it possible to have greater numbers of open-air dwellings, and they made a significant contribution to boating technology.

The weapons used in hunting had also become very different, although they derived out of earlier Cro-Magnon technology. In the dense

---

[8]Lewis Binford, "Post-Pleistocene Adaptations" in *New Perspectives in Archeology*, ed. S. R. Binford and L. R. Binford (Hawthorne, N.Y.: Aldine Publishing, 1968).

[9]Forager technology is described by J. G. D. Clark, *Prehistoric Europe: The Economic Basis* (Stanford: Stanford University Press, 1952).

Field Museum of Natural History

Bone fish-hooks. Different-sized hooks were designed to catch different species of fish.

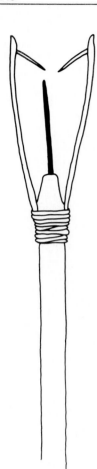

A leister. The center prong penetrates the fish. Side prongs hold the prey, preventing escape.

underbrush of the forest, the spear and the spear-thrower were almost useless. Spears would inevitably be deflected by bushes and trees. But the bow and arrow was uniquely capable of tremendous velocity in a limited space; it was exactly the right kind of weapon for use in a forest. The bows and arrows preserved in peat bogs are evidence of this new transition, which continued in many parts of the world into historic times.

Bone and antler were extensively available and were fashioned into a wide array of tools. There were bone needles, pins, projectile points, and fishhooks, and a surprising number of tools were made from antlers. Long splinters were removed from an antler with a burin, and a series of barbs was cut along one surface. Three such splinters grouped together formed an ingenious point called a leister. The barbs would separate very slightly when the point was impaled in a fish. The tension of the barbs would hold the point firmly in place. There were also antler scrapers and antler mattocks for digging roots, and a widespread use of antler projectile points.

The strategies of human technology had also undergone a significant change. There was the emergence, again, of the solitary hunter of game. Most of the big-game species were extinct after Cro-Magnon times. In their place were the animals of the expanding temperate forests. These prey were usually smaller and generally were solitary animals. There was little need for large-scale hunting and butchering expeditions. It *was* necessary, however, to have a detailed knowledge of plant and animal resources. An understanding of animal behavior and seasonal availability, as well as the usefulness of the various parts of an animal's body, were applied now to a large diversity of wilderness species. And wild plants were more a part of the diet than they had been in the Upper Paleolithic. Here too, it became necessary to discover the edible species and to devise very different methods of food preparation. The immediate result of these skills was a successful adaptation to the forest. But in the long run, they established a basis for revolutionary change.

But revolutionary change was scarcely perceptible in the wilderness at the end of the Ice Age. Across the European continent, a great forest had inherited the land. At first, there were pioneer species that sprouted along the disappearing tundra. The climate was becoming much warmer. The soil just below the surface was beginning to thaw. It was possible for the pioneer species to extend their tap roots down into the ground; the land was becoming dotted with occasional trees. There were willow, aspen, and birch—all of which require direct sunlight—and which spread quickly because of a fast rate of production. This made them ideally suited for colonizing the tundra and steppe, transforming most of Europe into a parkland. But by approximately 9,500 years before the present, the pioneers were all but replaced by a heavy forest. The warmer climate gave rise to elm trees, as well as oak, beech, pine, and hazel. They crowded out the earlier parkland; the ground became covered with blankets of leaves. Most of Europe had become a hardwood deciduous forest.

To the east, there was the vacant, desolate world of the Asian steppes, a land that was nearly empty of human beings. The tundra had shrunk to a fringe along the edge of the arctic ice. The Soviet Union and much of China were covered by grass. Water, forests, and game—and bands of foragers—were mostly along the rivers, the coastal regions, and the inland streams. And yet, there was one part of the continent very different in its appearance: the rainy tropical forests of Southeast Asia. Much of this region had been flooded by the final retreat of the glacier; the warmer climate had produced a growth of luxuriant jungle.

As for the wilderness of Africa, it was perhaps not so dramatically changed. Nonetheless, it was considerably different than it is today. The region of the Sahara was receiving more rainfall then; there was dry-loving shrub vegetation and open grassland. The Nile, which flooded annually, was a ribbon of forests and swamps with shellfish, gazelle, hippopotamus, crocodile, and fish. To the south of the Sahara grassland, was an equatorial tropical forest; below that was a seed-rich savanna: the African veldt. And the once-turbulent Great Rift Valley had now become a region of lakes. A population of hunters and fishers now lived on its shores.

Archeological traces of the foragers have occasionally left a lot to be desired. In some instances, all that we have is a pile of shellfish and animal bones; sometimes there is little more than a sprinkling of microlith tools. But the frustration itself is a challenge. Fragments of bones can often be identified, and we can learn of the animals in the diet. Analysis of pollen can reveal the plants that were available in the region for food. Determining the types of oxygen in shell-fish can tell us the season when a site was occupied. Through one technique or another there is much we can learn.

The coastline of Europe and the rivers of the interior have literally thousands of these small-scale sites. Often they are nothing more than vaguely circular mounds of shellfish: piles of refuse left by beachcombing groups of nomads. This shoreline adaptation is generally known as the Azilian. It is named for a site in France called Mas d'Azil.[10] This unusual dwelling place was a cave in the Pyrenees mountains, large enough so that a river ran through it. Hunters and fishers were camping here some 12,000 years ago, when the big-game hunting tradition was nearing its

The foragers of Europe

---

[10]Johannes Maringer, *The Gods of Prehistoric Man* (New York: Alfred A. Knopf, 1960).

Azilian pebbles. Johannes Maringer suggested that the stones were used by foragers in ancestor worship.

end. Among the shellfish deposits that were discovered at Mas d'Azil, there was also a large number of painted pebbles. Usually they were engraved or red-painted with points and lines; a number of the designs appear to be human forms.

Prehistorian Hugo Obermaier has noticed a strong similarity between many of the designs on the Mas d'Azil pebbles and rock paintings from the same period of time in southern Spain. Even as far away as Switzerland's Birseck Cave, 133 of the painted pebbles were found, and every single one of them had been broken to pieces. Johannes Maringer has speculated that this wide-spread pebble art was related to a prehistoric form of ancestor worship. Australian aborigines collect small pieces of wood and stone that they believe contain the souls of their dead ancestors. These churingas, as they are called, are also believed to have a special power: they transfer the personality of the dead one to the protector of the stones.

Conceivably, the Azilian pebbles were related to such a belief, but it seems likely that we will never know for sure. Did a hostile band of foragers smash their enemy's sacred stones? Was the Birseck site the remains of a desecration? Whatever their meaning, the pebbles are scattered throughout the shorelines of Western Europe. Archeologists continue to study their ancient designs.

A short distance from the Mediterranean coastline and the choppy waters of the North Atlantic, was the edge of the forest that dominated most of the continent. Within the tangled undergrowth and the hardwoods, there was a web of interacting human societies that combed the thickets and freshwater streams for plant foods and game. The excavations at the Star Carr site show us something of that foraging life, as it was lived in England some 9,500 years before the present. England, at that time, was not an island. It was connected by a belt of forested land to the remainder of Europe. Hunters and gatherers seasonally camped on its lakeshores and streams.

Archeologist J. G. D. Clark excavated the temporary campsite, which had been located at the edge of a lake, surrounded by birch trees.[11] The bones of red deer, roe deer, elk, ox, pig, and waterfowl were dug out of the layers deposited between the forest and the lake. There were also great quantities of antlers from elk and red deer of the region. Many of these had been shaped into leisters, as well as mattocks, scrapers, and frontlets. A frontlet is a section of the skull with a complete set of antlers attached. Two to four holes were usually drilled in each section, suggesting that the antlers were worn on someone's head. That someone was conceivably a *shaman: a religious practitioner in a hunter-and-gatherer society.* Very possibly, the antlers were worn as ceremonial dress. But the antlers

---

[11]Robert Rodden, "Europe North of the Alps," in *Varieties of Culture in the Old World,* ed. Robert Styler (New York: St. Martin's Press, 1975).

had additional significance for Clark's interpretation of the site: they were evidence that Star Carr was occupied during the winter. Antlers are fully grown during the winter months of the year. Red deer and elk do not shed them until sometime around April. F. C. Fraser and J. E. King have added evidence to Clark's interpretation, by pointing out that deer will devour their own shed antlers. If full-grown antlers are only available between the months of October and April, and if the animals promptly devour them as soon as they shed them during the spring, then this suggests that they could only be collected during winter months.[12]

But this interpretation has been recently challenged by British archeologist Mike Pitts. In the first place, there is no clear-cut evidence that deer normally devour their own antlers. The Norwegian archeologist Kjos-Hanssen has discovered that this form of behavior will only occur if the animals have impoverished diets. This means, as Pitts has suggested, that many of the antlers at the site could have been collected during virtually any season of the year. But the feature of greatest interest to Pitts was a rough platform made out of birch trees: a jettylike pile of logs that led out into the lake. Clark was unable to explain it. There was no direct evidence of fishing at the site. Why did the inhabitants of Star Carr create such a structure?

Probably, Pitts has suggested, because it was actually an industrial site: a place for the preparation of deerhides and worked-antler tools. The evidence for this is intriguing. Water is absolutely necessary for the removal of hair in the preparation of hide. If birchbark, moss, and bracket fungus are added to a pool of quiet water, the hides can be loosened and softened to make clothing and shelter. Preserved remains of precisely those plants were recovered from the mud that surrounded the birch trees. So it seems very possible that Star Carr was indeed an industrial site.

Such an industry, however, is pointless unless there is someone receiving the products. Star Carr is thus indirect evidence of a system of trade. We should not, I think, visualize these societies as isolated pockets swallowed up by a forest, but as an intricately connected network of early exchange.

A crucial factor in this interconnectedness was the use of boating technology. Post-Pleistocene hunters and gatherers usually kept fairly close to the rivers. Fish and game were naturally abundant, and there were edible plants along the banks. So the rivers became "roads that move"; they knitted together the scattered encampments of Europe. It is not surprising that Northern Europe, with its peat bogs that can preserve ancient wood, has been the region where the buried remains of these boats were discovered. At the Maglemose site in Denmark, which is roughly 10,000

---

[12]Mike Pitts, "Hides and Antlers: A New Look at the Gatherer-Hunter Site at Carr, North Yorkshire, England," *World Archeology* 2, no. 1 (1979). The site was originally described by J. G. D. Clark, *Star Carr* (Cambridge, Eng.: Cambridge University Press, 1954).

years old, the remains of a dugout canoe were preserved in the peat.[13] The site today is on the western coast of a barrier island on the east side of Denmark. At the time the canoe was carved out, this was a vast inland swamp. Red deer, elk, roe deer, wild pig, fish, shellfish, and a variety of water birds were killed and eaten by the early Danish foragers.

Daily life in this quagmire was probably a little damp: the Maglemosians put piles of compacted brush on top of the mud to create a higher and dryer place for building their huts. All along the coastline of Northwestern Europe, there are sites very similar to this one. Probably the waterways made frequent contact possible. Conceivably, they were natural routes for developing trade.

For the forest dwellers of Eastern Europe, sources of water were equally crucial. Their sites are almost always found near a river or lake. The hunter-and-gatherer camp at Zatyni, in northwestern Czechoslovakia, was close to where the Vltava River flows into the Elbe.[14] Between 5,000 and 7,000 years before the present, the region was thick with hazel, pine, and oak trees. Within this damp and temperate wilderness, there was roe deer and wild pig for the taking. Rabbits were shot with arrows or snared, and birds and turtles were eaten as well. The marten—a weasellike animal with sleek, brown fur and a long, bushy tail—was abundant in the thickets of pine and was part of the diet. Because of the nearby junction of rivers, there was shellfishing and fishing for carp. No hooks were ever found at the site, but carp can be easily netted. Possibly too there were stake-and-brush dams—fish weirs, they are usually called—to trap the carp as they swam through the shallower flows of the rivers.

Within the forests to the south of Zatyni, in what is now northeastern Yugoslavia, hunters and fishers were building their huts along the edge of the Danube. It was at the bottom of a limestone gorge, thick with birch trees, juniper, and pine, where foragers of 7,000 years ago set up an encampment. The site of Lepenski Vir had eight different habitation levels, the first two of which are the remains of a foraging tradition. Hunters and fishers built their houses on terraces cut into the sloping bank of the river. Usually the floor of the house was an oval pit scooped out of the ground. These were around 18 to 27 feet long and between 6 and 15 feet wide. They were never more than three feet deep, and their soils were saturated with ashes from the hearths. Occasionally the floors were plastered with limestone and surrounded by posts reinforced with stones. It is a remarkably permanent settlement for a foraging life. But this was probably because food was abundant. Red deer, wild ox, pig, roe deer, and a species of carp supported the hunters and fishers on the banks of the Danube. Carp was especially abundant and was probably netted at

---

[13]Rodden, "Europe North of the Alps."

[14]Ruth Tringham, *Hunters, Fishers, and Farmers of Eastern Europe* (London: Hutchinson University Library, 1971).

the site. Close to the edge of the river, was a whirlpool—still there to-day—which constantly churned up plankton that, in turn, fed the fish. No fishhooks were ever discovered, but there were stones at the Lepenski Vir site that had grooves ground in them, possibly for the attachment of nets. With plant foods, fish, forest animals, and a warm climate through-out most of the year, the Yugoslavian foragers flourished on the banks of the Danube.

Foragers of the Orient

Hunting a variety of animals, fishing, and gathering wild plants: in virtually every corner of the world, this strategy was now the basis of life. The Orient, in this regard, was markedly similar to the West; nomadic foragers wandered the coastlines and fished on the rivers. In the Manchu-rian Plain of northern China—east of present-day Mongolia—there were forests, grasslands, and rivers; the region was dotted with freshwater lakes. From 12,000 to 4,000 years ago, daily life on the forested plain was very similar to that of the hunters and fishers of Europe. There were fishing and shellfish gathering on the banks of the Amur River; deer and wild pig were hunted in the temperate forests. Along the coastal fringes of China, shellfish and waterbirds were collected and eaten. In estuaries, migrating tuna were caught in the shallows.

Japan, too, had a foraging tradition that intensely focused on its coast-lines and rivers: a 10,000-year adaptation that is called the Jomon.[15] The mountainous islands are something of a "test tube," as prehistorian Ches-ter Chard once expressed it. The Jomon appears to have developed in isolation from the cultural systems of the mainland, but its archeological record is especially rich. Chard has recently estimated that there are some 75,000 Jomon sites. Most of them are close to the shorelines or the deep river valleys of the islands; most reflect an increasing dependence on the river and the sea.

In the earliest sites, such as Natsushima at the mouth of Tokyo Bay, the piles of shellfish and animal bones are a reflection of change. The lowest deposits have shallow-water shellfish that were collected in marshes and flats but were replaced by deep-water species as the sea level rose. By 4,000 years before the present, Jomon was a fishing society; village life was developing along much of the coast of Japan. At Horinouchi, in To-kyo Bay, piles of shellfish shaped like a horseshoe enclosed a community of pit houses next to the ocean. Dugout canoes and paddles, bone fish-hooks, fish spears, and harpoons were now a critical part of an economy based on the sea.

If marine resources are abundant, fishing can lead to a sedentary exis-tence. The Jomon was a sedentary variation of the foraging life. At Fukui

---

[15]Chester Chard, *Northeast Asia in Prehistory.* (Madison: University of Wisconsin Press, 1974).

Cave, on the island of Kyushu, fragments of pottery were discovered that were radiocarbon dated at 13,000 years. This is a very early date for ceramics, and it marks the beginning of their pottery tradition. By the time of the later fishing villages, pottery was abundant in most of the middens: in a 12-by-15-foot area, many thousands of potsherds were found. Ceramics, of course, are not useful within a highly nomadic society. Large pots are clumsy to transport, and besides, there is nothing to store. The sheer quantity of the pottery in Jomon, then, suggests a strongly sedentary existence. By carefully adapting their technology to a resource that was local, abundant, and preservable, the Jomon fishers remained near their homes every month of the year.

The richness of Jomon archeology is striking when seen in contrast to the fragmentary record in the rain forests of Southeast Asia. Archeology here is often difficult because of the decay of organic materials. Still, a shadowy portrait of forest technology has begun to take form.[16]

Before the last of the glaciers retreated, Southeast Asia was probably twice its present-day size. From 23,000 years ago, until 12,000 years before the present, a wide continental shelf stretched out to the Pacific; but the plain was flooded as the glacier retreated; the ocean covered much of the land. Like the foragers in Europe and Northern Asia, the Southeast Asians lived close to the water. For a period of over 5,000 years, hunters and collectors lived on inland streams and rivers, surrounded by forests within the depths of the mountain valleys.

At Gua Kerbau, in western Malaya, archeologists were fortunate enough to uncover the extensive remains of a foraging tradition. The region was a game-laden forest, bordered on the east by low-lying mountains and on the west by the alluvial plain on the Strait of Malacca. Deer, monkeys, and porcupines were hunted in the thickets of the forest, tortoises and terrestrial snails were occasionally collected for food, and there were fishing and shellfish collecting on the edges of streams. Far to the north of Gua Kerbau, along the coastal fringes of Vietnam, Asian foragers were culturally adapted to the edge of the sea. Deer were hunted by these coastal inhabitants, but the great source of food was the ocean. Salt- and fresh-water fish, snails, crustaceans, and shellfish supported them for thousands of years on the South China Sea.

At first glance, it might be tempting to think that this was a region which changed very slowly, as hunters and gatherers were so closely adapted to their natural world. But post-Pleistocene Southeast Asia—the *Hoabinhian* it is sometimes called—has yielded archeological findings that challenge this view.[17] At Spirit Cave, in northwestern Thailand, Chester

---

[16]Chester Gorman, ''The Hoabinhian and After: Subsistence Patterns in Southeast Asia during the Late Pleistocene and Early Recent Periods,'' *World Archeology* 2, no. 3 (1971).

[17]The term *Hoabinhian* is still used today, but it is heavily criticized. Many specialists in Southeast Asian prehistory believe that the category is much too inclusive and obscures significant differences among the post-Pleistocene cultures of the region.

Gorman has discovered the traces of what were possibly the earliest cultivated plants in the world. Much more will be said of this later, but here it is important to note that pressures for change were reshaping society in this tropical world.

African foraging societies

The foragers of Southeast Asia and the African hunters and fishers have only been sketchily understood by archeological researchers. We know, at least, that the African landmass was significantly different than it is today, and there may have been contact with Europe and Southwest Asia. J. Desmond Clark has pointed out that the boundaries of the Sahara Desert were around 100 miles closer to its center than they are today.[18] There was grassland, scrub vegetation, Mediterranean forest on the highlands, and freshwater lakes where today there is little but sand. As there were no massive geographical barriers between Africa, Europe, and Asia, some archeologists have suggested a network of connections between them. Bone harpoons in the Kenya Rift Valley appear similar to those of Western Europe; North African microlith tools closely resemble those in Southwest Asia. But the evidence is still insufficient; dates of sites are not

Fish trap. After the Ice Age ended, traps and harpoons were extensively used by fishers on the lakes and ponds of Central Africa.

Field Museum of Natural History

[18]J. Desmond Clark, *The Prehistory of Africa* (New York: Praeger Publishers, 1971).

firmly established. There is much that remains to be done in this part of the world.

And yet, from a small number of excavations, we can trace the outlines of foraging technology, especially in the forest-rimmed lakes of the Kenya Rift Valley.[19] At Ishango, in the eastern Congo, archeologist J. de Heinzelin de Braucort discovered evidence of hunting and fishing in a rain-watered land. Possibly as early as 10,000 years ago, heavy rains fell often in this region. There were swamps and streams with gallery forests; there was Lake Edward and the Semliki River. Hundreds of bone harpoon points discovered at the Ishango site reveal that the African foragers stayed close to the water. The 12-foot-thick deposit was rich with fishbones and shell-fish remains. There were small projectile points, which suggest that the fish may have been shot with a bow. Along the upper Nile and the Congo River, the bow and arrow is still used for fishing. Conceivably, this is an ancient survival from foraging times. Fishing was also intensively prac-ticed at Khartoum, in the central Sudan, where the Blue Nile and the White Nile flow together on their route to the sea. A type of land snail today used as fishbait was found with harpoon heads and grooved fish-ing sinkers. Here again, there was a food-collecting life along the rivers and streams.

The world of the American foragers

The sweeping climatic and resource changes that transformed Europe and Asia also strongly affected the cultures of the ancient Americas. The extinction of the great Ice Age animals, some 10,000 years before the pres-ent, occurred when the temperature was warming and the countryside changing. With the final retreat of the glacier, the continental shelf off North America flooded. Estuaries appeared on the coastlines; the seas and rivers were teeming with fish. The region east of the Mississippi River was colonized by decidous and coniferous forest. Deer was an abundant resource, along with fish, raccoon, and opossum, as well as a wealth of small mammals and birds of the American woodlands. Acorns were gen-erally plentiful; there was a wide variety of nuts and seeds. Plant food became a significant part of the diet.

To the west of these sprawling woodlands, were the open reaches of the American plains. Modern-day bison—called *Bison bison*[20]—ranged from the Saskatchewan grasslands to the Gulf coast of Texas. Herds of deer were abundant, and the grasses had edible seeds. Scattered groups of hunters and gatherers lived close to the rivers and streams in rock shel-ters and open encampments, and sometimes in caves.

But it was in the Great American Desert of southwestern United States

---

[19]Sonia Cole, *The Prehistory of East Africa* (New York: Mentor, 1963).

[20]And sometimes *Bison bison bison*.

that the force of environmental change was most dramatically felt. Earlier it had been a grassland region where mammoths and bison were hunted. But by 10,000 years before the present, it was covered with sagebrush and cacti, one of the driest environments to be found in the ancient Americas. And yet, it contained variation. On the higher plateaus, there were forests of mesquite, juniper, and pinon trees. The slopes of the Rocky Mountains and the Sierra Nevada were covered with pine, spruce, and fir. Possibly too, there were cyclical changes in temperature and annual rainfall. Such subtle differences have long been a part of the American west.

Reminiscent of the Great American Desert was the Mexican Tehuacan Valley. This was the southerly extension of a region that is today called the Mesa Central, a plateau shielded by mountains from the coastal rain. Here too, there was surprising variation in a world that receives little rain. There were low-lying limestone foothills with barrel cactus, thorn trees, and yucca. But there were also humid river bottoms with gallery forests, fruit trees, and seeds. Deer, coyote, puma, bobcat, rabbit, opossum, reptiles, and birds provided meat for the nomadic foragers of the Mesa Central. Seeds and fruits were also collected during every season of the year. Broad-spectrum hunting and gathering were a part of survival.

Of the foragers in South America, much remains to be learned. This is especially true for the forests of the Amazon Basin. This humid, low-altitude region was covered by tropical jungle and laced with a network of alluvial rivers and streams. Its archeology is largely unknown, but prehistorians have begun to suspect that the jungle has advanced and retreated there for thousands of years.[21] Changes in annual rainfall may have shrunk the forest into isolated pockets. Grassland would have prevailed until the heavier rainfall returned. How did Amazon hunters and gatherers adapt to these large-scale changes? There are many conceivable answers—but we still do not know.

Along the coastal fringes of the continent, there were fishing and shellfish collecting that resembles the beachcombing life of the Old World Azilian. Nomads of Tierra del Fuego lived along the edges of the ocean and survived until European contact a century ago. Winter fogs of the Peruvian shoreline provided moisture for sparse vegetation that supported the foragers who lived in this great coastal desert. And on the Atlantic coast of Brazil, there are massive shell mounds called *sambaquis*: the accumulations of a shellfishing life between forest and sea.

To the north, near the lakes and the rivers of the eastern United States, the remains of the foragers' camps are abundant and deep. From these sites, archeologists have learned much about the hunters and gatherers of Eastern North America—an adaptation that is usually known as the

---

[21]Betty J. Meggers, "Vegetational Fluctuations and Prehistoric Cultural Adaptation in Amazonia: Some Tentative Correlations," *World Archeology* 8, no. 3 (1976).

eastern Archaic. The abundance of plants and animals throughout most of the eastern woodlands made it possible for hunters and gatherers to remain within the same region, shifting their camps to collect the foods of the different seasons. Over hundreds of generations, the adaptation grew more complex. Projectile points were shortened—better suited for bow and arrow—and fashioned into a wide variety of shapes. There were stone axes and adzes for clearing out the thickets, ground stone mortars and pestles for crushing up nuts and seeds, bone fishhooks and pronged fish spears for use on the lakes and streams, and baskets for gathering the plant foods that grew in the forest. Ultimately almost every food available in the woodlands was collected by the eastern Archaic peoples. This optimum adaptation—called *primary forest efficiency*—is evident in many sites of the eastern wilderness.[22]

Along a dried-up river channel in western Tennessee were the extensive remains of a forest-efficient tradition.[23] The Eva site is a natural levee, once covered by a walnut and hickory forest, where foragers lived some 7,000 years before the present. Deer were plentiful in the open woodlands, and the site was saturated with their bones. But shellfish, bear, raccoon, opossum, turkey, fish, and nuts also supported the population over thousands of years. There were 180 human burials at Eva, as well as 18 burials of dogs. Most of the human skeletons gave evidence of nutritional health; 13 individuals had even lived past 60 years old. But why were they burying dogs? Conceivably, because of their technological value. Dogs are marvelous tools for stalking, chasing, and, sometimes, retrieving animal prey. Their burial may be symbolic of their importance to life in the forest. Possibly too, it was simply a variation of burying humans alongside their tools. Dogs, like axes and spear points, would have been useful in the world beyond death. Not surprisingly, their burial is common in the eastern Archaic.

The foragers of North America

Many of the sites in the eastern woodlands—especially in the highland regions—are strongly similar to Eva in their material culture. But unique adaptations were possible in the New World as well as in the Old, and one was encountered by archeologists in an unlikely place.[24] Eighteen feet below Boylston Street, in the middle of downtown Boston, construction workers found the remains of an Archaic site. Archeologists later discov-

---

[22]The concept was first introduced by Joseph R. Caldwell, *"Trend and Tradition in the Prehistory of the Eastern United States*, Part 2" *American Anthropologist* 60, no. 6.

[23]Jesse D. Jennings, *Prehistory of North America* (New York: McGraw-Hill, 1968). Eva was originally discussed by Thomas M. N. Lewis and Madeline K. Lewis, *Eva: An Archaic Site* (Knoxville: University of Tennessee Press, 1961).

[24]Jennings, *Prehistory*. The Boylston site was first described by Frederick Johnson et al., "The Boylston Street Fish-weir," *Papers of the Robert S. Peabody Foundation for Archaeology* (Andover, Mass., 1942).

Milwaukee Public Museum

Birchbark canoes of the northern American woodlands. Forager societies were closely connected by systems of transport and trade.

ered that the remains covered roughly two acres. It is one of the largest North American fish-weirs that has ever been found.

Over 65,000 stakes, ranging from 4 to 16 feet in length, had been driven into the clay of the tidal flat region. Brush was stuffed between the stakes and flexible branches were woven between them. A wattlelike wall was created on the clay of the flats. This was probably shaped like a V, with the open end facing the ocean. High tide would sweep the fish toward the point of the V, where they were trapped inside a smaller enclosure of brush. Aside from the ingenuity involved in constructing the Boylston weir, there is a greater archeological significance bound up with the site. The ebb and flow of the tide undoubtedly damaged the weir. It had to be constantly repaired to be functional at all. This could only be possible, of course, if the Archaic fishers were constantly present, or in other words, if the Boylston site was a permanent settlement. Like the fishing societies of Jomon, the Boylston people did not move in a round. An abundant natural resource and a technology of specialization created a sedentary pocket on the coast of Archaic America.

Such abundance was totally lacking in the desert of the American West, but the descendants of the big-game hunters had changed and survived.

Field Museum of Natural History

Fragment of woven blanket. The dry soils of Danger Cave preserved many perishable artifacts similar to this that are usually lost.

Under the overhanging ledge of a cavern in the Great Salt Desert of Utah, small bands of foragers had seasonally camped for over 10,000 years.[25] The layers of refuse at the Danger Cave site had piled up to nearly 13 feet. In fact, Paiute Indians were still living in the cramped space that was left in the cavern at the time that Mark Twain made his journey through

[25]Jennings, *Prehistory*. Jennings first reported on the site in *Danger Cave*, University of Utah Anthropological papers, no. 27 (Salt Lake City, 1957).

the very same desert. The artifacts dug from this cavern reveal a technology that was virtually static from the time of the earliest foragers to the Paiute encampment.

The excavator Jesse Jennings discovered only the subtlest technological changes. Basketmaking slowly transformed from twining to coiling techniques; the baskets themselves were once made out of hemp and then later from bark. But the basic strategy of desert survival remained largely unchanged. Antelope and mountain sheep were occasionally hunted in the foothills; jackrabbit, bobcat, and fox were the game of the desert. At least 65 species of plants were regularly gathered in the region, and over 1,000 seed-grinding stones were dug out of the cave. A life of nomadic collecting meant survival in the Great Salt Desert. It was preserved through the centuries until it was shattered by the industrialized world.

Foragers in the Tehuacan Valley

Other dried-up regions of the Americas seem to be almost identical to this, but a closer look reveals that, in fact, they were far from the same. Southern Mexico's Tehuacan Valley is also a region of little rain. Sandwiched between the north- and south-running spines of the Sierra Madre mountains, this "rain shadow" valley is watered only by showers in summer.[26] But archeologist Richard MacNeish found that it was a valley of varied resources, where a prehistoric foraging life was about to be changed.

The oasis was a spring-fed region, with a water table higher than in much of the valley. As a result, its vegetation was lush, and it was constantly green. There were agave plants, opuntia fruit trees, amaranth seeds, and mesquite beans, as well as other edible fruits and seeds throughout the oasis. And there was a menagerie of meat for the diet: deer, peccary, skunk, raccoon, fox, gopher, and rabbit, as well as lizards, snakes turtles, iguanas, and a collection of rats. From a knowledge of these plants and animals—especially of their seasonal availability—it has been possible to sketch out the strategy of valley existence.

When spring came to the valley, there was new growth and the sprouting of seeds. Bands foraged together in this time of greater abundance. They collected cactus fruits, seeds, and wild maize; they combed the hills for avocado and herds of deer. With the rains of summer, the seeds and fruits were even more plentiful, and were gathered more intensely now than at any other season. Amaranth and chile seeds, mixta squash, and avocado filled the baskets of the foraging bands throughout the valley. In the cooler months of fall, the rain retreated from Tehuacan, and the bands

---

[26]Richard S. MacNeish, *The Science of Archeology?* (North Scituate, Mass.: Duxbury Press, 1978). MacNeish has also discussed the Tehuacan sites in his earlier book *The Prehistory of the Tehuacan Valley: Excavations and Reconnaisance*, vol. 5 (Austin: University of Texas Press, 1972).

prepared for the leaner times of winter. They walked through the thinning brush along the slopes at the rim of the valley, collecting acorns to
eat and store for the winter season. When frost arrived in the valley, the
bands broke up into smaller groups. They hunted peccary and deer, gathered the leaves of wild cacti, and ate the nuts that were stored until the
coming of spring.

The shifting bands of the Tehuacan Valley were closely adapted to the
flow of the seasons, yet their hunting-and-gathering life was about to
end. Here, as in other regions, the foraging pattern would slowly change,
and the change would revolutionize human existence.

Peruvian foragers

South of the Tehuacan Valley, there would be an equally great transformation: a food-collecting technology would come to an end. Along the
desert coast of Peru, fishing-and-gathering groups were shifting their camps
in a cycle bound up with the seasons.[27] Here the waters of the Humboldt
Current, chilled as they flow by Antarctica, meet a rainless desert that lies
between the sea and the mountains. The cold water and the heat of the
land create fogs in the middle of winter, and scanty vegetation appears
on the edge of the desert. Rivers stream down from the mountains, flow
across the coastal desert and into the sea. There are more than 40 of these
rain-fed rivers, bordered by thick vegetation, that have helped to support
human life in the Peruvian desert. Behind the desert, the land quickly
rises into upland regions of steppe. Higher still, there is Alpine tundra
and the snow-covered peaks of the Andes: a dizzying perch four miles
above the Peruvian coast.

In this patchwork quilt of environments, around 8,000 years before the
present, the glacially flooded Pacific met the rivers flowing down from
the Andes. Life flourished in the coastal estuaries; fish and shellfish were
taken from the sea. At Huaca Prieta, on the coast of Peru, a 45-foot pile
of shellfish still stands as a reminder of this earlier strand-combing time.
Yet not only were there marine resources, but wild gourds, squash, and
lima beans. Plant collecting was vital to life in this unusual terrain. Almost certainly these early Peruvians spent the winters on the coast near
the rivers, where the *lomas*—fogs from the ocean—fed the plants of the
lowlands. In the summer, when the *lomas* dried out, they probably migrated into the highlands to gather roots and seeds and kill an occasional
deer. Like the foragers of the Tehuacan Valley, the Peruvian bands lived
by schedules and seasons. Like them, their hunting-and-gathering technology would come to an end.

---

[27]Edward P. Lanning, "Western South America," in *Prehistoric America*, ed. Shirley Gorenstein (New York: St. Martin's Press, 1974).

The society of the foraging peoples

The hunting-and-gathering tradition was very different than the one just ahead. The very structure of human existence was about to be changed. Throughout the world, humanity existed in small, highly nomadic bands, shifting their campsites as the available resources changed. The tribe lingered in those regions where remnant herds were still the basis of life. But virtually everywhere else on the planet, the scattered and seasonally available resources caused a return to the band as the basic structure of human society. Archeologist J. Desmond Clark has studied the rock-shelter paintings of African foragers and synthesized these with recent studies of hunters and gatherers today. The result is a tentative portrait of a form of human society that was once shared by prehistoric people in many parts of the world.[28]

A hunter-and-gatherer band, on the average, could have numbered around 25 people, but in a time of abundance, the size could have increased to 200. Like contemporary food collectors, they may have ranged over 3,000 square miles; perhaps, too, there were territories claimed by particular bands. And they were not, as I mentioned before, tiny enclaves locked up in a wilderness; bands were undoubtedly aware of one another's existence. Amber amulets have been discovered on the European Mediterranean, though the amber from which they were made was from the shores of the Baltic. Hammered copper from the Great Lakes region made its way to the Gulf of Mexico, and conch shells from the Gulf Coast beaches have been found on the Lakes. Trade knitted the bands together into a wide-ranging network of exchange; this, too, would increase in importance in the time just ahead.

But the aspect of foraging society that is so different from our industrialized world is the absence of a permanent structure of political power. Chiefs did not rule these societies, and there was no cadre of nobles or assistants. Decisions were nonetheless made, in the way that bands make them today. There were discussion, argumentation, recall of experiences, and appeals to tradition. The advice of elders likely was heeded, for they remember what was done in the past. But the opinion of the elders can be challenged; it probably was.

We can drift too far in this portrait of an innocent age in our past. There were probably many optimum regions where hunters and gatherers lived in which all they needed was found in the natural world. As Marshall Sahlins once put it, they were the "original affluent society." Strategies, schedules, and nature met all of their needs. And yet, many forager burials near the rivers of our northerly states have skeletal lesions that tell of nutritional stress. The growth of young bone was arrested; tooth enamel was strikingly thin. Periods of hunger were part of their foraging life.[29]

---

[28]J. Desmond Clark, *The Prehistory of Southern Africa* (London: Pelican, 1959).

[29]The evidence will be discussed more extensively in Chapter 14.

Such studies are only beginning; they are needed in many parts of the world. Even so, our understanding of foragers is starting to change. The original affluent society concept is tempered by the realization that forager existence was not everything it has seemed. Climatic change at the end of the Ice Age brought abundance to many parts of the planet. But not every region was meeting humanity's needs.

In the foothills of Southwest Asia, the weather was becoming more dry. That world was no longer as rich as it had been in the past. There were northerly stretches of China changing from grassland to sage. In Southeast Asia, the jungle spread over the land. Mexico's grasses were waning; humid canyons and oases remained. A cycle of droughts may have begun in Peru.

Foragers who lived in these regions, like foragers everywhere in the world, were closely connected through intricate webs of exchange. The webs became especially critical as scarcity increased in their lands. Connections meant an easier life in a difficult world.

Out of these elaborate networks, came domesticated species of plants. Animals were raised for their meat and their shearings of wool. But the webs that created these changes forged permanent power as well; transformations occurred in the structure of political life. We will see, in the chapters that follow, the way this intricate process of change created the earliest rulers in ancient society.

Part Two / Farmers and Chiefs

8 / The Domestication Revolution: Theory and Excavation in the Eastern Mediterranean

July arrived in the desert, and there still was no rain. Clouds would sometimes gather in the heat of the afternoon, but they would quickly be blown away by the dusty winds. Sun Chief had gone to his cornfield as many as 25 times. He replanted the scattered seedlings uprooted by the blasts of sand. He chopped away all the weeds and set out traps for the rats. He watched the sky in anxious waiting. There still was no rain.

His friends no longer spoke to him when they met him on the road. They thought only about their crops and the empty sky. When Sun Chief went to his melon patch, he found that it was almost destroyed. Kangaroo rats had eaten about half of the seeds. He planted again and waited, but a windstorm covered the desert. He returned some four days later, dug the sand away from the seedlings, and built a wall of twigs to shield what was left of his crop. Then, one right after another, were three more storms of dust. A jackrabbit managed to eat a large number of seedlings.

Sun Chief and his people gathered together in the village in prayer. They captured wild hawks and strangled them, then buried them with ground corn. They asked the spirits of the hawks to fly home and send them some rain. He went back to his battered cornfield and planted a spruce bough in a hillock of sand. He prayed silently to the sun and to the stars. He sprinkled a path of meal on the ground. Then, at last, the sky was darkened. Sun Chief watched the boil of clouds. A few drops fell across the desert. Then there was rain.[1]

Sun Chief was a Hopi Indian concerned about his fields and his flocks. Without them, life as he knew it would have come to an end. For the last 10,000 years, much of humanity has shared his concern. We have domesticated animals and plants. We have produced our own food.

Anthropologists have often spoken of this development as a "revolu-

---

[1]Leo W. Simmons, ed., *Sun Chief: The Autobiography of a Hopi Indian* (New Haven, Conn.: Yale University Press, 1942), pp. 231–32.

Hopi snake priest. In marginal regions of the planet, religious specialists had significant political power.

tion." Sweeping changes did occur when the Pleistocene came to an end. They involved social and political behavior—and also religious belief. Even so, it is important to realize that revolutions are not all they seem. Behavior changes within a social tradition and is continuous with all that has been. In a sense, human societies simply strengthened what was already there. A matrix of kinship connections was likely extended to more human groups. There were more information and goods on the routes of exchange. The scale of decisions was heightened; old leaders were assuming new roles. Their actions affected more contexts in ancient society. Uncertainty, too, was increasing; leaders were threatened more than ever before. The cultural system of sharing soon evolved into a scheme of rewards. Sacred beliefs became part of political rule.

It is little wonder that social philosophers and the scientists of more recent times have been intrigued by this turbulent period of human existence. Their efforts are not simply the narrative of a problem in social research. They are a reminder of the intricate growing of science itself.

Many of the earliest speculations saw domestication as the work of the gods: supernatural power brought agriculture into existence. Humanity was deaf and sightless, until the Greek god Prometheus gave them senses. Then he showed them the art of cultivation and the "yoking of beasts." "Jupiter shortened the springtime," as the Roman philosopher Ovid explained it, and he "instituted a cycle of four different seasons. Then corn, the gift of [the god] Ceres, first began to be sown in long furrows, and straining bullocks groaned beneath the yoke of the plow."

With the spread of the Christian religion, the supernatural understanding remained. But agriculture was not a divine blessing; it was seen as a curse. Disobedience in the Garden of Eden led to exile and divine retribution. Adam would bring bread from the earth by the "sweat of his brow."

It was not until the 18th century and the advance of the scientific method that the causes of agriculture were no longer sought in the heavens. The French philosopher Condorcet saw the beginnings of cultivation as the natural result of the increasing use of our "reason." It was a popular explanation, one that was typical of his age, and it exerted a powerful influence for generations to come. Condorcet had replaced the gods with the mysterious factor of human "genius." A particularly bright individual once discovered that plants grew from seeds. This was the stuff out of which a social revolution was made. More will be said of this in a moment, but here it is sufficient to say that genius is almost as useless as the notion of gods.

The origins of domestication: The beginnings of theory

Yet the genius argument continued, reaching down to the 20th century, where it flourished in the writings of historian Arnold J. Toynbee.[2] In his massive *Study of History*, Toynbee searched out, and believed that he had discovered, the ultimate cause of domestication—and of cultural change. For Toynbee, the transformations experienced by human society were the result of a very small number of "heroic" individuals who responded in clever ways to a cultural challenge.

It was "challenge and response," in the great historian's view, that created agriculture and, subsequently, civilization. Human society is stable, but then its balance is suddenly disturbed, and this provokes creative genius into action. In the language of science, according to Toynbee,

Arnold J. Toynbee: A prehistoric challenge

> we may say that the function of the intruding factor is to supply that on which it intrudes with a stimulus of the kind best calculated to evoke the most potently creative variations.[3]

---

[2]Arnold J. Toynbee, *A Study of History* (New York: Oxford University Press, 1954), pp. 61–72.

[3]Ibid., p.63.

But the language of science was really of little importance to Toynbee's thought. Much more significant was the language he discovered in myth. "Let us shut our eyes," he pleaded, "to the formulae of science in order to open our ears to the language of mythology."[4] If we understand what different societies believed about their gods and heroes, then we can understand the ultimate cause of historical change.

Having explicitly rejected the use of the scientific method, he considered a highly restricted number of myths. There he found the recurrent theme of superhuman conflict—a collision between two forceful personalities. Disobedient Adam, Job, and the Devil all clashed with their Lord; the Greek and Scandanavian heroes all challenged their gods. These mythological conflicts are the echoes of actual events that—so Toynbee believed—have occurred in human prehistory. The collisions of super-personalities are symbolic of early crises that were successfully challenged by the heroes of ancient society.

From such mythological clues, Toynbee proposed that river valley regions were the centers where domestication had first occurred. The challenge that humankind faced was a change in the weather. As the ice sheets retreated northward, there were disturbances in rainfall patterns, which created deserts in Egypt and the Persian Gulf region of Asia. Archeologist V. Gordon Childe, who influenced Toynbee's opinion, also thought that humanity had been faced with a crisis of climate:

> Now we are on the brink of the great revolution, and soon we shall encounter men who are masters of their own food supply through possession of domesticated animals and the cultivation of cereals. It seems inevitable to connect that revolution with the crisis produced by the melting of the northern glaciers and consequent contraction of the Arctic high pressure over Europe. . . . Faced with the gradual dessication consequent upon the re-shift northward. . .three alternatives were open to the hunting populations affected. They might move northward or southward with their prey, following the climatic belt to which they were accustomed; they might remain at home eking out a miserable existence on such game as could withstand the drought; or they might—still without leaving their homeland—emancipate themselves from dependence on the whims of their environment by domesticating animals and taking to agriculture.[5]

So on the Tigris, the Euphrates, and the frail green thread of the Nile, there were intrepid hunters and gatherers who rose to the challenge. Wrote Toynbee,

> These heroic pioneers, inspired by audacity or by desperation, plunged

---

[4]Ibid., p. 60.

[5]V. Gordon Childe, as quoted in Arnold J. Toynbee, *A Study of History* (New York: Oxford University Press, 1954), p.69.

into the jungle swamps of the valley bottoms, never before penetrated by man, which their dynamic act was to turn into the land of Egypt and the Land of Shinar.[6]

Here is an attitude toward prehistory that generations have found inspiring, and it has certainly not been confined to the writings of Toynbee. We can inquire matter-of-factly: did agriculture really begin there? And more significantly: what can be said of this view of the past?

As for the river valley theory of agriculture, it can now be quickly dispensed with. There is no archeological evidence to support such a view. It was in areas well removed from the rivers (as we shall see a bit later in the story), where the transformation of human technology almost certainly took place. Besides, the "jungle swamps of the valley bottoms" were covered by thick wild grasses. Plowing would have been necessary to break up the sod. But small-scale agriculturalists have never made use of the plow. For this reason, river valley farming was much later in time.

Since Toynbee's theory of the emergence of agriculture collapsed like a house of cards, it is tempting to dismiss the whole venture as the failure of poetry. Exciting tales of heroes and gods were never meant to be a substitute for science. It is reckless to think that they accurately mirror the past. But embedded in Toynbee's thinking are other equally serious problems that have often interfered with the understanding of our own evolution.

Like many of his contemporaries, he underestimated hunters and gatherers by believing they had to discover that plants grew from seeds. However, a society that gains its living from wild plant and animal foods is well aware of what happens when seeds are covered by soil. Menomini Indians were careful, when they harvested wild grains, to scatter some seeds so they would never deplete their supply. The western Australian aborigine set fire to stretches of desert to increase the abundance of plants that grow over burned ground. For 3 million years, human beings gathered fruits, roots, and leaves. No hero was needed to tell them what a seed would become.

But the vision of an innovative hero faces another problem as well: it cannot explain why developments occurred when they did. It was not only in Southwestern Asia, but in other parts of our planet also, where totally independent subsistence transformations occurred. Between 10,000 and 4,000 BC, in northern China and Southeastern Asia, in southern Mexico and coastal Peru, cultivation was involved in the changes of human society. These events all happened within a time span that is a little more than 1/1,000 of the time that our species has been on the face of the earth. In other words, the domestication revolutions all happened at about the same time and in parts of the planet separated by thousands of miles. Is

---

[6]Ibid., p. 70.

this nothing more than coincidence? Was seed planting really an invention? Why did it occur in several different places at almost the same time?

There is a possible answer to these questions which is somewhat disturbing. Foragers throughout the planet were simultaneously challenged in one way or another, but only a limited number were creative enough to respond. This is, in fact, the way that Toynbee dismisses the Dinka and the Shilluk societies that live today by hunting and fishing on the Upper Nile valley.

> The forefathers of these people who now live on the margin of the Sudanese Sudd were living, in what is now the Libyan Desert, cheek-by-jowl with the founders of the Egyptiac Civilization at the time when these responded to the challenge of dessication by making their momentous choice. At that time, it would seem, the ancestors of the modern Dinka and Shilluk parted with their heroic neighbors and followed the line of least resistance by retreating southwards to a country where they could continue to live, without changing their way of life, in physical surroundings partly identical with those to which they were accustomed. They settled in the Tropical Sudan, within the range of the equatorial rains, and here their descendants remain to this day living the self-same life as their remote ancestors. In their new home the sluggish and unambitious emigrants found what their souls desired.[7]

The passage should sound familiar. Indeed, we have heard something like it before. It is an echo of Mark Twain talking about the American Indians. This is the hidden implication, then, of all such invention or genius theories: they imply that all stable societies are sluggish or stupid. But the stability of any human society, as I mentioned in the previous chapter, is more likely explainable in terms of an absence of stress. As we will see in the pages that follow, the rise of villages and civilizations, as well as the patterns of revolutionary change, have nothing to do with the presence or absence of heroes. The Toynbee view begins with mythology and, ironically, it ends there as well—with the myth of the unintelligent human society. Challenge and response, it would seem, tell us more about Toynbee's old British Empire than they do about the causes of prehistoric cultural change.

V. Gordon Childe: An adaptive explanation

But what of V. Gordon Childe, the archeologist who influenced Toynbee? Was his viewpoint simply an echo of challenge and response? True enough, Toynbee and Childe were in agreement about the climatic changes, but their understandings of human prehistory were far from the same. Childe was remarkably different from Toynbee and from his archeological

---

[7]Ibid., p. 71.

colleagues as well. He was a personality struggling to define both the past and himself.[8]

He was bookish. He was every inch the scholar. He had roamed the passageways of libraries from Australia to England. He had arrived at Oxford University with a scholarship to study the classics just as England and the rest of the world was preparing for war. Perhaps it was the waste and devastation of that conflict "to end all wars" which created a conflict in Childe that would last his lifetime.

It was a specific problem in classical research—the location of the ancient Indo-European language—that originally inspired him toward studies in human prehistory. Even 40 years later, as he reflected on those earlier days, there is the voice of an archeologist more excited by a book than a shovel. "Reading my Homer and my Veda," he said, "with the guidance of Schrader and Jevons. . .I was thrilled by the discoveries of Evans in Prehellenic Crete."[9] That excitement as such never left him; it helped shape the direction of his life. He would organize the scattered—and voluminous—accounts of the past.

But like many of his contemporaries, he was troubled by a question of value. He doubted his usefulness in a world that was broken by war. *"Is Prehistory Practical?"* he asked, in the middle of the Great Depression. He found it increasingly difficult to say that it was. Only two years before his death, he asked the same question again, and it was clear that Childe was still very far from an answer. He wrote,

> I am an archeologist and devote my time to trying to gather information about the behaviour of men long since dead. I like doing this and my society pays me quite well for doing it. Yet neither I nor society can see any practical application for the information I gather; we are indeed quite sure that it will not increase the production of bombs or butter.[10]

Childe seems never to have fully appreciated the importance of what he was doing or, for that matter, the role of the scientist in modern society. He thought of himself as the man who established a more accurate chronology for Bronze Age Europe, or as the chronicler of Oriental influences in later prehistory.[11] Toward the end of his life, he even defended

---

[8]The biographical sketch of Childe is adapted from P. Gathercole, "'Patterns in Prehistory': an Examination of the Later Thinking of V. Gordon Childe," *World Archeology* vols. 3 and 4 (1971); V. Gordon Childe, "Retrospect," *Antiquity* 32 (1958), pp. 69–74; Stuart Piggot, "The Dawn: and an Epilogue," *Antiquity* 32 (1958), pp. 75–79; and an "Editorial on Childe's Contributions," *Antiquity* 32, (June 1958) pp. 65–68. Many more interpretations exist. He was a highly controversial figure, and the sketch given here is only that. A brief overview of Childe interpretations is provided by Bruce G. Trigger, *Gordon Childe: Revolutions in Archaeology* (New York: Columbia University Press, 1980), pp. 7–19.

[9]Childe, "Retrospect," p. 69.

[10]"Editorial," Antiquity, pp. 65–66.

[11]These issues will be explored a bit later in the book.

a bizarre philosophy of archeology that viewed the excavator as a discoverer of "progress" in science. When we uncover buried evidence of the activities of early craftsmen, we are put directly in touch with a scientific view of the world. Craftsmen, he thought, were "the exponents of applied science" in human prehistory. Their "lineal descendants" were

> the natural scientists who from the days of Galileo and Newton to 1945 freely exchanged information and ideas by publication, correspondence, and visits regardless of political frontiers.[12]

But if archeology is primarily responsible for recovering the traces of science, then there is little reason for troubling with religious beliefs. Astonishingly, V. Gordon Childe, one of the world's leading prehistorians, found himself denying that these early beliefs could be known. Religious acts were "futile accessories, expressive of ideological delusions. It is just these that have been erased from the archeological record."[13]

There are multiple ironies and multiple misunderstandings here. Of course, Childe was never a determinant of the production of butter in Britain. And despite Childe and all other prehistorians, we still have our bombs. But when archeology was still a mosaic of local sequences and pottery tallies, he organized these data into a study of human behavior. From Karl Marx and Lewis Henry Morgan, he had learned of cultural evolution: of the constraints imposed by technology and the physical environment. This made it possible to better understand the transformations of human prehistory and the behavioral regularities that are part of our past. Here was certainly a contribution, and far from a minor one at that. In the prehistories of V. Gordon Childe, we could study ourselves.

But the record of early humanity is also a record of human beliefs. We need to know as much as we can about our ancient religions. Often the evidence is shaky; the reconstructions are mere speculations. But at times (as we will see a bit later), there is much we can learn. More to the point, it not only is possible—it is something that needs to be done. The ideological delusions are neither erased nor irrelevant knowledge. It is the very fact that they *were* mass delusions that makes them significant. As we will see in the chapters that follow, religion has been a powerful tool. It has often been used to intensify political power. Ideologies have been created and their content deliberately shaped to justify the despotic controls of the earliest states. An awareness of how this happens can help us recognize it happening today. Mass delusions are a central—and dangerous—fact of our lives.

Childe's defense of human prehistory was, I think, curious and misdirected, but his discussions of prehistoric events are still useful today. In *The Most Ancient East* and *Man Makes Himself*, he presented an eloquent

---

[12]V. Gordon Childe, as quoted in Gathercole, *"Patterns in Prehistory,"* p. 226.
[13]Ibid., p. 228.

outline of his theory of domestication in Southwestern Asia. It was a frankly speculative account, since little excavation had been done, and yet it was markedly different from the writings of Toynbee.

Here there was not any mention of ambitious or sluggish societies. Domestication for Childe was not the work of a hero. The drying-up of the eastern Mediterranean—Toynbee's prehistoric "challenge"—was for Childe only the beginning of a complex chain of events. The retreat of the northern ice sheets had created more than a desert. It had concentrated the resources of the hunter-and-gatherer world. Wrote Childe:

> Of course the process was not sudden or catastrophic. At first and for long, the sole harbinger would be the greater severity and longer duration of periodical droughts. But quite a small reduction in the rainfall would work a devastating change in countries that were always relatively dry. It would mean the difference between continuous grasslands and sandy deserts interrupted by occasional oases.
>
> A number of animals that could live comfortably with a twelve-inch annual rainfall would become a surplus population if the precipitation diminished by a couple of inches for two or three years on end. To get food and water, the grass-eaters would have to congregate round a diminishing number of springs and streams—in oases. . .And they would be brought up against man too; for the same causes would force even hunters to frequent the springs and valleys. The huntsman and his prey thus find themselves united in an effort to circumvent the dreadful power of drought. But if the hunter is also a cultivator, he will have

V. Gordon Childe's Oasis Theory. The explanation has not been supported by more recent archeological research. Even so, it introduced the question of the possible significance of climatic change in the evolution of plant and animal domestication.

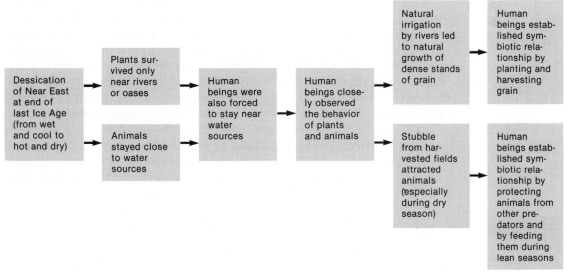

Adapted from V. Gordon Childe

something to offer the famished beasts: the stubble of his freshly reaped fields will afford the best grazing in the oasis.[14]

Ultimately there would develop a *symbiosis*, as later theorists have called it: an increasing mutual dependency between animals and humans. The earliest farmers could protect the animals.

> They could drive off the lions and wolves that would prey upon them, and perhaps even offer them some surplus grain from (their) stores. The beasts, for their part, will grow tame and accustomed to man's proximity. . . . Under the conditions of incipient dessication the cultivator has the chance of attaching to his menage not only isolated young beasts, but the remnants of complete flocks or herds. . . . If he just realizes the advantage of having a group of such half-tamed beasts hanging round the fringes of his settlement as a reserve of game easily caught, he will be on the way to domestication.[15]

Childe was probably as aware as anyone that this theory would have to be modified and, possibly, that it might have to be altogether abandoned. But it was not only a particular theory that was the critical issue here, it was the framework of thought within which the theory was built. People moved into the desert oases not because of any heroics, but because those regions had a greater supply of food. To supplement the available plants, they scattered the seeds of cereal grains, and they hunted the animals that grazed in the harvested fields. The entire transformation, then, was not explained in psychological terms but as the cultural result of a change in the physical environment. It was, in other words, an evolutionary explanation. Prehistory was beginning to move in a different direction.

Much of the oasis theory is now argued to be incorrect, but some aspects of it deserve our attention today. In reconstructing the environmental changes, a number of errors were made.[16] It is now known that, at the end of the Pleistocene, the eastern Mediterranean was not changed into the desert that it is today. Intensive historic agriculture, overgrazing the land, removing the vegetation for use as fuel: all of these are largely responsible for the Middle East desert. And just as later excavations did not support the river valley theory, neither did they support the theory of Childe. The environment of early agriculture—as I will explain very shortly—had very little resemblance to a desert oasis.

But *was* there some relationship between the end of the Ice Age and the beginnings of plant and animal domestication? And were there also

---

[14]V. Gordon Childe, *Man Makes Himself* (New York: Mentor, 1951), p. 67.

[15]Ibid., p. 68.

[16]Dexter Perkins, Jr., and Patricia Daly, "The Beginnings of Food Production in the Near East," in *The Old World: Early Man to the Development of Agriculture*, ed. Robert Stigler et al. (New York: St. Martin's Press, 1974), pp. 74–75.

Near Eastern oasis. V. Gordon Childe suggested that agriculture and animal domestication began in such areas.

resource "pockets"—even if they were not, in fact, oases—where animals and cereal grains were clustered together? These were the provocative questions that emerged from the writings of Childe. Later prehistorians would echo them and search for an answer.

The tattered slopes still carry the scars of too many harvests and too many herds. It is a land that has been nearly exhausted by settled existence. But in some of its more distant valleys, just after the spring rains, the slopes are as green as they probably were in the past. Herders still graze their flocks there on the tender shoots of the valleys. The animals water in the *wadis*—the spring-fed creeks of the region—and they grow fat as they follow the pastures into the summer.

Iraqi Kurdistan is just to the south of the Zagros Mountains and 150 miles north of the city of Baghdad. The region has been settled, farmed,

Robert Braidwood and the Mediterranean foothills

Foothills of the Zagros Mountains. After the Ice Age ended, this was a marginal resource region, but it also had scattered pockets of optimum land.

and plundered for over 8,500 years. Its rains still wash up broken pottery. Its fallen mud houses are grass-covered mounds.

It was probably in such a region, rather than a river valley or an oasis, where the long-sought domestication revolution occurred. The Iraqi archeologists themselves had suspected as much. They had excavated the small encampments of hunter-and-gatherer societies that often dwelled in the caves at the edge of the mountains. Bones of wild horses, gazelles, goats, and fish were found littered throughout these camps, along with microlith blades that were possibly for bone harpoons. These were the Mediterranean foraging people of around 10,000 years before the present. They were much like foraging societies throughout most of the world.

But what became of these hunters and fishers? Here, the record was virtually blank. The next sites were those of farmers in permanent villages. Somewhere in the 6,000 years that separated these two, food production had probably emerged in the Near Eastern hills.

But it was more than the local archeology that made the region seem so promising. There were also the resources that are found in the foothills today. The hills begin as a narrow spine on the eastern shore of the Med-

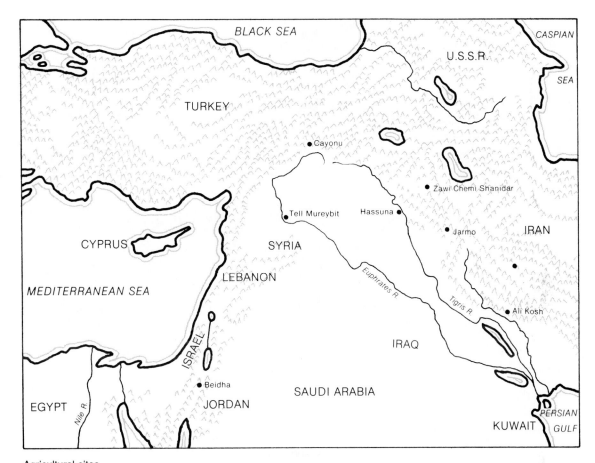

Agricultural sites.

iterranean. They curve eastward to form the fringes of the Taurus Mountains of Turkey, then southward following the peaks of the Zagros Mountains. Even today this range of foothills, known as the *Zagros-Taurus arc*, has resources that are noticeably different from much of the world. Closest to the Mediterranean, there are evergreen trees, shrubs, wild barley, and two different species of wild wheat. Following the great arc northward as it curves along the belly of Turkey, there are the vestiges of what was once a temperate forest. Here, the land is higher and cooler, flanking the edges of the mountains. There are oak and pistachio trees, edible fruits, and cereal grasses. Herds of wild sheep and goat still graze on the slopes. On the other side of the Taurus Mountains is the Anatolian Plateau. Nearly a mile above sea level, it was once a shimmering sea of wild wheat. Much of it had the look of a North American prairie. As the great arc curves to the south, approaching the shores of the Persian Gulf, wild

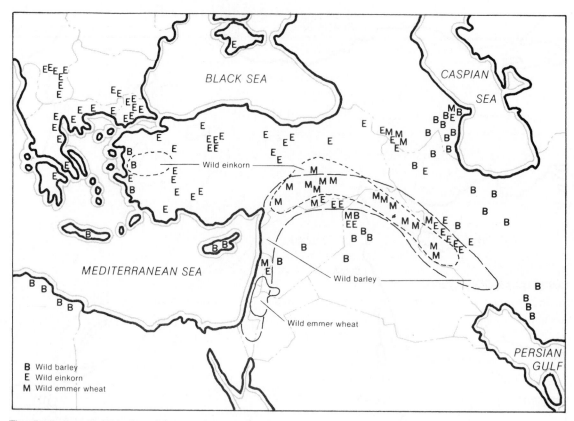

The distribution of wild barley, einkorn, and emmer wheat.

wheat becomes sparse along the slopes, but barley reaches down to the western shores of the Gulf. Prehistorians believed it was likely, then, that somewhere within this belt, food production had somehow emerged in Southwestern Asia.

"Somewhere" and "somehow" were the problems and they remain the problems today. But the strategies of archeology were beginning to change. Archeologist Robert Braidwood, who played a critical role in the changes, understood that the science of the past itself was evolving. He wrote,

> Until the end of World War II, the problem could still be framed only in its theoretical sense. Field archeology had done little to recover the necessary details of evidence, so that the compilers of ancient history and prehistory, like Childe, could rarely point up their theorizing with fact. Several distinguished excavators had concerned themselves with the more remote ranges of the prehistory of the Pleistocene (or "Ice Age") in the caves of western Asia. But the bulk of archeological excavation in the area had rather been concerned with the developed phases of con-

ventional ancient history. . . . Such sites as Babylon, Nineveh, Byblos, Megiddo, and Jericho were all excavated, but the intellectual frame of reference of their excavators was biblical or conventional ancient history. Occasionally narrow slit trenches or deep pits were driven down into the lowest levels of some of the great sites, and these operations yielded snatches of prehistoric material.[17]

Overlying these meager "snatches" were the tons of later debris. With a touch of irony, Braidwood noted that it apparently

> did not occur to the earlier archeologists to search for inconspicuous little sites which had not been occupied during the millennia following their prehistoric establishment. Therefore our comprehension of prehistoric village life was a thing of shreds and patches at best.[18]

So digging began on the Kurdistan hills in the spring of 1948, on a site that had no pretensions to classical glory. Jarmo was not a Babylon, nor was it a Jericho. It was a collapsed, mud village on the crest of a parched hill. Close by, there was a winding stream locally known as the Cham-Gawra Wadi. Hopefully, in the piled-up mud, there would be seeds and animal bones that would reveal the beginnings of our earliest farming existence.

There were four separate seasons of digging on the arid Iraqi hillside. Foundations of houses were found beneath the blanket of sand. Some 9,700 years ago, a small group of New Eastern farmers had built their first homes along the grassy crest of the hill. First, they had gathered up reeds, placed them on the ground in a line, and poured a course of mud—called *touf*—on top of the reeds. After the mud had dried out in the sunshine, another course was poured on the top. Quickly the mud-walled houses began to take form.

Over the years, these houses—there were usually about 20 at a time—would weather and weaken as rains fell over the country. Eventually they would collapse, but life in the village went on. New houses were built on top of the mud of the old ones. Reed foundations were replaced by stone, but the village of Jarmo changed little. It had always been about 20 or so houses, where perhaps 150 people had lived. They grew their crops of wheat and barley. They grazed their sheep and their goats on the hills.

The Jarmo mound, in other words, was not a site of technological change. It was an agricultural village from its earliest days. In the lowest of its 16 layers, there were ground-stone mortars and pestles for removing the tough outer husks of the cereal grains. Sickles of flint and obsidian were used for harvesting the wheat and barley. The microscope revealed the silicon polish left behind after cutting the stems. But the most convincing evi-

---

[17]Robert Braidwood and Bruce Howe, *Prehistoric Investigations in Iraqi Kurdistan*, Studies in Ancient Oriental Civilization, no. 31 (Oriental Institute, University of Chicago, 1960), p. 2.

[18]Ibid.

dence of all had been discovered in the houses themselves: the imprint of the actual grains pressed into the mud. To strengthen the walls of their houses, the farmers mixed the mud with some straw. Very possibly, the straw had been brought from the floor of a threshing room. The imprints were unmistakable: they were the traces of cereal grains—and they were noticeably different from the cereals that grow in the wild. Einkorn and emmer wheat, and a species of "two-row barley" were the crops that had supported Jarmo for hundreds of years.

The layers also contained sheep and goat bones, and—in the upper layers—the bones of pigs. For all three species, the skeletal remains were mostly of younger and smaller animals. Since herd animals are normally slaughtered when they are mature but still fairly young, it was likely that these were the remains of domesticated species.

The barren mound on top of the hill had left many questions still unanswered. The beginnings of farming and herding were nowhere in evidence at the Jarmo site. At the end of his third season of digging, Robert Braidwood candidly wrote that "how Jarmo came to be what it is still eludes us."[19] What Braidwood had discovered instead, were the remains of everyday village life, as it was lived in the hills overlooking the Kurdistan wadis.

> The people of Jarmo grew the barley plant and two different kinds of wheat. They made flint sickles with which to reap their grain, mortars or querns on which to crack it, ovens in which it might be parched, and stone bowls out of which they might eat their porridge. . . . Throughout the duration of the village. . .its people had experimented with the plastic qualities of clay; one type of human figurine they favored was that of a markedly pregnant woman, probably the expression of some sort of fertility spirit. They provided their house floors with baked-in-place depressions, either as basins or hearths, and later with domed ovens of clay. . . . Finally the idea of making pottery itself appeared, although I very much doubt that the people of the Jarmo village discovered the art.[20]

But perhaps the greatest significance of Jarmo was its role in the scientific process: it was both a discovery and an invitation to further research. Braidwood had discovered the earliest traces of plant and animal domestication in a region far removed from oases and rivers. But these were the earliest traces—not the earliest domestication. Jarmo had been a farming village from its earliest days. Where, then, did the transition happen? And, just as important, how? Braidwood believed that he had arrived at a part of the answer.

It now seemed to him very likely that the emergence of food produc-

---

[19]Ibid., p. 184

[20]Robert Braidwood, *Prehistoric Man*, 7th ed. (Glenview, Ill.: Scott, Foresman, 1967), p. 120.

tion had happened somewhere within the foothills of the Zagros-Taurus. Far better to dig in that region than in a floodplain or an oasis; that much, at least, had been learned from the digging at Jarmo. The sweeping arc of upland country, with its herds and cereal grains, was an appropriate natural environment—a *nuclear area*, he called it—where foraging people had settled down to a village existence. Probably they had experienced also an "era of incipient cultivation": a time of experimentation with the planting of grains.[21] But why had they experimented? Robert Braidwood's answer was intriguing: because of a human "tendency to be experimental."[22]

Now this is not very far from saying that English sparrows have a nest-building behavior because of an inherent tendency toward building a nest. The explanation, in other words, is circular. It really tells us nothing at all. What was it that caused the human populations in the nuclear areas across the world to change their good supply by deliberate planting? An experimental tendency is clearly not enough of an answer. We need to know the causes behind such experimentation.

The techniques of archeology were now directly focused upon the problem. There was more digging in the Zagros-Taurus than ever before. In a little less than a decade after the Jarmo excavation, traces of even earlier planting had been found in the hills. As Braidwood had predicted, there were more ancient sites than Jarmo in which gradual shifts toward food production were made. There were sites of nomadic foragers who collected wild cereal grains. Somewhat later, there were hunters and gatherers who cultivated part of their food. Out of this there evolved the villages of farmers and herders.

Foraging in the eastern Mediterranean

It was in the eastern Mediterranean wilderness, some 10,000 years before the present, where hunters first began collecting wild cereal grains. They lived in the mouths of caves and beneath overhanging ledges of rock. They gathered wild grain in large quantities and stored it. They hunted sheep, goats, gazelles, and wild pigs in the temperate forest. And they were fishers. Their dwellings were never very far from the sea. Often these foragers managed, because of the sheer abundance of wild foods, to build permanent dwellings and live in the same place all year round.

These Mediterranean foragers—the *Natufians*, they are usually called—have left behind traces of the grains that were part of their life. At Ain Mallaha in Israel, some 10,000 years before the present, we find the emergence of a sedentary pattern of living. Circular houses of stone, over 20 feet in diameter, were constructed in the Huleh Basin, where the wild grains were abundant. Wild pig and gazelle were hunted in the forested

---

[21]Braidwood and Howe, *Prehistoric Investigations*, p. 181.

[22]Braidwood, *Prehistoric Man*, p. 94.

reaches of the valley. Grains were collected and stored within clay-lined pits. And there were sickle blades at Ain Mallaha with their telltale silica polish, as well as ground-stone mortars and pestles for crushing the grain.

But it was at the campsite at Nahal Oren, on Israel's Mediterranean coastline, where excavators discovered the remains of the grasses themselves. Archeologist A. J. Legge used a "froth flotation" device to recover the carbonized traces of the cereal grain.[23] Samples of soil were sprinkled into an unusual bubbling concoction of water and chemicals, with a detergent for mixing the two. The heavier soil sank to the bottom, but the carbonized plants stuck fast to the bubbles. They were strained off the top and then microscopically viewed. The wild plants of the early Natufians now literally came into focus. Twenty thousand years ago, along the coast of the Mediterranean, wheat and barley were being collected by foraging bands.

Change at Nahal Oren was almost imperceptible through the years. The Natufian peoples camped there, and they gathered their wild grains. They hunted grassland cattle and pig and killed an occasional deer. And they intensively hunted the open-country gazelles. But the numbers of seeds in the layers are almost constant throughout the years. Farming and herding was probably never a part of their lives.

It was in the foothills of northern Iraq, not very far from the Shanidar cave, where there was a site that revealed the beginnings of adaptive change. Zawi Chemi Shanidar lay in the depths of a Kurdistan valley, surrounded by mountains over 5,000 feet high. Within the layers of sand that were nearly 11,000 years old, was a circle of stones that recalled the foundations at Jarmo. Ground-stone mortars and pestles were discovered throughout the site. There were storage pits filled with charcoal, snail shells, and butchered animal bones. But not a single cereal grain was ever found at the site.

It was instead the hundreds of animal bone fragments, scattered on the ground and tossed into trash pits, that reflected the emergence of technological change. Most of the bones recovered were those of immature sheep. This is not the sort of litter left behind in a hunting encampment. Hunters will usually kill both the adult and the immature animals, but herders will slaughter their animals at a particular age. Then too, the horns and the bones had a revealing cellular structure. The cells were wider than in the wild forms and separated by thinner walls: a more fragile structure found in domesticated species.

The domesticated grains themselves—direct evidence of the beginnings of farming—were eventually discovered some 300 miles to the south. At Ali Kosh in southwestern Iran, along the flanks of the Zagros Moun-

---

[23]A. J. Legge, "The Origins of Agriculture in the Near East," in *Hunters, Gatherers and First Farmers beyond Europe*, ed. J. V. S. Megaw (Leicester, Mass.: Leicester University Press, 1977), pp. 51–68.

tains, the elusive fragments of the ancient cereals were still in the ground.[24] Some 9,500 years ago, Ali Kosh was an open grassland. Alfalfa, clover, and cereals grew wild along the uplands. The hills sloped down to marshes that almost never went dry. The wheat and barley had probably been grown on the fringe of those marshes. Water—the critical variable—would almost always be there.

From a nearby quarry of red clay, the early inhabitants of Ali Kosh cut out slabs for building the walls of their houses. They mixed the red clay with mud and stamped the puttylike earth into a floor. Tiny houses sprang up among the grasses of the Deh Luran plain.

But had the villagers been planting the grain, or were they harvesting wheat that was naturally there? This was what Frank Hole and Kent Flannery—the archeologists who excavated the site—were trying to learn, as they screened through the tons of dry soil. Over 45,000 seeds were sifted out of the Ali Kosh layers: the remnants of approximately 40 different species of plants. But out of those 45,000 seeds, only 3 percent were domesticated cereals! Ninety-seven percent of the seeds were from wild plant foods. Here, finally, was the material evidence of the modest beginnings of planting—at the faintest stirrings of a hunter-and-gatherer technological change.

The early planters had also been herders, judging from the bones that were found at the site. From the very beginnings of Ali Kosh, there had been domesticated sheep and goats, yet the hunters still shot wild game at the edges of the wadis. Most of their meat, in fact, was from gazelle, wild cattle, and onager. Turtles and fish were caught in the marshes, where there were mussels and freshwater crabs. Ducks and geese were shot or, perhaps, netted. Pistachios and almonds were collected for food. The foraging pattern persisted, scarcely affected by the new plants and animals. The two traditions existed together for thousands of years.

And yet a critical problem remained: the question of causes. It was evident, from Ain Mallaha and, especially, from Nahal Oren, that hunters and gatherers had collected wild grains as part of their diet. On the southern stretches of the Zagros foothills, at sites such as Ali Kosh, foragers were scattering seeds along the edges of marshes. Here was Braidwood's "experimentation," then, with new strategies of human subsistence. But what was it that brought the experimentation about?

A recent attempt at an answer was not suggested by prehistory at all, but by technological changes in the world today. Industrialized nation-states, seeking out foreign markets, are blanketing the planet with the

The concept of population pressure

---

[24]Kent V. Flannery, "Origins and Ecological Effects of Early Domestication in Iran and the Near East," in *Prehistoric Agriculture*, ed. Stuart Streuver (Garden City, N.Y.: Natural History Press, 1971), pp. 50–79.

flow of manufactured goods. High-rise apartment buildings overshadow the dunes of the Sahara. There are traffic jams in the caravan towns of Libya. Transistor radios are carried by shepherds in the mountains of Afghanistan. There are television sets in the bamboo huts of Tahiti. In the remotest regions of the planet, the traditional ways of life are being changed. Almost everywhere, there are cultures in a state of crisis.

At the center of that crisis, there is the human population—swelling the villages and the ancient cities throughout much of the world. Sanitized clinics and hospitals, pharmaceuticals, and inoculations have made it possible for thousands to survive when they once might have died. But many technologically simpler societies never had such large populations. Less food is available for each person as the villages grow.

For over 200 million people, or one out of every 12 people in the world, the growing populations have given rise to agricultural change.[25] In Malawi, Zambia, Nigeria, the Philipine Islands, and Sierra Leone, the land is cropped more intensively than ever before. In these—and in many other—regions, there is *farming on temporary clearings in the forest,* a style of agriculture that is very descriptively called *slash-and-burn.* The 1 out of 12 people who practice it have often been viewed as heedlessly destructive: as ignorant farmers who persist in mysteriously wrecking their land.

A slash-and-burn field in Angola. Underbrush has resulted from a shortening of the fallow period.

Field Museum of Natural History

---

[25]W. M. S. Russell, "The Slash and Burn Technique," in *Man's Many Ways,* ed. Richard A. Gould (New York: Harper & Row, 1973), pp. 86–101.

For here indeed, there are no carefully plowed fields, rectangular gardens, or hillsides of clover: the familiar quiltlike farms of the industrialized world. Instead, there is a stretch of dense forest chopped down with axes and machetes, piled onto a heap, left to dry, and then fired with torches. After the fire is out, farmers walk through the piles of ashes, poking holes with a digging stick and planting their crops.

For all its apparent destructiveness, it is a remarkably balanced system. A patch of forest is only cultivated for one to three years at the most, then left to regenerate its growth—*lying fallow,* this is sometimes called— for a period of somewhere between 8 and 15 years. Because of this lying fallow system, neither the forest nor the soil is exhausted. In fact, the soil, through slash-and-burn farming, is actually enriched. After the dense forest cover is burned, bacteria convert it into organic matter; the reserves of nitrogen in the soil are gradually increased. Then, too, the piled roots of the trees contain phosphorus from deep in the subsoil. By burning these roots on the surface of the ground, it is cycled again. "I meant to teach these people agriculture," said Bishop MacKenzie after visiting Africa, "but I now see that they know far more about it than I do."

To be sure, it is a balanced technology—but it also has a critical requirement: the human populations that practice it must always be small. Yet in virtually every part of the world, as village populations are rising, the slash-and-burn system itself is being forced into change. The length of the fallow period is constantly being shortened, in order to produce more harvests from a single clearing. In parts of Sierra Leone, it has been reduced from 15 years down to 4. (In Nigeria, it has been drastically altered from 30 to 2!) Given no time to recover their nutrients, the soils have consistently deteriorated. Crops are less abundant. Erosion is destroying the land.

In a brief and controversial analysis, called *The Conditions of Agricultural Growth,* Ester Boserup suggested that such crises have happened before. The pressure of rising human populations—in both prehistoric and present societies—have forced cultivators to shorten their fallowing periods. Ultimately, what once was a forest is soon converted into grassland and bush: this is tough vegetation that requires a hoe or a plow. There seems to be little reason to doubt, according to Boserup on the prehistory of farming,

> that the typical sequence of the development of agriculture has been a gradual change—more rapid in some regions than others—from extensive to intensive types of land use. . . . Population growth is here regarded as the independent variable which in its turn is a major factor determining agricultural developments.[26]

[26]Ester Boserup, *The Conditions of Agricultural Growth: The Economics of Agrarian Change under Population Pressure* (Hawthorne, N.Y.: Aldine Publishing, 1965), pp. 17–18.

Social scientists' preconceptions had, abruptly, been turned upside down. Since the days of Thomas Malthus, a population theorist of the 18th century, it was believed that technological change had caused our numbers to grow. The human species had become agricultural. More food was suddenly available. The human population understandably exploded because of this change. But densely populated Third World villages suggested to Boserup a totally different picture. Rising populations were not seen as an effect; they were viewed as a cause. Archeologists were intrigued by the theory. Had an ancient population crisis forced a technological change? Had an increase in numbers compelled us to produce our own food?

Archeologist Lewis Binford, in a forceful theoretical argument, contended that Boserup's view was essentially correct.[27] It was necessary, he reasoned, for prehistorians to explain the chronology involved. How did it happen that independent regions, in widely separated parts of the planet, began experimenting with domestication at about the same time? The coincidence was almost certainly no accident, but instead was evidence of a special set of conditions that must have developed in the separated regions at about the same time.

A critical element in these special conditions is a region called an *ecotone: a borderline that separates two very different environments.* One of the two neighboring environments would have had plant and animal species that were amenable to manipulation by humans. That much, at least, is self-evident. Domestication is only possible in those limited regions of the world where there are plant and animal species which humans can control. But the other necessary region—a coastal environment rich in aquatic resources—existed only at the end of the Ice Age.

Such optimum coastal stretches had been created when the sea levels rose (see Chapter 7). Some were capable of supporting a highly settled existence. For the foragers on these food-rich coastlines, there was abundance—and increasing populations. Frequent mobility can take a toll through spontaneous abortions and infant mortality; in a more settled society, populations will generally rise.

There is a possibility, too, that edible grasses or roots along the coastlines may have directly contributed to a rise in the birthrate. It is a somewhat intricate theory and, almost needless to say, controversial. But it may help explain why populations increased where they did. Nancy Howell and Rose Frisch have pointed out that, among hunters and gatherers such as the !Kung, the delayed weaning of infants was a means of preventing conception.[28] Children in Bushmen society nurse for as long as five or six

---

[27]Lewis R. Binford, "Post-Pleistocene Adaptations," in *New Perspectives in Archeology,* ed. Sally R. and Lewis R. Binford (Hawthorne, N.Y.: Aldine Publishing, 1968), pp. 313–41.

[28]Gina B. Kolata, "!Kung Hunter-Gatherers: Feminism, Diet, and Birth Control," *Science* September 13, 1974, pp. 932–34. See also Rose E. Frisch and Janet W. McArthur, "Menstrual Cycles: Fatness as a Determinant of Minimum Weight for Height Necessary for Their Maintenance or Onset," *Science,* September 13, 1974, pp. 949–51.

Milwaukee Public Library

Kalahari San woman and child. Prolonged lactation in this society is a principle means of limiting births.

years. This means that a high amount of calories—approximately 1,000 per day—that would normally be stored in the mother, are consumed by her infant. Since the calories are lost to the nursing infant, the mother has only a small amount of body fat. But the body fat of a human female must be above a certain critical minimum for ovulation—the production of an egg—to take place. For this reason, if mothers nurse their children for a period of five or six years, the mothers' bodies will be low in calories; there will be little probability that ovulation—or conception—can happen.

What does this have to do with the diet? A hint of a possible relationship between lactation, diet, and population is contained in a harvesting experiment performed by Jack Harlan.[29] In a dense stand of wild wheat growing in the Anatolian Plateau of Turkey, he sheared the grain for an hour with a flint-bladed sickle. At the end of his work, he had over two pounds of edible grain; a family could harvest the area for three weeks and have over a ton. When the wheat was nutritionally analyzed, it was high in protein, carbohydrate—and calories; enough, perhaps, so that the birth control method would no longer work. Is it possible, in other words, that foragers eating cereal grains or starchy roots could have so drastically increased the calories in the bodies of their nursing females that lactation would no longer work in avoiding conception? Such failures, in fact, are occurring in Bushmen populations today, as cultural contact introduces more grain to the diet. Such a dilemma possibly occurred in human prehistory as well and was a contributing factor to the pressure on local resources.

So in time, these coastal environments would have faced the problem of too many people. Some families would have migrated out to the neighboring land. But in the neighboring territory, there were no resources from the rivers or the ocean. There were only thinner stands of wild grasses and small groups of plant-eating animals. Also, these sparser regions were already inhabited by other foraging groups. The available plants had to feed larger numbers of people. It was arguably out of such pressures that domestication ultimately emerged—as a deliberate means of increasing the local resources. Kent Flannery remarked that,

> This impression is reinforced by the fact that some of our most ancient samples of morphologically domesticated grain. . .come from "marginal" habitats well outside the present wild range of that plant. . . . It is possible, therefore, that cultivation began as an attempt to produce artificially, around the *margins* of the "optimum" zone, stands of cereals as dense as those in the *heart* of the "optimum" zone.[30]

The migration toward the margins—if we assume that it really occurred—could conceivably be related to animal domestication as well. Sheep and goats are eaters of stubble—the leftover stalks of the grasses. The harvested fields possibly supported their herds. In a time of relative abundance, there would be little need to capture these animals. But in a time of population pressure, they may have become more important. Exactly how was it done? That, probably, we never will know. Perhaps there

---

[29]Jack R. Harlan, "A Wild Wheat Harvest in Turkey," *Archeology* 20 no. 3 (1967), pp. 197–201.

[30]Kent V. Flannery, "Origins, and Ecological Effects," p. 60.

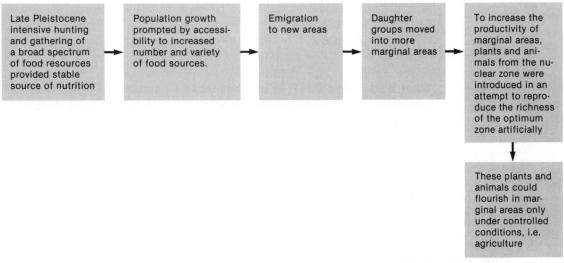

Adapted from Lewis Binford and Kent Flannery

The Binford-Flannery theory of the origins of agricultural society

were makeshift corrals to trap the animals in the harvested fields. Or possibly they were trapped in the gullies that abound in the region. However it happened, the animals became genetically changed by the process. Foragers spared the more docile, as well as the healthier animals. Such artificial control is the essence of domestication.

Is the theory reasonably accurate, or is it a fable about the past? The answer hinges on a great deal of work that remains to be done. For certain prehistoric agricultural regions, such as northern China or Southeastern Asia, there is only a meager amount of archeological data. And, in the case of Southeast Asia, the environment and the crops were both very different. Some particulars of Binford's theory may have to be changed. But perhaps the greatest difficulty of all is the buried remains of the prehistoric plants—the direct evidence which, all too often, is not very direct. "I wish I could explain to every botanist," Kent Flannery once said of this problem, "that while an archeologist looks the other way for one minute, a pack rat can bury an intrusive bean 50 centimeters deeper in his favorite dry cave."[31]

Then too, there has been a regrettable tendency to use sample sizes that are much too small. Botanists have been known to use the preserved remains of a single bean as "evidence" for the "fact" of domestication.

---

[31]Kent V. Flannery, "The Origins of Agriculture," *Annual Review of Anthropology* (1973), p. 272.

Under normal conditions, thought Flannery, such reconstructions would have never occurred. "But perhaps the search for agricultural origins is not a normal condition."[32]

Exchange and sedentism

That might have been an understatement. The reaction to Flannery's theory seemed out of proportion as well. This was an observation that he was among the first to concede. It had won an almost frightening acceptance in anthropological circles; but he had second thoughts. Could it be that his theory was wrong? He reflected on Southwestern Asia—on the dates and locations of sites. If he—and a bit earlier, Binford—had been correct in their ecotone view, then the sites should be densest in the middle of optimum land. After all, that was where populations had first begun their dramatic increase. From there, they should have budded out into the marginal lands.

But when he closely examined the region, a curious pattern was found. More sites were in the marginal regions than anywhere else! The "data (such as they are)

> do not show strong population increase in "optimum" areas like the Lebanese woodland, but the very opposite—some of the most striking increases are in "marginal" habitats like the Negev![33]

This contradicted common-sense notions as much as Boserup had earlier done. Were people ignoring the areas where they could easily find enough food and settling, perversely, wherever the food was most scarce? Such findings, at the turn of the century, might have triggered anthropological views of the quixotic, irrational nature of human society. As it was, the discovery meant simply that the theory was, possibly, wrong—and that population growth was more subtle than it earlier seemed.

Flannery considered a new possibility. Perhaps, all along, archeologists had been neglecting a critical problem: sedentary existence will leave a thick mound of debris. Archeologists, of course, understood this, but the implications were not always clear. Growth of the human population had meant counting the number of sites. It was a crude way of measuring population increase in the past. The formulas became complicated, but the counting was often involved. Was this a measure of growing populations—or the emergence of sedentary life? Conceivably, marginal peoples had been less numerous than in optimum lands. But they had remained in one place, and their litter was left in the ground.

More than that, there was a fresh implication about the sedentary pattern itself. If permanent clusters of houses were more frequent on the poorer terrain, it is conceivable there had to exist an adaptive reward. As

---

[32]Ibid.

[33]Ibid., p. 284. The Negev is a highland region in Israel.

Barbara Bender has recently argued, sedentism is a troublesome thing.[34] Even in a food-richened world, it is gained at a price. Structures must now become permanent for the storage of available food. More labor is involved in construction, as well as for the buildings' repairs. Pests are a problem; there is also the danger of raids. Human beings degrade the environment when they live in one place all the time. Vegetation is stripped, and the waters fill with run-off and waste. For this reason, many hunters and gatherers on the fringes of an agricultural world, though aware of such choices, will cling to their old way of life. If we recall that, beyond all these problems, there was the prospect of limited food, the early villages in marginal country make no sense at all.

Or do they? We need to remember the strategies that were probably involved. Possibly all ancient foragers were aware that sedentary existence, in a few generations, would lead to more mouths to feed. Mobility can lead to miscarriage, and, whether or not that was well understood, the simple fact of more-people-while-settled was easily seen. Frequent movement of foraging peoples kept the group from becoming too large. But opposing this game was the need for a web of exchange.

Trading networks had always existed, since the earliest humans (see Chapter 2). Much more was involved than the flow of material goods. Mates, alliances, services, and information about distant lands: all of these moved through the systems of ancient exchange. And yet, except for the nearest of neighbors, the flow was random and intermittent; it changed. Objects could travel great distances; information likely did much the same. But here were thousands of foraging peoples all involved in their seasonal rounds. Perhaps amber beads from the Baltic would be brought to a forest in France where there were only brush shelters; the people who lived there had gone. But this only meant that the trader would proceed to another part of the wood and, in time, would find a foraging group that had not moved away.

Such opportunistic connections seem, to me, the only possible way to knit together different scheduling systems over hundreds of miles. This meant that the foraging peoples—to regulate the net of exchange—would have had to remain in one place nearly all year. The tension between the two strategies—mobility or settling down—affected foraging societies in all the inhabited world. Every group likely struck its own balance—a special adjustment in terms of its needs. In a region of clustered resources— a patchwork quilt world—there was little reward in adopting a settled existence. Abundance, resource variety, and low populations would be possible, as long as they followed their seasonal round.

But people in the marginal regions were more in need of systematic exchange to buffer the food crises that could threaten their world. Even

---

[34]Barbara Bender, "Gatherer-Hunter to Farmer: A Social Perspective," *World Archaeology* 10, no. 2 (1978), pp. 207–8.

so, it was a dangerous gamble. They understood that their numbers would grow. The additional births would create a demand for more food. Only when, in time, it was possible for local food to be abundant and rich, could the marginal peoples abandon the foraging life. This, in itself, was probably the outgrowth of exchange—and genetics—as well. It was a process that occurred at different speeds, in different parts of the world.

At this time, it is simply not possible to compare, in any detail at all, the different realms of the planet where first domestication began. Some of these, like Southeastern Asia, are problematic and little-researched. Tropical-forest environments deteriorate organic remains. Sites have most often been covered by a canopy of dense jungle growth. Discovering one mound is a challenge; this, in itself, is a considerable remove from driving a jeep through the scrubland and counting the *tells*. Necessarily, global comparisons focus on Mexico and Southwestern Asia—two parts of the world where extensive research has been done.

The discoveries there are suggestive, in terms of people settling down. Southern Mexico—a scrubland mesa with human canyons, oases, and streams—was as marginal in its resources as Southwestern Asia. Here, too, there were foraging peoples that followed a seasonal round. But their settlement process required a much longer time. Plants were domesticated in Mexico long before villages ever appeared. In the Near Eastern region, these appeared at about the same time.

The difference points to an intricate weaving of human strategies and the natural world. Foragers in marginal regions, perhaps in several parts of the planet, were seeking to reduce the uncertainty of trade systems. The more time that was spent in one area, the greater likelihood that food, tools, or information would arrive from many parts of the land. This transitional, metastable system had effects on the genetics of plants. Fruits, roots, and grain that were traded were consumed—but a portion was saved. Cuttings and seeds were conceivably planted as well.

These were probably the tiniest of gardens, such as those in the tropics today. Many different kinds of plants would be grown in a small plot of ground. Too tiny and much too uncertain to be reliable food for the camp, the gardens were (and are) for experimentation with plants. This did not grow out of a tendency to toy with the natural world. Nor was it so simple as "having your own source of food." The plants in the gardens grew taller during the months of the seasonal round. Some food would be waiting when foragers came back to the site. But more than that, there could well be surprises—strange varieties that had never been seen. Cross pollination in gardens can generate hybridized plants. Larger, more nutritious varieties sprang from the ground.[35]

---

[35]A similar model of sedentism and genetic changes in plants has been suggested by Kent V. Flannery in "Archeological Systems Theory and Early Mesoamerica," *Anthropological Archeology in the Americas,* ed. Betty Meggers (Washington, DC: Anthropological Society of Washington, 1968), pp. 67–87.

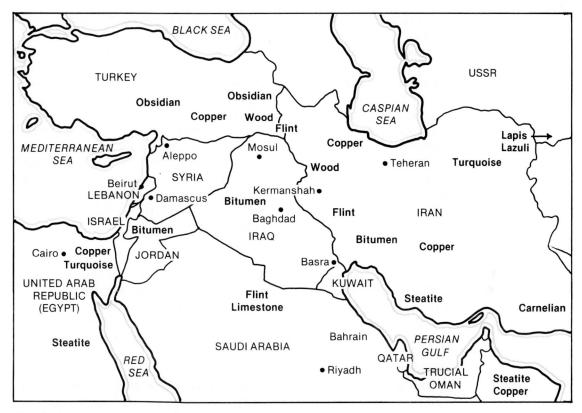

Near Eastern resources.

This meant that a camp-group of foragers could now remain longer at that site. They had local food, and they had the connections of trade. But perhaps something else was involved here beside production of food for the group. Perhaps the small gardens were also for use in exchange. Commonsensibly, all trading systems require variety—or they cannot exist. Wheat will never be traded for a basket of wheat. An exotic plant that sprang up in a garden was something that somebody else did not have. The plot was to extend one's connections in a web of exchange.

Depending on the size of the networks, frequency of connections, and the genetics of plants, the settlement process was brief—or required much time. Yet, no matter how long it required, when people finally remained in one place, the structure of human society experienced change. Opportunistic encounters had disappeared from the marginal lands. Settled existence had increased the volume of trade. Population was also increasing, but now there was locally available food. There were also imports arriving from distant societies.

Pressure mounted in the human community, but it was pressure of a much different kind. Every growth of village society had created more mouths to feed, and such growths were happening all over the marginal lands. Of course, this enlarged the system, but it was likely not as simple as that. As trade grew increasingly regular, it attracted more foraging groups. Emigrating into the villages, building houses and settling down, they reduced the uncertainty of their hunting-and-gathering life. There were other, more indirect strategies for adapting to a marginal world. Foragers acted as middlemen—as they do in some regions today. Like the Agta in the Philippine Islands, they settled near the fringes of farms.[36] Perhaps they had trading partners who lived in a village nearby. Foragers could circulate goods through a network of farms; or they could settle near a critical resource and then control it in a system of trade. Razor-sharp blades of obsidian were needed for agricultural tools. A rich deposit of the valuable mineral could be converted into baskets of food, traded for alliances and, perhaps, for information as well.

Social complexity, political power, and ritual

A web of connections was growing now—as well as the number of births. Complexity was changing the structure of ancient society. Every day, in this fabric of settlements, thousands of decisions were made. What did the community need? What could it conceivably spare? What were the needs and the products of outlying farms? Even more: was there hope of assistance as the harvest drew near? Had there been early snow from the clouds that lay off in the hills?

The management of service agreements, of production, information, and trade required more time for decisions than ever before. A traditional pattern existed for the direction of public affairs. Since the days of the hunting societies, foraging peoples had united in tribes. The strategy had proven its value for thousands of years. It had been an episodic arrangement—a gathering together to hunt. Bands went their separate ways throughout most of the year.

But this established, in ancient society, a tradition of political power being vested in persons who were able to capture more food. It was not simply skill with a weapon, but kinship connections as well, that enabled these leaders to provide for the needs of the tribe. These linkages led to alliances that were useful in a large-scale hunt. The leader of the tribe was the provider. His connections were wide.

But there, perhaps, was another tradition with its roots in this earlier time. Every known human society, more than likely since Neanderthal days, was closely bound to the world of religious belief. The spaces that surround our existence—before birth and then after we die—had troubled a species able to reflect on its life. And there were troubles that were

---

[36]See Jean T. and Warren Peterson, "Implications of Contemporary and Prehistoric Exchange Systems," in *Sunda and Sahul*, ed. Golson et al. (New York: Academic Press, 1977), pp. 533–64.

Field Museum of Natural History

Ceremonial costume of a Kwakiutl chief, American Northwest Coast. Elaborate systems of exchange contributed to the emergence of chiefs in many parts of the world.

much more immediate, woven into the everyday world. Sickness, accident, famine, the real dangers that threaten our days, were feared—and were pondered—for thousands of years.

Some people are more reflective than others—it is uncertain why this is so. Paul Radin simply called them philosophers, and he said they exist everywhere.[37] For Claude Levi-Strauss, they were mad—and "addicted to dreams."[38] They are *shamans:religious specialists who use charisma and sleight-of-hand skills to create the appearance of a link with the supernatural world.* When a shaman goes into action, as anthropologist William Howells once noted, the result is a drama—a burst of ceremonial life.

> A typical performance is a summoning of spirits, and is carried out in the dark (for the same reasons as among ourselves—i.e., to hide the shenanigans), in a house, a tent, or an Eskimo igloo. The people all gather, and the shaman says what he is going to do, after which he puts out the lamps and the fire, being sure that there is little or no light. Then he begins to sing. There may be a wait, and he beats his tambourine drum first of all, an immediate dramatic effect. The song starts softly. The sense of the song is of no consequence as far as the listeners are concerned; it is often incomprehensible, and may have no words at all. . . . As the singing goes on, other sounds begin to make themselves heard, supposedly made by animal spirits and said to be remarkably good imitations. The shaman may announce to the audience that the spirits are approaching, but he is apt to be too absorbed or entranced himself to bother. Soon voices of all kinds are heard in the house, in the corners and up near the roof. The house now seems to have a number of independent spirits in it, all moving around, speaking in different voices, and all the time the drum is sounding, changing its tempo and its volume; the people are excited, and some of them who are old hands help the shaman out by making responses and shouting encouragement, and the shaman himself is usually possessed by a spirit or spirits, who are singing and beating the drum for him. The confusion of noises goes on increasing in intensity, with animal sounds and foreign tongues as well as understandable communications (among the Chuckchis, the wolf, the fox, and the raven can speak human language), until it finally dies down; the spirits give some message of farewell, the drumming ceases, and the lights are lit. Often the shaman will be seen lying exhausted or in a faint, and on coming to he will assert that he cannot say what has been happening.
>
> This is all a combination of expert showmanship and management and of autohypnosis, so that while the shaman knows perfectly well he is faking much of the performance he may at the same time work himself into a trance in which he does things he believes are beyond his merely human powers.[39]

Such behavior once smacked of possession—of a human being out of

---

[37]The view was expressed in Paul Radin, *Primitive Man as Philosopher* (NY: Dover Publications, 1927), and many of his other writings.

[38]Claude Levi-Strauss, "The Social and Psychological Aspects of Chieftainship in a Primitive Tribe: The Nambikuara of North-western Mato Grosso," *Transactions of the New York Academy of Sciences* 7 (1944), pp. 16–32.

[39]Excerpt from *The Heathens* by William Howells. Copyright 1948 by William Howells. Reprinted by permission of Doubleday & Company, Inc.

control. For the people in industrial cultures, these were witch doctors doing their work. And the work that they did seemed to have little purpose at all. But, in time, anthropologists realized the meaning that these rituals have: they serve as a powerful system of social control.

That meaning is especially evident in those threatening parts of the world where care must be taken, or people will never survive. Anthropologist Asen Balikci, in the chill of the Canadian Arctic, was a witness to this critical function of social control:

> At the winter sealing camp, built on the flat ice, a young girl had a hole in her boots, repaired them, and thus broke a sewing taboo. Soon followed an extraordinary snow storm; the ice started cracking and breaking, endangering the whole camp. The people, terrified, gave presents to the *angatkok* (shaman) and begged him to stop the oncoming disaster. The seance took place in the *kagske,* the large ceremonial snowhouse, after putting down all the lamp lights. The *angatkok,* in trance, cried, "It is coming," pointing to a young caribou (a spirit) he saw running about. Everybody except the young girl started confessing, admitting breaches of taboo. When the spirit came near enough to be seen by the girl, she admitted her fault, and the ice cracking stopped.[40]

Such rituals were probably practiced in many marginal parts of the world. The skills of the shaman uncovered the broken taboo. At times, the prohibited actions were adapted to the natural world. Certain game were taboo in a time when that species was scarce. But the prohibitions that seemed to be frivolous—it being wrong to mend a hole in a boot—were a means of assessing the extent of religious control.

Suppose I am charged with very powerful magic. I say the gods think it is wrong for you to bring a lighted match in a room where they store gasoline. The obvious survival strategies—these are easy enough to obey. And such practical guidance was part of shamanic control. But, more than that, was religion effective? Did the audience *really* believe? This was something a magic specialist needed to know. And so the frivolous, trivial restrictions were actually a monitoring system of sorts. If you followed these laws, it was certain you deeply believed.

This subtle, elaborate process was probably in use in tribes that were adapting to the marginal regions through widespread exchange. Indeed, it might have been possible—at least in those parts of the world—that shamans were becoming more powerful than ever before. In Mexico and Southwestern Asia, the experience of climatic change had created pockets of scrubland where once there was plant food and game. This meant that tribal leaders were powerful, because they managed the flow of exchange. But the power of the shamans was likely increasing as well. Through persuasion, illusion, and ritual, they enforced the proper shar-

---

[40]Asen Bailikci, "Shamanistic Behavior among the Netsilik Eskimos," *The Southwestern Journal of Anthropology* 19, no. 4 (1963), pp. 380–81.

ing of goods. They made it right to produce and, perhaps, to be skillful at trade.

Tribal leader and magical shaman: two traditions were at work in the world. A conflict was growing in the structure of human society. At the center of the cultural crisis, were the workings of a magical mind—of thinking that blended together intuition and dreams. You could never really count on the shaman to behave in a particular way. And so a figure of uncertainty had power in an uncertain world. More than that, the two roles were autonomous: they were independent systems of sorts. Because the scale of decisions was growing, the chances increased every year that disagreements would occur between a shaman and the head of the tribe.

The result was a remarkable melding of economy and religious belief. The range of economic decisions increased with the passing of time. Tribal leaders, directing their networks, had less time for producing their food.

A chief in ceremonial costume (Samoa). The position of chief was permanent and was inherited within a kin group. It was reinforced through redistribution and religious belief.

Milwaukee Public Museum

Beyond that, a new option existed in the elaborate webs they controled: *a portion of the incoming goods could be kept for themselves*. This "theft," as Proudhon once called it, now supported the head of the tribe.[41] It could also be used for supporting immediate kin. The property was also a buffer—very useful in a marginal land. It provided relief from a famine anywhere in the web.

Most of all, it was positive sanction—a reward for supporting one's ruler. Suddenly, our magical systems were never the same. Tribal leaders rewarded the shamans—and they gained their support in return. Political power was fused with religious belief. In Southwest Asia and Mexico, as we will see in the chapters to come, the remnants of political change are preserved in the ground. Altars and fragments of icons, cleared plazas, ceremonical sherds: this complex appears in the villages for the very first time. Beyond that, there are living societies that have reflected this change in the past. Anthropologist Irving Goldman discovered a pattern in Pacific societies that conceivably hints at this ancient political change.[42] He noticed, throughout Polynesia, that less politically centralized groups had

The theory of agricultural society proposed in this chapter.

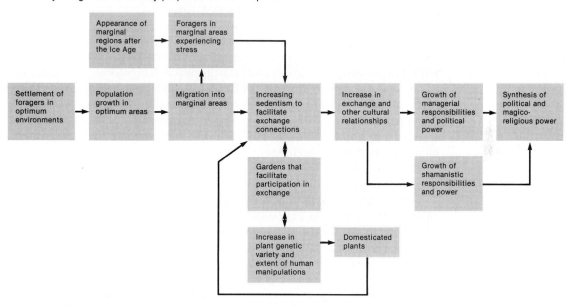

[41]Pierre J. Proudhon, *What Is Property? An Enquiry into the Principle of Right and of Government* (New York: Howard Fertig, 1966), pp. 250–59. The discussion, though highly polemical, was an attempt to explain private property as the outcome of decisions (reason) and growing social complexity. The way in which Proudhon's contribution suffered from his conflict with Marx is suggested in the entertaining book by Robert L. Heilbroner *The Worldly Philosophers* (New York: Simon & Schuster, 1972), p. 148.

[42]Irving Goldman, "Status Rivalry and Cultural Evolution in Polynesia," *American Anthropologist* 57, no. 4 (1955), pp. 680–97.

specialists who dabbled in the powers of a magical world. But on the islands with powerful rulers, politics had been combined with belief. There was a cadre of permanent specialists—a priesthood—controlled by a chief. Magic and ritual were fused with political rule.

A theatrics of sorts was involved here—with repercussions that endure to our day. All ritual is an acting-out process; it is a drama of the society's life. The way you should farm, go fishing, treat your neighbors, or behave toward kin: each could be mirrored in dance, recitation, and prayer. In a sense, then, the ritual process can be a detailed map of the world. It can tell you of the people (and place) within which you were born.

But consider: the marginal regions, knit together by threads of exchange, were worlds unlike any that had ever existed before. New foods, information, and customs were being carried on the fabric of trails. The world was becoming much larger—almost overnight. Human beings, within our own century, have been confronted with turbulent change. Alternative ways of believing, new customs, behaviors, and tools have threatened the predictable patterns of traditional life. What is right? What should one believe in? These are the dilemmas of cultural change. Anxiety is likely a part of any widening world.[43]

Ritual, within this dilemma, can keep society from falling apart. That role was an aspect of political power as well. Remember the nature of ritual: the process is a map of our cosmos. This means it is a critical feature of cultural change. When our surroundings seem confused and bewildering, a ritual can give comfort and peace. Ceremony, charisma, and music will prepare us for a set of beliefs. A ritual will tell us those things that are "true" of the world. And then, crucially, *the map is made simple;* our surroundings can be understood.[44] A collection of easy, pedestrian formulas is imparted to people as truth. An existence with frightening changes can now be endured.

This process may have had its beginnings among the first agricultural peoples. It would become a great danger in the time of the earliest states. Wherever such rituals happened, information was being destroyed. All rituals had once been canonical—detailed maps of surroundings. When attending them, all the believers had learned to think in the subtlest of ways.[45] Their logic, like the cosmos around them, was highly complex. But when their map of the world became simple, inner peace had been

---

[43]This has been examined by (among many others) Anthony F. C. Wallace, *Culture and Personality* (New York: Random House, 1966), pp. 120–63.

[44]The "simplifying" function of ritual during a period of rapid cultural change is discussed by John McManus, "Ritual and Human Social Cognition," in *The Spectrum of Ritual: A Biogenetic Structural Analysis,* ed. Eugene G. d'Aquili et al. (New York: Columbia University Press, 1979), pp. 234–35.

[45]"Canons" as maps or copies of something are described by Douglas R. Hofstadter in *Escher, Godel, and Bach: An Eternal Golden Braid* (New York: Vintage Books, 1980), pp. 1–81. The book is an enjoyable, sometimes baffling, introduction to logic and information theory.

Field Museum of Natural History

Flute priest of Southwestern Indians tracing picture of a cloud on the ground. In egalitarian societies, ritual was highly canonical: it was a detailed map of the cultural and natural world.

gained at a price. Things were now "good," or were "evil." Such ideas were only vaguely defined. This made it easy for centralized rulers to manipulate human belief. The menance of the ritual process was growing through time.

A tribal leader, his immediate kin group, and a permanent collection of priests: this core was the political center of village society. With its control of religious behavior, and the elaborate flows of exchange, this center held permanent political power through time. Such power could now be inherited—transmitted to immediate kin. Hierarchies had now become part of a community's life. The *chiefdom* was a *ranked society,* the very first of its kind to evolve. *The chief, in an inherited office, managed everyday public affairs. His power was based on reward and religious belief.*

In time, as we will see in the story, these systems would experience change. Slowly, populations were growing and, in some regions, depleting the land. Pioneers would abandon their chiefdoms and build their homes in unsettled terrain. But others would follow. Pioneers were not left to themselves. This restlessness—budding and settlement—would crowd the inhabitable world. Soon, there would be a lattice of chiefdoms where once there had been nomadic bands. That matrix in time would give rise to the earliest states.

9 / Seedtime and Harvest: The Old World and the New

The hunters of Northern Asia had long been familiar with powerful winds. With no trees or mountains to stop them, the Arctic gusts had howled through the tundra. The hunters dug into the earth and stayed close to their fires. For hundreds of generations, as the last of the glaciers retreated, the powerful winds had crossed the steppe and tundra of Asia. The winds gathered dust as they traveled and carried it for thousands of miles. Then the winds began to lose their power, as they gusted through China. The dust had settled like a gentle powder along the banks of the Huang Ho River that flows eastward across northern China toward the Pacific. In places, this *windblown soil*—or *loess*, as geologists call it—has grown into mounds sometimes a hundred feet thick. Some of it has always been lost to the current of the Huang Ho River, the Yellow River that is murky and rich with its burden of silt.

The millet growers of northern China

The loess of China has remarkable properties. It has a fine, powderlike texture, which means that it is easily tilled. A digging stick is all that is necessary to loosen the soil. Then, too, it is an alkaline soil suitable for the growth of sagebrush and, more significantly, for cereal grains. The tiny holes left in the soil by the decay of surface vegetation cause minerals to slowly rise upward by capillary action. This is the same physical process that causes water to rise upward through a sponge. It draws minerals from the lower deposits to the top of the land. If rain fell often enough along the river, these minerals would soon be eroded away. But most of the loess deposits are outside the heavy-rainfall regions. There is usually only 10 to 20 inches of rainfall a year. Most of those scanty showers occur in the summer months, when the higher temperature quickly evaporates the water from the soil.

Wild millet flourished in these loess lands, probably back into Pleistocene times. Like barley and wheat, it can support a settled society. Our best evidence of early cultivation and the emergence of permanent villages is near the Wei River, a tributary of the Huang Ho.[1] Here, some

---

[1] Kwang-chik Chang, "The Beginnings of Agriculture in the Far East," *Antiquity* 54, (1970); and Judith Treistman, "The Far East," in *Varieties of Culture in the Old World*, ed. Robert Stegler *et al.* (New York: St. Martin's Press, 1975).

Agricultural sites in
China

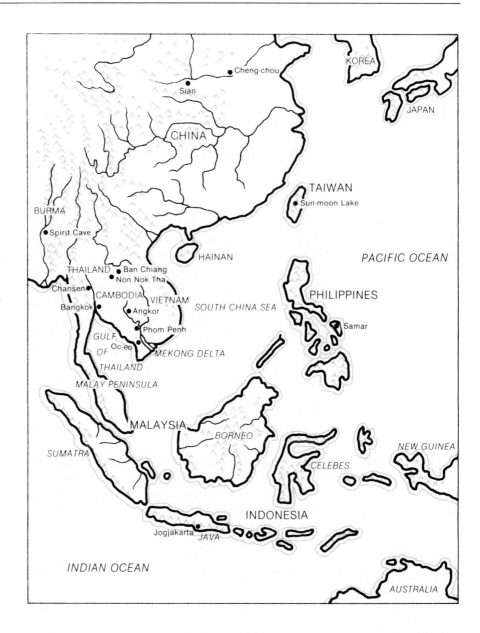

6,000 years ago, villages were built along the banks of the river. The loess
was tilled. The millet was planted. When the fuzzy, caterpillarlike seeds
were harvested in the fall of the year, they were stored in vessels and
pits before the coming of winter.

On a tributary of the Weishui River, the remains of an early settlement
were preserved in the soil. Pan-p'o, at 4000 BC, was a village of over 200
dwellings, surrounded by a ditch and covering seven acres of land. The

buildings were wattle-and-daub—a style which later would appear in Western Europe: walls of woven grass that were plastered over with mud. To keep out the harsh northern blasts, the houses were partially sunken in the ground. Houses of the village were grouped around a large central building.

Inside the dwellings were traces of center posts—the supports for a possibly conical roof—and storage pits and tapered clay jars for holding the grain. Thirty-one excavated dwellings were circular, while 15 were rectangularly shaped. The large building at the center of the village was possibly designed for community meetings. To the north were the cemetery and most of the village's wells. Just to the east of this early community, which might have had 600 inhabitants, were pottery kilns where vessels were molded and fired. There is a possibility that Pan-p'o was something more than a farming community: it may have been involved in specialized manufacture and trade.

The Pan-p'o village is a record of early domestication in China—a record that, unfortunately, does not take us back far enough. Foxtail millet, Chinese cabbage, pigs, dogs, vegetables, and fruit trees were all in a fully domesticated state at the site. But what brought about this transformation? Was it a growth in the human population? For the moment, there is very little evidence to support *any* theory.

Yet there is reason for a cautious optimism. The historian Ping-ti Ho has argued, on the basis of several different types of evidence, for a significant change in the Chinese climate as the Pleistocene ended.[2] Soils in the highland regions of China increase in alkalinity in those layers closest in time to the end of the Ice Age. Animal bones buried in these layers are mostly from species of rodents. The pollen shows that drought-loving sagebrush was covering the land. In other words, there is developing evidence that China was becoming hotter and drier at precisely the time when domestication probably emerged. But in the regions that were nearest the rivers, the water table was constantly high. Beyond that, the capillary soils would have kept moisture close to the surface. The country near the streams was most likely an optimum land.

It is possibly for this very reason that early evidence of settled existence has not been discovered on the tributaries near the Huang Ho. In a way, it was somewhat comparable to Flannery's Lebanese woodland, while the hinterland regions were conceivably like the Negev. Perhaps the foragers removed from the rivers, as the land evolved slowly to sage, adapted by designing elaborate networks of trade. Only later did pioneer settlers move into the riverine lands, possibly long after village existence began. Such a theory seems plausible—but the digging remains to be done. As archeol-

---

[2] Ping-ti Ho, "The Loess and the Origin of Chinese Agriculture," *American Historical Review* 75, no. 1 (October 1969), pp. 1–36.

ogists continue to sift through the cocoalike soils of China, there is hope that the answers to these questions will someday be found.

Adaptations in the Asian triopics

Far to the south of the Chinese loess lands are the rain forests of Southeastern Asia. Archeology in this area is difficult, and it will probably always be so. Organic materials deteriorate quickly in rain-drenched tropical soils. Direct evidence of plant foods is often difficult to recover. When such evidence *has* been found, it is often a small sample or highly eroded. Archeologists have been heatedly accused of not being "able to tell a pea from a palm."[3] That was harsh—but the problems of identification are real.

Not only this, but the techniques of cultivation are usually very different in the tropics. They are strategies that can leave almost no evidence of human disturbance. There is root propagation, for example, a method that is widely used in the rain forests. To increase the yield from a crop such as yams, the farmer plants pieces of the root. Trees too are grown for food in the tropics. Almond trees and betel nut palms grew wild in the evergreen forest. The wild nuts can be collected, or they can be planted for food. These are obviously subtle transformations, a cultivation that is scarcely different from collecting. No wonder it is hard to distinguish it from a foraging tradition.

Even so, archeologists are trying, and they are beginning to meet with success. At Spirit Cave in northwestern Thailand (see Chapter 7) Chester Gorman found evidence of what might well be plant domestication.[4] Two thousand feet up the steep face of a limestone cliff in the jungle, it is a rock shelter located just above the Khong Stream. Some 9,000 years before the present, foragers were camping in this cave and preparing their food. The four layers on the floor of the shelter were, altogether, over three feet deep. Seeds were discovered in the deepest of the four deposits. Almonds, betel nuts, beans, peas, bottle gourds, and Chinese water chestnuts were screened from the soil in the oldest layer of the cave. Traces of charcoal from the middle of the deepest layer were dated at around 11,000 years before the present.

Were the plants wild or domesticated? Archeologists are not at all in agreement. The debate will undoubtedly continue until more work has been done in the region. Nonetheless, there is a good possibility—based on archeological evidence and contemporary Southeast Asian cultiva-

---

[3]Jack R. Harlan and J. M. J. de Wet, "On the Quality of the Evidence for Origin and Dispersal of Cultivated Plants," *Current Anthropology* 14, no. 1 and 2 (February–April 1973), p. 52.

[4]Chester Gorman, "Hoabinhian: A Pebble-Tool Complex with Early Plant Associations in Southeast Asia," *Science*, February 14, 1969, pp. 671–73; and Chester Gorman, "The Hoabinhian and After: Subsistence Patterns in Southeast Asia during the Late Pleistocene and Early Recent Periods," *World Archeology* 16, no. 9 (1970), pp. 300–17.

tion—that the foragers at the shelter were experimenting with plant domestication. Said archeologist I. C. Glover,

> the botanists all seem to accept that it is very difficult to distinguish wild from cultivated varieties of these plants, but to my mind the most significant point is that this list represents plants, most of which, later are certainly domesticated, and that it includes virtually nothing which remains wild, occasionally utilized, or altogether abandoned. This is remarkable when we think of how many useful, but not domesticated, plants have been found in archeological sites in Europe and the Near East.[5]

If plant domestication did in fact occur here, there was little else in the technology that changed. Most of the remains in the shelter are those of a foraging tradition. A wide range of wild animal species was collected in the jungle near the cave. Bones of langurs, squirrels, porcupines, rats, birds, bats, reptiles, and fish were found in the same layers as the possibly domesticated plants. The stone tools, too, are unspecialized—and very suitable for hunting and gathering. Made of quartzite, they have been modified by breaking off irregular flakes. Either one or both faces of pebbles have been worked in this way. They are tools we might expect to find among groups of hunters and gatherers who technologically capture about as much energy as they expend (see Chapter 3). Archeologist Karl Hutterer viewed these tools from just such a standpoint and pointed out:

> The energy invested in the procurement of raw materials and the manufacture and. . .carrying. . .of tools must be balanced against the energy gained through the use of these tools. Since any one of them may be used only occasionally and under special circumstances, energy investment has to be kept to a minimum. . . . The manufacturing process calls for (stone) tools with very limited requirements: sharp edges of certain configurations and sharp points. Such tools can be created at a moment's notice and from a variety of raw materials, thus further reducing energy outlay for procurement and maintenance.[6]

The pebble tools, then, and the animal remains reveal a rain-forest foraging pattern; the plant remains suggest the possible beginnings of domestication. If, in fact, it turns out to be true that plants were being grown near the site, then what led to this technological change?

Before the Pleistocene ended, Southeast Asia had been a much larger region. Freom 23,000 to 12,000 years ago, before the last of the glaciers retreated, this part of the world was at least twice its present-day size.[7]

---

[5]I. C. Glover, "The Hoabinhian: Hunter-Gatherers or Early Agriculturalists in Southeast Asia?" in *Hunters, Gatherers, and First Farmers beyond Europe,* ed. J. V. S. Megaw (Leicester, Mass.: Leicester University Press, 1977), p. 158.

[6]Karl L. Hutterer, "An Evolutionary Approach to the Southeast Asian Cultural Sequence," *Current Anthropology,* vol. 17, no. 2 (1976), p. 225.

[7]The discussion of post-Pleistocene environmental changes in Southeast Asia is taken largely from Glover, "Hoabinhian," pp. 160–63.

But as the melting glaciers flooded the oceans, the rising waters crept over the land. Scattered groups of hunters and gatherers would now have been forced to live closer together. A vast out-of-doors was shrinking. Old encampments lay under the sea.

The climate, too, was becoming different and causing surface vegetation to change. For millennia during the Ice Age, the climate was unstable, perhaps even erratic. At least some of this instability had been due to the prevailing winds. There are trade winds from the northeast and the southeast that are still found in the tropics today. They meet somewhere around the equator—the intertropial convergence zone—and they thrust upward: huge columns of air reaching out toward space. This zone—a heavy rainfall belt—shifts a little from season to season, but it rarely wanders any great distance away from the equator. The zone, then, is relatively stable. But it has not always been so. It once swept in great movements back and forth over Southeast Asia.

As long as this zone had been on the move, Southeast Asia had been a region with great fluctuations in average temperature and rainfall. The natural world has adapted itself. Deciduous woodland and open savannas—excellent foraging environments— were especially suited to these rainfall and temperature changes. But by 12,000 years ago, the convergence zone retreated to the south. Savannas and woodlands that escaped the flooding became covered by jungle.

The lushness of these tropical forests has, at times, been misunderstood. Dense foliage suggests a region with abundant foods and game. But these forests, more often than not, are a marginal world. Wild game is much harder to find here than in the grasslands or deciduous woods. Plant foods are not easily stored as a buffer against difficult times. Floods cover much of the jungle floor in the wake of a tropical storm. Diseases and pests take a toll of available foods. And so—possibly—at the end of the Ice Age, as jungle covered over the land, the human populations were faced with an uncertain life. Perhaps, like the Amazon foragers they formed elaborate links of exchange. Natural products from foodstuffs to poisons, from fish to baskets, from taro to tools may have moved between tropical peoples for hundreds of miles. Spirit Cave, we may one day discover, was one node in an intricate web. Our understanding of tropical Asia has only begun.

Domestication in Africa

There is probably no place on the planet that hides more of the archeological record than the great sea of gravelly dunes called the Sahara. It is over 3 million square miles of desert—a region the size of the United States. Thousands of archeological sites are buried under the sands. The Fahrenheit heat of its surface is often well over 100°. A single inch of rain may occur in the space of 10 years. Its days are often punished by sandstorms; its sunsets bring shivery nights. It is hardly a wonder that the region is so little known.

H. Armstrong Roberts

The Sahara. Evidence of early agriculture has been found on its eastern margin. A later herding tradition connected its scattered plateaus.

Fred Wendorf and Romuald Schild, while exploring the Egyptian Sahara, discovered the penalties of work in this part of the world. Their trek to the site of Tarfawi

began early one morning with a convoy of 10 vehicles, including a large lorry that caried most of the camp gear and food, a gasoline tanker, several small trucks, and two jeeps. We expected to arrive at Bir Tarfawi late that evening, but we had moved only 20 kilometers when the first "event" occurred—the big lorry broke an axle. This took the rest of the day and a night to repair. It was late January, and the night was cold, near freezing, and no one was very comfortable, but we did have our bedrolls. The next event was near Bir Dibis, about noon the following day, when the jeep we were riding in threw a rod. It had to be abandoned there to be picked up later.

At this point the trucks were still traveling as a group, but as evening came on, the convoy began to scatter as the faster vehicles reached the sand sheet 150 kilometers south of Bir Tarfawi. The going that day had been unexpectedly hard. Many of the vehicles overheated, and much of the drinking water had been used to refill the radiators. One of the trucks left behind was the gasoline tanker, which ran on diesel fuel, of course. As night approached, everyone began to worry about the tanker. It was then that we discovered that the diesel fuel for the tanker was packed on the large lorry. The tanker was somewhere behind us and out of fuel, but none of the vehicles had enough gasoline to return to the tanker. The last reserve jerry cans had long before been emptied into the vehicles. Only by draining the gas from several trucks and combining the fuel into one could that vehicle go back with diesel fuel for the tanker. Yet another night had to be spent without shelter on the desert, and this time there was no drinking water.

The next day saw the final push to Bir Tarfawi, and the first vehicles arrived shortly before noon, only to find the well contaminated with decayed vegetation and filled with sand. On this occasion even the camp manager took his turn with the shovel and bucket in the effort to clean the well. He had to, because otherwise he would have been last in line for water.[8]

Out of this has come remarkable evidence of an ancient technological change. Domestication may have been earlier here than anywhere in the world. But more than just sheer antiquity is at issue in Saharan research. We need to know what created this process. What, exactly, was involved in this change? Some possible answers already have begun to emerge.

In southern Egypt, near the Sudanese border, a short distance to the west of the Nile, there were dune-covered traces of early agricultural life. The debris at Wadi Kubbaniya was some 18,000 years old.[9] In those years, the Nile had been higher, seeping into the nearby dunes. For hundreds of miles down the river, the countryside was dotted with ponds. Gazelle, hippopotomi, hartebeest, and wild cattle ranged through the grass. For miles on either side of the river was a network of life.

And yet, it likely was a marginal region, drying up with the passing of time. Wadi Kubbaniya's layers contained fragments of tamarisk and acacia. These are dry-loving shrubs found in Mediterranean lands. The region was possibly a scrubland dotted by river-fed ponds. From very early times, it was threaded by a webbing of trade.

The hints of this cultural network were at Wadi Kubbaniya itself. Flint burins, endscrapers, and denticulates were dug out of the layers of silt. The techniques of tool manufacture were not unique to this spot near the river. Strikingly similar tools were discovered in Sudan, to the south, and at Isna, near the river, some 93 miles to the north. More than that, the flint used to make them was the same at Kubbaniya and Isna. Cultural circuits connected the sites near the Nile.

Within this elaborate nexus, were the stirrings of technological change. Grains of domesticated wheat and barley were found in Wadi Kubbani-

---

[8]Fred Wendorf and Romuald Schild, *Prehistory of the Eastern Sahara* New York: Academic Press, 1980), p. 81.

[9]*Ibid.*, pp. 274–76.

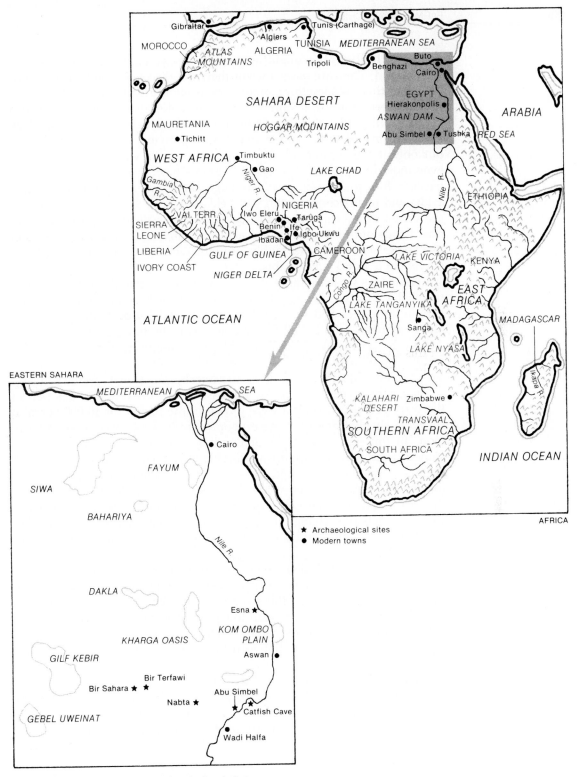

African geographical features and agricultural sites.

ya's soils. In itself, this might not seem unusual, except that these grains were so old. They are more ancient than any discovered in Southwestern Asia. But there is something more curious about them: they should really not be there at all! It is "almost unconceivable" that scrub-country hills near the Nile had a climate suitable for growing such cereal grains.[10] Jack Harlan admitted with caution that barley growing was possible there— but only if the summers were cool and the soils were moist. Wheat is even more of a problem because it lives in a narrower range. From north-western Iran to Turkey, south to Yugoslavia, Bulgaria, and Greece is a colder and rainier country with vast fields of wheat. So neither grain would grow well in the climate, and there is another difficulty as well. The annual floods of the river are not exactly the same every year. The crests of the floods will vary in a highly unpredictable way. Barley can seldom survive in a world such as this.

Perhaps, as we learn more about it, we will find that these cereal grains traveled south through a web that extended for hundred of miles. Foragers in the pond- and scrublands that stretched out on both sides of the Nile may have been linked in exchange with the foragers of the Levant. Across the brief neck of the Sinai, the grains might have made their way south. Some were planted near the ponds of the river; a portion circulated in trade. Mutations increased; the cereals, very slowly, were changed.

As it happened, it was nearly impossible to grow cereal in this part of the world. And yet, cereals were grown in the region for 10,000 years. It seems likely that grain for these peoples, at its best, was an emergency food. In times of drought or of flooding, the available grain was consumed. Then too, because it was storable, it created a more certain world. Societies near the river could cope with unpredictable change. Probably, for that very reason, grain was a valuable item of trade. More than that, the exotic varieties that grew up on the fringes of ponds were especially valued in nets of exchange. Larger-grained, tougher hybrids—richer, but less fragile as well—would circulate quickly in the scrub-country dunes near the stream.

The growth of this elaborate system, at the moment, is not well understood. In a very real sense, it is a guess at what occurred in the past. Cereals were grown near the river for, probably 10,000 years. But the critical sites of that period remain to be found. Layers at Wadi Kubbaniya held the fragments of cereal grains. Wheat and barley were also discovered at a site called E-75-6. Between the two is a gap nearly 10 millennia long.

What happened to the sites of that period? Perhaps, very simply, they drowned. The Sahaba-Darau aggradation—in plain English, a flood of the Nile—covered a great many sites in the marginal lands; then the waters slowly receded, some 9,000 years in the past. The old channel and the

---

[10]*Ibid.*, p. 276.

ponds near the river became much like an earlier time. But that moment was fleeting. The country grew ever more dry. The river shrank in its traditional channel. Mud dried up and cracked in the sun. Ponds fed by the Nile became swales of sand.

I suspect that those 9 millennia had a powerful effect on the lives of the foragers and planters that lived in the marginal lands. Through the years, as the Nile crested higher, the settlements continued to shift. The banks of the Nile, the floodponds, and the intricate systems of trade all were pushed farther and farther out into the desert. There was something akin to this process in a very different part of the world. Early peoples who settled New Guinea had acquired a foothold of sorts. They made tentative, short-distance voyages out to the sea. Flocks of birds, the smell of vegetation, and reflections of landforms on clouds: from clues such as these, the locations of islands were found.

The islands of the ancient Sahara were its moister, more verdant plateaus. One of these massive formations is known as the Gilf el Kabir. Stony mesas dissected by canyons—and all of it enveloped by sand—it is some 400 miles to the west of the present-day Nile. Humans reached it about 7,500 years ago, perhaps for the very first time. They brought cattle, sheep, and goats to the mesas where, then, there was water and grass. Other desert plateaus were first settled at about the same time.[11]

As the desert around them grew drier, and the Nile's waters began to recede, a new strategy was opened to the people who found the plateaus. They could follow that once-flooded river as it settled back into its banks. Many desert dwellers probably did this (they abandoned the Gilf el Kabir), but many others could now find their way through an ocean of sand. Like the islands off the coast of New Guinea, the first plateaus to the west of the Nile were a home for the probers exploring the gravel and dunes. And like the navigators of the Pacific, they used their collections of clues. The tiniest, most distant plateaus were eventually found.

What caused them to take such a gamble? Were they curious about the world to the west? I suspect the migrations were never as simple as that. Perhaps here, as throughout the Pacific, populations were building through time. On the islandlike mesas, there was pressure on available food. Families kept sheep, goats, and cattle—and they planted their cereal grains. But the strategy was growing more fragile as centuries passed.

The animals they kept near the mesas competed with people for food. Land useful for grazing was needed for cereal grains. Tension increased— and a new adaptation was born. Families left, with belongings and cattle, for plateaus in Libya and Chad. A network of herding societies was coming to be. Distant uplifts out in the desert were the pastures for grazing

---

[11]Pollen evidence for the verdant environment at the fringes of Saharan plateaus is discussed by Brent D. Shaw, "Climate, Environment, and Prehistory in the Sahara," *World Archaeology* 8, no. 2 (1975), pp. 133–49.

the herds. Beyond that, they were nodes in the network—meeting places for gossip and trade. Desert peoples were closely connected by bonds of exchange.

From the flood and retreat of the river, two separate traditions were born; but connections between them continued for thousands of years. The nomadic pastoral societies required agricultural foods. Farmers near the Nile needed milk, meat, and products of trade. The river would become an exchange place where the separate traditions could meet. Out of this growing complexity would come political change on the Nile. The chemistry of desert and river would generate kings.

Domestication in the Americas: The Mexican Mesa Central

Since the days when the big-game hunters killed off the last of the American mammoth, the New World has been evolving independently of the Old. Even so, there were strong similarities between the world left behind and the Americas. Because the big-game hunting tradition had been imported from the Asian tundra, it had contributed to extinctions here as in the rest of the world. Then, too, the global changes in climate that followed the end of the Ice Age played a role in animal extinctions all over the planet. So like most of the world, the Americas became a vast region of resource diversity. Prehistoric Americans were committed to a foraging life.

It is important to revisit these events. Occasionally they are ignored or forgotten. The fact that American Indians, like other societies, were involved in a foraging tradition helps explain domestication in their part of the world. That, in turn, goes far toward explaining the emergence of American Indian complex societies. There was no necessity, in other words, for colonists from ancient Egypt to land on these shores with the idea of civilization. And even if such contacts were made, they were certainly not the critical factor. Civilization requires a technology that captures a tremendous amount of energy. Such a technology had been building in the Americas for thousands of years.

From the Mexican Mesa Central (see Chapter 7) archeologists have uncovered the evidence of subtle changes that in time would culminate in cities and states. At Coxcatlan Cave in Mexico's Tehuacan Valley, Richard S. MacNeish found the buried remains of a "cultivation" that was scarcely distinguishable from a foraging life.[12] The cave was a seasonal camp for hunters and gatherers in the foothills of the Sierra Madre. The gravelly hills are covered by thorny trees and patches of grass. Scattered fruit trees grow at the edges of streams and in seasonally wet gullies. Spring and

---

[12]Richard S. MacNeish, "Ancient Mesoamerican Civilization," *Science* 143 (1964), pp. 531–37. See also Richard S. MacNeish, *The Science of Archeology?* (North Scituate, Mass.: Duxbury Press, 1978); and Richard S. MacNeish, "Speculation about How and Why Food Production and Village Life Developed in the Tehuacan Valley, Mexico," *Archeology*, October 1971.

The excavation at Coxcatlan.

Courtesy of the R.S. Peabody Foundation, Andover, Massachusetts

summer were the most plentiful seasons. Fruit trees and grass seeds were ripening. There were rabbit, opossum, pecarry, and other small game. Above all, in the spring and summer there was life-giving rain. In the fall and winter there was less plant-food collecting. Rabbit and deer were hunted in the valley. The cycle would begin again with the coming of spring.

At Tehuacan, the Valley of Oaxaca, and probably in other parts of southern Mexico as well, foragers followed such schedules 9,000 years before the present. But some 2 millenia later, native plants were deliberately grown. There were cultivated beans, squashes, tomatoes, avocados, pumpkins, amaranths, and chiles. Conceivably, these were grown from seeds planted in spring. Possibly, too, they tended prickly pear, maguey (this is sometimes called a century plant) and the zapote, a semitropical fruit tree of the Mesa Central. Yet, none of these would later be as important as maize, or Indian corn. Eventually this plant would become a staple of ancient Mesoamerican civilization. Ironically, its origins are still not well understood.

Maize and its origins

It may have been a weedy grass, called teosinte, that ultimately evolved into maize, but where—and even *if*—this happened has been hotly debated.[13] Today, teosinte is a maizelike pioneer plant in the dry country of Mexico and Guatemala. It takes over abandoned corn fields or any ground that has been disturbed; it colonizes gullies and ditches in the landscape. Intriguingly, wild squash and runner beans are often found with it, the beans twining around the stalks of teosinte. Very possibly the combination of maize, beans, and squash in the diet was something the Mexican Indians took from nature.

But not everyone is in agreement with the teosinte theory. A different grass, or even a primitive corn itself, may have been the ancestor. There

The earliest maize was considerably smaller than corn that is grown today. An early Tehuacan cob is on the extreme left. A modern maize cob is on the extreme right.

Courtesy of the R.S. Peabody Foundation, Andover, Massachusetts

[13]The discussion of the corn controversy is taken from Kent V. Flannery's summary in "The Origins of Agriculture," *Annual Review of Anthropology*, 1973. It is a highly complex and unsettled controversy. Interested students might investigate the references provided in Flannery's article.

is a wild grass, called *Tripsacum*, that is distantly related to Indian corn. It grows in dry scrub valleys not far from where teosinte is found. At one time it was thought that maize and *Tripsacum* had hybridized and given rise to a more nutritious tripsacoid corn. But *Tripsacum* is a stubborn grass that does not easily hybridize. For this reason it seems unlikely that it was ever crossed with anything. One could hardly say it was amenable to domestication.

There are difficulties, too, with the ancient maize theory—the idea that corn's wild ancestor was corn itself. The crucial archeological evidence is some 60,000-year-old pollen found in a core sample in the Valley of Mexico. Was it maize pollen or teosinte? Archeologists are still divided. But there is good reason for suggesting it was teosinte. When the sample was first discovered, it was believed that the pollen from maize was larger than that of teosinte. The pollen in the sample was, in fact, larger than known teosinte pollen. The verdict was logical enough: it was ancient maize.

But teosinte revealed itself to be more complicated than that. Later excavations produced varieties with pollen that is smaller than Indian corn, other varieties with pollen that is approximately the same size, and one variety in which the pollen spores are larger! So size alone was not enough to make the core sample very ancient corn. The debate was at last appealed to a scanning electron microscope. The maize and teosinte pollen showed almost identical surface appearances. Thus the ancient maize in the core could very well have been teosinte.

Richard MacNeish and the Tehuacan Valley

An understanding of the complex relations that led to domestication in Mesoamerica is slowly growing out of research in the Tehuacan Valley. Richard MacNeish has spent many seasons in the valley's thorn forests and canyons. He has excavated forager campsites and recorded their changes in size through the years. He has found evidence of strategies for coping with a marginal world.

One kind of encampment he encountered was large and had multiple hearths; perhaps 100 foragers lived at each of these macroband campsites. The other kind of site is smaller. It has fewer hearths and much less debris. Perhaps two or three related families—about 15 people in all—lived for only the space of a season in these microband camps.

Beginning some 12,000 years ago, foragers in the valley lived in microband camps. They were mostly hunters. Seventy percent of their diet came from meat. They hunted antelope, deer, and wild horse along the grass of the valley. But around 9,000 years ago, the climate in the valley grew warmer. Grasses became thinner. Cacti flourished on the sand. There was now

a greater diversity in seasons, a drier and warmer climate, a diminution of grassland steppes and water holes, as well as an expansion of the thorn forests on the alluvial slopes. . . . Although climatic changes and changes in the ecosystem had probably occurred previously in the Tehuacan Valley, apparently never before had they coincided at a time when men were ready with exactly the right variety of eco-subsistence knowledge crucial to cause a major culture change.[14]

With the drying up and warming of the valley, it became a more diverse region than ever before. The big game was gone, the climate was hotter, water was scarcer, and plant food was more critical. Certain parts of the valley became easier to live in than others. There were humid canyons where the plant food was richer. In springs near the Rio Salado there was water and food. Stream gullies not far from the cave nourished grasses and the century plant. Nomadic bands moved into these pockets. They stayed there during the wet season, gathering fruit and wild seeds. With a more stable existence, the size of the population could grow. MacNeish's estimates for population, based on the total number of different kinds of campsites, suggests that it had tripled in the valley since the days of the earliest hunters.[15]

Foragers were settling down in the pockets where there was more wild plant food and game, and this made possible more recurrent connections of trade. At El Riego Cave in Tehuacan, imported obsidian was found. It was mined outside of the valley, imported, and chipped into flakes. This hints at a not-yet-stabilized web of exchange.[16] Chili peppers, avocados, squash, amaranth, and wild corn seeds probably circulated between the encampments of the Mesa Central. There may have been hundreds of species involved in the system of trade. But at least two, as Kent Flannery notes, were remarkably different. Maize and beans were genetically plastic: they could undergo rapid mutations. As it happened, they did—which transformed the entire technology. Wild beans, because of chance mutations,

> became more permeable in water, making it easier to render them edible; and developed limp pods which do not shatter when ripe, thus enabling the Indians to harvest them more successfully. Equally helpful were the changes in maize, whose genetic plasticity has fascinated botanists for years. While. . .other grasses remained unchanged, maize underwent a series of alterations which made it increasingly more profitable to harvest (and plant over wider areas) than any other plant.
>
> Starting with what may have been (initially) accidental deviations in the system, a positive feedback network was established which eventu-

---

[14]Richard S. MacNeish, "Speculation."

[15]Richard S. MacNeish, *Science of Archeology?*, p. 145.

[16]Richard S. MacNeish et al., *The Prehistory of the Tehuacan Valley, vol. 5: Excavations and Reconnaisance* (Austin: University of Texas Press, 1972), p. 24. The role of exchange in Tehuacan domestication has been specifically emphasized by Warwick Bray in "From Foraging to Farming in Early Mexico," *Hunters, Gatherers, and First Farmers*, p. 239. His model strongly influenced my views.

ally made maize cultivation the most profitable single subsistence activity in Mesoamerica. The more widespread maize cultivation, the more opportunities for favorable crosses and back-crosses; the more favorable genetic changes, the greater the yield; the higher the population, and hence the more intensive cultivation. There can be little doubt that pressures for more intensive cultivation were instrumental in perfecting early water-control systems, like well-irrigation and canal-irrigation. This positive feedback system, therefore, was still increasing at the time of the Spanish Conquest.[17]

It is a breathtaking chain reaction, there can be little doubt about that: a few mercurial genes giving rise to a civilization! But little changes in well-knit systems *have* produced large-scale effects. A new kind of axe once destroyed an entire society.[18] And beans and maize, as Flannery states, can be improved by genetic mutations. Maize, especially, can hybridize easily with other types of grasses.

The strategies at work in the valley had remained balanced for hundreds of years. New varieties of maize and beans did not, at first, generate enough food to support the populations of settled—and growing—societies. But some stability was nonetheless needed to stabilize the links of exchange. By 7,000 years before the present, plants were tamed for some 2,000 years. But valley peoples were settled for only six months of the year. Not until 5,500 years ago did houses appear in the valley. Perhaps, by then, the subtle interplay of genetic mutations and trade had made permanent settlement possible in the Mesa Central.

Far to the south of the Tehuacan Valley is the snow-crested summit of the Andes, a spine of mountains that rises like a wall between desert and jungle. On the Peruvian coast west of the mountains, the tides of the Pacific meet the shores of a desert, relieved only by rivers that flow from the Andes to the sea. Dry-loving shrubs and cacti are abundant on the coastal sand, eventually merging with the grasses that climb the lower slopes of the mountains. East of this massive divide, there are lowlands covered with rain forest. Flying over that dense green canopy, one can spot occasional clearings below. Jungle villagers hunt and fish in the wilderness east of the Andes. They grow small gardens as they probably have for thousands of years.

In some way that is not yet understood, domestication began in the Andes. The earliest cultivated plants in the New World may have come

Domestication in the Andes

[17]Kent V. Flannery, "Archeological Systems Theory and Early Mesoamerica," *Anthropological Archeology in the Americas,* ed. Betty Meggers (Washington, D.C.: Anthropological Society of Washington, 1968), pp. 80–81.

[18]Primarily because it had social as well as technological significance. The story has been told by Lauriston Sharp in "Steel Axes for Stone Age Australians," *Human Organization* 2 (1952), pp. 17–22, which is a good introduction to the ideas of "systems theory."

from this region. But it is one thing to excavate a seed which might have been grown in a very ancient garden; it is quite another to find evidence of what brought the whole process about.

For the moment, there are only scattered excavations, like the pages torn out of a novel. The connections between them are still very poorly understood. The coastal desert to the west of the Andes has been a focus of archeological activity.[19] Seven-thousand-year-old settlements have been found on its rivers. In the Lurin Valley, not far from the Pacific, hunters and gatherers lived in sedentary communities. All the food they required was less than an hour's walk from their homes. There were fish and shellfish from the ocean and rivers, sea lions that were hunted in the summer, and vegetation that was nourished on the desert by the thick winter fogs.

Just as in the eastern Mediterranean, there was settled life without domestication. But 4,500 years before the present, these communities changed. No longer did they gather the plants that flourished when the fog drifted over the desert. They moved still closer to the rivers and the sea. Fishing communities grew. At this time too, there were cultivated plants from some unknown source in Peru that were carried down to the coast along routes that are still undiscovered. Squashes and lima beans were traded into the coastal communities and then grown along the banks of the rivers as a new source of food.

Were all of these changes related? Some archeologists believe that they were. But there is strong disagreement about what happened in coastal Peru. Archeologist Edward P. Lanning argued that the climate along the coast was changing.[20] Higher temperatures were slowly displacing the winter fog. Vegetation on the desert became sparser; hunters and gatherers had less food to eat. In time, they shifted their communities closer to the edge of the sea. Yet geographers have remained unconvinced. They find little evidence of a climatic change along the coast. Perhaps it was the foragers themselves that brought an end to the fog vegetation. Anthropologist Mark N. Cohen has recently suggested that this is what happened.[21] Rising populations may have stripped the vegetation from the desert.

But however they happened, these coastal changes do not really tell us about another puzzling matter. Who was growing the squash and the beans that came down from the Andes? Were there gardeners higher up in the mountains or in the jungles that lay to the east? At Jaywamachay Cave in the Andes, Robert MacNeish found a seed of *achiote*—a source of

---

[19]Thomas C. Patterson, "Central Peru: Its Population and Economy," *Archeology*, October 1971, pp. 316–21.

[20]Edward P. Lanning, "Fog, Folly, and Fuzzy Thinking," *Anthropology*, December 1977, pp. 158–64.

[21]Mark N. Cohen, "Population Pressure and the Origins of Agriculture: An Archeological Example from the Coast of Peru," in *Population, Ecology and Social Evolution*, ed. S. Polgar (The Hague: Mouton, 1975), pp. 79–122.

Photos by Dr. Thomas F. Lynch, Department of Anthropology, Cornell University

Guitarrero Cave. View of the Andes from within the cave (top), and the entrance to the cave, seen from the northeast (bottom).

red pigment that grows wild in the Peruvian jungle. It has always been overly tempting to draw too many conclusions from a seed. But there are other findings that are calling attention to the Amazonian slopes.

At Guitarrero Cave, 1.5 miles above sea level, Thomas Lynch found plant remains that might originally have been domesticated east of the Andes.[22] The cave was located near a spring and was less than an hour's walk from the Rio Santa. Dry-weather shrubs and cacti surrounded the mouth of the cave. Probably the shelter was abandoned every year during the dry summer months. The dwellers probably moved downslope to be closer to the river. Migratory groups had lived there since 12,000 years before the present. But in time, they were supplementing their diet with domesticated plants.

From deposits in the floor of the cave that were about 10,600 years old, Lynch screened out the remains of specimens of common beans. Lima beans too were encountered from an 8,800-year-old deposit.[23] Wild ancestors of lima beans grow today in the jungles to the east of the mountains. So, it is possible that the Amazonian forest dwellers were experimenting with gardens and then trading their crops across the peaks of the Andes.

C. Earle Smith said that these findings

> show the progression from wild forms to a cultivated plant that might be expected in such a long chronological sequence. . . . Therefore the archeological sequences showing the progression from wild to cultivated. . . must be sought east of the Andes.[24]

But where are the sites of the Amazonian gardeners? How old are their gardens? What brought them about? Archeology, for the moment, has little to say. It seems plausible that changes in climate may have played a significant role. As the grasslands yielded to tropical forests at the end of Pleistocene times, hunters and gatherers may have turned to gardening to meet their needs for more food. The process might have been very similar to the early experiments in Southeast Asia. But the answers to all of these questions remain to be found.

In many different parts of the planet, foragers in marginal landscapes adapted with resilient systems of widespread exchange. Staying in camp long enough to stabilize a web of connections, they slowly became causes of change in the natural world. More food—and more intricate systems—made it possible to stay in one place. Managers controlled the commodities that flowed through the network of trade. Communities were growing in the midst of the marginal lands.

---

[22]Thomas F. Lynch, "Preceramic Transhumance in the Callejon de Huaylas, Peru," *American Antiquity* 36, no. 2 (1971), pp. 139–48.

[23]Site chronology is presented by Lynch in "Stratigraphy and Chronology," in *Guitarrero Cave: Early Man in the Andes* (New York: Academic Press, 1980), p. 38.

[24]C. Earle Smith, Jr., "Plant Remains from Guitarrero Cave," in *Guitarrero Cave*, p. 118.

For most of the world, these great transformations remained far away and little known (if at all). Hunters, fishers, and plant collectors ranged through the forests and caught fish in the streams. Granaries, mud houses, or bread did not concern them at all. Yet in time, in the thickets of the wilderness, there were new sounds and more people—a stirring. Birds were startled into flight by the thud of stone axes in the trees.

10/Warriors and Farmers in Anatolia and Europe

There is a place on the west coast of Ireland where cliffs drop down to the sea. A steep, narrow road leads up the face of a rocky hillside. There are no villages along that road. There are no people—only a scattering of sheep. At the top of the hill, there is no sound except the wind.

I once drove to the end of that road in a tiny European Ford. Even in low gear the car had difficulty making the climb. But at the very top where the road finally ended, there was the sign of a much earlier visit. A massive rock at least 8 feet tall and weighing a few thousand pounds had been pushed up the hill and mounted in the earth at the summit.

They are found all over Ireland, these remarkable standing stones. They are found in England, France, and the Mediterranean coastline of Europe.

European megalith (Carnac, Brittany). For centuries the subject of fantasy, these structures are now much better understood.

Field Museum of Natural History

For the local people, they are often curiosities or the survivals of a super-natural time. There are four standing stones on the River Clun in the border country of Wales, where the villagers say that four women once danced with the Devil. There are other stories of rocks that bleed when you stick them or that drink from rivers at the first light of dawn. In some villages, they say that the stones were the playthings of giants.[1]

It is easy to smile at the fantastic and less easy to explain the stones. But, as I hope to show, there is much about them that we now under-stand. The most critical part of that understanding involves viewing them in the context of time. For the massive stones are only one aspect of the great changes in European society that occurred when the first farms and villages sprang up in the land.

In the generations that followed the Ice Age, a vast tract of forest dom-inated Europe.[2] In the northerly regions, there were remnant stretches of tundra. In campsites deep in the forest, hunters and gatherers lived for thousands of years. At Maglemose Bog in Denmark, they fished and hunted waterfowl and pigs. At Star Carr in England, they skinned freshly killed deer and tanned the hides for trade with other foragers. On the Mediter-ranean beaches, they combed the shoreline for shellfish and crabs.

Today those hunting-and-gathering societies have totally vanished from the European landmass. Most of the forest has gone with them, and in its place are fences and farms. How did the transformation happen? Why did Europe become a village society? In the search for an answer, we should look at the continent itself.

The changing European woodlands

Europe is small, although this might seem surprising. Because of our European heritage, we are sometimes tempted to think that it is large. But Africa is about three times greater; each of the Americas is around twice its size. And Asia—at least four times as vast—so overpowers the land to its west that Europe seems little more than a peninsula embracing the Mediterranean Sea.

But if Europe is a diminutive peninsula, it is also a continent of striking differences, of geographical features that themselves were evolving through time. Some 7,500 years before the present, the continent began to grow warmer and wetter. Its plants and animals, it lakes, and even its soils

---

[1]Jacqueline Simpson, *The Folklore of the Welsh Border* (Totowa, N.J.: Rowman & Littlefield, 1976), pp. 19–23.

[2]The discussion of the European physical environment is taken from H. T. Waterbolk, "Food Production in Prehistoric Europe," *Science* 162 (1968), pp. 1093–1102; Karl W. Butzer, "The Significance of Agricultural Dispersal into Europe and Northern Africa," in *Prehistoric Agriculture*, ed. Stuart Streuver (Garden City, N.Y.: Natural History Press, 1971), pp. 313–34; Robert Rodden, "Europe North of the Alps," and "The Mediterranean," in *Varieties of Culture in the Old World*, ed. Robert Stigler et al. (New York: St. Martin's Press, 1975), pp. 49–105.

were changed. A glacier covering much of Scandanavia disappeared into the waters of the North Sea. The ocean rose. For the very first time, there was salt in the Baltic. The northern tundra, always a fragile environment, retreated as the temperature climbed. Oak trees and hazel took root in the warmer, thawed soils. Berries and fruits were now flourishing in this curious, new Scandanavia. Mediterranean grapes grew wild in the forests of Sweden.

For the big game in these northerly regions, the changes were a threat to survival. The shady woodlands were lacking in pasture for the large grazing animals. The aurochs, the elk, and the red deer, so abundant in Pleistocene times, were now harder to find—and so the hunters moved away to the sea. At the Vedbaek site north of Copenhagen, there were scattered bones of deer and wild boar. But there are also the remains of porpoises, codfish, and seals.

Much of Europe to the south of Scandanavia became covered by the temperate woodland. Open grassland was colonized by oak, elm, ivy, and alder. Here too, the big game grew scarce as the grasslands were covered by trees. The spreading of this immense, deciduous forest brought a blanket of litter to the ground. Dead leaves and branches settled over the floor of the forest. The deeper levels of decaying matter were dissolved into the soil with the rain. The ground became more acidic. Minerals were leached down to lower depths. The rich, loess soils of Northern Europe had become degraded.

Rainfall came more often to the evolving countryside of Europe. Slowly the ponds and lakes began to change. Leaves and branches fell in their waters and quickly settled down to the bottom. Wet-loving vegetation

European temperate woodland.

Milwaukee Public Museum

now grew thicker along the shore, and when it died, it created deposits within the shallows. Over the years, the litter on the bottom climbed higher toward the surface. Ponds and lakes were changed into bogs. Fish and waterfowl died.

As the world around them changed, the hunters and gatherers abandoned their forests. Like the Scandanavians, they probably shifted their camps to the sea. There were isolated pockets of stability—the fringes of the Alps and the Jura Mountains—where foraging life went on as it always had. But most of Northern and Central Europe had become empty of human beings. A wave of forest had driven the foragers out of the land.

To the south along the Mediterranean, rainfall was scantier, and the woodlands were different. Much of the coastline was mountainous, with jagged cliffs that plunged down to the sea. The outlying stretches of the Pyrenees, the Alps, and the Balkan Highlands made the southern fringe of Europe a ribbon of valleys and forested peaks. For about half a mile above sea level, there were evergreen oaks and pines. On the drier slopes, there were thickets of brush known as *maquis*. Higher up than about half a mile, the woodland turned into a deciduous forest. Chestnut, oak, and ash grew thick on the slopes. If you climbed still higher to a mile above sea level, you would find yourself in open, grassy meadows. In this colder world, there were stands of evergreen forest.

The rough landscape of Mediterranean Europe helped make it a region of diversity. But it was a land with significant problems for the farmers of Europe. The rugged coastline was created many millions of years in the past when sedimentary rocks bulged upward, forming mountains. But such rocks are prone to erosion, and the region has been eroding for millions of years. The slopes became steep, and the soils left on them were thin.

Rainfall was not as frequent here as it was in the lands to the north. It more closely resembled the dry climate of the Levant. Spring and autumn were the seasons of rain, and the summers were especially dry. Almost all of the rivers evaporated, and their beds turned to mud. The thin soils could hold little water during the hot Mediterranean summer. Natural springs and wells in the stream beds held what water there was. Only on the mile-high slopes, rich with streams that never went dry, was there abundant water during the hottest months of the year.

The technology of the European farmers

To a land that was being changed by nature, humanity brought even greater change.[3] The woodlands of Europe had to be cleared before farmers could plant in the soil. Like the cultivators of Southeast Asia, the ancient Europeans burned and planted in the ashes. Ground-stone axes

---

[3]J. G. D. Clark, *Prehistoric Europe: The Economic Basis* (Stanford, Calif.: Stanford University Press, 1952), pp. 91–107.

The rocky slopes of Mediterranean Europe.

Milwaukee Public Museum

were part of that technology as the settlements moved across the face of Europe. The blades of these axes had been formed of stone rubbed by another stone to make an edge. More time was required to produce them than the blade tools of the Upper Paleolithic. But the stones would not shatter. Mounted in a handle, they proved extremely effective.

Archeologist K. Jacob-Friesen once put two kinds of early axes to a test. Using a chipped-flint axe similar to the woodworking tools of European foragers, he cut through the trunk of a pine that was about 6.5 inches in diameter. It took him about seven minutes to cut through the tree. But by using a ground-stone axe, he finished the task about two minutes faster. Such a difference might seem of little consequence, but we should remember that this was only one tree. For a group of families chopping out a tract of forest, this could mean a difference of many labor-hours. The new axes became widely adopted as the continent changed.

But technology was much more than axes: it was behavioral strategy as well. Patterns of land-use became very different from those of the Levant. The pollen spores preserved in the soil have revealed at least part of the story. Pollen provides us with a vegetation profile—a record of the trees and shrubs that once grew on the land. Layers of ashes are the clear-cut evidence of when the woodlands were burned. Since botanists know the length of time it takes for certain types of trees to grow back, we can learn something of the cycles of slash-and-burn farming in Europe. At the site of Bylany in Czechoslovakia, about 72 acres of forest were burned off and planted in cereals for three or four years. Probably

Courtesy of the American Museum of Natural History

Stone axes like these were used in Europe for forest-clearing and construction of dwellings.

there were three such burnings during the lifetime of the settlement. After some 14 years it was abandoned, and the farmers moved on.

A more detailed picture than this has been discovered in the remote corners of the world where temperate-forest farming has lived on until industrialized times. In the Volga-Kama region of the Soviet Union, to the north of the Caspian Sea, Wotjak farmers, like the people of Bylany, set the forests into flame. In the spring of the year, they grubbed the smaller trees and chopped a ring around the larger ones with an axe. A few months later, the larger trees would die because the sap could not rise. Just before the rainy season began, the vegetation would be piled up and burned. The heavy rains would drive the layers of ashes—containing the valuable fertilizer potash—deeper into the soil. Here they planted their crops of rye until the farmland became exhausted. Then the devastated soil was abandoned, and they sought out new ground.

This slash-and-burn farming in Europe—*brandwirtschaft* it has sometimes been called—was significantly different from the variety in Southeast Asia. For one thing, the vegetation was different: it grew much slower than the plants of the tropics. Much more time was required for the forest to recover the land. In the tropics, when the last field was abandoned, the original clearing would be replenished again. But in Europe, it would be covered by underbrush, stumps, and dead trees.

Besides this, the European crops were wheat, barley, and other cereal grains. These are plants which make heavy demands upon soil fertility. For such agriculture to be successful, it had to steadily be on the move, laying waste to the virgin woodland with fire and axe. This is a pioneering mode of technology. It thrives at the margins of unsettled land. But when the frontier is gone, the pioneers are left with a crises.

To tell of that crisis in detail and the behavioral change that it brought is to move ahead of our story of the transformation of Europe. How did the wooded peninsula become a network of villages and farms? Was Europe invaded by cultivators and herders? What caused European society to change? These questions have not been as easy to answer as they might first appear.

Anthropologists very early in this century were speculating about the settlements of Europe.[4] For them it was largely a question of migrations versus independent change. Since laboratory dating techniques would not be developed until a later generation, the prehistorians resorted to the use of the information they had. One of the methods that they used is typological dating—matching an artifact with another of the same type for which the date can be found. The way that this worked some 70 years ago involved beginning with historical records, such as Egyptian records that chronicled the lives of their rulers. Since there is sometimes a passing reference to a comet or an eclipse in the heavens, astronomers could precisely identify the time of a king. In this way, the Egyptian records could be dated back to 1900 BC. And there were guesstimate dates for some 1,000 years before that. Now if a stone figurine or a copper dagger was discovered somewhere in Europe, it was compared with the same type of artifact discovered in Egypt. Since the one in Egypt could be dated, the

Theories of global migrations

---

[4]The account of the controversy concerning the prehistory of agricultural Europe is drawn largely from Colin Renfrew, *Before Civilization: The Radiocarbon Revolution and Prehistoric Europe*, (New York: Alfred A. Knopf, 1973).

one from Europe could be located in time—allowing enough years for it to travel from Egypt to Europe.

And there—at the last—is the rub. A demon was lurking within the method itself. Egypt provided early archeologists with a series of dates for the past. But the dates were for Egypt and not for the rest of the world. To date the artifacts discovered in Europe, archeologists began assuming that they were later in time than the same kinds discovered in Egypt. From there it was only a short step to saying that the *artifacts had come out of Egypt.* What began as a method had turned into a scheme of prehistory.

Archeology's darkest hour

The 20th century had scarcely begun when the Swedish archeologist Oskar Montelius portrayed all of Europe as a cultural backwater settled by Egypt. Like many prehistorians who would follow him, he was impressed by *giant stone architecture,* the *megaliths* of wonder and fable found throughout Europe. With as much emotion as logic, he argued:

> one does not have to probe deeply into a study of the. . .conditions here in the north during the stone age. . .to see that the original homeland of the dolmens (megaliths) cannot be sought in north Europe. They could not have spread from here to the southern shores of the Mediterranean, to Palestine and to India. The entire discussion shows that this would be absurd. So powerful a movement, able to influence the burial customs of so many and widely distributed peoples, simply cannot have originated here, thousands of years before our era. It is indeed remarkable enough that, originating in the orient, it should already have reached us here in so early a date.[5]

But the work of Montelius was merely an overture for the thundering productions of Grafton Elliot Smith, the British anatomist who thought that all civilization was the work of Egyptians. "Children of the sun"—Egyptian explorers—had traveled to every continent except for Antarctica and prodded the local inhabitants into civilization. Mummies and megaliths, for Smith, presented

> so many peculiar and distinctive features that no hypothesis of independent evolution can seriously be entertained in explanation of their geographical distribution. They must be regarded as evidence of the diffusion of information, and the migration of the bearers of it, from somewhere in the neighborhood of the east Mediterranean, step by step out into Polynesia and even perhaps beyond the Pacific to the American littoral.[6]

There is a dark underside to such theories, as I suggested earlier in the

---

[5]Ibid., pp. 32–33.
[6]Ibid., p. 33.

story. It did not take long for prehistory to become propaganda. What Elliot Smith had done for the Egyptians could as easily be done with any other society. Similar artifacts could "prove" there were migrations in any direction. The German nationalist Gustav Kossina, seeing that anyone could play at this game, held that all civilization had come from Germany to the rest of the world:

> The Germans were a heroic people and have always remained so. For only a thoroughly manly and efficient people could have conquered the world at the end of the Roman Empire. And how was it two to three thousand years earlier?. . .The great folk movements then went out, in the third millinium BC from north-central Europe, from this side of the Baltic and beyond, and then further, from the middle and lower Danube, populating all Europe, and especially southern Europe and the Near East, with the people who speak our tongue, the language of the Indo-Germans. Everywhere people of central European blood became the ruling class. . .and imprinted at least our language, as an external symbol of the world-historical vocation of our race, indelibly upon those lands.[7]

Such a view was deeply congenial to the rise of fascism in Germany. Gustav Kossina and Adolf Hitler discovered one another. Kossina began to quote the Fuehrer at length in later editions of his writings. In a short while, Heinrich Himmler, the Nazi minister of the interior, was sponsoring archeological excavations with Kossina in mind. Hitler, in the beginning, was dubious: "Himmler is starting to dig up these villages of mud huts and enthusing over every potsherd and stone axe he finds."[8] But his own views became very similar. Ancient Greece, in his personal opinion, was a society close to perfection but only because of Germanic immigrants that came from the north. The frightening episode reached its climax in the pronouncement by Himmler that "Prehistory is the doctrine of the eminence of the Germans at the dawn of civilization."

The nature of human invention

There are probably a great many archeologists who would prefer to forget that this happened. In any event, Kossina and his colleagues have been all but forgotten.[9] Does revisiting them serve any purpose? Possibly it does. At the very least, it leads us to consider what we know about human inventiveness. And what we know does not correspond with Elliot Smith or Kossina. Anthropologists have known for some time now that the same discoveries can happen in many places. Not only that, but very often they can happen at almost the same moment. In recent cen-

---

[7]Ibid., p. 35.

[8]Albert Speer, *Inside the Third Reich* (New York: Macmillan, 1970), p. 113.

[9]The exceptions include the valuable historical discussions in Renfrew's *Before Civilization* and Daniel's *Idea of Prehistory*.

turies, there have been a great many instances of inventors who were unaware of one another's existence but who nonetheless discovered the same thing at about the same time. Telescopes, for example, were invented at three different places in 1608. Sunspots were independently discovered by four different people around 1610. The elements nitrogen and oxygen were each discovered by independent scientists, and in each case the coincidence happened in the space of a year. More recently, the telephone and the airplane, regardless of what we were all taught in school, were simultaneous inventions that happened in different parts of the world.

How can we explain such coincidence? Actually, it is not a coincidence at all. More than anything, it is simply a matter of social preparedness. As Peter Farb has put it,

> There is no way in which any culture can be explained in terms of one or more of its great men, whether they be Pericles, Augustus, Charlemagne, Ghengis Khan, Franklin Roosevelt or Hiawatha. The great man is not the culture's prime mover; he is its manifestation. If Newton had spent his life being a lowly tavernkeeper instead of going to Cambridge, it is certain that someone else would have discovered the law of gravitation—because the culture of the time demanded that such a discovery be made and because the intellectual groundwork for the acceptance of that discovery had already been laid. No great intellectual leap was required for the invention of the steamboat: Steam is a principle known to ancient man and knowledge of the boat also goes back thousands of years. The combination of steam and the boat took place at a time when European civilization was receptive to new ideas and when its technology was sufficiently advanced for a workable steamboat to be made. If the actual inventors had not performed the cultural synthesis of these two ancient ideas, then other people would have done it.[10]

What we know of the discovery process, then, makes a shambles of Elliot Smith and Kossina. Similar artifacts, much of the time, are independent inventions. In their theories we find a slightly different version of lazy people or sluggish societies—of people too dull to discover anything for themselves.

It was this last point that fit so neatly into the nationalist views of Kossina. If archeology proved that the Germans had brought civilization to everyone else, then it demonstrated that they were superior to the rest of the world. Could such abuses happen in the present? At times I am afraid that they might. There are "Elliot Smiths" popular even today.

Erich von Daeniken, for example, has argued that most, if not all, civilization was the result of extraterrestrials who inspired our planet. His approach is fundamentally silly because it never evaluates alternative views. And in themselves, the books he has written do little serious harm. What

---

[10]Peter Farb, *Man's Rise to Civilization* (New York: Avon 1968), pp. 133–34.

bothers me more than his spacemen is the great popularity of his views. This is evidence that the slipshod thinking found in Elliot Smith or Kossina is still totally acceptable to many people in our society. We are fortunate that von Daeniken's "heroes" are extraterrestrials—and not Anglo-Saxons. Clearly, the need for responsible prehistory is greater than ever.

The awareness that these globetrotting theories had serious anthropological limitations was growing even at the time of their greatest popularity. V. Gordon Childe, in several detailed treatments of Western European prehistory, deliberately sought to avoid the extremes of Elliot Smith and Kossina. In *The Dawn of European Civilization* and *The Danube in Prehistory*, he presented massive archeological evidence for the colonization of Europe. It was a detailed and complex argument, more modest in its view of migrations. European society had changed because of colonists from the Near East. Traveling by boat across the Mediterranean and chopping their way through the forests of the Danube, "Oriental" immigrants had brought farming and stone architecture to Europe.

V. Gordon Childe and a scientific crisis

Childe knew that on the coastline of Spain were ancient megalithic tombs that closely resembled structures on the island of Crete. He knew there were fortifications at Los Millares, near the southern coast of Spain, strikingly similar to fortifications in the Aegean. And he was impressed by the close resemblance between pottery and figurines from the Danube to those that were dug out of Troy on the west coast of Turkey. Bringing all of these threads together, he argued that urban societies in the eastern Mediterranean moved westward, over land and by sea, into the woodlands of Europe. Mesopotamians and Egyptians, he thought, made their way into the nearby Aegean. From there the two pathways were taken, and the world had been changed.

He thought of it as his greatest achievement, this deciphering of the prehistory of Europe. But part of his edifice began to grow shaky as archeology changed. The house that Childe built was constructed to a large extent upon the writings of the Egyptians. They were the only way of dating the events he described in his books. But with the development of carbon-14, archeology was suddenly changed. Sites could be dated from their organic materials. Chronology would be more precise than it ever was before. When the European sites were dated, the results were in fairly close agreement with Childe. There were occasional grumblings, but for the most part he appeared to be right.

Yet in a short time, the grumblings grew louder. There was something wrong about the dates. The stone tombs in France, according to the laboratories, were 500 years older than Childe had suggested. Yugoslavian artifacts were older than those in the Aegean. And when historically dated

Egyptian materials were cross-checked by carbon-14, there was a discrepancy of several centuries between the two dates. Which was right—archeology or physics? The debate grew complicated—and heated. Where are we? asked one prehistorian:

> We are at a moment when some of us at least are uncertain how to answer this question: when is a carbon-14 reading an archeological fact?[11]

Here was a moment when the prehistory of Europe—and prehistory itself—was caught in a crisis. If carbon-14 could not be relied upon, then the chronology it produced was an illusion. But if it *was* reliable, then the traditional understanding of Europe was wrong. As it happened, the nettlesome technique had been right—but only up to a point. The problem was resolved in the White Mountains of central California.

Every child who grows up in the country knows that you can count the rings in a stump and figure out the age of the tree when the axe cut it down. Although there is a good deal more to it than that, it was this fundamental technique that evolved into the tree-ring dating of the American West. Using bristlecone pines of that region, archeologists with the tree-ring method can date materials that are somewhat more than 8,000 years old. Carbon-14 was checked against this method. The effects of that experiment are still being felt. It turned out that carbon-14 is accurate back to 1,500 BC. Earlier than that, it becomes more erratic. For objects that are actually 4,500 years old, carbon-14 would show them to be only 3,800!

For Turkey, Egypt, and the eastern Mediterranean, the correction did not result in much change. But to the west of that accurate region—in Portugal, Spain, and France in particular—the new dating forever altered European prehistory. The massive stone structures of Europe were not inspired by Egypt or Mesopotamia. They could not have been. They were the earliest stone monuments ever built.

This was more than a technical consequence and more than a "wonders of the world" observation. It effectively ended the archeological practice of explaining customs in terms of migrations—of saying that a people did something because they had learned it from others. After this, much more attention was given to understanding what had *first caused* the custom and, *if* it had spread, what had caused another people to accept it and keep it. Beyond this, archeology had confirmed what cultural anthropologists had long been maintaining: that inventiveness was universally a part of the human condition. Preliterate people, said the British Lord Raglan, "never invent or discover anything." But the California tree-rings had shown how that was not true.

---

[11]Cited in Renfrew, *Before Civilization*, p. 58.

Over 20 years have gone by since the controversy over Childe's *Dawn*. Since those days, a great deal has been learned about villages and early farming in Europe. And, as in most of the world, there is much that remains to be done. Yet in no sense are European prehistorians faced with a problem of beginning from scratch. Childe had been wrong about the European megaliths being the creations of colonists from cities, but he was right when he emphasized that Europe was changed by migration. Cultivators from the eastern Mediterranean, bringing their herds and domesticated grains, had migrated westward into the European woodlands. There is no evidence of cereal-grain farming in Europe earlier than in the Near East. Nor are there traces anywhere on the continent of experimental manipulation of plants. The corrected dates for the European farming villages suggest instead a gradual migration out of the Mediterranean foothills ever deeper into the forests of Europe.[12]

Migrations into Anatolia

The driving forces behind that migration were probably soil exhaustion and war, as the early farmers and fighters pushed west in the search for more land. In their wake they left fortified villages with stacks of stones: the ammunition for slings. Their burials were mostly women and chil-

Chronology of European agricultural migration.

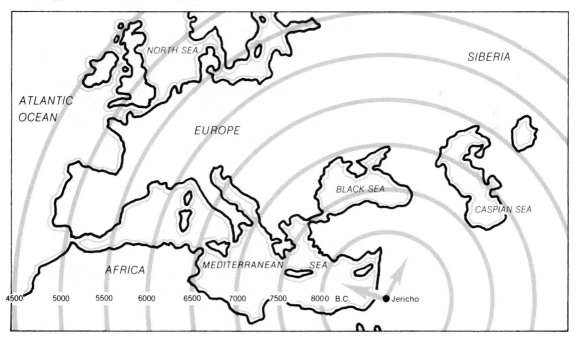

---

[12]A. J. Ammerman and L. L. Cavalli-Sforza, "A Population Model for the Diffusion of Early Farming in Europe," in *The Explanation of Culture Change: Models in Prehistory*, ed. Colin Renfrew (Pittsburgh: University of Pittsburgh Press, 1974) pp. 343–59.

Agricultural sites in
Europe.

dren; men were probably left where they were slain. This process moved
very slowly through Anatolia to Europe.

On the left bank of the Jordan River, in a stony desert to the north of
the Dead Sea, Kathleen Kenyon discovered the remains of organized conflict.[13] This is the Jericho of biblical legend where Joshua of Israel "burnt
the city with fire." But long before that, the village had been building for
war. Jericho began almost 10,000 years ago as a small group of circular,

---

[13]Kathleen Kenyon, "Ancient Jericho," *Scientific American*, April 1954.

mud-brick dwellings. It was unfortified and tiny, much like Ain Mallaha to the west. They grew their grain and kept their flocks near the village where there was a supply of fresh water from a spring. But a thousand years later, the settlement was braced for defense. A large tower was constructed near the village, which was totally surrounded by a wall. The dwellings inside it were now rectangular—which, perhaps, was an adaptation to war. Unlike the earlier circular houses, the new dwellings could be quickly enlarged. As the kin group increased, it was a matter of tacking on rooms. Very likely, in this fortified settlement, adult males remained with their kin. Women left home as they married into other societies. This meant that a collection of warriors would remain close to home at all times. More than that, because they were kinsmen, their behaviors were strongly cohesive. Individual strengths, weaknesses, and curious personality traits were well understood by every man in the group. A sharing of cultural tradition, and intimate information as well, made lineages of males a powerful weapon of war. For that reason, it is not surprising that villages in more recent times frequently have such a social arrangement when there are ongoing raids.[14] It explains why the new style of dwelling appears within fortified sites in Anatolia, Europe, and much of northern China as well. Soil exhaustion and a rising birthrate were putting pressure on arable land. Competition for resources was transforming Middle Eastern society.

Pressures of conflict led to migration, to a search for fresh soils, new fields. It drove migrants to the edges of the Taurus in southern Anatolia. In that region, some 8,000 years ago, farmers settled along the banks of a river that once flowed from the Taurus Mountains toward the plains to the north.[15] They grew cereal grains, peas, and lentils. Cattle grazed along the foothills. The settlement of Catal Huyuk prospered and became one of the largest such sites ever known. At its height, it covered 32 acres—larger than many towns of the industrialized world. Within this village there were craftsmen, artists, religious specialists, and merchants. It was a center of material abundance and of crafts and creation.

Wild nuts, berries, and fruit trees grew within easy reach of the villagers. Within a three-mile walk from the site there were soils that may have been suited for the growing of melons, sugarbeets, and cereal grains.[16] Even so, it was a marginal region. It was a countryside of scanty rainfall, scattered swamps, and poorly drained soils. Evaporation of surface moisture left soils that were highly saline. Pollen spores of salt-loving plants were recovered from the village's layers. This community never emerged

[14]Melvin Ember and Carol R. Ember, "The Conditions Favoring Matrilocal versus Patrilocal Residence," *American Anthropologist* 73 (1971), pp. 571–94.

[15]James Melaart, "A Neolithic City in Turkey," *Scientific American*, April 1964.

[16]Ian A. Todd, *Catal Huyuk in Perspective* (Menlo Park, Calif: Benjamin-Cummings, 1976), pp. 123–24.

in an optimum land, yet its citizens were generally healthy. Their skeletons bear little trace of disease. More than likely the village prospered, not because of what was locally there, but because it was the center of an elaborate network of trade.

At every level of the settlement there is evidence of religious activity, rituals, and beliefs that were finding expression in art. Out of some 200 rectangular buildings uncovered by James Melaart, at least 40 were shrines, the sacred centers of burial and belief. The walls of these shrines were decorated with painted murals and sculptures in relief. Bulls' heads were mounted in the walls, covered with plaster and probably painted. Women's breasts were sculpted out of wet plaster in relief. Some of the walls were painted in murals: one showed the capture of a wild bull; another portrayed a dancing procession; a third depicted the headless bodies of humans being ravaged by buzzards.

The morbidity of that final mural is echoed throughout much of the art. Perhaps it is better to call it an opposition between life and death. The west walls of the shrines were decorated in a manner suggestive of life. They were painted partially in red—a color associated with blood. This formed a backdrop for statuettes, usually around 8 inches tall, of human females giving birth to a bull or a ram. The east walls were black,

Artist's reconstruction of a shrine at Catal Huyuk. There is no archeological evidence that chiefs ever ruled the village. Perhaps, as among the Pueblo, social control was achieved through ritual.

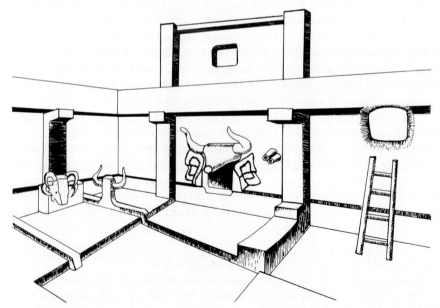

and it was here that the headless humans were painted. On these same walls there were sexual sculptures, but even they had a deathly aspect. The remains of vultures, boars, foxes, and weasels—all of them scavengers or devourers of corpses—were worked into wet plaster that was shaped into the contours of breasts.

Catal Huyuk has been a mine of riches (a mother lode?) for matriarchial theorists. But the paintings and sculptures can be interpreted in many different ways. The female forms, often said to be symbolic of women rulers of agricultural society, could as easily symbolize procreation and the mystery of life. Just as significant, in my own opinion, is the large number of shrines at the site, and the fact that human burials were usually underneath their floors. Religious observances, judging from this, were not shared community behavior; it seems more likely that each kin group within the village had its own shrine. There they would worship and celebrate the harvests (burned grains have been discovered on the altars), and they would bury their dead underneath the floor of their shrine. Such behavior is often found among more permanent kin groups—such as lineages—that have their own rituals, costumes, and property that are not shared with others. On the last point it is interesting to note that clay seals were discovered at the site, which could possibly have been used for property identification. Each seal had its own raised design, very comparable to the rubber stamps of today. Conceivably, they were used for marking the side of a jar. Melaart found them on the floors of the houses— which had rooms for the storage of grain—and he discovered that each house never had more than one kind of seal. Very possibly, this could be evidence of economic and political change—of permanent groups with private property in human society.

There was little archeological evidence that the village was every successfully raided. This is, of course, not the same thing as saying it was never at war. The entire village was built in such a way as to be easily defended from enemies. Houses were constructed without doors or windows; they were entered through a hole in the roof. This meant that enemies facing the village would be confronted with a solid wall. The houses themselves could be defended from a rooftop position. The burials at Catal Huyuk are mostly of women and children, which is what we might suspect for a society often in battle. The few men buried in the village were placed into graves along with their weapons: maceheads, arrowheads, spearheads, and daggers of flint.

But Catal Huyuk was something other than a warrior-farmer society. Much of its wealth was the result of a network of trade. Some 50 miles away from the village was obsidian, or volcanic glass. This was often used for cutting-tools and mirrors throughout much of the region. Chemical analyses of obsidian have indicated that it was exported for hundreds of miles, from southern Turkey down to the farming villages in the Levant. But exchange involved more than obsidian. Flint, marble, alabaster, limestone, slate, mica, chalk, pumice, coral, greenstone, copper ore, manganese, and other exotic items as well: all of these, along with foodstuffs, were imported at Catal Huyuk. The village directed an elborate system of trade.[17]

The site is far from completely excavated, but enough has already been learned to see it as a reflection of changes in human society. Growing up in a marginal region, the village might have always survived through the trading connections in the Anatolian plains. But life in such a region has dangers: villagers were threatened by raids. More than likely, there were warrior lineages emerging at Catal Huyuk who enhanced their power by controlling their nets of exchange. At the moment, there is not any evidence of power any different than this. We discover no houses or burials more elaborate than all of the rest. There was not any centralized area in which stategic resources were stored, nor a standardized structure of the village's ritual life. There may not have been chiefs in this village; life perhaps was too uncertain for that. Droughts, the danger of raiding, and poor soils throughout much of the region all placed limitations on webs of exchange. Amassing strategic resources was difficult within such a region. Political power was shifting and fluid through time.

Perhaps, throughout all its existence, village kin groups competed for power. But over the years, as the soils grew poorer, Anatolians sought out other lands. Trading connections were weakened. Catal Huyuk was abandoned as well.[18] Agricultural peoples were discovering a world to the west.

Mediterranean farmers

In time, the search for new soils brought migrants toward the mountains of Greece.[19] Hunters and gatherers had been camping there in caves overlooking the sea. Whether these foragers withdrew into the forest or whether they were violently driven from their homes is something that we still do not know about the ancient Aegean. But the deposits in Francthi Cave in a hill overlooking the Gulf of Argolis reveal a sudden interruption of the hunting and gathering life.

For 20,000 years the cave had been a home for hunters and fishers. They gathered land snails and shellfish and hunted deer in the forests near the cave. The Mediterranean crept higher on the hillside; the foragers turned to the sea for their food. Nine thousand years ago, they caught bluefin tuna, a fish that can weigh over 1,000 pounds. They traded for obsidian on the island of Melos, a 90-mile voyage across the open sea. But with the coming of farmers and herders, their way of life ended. In the deposits of 8,000 years ago there are suddenly wheat and barley re-

[17]Todd, *Catal Huyuk*, p. 126.
[18]This site was apparently occupied for a total of about 2,000 years, beginning around 6500 BC. Todd, *Catal Huyuk*, pp. 104 and 118.
[19]Thomas W. Jacobsen, "17,000 Years of Greek Prehistory," *Scientific American*, June 1976.

mains. Bones of domesticated sheep and goat, ground-stone axes, mill-stones, and sickle blades were found in layers directly above those of the seagoing foragers.

The migration continued westward, along the shores of the Mediter-ranean sea. Farmers and herders settled along the coastline, then moved deeper into the woodlands of Europe. In Switzerland, southern Ger-many, and southern France they often built lake-side villages—houses of timber and bark on damp ground near the reeds of the lake. Wheat, peas, beans, and lentils were grown. There were wild plums and apples as well. Sheep and goat were still grazed near the villages, but cattle and pigs were more often kept. No one is exactly sure of when the latter two were first tamed by humanity, but certainly they were both well adapted to the forests of Europe. Cattle browsed on the tender shoots of the woodlands and grazed on the open pastures of the highlands. Pigs were

Reconstruction of a Swiss lake dwelling.

Field Museum of Natural History

descended from wild boars, and were probably long adapted to the forest. They fed on acorns and beechnuts in the woodlands, as well as on food scraps discarded in the villages. From the cattle came milk, butter, cheese, cowhide for straps, and horns for carving into spoons. Pigs were marvelous meat producers because of their large litters and very rapid growth. Bacon, belly-meat, sausages, and hams were probably smoke-dried and hung up near the houses to provide enough meat for the village to live through the winter.

First farmers in Central Europe

As the farmers followed the Mediterranean coastline, still others cut through the forests of the interior. Unlike the grassy plains of Anatolia, Central Europe was thick with elm and oak. Grass was sparser, and the winters were cold and snowy. No longer were there mud-brick dwellings; the European houses were wattle-and-daub. Logs were used to make the framework of rectangular walls and gable roofs. Branches were wedged in between the logs and plastered over with mud and clay. Such houses were better suited to the colder and wetter European climate, and the materials had come from clearing the forest itself.

In the Maritsa Valley of southern Bulgaria, bulging up from the level, plowed fields, there is a mound left behind by early farmers north of the Aegean.[20] The layers of the Karanovo mound have piled up over 40 feet high. The wattle houses collapsed and were rebuilt for many thousands of years. Farmers first moved into the valley some 8,000 years before the present. They cleared the forest and built their daub houses, usually about 50 or 60 at a time. They gathered grain with deer-antler sickles that had flint blades. Most of the houses were rectangular dwellings about 15 feet on a side. They had only one room, with a dome-shaped clay oven at one end. There was no separate area for storage; grain was kept in large jars in the room. As many as 300 people probably lived in the Karanovo village.

To the north in Czechoslovakia lay a group of sites known as Bylany, in a region that was farmed for probably 600 years. Farmers here had a cyclic movement: they burned the forest, planted their crops, and then probably abandoned a settlement after living there for some 14 years—the forest was cleared again and wattle houses sprang up on the land. A way of life very much like this moved into Germany and Holland as well. Koln-Lindenthal on the banks of the Rhine would in time become the city of Cologne. But in the beginning, it was 21 wattle houses built in a clearing. And at Sittard, a site in the Netherlands, at least 21 timber houses were built. Logs were mounted in a trench, and the walls were over 80 feet long.

As in the eastern Mediterranean, it is very possible that the remains of

---

[20]Stuart Piggot, *Ancient Europe from the Beginnings of Agriculture to Classical Antiquity* (Hawthorne, N.Y.: Aldine Publishing, 1965).

the houses are evidence of adaptive changes in human society. At the outset of the European migrations in the Aegean and in early Karanovo, the dwellings are small; there is just enough floor space for a family of five. Similar to them are the lakeside houses built by the first farmers in Switzerland. The Swiss houses remained very small throughout most of prehistory. What do these regions have in common? They have abundant resources, more than anything else: enough food to circumvent the danger of raids. The lakeside villages in Switzerland had a constant supply of water, virgin forest for farming, and high-altitude meadows for their herds. Then, too, the Swiss lake region had more food-rich forests than Northern Europe. The old foraging strategies continued side by side with farming and herding. They caught fish from the lakes and hunted game in the forest; they gathered wild apples, plums, berry seeds, hazelnuts, and mushrooms. Their communities remained small, while all around them the continent changed. Early Karanovo was like this—but only for a time. For 2,000 years that settlement had farmed in the forest clearings. Virgin land was abundant; all of the houses were small. But over the years, the forest around them began filling up with people. New stretches of forest were probably scarce; old clearings were producing less food. Kin groups responded to the dilemma by keeping adult males at home. A warrior force was on hand to protect the households. Scarcity was triggering change throughout European society. By the time Karanovo was abandoned (at around 2000 BC) the houses were 45 feet long; they had tripled in size. Additional rooms were being tacked on, just as in the eastern Mediterranean. Each room was usually large enough to accommodate four or five people. Usually each one was equipped with its own clay oven.

As the farmers moved across the woodlands, the adaptation became a tradition. The fine loess soils of Germany and Holland were held together by the roots of the trees, but they eroded swiftly with slash-and-burn agriculture and wintertime rains. Livestock too became a problem. They were food—but they were destructive as well. The early farmers probably allowed the cattle to range freely throughout the forest. This meant the herds could grow fat by browsing on the tender shoots of the woodlands. It also meant that they could interfere with regeneration of the forest by eating up the seedlings of trees as they sprouted in the fields. Out of necessity, the northern Europeans maintained warrior households as they migrated west. At Koln-Lindenthal, Bylany, and Sittard on the flatlands of Holland they built wattle-and-daub houses that now were a hundred feet long.

As they steadily exhausted the land, Europeans were moving toward a crisis much like the one faced in the Levant. This seems strong, but as Grahame Clarke said, "One might put it more strongly."

> It has long been appreciated that the closing stage of the neolithic (domestication) phase was an uneasy one over temperate Europe as a whole: instead of peaceful peasants. . . one finds warriors, some

equipped with battle-axes, others relying on their bows, but all intent on commerce, war and domination, moving at times rapidly, and themselves depending more on pastoral activities and rapine than on agriculture, a veritable scourge to the older peasantries into whose territories they irrupted. Prehistorians have indeed vied in emphasizing the contrast between the early peasants and the later warriors, without, however, offering any very satisfying explanation. Yet, surely one is dealing here with the effects upon human history of an immense ecological change wrought unthinkingly by the neolithic farmers and their livestock. The crisis came when it extended far beyond the sphere of animals and plants and involved not merely the economic basis, but the whole outlook of large segments of the populations of prehistoric Europe. In many parts at least the fat times of forest farming were over for good and all. The stored up fertility of the virgin soil had been taken and the potash from the burnt woodlands had been absorbed.[21]

Out of this crucible of scarcity and conflict, new complexities of society were born. Moving westward and devouring the woodlands, the migration ultimately ground to a halt. It met up with what British prehistorians have sometimes called the Atlantic facade—a network of foraging societies along the seacoasts of Europe. The lands behind the farmers were settled and ravaged. Before them lay an unknown sea. With nowhere to turn, the villagers of Europe sought an answer in war. Out of that crisis emerged social change—a new political system. Power in European society—once evanescent, hardly present at all—became permanent, inherited, and valued—like an heirloom through time.

The megaliths of Europe

In a very real way the European continent had contributed toward its own changes. The higher temperatures and heavier rainfall that drove the foragers from Northern Europe made possible an open forest easily cleared by the migrating farmers. This meant too that hunters and gatherers, after they abandoned the northerly forests, became closely adapted to the coastal fringes of Europe. It was only a matter of time, then, until forager and farmer would meet. The seaside fringes of Europe were suddenly crowded.

What is most striking about that coastline is its archeological richness in the enormous stones that have long been objects of theory and wonder. They are found on the islands of Sardinia and Corsica, and on the Mediterranean coastline of Spain; they are in Portugal and western France, and on the Bay of Biscay and the edges of the Baltic; they are on the western coast of Great Britain and the rain-swept pastures of Ireland. Prehistorians for the last 200 years have tried to explain them.

Radiocarbon and tree-rings have cleared away much of their mystery.

---

[21] Clark, *Prehistoric Europe*, p. 97.

We now know that they were the earliest large-stone structures in the world. The first megaliths were built on the island of Malta around 6,000 years before the present. The Maltese temples, as they are usually called, are buildings with walls of stone slabs. Probably they were roofed with timbers covered by thatch. One of the largest of them all is Hal Tarxien, a multi-roomed monument with rock-cut designs, excavated by the wonderfully named Themistocles Zammit.[22] Its walls were of close-fitting slabs, many of which were decorated with spirals. A central passageway over 100 feet long had transcepts leading out from its sides. Female figurines were recovered from the floor of the temple. It is possible that Hal Tarxien was used for both meetings and worship.

Only a few centuries later, in Portugal and coastal Spain, there were rock-walled "chamber tombs" dug into the earth.[23] They were built by a method called corbelling, which created an early form of the arch. Slabs of rock were placed atop one another, each one slightly off-center; a final stone was carefully fitted in the middle, completing the arch. The corbelled tombs were essentially a tunnel leading down to a dome where the burials were placed. At Los Millares in southern Spain, there were 75 of these tombs, surrounded by a protective wall with semicircular bastions. The suggestion of conflict at Los Millares is echoed at nearby Almeria, a chamber tomb where burials were discovered along with implements of war. Stone axe heads, arrow heads, daggers, and pressure-flaked knives were found along with pottery, stone figurines, and clay plaques.

Over the years at least 40,000 of these underground chamber tombs were built across Europe. At Maes Howe in the Orkney Islands, and New Grange on the outskirts of Dublin, the rocks were quarried, and the great tombs were built, then covered with earth. But the culmination of megalithic art was in the *great standing stones*—the *henges*—some of the grandest of which were constructed on the plains of southern England.

One of them was discovered by a fox hunter on a January morning three centuries ago.[24] He was "wonderfully surprized" by the Avebury megaliths and the ditches and mound of earth that enclosed them. Much of the structure still stands today—one of the largest megaliths in the British Isles. A flat-bottomed ditch a quarter-mile long, around 25 feet deep, and over 20 feet wide surrounds three circles of stones built on the crest of a hill. Over 190 stones, some of them weighing as much as 47 tons, were mounted upright in the chalky soils of the Salisbury Plain. Some 4,000 tons of stones made up the structure itself, while about 200,000 tons of chalk were removed from the ditch.

---

[22]Glyn Daniel, *The Megalith Builders of Western Europe* (New York: Penguin Books, 1958), p. 85.

[23]Piggot, *Ancient Europe*, pp. 44–64.

[24]Aubrey Burl, *The Stone Circles of the British Isles* (New Haven, Conn.: Yale University Press, 1976), pp. 320–29.

The Bettman Archive, Inc.

Stonehenge, near the Avon River. The monument was under construction for nearly 2,000 years.

A short distance south of the Avebury site is Stonehenge on the Avon River, a monumental structure that required over 17 centuries to build. A circular ditch over 300 feet in diameter surrounds two circles and two horseshoes of stones. Several were bluestones weighing up to 4 tons each; the closest quarry for these stones is 135 miles away. Remarkably, the upright stones have been shaped to conceal the effect of perspective. When seen up close, they do not appear smaller at the top. This is an architectural illusion called *entasis,* sometimes credited to the ancient Greeks. But the builders of Stonehenge were the first in the world to employ it.

Is there any way that archeology can explain how and why such monuments were built? Only, it would seem to me, if we remove the miraculous. We need to recognize that the structures were the work of ancient Europeans, that no superhuman forces were required to put up the stones. It is true that the monuments were impressive, but they were built over a long period of time. The largest of them, like Stonehenge, were under construction for nearly 2,000 years. Then, too, there was nothing about these structures that was impossible for an agricultural society. There were blade tools and wedges for cutting out the stones (many of which had straight fracture lines), logs for rolling them, and rafts for floating them to the site of construction. Levers could have been used to lift the cap-stones, if a crib of timbers was placed underneath them.[25] There is every reason to believe that they were built by European farmers. Indeed, the Kelabit farmers of northern Borneo have a living megalithic tradition: they build large stone tombs for the burial of their powerful kinspeople.

Megaliths, power, and trade

The engineering of megaliths is one thing; the causes behind them quite another. Prehistorians have debated for years as to why they were built. Burial of the dead seems a logical answer, but this is true for only some of the sites. The standing stones and the elaborate temples had some other function. Conceivably, the isolated stones might have served as ter-ritorial markers. Perhaps the temples as well as some of the tombs were used for meetings and worship. Added to all of these unsettled questions are the speculations of astroarcheology—the view that megaliths were used for predicting events in the heavens. This last point of view in particular has gained much attention and some notoriety. Astroarcheologists have noted that the axis defined by the horseshoes of Stonehenge is aligned with the summer and winter solstices of the time it was built. Beyond this, they have gone on to postulate a megalithic mathematical system derived from surveys and measurements that themselves have been open to question.

I believe that all of these viewpoints—some of which are more persua-sive than others—leave unanswered the problem of human energy in-volved. Burials can be marked by pebbles as well as by gigantic boulders. People can meet in wattle-and-daub houses as well as stone temples. The position of the midsummer sunrise can be easily recorded by two little stones. Why, instead, did they use 4-ton slabs from 135 miles away?

To answer these questions we need to remember the technological and social conditions which probably existed at the time and the place mega-liths were built. For the most part the great stones are found near the Atlantic and Mediterranean coast, where the migrating farmers met with a foraging tradition. In all probability, population pressure would have been greatest, then, on the fringes of Europe. Conflicts between foragers and farmers, as well as between the farmers themselves, would have be-come more intense as the pressure on resources grew.

But it was likely not the straightforward process of a meeting that led to a war. It more probably involved the creation—and collapse—of ex-change. Today in the Philippine Islands, foragers live near the fields of farmers. So too do the Zaire Mbuti—and foragers in many other parts of the world. These neighboring, very different societies have designed an

---

[25]Renfrew, *Before Civilization*, pp. 129–31.

exchange adaptation: a system of trading that meets complementary needs.[26] Hunters and gatherers, more often than not, are lacking in storable foods. This is especially critical in regions where winters are long. Farmers have storable grains; they may, in fact, have more than enough. But they have less time for hunting. They need to have stores of fresh meat.

The situation is a striking example of the basis for human exchange. Foragers become "professional primitives," providing farmers with freshly killed meat. Farmers respond with large portions of storable grain. More than that, hunter-and-gatherer peoples help farmers with the harvest in fall. And farmers give foragers the products of specialized crafts.[27]

If enough grain and game are available, the system works remarkably well. It can also bring into existence political change. Success is its own advertisement—and the web becomes ever larger. Foragers, receiving their foodstuffs, have themselves gained an item in trade. It can be passed down the line to other hunter-and-gatherer groups. Strategy is nested in strategy, and the system grows ever more large. But at its center is the farming community which is directing the flow of exchange. Settled in the same location, providing the most critical food, the farmer is the node of the elaborate network of trade.

Productive European kin groups discovered in no time at all the intimate relation of trade and political rule. Food was a reward for alliance. It buffered famine in difficult times. By managing the trading of foodstuffs—and manufactured items as well—agricultural peoples increased their political power. For these groups at the heart of the system, their existence became more secure. The network was strengthened through the use of religious belief.

Exchange becomes more dependable when trading itself is a rite. The farmers directing the networks—the first chiefs of agricultural Europe—were likely aware of the power of ritual life. By presenting themselves as sacred, or at least closely in touch with the gods, they could easily regulate their systems of trade. The trek along the forested footpath, the journey of a boat down a stream—for foraging peoples these acts were infused with belief.

The strategy not only succeeded—but bore the seeds of enhancing itself. Foragers, directed by farmers, could quarry and transport the stones that, in turn, would be used for the sites of ceremonial life. The constructions became symbolic of the strength of political rule. Every stone that was brought from a distance and mounted on the land of a chief was, at

---

[26]Jean T. Peterson and Warren Peterson, "Implications of Contemporary and Prehistoric Exchange Systems," in *Sunda and Sahul: Prehistoric Studies in Southeast Asia, Melanesia and Australia*, ed. J. Allen et al. (New York: Academic Press, 1977), pp. 533–64.

[27]A similar interpretation of European agricultural society is presented by Sarunas Milisaukas in *European Prehistory* (New York: Academic Press, 1978), pp. 88–91.

first, a behavior done out of religious belief. But for forager generations that followed, they derived from a magical time. The lineage of a chief could present them as work of the gods. Labor on them became honorific—and it dramatically increased through the years. Temples, tombs, property markers, and "astronomical" henges had each begun in an ancient, miraculous time.

This fusion of monumentality, trade, technology, and religious belief survived in the European forests for thousands of years. Yet the "crisis" Clarke told of was growing; it had never been solved through exchange. The problem was worse in the regions not far from the sea. Degraded soils and larger populations were taking their toll of the land. In time, there was not any grain to be used in exchange.

The system began falling to pieces—exploding into ongoing raids. Farmers, facing critical shortages, may have attacked other farmers nearby. And, more than likely, they suffered as well from the foragers' raids. Weakened by poorer nutrition and the stresses of incessant war, European farmers fell victim to the spread of disease. Smaller populations of foragers grew sparse and in time disappeared. Diminutive Europe was a patchwork of fortress and farm.

As Sarunas Milisaukas has shown, remains of this turbulent time suggest that something like this might well have occurred in the past. Europe's first agricultural settlements bear the evidence of wide-ranging trade. Mediterranean *spondylus* shellfish, flint, pottery, and obsidian blades were traded through Europe over distances of hundreds of miles. The settlements containing these artifacts have the traces of political change. At Nitra, a Slovakian cemetery,

> the artifacts associated with burials indicate that status differences were based primarily on age and sex. *Spondylus* shells and other artifacts made of nonlocal raw material are strongly associated with old males. This may indicate that the older males were more important in the community and participated in an interregional exchange system.[28]

And, as we might expect of this period, there is very little evidence of war. Graves seldom contain any weapons, unlike the burials of subsequent times. Skeletons do not bear the scars that result from disease.

But beginning some 5,000 years ago, the sites were remarkably changed. Certain graves were elaborately furnished with the trappings of social prestige. Burials of males especially were accompanied by weapons of war. They also had the copper and obsidian of widespread exchange. Megalithic sites of this period—the temples, the henges, the tombs—were far more spectacular than those of the earlier time. Then too, the practice of warfare left its mark everywhere in the ground. Not only were there weapons in burials, but there were fortifications as well. Sites were con-

---

[28]Ibid., p. 113.

structed on hilltops, behind ditches, and inside a fortress of logs. Skeletons often bear scarrings of hand-to-hand fights. Not only that, but the bones of the burials very often have the marks of disease. The later days of agricultural Europe were a violent time.

The theory makes sense of the findings, but a great deal still remains to be done. Foodstuffs—the critical item—seldom leave any trace in the ground. We need to "diagnose" better the causes of ancient disease.[29] Yet it does seem that ancient Europeans faced problems that never were solved. Poor soils and ongoing warfare would continue through the time of the Celts. Chiefdoms still fought in the days of the legions of Rome.

---

[29]Skeletal lesions from malnutrition can be similar to those from venereal disease. This problem is directly related to the reconstruction presented here, as well as to the discussion of Hopewell in a subsequent chapter.

11 / Iron, Trade, and the African Kingdoms

The Fulani had come with their cattle, the shuffling hooves kicking sand. The herd lumbered into the lake bed that had turned into cracked mud and weeds. Songhay villagers quietly watched from the shade of their huts. There often were troubles between them, mostly because of the herds and the fields. Fulani needed the lakeshore salt lick and the watering place for their herds. But Songhay often planted their crops in the trail they used. The cattle would trample the millet. Was it deliberate? No one could be sure. The raw-boned cattle moved closer to the edge of the lake.

But now the Fulani were shouting. A large cow that was almost a skeleton had fallen over in the mud near the lake. They tugged and pulled at the animal, but it splashed back into the mud. Finally a Songhay villager helped the men get the cow to its feet. But its legs buckled under; it fell for the very last time. The Fulani left it; they watered their cattle. The Songhay villager went back to his hut. Shadows grew long in the village. The Fulani disappeared down the trail. Hide-covered bones lay behind them in the mud of the shore.[1]

Ancient patterns endure on the grasslands to the south of the African wastes. Such meetings and tensions occurred in much earlier days. Between the dunes of the sprawling Sahara and the forested lands to the south, there is a woodland-savanna that extends from the west to the east. The Fulani and Songhay of West Africa live there within an intricate system that probably evolved many hundreds of years in the past.

From Senegal on the west coast of Africa to Sudan and the Blue and the White Nile Rivers, the ribbon of grass is the homeland of farmers and herds. But, of course, it was not always like this. The ribbon has evolved through the years. In millennia past, it was likely a rainier world. As early as 10,000 years ago, clouds gathered over this land. Rains fell often; the country was dotted with lakes.

For the foragers who lived in this region, there was abundance through

Domestication south of the Sahara

---

[1]This incident in Upper Volta is described by Carole E. Devillers, "Oursi, Magnet in the Desert," *National Geographic* 157, no. 4 (April 1980), pp. 512–25.

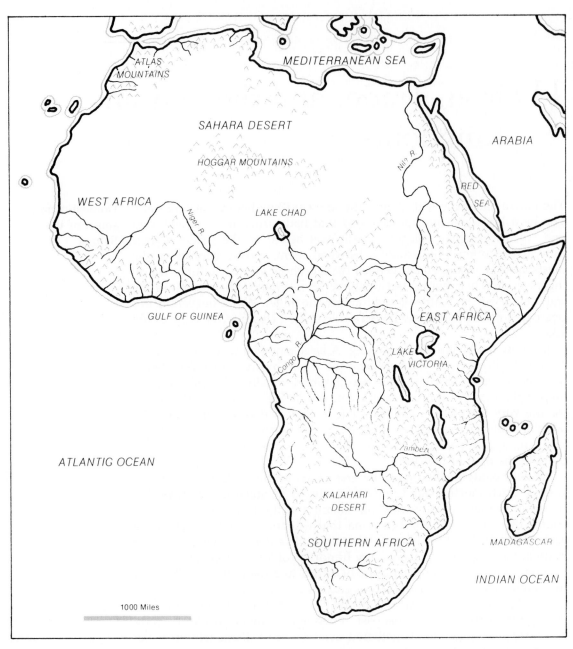

Africa.

all of the year.[2] Everywhere, there were edible grass seeds. There were herds of antelope and gazelle. But, more than anything else, there were fish in the rain-watered lakes. Lake Edward in the Congo was one of them, and some 10,000 years in the past, there were hunters and fishers who lived through the year on its shores. Bone harpoons at the site of Ishango are the remains of this earlier time. Middens were rich with bones of the fish that were speared. Hippopotami also were hunted, although no one is sure how this was done. It may be that these mud-loving creatures were taken, like the fish, by harpoons. Hunters on the banks of the Niger still kill them in exactly that way. "Sometimes over a hundred hunters," archeologist Sonia Cole once recalled, "pelt the animals with harpoons" until they become meshed in the lines.[3] The teeth of Ishango skeletons are often worn very close to the gums, perhaps from chewing and softening the lines that were used for harpoons.

Hundreds of miles to the east, in Sudan, where the White Nile flows into the Blue, fishers lived near the rivers and ponds at the site of Khartoum. Harpoon points, grooved-pebble sinkers, and the remains of innumerable fish all were found in the middens near the lakes and the streams. There also were fragments of pottery "combed" by the spines from the fish. The shards are the telltale vestige of foragers with a settled life. The watery ribbon of Africa had thousands of encampments like this. For centuries, this plentiful country met the foragers' needs.

Archeologist J. E. G. Sutton has called it "water stone age."[4] But some 5,000 years in the past, it was nearing its end. At Esh Shaheinbab in central Sudan, downstream from the site of Khartoum, there was a small heap of litter unlike those of earlier days. Pollen and bones from the trash heap revealed that the country had changed. Ponds and lakes were drying

"Combed" pottery, fishhook, and harpoon barb from Esh Shaheinbab.

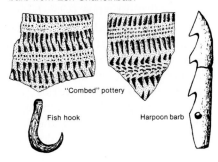

"Combed" pottery

Fish hook   Harpoon barb

---

[2]Environmental and site descriptions are taken from Sonia Cole, *The Prehistory of East Africa* (New York: Mentor, 1963), pp. 245–72.

[3]Ibid., p. 249.

[4]J. E. G. Sutton, "The Aquatic Civilization of Middle Africa," *Journal of African History* 15, no. 4 (1974), pp. 527–46.

up in the region. The ribbon was now covered with grass. There were dry-country shrubs and occasional patches of trees; yet the fishing tradition continued on the lakes that remained in Sudan. But the fishers were gathering plants—and they kept goat and sheep. It began as the subtlest of changes; we should not make it more than it was. A. J. Arkell discovered that bones from the tamed goat and sheep amounted to about 2 percent of the skeletal finds. Other bones were from duiker, monkey, lion, oryx, and ground squirrel as well. The herders still tracked wild game as they had in the past.

Evidence of more striking changes has been found in a site up the Nile. Kadero is a mound of debris about 12 miles to the north of Khartoum. Lech Krzyzaniak dug from its soils over 1,200 fragments of bones.[5] Nearly 90 percent of the fragments were from domesticated cattle, goat, and sheep. More than that, there were broken-up grindstones used for processing seeds. Impressions of seeds on the pottery revealed that sorghum and millet were there. But whether they were domestic or wild we still do not know.

So it does seem that 5,000 years ago, this region was experiencing change. And archeologists are beginning to see how this might have occurred. As I mentioned earlier on in the story, the vast country that lay to the north had been gradually turning to desert for thousands of years. Near the Nile a scrub-country network was trading tools and, conceivably, plants. Eighteen thousand years ago—before any other part of the world—domesticated grains were being grown not far from the Nile.

Much of what happened afterward has been lost to the silts of the river. Perhaps when the Nile was swollen—as it was for some 10,000 years—cattle raisers and farmers were pushed farther out to the west. That led them to discover the mesas, as the desert grew ever more dry. Plateaus in the African desert were surrounded by pasture and swamp. A network of herding societies began to appear.

Yet, not until 3,000 years later were cattle ever brought to the south. All at once we find horns, hooves, cattle, sheep, and goat bones, and cereal grains. What occurred in those earlier millennia we still do not know. But what is understood of the African landscape, and of its changes that occurred in those years, suggests an intricate—and deadly—interweaving in the natural world.

Anthropologists have often suggested that malaria played a critical role.[6] Agriculturalists, stripping the topsoil, exposed harder, deeper layers of earth. These soils, in the rainy season, would hold water for a very long

---

[5]Lech Krzyzaniak, "New Light on Early Food Production in the Central Sudan," *Journal of African History* 19, no. 2 (1978), pp. 159–72.

[6]This was suggested by Thurston Shaw in "Hunters, Gatherers, and First Farmers in West Africa", *Hunters, Gatherers, and First Farmers beyond Europe*, ed. J. V. S. Megaw (Leicester, Mass.: Leicester University Press, 1977), pp. 69–125.

time. *Anopheles* mosquitoes would hatch there and spread malaria—a fatal disease. Farmers learned from this tragic experience to avoid the wetter lands to the south. Agriculture remained in the north for many thousands of years.

But I think that this view of Africa is more accurate for a much later age. The farmers of 5,000 years ago were very different than those in more recent times. Grain growers of the Nile and Sahara likely scattered their seeds on the ground. Draught animals, the plow, and erosion belong to a much later day. The deadly mosquito was present but might not have been a serious threat. Only later, when soils were plowed, did the danger emerge.

Sleeping sickness—trypanosomias—conceivably took more of a toll.[7] The protozoan that causes this malady lived in Africa for thousands of years. It is carried in the bloodstream in antelopes and in other hooved beasts of the south. These animals are not harmed by its presence—this enables them both to survive. A protozoan that killed an antelope would be killing the world where it lived. This parasitic relation has endured for a very long time.

The protozoans are carried to humans by an insect—the tsetse fly. Buzzing in the tree-shaded woodlands, it makes darting flights out to the grass. It sucks blood—and protozoans—from antelopes, then carries them to people and food. The victims grow drowsy; they lapse into coma and die. This malady, though it always had been there, had not been an epidemic disease. Humans and hooved wild animals were very seldom in contact at all. Only in the hours of hunting was there danger of meeting up with the fly. Sleeping sickness very seldom endangered the rain-watered lands.

But with the coming of northern cattle, the pattern was remarkably changed. The flies darted from woodland to antelope, and from antelope to cattle as well. Because herders stayed close to their cattle, they encountered the fly—and disease. The sickness could well have affected both humans and herds. More than likely, generations of herders some 8,000 years in the past had been curious about the rain-watered pastures that lay to the south. Verdant and pond-dotted country was more appealing than desert plateaus. But every trek to the south had almost always brought death and disease. Schooled by this lethal experience, they had remained in their northern world. And then—5,000 years before the present—the danger was gone.

The land that was drenched by rainfall was now becoming drier.[8] Lakes

---

[7]The disease and its devastating effects are briefly discussed by Rene Dubos, *Man Adapting* (New Haven, Conn.: Yale University Press, 1965), p. 174.

[8]The chronology and geographical extent of grassland-forest development in sub-Saharan Africa is taken from D. W. Phillipson, *The Later Prehistory of Eastern and Southern Africa* (London: Heinemann, 1977), pp. 56–70.

Sorghum.

H. Armstrong Roberts

became ponds through the centuries; ponds vanished into swales of grass. The woodlands—home of the tsetse—became shrunk into islandlike groves. The country was covered by stands of wild cereal grains. Such grasses had always been present but were more abundant now than ever before. Millets, guinea rice, ensete, fonio, teff, sorghum grew in the region where once there were rain-watered lakes.

For pastoralists north in the desert, the danger of the tsetse was gone. There was food for their herds in the region, as well as food for supporting themselves. But foragers who lived in that country also required the cereals. Fishing was not as rewarding as it was in the past. Many strategies were suddenly opened; conflicts might well have occurred. Pastoralists might simply have captured the foragers' lands.

But more enduring than cultural conflict were stabilized links of exchange. Foragers, now turned cultivators, provided grain for the pastoral groups. Herders brought meat, milk, hides, and the products of trade. The grasslands south of the desert became the homeland of middleman groups. Wood and ivory from southern forests, and salt brought down from the north flowed through elaborate systems of trade. Out of this net of connections, new patterns of power emerged. Grassland towns were the home of the African kings.

Village in Guinea. Early agricultural communities in Africa probably looked much like this.

To the east of the upper Nile River, 100 miles to the north of Khartoum, wrecked buildings of stone are surrounded by rubble and sand. The ruins, which are known as Naqa, are some 2,200 years old. They date from a time when the wasteland was dotted with trees. In the wreckage was a curious megalith with a figure carved out in relief. The twisting body of a serpent wound its way up the length of the stone. It became, abruptly, the torso of a human with the head of a lion.[9]

The lion figure is often discovered in the Sudanese sites of that time. Visitors who came to the region believe it represented a god. The animal itself may have guarded the house of the king. What is striking in the form of expression is the suddenness with which it was born. For 3½ long centuries, artists in this African region simply echoed the themes of Egyptians that lived to the north. Pyramids were built in the woodlands. Local pharaohs ruled over the land. Rituals and gods had their roots in the cities downstream. And then, 2,200 years ago, was an explosion of Sudanese art. Lion symbols–never common in Egypt—were now carved into towers and walls. There were elephants and serpent motifs. Hieroglyphics were gone.

Archeology and the African kingdoms

---

[9]Naqa art is discussed and illustrated in Roland Oliver and Brian M. Fagan, *Africa in the Iron Age* (London: Cambridge University Press, 1975), pp. 36–38.

The ruins at Naqa.

Art is often a sensitive symptom of transformations in our cultural lives. Politics and trade were evolving in the world of Sudan. What once had been a southerly outpost of the god-kings that ruled on the Nile was now independent—creating its own style of life. Perhaps the distinctive emergence of the kingdom known as Kush can be traced to political change that occurred down the Nile. Egypt was ruled by the Ptolemies, who, in fact, were not Egyptian at all. They had accompanied Alexander of Macedon as he invaded the towns on the Nile. In a flash of military authority, they had come to the throne. Egypt was weakened by warfare and was now clumsily governed for years. Its control of the Sudanese people was dwindling away.[10]

But there may be much more to this story than the failures of parvenu kings. In the ruins of the Sudanese settlements, there are odd-looking piles of debris. They are slag—the impurities produced by the smelting of iron. That mineral— and a lattice of commerce—were both appearing in the kingdom of Kush. Iron would play a critical role in political life. Fashioned into swords, hoe blades, and ornaments for widespread exchange, it figured very strongly in the power of the African kings. It was iron as much as the Ptolemies that made possible the rise of Sudan. And these changes were echoed all over the African world.

It is mostly within this century—especially within the last 20 years—that archeologists have worked in the ruins from Senegal to Sudan. Before that, the prehistory of Africa meant Egyptians that ruled on the Nile. The chain of remarkable kingdoms that had emerged to the south of the desert had remained unexplored—the old settlements were covered by sand. Often it was stated by scholars that the Africans never had changed. They were simple societies that somehow were frozen in time. Of course, the white settlers in Africa encountered curious sights in the land. There were great walled ruins in Rhodesia, in Ghana, and the Ethiopian plains that seemed to be relics from kingdoms of earlier times. But like Avebury and Stonehenge, migrations soon explained them away. Eliot Smith's ubiquitous tourists had made a pass through this country as well. Kingdoms popped up as the "Sun Children" slipped out of sight.

So prejudice mingled with fantasy has obscured much of the African past. But today we have a far clearer view of this part of the planet. Even so, there are difficult questions. What caused agricultural villages in the grasslands below the Sahara to evolve into kingdoms with wide-reaching systems of trade? What caused the collapse of these kingdoms? Was it raiding or problems with trade? Or were the kingdoms at dangerous odds with the natural world? More technically, what about iron? Was it local or gained through exchange? How was it related to the rise of the African kings?

---

[10]The interpretation of the emergence of Kush resulting from ineffective government in Egypt is presented by Basil Davidson, *Africa in History: Themes and Outlines* (London: Weidenfeld and Nicolson, 1968), pp. 30–33. Though not always agreeing with its arguments, I found this a valuable and well-written book.

**East Africa:
Kush and
Axum**

When the ribbon of lakes dried and vanished from the south of the spreading Sahara, embryonic political power emerged. Herders came down to the region, as the threat of disease was now gone. Agricultural hamlets were linked to the desert in trade. Forest peoples to the south of the grasslands were connected to the net of exchange. The elaborate matrix extended for hundreds of miles.

For the villagers along the savanna, this was strategy for a more stabilized life. Drought is no stranger to grasslands, and famines can occur there as well. Through the intricate web of connections, existence could become more secure. This meant, as in many other regions, that power was evolving as well. Kin groups with dependable contacts could punish, assist, and reward. Their control over village society was growing through time.

It was likely—and almost inevitable—that the chiefs in this region of grass would seek out every possible item for use in exchange. Iron, especially, was valuable—and quickly spread through the middleman land. At one time it was strongly suspected that the ore was brought in from the steppe. Warriors from the Iraqi highlands—Assyria, as it was called in the past—had carried weapons of iron as they raided the towns on the Nile. Out of this bloody experience, the new metal had spread to Sudan. It was traded to the west, through the grasslands, as far as the sea.

But there is at least as much reason for thinking that the ore was discovered and used generations before the Assyrians and their African raid.[11] There were surface deposits of iron from Mauritania east to Sudan. Deep mineshafts have never been needed to recover the ore. Patches of trees on the grasslands were adapted to months of no rain. Such dry-loving wood, when kindled, is a fuel of remarkable heat. The savanna, in a way, was adapted to the smelting of ore. Furnaces may have had their beginnings heating pottery or as ovens for bread. The technology was readily adapted to metals as well.

Slag heaps along the savanna are the relics of technical change, which was appearing on the grass near the desert almost overnight. It may be that the discovery was happening in many villages at about the same time. Chiefs in this marginal region saw iron as an item for trade that could yield them considerable power in the webs of exchange. It was closer than the iron in Asia; a supply of it was always on hand. And its quality was probably the best there was at that time. Heated in contact with charcoal, it was actually a crude form of steel. It was fashioned into durable swords, axes, adzes, and hoes. This and control of the quarries meant a significant advantage in trade. High prices were probably paid for the weapons and tools.

---

[11]The "Assyrian" theory of iron is presented by Davidson, *Africa in History*, p. 31. An argument for African origins is found in Nikolaas J. van der Merwe, "The Advent of Iron in Africa," in *the Coming of the Age of Iron*, ed. Theodore A. Wertime and James D. Muhly (New Haven, Conn.: Yale University Press, 1980), pp. 463–506. The latter article describes smelting extensively but it does not have a single illustration!

The ruins of Meroe.

Courtesy of the Oriental Institute, University of Chicago

The repercussions of metal and trading were experienced first in Sudan. Temples grew up on the grasslands, near the joining of the Blue and the White Niles. Kush—the first of the kingdoms—at about 200 BC controled systems of trade that stretched out to the cities of Rome.[12] Gold, ivory, skins, feathers, and slaves captured from lands to the south were sent north to the Mediterranean Sea. And iron moved out on the caravans—tools and weapons for Romans and Greeks. Smoke from the furnaces rose over grass-covered hills.

What is left of the capital city tells us something of this bustling time. At Meroe, to the east of the Nile, there were pyramids and temples of sandstone. Hills of iron slag were on the south and west sides of the town. Very likely, the elaborate temples were the homes of the ruling elite. Farmers, and perhaps ironworkers, lived in houses of wattle-and-daub. Beer pots and fragments of grindstones were scattered through much of the settlement. The grassland farmers were ruled by a tiny elite.

The Roman writer Diodorus Siculus witnessed Kush at the height of its power. He discovered a mixing of rule and religious belief:

> As to the customs of the Ethiopians [a loosely applied word in those days] not a few of them are thought to differ greatly from the rest of mankind, this being especially true of those which concern the selection of their kings. The priests first choose out the noblest men, and which-

---

[12]Kush is described by Phillipson as "Meroe," *Later Prehistory*, pp. 86–91; and by Oliver and Fagan, *Africa*, pp. 33–42.

ever from this group the god may select, as he is borne about in a procession in accordance with their practice, him the multitude take for their king, and straightway it both worships and honours him like a god, believing that the sovereignty has been entrusted to him by the divine providence. And the king who has been thus chosen both follows a regimen which has been fixed in accordance with the laws, and performs all his other deeds in accordance with the ancestral customs. . . . They also say that it is customary for the comrades of the kings to die with them of their own accord. . . . And it is for this reason that a conspiracy against the king is not easily raised among the Ethiopians, all his friends being equally concerned both for his safety and their own.[13]

Diodorus's intriquing description suggests a ruler who was thought of as god—and yet came to the throne by charisma and public acclaim. There is little doubt that when this procession made its way through the houses of thatch, the most capable claimant was likely perceived as divine. Through this strategy, a ruling kin group could minimize internal conflict and, hopefully, place the most competent heir on the throne.

Even so, 300 years later, something began to go wrong. By AD 200 the pyramids were constructed much smaller in size. Workmanship, too, was now poorer—and stone carvings were less often done. Although the kingdom had 22 rulers before the very last of its days, only about half of their names have survived to our time. This is because there was much less writing that chronicled the lives of their kings. For some reason, scribes and specialists were disappearing in the kingdom of Kush. And the graves of that time tell a story of vanishing trade. The 22 royal burials are not like those of earlier days. Artifacts from the Mediterranean have disappeared from the tombs of elites. Distant connections were lost in the passing of time.

Warriors southeast of the kingdom were watching as its power declined. Then they plundered what was left of its towns in its final days. They were led by a king named Ezana who ruled over the towns of Axum. A new center of power was growing in the Ethiopian plains.

A plateau veined by rivers sloped down toward grass-covered flats.[14] Cedars and palm trees clustered near the springs and the streams. To the east, the Red Sea waters were a connection with the rest of the world. Here, for many generations, chiefs of agricultural villages were building their power by slowly increasing their trade. All along, their closest competitor had been the neighboring kingdom of Kush. But after Ezana, there was only the rule of Axum.

---

[13]Oliver and Fagan, *Africa*, p. 39.

[14]The sketch of the Axum environment and information about trading connections is derived from Karl W. Butzer, "Rise and Fall of Axum, Ethiopia: A Geo-Archeological Interpretation," *American Antiquity* 46, no. 3 (July 1981), pp. 471–95.

In fact, shortly after his victory, the kingdom reached the height of its power. It was linked with interior trade and sea-going exchange. Ivory and the horns of rhinocerous were carried on trails to Axum. Hides were exported—and there also was traffic in slaves. Thousands of exchange transactions occurred daily in the port of Adulis—a Red Sea town that was a center of maritime trade. The town was a gateway community— connected with the oceans and the plains. Interior traders met merchants that came from the sea. Prehistorian Y. M. Kobishchanov has found in the accounts of Axum the description of a web that extended for thousands of miles.[15] It stretched out to the Black Sea communities, India, China, and Spain. It brought cloth and dyed cloaks out of Egypt and flint glass manufactured in Thebes. It brought olive oil from the Mediterranean, along with brass, copper, pots, silver, and gold. It linked the African peoples with the east and the power of Rome.

Relics of its temples and monuments are reflections of that earlier time.[16] In the town of Axum—the capital—over 100 great stones had been raised. Many, now fallen, were over 100 feet tall. They had been carved to resemble large buildings—doors and windows chiseled in relief. Stone palaces were likely the homes of the local elite. More than that, in its rubble were traces of agricultural and industrial wealth. Remains of water storage basins and dams were discovered in the African settlement. Upland water was channeled and stored for the grain in the fields. Bronze and copper were worked in the community and, very likely, local iron as well. Wood from the dry-loving forests provided the fuel.

Axum was still a powerful kingdom when Gothic warriors were ransacking Rome. But after about 650 AD, it was never the same. Like Kush many centuries earlier, its old trading connections were gone. Herders on its borders were raiding its farmers and fields. One hundred and fifty years later, it was crumbled to sand and debris. A few standing stones in the rubble looked out over sun-heated dunes. Axumite rulers had vanished from the African plains.

Axum had found its way into legends carried through the African grass. Yet even as its buildings were crumbling and its memories were being richened by myth, other kingdoms were growing in grasslands that lay to the west. By that time, about 1,000 years ago, when the Normans crossed the channel from France, there were rulers on the Niger believed to have powers of gods.[17]

The West African grassland kingdoms: Ghana, Mali, and Songhay

[15]Y. M. Kobishchanov, *Axum*, trans. and ed. L. T. Kapitanoff and J. W. Michels (University Park: Pennsylvania State University Press, 1979), p. 175.

[16]Axumite archeological descriptions are taken from Phillipson, *Later Prehistory* pp. 91–98; and Oliver and Fagan, *Africa*, pp. 42–48.

[17]For the descriptions of Ghana, Mali, and Songhay, I relied upon Davidson, *Africa in History*, pp. 74–91; and Oliver and Fagan, *Africa*, pp. 157–79.

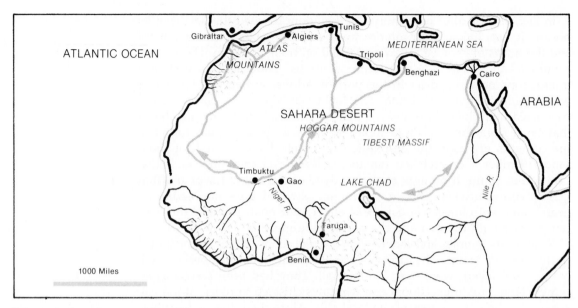

Saharan trade routes.

For generations the kingdom of Ghana flourished in the scrub-country plains between northerly desert and forests that lay to the south. Its towns—Awdaghast, Kumbi, and Timbuktu to the east—were alive with the dust and the color of regional trade. Swords were brought in from Arabia and from Southern Europe as well. There were horses from Egypt and slaves captured far to the south. Salt was carried down from the desert, and there was ivory from nearby forests. But most important of all were its caches of iron and gold.

The deposits were close to the surface; the minerals were traded to much of the world. Furnaces in Atwetwebooso were smelting the African ore before the time of Ezana and the final destruction of Kush. Its gold reached Europe and Asia, and it rewarded the court of the king. The ruler of Ghana controlled a great lattice of trade.

He was a *mansa*, a godlike figure, who ruled over the territorial towns. Inside his *Kafu*, or territory, perhaps 10,000 citizens lived. The Andalusian scholar al-Bakri came to Ghana in 1067. He scribbled in his journal as he witnessed the pomp of its king:

> On his head he wears gold-embroidered caps covered with turbans of finest cotton. He gives audience to the people for the redressing of grievances in a hut, around which are placed 10 horses bedecked with gold caparisons. Behind him stand 10 slaves carrying shields and swords mounted with gold. On his right are the sons of his vassal kings, their heads plaited with gold and wearing costly garments. On

the ground around him are seated his ministers, while the governor of the city sits before him. On guard at the door are dogs of fine pedigree, wearing collars adorned with gold and silver knobs, which rarely leave his presence. The royal audience is announced by the beating of a drum. . . . When the people have gathered, his fellow pagans draw near upon their knees, sprinkling dust upon their heads as a sign of respect, while the Muslims clap their hands as their form of greeting. Their religion is paganism and the cult of idols. When the king dies, they construct a large hut of wood over the place of burial. His body is brought on a simple bier and placed in the hut. With it they put his eating and drinking vessels, a supply of food and drink, and those who used to serve him with these things, and then the entrance is secured. They cover the hut with mats and cloth, and all the assembled people pile earth over it until it resembles a considerable hill. Then they dig a ditch around it, allowing only one means of access to the heap. They sacrifice victims to their dead, and offer them fermented drinks.[18]

But the documents of scholars and travelers tell us too that this came to an end. Berber peoples from the western Sahara invaded north of the Niger. By 1204, the old kingdom of Ghana was gone. Yet the collapse of an intricate system, here as in other parts of the world, was a process that nourished the growth of new centers of rule. A kin group known as Keita, through warfare and bargains of trade, created the kingdom of Mali where Ghana had been.

One *Kafu* after another was brought into its powerful realm. Unlike the old rulers of Ghana, it managed a riverine trade. The entire bend of the Niger, and the streams that flowed from it as well, became pathways in Mali for flourishing regional trade. Yet there also were distant connections. Mali imported wool, leather, wax, horses, and fruit from North Africa. Slaves, elephant ivory, and skins were brought in from Sudan. To almost all of these clients went gold from Bombuk and Bure. Seldom before in prehistory was this metal so abundant in trade.[19] A Mali ruler, when visiting Cairo, lavished so much gold on the way that its value declined in the webs of Egyptian exchange.

Prehistorians often cite with approval the special quality of life at that time. "A long period of effective government," Brian Fagan and Roland Oliver write, established "law and order" throughout every part of the land.[20] A caravan traveling through Mali could journey for 800 miles without any danger of plunder. "A golden age," Basil Davidson called it, of prosperity and also of peace.[21] But this kingdom may have been very different from what it has seemed.

---

[18]Oliver and Fagan, *Africa,* p. 164.

[19]Gold sources and possible trade routes are discussed by Merrick Posnansky, "Aspects of Early West African Trade," *World Archeology,* 1973, pp. 149–62.

[20]Oliver and Fagan, *Africa,* p. 175.

[21]Davidson, *Africa in History,* p. 85.

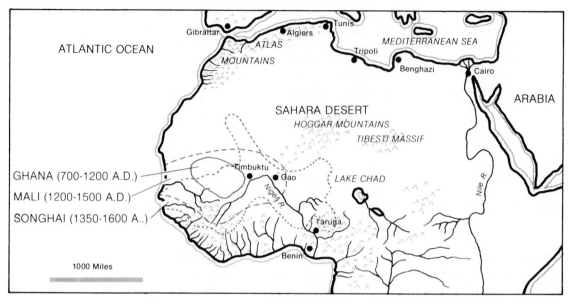

The African kingdoms.

We know that, about 1260, Mali was conquering neighboring lands. A little over a century later, it fell victim itself to Songhay. Mali ruled over captives of war for some 100 years. In one century, it is very unlikely that the subjects accepted such rule. They were peoples with different traditions, their own languages, customs, beliefs. Law and order was the shallow veneer of an unstable world. Seen this way, the acts of its rulers can more easily be understood. Captured peoples were forcibly settled in villages near the banks of the Niger. This stream was a major pathway for the flow of information and trade. If rebellions occurred, they could quickly be seen and subdued. To make insurrection unlikely, captive women were kept near the throne. Forced nudity made them conspicuous; it was difficult for them to flee. They amounted to a kind of insurance against rebellions that imperiled the crown. Captive peoples who threatened the ruler would also have endangered their kin. This strategy of hostage protection would be used by the Inca as well. It can quiet a volatile kingdom—at least for a while.

Deceptive law and order was shattered when the Songhay rebelled in the east. Ancestors of herders and planters who carry their name to this day, they began the rebellion that ended a hundred-year rule. Fleets of canoes brought their warriors along the heart of the realm. Word of insurrection was spreading to every part of the land. The Tuareg and the Soninke seized the moment and joined the Songhay. In time, when the battles were over, the sudden kingdom was broken and gone. In the cen-

Iron staff manufactured in Mali. This metal, in addition to gold, was a major item of African trade.

turies that followed these troubles, the Songhay had control of the realm. But it remained a disorganized kingdom, a shadow of an earlier time. The powerful elites of the grasslands belonged to the past.

Environment, iron, and kings

"The will to rule subsided and the will not to be ruled increased."[22] For Roland Oliver and Brian M. Fagan, this explains the revolt of Songhay and trajectories followed by earlier kingdoms as well. But I doubt that elites on the grasslands lost their will to remain on the throne. Rulers enjoy their positions and the prestige and rewards they receive. For that reason, they cling to their status—and occasionally they forfeit their lives. Elites of the past are akin to the ones of our time. And true enough, rebellious peoples were a threat to the African kings. But we need to know more about why these rebellions occurred.

It is useful, perhaps, to remember that these intricate systems emerged in that long belt of grass that extends from the west to the east. This made cereal growing possible. It provided food for supporting the herds. Little wonder that villages stretched from Senegal to Sudan. More than that, the great stretch of savanna also had deposits of iron, which could be smelted and hammered for use in exchange.

But the grasslands were slowly changing, as the climate became ever more dry. The transformation was long and erratic; it lasted for a good thousand years. Dry centuries along the savanna would be followed by epochs of rain. Even so, there was a large-scale pattern: the grasslands were turning to sand. That pattern was changing the structure of African life.

There are hints that the climatic changes began at 500 BC. Napata, the old Kushite capital, was abandoned very close to that time. Shortly before its desertion, water reservoirs were built everywhere. But the strategy failed, and its people moved to the east. Yet in Meroe, the new ruling settlement, the same problem was occurring again. Collapse of the trading connections, careless architectural style, and water reservoirs all appear in the last of its days. Roman spies reported to Nero during the first century AD that conquering this kingdom was probably not worth his time.[23]

The crisis very likely contributed to the subsequent rise of Axum.[24] As Roman spies snooped about in Meroe, Ethiopia was gifted with rains. There was a long growing season; two crops could be raised in a year. The good fortune, when viewed in a lifetime, seemed something that never would end. Seven centuries passed, and the bountiful rains were

---

[22]Oliver and Fagan, *Africa*, p. 179.

[23]D. W. Phillipson, *Later Prehistory*, pp. 86–98.

[24]Karl W. Butzer, "Rise and Fall," pp. 471–95.

now gone. In those drier, more difficult decades, Axum lasted 70 years. New kingdoms—and ancient dilemmas—emerged to the west.

Here too, there was no escaping the inexorable process of drought. Beginning perhaps 1,000 years ago, when Ghana dominated the land, the rainfall had slackened; the country was becoming more dry.[25] The drought continued for centuries. It endured through the time of Songhay and it gave rise to a striking—and futile—technological change.

As Candice Goucher has recently argued, the sub-Saharan African lands presented a crisis that worsened through time. As grass became sparse in the region, new strategies of survival emerged. Extensive deposits of iron—sometimes copper and other metals as well—could be smelted in furnaces and sent out as items of trade. Not only would this process engender the emergence of local elites, it could also bring food through the intricate nets of exchange. The strategy was especially obvious in a country becoming more dry. Relic forests along the savanna furnished fuel that was just the right kind. High in alkali and silica content, it remains hot for a very long time. Forests and metals were an answer to the deepening drought.

The strategy, in each one of the kingdoms, succeeded—at least for a time. It persisted until the last of the dry-loving forests were gone. There are descriptions in travelers' records of how the African smelting was

African iron-smelting furnace. The fueling of the furnaces contributed to deforestation.

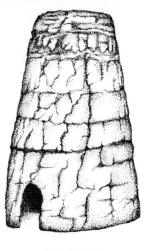

```
0        1'       2'
```

Illustration by Gail Delicio

[25]Candice L. Goucher, "Iron Is Iron 'Til It Is Rust: Trade and Ecology in the Decline of West African Iron Smelting," *Journal of African History* 22, no. 2 (1981), pp. 179–89. This article strongly influenced my interpretation of the African kingdoms.

done; there are furnaces and slag left behind on the grasslands today. From these, Goucher calculated that 26 mounds of slag at one site resulted from the burning of 300,000 large trees! We should also remember that these dry-loving species often grew slowly. Old forests were being destroyed and were never replaced.

The catastrophe had repercussions on every aspect of African life. Disappearance of the dry-loving forests brought erosion to much of the land. The soils were dust, and the crop yield continued to fall. Karl Butzer has excavated deposits that date from the end of Axum. He has found evidence of widespread erosion, of soils spilling down from the hills. In these upland Ethiopian regions are tiny patches of dry-loving trees. They likely remain from the forests that were cleared in the past. The loss of the African forests meant decline of metal working as well; and the loss of the metals disturbed the old balance of trade. Rulers, in desperation, conducted wars with neighboring peoples. They needed more forests and iron, more food, and more slaves. Captive groups were coerced into labor in an attempt to bring food from the soil. But climate and iron had taken their toll of the land. Little wonder that peace was illusory, that kingdoms were destroyed overnight, or that rulers could never sustain their industrial age.

12 / Highland Traders and the Passage to Indus

People were moving with sheep, goats, and cattle to settle in new parts of the world. There were mud houses and smoke from ovens where once there were hunters. On the low, rounded hills of northern Iraq, and in the swampy lowlands near the Persian Gulf, there were small nests of houses on the edges of rivers and streams. Migrating families settled along the Indus—a turbulent river in Pakistan—and they cleared away the forests near the Yellow River in China. In time, the Pacific islands, still untouched by the human experience, were discovered by boatloads of farmers who had set out to sea.

To tell the story of agricultural villages as they developed and spread throughout Asia is also to tell of the emergence of urban communities. Cities, of course, never sprang up like toadstools, but were an outgrowth of the village itself; they were a product of the material conditions of late agricultural society. In a real sense, then, we are involved with much more than the changes in the Asiatic villages. We are considering the forces that in time produced civilization.

Because the later villages and the earliest cities were often found in the same parts of the world, the archeology was often done with little sense of proportion. Archeologists of earlier years were so concerned with digging up ancient cities that they neglected the smaller village sites. In the *Tigris-Euphrates region of Southwest Asia*—usually known as *Mesopotamia*—that imbalance is felt by archeologists even today. Said Robert McC. Adams,

> It is. . .unfortunate that the traditional sources on the growth of early Mesopotamian civilization are urban-centered and consequently ill-adapted to formulating a more balanced regional view. . . . The prevailing emphasis has been not on the living arrangements of the mass of the population but on public buildings and their associated archives and works of art.[1]

---

[1]Robert McC. Adams, "Patterns of Urbanization in Early Southern Mesopotamia," in *Man, Settlement, and Urbanism*, ed. Peter J. Ucko, Ruth Tringham, and G. W. Dimbleby (London: Ducksworth, 1972), p. 736.

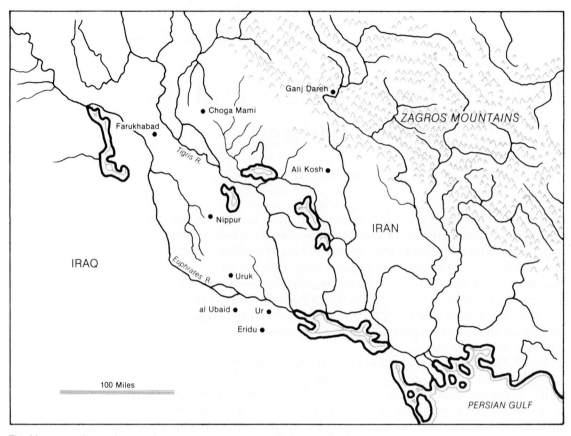

The Mesopotamian region.

It is true enough that much was neglected, but a great deal was created as well. There is considerable value in seeing archeologists in the light of their times.

Leonard Woolley and the emergence of method

For a taste of archeology's flavor in the earlier part of this century, there is no better example to be found than Sir Charles Leonard Woolley.[2] To begin with, he was never called Charles; he did not like the name. Perhaps it had a certain formality that he did not find pleasing. Formality, in fact, became an issue in much earlier archeological thought. But all of this is getting a little bit ahead of the story.

---

[2]The biographical sketch of Leonard Woolley is taken from *Current Biography*, 1954, pp. 662–64.

The proper beginning is Oxford University, when this century had scarcely begun, and when a nervous Leonard Woolley was summoned before the warden of the college. Asked abruptly if he had made up his mind about what he was going to do with his life, Woolley respectfully answered that he was thinking of becoming a schoolmaster. The warden became sarcastic: "Oh yes, a schoolmaster, really. Well, Mr. Woolley, I have decided that you shall be an archeologist." As Woolley remembered it later, he had only a fuzzy idea of what archeology was. He knew that it had some connection with dead people and museums. He felt disappointed. He had always preferred to spend time out-of-doors.

In this bewilderment he could never have realized that his entire life was to be spent outdoors; that he would help establish the image of the archeologist in the popular mind. His life became almost a scenario from some of the movies that were made at that time. He excavated a Roman ruin in the chilly Northumberland country and then joined an expedition that was digging in the lower Nile valley. There he grew impatient with himself because he was unable to read hieroglyphics. He threw his energy into learning as many languages as he possibly could. He became competent in Latin, Greek, French, Italian, German, and Arabic—and all of this while commanding a new expedition to Turkey. There he dug beside Lawrence of Arabia, then went to Sinai, and then went to war. He was captured by the Turks in 1916 and was in and out of prisons across the Levant. He was freed, went home, was decorated, and—in a year's time—was digging again. He dug in Turkey, Iraq, and Syria; he found time to go back to Egypt. And then—the decisive move of his life—he went to Mesopotamia.

Ur was a city described in the Bible—and Woolley discoverd its actual location. Its houses and temples were slowly dug out of the sand. When the royal tombs of the city were opened they became a journalistic sensation. The America of the 1920s was dazzled by lapis and gold. It was probably out of digs such as these that the romance of archeology was born: khakis, pith helmet, British accent, and mysterious tombs.

What was this era's greatest accomplishment? Something, I think, that cannot be understated: a greater attention to method in archeological research. A short generation before Woolleys time, archeology was–often literally—a picnic. For fashionable lords and ladies it was little more than a sport. Wrote an upper-class Briton in the 1850s,

> We were rowed several miles down the river which is here picturesque and . . . tortuous to the place of landing. A plentiful supply of provisions had been procured for picnicing on the hill, and we remained by the barrow all day, watching and directing the operations. Unfortunately it was one of those large barrows which do not repay the labor of cutting through them. . . . The mound was 20 feet high . . . and the workmen had imprudently cut the walls of the trench perpendicular;

Field Museum of Natural History

Excavation of Inghara Ziggurat, Iraq, at the time of Leonard Wooley's research. Increasing emphasis on method was making possible the comparison of sites. This would ultimately lead to classification and the emergence of theory.

the consequence of which was that in the afternoon of the fourth day the upper part of one side fell in, and one of the laborers escaped narrowly with his life.[3]

Destructive antics such as these—a kind of aristocratic slapstick—were all too often the only approach brought to the past. But at about the time that Leonard Woolley as being called into the warden's office, a very different archeological book had just come off the press. The author was Flinders Petrie, who had directed excavations in Egypt. But the book was not a chatty discussion of romps in the desert. *Method and Aims in Archeology* was a quiet title for an angry book. Here was writing that would influence Wooley and a whole generation. Petrie snorted:

To attempt serious work in pretty suits, shiny leggings or starched collars, would be like mountaineering in evening dress. . . . The man who cannot enjoy his work without regard to appearance, who will not strip down and go into the water, or slither on slimy mud through un-

[3]Glyn Daniel, *The Origins and Growth of Archeology* (New York: Penguin Books, 1967), p. 223.

Center for American Archeology, Northwestern University

Removing muck from an Illinois site. "To attempt serious work in pretty suits . . . would be like mountaineering in evening dress. . . It may be amusing, but it is not business. And whatever is not businesslike in archeology is a waste of the scanty material which should be left for those who know how to use it."

known passages, had better not profess to excavate. . . . To suppose that work can be controlled from a distant hotel, where the master lives in state and luxury completely out of touch with his men, is a fallacy, like playing at farming or at stockbroking: it may be amusing, but it is not business. And whatever is not businesslike in archeology is a waste of the scanty material which should be left for those who know how to use it.[4]

---

[4]Ibid., pp. 232–36.

And he was right. The fiery words—they were first written in 1904—are no more out of date in the present than they were at that time. We still have the afternoon dilettantes who destroy archeological sites and—as a consequence—diminish the knowledge that we have of the past. One hopes that, if there is more public involvement in professionally led excavations, this destruction of our cultural resources might come to an end.

With Woolley, Petrie and many others, archeology became systematic. There was a set of procedures for digging archeological sites. Beyond that, it now was required that the procedures and findings be recorded. Other scientists could draw their own conclusions from what was done. This in itself helped to make archeology into a communicating body of scientists. That led to classification of the findings—and emergence of theory. In a sense, then, what these workers had done was to view digging as a form of observation, affecting the meaning (or the meaninglessness!) of the things we observe.

The early settlement of Mesopotamia

The turn-of-the-century archeologists overlooked much that we think is important. They sought out temples, not farming villages; works of art, not seeds and goat bones. This means that archeologists working in the area today need to know much more about what the environment was like in the past. Pioneers inevitably suffer from the values of their own descendants. Future archeologists will likely find fault with today's perspectives. Fortunately, we have a least some understanding of the Mesopotamian countryside and of how the human community changed in that part of the world.

The land that was Mesopotamia—literally the "land between the rivers"—was a gently rising plain between the Tigris and the Euphrates.[5] Today it is desert country, but some 8,000 years ago it was a nearly uninhabited region of grassland and marsh. In the north, nearer the source of the rivers, were the grassly uplands—the flanks of the Taurus. Here, as in much of this region, rainfall was scanty; surface water was scarce. Settlements were close by the rivers or at the edges of wadis. But below the present-day area of Baghdad there were low-lying marshlands, mud flats, and streams; it was a humid region flooded every year with silt from the rivers. And those two rivers, so close to one another, were more different than we might first expect. They were by no means equally suitable for colonization. The Tigris River, the shorter of the two, has higher banks and a swifter current. Its flooding is often more violent than that of its neighbor. The high banks in particular pose a problem for digging an irrigation system: canals must be deeper and large enough to channel

---

[5]M. E. L. Mellowan, *Early Civilization in Mesopotamia* (London Thames & Hudson). See also Robert McC. Adams and Hans J. Nissen, *The Uruk Countryside: The Natural Setting of Urban Society* (Chicago: University of Chicago Press, 1972), pp. 1–5.

the flood. Probably for all of these reasons, early settlers largely avoided the Tigris. Villages grew on the banks of the calmer Euphrates. Canals were more easily dug there; it was less likely that a flood would destroy them. It was safer for boats, which meant that it was suited for trade.

Commerce, in fact, became a critical feature of the early settlements in Mesopotamia. The region has often been described in terms of what was *not* there. There was not, for example, much wood; minerals and metals were virtually absent. To acquire them, Mesopotamians resorted to networks of trade. As we will see a little later in the story, these strategies were a significant factor in the emergence of complex society between the two rivers.

At the moment there is little or no evidence of a hunting-and-gathering life in this region.[6] The most ancient sites are of farmers and herders. Of course, this might well be the result of the Tigris-Euphrates environment itself. In Mesopotamia the dunes are often so deep that entire cities were buried. It is little wonder that the campsites of foragers have seldom been found. And, for that matter, there is very little certainty about the homeland of the earliest settlers. Where did they come from—and why? We still do not know.

But archeologists have discovered that the oldest villages appeared in the north—in the grassy hills that in a much later age would be known as Assyria. It was a countryside with winter rainfall and oppressive heat in the summer. At some 8,000 years before the present came its earliest settlers. Mounds of earth from their collapsed clay houses dot the hills that are nearly a desert. Archeologist Diana Kirkbride discovered 87 sites in the region. Some 40 of these were left behind by the earliest migrants.

One of the sites—called Umm Dabaghiyah—was excavated to its deepest layers.[7] Small, mud-plastered houses had been built on the vacant grasslands. The rooms were small—around four feet by six feet—with fireplaces connected to ovens on the outside of the wall. The tiny houses had no doors or windows and shared common walls as in Catal Huyuk. Using toe-holes in the plaster, the residents came and went by the rooftops.

On the walls of some of these dwellings were mural paintings of wild asses. The animals were shown running toward netting that was staked on the ground. Buried in the soil on the outside of the houses were butchered bones of wild ass and gazelle. They amounted to nearly 90 percent of the bones that were found. Close by, there were rows of tiny rooms—too small for anyone to have lived in—but the right size for storing large numbers of animal skins. Like the Star Carr of an earlier time, Umm

---

[6]Archeologist Joan Oates has made note of the possible exceptions to this in the "apparently non-agricultural villages of the upper Euphrates" in "Prehistoric Settlement Patterns in Mesopotamia," Ucko, et al., *Man*, p. 299.

[7]Seton Lloyd, *The Archeology of Mesopotamia: From the Old Stone Age to the Persian Conquest* (London: Thames & Hudson, 1978) pp. 70–73.

Dabaghiyah was a processing center. The animal skins were probably exported to other communities.

The architecture of Umm Dabaghiyah hints strongly of conflict as well. Entrances built in the rooftops meant that the village was a fortress of sorts. Possibly, in this marginal country, there was the danger of not enough food. The strategy of specialized exports made life in the hills more secure. But goods that were being exported had to be protected from raids. It is possible that chiefs were managing community defense and the flow of exchange. Yet, that system is not inevitable. Villagers at Umm Dabaghiyah may have experienced a ritual life. This is possibly the reason for the paintings that were found on the walls. Social responsibilities could have been dramatized through dancing and prayer. There may not have been pressure for centralized political rule.[8]

At the same time that trading villages were appearing in Mesopotamia, farming communities were moving deeper into the northern uplands. The village of Hassuna, some 8,000 years ago, was a cluster of small, clay houses, most of them with grain-storage areas and courtyards for animals. Flint-toothed sickles for harvesting the crop and baked-clay trays for winnowing grain were discovered along with spear heads and arrow heads for hunting. In Hassuna, as in many other villages, Asian farmers still stalked wild game. Hunting had by no means disappeared with the coming of crops.

For anthropologist Michael Harner, mixed technologies of hunting and farming are indirect evidence of the pressures on available resources.[9] He has reasoned that hunting persisted in those early agricultural villages where farming and herding alone did not provide enough food. In this northerly grassland country, water was a critical resource. It was much more limited there than in the marshy regions to the south. Families could settle close by the rivers, near small streams, by spring-fed wadis, or in a dry-land area if the water was close to the surface. In the dry places life would have been possible if the soil had a loose enough structure to bring deeper water to the surface by capillary action. Limited to these special areas, the population grew and budded off to the south. Farmers were coming closer to the marshes of southern Mesopotamia.

Only a short 500 years after cultivators first settled in the north, villages emerged along the southernmost margins of the grasslands. Here the hills disappeared into flatlands. Dry grassland became humid marshes. And the settlements grew on the edge of the uninhabited lowlands. One

---

[8]The effectiveness of ritual behavior in the "management" of community life is briefly discussed in relation to North American complex societies by Michael E. Whalen, "Cultural-Ecological Aspects of the Pithouse-to-Pueblo Transition in a Portion of the Southwest," *American Antiquity* 46, no. 1 (1981), pp. 75–92. This argument will be revisited at a later point in the story.

[9]Michael J. Harner, "Population Pressure and the Social Evolution of Agriculturalists," *Southwestern Journal of Anthropology* 26 (1970), pp. 67–86.

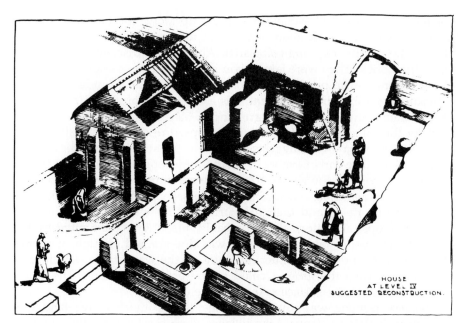

Reconstruction of a Mesopotamian village dwelling.

HOUSE
AT LEVEL IV
SUGGESTED RECONSTRUCTION.

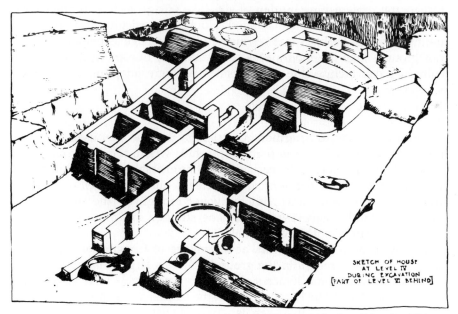

SKETCH OF HOUSE
AT LEVEL IV
DURING EXCAVATION
[PART OF LEVEL VI BEHIND]

Courtesy of the Oriental Institute, University of Chicago

of these villages—Tell-es-Sawwan—grew up along the banks of the Tigris.[10] There was much about it that was different than the villages that lay to the north. Iraqi archeologist B. Abu-al-Soof discovered houses of sun-dried brick. They were larger than in earlier villages—sometimes they had 14 rooms—with private grain-storage areas and burials under the floors. Surounding the entire settlement was a brick wall protected by a ditch. Fortifications and conflict were growing in Mesopotamia.

Like the villages in Anatolia and Europe, the structure of the settlement at Tell-es-Sawwan suggests changes in the structure of later agricultural society. The early farmers in northern Mesopotamia were not free to settle anywhere on the grasslands; they were limited—especially in summer—by the available water. They had to search out lakes, ponds, and wadis, or the rivers and their tributaries to find water enough for their animals, crops, and themselves. Probably, too, they were limited by the soil and the water table. If the soil was fine-grained enough, it would hold the moisture of the wintertime rains. If the water table was close to the surface, then the ground could be loosened with a hoe. The water would diffuse to the surface and water the crops.

Because farming was confined to small areas, much of the land was probably depleted. Many of the villages were too far from the rivers to receive the replenishing burden of silt. Like village society in other parts of the world, Mesopotamia changed. Houses of agriculturalists now had multiple rooms. Perhaps males remained in the village as permanent warrior groups. Like the longhouses constructed in Europe in its later agricultural days, architecture—and residence—were adapting to the pressure of raids.

The marshlands and irrigation

Throughout the dry northern grasslands, the hoe was used to loosen the soil, especially in those parts of the hills where the water table was high. When the settlements reached low-lying marshlands, the old strategy was brought to that region. Clogged creeks and the edges of marshes were broken up into clods. But the water brought to the surface came more abundantly than ever before. The strategy did more than simply moisten the surface: it created canals.

Southeast of Tell-es-Sawwan, at the village of Choga Mami, traces of early irrigation were still in the ground.[11] It was larger than most earlier villages, covering some 15 acres of land. Its households were large: some of the homes had 10 to 12 rooms. From the earliest years of the settlement, Choga Mami had irrigation canals. Archeologist Joan Oates discovered ditches dug into virgin soil. Unlike many of the earlier settlements, the

---

[10]Lloyd, *Archeology of Mesopotamia.*

[11]Lloyd, *Archeology of Mesopotamia;* and Joan Oates, "Prehistoric Settlement Patterns in Mesopotamia," Ucko et al., *Man,* pp. 303–6.

village did not follow the natural bends of a stream. It was built at right angles to the current, and parallel to the ditches. It is likely, then, that the first houses and the ditches were built at about the same time. Choga Mami seems to have been built to a plan from the days of its earliest settlement. Centralized rule—or perhaps the power of ritual—was being brought into the low-lying lands. In the new region there was both technological and cultural change.

Swampy, humid lowlands were now opened to colonization. In the floodplain of southern Mesopotamia, the land was flat and the water table was high. Farmers moved into the region, drained, and settled it for 2,000 years.

Susan Lees and Daniel Bates have suggested that this spread of early irrigation systems may have contributed to the emergence of pastoral socieites.[12] *Pastoralism*, unlike agriculture, is a *form of technology that almost totally involves the herding of animals. It usually does not emphasize plant collecting or cultivation.* Pastoralists often acquire their plant foods through raids or exchange.

Since the days of the earliest seed crops, domesticated animals had been managed by farmers. It seems very likely, as Childe once suggested, that animals grazed in the harvested fields, and that plants and animals were tamed by humanity at about the same time. But as the farmers moved out of the foothills and pushed into the lowland flood plains, irrigation brought options that had never existed before.

In the rainfall-dependent regions, humans consumed most of the grain. A small number of animals grazed on the stubble in the fields. But irrigation in the riverine regions made possible more plentiful food. This meant that a large herd of animals could be taken to pasture in the spring and fed from a surplus of grain when they returned in the fall. It was a resilient—or flexible—strategy that could help every household survive. Not only was there grain from the harvest but also meat, milk, and hides. Any of these resources could also be used in exchange. More than that, the traveling herders created links with other parts of the world. They connected sedentary farmers with clients in a network of trade. This made possible marriage alliances that, in turn, could make life more secure. But the intricate system, at times, had its dangers as well.

Suppose it had been a dry winter and there was less melt from the mountains in spring. Rivers were lower; less water was in the canals. Perhaps enough grain would be harvested to meet the needs of the farmers alone. There would be very little left over for the groups with their herds. Requiring grain for the winter, pastoralists would be forced into raids. More than likely, such crises occurred many times in the past. This strategy—sometimes explosive—evolved in several parts of the world. In time,

---

[12]Susan H. Lees and Daniel G. Bates, "The Origins of Specialized Nomadic Pastoralism: A Systemic Model," *American Antiquity*, April 1974.

as we will see a bit later, it may have played a significant role in the evolution of urbanized states near the rivers of Asia.

Southern Mesopotamia: Systems of exchange

But those days were still in the future. For the moment, Mesopotamia was still a land of mud-brick villages growing up on the marshy flats of the southern floodplain. One of those villages, called Al Ubaid, was dug by Leonard Woolley himself.[13] It was a small mound littered with broken pottery, much of it poorly fired. For the most part the scattered fragments had simple rectilinear and curvilinear designs, but a small number were decorated with patterns resembling plants and trees. And it was not only the pottery that suggested how the Al Ubaid region once looked. There were also the remains of the village's earliest homes. The dwellings had been built out of reeds woven together to make walls and a roof. In recent times, the marsh dwellers of Iraq have lived in such homes. Eventually the reed houses were replaced by more traditional mud-brick dwellings. As the generations passed, the marshlands were filling with people.

To the south of the Al Ubaid village was the settlement of Eridu, another farming community built along the edge of the marsh. Later Sumerian writings portrayed it as a "city" on the "shore of the sea" but this was more of a literary flourish than geographical fact. The location of the ruins themselves, the buried reed structures, and the illustrations on seals reveal an environment very much like Al Ubaid to the north.[14]

As archeologist Seton Lloyd has suggested, the village was probably "connected to the sea" by a network of tidal lagoons that stretched away to the south. It was here, some 6,500 years ago, after the mud-brick village was built, that Mesopotamians constructed one of their earliest temples. This temple was little more than a box; it was slightly over 9 feet on a side. With its small niche and its offering table, it looks more like a shrine. But its very compactness offers an insight into the village's religious behavior: the original number of its religious specialists was probably small. Yet over the next thousand years, the structure became a more intricate place. In time, there was a central sanctuary with an offering table and tiny rooms on the sides. It seems very likely that there was an emerging religious elite.

A short distance southwest of the shrine was the cemetery of the Eridu village. This burial area might well have contained over 1,000 graves. Bodies were placed in rectangular shafts that were lined—like the dwellings— with courses of mud-brick. Painted black and brown pottery was placed

[13]Lloyd, *Archeology of Mesopotamia.*

[14]The illustrations were done on cylinder seals, which were being made at the time of the Urban Revolution, some 1,500 years after the first settlement of Al Ubaid. There were cylinders of stone or pottery, decorated with recessed figures which, when rolled over clay, left behind a permanent impression. I will talk about these seals in more detail in a later part of the story.

The University Museum, Philadelphia

Mesopotamian Ziggurat.

in the graves. Ceramics very similar to these have been found to the east and the northwest of Eridu. It is very likely that the village was connected to a network of trade. The possibility is especially evident when we take notice of other grave furnishings. There are male and female figurines made of earthenware, and the lizard-shaped heads. The headdresses that adorned the figurines were made out of asphalt. Knives and hoes chipped out of flint had sometimes been placed in the graves, but there were also nails, sickles, and axes that were made out of clay.[15]

Of course, these systems of exchange, in order to function on a regular basis, were now demanding greater complexity in human society. It is true that trade has existed probably as long as there have been human beings. But it is also true that trade was now becoming more complex. The growing populations of sedentary villagers were often lacking in critical resources. The need for them was constant and could not be met by intermittent exchange. So there had to be specialized producers—of asphalt, flint, and raw metals—who could make these resources available on a regular basis. And not only this; it was also necessary to manage the

---

[15]These were conceivably models of the originals that had funerary functions in Mesopotamia.

exports and imports themselves. Suppose, for example, that a village had some asphalt, either locally available or traded into the community. That village could follow (at least) four possible strategies. It can *use* the asphalt: the black, sticky substance can patch up roofs and the bottoms of boats. It can bind handles to blades and can even be shaped into sculpture. Or the village can *export* the asphalt in exchange for something else it needs more. Perhaps it needs food, and another village has a surplus of grain. Then again, it is sometimes more prudent to *store* the critical resource. There might be some time in the future when the grain supply is dwindling. At that time, then, the stored asphalt can be traded for grain. And of course, it would rarely be the case that these three possibilities would happen so neatly. So a fourth strategy might very well involve a *combination* of the three.

Managing the movements of goods, then, was becoming much more of a problem.[16] Beyond this, the movements themselves could be a dangerous business. As cereal grains and other precious commodities made their way across Southwestern Asia, they were vulnerable to plunder by anyone who needed those goods. So, in all likelihood, groups of warriors were needed to protect the travelers. Exchange required producers and merchants, and it needed defense.

The size of communities was growing; the scale of decisions was growing as well. It is not surprising that we discover the traces of a religious elite. Management of local production, the problem of raiding, and widespread exchange were likely bringing into existence more centralized rule. Kin groups with extensive connections were assuming a permanent leadership role, not only because of exchange, but information as well. Their linkages made it possible to buffer shortages in difficult times. More than that, their control over commerce made possible the support of their group. This freed their personnel from production for the decisions that had to be made. Information about weather, raiding, crop failures, surpluses, and disease was brought to the group with the goods gained through exchange. Long hours of debates—and decisions—would further polish their systems of trade. Their power and prestige was increasing. It may have been strengthened by ritual life. If these kin groups were thought of as sacred, then their position became more secure. Remarkably, as distant connections became vulnerable to hazard and raid, the chiefs that controlled them experienced a stabilized rule.

---

[16]It was almost certainly the case (though the archeological evidence is slim) that *services* were involved in exchange and not just commodities. We might consider the pastoralists in India who corral their sheep in an unplanted field, thus "fertilizing" a farm family's land in exchange for their goods. Such examples are a vivid reminder of the probable complexity of early exchange and of how much of it has not been preserved in the archeological record. See Bridget Allchin, "Late Stone Age Settlements in Western and Central India," Ucko et al., *Man*, pp. 117–18.

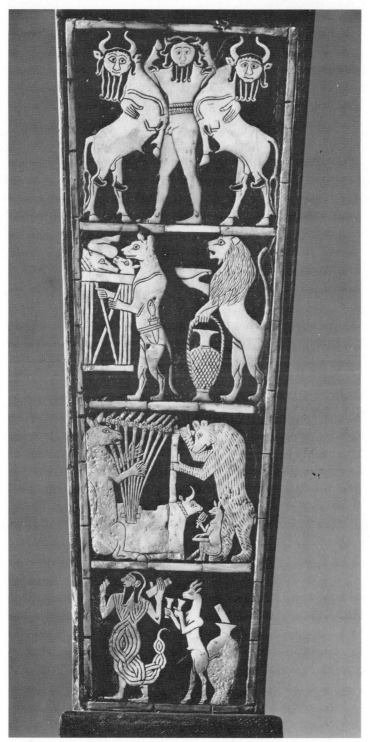

Mesopotamian mythical figures on blue lapis lazuli. The mineral was a major item of Near Eastern trade.

**The Southwest
Asian highlands:
A passage to the
Indus**

Among Iranians it is called the *sardsir*—the "cool country" that lies to the north. It is a land of sharp seasons and cold streams, meadows for the flocks, and relic forests of maple, ash, and elm. Summers are warm along the *sardsir*, with dry days that give way to chilly nights. But in the fall of the year, the gentle world of the uplands is changed. Humid air from the Mediterranean blows eastward across the foothills. The breezes climb the slopes and drift upward into the mountains. Along the way the moisture condenses, and the uplands are washed with rain. Near the Caspian Sea, 40 inches can fall in a year. The cold drizzle stretches on into winter, chilled by winds from the grasslands of Asia. Frost glazes the hills, and the skies become heavy with snow. Sheep huddle close to the villages. Smoke rises in the winter night. Snow and ice lay deep along the foothills until the coming of spring. It is not until March or April that a thaw comes into the uplands. The damp ground is warmed by the sun, and the pastures are green. The villages are stirring with life now, as the herds pick their way up the slopes. Another year has passed in the highlands of Southwestern Asia.

The rhythms of life along the *sardsir* are only a part of a much larger system that stretches from the Zagros Mountains towards the lands of Southern Asia. It was on the fringes of this kind of country where the

The Iranian Plateau.

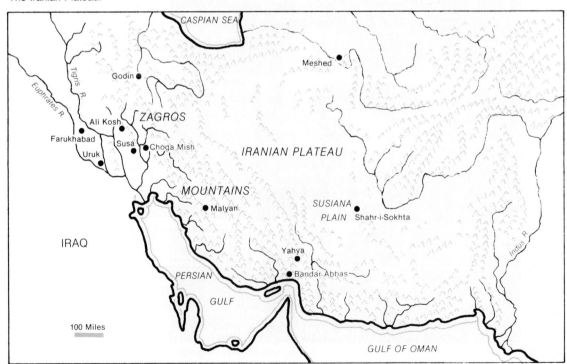

earliest cereal grains were probably grown. But the country extends a great distance beyond Ali Kosh. It is a chain of foothills and snow-fed streams with patches of forest and highland pastures and it connected the people of Southwestern Asia with the world to the east. It curves northward, following the Zagros, to the southern shores of the Caspian Sea and bends eastward, on the edges of the Alborz, toward Turkemenia. Then the snakelike curve of the foothills becomes the flanks of the Kopet Mountains that stretch to the south and connect with the Afghani ranges. And there, in western Afghanistan, was a ribbonlike network of streams fed by the melting snows of the Hindu Kush. The streams, of course, flowed away from the mountains, then into southern Afghanistan. Others flowed into Pakistan and became the Indus River.

Much of this highland country was a corridor of abundant life, hemmed in by deserts and mountains for most of its length. The uplands of western and northern Iran curved around a semiarid plateau, and on their outer fringes were the Zagros and Alborz Mountains. In the region that is Turkemenia, the Karakum Desert lay to the north, while on the south was the hot, vacant land of the Dasht-e Kavir. The cultivable soils of northern Afghanistan were found beside snowmelt rivers that churned beneath the slopes of high mountains for hundreds of miles.

Farmers had settled in these uplands shortly after domestication began. As their villages grew, they searched for new land on the hills. Probably they planted their crops in the muddy floodplains of the rivers, after the waters had crested in spring and begun to subside. Over the years, this gradual movement brought them ever deeper into Asia, until villages dotted the banks of the turbulent Indus. So the highlanders, through their migrations, in time created a cultural circuit that would link together two centers of civilization. Cities of Indus and Mesopotamia would send their products across these uplands. Middlemen who lived in the hills would become part of the trade. The highlands of Southwestern Asia would become something other than a region of farms—the great bridge of buckled earth would be a road for exchange.

Since the early part of this century, archeologists have dug in the highlands, tracing out the trajectory of movement into the east. In the hills southwest of Tehran, where the Zagros chain bends east to the Elborz, two mounds were discovered near a spring in a modern oasis. Today, these foothills are arid, sloping down to parched Dasht-e Kavir. In the past, there were springs, streams, lakes, fish, wild plant foods, and gazelle. Possibly as early as 7,000 years ago, farmers settled at Tepe Sialk.[17] They built small, clay-walled huts and grazed their cattle, sheep, and goats

Tepe Sialk and the making of metals

---

[17]Walter A. Fairservis, Jr., *The Roots of Ancient India* (New York: Macmillan, 1971), pp. 107–8.

on the hills. The village grew through the centuries, and the settlement spread out to the south. Dwellings were larger and made of mud-brick; stamp-seals have been discovered within them. Possibly these were used for marking pottery intended for trade.

It is very possible that Tepe Sialk was part of a larger industrial pattern followed by hundreds of communities found in the uplands. As villages grew ever larger, the better lands became harder to find. Settlements had to stay close to the springs and the streams. For many households, this forced a decision to leave the village and search for more land: to follow the narrow path between the mountains and the Dasht-e Kavir. But there were others who probably realized that the outcroppings of copper in the foothills held out the possibility of a living gained through exchange. Since the earliest days of Tepe Sialk, copper had been hammered into ornamental pins; but hammered copper is brittle and less valuable as an item of trade. Then again, if the metal is heated—how this was discovered, we still do not know—it becomes softer, more easily worked, and the product is stronger.[18] It is likely that the critical factor was the ovens of the farming villages, in which pottery had been fired since 9,000 years before the present. Perhaps mixtures of copper and clay had been put into the

Bronze chisels and needles. A network of metal working villages extended from Anatolia to the Iranian Plateau. Their products were often exchanged for agricultural goods.

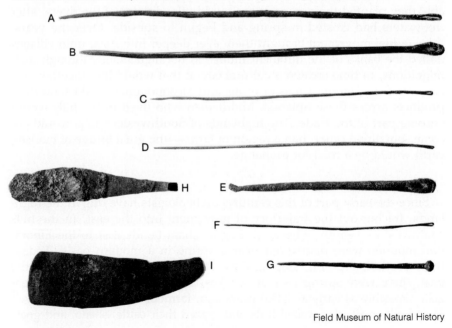

Field Museum of Natural History

[18]Theodore A. Wertime, "Pyrotechnology: Man's First Industrial Uses of Fire," *American Scientist*, November–December 1972, pp. 670–82.

pottery ovens; the heated copper was found in the ashes and the process began. With dry wood gathered on the foothills—here as on the African grass—the fire in the ovens was hot enough to melt copper ore. The color of the clay in these ovens is an ancient thermometer of sorts. It is a record of the temperature produced by the fire inside. In the ovens at Tepe Sialk, the threshhold was apparently reached: at 1083 centigrade, the copper ore melted down.

Experiments like these were occurring all across the uplands of northern Iran in a copper belt that stretched to the south of the Anatolian Plateau. The very fact that the deposits *were copper*—and not lead, for example, or tin—caused the manufacture of metals to develop at a quickening pace. The melting points of many of the others (iron is an important exception) are lower than copper, and this had an important result. It meant that a new technology was not necessary to melt the different metals. The ovens in the highlands, for the most part, could handle them all. Gold, silver, antimony, and tin could be melted and combined into alloys. Bronze, the most valuable of these, was a mixture of copper and tin. Used for making weapons and ornaments, it was traded out to much of the world. It was one of the most desirable items of ancient exchange.

For many of the households at Tepe Sialk, the heated metal acquired new meanings. It could be traded out to other communities for textiles and grain. Metal tools could be easily manufactured, and they would never spoil or perish from drought. At any time, they could be easily "converted" into grain from the lowlands. So it is hardly surprising that many of the villagers who lived in the Asian highlands began devoting more time to specialized manufacture and trade.

Djeitun: The land in-between

And yet, it was not every village that had this particular fortune of being located close to a strategic resource for exchange. Cultivators settled a region because of its soils, its water, and its pastures; probably too, they preferred higher ground as protection from raids. As communities in time became crowded, there was little to do but move on. The farmers pushed east, toward the foothills of the Koppet Dagh Mountains.

Archeologists have described this region in phrases usually reserved for advertising a honeymoon package to Costa del Sol. For anthropologist R. O. Whyte it was a "prehistoric Cote d'Azure," a "playground for the idle rich" of hunter-and-gatherer times. Archeologist William Allan, catching the infectious spirit of Whyte, has suggested that the region was the model for the Garden of Eden. In both of these playful comparisons,[19] there is

---

[19]They appear in William Allan, "Ecology, Techniques, and Settlement Patterns," Ucko et al., *Man,* p. 212.

an element of probable truth: the richness of the natural world along the Caspian Sea. Its low hills were veined with deep rivers filled with sturgeon and carp; there were poplar and maple woodlands where hunters stalked wildcat and fox. Wild barley was native to the region; wild sheep and goats grazed along the slopes. Gazelles and cattle had fed in the open grasslands for thousands of years.

But the wilderness to the east of the Caspian was a world that was narrowly bounded: to the north and the east was the Karakum Desert; on the south were mountains. In this region—which is called Turkemenia—could there have been hunter-and-gatherer pressures on the fringes of this pocket as there were in the ancient Levant? Is it possible that marginal peoples to the east of the Caspian Sea were circulating foods through elaborate systems of trade? In the caves just to the east of the Caspian, no plant remains have been found, but perhaps the crucial sites are closer to the rim of the desert. We *do* know that by 7,000 years ago, there were farming settlements on the banks of the rivers. But there is much that we still need to know about how they began.

Whatever the causes may have been of village life in the hills of Central Asia, there can be little doubt about the role it eventually played. For travelers moving over the highlands, Turkemenia was the middle of the journey: a "gateway" between the civilizations to the west and the east.[20] Mesopotamian merchants would meet with traders from the Indus Valley. Commercial communities would grow up on the flanks of the mountains.

But its role was only an outgrowth of the patterns of earlier times: of the social connections in the days of its most ancient farmers. The Turkemenian site of Djeitun began as a village of clay-walled houses on the edge of a stream that flowed down from the Kopeh Dagh.[21]

Villagers here, some 7,000 years ago, grew cereal grains near the edge of the desert. They herded sheep and goat and still hunted gazelle in the uplands. As the village continued to grow, it made contact with other communities. Fragments of decorated pottery have been dicovered in Tepe Sialk that are very similar to the later ceramics made at Djeitun. Microlith tools and sickle blades uncovered in northern Afghanistan strongly resemble the ones found in southern Turkemenia. Perhaps as the plots of farmland followed the rivers of this hemmed-in region, cultivators flowed out of Djeitun to the west and the east. If they did, then they established connections that would be a basis, somewhat later in time, for the management of commerce in an era of cities and kings.

---

[20]For the concept of *gateway communities*, see Kenneth G. Hirth, "Interregional Trade and the Formation of Prehistoric Gateway Communities," *American Antiquity* 43, no. 1 (1978), pp. 35–45.

[21]Fairservis, *Roots*, pp. 108–11.

To the south of the Hindu Kush mountain, there is a network of narrow river valleys that led migrating farmers to the floodplain of the Indus Valley. Archeologists are still far from knowing the exact pathways that the migration followed, but there is little doubt that it flowed to the southeast from the Turkemenian highlands. Where the rugged fringes of the Hindu Kush stretch across northern Afghanistan, rivers and streams branch out like unraveling threads. The Helmand, the Kaj, the Arghandab, the Tarnak and the Arghastan: along many, probably all of these rivers, the migration moved.

One of these rivers, the Helmand, is a wide and powerful stream that begins in the mountains of eastern Afghanstan. It flows south through the Registan Desert and then bends sharply toward the west, where it spills out into shallow Lake Helmand in eastern Iran. The armies of Alexander the Great in time would march through the valley of the Helmand. Medieval caravans would follow its waters after leaving the desert. But some 4,000 years ago, in a valley near the source of the river, the great stream was discovered by nomads who camped in the valley. No traces of houses have ever been found in the most ancient layers of the Mundigak site. Perhaps it began as a stopping-place where pastoralists could pitch their tents as they moved from pasture to pasture on the banks of the river. But in time, there were clay-walled houses where once the nomads had camped and, later, houses of mud-brick built upon stone foundations. Downstream from the Mundigak site was another spreading web of mud houses; the small village of Shahr-i-Shokhta on the shores of Lake Helmand.[22]

The two villages grew up together, aware of one another from the start, in a network of trade that extended for hundreds of miles. Italian archeologist Maurizio Tosi found fragments of pottery at the Sokhta site that were strikingly similar to fragments in the Mundigak layers. And when these two collections were later compared with pottery fragments in southern Turkemenia, many of the ceramic designs were almost the same. It is hardly surprising, in Tosi's opinion, that the two villages were so closely linked. They depended upon one another—and they probably knew it. The Mundigak people were living upstream on the banks of the life-giving Helmand, at a strategic location where the river flows south to the desert. Village life to the south

> would not have been possible if upriver where the flow was easily directed or interrupted. . . a friendly and culturally similar people had not been established.[23]

Mundigak and Shahr-I Sokhta: The subtleties of exchange

---

[22]Sokhta is discussed in "Dynamics of an Early South Asia Urbanization: First Period of Shahr-i-Sokhta and Its Connections with Southern Turkemenia," in *South Asian Archeology*, ed. Norman Hammond (London: Duckworth, 1973. Mundigak is described in Fairservis, *Roots*, pp. 122–34.

[23]Maurizio Tosi "Early Urban Evolution in the Indo-Iranian Borderland," in *The Explanation of Culture Change*, ed. Colin Renfrew (London: Duckworth, 1973), p. 439.

But there is more: buried deep in the sands that washed across the Sokhta site were fragments of lapis lazuli—a precious stone. The blue mineral is usually found embedded in chunks of limestone in deposits far to the northeast in the Hindu Kush mountains. At Sokhta there were workshop areas where the limestone was chipped away; the lapis lazuli was worked into beads, a valued item of trade. Fragments of half-finished beads and tiny flint drills with the lapis still on them appeared upon the fine-mesh screens used at the site.

From Sokhta the beads went west, across the desert, to Mesopotamia. Raw lapis went north to the workshops of southern Turkemenia. Perhaps because Sokhta had grown along the shores of a desert-ringed lake, the villagers had begun exporting lapis and importing grain. As their trade flourished, they became more dependent upon the village of Mundigak, located upriver directly on their route to the north. But Mundigak depended on Sokhta to give it its commercial importance, as a link in a chain that extended to the Caspian Sea.

We are only now discovering a fraction of such subtle and intricate relations that bound together the settlements on the rim of the Iranian desert. It was very likely *not* just a matter of a simple exchange of commodities. Settlements could well have been connected in a number of ways. Some villages were resource centers that exported raw copper or lapis. Still others were manufacturing points where the final products were made. Another village's critical importance might have been the location itself: halfway between cities, on a river, or near an oasis. Or if a village had a large group of warriors, it might offer protection for travelers and their goods in exchange for textiles, luxury items, or cereal grains. In all these ways the South Asian villages became closely bound with one another—and formed a bridge between Mesopotamia and the peoples to the east.

The environment of the Indus Valley

Somewhere in the Ganglingshan Mountains in the shadow of the Himalayas there are two mountain streams that rush together and flow to the west.[24] Fed by the snowmelt and the glaciers of this almost unearthly region, the river tumbles through desolate country for hundreds of miles. Tibetan herders, bundled in wool to survive the cold at nearly 20,000 feet, bring their herds down to drink from the sharp, chilling water of the river. It flows on through the wind-whipped country, gaining in strength as it moves, as river after river rushes into its turbulent current. On the flanks of the Hindu Kush Mountains it plunges down a 10,000-foot gorge, and in the mountains of northern Pakistan, it bends to the south.

The Indus River cuts a furrow through the mountains, and then it widens in the warmer lands. It is a powerful—even dangerous—river and

---

[24]The Indus environment and sites are described in Fairservis, *Roots*, pp. 1–28, 166–17.

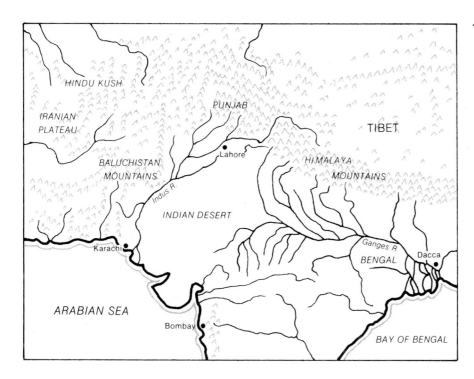

The Indus Valley.

always has been. Melting snow and mountain rivers feed into it for a distance of over 300 miles. Its flow is 3 times that of the Nile, 10 times the Colorado. Carried along from the mountains to the plains is its soil burden—the silt within the river. The Indus is heavy with soil, twice as much as the Nile. In Pakistan it is known as *kacho*—a light, loamy, mineral-rich sediment. Villagers have dug and planted in the *kacho* for thousands of years.

But the villagers have also discovered that the sediments are not a simple blessing. So rich and so thick are these soils that they quickly settle down to the bottom—more so than in the Nile or in most other rivers of the world. The muddy loam builds in the bottom of the river—especially in the eddies where the Indus makes a turn—until the bed becomes so high it pushes the river out of its banks. Once it floods, there is little to stop it. The Indus Vally is a low, level plain. It is land that rises only nine inches if you travel a mile. So a sudden thaw or a snowslide in the mountains might raise the Indus by 15 feet and drown villages and crops that are 10 miles away from the river.

The quirky behavior of the Indus has been a problem for thousands of years, but it has also been the basis for much of the life of the region. Because it sometimes spills over its banks, shifts across the plain and cuts out new channels, the soils across the valley stay moist; the water table is high. Without the river, much of this country would have been a desert, or a grassland, at best. Rainfall is scanty: as little as 10 inches might fall in a year. It is a region that is "superheated," as Walter Fairservis once said. The Himalayas and the Hindu Kush rise up like a giant wall to block the cold winds that blow across the Asian grasslands. Because of that wall, the lands to the south are heated by an equatorial sun. The climate on the Indus is warm throughout most of the year. The hot climate is a low-pressure region that attracts winds from the Indian Ocean. But these blow across the valley and shed their rain in the north and the east. Life on the Indus, then never depended on the clouds that scudded over the valley. It was the river itself that brought moisture and life to the land.

It is likely that the earliest farmers, moving out of the highlands and into the valley, discovered a tropical forest that flourished in the well-watered earth. Beyond the forest, as the soils grew drier, grassland faded into desert. But the land near the river was a wilderness of fish, fruit, and game. There were date palms, plumlike jujubes, deer, antelope, wild cattle, and elephant; there were rhinocerous, gazelle, wild ass, soft-shelled turtles, and fish. Generations of farming and clearing would shrink the forest into isolated pockets. Irrigation canals would turn the moisture-laden soils to dust. But to the settlers moving in from the highlands, the river valley was a rich, loamy region—replenished every year with soils that came down form the north.

Early settlements in the Indus Valley

Even before they reached the Indus, farmers had adapted to life in the lowlands by settling along the streams west of the river itself. They built houses of clay and mud near the banks of the Hannah River in western Pakistan, planting their wheat in the moistened earth of the Quetta Valley. One of these villages, Kile Gul Mohammed, is a little over 5,000 years old. It was a cluster of huts with walls of clay and mud; possibly some huts were of wattle-and-daub. Bones of sheep, goat, and cattle were discovered in the deepest layers of the site. A few sickle blades were found there too, along with stones for grinding up grain. Kile Gul Mohammed and a score of other sites discovered closeby in the valley are much like the earliest villages in sothern Mesopotamia. For here too there were farmers and herders in a world where land was abundant. If the village grew crowded, there were always new streams and other rivers.

It was not long before the migrating farmers settled along the Indus itself. For the first time there were mud-brick villages on the flat, humid plain. At the site of Amri, on the southern part of the Indus, the earliest foundations were still in the ground: tiny houses on the loamy, wet *kacho* near the banks of the river. The early settlers dug trenches in the soil, filled them with gravel, and built their houses on top. This was probably a way of adapting to the less-than-solid ground near the Indus, where a shift in the mud could crumble a house overnight. In later years, the dwellings were mounted—or so it appears—on top of mud-brick supports: early evidence of a long-term struggle with the floods of the river.

On the east bank, and to the north of Amri, the farmers in the village of Kot Diji built massive constructions to stop the unpredictable floods. The walls of the houses themselves were 5-foot-thick barriers of brick, and the village was surrounded, since its very early days, by a wall. At its base were limestone blocks, piled on one another some 10 feet high. On top of the blocks there was a 14-foot wall of mud-brick. Outside were limestone structures that were probably small-scale dams. Within these river-threatened ramparts, the settlement grew.

All along the geat murky river, the valley was dotted with villages and farms. Wheat grew on the flatlands where once were rhino and deer. How did it happen that these clusters of houses in time became a civilization? Here, as in Egypt, there is much that we still do not know. At around 5,500 years ago the Indus Valley was a chain of growing villages. Thirteen hundred years later it was a network of cities. What happened in the time in between? It is a difficult question to answer. But I will offer a suggestion a bit later on in the story. For the moment, it is enough just to say that the river has devoured much of its own history by flooding the very layers that would tell us the most. And yet, not all has been lost—although the evidence we do have is meager. There are places on the Indus that time and the river have spared. I think it will not be very long before we understand much more of this region and of how civilization developed along that powerful stream.

13 / The Exploration of the Pacific

A misting rain settles over the village and turns the earth near the huts into mud.[1] There is a chill in the forest with the final light of the sun. Rain percolates down from the treetops and flows softly down vine-covered trunks. The sounds from the heavier drops, when they splatter on the fan-shaped leaves, are like a delicate tapping of fingers on the skin of a drum. There is hardly a sound in the village. Almost no one is outside in the rain. But in one of the huts there are murmurs and a mingle of voices.

The day before, the village had been horrified by what Aang-the-widow and Tieng had done. They belonged to the same kin group—the Cil—and they had slept with one another. It was not something that could pass unpunished. You could not seek a mate from among your own kin. Out of that would come conflict and jealousy. Kin would be set against kin. Work in the fields would soon go undone. The rice would wither and die. In no time at all the rain-fed jungle would sprout back among the emptied-out huts. Seasons would pass—and the huts would be covered by forest.

And so, only a few hours before, the villagers had stood in the drizzling rain and had watched as Aang-the-widow and Tieng waded into the river. Her brother had squatted in the mud while he sang a prayer to the Spirit. Aang and Tieng had brushed the water across their bodies. And now, in Chaar-Rieng's house, there is laughter, prayers, and beer. The Spirit watching over the forest would protect them again. Outside the misting rain is still dripping from the bamboo eaves. It forms puddles around the village and trickles down the slope of the hill. Slowly it washes the footprints from the edge of the river.

The Mnong Gar have lived for centuries in the central highlands of South Vietnam. They grow rice on the hills, hunt, and fish in the tropical forest. Throughout most of Southeast Asia, there are highland people with similar lives. From the Bay of Bengal to the Gulf of Tonkin, from southern China down to Singapore, there are people much like the Mnong Gar at the rim of the mountains. Their lives are a vivid reminder of something

Agricultural society in Southeast Asia: The two kinds of forest

---

[1]The story of Aang and Tieng is told by George Condominas, "The Primitive Life of Vietnam's Mountain People," in *Man's Many Ways*, ed. Richard A. Gould (New York: Harper & Row, 1973), pp. 199–227.

Northern China.

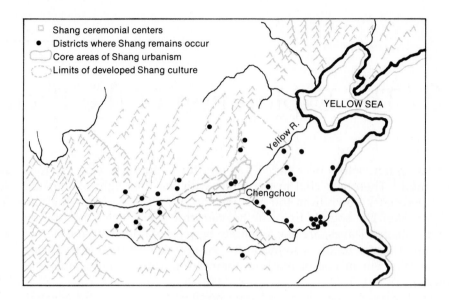

that is too often ignored: the tropical country of Southeast Asia is not all the same.[2] It is a region of natural diversity, of forests that are not all alike. If we know this, we can understand better its ancient societies.

Much of the jungle is actually highlands along the fringes of mountain chains. The jungles of central Burma are tucked between western and eastern foothills. Most of Laos is upland country. So is northern Thailand and central Malaya. Vietnam is a long chain of hills that slope down to the sea. Here are evergreen forests and rain that falls every month of the year. Dense columns of tropical trees push up to the sky. And because of these broad-leaved evergreens, the ground is shaded from the light of the sun. Shrubs and grasses are sparse along the floor of the forest. The temperature of the dampened ground is almost the same every season of the year. So, the clearings of slash-and-burn gardens are almost hidden by the soaring forest, constantly warm, and not taken over by grass.

Up in the trees, there are bunches of fruit, edible leaves, and animal life. There were forests like these, long ago, throughout much of the planet. Monkeys, squirrels, bats, and birds inhabit the world up above the ground. Below them are jungle cat, leopard, panther, and tiger. The highland forests are rich in diversity, well watered, and teeming with life. There are foragers who can easily live there, even today.

---

[2]Charles Higham, "The Economic Basis of Prehistoric Thailand," *American Scientist*, November/December 1979, pp. 670–79. I have found this article to be highly useful in synthesizing mainland Southeast Asian prehistory.

But the lowland forests are different. They have been different for thousands of years. Here the rainfall is not as abundant; the seasons are less kind. Very often, especially in Thailand, a row of hills to the west stops the *moisture-bearing winds*—the *monsoons*—that blow in from the sea. Rainfall in the lowland jungle is much less than in the upland forest. In some places there are droughts that might last for half the year. Deciduous trees, adapted to the dryness, grow wild in the lowland plains and are not at all like the broad-leafed trees of the evergreen forest. Fruit and edible leaves are scanty in this lowland canopy, and so the fruit- and leaf-eating animals are harder to find. Then too, the sun of the lowlands is not screened from the floor of the forest. Underbrush grows in the soil. There are deep stands of grass. Animal life is less plentiful, except where water can always be found. Near the permanent lakes there are elephant, rhino, and deer.

Eleven thousand years ago, there had been foragers living in the highlands. In the low country, where the food was less abundant, the population was sparse. The upland hunters and gatherers—like the people at Spirit Cave—lived off animals and plants in the evergreen forest. And Spirit Cave was one camp out of many; there were other clearings at the edges of streams. The foraging tradition persisted in some of them for thousands of years. Steep Cliff Cave is in northern Thailand, a little to the south of Spirit Cave, in a river valley where foragers lived for 2,000 years. Some 7,500 years ago they hunted in the game-rich forest. There were bones of water buffalo, cattle, deer, pigs, monkeys, and squirrels. Fruits, nuts, wild peas, and beans were discovered here, as at Spirit Cave. Daily life in both of the campsites was almost the same. And in Banyan Valley Cave, which lay to the east where a jungle stream plunges down into a gorge, there were foragers after the world's earliest cities had long diappeared.

The silent millenia

Yet the matter was not so simple; there were probably pressures as well. In many of the caves and the chopped-out clearings there were the workings of change. A layer of soil in Spirit Cave about 8,000 years old was very different from the litter of foragers buried beneath it. In that upper layer, Chester Gorman discovered fragments of pottery along with adzes and knives, the evidence of sedentary life and technological change. Pottery is that sensitive indicator of people who are settling down. And the knives? We know that Madeline Colani had found similar ones on the island of Java. To this day they are used by the Javanese when they harvest their rice.

So it looks as though, 8,000 years ago, there were changes at work in the highlands. Wet-rice cultivation was spreading. That seems evident from the Spirit Cave finds. But did it spread by word of mouth and imitation? Or were there actual migrations involved? Where did rice cultivation begin? And—for that matter—what brought it about? The answers are buried in the forest. They have not yet been found.

We *do* find rice cultivation much later in the lowland regions of Southeast Asia. But it is *too* much later to tell us about how it arrived. In fact, there is a span of some 2,000 years between the telltale knives at Spirit Cave and the most ancient sites that we have for the lowland jungles. It was during those 20 centuries—Southeast Asia's "silent millenia"—that people probably moved down into the lowlands for the very first time.

Archeologists, like the angels, do not tread everywhere they might. For theories about Southeast Asia there is a good measure of risk. Even so, Charles Higham has proposed a well-reasoned theory of rice cultivation and of the migration of farming populations down into the lowlands. For Higham, the very settlement of the lowlands does not make a great deal of obvious sense. The forest resources are poorer, there is a dry season for much of the year, and the swamps and river deltas are the home of the malaria mosquito.

Higham is intrigued by the scattering of lakes that dot the fringes of the highland jungles where the land slopes down into swamps and deciduous forest. It might have been that along these lakes foragers once collected the wild rice that springs up in the mud when the water level falls in the summer. The rice is large-grained and abundant; it might have made a sedentary life possible. In this rich pocket of rice, the population would have continued to grow.

As they settled farther away from the lakes, they sought out new rivers and streams. Perhaps it was just such a strategy that brought farmers to the edge of the Khong, meeting foragers and gardeners in the home that was called Spirit Cave. There is little doubt that most of these farmers would have now preferred the lands to the south: the muddy deltas, the rivers, and the swamps that were suited for rice.

Here we have archeological evidence—the early sites in the northern lowlands. They are in rain-shadowed deciduous forest called the Khorat Plateau.[3] One of the sites was a low burial mound only about 5 feet high, a gentle hill of earth a short distance from the Chi River. The lowest layers of Non Nok Tha are, possibly, 6,000 years old. They contained human burials, pottery, and deposits of animal bones. Pottery from these most ancient layers was made of clay mixed with rice chaff—very likely a "temper" to prevent clay from shrinking while firing. This suggests, of course, that rice was being grown in the area, but whether it was wild or domesticated we still do not know. One thing is evident: the earliest settlers still hunted wild game in the forest. The deepest layers have bones of deer, tiger, and some wild cattle. And yet, a serious problem remains:

---

[3]The Khorat Plateau is an unfortunate name for what the Thai people simply refer to as northeastern Thailand. It is really not a plateau at all, but a gently rolling plain that slopes down to the coast, and is seldom as much as 650 feet above sea level.

can we be sure about the age of these layers? Radiocarbon dates have provided more confusion than anything else. Some of them indicate that the deepest layers are 6 millenia old; other dates suggest that the layers are only 2,000!

But around 110 miles to the northeast, a less-frustrating site had been found—the Ban Chiang mound near the source of the Songkhram River. Over 100 human burials were found there, along with pottery and animal bones. The layers of the mound covered a time span that began nearly 6,000 years ago and only ended shortly after the settlement of Colonial America. As archeologists dug through its layers and brushed off the dirt from the pottery and bones, the story of lowland settlement was slowly revealed.

Ban Chiang, 5,600 years ago, was in a country of lakes and clear streams. Evergreen forests followed the rivers, but that was only where the soil was damp. Away from the water, there was the tangle of deciduous forest. The earliest people who lived there brought domesticated cattle and dogs, but they still hunted wild cattle and pig in the brush of the jungle. Yet, this was a lowland forest; game was scarcer than up in the highlands. And during a seasonal drought food was harder to find. Because of this, it is hardly surprising that we find very early traces of rice. Probably they grew it on the edges of the lakes as they had in the highlands.

As the population continued to grow, they needed more rice and more fields. They slashed away at the swampy forest around them, piled up the debris, and set fire to the heap. Where a jungle once flourished, there soon was a hillock of rice. Charles Higham, looking over the animal bones, found a dramatic increase in wild cattle and deer: grass- and bush-eating animals that thrive when a forest is burned. Slash-and-burn planting can lead to erosion as root cover is removed from the hills; the streams grow muddy, and the fishes and frogs in them die. Here again, the bones told a story: the fish and frog bones become ever more scarce. The earliest settlers probably burned the swampy forests and planted their rice.

Rice paddies and exchange adaptations

As long as there were swamplands around them, the strategy worked very well. The soil below the ashes was wet enough for growing their crop. But when the villages grew and there were no more swamplands— and when drought became more of a threat—water had to be captured and held so there would be enough food. Probably just this dilemma, some 3,600 years before the present, led to that remarkable invention— the paddy of rice.

Like irrigation in southern Mesopotamia, it probably grew out of an earlier system: a way of trapping water in an attempt to create a new swamp. Ridges of mud built along a slope can bottle up rainfall or the flow of a stream, as they do in many parts of Southeast Asia today. Microscopic algae live in the paddy and add nitrogen to the shallow water;

insects and frogs are abundant and fertilize it as well. So it is a highly productive system which does not lie fallow like the fields of dry land. Less than a square mile of paddies in Java can support 2,000 people.

The rice paddy brings other changes as well to human society and the natural world. With the spread of the paddies, the tropics were never the same. In the first place, they cause the dry season to be even harsher on the rivers and streams by trapping the rains that would normally supply them with water. This means that when the dry season comes, the streams are much lower than they normally would be. So sometimes where there once was a stream, now is a bed of cracked mud. Then, too, the rice-paddy farmers let surplus water flow down to the streams; the current becomes muddy, and the fish in the streams often die. In the layers of Ban Chiang that are 3,600 years old, Higham discovered that the remains of fish were becoming more scarce.[4] In the same layers were bones of water buffalo that were noticeably enlarged, perhaps from years of selection for plowing the paddies. Dry, open-country animals, such as the mongoose, had almost disappeared.

If Higham is right in his theory—and only later excavations will tell—it might explain a great deal about changes in the lowland societies. Rice paddies meant a surplus of food, but they presented difficulties as well. Once again, we are involved with the complexities of early exchange. Rice growing is labor-intensive, especially during harvest time. A large num-

Water buffalo plowing a paddy. Upper layers at Ban Chiang contained the bones of these animals. Their large size may have resulted from human selection for use in such labor.

Field Museum of Natural History

---

[4]The discovery was the result of an analysis of excavated materials. The excavation itself was directed by Chester Gorman and Pisit Charoenwongsa.

ber of people is needed to gather the grain. Today, in parts of Southeast Asia, hunters and gatherers help with the task—a *service* in exchange for the products of a farming society. The foragers who live in the highlands can provide farmers in the lowlands with meat—a valuable source of protein and a change in the diet.

Archeologists Jean and Warren Peterson have found that such systems of exchange are still being practiced today in the Philippine Islands.[5]

Painted vessel from Ban Chiang. Ceramics are a sensitive indicator of increasingly settled life. At Ban Chiang this was likely the outgrowth of rice agriculture and systems of exchange.

The Art Institute of Chicago

[5]Jean T. Peterson and Warren Peterson, "Implications of Contemporary and Prehistoric Exchange Systems," in *Sunda and Sahul: Prehistoric Studies in Southeast Asia, Melanesia, and Australia,* ed. J. Allen, J. Golson, and R. Jones (New York: Academic Press, 1977), pp. 533–65.

Hunters and gatherers in northeastern Luzon help in the harvest of manioc and yams. Farmers give them a portion of the cultivated crop in return. For the farmers, it is a way of obtaining additional labor and animal protein. For the foragers, it is a system that provides them with storable food.

The Petersons suggest that these systems may extend far back in the past—an "exchange adaptation" to the problem of rising populations. As agricultural settlements grew and farmers were confronted with dwindling food, they may have encroached upon hunter-and-gatherer lands. But instead of pushing out the foragers, farmers resorted to systems of trade. Less destructive than ongoing warfare, the system also increased the variety of food. It has been a stable adpatation in the lands of the tropical East.

It would be convenient if these intricate systems survived perfectly intact in the ground. Unfortunately, archeologists are only left with their durable remnants. These may have been of only minor importance; all the same, they are often all we have when we attempt to reconstruct a network of prehistoric exchange. In the highland country of Southeast Asia, archeologists have found objects of bronze. Copper and tin were rare in this country where the hunters and gatherers lived. There was no technology in the highlands for the smelting of bronze. But on the edges of the Khorat Plateau, where the rice-growing lowlanders lived, there were copper and tin deposits—and metallurgical ovens. The technique of manufacturing bronze was discovered by the lowland dwellers almost as soon as they migrated into the region. Bronze anklets, bracelets, and a spear head were unearthed in Ban Chiang's deepest layers (the ones that dated back to the time of the earliest settlement). And yet—though the technology existed—the richest caches of bronze manufacture are first found in those layers where we have evidence of rice-paddy farming. There could well have been a similar pattern in the lowland deltas of North Vietnam. Here too, there was rice paddy agriculture and a local tradition of working in bronze.[6] But over the years, as population grew and wet-rice farming expanded, the region became a center of bronze manufacture and trade.

So it is conceivable that the lowland farmers sent their metals up into the highlands in exchange for wild meat and, possibly, help with the harvest. Of course, it was not all that simple; unquestionably, there was much more involved. We hope to learn more about the region in decades to come.

---

[6]Archeologist William Watson has recently disagreed with this view, suggesting that the bronzes are as recent as ca. 100 BC and were exported into Vietnam from southern China. But increasing archeological research (and the radiocarbon dates) in north Vietnam indicate a bronze metalurgical tradition dating back to ca. 2000 BC in the Red River Valley, long before there was significant Chinese influence in Southeast Asia. The controversy is discussed in Peter Bellwood, *Man's Conquest of the Pacific* (New York: Oxford University Press, 1979), p. 189.

Field Museum of Natural History

Bronze drum from northern Laos. These, and other bronze objects, were likely traded to tropical foragers. In return, they may have provided fresh meat and help with the harvest.

North of the Asian tropics were the loess-banked rivers of China. Here too, as in much of the world, farming villages may first have appeared in fertile areas that faded away to less favorable lands. Exactly how that happened in China is something we still do not know. For Ping-ti Ho, the beginnings of agriculture—indeed, Chinese civilization itself—were triggered by the slow drying of the lands of north China.

Village life on the rivers of China

But the truth is that we know next to nothing about the emergence of farming in China, of the processes that led to villages such as Pan P'o. For that matter, the *later* settlements—in the millenia that followed Pan P'o—were not well understood until recently. But much recent archeology in China has been concerned with classification—the comparison of hundreds of later sites in different parts of the land. This is tedious and not always exciting, but it is the raw material of prehistory itself. Because of these cross-comparisons, we know what the later villages were typically like. We know the pathways the cultivators followed as they moved across China.

It is very likely that along the Huang Ho (where the earliest farming villages were found) the communities were growing too large for the available land.[7] Archeologist K. C. Chang suggested that the pressures of growth possibly caused early villagers to migrate south and east. Like the farmers of Southwest Asia in their migrations toward the Indus, many of the Chinese cultivators followed the rivers. There they could plant their crops in the fresh silt when the flood had receded. When the village grew large, there was always more room down the river. On the Han Shui and the Yangtze Rivers, and on the streams that flow into their waters, archeologists have discovered the villages of riverine farmers. At one of the settlements—Ch'u-chia-ling, which is probably 6,000 years old—the walls of the houses contained evidence of technological change.[8] Carbonized grains and tiny straws of rice had been worked into the mud plaster of the walls; it is some of the best evidence we have for rice cultivation. At other villages not far away, rice-harvesting knives were discovered along with axes, adzes, and the bones of dogs and domesticated pigs.

But the settlement along the rivers was much more than just simply migration. Processes of social change were occurring as well. In the later years of these waterway villages there are the signs of disturbances— conflicts. Many villages were surrounded by massive walls of rammed earth. Spears, arrow heads, and daggers were discovered in many of the burials. Some of the skeletons had the marks of scalping; others were headless.

And there was the stirring of diversification—of specialized groups in the villages who were involved with manufacture and trade, perhaps with religion. The pottery is no longer crude but well made and probably thrown on a wheel. Often it is black and lustrous; sometimes it has painted designs. Perhaps, as Chang has suggested, there were now specialized groups of craft workers producing the vessels for the village or, conceivably, for trade. Then too, there are the incised shoulder blades of domesticated pig and sheep: artifacts that in Chinese tradition are called *oracle bones*. Religious specialists apply heat to these bones, sometimes with a glowing piece of metal, which splinters the surface of the bone into a maze of cracks. In historic times, the Chinese have believed that a specialist could read the cracks and discover in their patterns the events that lay in the future.

So there is little doubt that Chinese society was caught up in the pressure of change. But what led to these changes? At this time, it is not easy to say. But it seems possible that an earlier strategy was encountering new limitations as the available land near the rivers in time disappeared. The migration to the south and southeast had been a push into warmer

---

[7]K. C. Chang, *The Archeology of Ancient China* (New Haven: Yale University Press, 1979), p. 152.

[8]Site descriptions are taken from ibid., pp. 144–84.

lands, where the rainfall was greater than along the Huang Ho. The current of these rivers was slower, and they meandered more than in the north. The land was more level, and some of it was dotted with swamps. It is little wonder that rice growing spread, as the migration followed the rivers. The cereal was probably grown near the streams or at the edges of swamps.

Such a system was highly productive for pioneer settlements in the south. But when wet soil near the swamps and the rivers was converted into stands of rice, new fields could only have been created away from the water. It was probably this situation that had led, in Southeast Asia, to the development of rice-paddy farming in the lowland jungles. But in the southerly country of China, the process was probably different. The region of greatest productivity where, eventually, cities would emerge was not in the lowlands but in the north along the Huang Ho. Perhaps one reason for this was the technology of rice agriculture and the need it created for a suitable beast of burden.

From the scanty archeological studies of the later villages of China, it appears as though cattle were the beasts of burden in the south. These animals are valuable for plowing, especially if the ground is soft. But there are other kinds of tasks for which cattle are not of much use. These are the very tasks necessary for the development of rice-paddy farming: pulling away the chopped-down trees from the site of the future paddy; dragging a harrow along the ground to clear away the brush; and, once the field has been cleared, a heavy, metal plow must be pulled through the ground to tear apart the roots so the soil can be planted in rice. The bones of cattle are inadequate for performing this kind of work, and the structure of their hooves does not provide enough traction.[9] But water buffalo are well suited for clearing out the forests for paddies. That is the way this animal is used in southern China today.

Where was it first used in the past? No one seems to know the answer. As Peter Bellwood has remarked, its history is "an open question."[10] We *do* know that there is very little evidence of water buffalo in the riverine south. Most evidence of the animal's early use appears in the north.[11] Conceivably, this was one of the reasons why the villagers in the warm, rainy southlands were building walls of rammed earth and were beleaguered by violence and raids. Without a suitable beast of traction, they were effectively confined to the rivers or to the margins of swamps where they could scatter their seeds of rice. As the size of the villages grew,

---

[9]Higham, "Economic Basis," p. 676.

[10]Bellwood, *Man's Conquest*, p. 151.

[11]In discussing the Shang civilization of northern China, Chang notes: "In the domestication of animals the Shang carried on the neolithic heritage (pigs, dogs, cattle, sheep, horses, and chickens) with some additions (water buffalo) and modifications (such as the use of dogs, cattle, and sheep for sacrifice and horses for chariot warfare)." Chang, *Archeology*, pp. 289–90.

there could well have been pressure on such limited land. Scarcity might well have been the basis for strategies of trading and raids. And it might have created more powerful groups in the village societies.

These may have been households of kinfolk with extensive connections of trade. Perhaps the kin included craftworkers producing painted black pots for exchange. Commodities that flowed through the networks could be traded for alliance as well—for military assistance that protected the system from raids. And here, as in other societies, political power was reinforced by belief. Heated bones found in the villages suggest there were diviners at work. The ritual was a powerful tool of political life. Prediction of a conflict with neighbors could generate suspicion that would make it come true. Forecasting a seasonal shortage could lead to more products manufactured for trade. Divination is a flexible instrument well adapted to political rule. It endured on the rivers of China for hundreds of years.

Humanity goes to sea

There was still an uninhabited region—a place our species had never experienced. People lived on its fringes, knowing little of what it was like. For thousands of years the Pacific was the water that stretched out to the sky. What lay beyond that haze in the distance had never been seen. For the dwellers along the shoreline, it had remained a predictable world: the quickening pulse of the tide that was the sign of a gathering storm; the coldness that came into the air as it blew from the sea; the clouds that hung over the ocean had dark bellies heavy with rain; there were the filaments of distant storms and the mutter of thunder. But this was only the mere edge of a world that humanity had not yet discovered. It is one of the last great reaches of the planet to be explored.

But we should not be led into thinking that humans were total strangers to the sea. For thousands of years they fished in lagoons and set out on the waves. Francthi Cave in Greece had the bones of tuna that must have been caught in deep-sea waters. In fact, the Aegean Islands could only have been reached by voyaging craft, and the same was probably true of Australia and New Guinea. Perhaps the very earliest boats might have been built in big-game hunting times. Animal skins stretched over a frame—much in the manner that some of the houses were built—might have followed the coastline from Asia toward the Americas.

But these voyages, important as they were in the evolution of sea-going craft, were tiny ventures, a matter of miles or of a day's time at the most. The earliest boats (dugout canoes and, conceivably, skins-over-a-frame) could never have survived the punishing waves far out at sea. Yet, somehow, the water was crossed. Our species settled the ocean. More exactly, we colonized the islands scattered across the Pacific. How did it happen? What brought it about? What routes did the voyagers take? Today, archeologists are discovering much of that story.

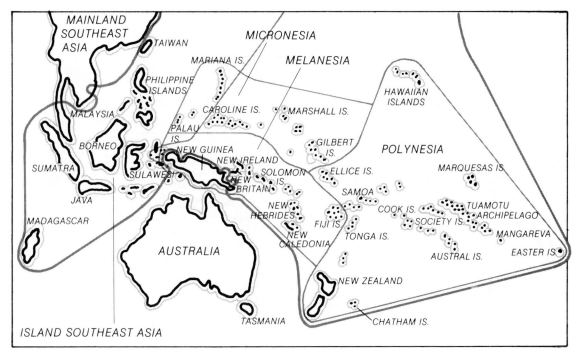

The Pacific Islands.

A serious problem in telling the story has been the nature of the Pacific itself: the distances to its islands; the direction of the prevailing winds. The southeastern and northeastern trade winds rush together and blow to the west. But the earliest settlers who reached the islands almost certainly came out of the east. This means that these ancient seafarers must have sailed against the wind. For many years archeologists doubted that this could have been done. Andrew Sharp saw the colonization as a great accident in human prehistory. A boatload of islanders close to the mainland were, perhaps, blown off their course in a storm. Luckily, they survived the mishap and were washed ashore on a Polynesian beach. Conceivably, other boatloads had been banished from their homes on the mainland. Many of these exiles went to the bottom, but others survived. Such random events, over the centuries, scattered people across the Pacific in much the same way that birds were once blown to the Galapagos Islands.

But there seems to be no convincing evidence that the exploration happened that way. More than likely, the Pacific islands were deliberately settled. Many of the sites in the islands have been dated by carbon-14. Often it is possible to tell when they first were discovered. When the

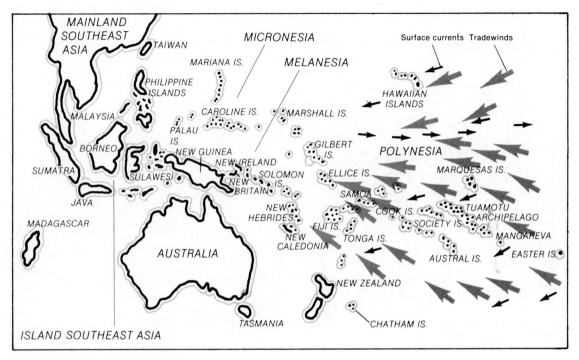

Tradewinds and currents of the Pacific.

dates are plotted on a map, they fall into a logical pattern.[12] They do not have the randomness that we would expect from the accident theory. The most ancient sites are in Melanesia, to the east of the New Guinea coast. They are followed by Fiji, Samoa, Tonga, the Marquesas, and the Society Islands. Last of all are the very distant landfalls: Easter Island, Hawaii, and New Zealand. This looks like an evolving system, rather than the aftermath of banishment and storms. Polynesian settlement seems not to have been an accident but a human design.

Very possibly, there were Melanesian mariners skillful enough to sail the high seas but perhaps lacking the technology to sail toward a small target. From floating branches and driftwood they were aware of island groups somewhere to the east, as well as from waves deflected off islands and reflections on clouds. By sailing in the direction of these clues, they were actually moving toward a large target. It is misleading to think that small islands are lost in the sea. As archeologist Ben Finney has noted, most of the islands are found in long chains.[13] When one part has been

---

[12]This is illustrated in the introduction by Jesse D. Jennings to *The Prehistory of Polynesia*((Cambridge, Mass.: Harvard University Press, 1979), p. 3.

[13]Ben R. Finney, "Voyaging," in *Prehistory of Polynesia*, pp. 323–52.

found, short voyages can discover the rest. In a certain sense, the islands are connected; they are not just dots in the sea. This means that the discovery of the Fijis, far from being an unlikely event, was comparable to sailing toward an island the size of New Mexico.

It was probably by repeating these methods that the other Pacific islands were found. For nearly 2,000 years, the mariners crisscrossed the heart of Polynesia. They found Tonga, Samoa, the Marquesas, and the Society Islands. All the while, their navigational knowledge and sailing behavior became more complex. Eventually, it was possible to make the longest voyages of all. These began about 400 AD and ended 400 years later. The three distant outliers of the Pacific—Easter Island, Hawaii, and New Zealand—were discovered by sailors who could travel over 2,000 miles.

These final colonizing voyages are the most remarkable of all. How did they know something was out there? How did they find it? I think it is very unlikely that they knew of these outlying islands. The great distances involved meant a lack of reliable clues. Floating debris from these islands, by the time it reached the rest of Polynesia, could have been scattered by shifting currents all over the sea. Such signs as changes in wave patterns, birds, reflections, and the smell of land only happen when a sailor is much closer than 2,000 miles.

The settlement of the Pacific.

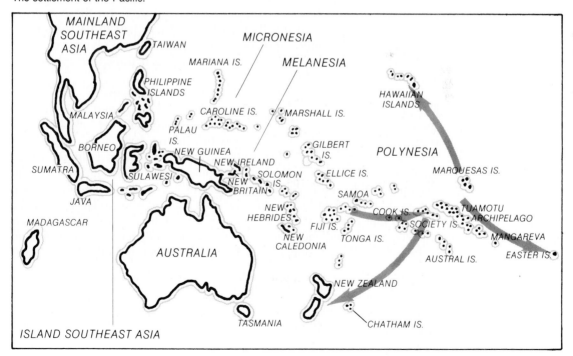

I suspect that these last three discoveries were experimental probes of a sort. Pressures were building in Polynesia—which I will talk about a little bit later—and pushing islanders outward in an attempt to discover new lands. The critical strategy probably involved in this last stage of exploring the ocean was the technique of sailing a boat in a constant direction. This strategy depended strongly on a detailed knowledge of the heavens: the sun by day and the locations of the stars at night. A great deal more was involved here than simply selecting a star and then sailing toward it. The stars, of course, rise out of the horizon, move across the sky, and then set.[14] Any particular star is only on the horizon for a very short time. So the ancient Polynesian navigators had to memorize a succession of stars that rose out of the same location on the distant horizon. This made it possible to keep a constant direction, whether sailing by day or by night. The most visible linkage between those two periods was the morning and evening star. The location of Venus may have been of great aid in Polynesian discoveries. It is conceivable that, using these methods, the ancient islanders sailed out to sea. They traveled for hundreds of miles, turned around, and went home. Soon there was another probe— this time in a different direction. Eventually—almost inevitably—the outliers were found.

Since, after all, these people were colonists and were not traveling the ocean for pleasure, their boats were built for the transport of cargo across the high seas. Families were moving with possessions, including food and supplies of fresh water. They brought pigs along on these voyages and introduced them to the Pacific islands. There had to be shelters on the boats for the families and the cargo they brought. Polynesians of recent centuries have used the *double canoe* for such transport: *two parallel canoes with a platform of logs on the top.*

There is a muck deposit in Tahiti where the remains of such a boat have been found. Double canoes appear to have changed little through the course of the years. They were probably about 40 feet long—judging from the ones in historic Hawaii—with a triangular sail, a rudder, and five paddles on a side.[15] The hulls of the canoes were bulging, which increased their carrying capacity but could also have led to problems in maneuverability. Because of their size and water displacement, the two canoes often worked independently: they pushed and pulled against the lashings that held them when they were struck by the waves. If the craft was swamped, and the canoes were both flooded, both the hulls had to be bailed together. If one was bailed out first, then the other would sink

---

[14]At least they do from an earthling's point of view. The actual relationship was not understood until the 16th century AD, but this "earth-centered" viewpoint is still useful in navigation today. A well-written account of traditional sailing practices on Puluwat, to the north of New Guinea, is Thomas Gladwin, *East Is a Big Bird: Navigation and Logic on Puluwat Atoll* (Cambridge, Mass.: Harvard University Press, 1970).

[15]Finney, "Voyaging," pp. 323–52.

Field Museum of Natural History

Double canoe with sail at the time of Captain James Cook.

even deeper. But such a craft could carry humans and cargo, including penned-up domesticated pigs. In the center of the platform, there were sleeping shelters and animal cages.

Ben R. Finney once built a replica of an ancient double canoe and sailed it from Hawaii to Tahiti in 32 days. The experimental voyage covered a distance of over 3,300 miles. Finney often had to move the sail so the boat could travel against the wind. He took advantage of the occasional breezes that were blowing his way. Very probably, in boats such as these, using strategies like Finney was using, the ancient voyagers settled the islands throughout the Pacific.

Early pressures and the settlement of Melanesia

But where did the islanders come from? And why did these voyages ever begin? The two questions are closely related, and they involve a special part of the world: New Guinea and the islands to its east—the realm of Melanesia. It is here that we discover the beginnings of a pressure-and-movement cycle that would be repeated to the remotest islands of the central Pacific.

At the moment, we know only a little about the *very* first ventures out into that ocean. These attempts were likely short journeys of 30 or so miles at the most. People sailed from somewhere in Indonesia and headed east to New Guinea. This was 25,000 years ago: an age that still belonged to the hunters. Far to the north, there were mammoth and caribou on the tundra and steppes. What caused voyages at this early date and what became of the voyagers are problems that, for the moment at least, are not well understood.

On a slope overlooking a swamp over 5,000 feet above sea level, thin deposits of stone tools and charcoal were discovered in a forest.[16] The tools were small flakes and hand axes littered over a small patch of ground—the debris often left behind by a foraging band. Conceivably, people at Kosipe, New Guinea, found fruits, leaves, and game in the swamplands. Pandanus trees with edible leaves and storable fruit were growing there. Archeologists are looking closely at samples of soil from where the swamp was once found. Pollen spores may reveal how the swamplands were changed by the settlers.

The story of this early adaptation is really little more than a shadow. Only much later is there detailed evidence of how the island was changed. There is a marshy valley in the central highlands of eastern (Papuan) New Guinea that is revealing changes and probable pressures in the island's prehistory.[17] The Kuk site is in a poorly drained valley some 5,000 feet above sea level. Archeologist Jack Golson discovered that the site had thick deposits of peat created over thousands of years by the swamps in the region. He noticed, too, that the peat was changing—as early as 20,000 years ago. Clay was washing into the peat from the hills to the south. It was a subtle disturbance at first, but it increased over the years. By 9,000 years before the present, the erosion quadrupled. At almost the same time that this happened, ditches were dug along the edges of the swamp, connected by gutters, and leading into basins and creeks. In recent times, throughout much of the Pacific, such ditches were dug for the growing of taro. This starchy, tropical fruit is related to the "elephant ear." Grown for its edible root, it needs a constant supply of fresh water. Very often, it is planted in a mound between two flooded ditches.

The ditches and the clays tell a story of an island that was being transformed as the meager populations in the forest continued to grow. New Guinea, as Jack Golson has put it, is an island with "no room at the top." More exactly, it is a place where there are hazards both above and below. Running east to west across the island are the peaks of the central highlands. Rising 10,000 feet in the air and often covered by ice, they slope down to the lowlands that are covered by tropical swamps. The higher up on these slopes that you travel, the more different the world around you becomes. The jungle turns into cold-weather trees which disappear into grasslands. Much lower, near the bottom of these slopes, is rugged jungle terrain. There are seasonal droughts and the ever-present threat of malaria.

So as populations grew on the island, they found themselves squeezed in the middle. They were confined to the mountain valleys that had fresh

---

[16]J. Peter White, "Melanesia," Jennings, *Prehistory*, pp. 352–78.

[17]"No Room at the Top: Agricultural Intensification in the New Guinea Highlands," in *Sunda and Sahul*, pp. 601–39.

Field Museum of Natural History

A flooded taro field. Plants such as these were probably grown alongside the ditches at Kuk.

water, plant food, and game, and to a vertical zone that was only 2,000 feet high. It was nearer the top of that zone, where the tropical vegetation is scanty, that the pressures of crowding in New Guinea began to be felt. Here, when the forests were cleared and the gardens were planted in crops, it took much longer for the cold-adapted trees to grow back on the land. Beyond that, there is a good possibility that the early farmers were shortening their fallow: planting more often in order to increase their yields. This meant that the land near the top was overplanted and stripped of vegetation. Soil washed down the slopes and spilled out into the swamplands. At the fringes of these clay-flooded marshes, drainage ditches and basins were dug—to irrigate the taro and to dry out the swamps for new land.

It is almost certain that, under such pressure, some people had to leave the island. More than likely, there were kin groups who loaded their belongings on a double canoe and paddled out to the scattering of islands that lay off the coast. Melanesia, as these islands are called, was apparently settled from the west to the east.[18] The oldest sites on any of these islands are located closest to eastern New Guinea. They are around 3,600

---

[18]*Melanesia* as a geographical term includes New Guinea and the islands to its east, stopping just short of Fiji, Tonga, and Samoa.

years old, or about as old as those layers at Kuk that have strong evidence of drainage, erosion, and deforestation. On these tiny volcanic islands, there were new forests and uncultivated ground. And they were close enough to one another for a network of trade.

Although they may not have been aware of it, these travelers were sailing to a very different world. It is true enough that they and their ancestors had lived for thousands of years on an island, but that experience had not really prepared them for what was to come.[19] The dark lines of trees that lay off in the distance belonged to islands much smaller than their homeland. The ones that are closest to the shores of New Guinea can be as much as a hundred miles long, but the islands become smaller the farther that you go to the east. Often too, because they once were volcanoes, they have a ridge of steep hills near the center. On these slopes there is greater erosion, so the centers of their islands are less suited for planting.

The earliest inhabitants of Melanesia probably sought the best lands they could find. Often these were stretches of lowlands, a short distance away from the beach, that were watered by streams flowing down from the volcanic hills. Whenever possible, they chose a location near an offshore reef or a protected lagoon. There they could fish and bring back the catch to the village. But even here, in the Melanesian lowlands, there was swampy country where no one could settle. They built their villages in the better-drained pockets close to the sea.

Archeologists now better understand what ancient life in Melanesia was like. But the picture is a sketch; many unanswered questions remain. It is probable that most of these islanders lived from their gardens and from fishing the sea. Pigs and chickens were brought to Melanesia, and taro from the old gardens was brought along with them. At the moment, there is no direct evidence of gardening in the Melanesian islands, but good indirect evidence exists for suspecting that it was probably there.[20] Village sites were usually located in parts of the islands most easily farmed. Shell scrapers and peelers have been found; they may have been used in the preparation of food. Cooking ovens have been discovered, as well as large pits dug into the ground. Today the Melanesian islanders use these pits for the storage of taro. It is a technique that might well have been practiced for thousands of years.

And of course, there was the ocean itself, where food was just below the surface. But locating that food was a strategy learned over time. The layers of the Melanesian sites are thick with shellfish and sea turtle bones.

---

[19]I am referring here to the New Guinea migrants. In all likelihood, voyagers reached Melanesia from other points near the Asian mainland. Ross Clark, on linguistic grounds, identifies the homeland of the Melanesians as "inside the triangular area defined by Taiwan, Sumatra, and New Guinea," in Jennings, *Prehistory.*

[20]Patrick V. Kirch, "Subsistence and Ecology," in Jennings, *Prehistory,* pp. 286–308.

Field Museum of Natural History

Domestic pigs in Siar, New Guinea. The animals were brought by humans from Melanesia into the Pacific.

There are bones of porcupine fish, eels, sharks, parrotfish, and sea basses. Archeologist Roger Green has pointed out that these are mostly "reef and shallow-water lagoon fish."[21] They are usually speared or netted; very seldom are they caught by hook and line. But this is really what might be predicted for new colonists arrived in the Pacific. In the beginning, they fish the shallow waters, perhaps by forming a line in the surf and then moving forward to drive the fish into a net. Only later, with improvements in their boats and a better understanding of the sea, would they sail far away from the islands for the deep-water fish.

The settlement of Melanesia was the beginning of a long exploration: paddling and sailing for hundreds of miles in the search for new islands. I doubt that it was simply curiosity that brought canoes into the central Pacific. Here, as in much of the world, it was a question of food. The small size of most of these islands and their smaller patches of habitable land meant that population pressure could quickly be felt. The earliest settlers moved out to the islands around 4,000 years before the present.[22] Only 1,000 years later, they had reached the western edge of Polynesia.

---

[21]Roger Green, "Lapita," in Jennings, *Prehistory*, pp. 27–61.

[22]This is the approximate date of earliest settlement as determined from sites in Melanesia with Lapita ceramics. It is very possible that an earlier migration into Melanesia took place, but this appears to have been largely confined to the immediate east of New Guinea. The best evidence of the earlier migration is the Balof rock shelter on northeastern New Ireland, which may be as much as 7,000 years old. J. Peter White in Jennings, *Prehistory*, p. 356.

The islands may have filled up with people because of wave after wave of migrations, but there is little convincing evidence that this was the case.

There is striking physical variation among the populations that live in these islands, and hundreds of very different languages are found there as well. While many migrations could be partly responsible, there is also a good possibilty that isolation on the islands was a strong contributing cause. Small groups that "splinter off" into islands can develop noticeable biological differences.[23] Their dialects can change until they become different language communities. So at the moment we do not really know if there was wave after wave of migrations. But population pressure would quickly have developed in any event. On the limited land they had, it is probable that starchy, root crops were grown—especially taro—judging from the large storage pits that were found. The crops and the fish that they caught made a sedentary existence possible. Our numbers often climb when we settle down to live in one place.

The ventures out into the Pacific probably grew more frequent through time. The outlying Melanesian islands were even smaller, with fewer resources. The farther east the voyagers sailed, the less they found. Yet, it was this very scarcity that played a role in later discovery. As the settlements grew in these islands, trading canoes became a very common sight. Flint, obsidian, produce, and pigs were exchanged all across Melanesia. Over the years, as the trading continued, navigation improved. Out of these pressures, some 3,000 years ago, came journeys that were longer than ever before. An open expanse of Pacific—some 500 miles of deep water— was crossed by the voyaging canoes. They had reached Polynesia.

The paradise that never was found

Here were islands that, generations later, would haunt the imagination of the industrialized world. Pushed by crowds in noisy, city streets, pressured by business, and breathing foul air, humanity created a dream that was called Polynesia. Musicals turned it into jingles; novelists made it a romantic escape. At least one stockbroker abandoned his profession to seek an Eden-like world in the islands. He found diseases, social conflicts, taboos—and died in despair.

So if this was *not* the real Polynesia, then what was Polynesia actually like? Long decades of digging in the islands have suggested an answer.[24] They are islands that have much in common, although certain differences are obvious enough. There are coral formations, for example, as tiny as

---

[23]Peter Bellwood, "The Prehistory of Oceania," *Current Anthropology*, March 1975, p. 10.

[24]Patrick V. Kirch, "Subsistence and Ecology," in Jennings, *Prehistory*, pp. 286–308; and "Polynesian Prehistory: Cultural Adaptation in Island Ecosystems," *American Scientist*, January/February 1980, pp. 39–48.

The Museum of Modern Art/Film Studies Archive

Tyrone Power succumbs to Gene Tierney in a Hollywood Polynesia. The belief that the Pacific Islands were a carefree, Eden-like setting is a remarkably durable myth of the industrial world.

Key West or Long Island, while New Zealand—which is really three islands—is the size of Colorado. And, of course, it is true that the islands are scattered across much of the Pacific. The difference in lattitude between Hawaii and New Zealand, which amounts to some 60 degrees, is about the same as between Mexico City and the Argentine Andes. But probably the most remarkable differences are between the high islands and the coral atolls—differences that have a good deal to do with the way they were formed. The high islands are ancient volcanoes—the peaks of mountains mostly under the sea. They are covered with mineral-rich soils and a dense community of tropical plants. Away from the beach, these islands are a rugged landscape of hills and ravines where the sounds of the waterfalls are mixed with the chatter of birds.

The atolls are strikingly different, although they began in very much the same way. Like the high islands, they began as volcanoes that burst through the surface of the sea. As they cooled and the centuries passed, they were colonized by tangles of coral that grew along their watery fringes like a natural wreath. Then the volcano trembled again and sank down to the ocean floor, leaving only the fringes of coral and fragments of mountain. Almost all of these atolls are low, and they are dangerous in hurricane season. They have little, if any, fresh water; their soils are sandy; their resources are poor. Many of the Pacific atolls were never colonized by human beings at all. Others were settled for a time, but they are uninhabited today; prehaps the people starved, or abandoned the island, or were drowned in a storm.

Yet, different as many of them were, the islands were alike in a number of ways. Most of them were smaller in size than the tiny islands to the east of New Guinea. They were scattered across the ocean; distances were greater between them. This meant that longer voyages were necessary to carry on trade. And because the Poynesian islands are so far from the Asian mainland, they have a much smaller number of animals and tropical plants. Wild relatives of the Pacific crop plants never spread east of Melanesia. Most wild plants native to polynesia are not useful as food. Reptiles are not abundant; edible mammals are scarce in the islands. There was little possibility for a hunting-and-gathering life.

In other words, survival in Polynesia was a matter of fishing and intensive cultivation. There were no hunting-and-gathering resources to fall back upon. As archeologist Patrick Kirch has shown, we discover throughout the islands buried evidence of specialization in fishing and gardens. Slash-and-burn agricultural methods were brought into the Polynesian realm, but through time the cultivation strategies became more diverse. Terraces were cut into hills, flooded by streams, and then planted in taro; or the crop was grown on the banks of muddy ditches that drained out the swamps. Orchards of breadfruit, Tahitian chestnut, Polynesian apple trees, and coconut palms were planted and tended along with the irrigated taro.

Fishing, too, became much more specialized: it was the only other source of food.[25] Humanity changed its tools and its strategies to adapt to the sea. Crab and shellfish were collected along the beaches; fish were driven into nets in lagoons. Turtles were hunted in shallow salt water; larger fish were speared near the reefs. There were probably angling expeditions that set out to sea.

The fishhooks themselves are a record of the patterns of technological change. They were usually carved out of bone into different thicknesses, sizes, and shapes. It seems likely that the hooks were designed for different species of fish. In Hawaii, Easter Island, and New Zealand, the hooks were made of two pieces of bone, very likely to keep them from breaking with the weight of the catch. Throughout Polynesia—and over the centuries—the specializations became more complex. The islanders survived from their gardens and the food in the sea.

---

[25]Other than the small number of wild plant and animal species (including birds) which never played an important role in the diet.

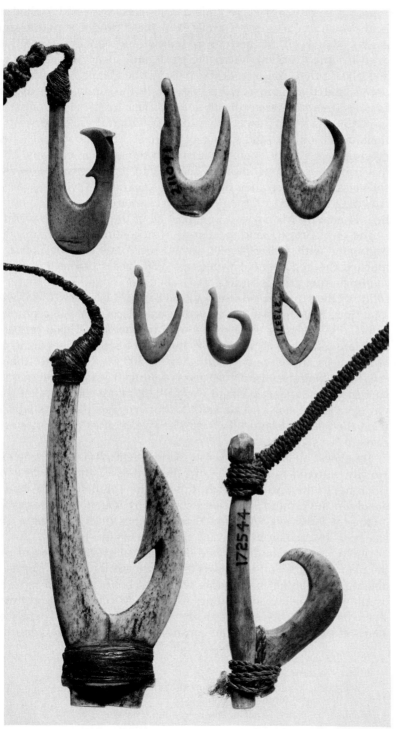

Polynesian fishhooks
of bone and stone.

Field Museum of Natural History

Not only did they have limited resources; they had limited available land. Much of Polynesia is atolls, and these cannot support large populations. Yet, even on the high islands, there were pressures that developed in time.[26] Polynesians were gardening socieities, seeking whatever good lands they could find. On most of the Pacific high islands there is only a limited amount of cultivable soil. In the sandy earth just above the beaches, the islanders probably tended their trees, while root crops were grown in the valleys away from the sea. Often these valleys are radial— they branch out like the spokes of a wheel. The hub of that wheel is the mountainous interior, totally unsuited for the growing of crops. This meant that rising populations, moving deeper into the valleys, discovered poorer soils at a time when they needed rich soils most. Over the years, as the crowding increased, all the Polynesian islands were searched out and settled. Humanity had arrived in almost all of the inhabitable world.

The great pressure-and-movement cycle continued for some 2,000 years, beginning with that 500-mile voyage from eastern Melanesia. Canoes touched the beaches of Fiji perhaps 3,300 years before the present; two centuries later, the islanders had sailed to Tonga. From there, about a century later, they sailed north to the Samoan Islands. And it was there, for a time, that the islanders stayed in one place. Some 13 centuries passed before other islands were discovered and settled. These probably were the Marquesas, which were far to the east of Samoa. They lie in the heart of Polynesia and were first settled about 300 AD. Soon after their discovery, the remainder of Polynesia was found. It was only about a century later that remote Easter Island was settled, and a century after that when voyagers sailed north to Hawaii. A short voyage 100 years later encountered the Society Islands. Two hundred years after that, Polynesians discovered New Zealand.

On almost all of the Polynesian islands, beneath a riot of tropical plants, are the battered foundations and the burials of those earliest days. At Huahine, in the Society Islands, litter of the Tahitian settlers had sunk so deeply in the ground that it was covered by water.[27] The soggy evidence of ancient Polynesia was only about 8 inches thick, and yet a great deal has been learned from this site about life in the islands.[28] Archeologist Yosihiko Sinoto soon discovered that this waterlogged site had preserved the plant remains and the wood that are normally lost. In four seasons of digging at Huahine, he found a wealth of bone and shell tools probably used for the peeling and grating of plants. As Sinoto dug on through the layer, he found the remains of the plants themselves. There were fragments of pandanus, kava, and coconut palm, and pieces of gourd embed-

---

[26]Kirch, "Subsistence and Ecology."

[27]The carbon-14 dates for the Huahine site extend from AD 780 to AD 1270. More secure dates are anticipated for the site in the future.

[28]Kenneth P. Emory, "The Societies," Jennings, *Prehistory,* pp. 200–22.

ded in the mud below a mantle of coral and sand. Pig bones were never encountered there, but chicken and dog bones were littered about. Rat bones were discovered there too, but this was hardly a cause for surprise; the furtive rodent has managed to hitchhike around most of the world.

The remains reveal a tentative picture of a cultivating life on the island. Root crops were not found at Huahine, but the site was located near a swamp. Taro could easily have been grown at the edge of the marshes. Then, too, in the southern part of the layer, there were sunken posts and pieces of floorboards from four small buildings that may have been used for the storage of yams. Structures like the ones at Huahine are used to store yams in the Melanesian islands; conceivably, in the past, they were used in Tahiti as well.

Scattered through the boggy deposit were harpoon points and pearl-shell fishhooks. The islanders gardened and tended their orchards, but they still fished the sea. It was here, preserved by the water, that part of a double canoe was discovered: the end of the platform and the steering paddle were still in the ground.

At Huahine, and across Polynesia, the islanders cultivated their plants, and they fished. The years passed, the populations grew, and they filled up the valleys. Long before the Europeans arrived, the Polynesians had created a crisis: the islands were pressured with people and there was no place to go. Out of this came raiding expeditions, political rivalry, and a struggle for food. Scarcity and organized conflict, like rats on the double canoes, had followed humanity's trail across the Pacific.

The end of pre-historic Polynesia

Eighteenth-century Hawaiians were as shocked "as Cedar Rapids would be if a party of Martians in a space ship landed on the roof of the Quaker Oats plant."[29] This was the way that J. C. Furnas, a little less than 50 years ago, described the impact of Captain James Cook when he arrived in the Pacific. By all accounts, the meeting *was* eventful—and it ended tragically for everyone involved. But perhaps it was a good deal less shocking than is sometimes suspected.

What happened? On the 18th of January, 1778, the captain sighted a flock of birds while he was sailing northward. "These are looked upon," he recorded, "as signs of the vecinity [sic] of land." Kauai Island rose up east-northeast of the ship. Hawaiians sent out reconnaisance canoes and then climbed over the side of the boat. They began removing the metal and cloth found on the deck. Iron nails could be made into fishhooks, and the only form of cloth that they had was pounded out of the pulpy inner bark of the mulberry tree. For the Europeans it was simple theft, and they shot one of the Polynesians dead. Over and over, this pattern would happen at the end of prehistory.

[29]J. C. Furnas, *Anatomy of Paradise* (New York: William Sloane, 1937), p. 109.

The weeks that followed saw dreary episodes of exploitation, violence, and disease. James Cook and his crew helped themselves to all the food on the island, loading up the boat with provisions, and then asking for more. They sought out Polynesian women. Venereal disease became rampant. As they sailed to other islands, they encountered epidemics and death. The final outrage happened in February 1779 when it looked as though Cook was leaving, but a mast was broken at sea and he returned for repairs. By this time, enough was enough—even for the god which they believed him to be. There was a scuffle shortly after he landed, and James Cook was killed.

But I wonder if he actually astonished them and how awestruck they really were by his visit. Perhaps he was less of an anomaly than we have sometimes believed. It was not really the same thing at all as a Martian landing on an Iowa factory. For one thing, belief in the supernatural was deeply woven into everyday life. There was sacredness found in fishhooks, in freshwater ponds, and in parts of the forest. There were powerful rulers in Hawaii who claimed to be gods. Then, too, it was nothing unusual to surrender your food to a powerful figure. And, like a typical chieftain, James Cook kept a lot for himself. Even the violence—tragic as it was—was not a stranger to life on the islands. Hawaiian rulers, on occasion, took the lives of some of their subjects. So perhaps it was this very feature—that he fit so well into the scheme of things—that made it possible for Cook to thoroughly exploit the Hawaiians. When they finally *did* decide to kill him, they burned his body and returned his bones to the crew—a ceremony practiced in Hawaii at the death of a chief.

What created these traditions of conflict and the emergence of powerful elites? For Polynesia, much of the answer is now reasonably well understood. As in many other parts of the planet, it is the story of war and exchange—and of the role they played in transforming political life. Hawaii and the rest of Polynesia were societies caught up in a crisis, long centuries before Cook dropped his anchor near the beaches of Kauai.

From the very earliest days of settlement, the islands had presented severe limitations. Land mammals were scarce in Polynesia; the tropical plants were mostly not edible. A foraging population in the islands would not have survived. This meant that, in terms of technology, there was never a back-up system. If the crops died of drought, there was no wild plant food or game. So Polynesians had little alternative except cultivation and fishing the sea. And even the great Pacific was, perhaps, not always a bountiful world. It is, after all, an environment with migrations and changes of season. It seems unlikely that fish were abundant every month of the year. In any case, they are only a meat source—more protein than anything else—and they spoil very quickly; there is no evidence that they were ever stored. In other words, the island societies were heavily dependent on the crops they grew. As the population climbed, the pressure on food was severe.

Archeologist Patrick V. Kirch believes there was probably population pressure in almost every inhabited part of the Polynesian islands.[30] Excavations in the Hawaiian chain have uncovered agricultural villages; the living floors of many of the houses have been measured and dated. From the reading of historic documents and the study of living Polynesian societies, it is possible to estimate how many people once lived in a house. In this way, archeologists have discovered a steep rate of growth in Hawaii that continued for 600 years after the island was settled. For Kirch, it has become very clear that Hawaii was "saturated" with people "at least two centuries prior to European contact."

In many other Polynesian islands, the pattern was probably very much the same. On Easter Island, slash-and-burn agriculture deforested the entire land surface. When the Europeans arrived, the small island was ravaged by war. In Samoa, the expanding villages were filling up the fertile inland valleys. Fortifications were built as conflict spread through the islands. And New Zealand, although very distant, did not escape the chain of events. Its islands are so far to the south that it has a temperate climate. The cooler weather meant poor growing conditions for taro and yams. So the sweet potato was brought to New Zealand and planted by the islanders known as Maori. Woodlands were burned to provide more arable land. By the time the Europeans arrived, many of the forests on the island were gone. At Pallister Bay in North Island, the sides of the hills were eroding away; soil flowed down from the gardens and into the sea. Thousands of fortifications were constructed to protect the croplands. Ninety-eight percent of them were built where the gardens were found.

Warfare and limited food brought more than technological change. They affected the structure of ancient Polynesian society. Here, as in other environments, villagers were connected by a lattice of trade. But the system may have been very different from much of the world. There was not a wide array of resources that could flow through a web of exchange. Fish, the food from the gardens, and, conceivably, stone to make tools circulated by trading canoes through the ancient Pacific. There were no herders, no metal workers, and no foragers that lived in these islands. Pacific peoples had a limited number of products for trade.

This closed and inflexible system grew more troubled as the centuries passed. Islands were filling with people; there was no solution to be had in exchange. The same strategies and much the same products were found in every part of the realm. Amid scarcity you discovered that others faced exactly the same dilemmas as you. Many islanders' yields were declining at about the same time.

The only (temporary) solution was to increase the resources at hand.

---

[30]Kirch, "Subsistence and Ecology."

Maori club. The limitations of island environments led to chronic war in the Pacific.

There was a shift to greater intensification: deriving a large amount of food from a small plot of land. Terraces were cut into hills and irrigated by inland streams; stone-lined canals brought water downslope to the fields. Stone walls were built out from the beaches to enclose the shallow offshore reefs. Fish were trapped in these artificial ponds and then grown for food. For islands that were part of this system, shortages could be buffered, at least for a time. But the pressure on available resources continued to grow.

The demands of intensive technologies required larger permanent groups. Sons and daughters remained in home villages to labor on the beaches and fields. Kinship became *cognatic—traced along either male or female lines.* More than that, the kin groups—or ramages—very often were internally ranked. Cadet groupings with the same ramage received varying rewards from the chief. Rivalry for rewards from their leader made each group in the system work harder. And the competitive strategy was strengthened by religious belief. In Hawaii, a chieftain was sacred. He was closely in touch with the gods. Commoners bowed down in the dust whenever he came through the village. To labor for rewards from such persons in a sense was becoming a rite. The effects of that powerful system are standing today.

Probably the most enduring evidence of competing elites in the islands is the massive architecture found all across the Pacific. More than 600 standing "stone heads" have been discovered on Easter Island; the largest one encountered so far weighs 82 tons.[31] On occasion, cylindrical top-

The megaliths of Easter Island. These constructions, here as in Europe, intensified the political power of chiefs.

Milwaukee Public Museum

[31]Patrick C. McCoy, "Easter Island," in Jennings, *Prehistory,* pp. 135–67.

knots, weighing up to 11 tons, were carved out of a quarry and mounted on top of a statue. In Hawaii, there were cobblestone temples with several platforms and high, standing walls.[32] King Kamehameha was supervising such a project in 1791. South of Hawaii, in the Society Islands, there is abundant evidence of the stonecutter's art. Religious structures—known as marae—were pyramids of stone overlooking a plaza, which itself was enclosed by a wall made of cut stone.[33] By the time the Europeans arrived, Tahitians were constructing archery platforms. These enormous foundations of stone, requiring thousands of hours of labor, were used in archery competitions among the elite. Bowmen would stand on the platform and shoot their arrows in a distance competition. The massive platform simply marked the location from where the arrow was shot.

Here, as in Western Europe, kinfolk labored to mount the huge stones in anticipation of generous rewards from the chief. For the chief, it was proof of his power—a symbol of the large ramage he ruled. And, of course, as these works grew larger, the proof was more convincing as well. Power, rewards, and architecture were a circuit through time. And conceivably, it might have been possible to see the stones through the eyes of belief. Constructed over generations, they could be thought of as inceptions of gods: a divine undertaking that humans now had to complete.

Yet in the end, all the strategies failed. Production throughout the islands likely declined on the overworked lands. Populations were growing; Polynesians resorted to war. And enemies on neighboring islands were not all that the chiefs had to fear. Less food for rewarding the subjects meant that rebellions were increasing through time. Chiefs were not even secure among those whom they ruled. Uncertainty grew through the seasons as the islands were troubled by raids. The gods themselves took notice—or, at least, so it probably seemed. Whether the vision meant rescue or punishment, no islander could really be sure. But the mast of a curious boat was sighted far out at sea.

---

[32]H. David Tuggle, "Hawaii," in Jennings, *Prehistory*, pp. 167–200.
[33]Kenneth P. Emory, "The Societies," in Jennings, *Prehistory*, pp. 200–22.

14 / Chiefs of the Eastern Woodlands

A hundred years ago the woods were full of them. Idle rich that were floated down the Ohio or brought across the valley in a rickety stage, they were shoveling with destructive abandon into America's past. Like their counterparts in England at the time, they understood little of what they were doing. American prehistory was a picnic, a fantasy—rarely anything else. They probed and picked into any site they could find, but what excited them more than all other relics were the thousands of mounds they encountered from Illinois to Ohio.[1]

In some parts of the Ohio River Valley, they were almost everywhere that you looked. Five hundred were discovered in southern Ohio alone. Within the mounds were human burials placed in log-lined tombs. Stone pipes in the shape of birds, a sheet of mica cut in the form of a claw: these and a thousand other curious objects were found in the graves. Yet sometimes there were hardly any burials, and the mound itself had been shaped into art. In the forests of Adams County, Ohio, earth was banked several feet above the ground into the shape of a serpent over a quarter mile long. Even well to the north in Wisconsin, a mound had been shaped into the form of a bear; another in that state bore a resemblance to a two-headed man. Near the town of Chillicothe, Ohio, they were built into circles and squares. Some of these might have been fortifications, but no one was sure.

Of course, this far along in the story, you know as well as I do what happened. They were built by Atlantans, Phoenecians, Egyptians, Lost Tribes, Scandanavians, and Mu. They were built by Scythians, Chinese, Moluccans, Ethiopians, Polynesians, and the Hindu. The fantasies flourished like mushrooms—rootless, puffed-up, and surviving on air—and eventually led to the rise of the "Mound Builder" myth. In this last, and most popular, version, there was an invasion of an unknown people. There was a Golden Age when their genius flowered. Then they all dis-

Mythology along the Ohio

---

[1]The story of the early mythologies relating to Midwestern earthworks is told in the highly readable *The First American: A Story of North American Archeology* by C. W. Ceram (New York: New American Library, 1971), pp. 176–222.

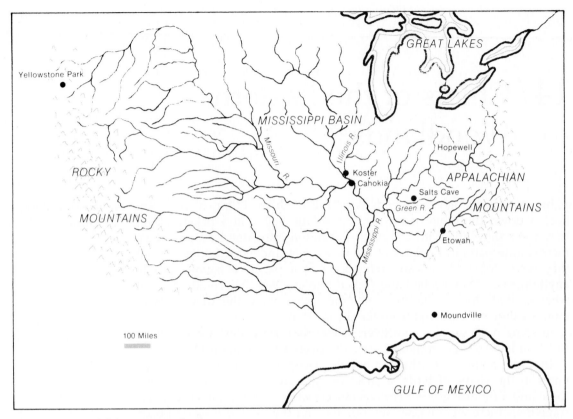

Agricultural sites of the eastern woodlands.

appeared. Explanations had canvassed the planet as a means of explaining the mounds. But one possibility was almost never suggested. This was the notion that the mounds had been built by the people who lived in the valley: that they had not been the work of outsiders but of the American Indian.[2]

All along, there had been a few heretics who suspected that this might be the case. Thomas Jefferson, surveyor and president, excavated a mound at Monticello and concluded that Native Americans originally built it. The archeology of the eastern woodlands has given strong support to this view. There is no evidence at all for an invasion of mound-building people. In the days of eastern woodland foragers, some 5,000 years before the present, burial mounds like those in the valley had begun to appear. On Morrison's Island in eastern Ontario, in Newfound-

---

[2]Racism was probably a factor in the rote dismissal of this possibility. It was a prevalent feature of much 19th-century thought.

land, Quebec, and on the southern Great Lakes, there were low burial mounds containing weapons, charms, amulets, and tools. The thousands of mounds in the Ohio River Valley were not a development that arose out of nothing but an intensification of an earlier—and ancient—tradition.

But why was there an "intensification"? Why did native Americans build so many mounds? To understand this, we will have to consider the changes in ancient American society brought about by the development of settled agricultural life. In the Ohio Valley and the American Southwest, in the Mesa Central and in highland Peru, human society was adjusting to the conditions of village existence. Out of these conditions came mounds, pueblos, and villages in Mexico and on the slopes of the Andes. Greater social complexity was becoming a part of prehistoric America.

Adena: Early transformations

Long centuries before the Europeans, there were changes at work in North America. On this continent, as in the Old World, there were regions of abundant resources where populations were collecting a spec-

The Midwest-riverine region had plant food and abundant game. But the winter season was often the "hungry time."

Center for American Archeology, Northwestern University

trum of available foods. One of these regions was the Ohio River Valley, some 2,800 years before the present—a countryside where game was abundant and food plants grew wild. The river flows from southwestern Pennsylvania below Ohio and toward the Mississippi, forming along the way the northern boundary of the state of Kentucky. It is a region of cold, snowy winters—a time when animal and plant foods are scarce—but the woodlands are remarkably different with the coming of spring.

With the thawing and greening of the valley, there was a blossoming of edible plants.[3] Wild persimmon, pawpaw, red mulberry, blackberry, elderberry, plum, and wild grape all flourished in the rich valley bottoms in the early part of the year. White-tailed deer were abundant in the region, and there were turkey, fox, squirrel, and raccoon. The tributaries and the marshes of the valley were teeming with fish. In the fall of the year, the nut-bearing trees furnished quantities of storable food. Walnut, butternut, and hickory trees grew in thickets along the courses of the rivers. It was a valley remarkably suited for a foraging life.

Yet there was more: for those hunters and gatherers who lived on the bends of the Ohio, the environment offered the possibility of domesticated plants. The low, marshy flats that followed the river were flooded by the spring thaw.[4] It was a meandering river; the water table was constantly high. Everywhere on the Ohio flatlands, edible plants had sprouted in the soil. Pigweed, goosefoot, knotweed, marsh-elder, canary grass, and sunflower were seed-bearing species that thrived in the mud near the river. The pigweed plant in particular was thick with clusters of edible seeds concentrated at just the right height to be easily picked. Foragers and gardeners, some 6,000 years ago, grew pigweed in the Tehuacan Valley. It may have yielded more food than many varieties of domesticated corn.

As populations increased near the river, the seed plants flourished more than ever before. These are plants expecially adapted to soil that has been recently disturbed. Clearing away the brush and weeds near a village; visiting and playing; tossing out the trash: these created a fertile environment for the seed-bearing plants. There was another possibility as well. The rich alluvial flats of the valley were more protected than the outlying bluffs. For four months of the year, there was little danger of frost. This is the minimal frost-free period essential for the growing of

---

[3]The description of Midwest riverine ecology is largely taken from Patrick W. Munson, Paul W. Parmalee, and Richard A. Yarnell, "Subsistence Ecology of Scovill, a Terminal Middle Woodland Village," *American Antiquity* 36, no. 4 (1971), pp. 410–31.

[4]Climatic conditions and the cultivable plants of the region are discussed briefly by Stuart Streuver, "Woodland Subsistence-Settlement Systems in the Lower Illinois Valley," in *Perspectives in Archeology*, ed. Sally R. Binford and Lewis R. Binford (Hawthorne, N.Y.: Aldine Publishing, 1968); and at length by Stuart Streuver and Kent D. Vickery, "The Beginnings of Cultivation in the Midwest-Riverine Area of the United States," *American Antrhopologist* 75 (1973), pp. 1209–20. I additionally consulted Richard A. Yarnell, "Early Woodland Plant Remains and the Question of Cultivation," *Florida Anthropologist* 18, no. 2 (1965), pp. 77–83.

Center for American Archeology, Northwestern University

Marsh-elder. This, and other seed-bearing species, thrived on the mud of the
Midwestern rivers.

corn. As it happened, there was no corn in the valley. But that was a
matter of time. Populations in this riverine country had the opportunity
to gather plants that matured in the mud of the streams in the fall of the
year. By disturbing the ground near their settlements, they could easily
have increased their yield. Such casual manipulation is occasionally practiced today by groups following a hunter-and-gatherer life.[5] For people
on the Midwestern rivers, the disturbance provided more food; it would
feed them in winter—a time when resources were scarce. This strategy
allowed greater stability and more frequent connections of trade. Plant

[5]Western Desert Australian aborigine set fire to stretches of desert to provide a "fertile"
area for food plants that live on burned ground.

foods from distant regions—the gardens of Mesa Central—could eventually be traded into the riverine north.

Through the years, the Ohio region attracted team after team of archeologists. Even so, there is much about the valley only now being learned. Early cultivators who lived near the river—Adena people, they often are called—are not yet understood to the degree that we might have expected. One of the reasons for this is an echo of Adams's remark about Mesopotamia: the more grandiose remains were explored and the rest was neglected. But archeologists are not totally to blame here; the Ohio River has taken a toll. Many of the sites have been covered over and concealed by nearly 10 feet of silt. True enough, people lived on the high ground, but there were houses near the mud-flats as well. Don Dragoo has remarked,

> These sites have been covered by many feet of silt—often six to eight feet in the Ohio Valley proper. We know very little about the settlement patterns that may exist at these sites and their relationship to the high ground burial mound sites. We do know that there were structures under and adjacent to many of the mounds. However, there is not one Adena site where we know the entire settlement pattern.[6]

Yet Adena is not a total enigma. In fact, the study of adaptation in the valley is at a quickening pace. Perhaps the most developed picture so far has come from Salts Cave near Kentucky's Green River, where dry soil has preserved fragments of plants that are normally lost. In a witch hazel and hickory forest is a deep sink that leads down to the entrance—a web of dark passages that is part of the great Mammoth Cave.[7] Fifty years ago, it was open to tourists; before that, it was a haunt for spelunkers. Twenty-five hundred years earlier, Woodland Indians lit bundles of cane and followed passageways back to their camp where they lived in the winter. The walls are a stained and scarred record of prehistoric Indians and tourists of the 1930s—a crazy fresco of smoke from cane torches and Depression graffiti.

Patty Jo Watson and Robert J. Hall excavated the cave in the dead heat of August. The litter of the Ohio Valley Indians was still on the floor. They found fragments of weedstalks and cane that were bound with fiber and lit to make torches. There were fiber-woven moccasins, hickory nuts, and fragments of gourd. In almost every part of the cave, the passageways had been battered by limestone to remove gypsum and mirabilite minerals crystallized in the walls. Conceivably, gypsum was used either as a medicine or a pigment for painting. It is possible that mirabilite, too,

---

[6]Don W. Dragoo, "Adena and the Eastern Burial Cult," *Archeology of Eastern North America* 4 (1976), p. 3.

[7]Patty Jo Watson and Richard A. Yarnell, "Archeological and Paleoethnobotanical Investigations in Salts Cave, Mammoth Cave National Park, Kentucky," *American Antiquity* 31, no. 6 (1966), pp. 842–49.

The banks of the Illinois River. Recurrent springtime floods have covered many Adena settlements. Adenans probably lived very close to the rivers.

had medicinal value. More significant than either of these were the plant remains found in the cave. Forty-five percent of the seeds and fragments belonged to domesticated species. Gourd, squash, sunflower, and marsh-elder were deliberately planted by the Salts Cave Indians. If goosefoot was also domesticated—and Richard Yarnell suspects it possibly was— then 66 percent of these remains were from domesticated plants. The cave is probably the best evidence we have of an eastern agricultural complex: river-flat gardening that developed in the Ohio Valley.

More than likely, there are many other caves and rock shelters not yet explored, but which hold caches of detailed evidence of life on the river. Yet the caves have never seemed quite as captivating as the hundreds of burial mounds built by these hunters and gardeners of the riverine bluffs. At Robbins Mounds in northern Kentucky, just southwest of Cincinnati, Ohio, 52 burials were discovered in a cluster of mounds. In one instance, a large mound at Robbins was built over the ashes of a house. Perhaps the dwelling was burned when the leader of a kin group died. Many of the burials were placed in log tombs roofed over with a covering of bark. Some individuals had been placed in clay basins, and the bodies were burned. From southern Illinois to the south of Ohio, the mounds have been explored along tributaries and bluffs of the valley. They are often similar, which is what we might expect of interacting communities.

Burials within the mounds are almost never elaborately furnished. An Adena grave might very well contain a rectangular stone known as a gorget which was probably threaded with leather and worn as a pendant. Or it might contain a flat stone tablet with a stylized bird or geometric design. But rarely do any of the burials have the rich caches and the unusual furnishings that would suggest the emergence of ranking in Ad-

Adena gorgets. These, and flat stone tablets are frequently found in Adena graves. But there are no elaborate furnishings that would suggest a ranked society.

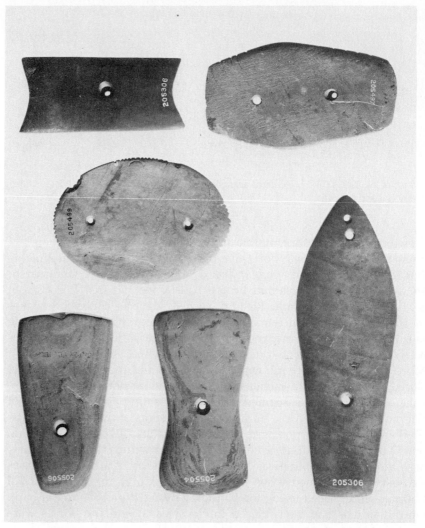

ena society. The mounds were possibly boundary markers for territories of gardeners and foragers. Little evidence of prestigious kin groups has ever been found.

It was a society with trading connections—with exchange that stretched far to the south. Squash and gourd had been brought to the valley from the Mexican Mesa Central. The exact trail they followed is something we still do not know. Fragments of these cultigens were found along the dried floor of Salts Cave. Seeds of squash were excavated from Florence Mound in southern Ohio. From remains such as these, it seems likely that by 2,500 years before the present, Mexico and the Midwest were connected by a network of trade.

Along the rivers in these midwestern forests, some three centuries later in time, there developed an intricate system of ancient exchange. Even more, the exchange was one facet of changes in society, perhaps even belief, that developed and spread through the region and then disappeared. Archeologists know it as Hopewell—this curious complex of cultural changes. Debates about it are apt to continue for generations to come.

Hopewell and the Hopewell debate

What was Hopewell? One part of the answer is to say it was a network of trade. Commodities were exchanged over distances of hundreds of miles. Lake Superior copper, Minnesota pipestone, Appalachian mica and obsidian, as well as tortoise shells, alligator teeth, meteoric iron, shark teeth, beads, seashells, wolf canines, and grizzly-bear jaws were passed along trails and rivers from the lakes to the Gulf. Yet the exchange was not a straightforward matter of six bear teeth for an ornament of copper. There were specialized manufacture and markets for regional trade. Certain sites in the midwestern woodlands were stone-pipe manufacturing centers. Carved into the shape of a heron, a hawk, an eagle, a beaver, or toad, the little pipes were exchanged out of Hopewell across the Midwest. They emanated from centers like Mound House, a 20-acre site in southwestern Illinois, where once there were the crowds and the bustle of regional trade.[8] All over the surface of the site were copper earspools and stone-pipe fragments, pieces of mica and obsidian, marine shells, and the drilled teeth of bears. Hopewell, at the very least then, was a coordinated web of exchange involving traders and specialists in many different parts of the land.

It was a remarkably diversified culture with its traders, craftworkers, and farmers; it was a society with differences in power and social prestige. No longer were almost all of the burials accompanied by a hoe or a tablet of stone. Some graves were richly furnished; in others, there was nothing at all. Archeologist Joseph Tainter compared some 500 Hopewel-

---

[8]The site is described in Streuver, "Woodland Subsistence."

Hopewell artifacts.

Field Museum of Natural History

lian burials and discovered 6 hierarchical groupings in Woodland society.[9] Trade, specialized manufacture, agriculture, and systems of ranking all were in some way connected in Hopewellian times. What brought it all into existence? Why did it flourish and then disappear? There is hardly an American archeologist without an opinion.

Many have thought of it as a prehistoric *ethos*—a *widely shared cultural value*—and an intensification of behavior related to death. For archeologist Joseph Caldwell it was a widespread "funerary cult": a flurry of tomb-building, burying, and fashioning items for graves. Hopewellians, said

---

[9]Joseph Tainter's results are discussed by John E. Pfeiffer, *The Emergence of Society: A Prehistory of the Establishment* (NY: McGraw-Hill, 1977), p. 422. Alternative analyses of burial practices to derive information concerning hierarchical groups is discussed by Joseph Tainter, "Social Inference and Mortuary Practices: An Experiment in Numerical Classification," *World Archeology* 7, no. 1 (1974), pp. 1–14.

Hopewell effigy pipes.

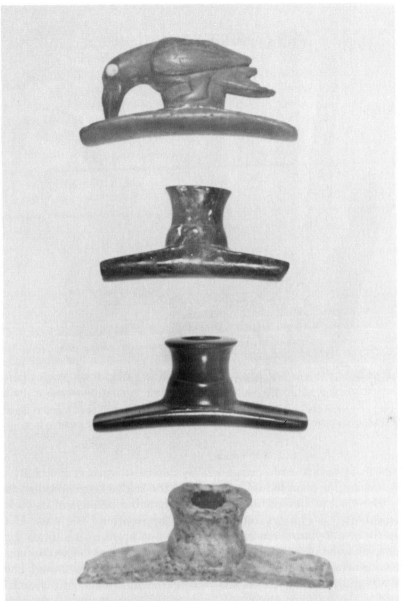

Field Museum of Natural History

Richard G. Forbis, were expressing their "concern for the dead."[10] Only after many generations did this value slowly begin to change. That was

---

[10]Richard G. Forbis, "Eastern North America" in *North America: St. Martin's Series in Pre-history*, ed. Shirley Gorenstein et al. (NY: St. Martin's Press, 1975), pp. 91–92. Forbis is undecided between psychological, climatic, and exchange explanation of Hopewell decline.

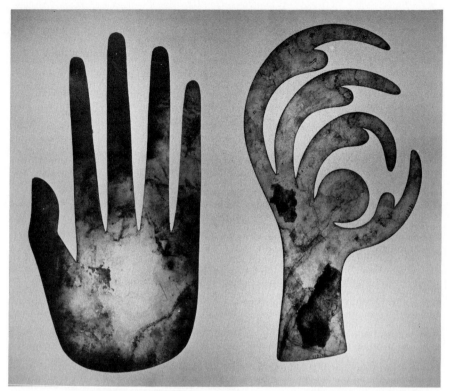

Hand and eagle-claw effigies. Because such artifacts have often been found in burials, some archeologists have suggested there was a Hopewell obsession with death.

rebirth—psychological springtime—as the great wave of morbidity passed. A "desire for plain living" returned to the midwestern woodlands.

Here is a picture of human society changing because of its view of the world. It is a strategy often used for approaching the past. Historians speak of a *Zeitgeist,* elusively defined as a "spirit of the times." Anthropoligsts write of "world views" or of "cultural values." The concepts might be a bit cloudy, but by no means are they empty of meaning. There was a Navaho belief in "perfection" expressed in artifact, music, and prayer and a Crow Indian theme of "individual acquisition of knowledge." In Maya and Aztec societies there was "concern with calculation of time"; in Renaissance Europe was a "celebration of everyday life." Modern America has its own special ethos—a curious idea known as "progress," an intellectual invention only three centuries old.

But the problem with such explanations—indeed with much intellectual history—is that the origins of the cultural values are left unexplained. If Hopewell really was an expression of intensive concern with the dead, then how did this preoccupation come into existence? Why, several hundred years later, were the traditional values abandoned? Ideas, of course, are important, and have an impact on human society. Just as important are the causes behind the ideas.

Other archeologists have been less convinced by the inroads into Hopewell psychology and have emphasized that artifacts were not always buried in graves. The items traveled over considerable distances, changed hands, and had a functional life. Hopewell was more than a cult focused on death. For Tainter the intricate webwork of artifact pathways suggests an equally intricate system of economic exchange. Perhaps ranking in Hopewell society was connected with redistribution. Tainter has recently discovered that high-status Hopewellian burials had little evidence in their bones of childhood nutritional stress.[11] Beyond that, their bones did not indicate that the experienced much physical labor. The exact opposite was true of the bones of the low-status people. For Tainter it is tentative evidence of an elite with good diets and leisure—very possibly because they were controlling the movement of goods.

Hopewell as exchange adaptation

If it was a redistributive system, then why did it emerge in the region? Why did it flourish for 600 years and then slowly diminish? I believe that a possible answer is suggested by the region itself—that mosaic of forest and stream which was the Ohio Valley. Hunters and gatherers had lived in that country since the beginning of the foraging tradition. Fish were plentiful in the creeks and the rivers; there were berries and grapes. And yet, one can drift a bit far in such a picture of the Ohio Valley. The abundance was seasonal—confined to the warm months of the year.

In the bone-chilling midwestern winters, food was scarce; it was the "hungry time."[12] The low hills and the flats near the rivers were covered with snow. There was very little in that season to live on, other than waterfowl or occasional deer. Supplies of meat in time would diminish; fruits and berries would quickly have spoiled. Nuts, of course, are a storable resource, but their value is open to question. They may not have been as important a food as they were cracked up to be. One problem is that nut-bearing species do not always bear a crop every year. White oak trees produce their acorns once every 7 to 11 years; shagbark hickories yield up their crop on alternate years. It is possible, but not yet certain, that a grove might have been synchronized—all of its trees producing in

---

[11]Joseph Tainter, "Behavior and Status in a Middle Woodland Mortuary Population from the Illinois Valley," *American Antiquity* 45, no. 2 (1980), pp. 308–13.

[12]Jane E. Buikstra, "Biocultural Dimensions of Archeological Study," in *Biocultural Adaptation in Prehistoric America*, ed. Robert L. Blakely (Athens: University of Georgia Press, 1977), pp. 67–84. I have found this to be a very valuable summary of the Midwest-riverine adaptation.

Center for American Archeology, Northwestern University

Views of the Koster site. This Illinois excavation has contributed much to our knowledge of environmental and cultural changes in the riverine north.

Center for American Archeology, Northwestern University

A nutting-stone. Walnut and hickory groves may have been thinning in the Midwest. This could have contributed to increased riverine farming.

one year and barren the next. Then too, the walnut and hickory groves may have been thinning in the Ohio Valley—apparently at about the same time that agriculture began.

Perhaps this is one of the reasons for cultivation among the Adenans: the trees could not furnish enough storable food for the winter. Goose-foot, knotweed, smartweed, marsh-elder, and sunflower seeds provided food through the deep winter months until the coming of spring. For generations the Adena people planted and hunted in the Ohio Valley. But about 200 BC there were the beginnings of pressure and change. With the emergence of agriculture, the population had probably grown. To provide more food, cultivation had spread through the mud-flats. Hoe and digging-stick agriculture demanded more time and more labor for planting, weeding, and guarding from pests until the harvest in fall. This meant that less time was available for hunting in the oak-hickory forests, or for the mass fishing done in the fall when the harvest was due.

In other parts of the world under a similar set of conditions, humanity has adapted by creating a net of exchange. Today in the Philippine Islands—and other parts of Southeastern Asia—hunters and gatherers live on the fringes of agricultural groups. They practice what Jean and Warren Peterson have called an *exchange adaptation* —a strategy for meeting their

Center for American Archeology, Northwestern University

Screening at Koster. Careful recovery of botanical materials, here and at other sites, has provided evidence of an Eastern agricultural complex.

resource and labor requirements.[13] Foragers need storable plant foods for their times of seasonal shortage.[14] Farmers need meat; there is less time from them to hunt it themselves. So foragers become professional primi-

---

[13]Jean T. Peterson and Warren Peterson, "Implications of Contemporary and Prehistoric Exchange Systems," in *Sunda and Sahul: Prehistoric Studies in Southeast Asia, Melanesia and Australia,* ed. J. Allen, J. Golson, and R. Jones (New York Academic Press, 1977), pp. 533–64.

[14]Problems of forager storage are discussed by Elizabeth Colson, "In Good Years and Bad: Food Strategies of Self-Reliant Societies," *Journal of Anthropological Research,* Spring, 1979, vol. 35, pp. 18–29.

tives, as anthropologist Karl Hutterer has called them: they specialize in hunting large game that they give to the farmers. Cultivators provide storable plant foods and manufactured items as well; they allow hunters to shoot wild game along the edges of fields.

I believe that such a system existed throughout the forests of the Ohio Valley. It emerged as agriculture became more intense on the rivers. At Peisker in the lower Illinois Valley, a wide range of forest animals was hunted. This is true throughout much of the Midwest until 200 BC.[15] But when cultivators began hoeing the mud-flats, hunting patterns become strikingly different: there was specialization in larger species of game. At Scovill and Apple Creek, Illinois, deer and turkey were shot by the hunters; other game, although abundant, were "relatively ignored."[16]

As the process became more intricate, distant regions were involved in exchange. If a group had access to copper, deposits of mica, or outcroppings of stone, these were resources easily converted into storable food. Or they might be delivered to specialists who would fashion them into ornaments and tools. Perhaps, as in the New Guinea highlands, information was also exchanged: magical knowledge believed to have influence on the supernatural world.

Here, as in other parts of the planet, there was power to be had in connections: in linking up one's scattered relations into a network of trade. The kin groups directing the traffic provided their clients with valuable items from distant locations, other territories, and other societies. If such power were inherited by descendants, then very likely there were midwestern chiefdoms at the centers of these far-ranging networks of Woodland exchange.

Collapse of Hopewell exchange

It might have endured for millennia, but there were dangers built into the system. Like any other matrix of trade, it involved trivial and critical items and thousands of items that existed on a range in-between. If stone pipes had disappeared from the world, that (perhaps!) would not have ended the system—even though they were probably valuable for ritual use. Food was another matter entirely; it may have been here that difficulties began—as the farming populations expanded on the riverine flats.

All along, the Hopewellian farmers had to live close to the rivers, where the water table was high and the crops could be abundantly grown. Farming had not spread randomly, but had expanded from mud-flat to mud-flat. The density and the number of sites noticeably increase at about 450 AD.[17] Populations were filling up the pockets of the riverine north. Settlements after this time extended farther away from the rivers, toward the marginal

---

[15]Streuver, "Woodland Subsistence."

[16]Munson, Parmalee, and Yarnell, "Subsistence Ecology."

[17]Jane E. Buikstra, "Biocultural Dimensions."

backwater ponds and meandering sloughs. Don Dragoo suggests the possibility that the soil was becoming exhausted.[18] Populations were moving to the margins of arable land.

If cultivators had declining crop yields, this would have jeopardized a system of trade. When the harvest was consumed, there was little left for exchange. Hunters and gatherers, of course, could retaliate by reducing their contributions of protein. For foragers and farmers there was a decline in available food. Physical anthropologist Della Cook has examined skeletal remains excavated from burial mounds at the edge of the floodplain.[19] She has discovered that many of the skeletons from the last years of Hopewellian times bore the telltale markings of disease and nutritional stress. They had high-carbohydrate diets, probably from consuming the food that they grew—and their bones bore the evidence of protein malnutrition.

In the last 600 years of Hopewell, until about AD 1000, chronic warfare spread across the valley as the network collapsed. Farmers conceivably fought one another as their crop yields continued to fall. And they might well have fought hunters and gatherers, since, beginning at AD 800, the agricultural settlements were encroaching on the forested slopes. Stockades now dotted the valley. There were burials with arrow wounds. Hopewell interaction was becoming a network of war.

As raiding increased on the rivers, political systems might also have changed. There may have been an increase in the number of ranked social groups. Jane Buikstra has suggested that the burials from the last days of Hopewell reflect such a change.[20] But more comparisons remain to be done, so we still do not know. If there really was such a transformation, it would have been an understandable one, and similar to what we have seen in many other societies. Scarcity—as Michael Harner has noted—is closely related to political power.[21] Lingering groups that, at the end of Hopewell, were still managing to regulate trade, may have become more politically powerful than even before. Intriguingly, the effigy mounds—those rambling structures of piled-up earth—were built in this period of chronic malnutrition and raids.[22] Conceivably, the mounds were symbolic of the power that a chiefdom possessed—the human resources still available for commerce and war.

[18]Don W. Dragoo, "Some Aspects of Eastern North American Prehistory: A Review 1975," *American Antiquity* 41, no. 1 (1976), p. 16.

[19]Della C. Cook, *Pathologic States and Disease Process in Illinois Woodland Populations: An Epidemiologic Approach*, Ph.D. dissertation (University of Chicago Department of Anthropology, 1976), pp. 1–8.

[20]Jane E. Buikstra, "Biocultural Dimensions."

[21]A recent formulation of his view is "Scarcity, the Factors of Production, and Social Evolution," in *Population, Ecology and Social Evolution*, ed. Steven Polgar (The Hague: Mouton, 1975). See also the earlier discussion in Chapter 8.

[22]James B. Griffin, "The Midlands and Northeastern United States," in *Ancient Native Americans*, ed. Jesse D. Jennings (San Francisco: W. H. Freemn, 1978), pp. 255–56.

At about 1,000 or so years ago, the system had at last disappeared. Malnutrition, ongoing conflict, and stress-related diseases as well took their toll from the last of the chiefdoms of the riverine north. Small groups abandoned their villages, hunted, and gardened in the forested hills. The remarkable system called Hopewell had faded and gone.

A commonplace of social evolution is that deterioration is also emergence: one society's decline can be a part of another's growth. I think this was especially true of the southeastern woodlands of North America during the centuries of diseases and conflicts on the midwestern rivers. Here were societies of growing complexity at the very period of Hopewell decline: ritual centers, large villages, and a developing network of trade. This seems more than just a simple coincidence or a mysterious shift in the location of power. The two regions may have been closely related in intricate ways.

The emergence of social complexity in the American Southeast

Social relations that knit the Hopewellians with the societies of the southeastern woodlands connected the north with a wilderness visibly different. To the south of the Appalachian Mountains, the climate was warm throughout much of the year. The hungry time of deep-winter months was less of a problem in the southeastern woodlands. Forager territories were not covered for months with a mantle of snow. Yet the wilderness had its diversity. There were stretches almost empty of people and other parts of the forest where villages grew into towns. In the foothills below the Appalachians and in highland uplifts throughout the deep south were dense forests with abundant wild plant foods, turkey, and deer.[23] It was here and along the deep rivers—especially the murky, twisting Mississippi—where southeastern Indians had settled for thousands of years. Much of the southland that sloped to the ocean was a desolate "pine barren" country—a "green desert" of coastal-plain pines that was almost abandoned.[24]

By as early as 3,000 years ago, complex society had emerged in the southlands—on the high bluffs overlooking the floodplain of the lower Mississippi. Poverty point was six earthen embankments, octagonal, and concentrically nested; attached to its outermost ridge was a bird-shaped mound. It is possible that about half of the structure may have been lost due to river erosion. Nearby, in the Louisiana countryside, village sites are on the rims of the bluffs and near the edges of bayous that snake through the mud of the floodplain. Perhaps as many as 10,000 people lived in this basin of ridges and mud-flats, controlling the trade goods

---

[23]Bruce D. Smith, "Middle Mississippi Exploitation of Animal Populations: A Predictive Model," *American Antiquity* 39, no. 2 (1974), pp. 274–91.

[24]The "green desert" is extensively discussed by Lewis H. Larson, *Aboriginal Subsistence Technology on the Southeastern Coastal Plain During the Late Prehistoric Period*, Ph.D. Dissertation (Ann Arbor: University of Michigan, Department of Anthropology, 1969).

that flowed along six major rivers. Archeologist Jon Gibson has analyzed 19,000 artifacts from the site and discovered 3 ranking groups buried at Poverty Point.[25] The site may have been, he has argued, the very first North American chiefdom—emerging on the rivers and managing a network of trade.

But Poverty Point was only the beginning. There were other chiefdoms along other streams. Southern chiefs were emerging and controlling the circulation of goods. A thousand years after Poverty Point there was Marksville in Louisiana, with its burial mounds and its system of local exchange.[26] And in the years when the Hopewellian networks were broken by diseases and war, there were elites in the south gaining in political strength. At Kolomoki in southwestern Georgia, six miles from the Chattahoochee River, a temple mound and a plaza were a community's ceremonial center. On a tributary of the Chattahoochee River, the site was dotted by mounds; one was flattened on top and was approximately 50 feet high. Several of the burials in the mounds were furnished with animal-effigy vessels. Kolomoki was home for a rising southeastern elite. Weeden Island in gulf coastal Florida was a rich ceremonial complex at a time when Hopewellian interaction was falling to pieces.

Many of these southeastern chiefdoms—like the ones in the riverine north—may have tended the plant foods that flourished on the alluvial bottoms. Pigweed, goosefoot, smartweed, sumpweed, ragweed, and wild millet could all have been grown on the mud-flats of Poverty Point. Even so, there has been some reluctance to envision an agricultural complex, not only for Poverty Point but for the other chiefdoms as well. Archeologist Richard Ford has argued that the villagers were not cultivators at all; that wild foods were abundant and were part of their systems of trade.[27] But evidence on the question is meager. Many of the sites were dug decades ago, when pottery seemed more important than a sample of riverine plants. Of course, it is this very evidence that might tell us of the chiefdoms themselves, of how they emerged from a southeastern foraging society. Did plant-food gathering on the rivers become more labor-intensive through time? Did this lead to the emergence of a southern exchange adaptation? Such questions are beginning to refocus archeology in the American South. There is much to be learned of how these riverine chiefdoms began.

Whatever might have been their beginnings, they were flourishing at exactly the time when the intricate midwestern system was falling apart. Conceivably, as I mentioned earlier, the two processes were closely related—both part of a larger system of changes in the forested east. Hope-

[25]Jon L. Gibson, "Poverty Point: The First North American Chiefdom," *Archaeology*, April 1974, pp. 97–105.

[26]Marksville and related sites are discussed by Jon D. Muller in "The Southeast" in Jennings, *Ancient Native Americans*, pp. 281–325.

[27]Richard I. Ford, "Northeastern Archeology: Past and Future Directions," *Annual Review of Anthropology* 3, 1974, pp. 385–413.

wellian commercial connections had reached far into the American South. Burials and pottery at sites such as Marksville reflect the Midwest. Southern elites along the Mississippi, the Yazoo, or the Chattahoochee Rivers received trade items from the shores of the lakes or the edge of the Rockies. From the hamlets in the woodlands around them, they collected goods to be exchanged farther north. Then the valley of Ohio fell victim to malnutrition and raids. As Jon D. Muller has suggested, the southeastern "volume of trade" was probably reduced as the Hopewellian system collapsed.[28] If so, it might have been an opportunity for chiefs throughout the southeastern woodlands to become more politically powerful than before. If the obsidian supply out of the Rockies was reduced to little more than a trickle, then obsidian would have become more valuable than it was in the past. The chief who had maintained a connection—or a personal cache of obsidian blades—could probably accelerate his power within the society. The blades would have a higher exchange rate in terms of local plant foods, ornaments, or meat—or in terms of secret information, alliances, and new trading connections. The same effect was probably true of other items now growing scarce. The plight of the Hopewellians was affecting political power.

Out of this emerged greater complexity and more conspicuous social prestige. The centuries that followed in the southlands were an epoch of powerful chiefdoms still in existence when the Western Europeans arrived. The evolution of agricultural systems was a critical contributing factor but, as I hope I have suggested, there was probably much more involved. Before corn was ever planted on the bottom lands, there were elites along the southeastern rivers—waxing powerful because of the crisis in the riverine north.

The Mississippi chiefdoms

Hopewell was already a memory when the South was a constellation of chiefdoms—communities grown up on the flats and the bluffs near the rivers. Corn, beans, and squash were cultivated on the flood-richened mud of the bottoms. Deer and wild turkey were hunted in the woods near the streams. Nuts, wild plants, grapes, and berries were collected in the woodland thickets. The southeastern chiefdoms had food throughout most of the year.

Never far from the banks of a river, the southern settlements were very much alike.[29] Late prehistoric southeastern chiefdoms—or Mississippians, as they are usually called—were ceremonial centers embedded in a network of hamlets. The center itself was often surrounded by a stockade of vertical logs. Inside that enclosure was usually a large earthen mound. It was in the shape of a flat-topped pyramid with steps leading up on one side. On

---

[28]Muller, "The Southeast," p. 305.

[29]Mississippian site descriptions, except when otherwise noted, are from Muller, ibid.

Center for American Archeology, Northwestern University

Most Mississippian farmers inhabited dwellings very similar to this.

the top there were probably houses for chief and his immediate kin. Perhaps, too, other powerful kin groups made up of warriors, traders or priests lived in this summit overlooking a ceremonial plaza. From what we know of the southeastern chiefdoms still in existence when Europeans arrived, it is likely that the pyramid was a focus of religious behavior. People from the countryside gathered at its base in the ceremonial plaza to observe the enactment of ritual that bound them together. On one occasion, in Louisiana, the group of observers included a Frenchman. The account by Le Page du Pratz of the burial of Natchez chief Tattooed Serpent is a restrained—and powerful—portrait of ceremonial life:

> I have said elsewhere that the temple, the house of the great chief, and that of the Tattooed-serpent were on the square; that of the great Sun was built on a mound of earth carried to a height of about 8 feet. It was on this mound that we placed ourselves at the side of the dwelling of the great Sun, who had shut himself in in order to see nothing . . . .
> At the appointed hour the master of ceremonies arrived, adorned with red feathers in a half crown on his head . . . . He entered the house of the great Sun in this dress to ask him, without doubt, for permission to start the funeral procession. We were not able to hear what reply was made to him, because this sovereign ordinarily spoke in a very low although serious tone . . . . As soon as the master of ceremonies went to

the door of the deceased he saluted him, without entering, with a great *hou*. Then he made the death cry, to which the people on the square replied in the same manner. The entire nation did the same thing and the echoes repeated it from afar . . . . The Tattooed-serpent . . . was placed on a litter with two poles, which four men carried. Another pole was placed underneath toward the middle and crosswise, which two other men held, in order to sustain the body. These six men who carried it were guardians of the temple. The grand master of ceremonies walked first, after him the oldest of the war chiefs, who bore the pole from which hung the cane links. He held this pole in one hand and in the other a war calumet, a mark of the dignity of the deceased . . . . Finally the body reached the temple, and the victims put themselves in their places as determined in the rehearsals. The mats were stretched out. They seated themselves there. The death cry was uttered. The pellets of tobacco were given to them and a little water to drink after each one. After they had all been taken [each victim's] head was covered with a skin on which the cord was placed around the neck, two men held it in order that it should not be dragged away [to one side] by the stronger party, and the cord, which had a running knot, was held at each end by three men, who drew with all their strength from the two opposite sides. They are so skillful in this operation that it is impossible to describe it as promptly as it is done. The body of the Tattooed-serpent was placed in a great trench to the right of the temple in the interior. His two wives were buried in the same trench. La Glorieuse was buried in front of the temple to the right and the chancellor on the left. The others were carried into the temples of their own villages in order to be interred there. After this ceremony the cabin of the deceased was burned, according to custom.[30]

Beyond the stockade was the everyday world of tiny villages and fields of maize, where cultivators hoed and weeded in the summer heat. The square-shaped houses they lived in were vertical poles covered with mud. The roof was of thatch; there was a hearth in the center of the floor. Often, the villages were built between the forest and the flats of the river; wild foods and the cultivated fields were a short walk away.

Many of the mounds have survived to the present, looming over the 20th-century towns—imposing evidence of the powerful chiefs of Mississippian times. Lake George, Greenwood, Anna, and the so-called Grand Village of the Natchez were riverine agricultural communities in western Mississippi. At Moundville, Alabama, Etowah, Georgia, and Irene Mound at the edge of the savannah, ceremonial centers were surrounded by small farming hamlets. But probably the most powerful of all was a chiefdom in East St. Louis, Illinois—a large village and a center of trade—the Cahokia site.

---

[30]Le Page du Pratz, cited in John R. Swanton's *Indian Tribes of the Lower Mississippi Valley and Adjacent Coast of the Gulf of Mexico*, Smithsonian Institution, Bureau of American Ethnology Bulletin 43, (Washington, D.C.: U.S. Government Printing Office, 1911), pp. 148–49.

Some 14 centuries ago several small villages were built in a valley, in a land of mineral-rich soils called the American Bottoms. The Mississippi, the Illinois, and the Missouri Rivers flow together where the village emerged. It became possible to establish connections with the entire Midwest. At about AD 1000 Cahokia was indeed at the height of its influence: an agricultural chiefdom coordinating riverine trade.

The Cahokia site. At the junction of three major rivers, it was a center of Mississippian exchange.

Photos courtesy of Melvin L. Fowler, Archeological Research Laboratory, University of Wisconsin—Milwaukee

Five hamlets had become a community where perhaps 30,000 people were living. On its outskirts, beyond the stockade, the country was dotted with about 48 villages, many of which were clustered very close to ceremonial mounds. The great mound in Cahokia itself—Monks Mound, archeologists call it—covered nearly 14 acres and was constructed 100 feet high. A burial mound was aligned with this structure on the north-south axis of settlement. It was here that Melvin Flower excavated a male burial on a platform of beads.[31] Nearby were "bundles" of bones and a bit farther away, six separate tombs.[32] Copper, stacks of mica sheets, highly valued precious stones, and some 800 arrow heads had been placed in the graves of the men found near the beads. Most remarkable of all were burials of 50 young women. All about the same age and size, their bodies arranged into rows, they probably were ritually sacrificed and placed with the chief. In America, as in the Pacific and Europe and in many parts of Africa and Asia, authoritarian political power was a fact of existence. Sumptuous burials, the mounds themselves, religious ceremonies, and the taking of lives all were privileges and rights of a southeastern chieftain.

Between a tyrant or usurping chief and any
outlawed man or errant thief
It's just the same, there is no difference.
                    Geoffrey Chaucer

**Moundville,
information,
and chiefs**

There is insight in these cynical lines—touching both ancient times and ourselves. The chief, like society's outlaw, could be abusive—even lethal—at times, could commandeer property, and could force others to yield to his wishes. But of course there is one important difference: the chief, ironically, is playing by the rules. His deeds do not make him a fugitive; they make him esteemed. Why was it that, despite their excesses, chiefs could somehow inspire respect? How was power maintained in the ancient North American chiefdoms?

It is a question we have looked at before but should briefly consider again—especially in connection with the chiefs of Mississippian times. As I mentioned earlier in the story, I believe that the power of a chief was largely the result of his role in a redistributive system. Villages in different territories could deliver their goods to a chief. He could parcel them back to the villagers on the basis of their critical needs. He could provide more for the ones who were loyal and punish those who were not. A portion would be kept for himself and for the members of his kin group as well. And there would be a bit more beyond that—conceivably the goods that

[31]Melvin L. Fowler, "A Pre-Columbian Urban Center on the Mississippi," *Scientific American,* August 1975.

[32]The "bundles" were possibly reburials of individuals who had died earlier and were subsequently exhumed to be placed alongside the elite.

were in scarcest supply. These could be exchanged for other materials, information, or military alliances. They were a bank that was actually a store of political power.

This is not the only theory of a chiefdom, though perhaps it is the predominant one. Christopher Peebles and Susan Kus (among others) have recently suggested an alternative view.[33] Were the chiefs really redistributors? Or were they powerful for a very different reason? Perhaps our theories about these overbearing ancients should be examined again.

Over 200 burials from Moundville—a Mississippian site in Alabama—were analyzed by Peebles and Kus to determine their ranking. Prestigious artifacts, everyday items, and the location of the burials themselves all were used to find evidence of social prestige. The clusters of these characteristics suggested three hierarchical groups. And at the pinnacle of Moundville society, of course, was the chief. What was the basis of his political power? They deny that it was redistribution. Chiefs did not channel the movement of goods—they controlled information.

Peebles and Kus have suggested there was little need at sites such as Moundville for a centralized authority to control a system of trade. Villages were within easy reach of the river and the forested bluffs. All the resources that one would require were a short distance away. Trade existed but was not centralized. Casual exchanges between two territories involving kin or, perhaps, trading partners were more than likely the economic system of chiefdom societies.

Why was there a chief at all? Perhaps, more than any other reason, because of the knowledge he acquired and the decisions he made. Conducting a tour of his territory, he would converse with the village authorities. They would talk about the weather, the crops, or the possibility of raids. Through such visits, done over and over, he would learn much about the chiefdom he ruled. Indeed, he would understand it better than anyone else. This information was the key to his power. Decisions, such as when to plant, when to gather your warriors, and perhaps, when to harvest your crops, when made by the chief, were most often correct. He was rewarded with prestigious items, treated as something akin to a god. Knowledge—not commerce at all—was the basis of power.

It is an elegant and forceful analysis—and I have only sampled it here. But perhaps it is a valuable idea taken too far. It is true that the Moundville hamlets were never very far from the forest and that they were only a short walk away from the crops near the river. But—as Peebles and Kus have suggested—their populations were growing through time. They admit that the villages "fissioned," but they never say where the villagers went. Conceivably, since the best lands were occupied, people moved into marginal country, away from the river to where crops were less easily grown.

---

[33]Christopher S. Peebles and Susan M. Kus, "Some Archeological Correlates of Ranked Societies," *American Antiquity* 42, no. 3 (1977), pp. 421–48.

In my view, this is the critical problem that Peebles and Kus have ignored: the movement of agricultural populations out of optimum lands. Such migrations are not a smooth process, like ripples flowing out from a center. They are movements into scattered, distant pockets of arable soil. Informal trade across territorial boundaries is no longer an exchange with rich neighbors. Adjacent marginal societies have little to offer one another. This is why it would seem more adaptive to pursue a strategy of centralized trade, coordinated by a kin group inhabiting an optimum area. Resources are more equally distributed; the process is formalized and highly predictable. This explains why chiefdoms make their appearance when agricultural populations become scattered in Southwest Asia, Europe, the Pacific, and Eastern North America. It explains why Joseph Tainter discovered that chiefs had better diets than their subjects. The clear implication is privileged access to a wide range of food. Of course chiefs could give advice to their subjects, and almost certainly many of them did. But this was a means of enhancing their power. It was not the entire basis for rule. The inhabitants of distant, marginal lands could not eat information.

It is impossible to say with any certainty what the Mississippian might have become. Powerful chiefdoms, vast regional trade, craft specialists, and bustling villages were all in existence at the time the Europeans arrived. Many of the villages were often at war, but the chiefdoms were, perhaps, not collapsing. Indeed, war can contribute to nucleation—more densely populated communities—to the increase of centralized power, and to the rise of the state. And we still do not know enough about them to say with certainty why they were fighting. Possibly in many parts of the southlands, marginal communities began raiding one another—especially if a centralized chief could not provide for their needs.

The end of the Mississippian

Lewis Larson at one time suggested that the raids of Mississippian times evolved out of the pressures on limited arable lands.[34] Easily tilled bottomland soils were becoming increasingly scarce. Such soils, however, were needed if villagers were to have enough food. Because of this pressure, Mississippians were often at war.

But Jon L. Gibson suspects there was never a crisis over soils and food.[35] Warfare grew out of the structure of political life. Like the Natchez that Du Pratz once visited, Mississippians were hierarchically ranked. If you were born into a high-ranking kin group, your prestige would be fairly secure. But you were required to take a mate from a group lower than yours. This would lower your childrens' prestige; for their offspring, it

---

[34]Lewis Larson, "Functional Considerations of Warfare in the Southeast during the Mississippian Period," *American Antiquity* 37, 1972, pp. 383–92.

[35]Jon L. Gibson, "Aboriginal Warfare in the Protohistoric Southeast: An Alternative Perspective," *American Antiquity* 39, 1974, pp. 130–33.

was lowered again. Theoretically, almost all the society was "marrying-down."

Cross-cutting this unbalanced system was the acclaim acquired through war. Successes in fighting an enemy could elevate a person's prestige. He was accorded high rank, and the process began over again. Equilibrium—or simply, a balance—was restored to the systems of kin. To maintain that balance, the warriors set off on their raids.

I believe that there is something persuasive about *both* of these views of the past. Ranking systems among Mississippians had a built-in decline of prestige—an imbalance that was only corrected by achievements in war. But why was this system created? Perhaps, as Bruce Dickson has argued, the shortage of available land gave rise to societies that rewarded military success.[36] You were fighting to better your status—but this affected the natural world. It put distance between warring villages; Mississippians were dispersed on the land. Unsettled territory, in a sense, was a natural preserve.

What that strategy in time might have led to is something that we never will know. French, Spanish, and English "discoveries" all successively took a great toll. Smallpox and other diseases became American plagues. Today, four centuries later, little is left but the names of the rivers. Garish drawings of Indians and tomahawks adorn souvenir shops near the roadside. The ancient mounds stand vacant above the hum of the industrial South.

---

[36]D. Bruce Dickson, "The Yanomamo of the Mississippi Valley?" *American Antiquity,* October 1981, p. 913. This article also suggests that the development of stockade defenses created a military stalemate in Mississippian society. Stockades—and the lands around them—could rarely be captured and held. This state of affairs ended abruptly when Europeans arrived.

15 / Ritual and Trade in the American West, Mexico, and Peru

It is more than just cacti and rattlesnakes—although, in fact, it has plenty of those. The American Southwest is a tapestry of landscapes and life.[1] Just to the north of the Mexican border, from southern Arizona to south-central New Mexico, sparse cacti and shrubs are scattered across the flat desert floor. Rainfall is scanty, and yet there is water. The Gila, the Santa Cruz, the San Pedro, and the Rio Grande rivers stream down from the northerly highlands out into the desert.

Land lifts higher as you move to the north and becomes a woodland of juniper trees. Pinyon, mahogany, and oak forests cover the slopes. Warm air blowing north from the desert climbs the hills and there is thunder and rain. It is the richer, transitional world of the Mogollon Highlands.

Close to the Little Colorado River and not far from Flagstaff, Arizona, this forested, high country becomes the Colorado Plateau. It is a vast geological masterpiece, an intricate artwork created by time. Long before humanity existed, great formations of sedimentary rock were covered over as waves of hot lava burst out of the ground. Later, when the lava had cooled, the Colorado River cut its way through the land, carving deep below the surface down into the softer formations. Today it is a bewildering complex of mesas, peaks, canyons, and valleys. The Colorado River still churns between steep rocky walls. The plateau covers much of Utah and stretches out into western Colorado. It is rugged and changeable country; it always has been. Willow and cottonwood grow in the canyons near the edges of rivers and springs. Shrubs and grassland cover the ground at the low elevations. But if you can manage a climb up the slopes, you make your way into forests of pine trees. If you can scale the very highest peaks, you find cold-loving spruce.

---

[1] The description of southwestern ecology is derived from William D. Lipe, "The Southwest," in *Ancient Native Americans*, ed. Jesse D. Jennings (San Francisco: W. H. Freeman, 1978), pp. 327–401.

The American
Southwest.

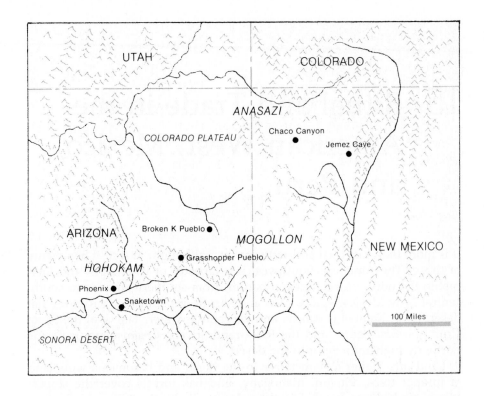

We have seen much earlier in the story that this country was discovered
long ago by big-game hunters moving down from the Canadian tundra.
In the days when the deserts were grassland, they hunted mammoth until
the mammoth was gone. They drove bison over the edges of arroyos and
stripped the meat from their bones. Then the grassland turned into desert;
lakes and marshes dried up into ponds. The herds disappeared; in the
west there was a new way of life. Now there were small scattered bands
that gathered plant foods and seeds on the desert. They scraped out the
insides of cacti and hunted rabbit and deer. Many of them would continue
as foragers when European settlers first arrived in the west. But groups
along the rim of the mountains were a circuit of change.

Perhaps as early as 4,000 years ago, corn and squash were being grown
in the highlands, in an area that today is the New Mexico-Arizona border.
The Southwest, like eastern North America, became a theater of cultural
change. Archeologist Emil Haury suggested that a web of cultural connections brought these crops northwest from the Mesa Central. Following
the highland edge of the mountains, they spread into northwestern New
Mexico, transforming the lives of the foragers who lived in that region.
Archeologist Cynthia Irwin-Williams has found that the size of forager
camps was increasing. Hunter-and-gatherer populations were growing in
the stream-fed hills.

The Arizona State Museum, The University of Arizona, E.B. Sayles, Photographer

A.V. Kidder. A product of New England society, he became enamored of the American West. His concept that archeology could be a synthesis of multiple sciences has become a philosophical principle for researching the past.

Archeologists have worked in this country before this century even began, picking and probing their way on the slopes of the mesas. Out of those days of pack horses and dust storms, of Indian guides and chilly nights on the desert, a past was discovered; a science was slowly created. It is true enough that American archeology was a product of many different regions. But it is also true that a great deal of it was born in the American west.

A. V. Kidder and the discovery at Pecos

There was nothing of the cowboy about him—at least when he first saw the canyons.[2] His world had been New England colleges, three years in a Swiss private school, the soccer team at Harvard, and bird watching on the campus at Cambridge. There was little doubt about where he was headed: a career in medicine was carefully planned. But when the time came to make the decision, he had started to waver.

Alfred Vincent Kidder was just 22 then and deciding what to do with his life. (Charles Darwin had faced the same question at precisely that age.) The exact chemistry that led him to abandon a medical career for the southwestern mesas was something that perhaps even he did not quite understand. It may have had something to do with the old books in the library at home: long government reports about the customs of the American Indian. Or perhaps the spark was ignited when he hunted arrowheads as a boy. Whatever the cause, he joined an expedition going west.

The experience was a transformation. Exhausted by the heat of the canyons, footsore from the treks up the mesas, he discovered something that may have been in him from his earliest years. "None of us," he remembered it later, "ever viewed so much of the world at one time." He had never seen "so wild and barren" a country as this. The weeks in New Mexico were a trial by fire of skittish horses and mazes of canyons. He was decided. He would be an archeologist for the rest of his days.

The ink was hardly dry on his doctorate when he was back digging in the Arizona heat. His skin darkened in the hot sun of Utah; he cultivated a beard. Now that he had made up his mind, he put all of his energy into the West. He met others who were sharing his passion: people with ideas that had barely been tried. The dry canyons turned into a center of intellectual change.

A New Mexico ruin called Pecos became a laboratory of method and theory. New ideas of reconstructing prehistory were put to the test. N. C. Nelson showed how cultural deposits placed the materials of a site into sequence. He showed how pottery types in layers increased and diminished through time. This made it possible to compare different sites and learn more of the region. An astronomer named A. E. Douglass insisted that the wood preserved in the desert would provide evidence of how old something was and of how climate had changed. Kidder himself was endlessly speculating about what archeology might well become: a science that explains how our behavior has changed in the past.

In later years he dug in other places, and yet somehow it was never the same.[3] The excitement of the days in the canyons was never rekindled.

---

[2]The biographical sketch of A. V. Kidder is taken from Robert Wauchope, "Alfred Vincent Kidder, 1885–1963," *American Antiquity*, October 2, 1965, pp. 149–66. I also profited from criticism offered by Richard B. Woodbury.

[3]He experienced a productive career as a Mayan archeologist, during which time many Pecos ideas were put into effect.

When he traveled back 30 years later, the old memories returned in a flood. He saw "the gray curtains of the summer storms trailing far off across the Big Prairie"; he savored the smell of the first drops of rain on the parched desert ground. For Kidder, "it was all most upsetting." For years, he had been struggling, he said, to get the "Southwestern virus" out of his system. Now it was back again and it was "worse than ever." The "virus," as he called it, never left him; it was with him until the last of his life. He could never recapture the feeling of the years out at Pecos.

I think what came out of those days was a challenging view of archeology—but it was a challenge inevitably faced by a developing science. Kidder knew that archeology required a pan-scientific attack—that it is not possible for an experimental science to go it alone. Techniques of chemistry and physics were needed to determine the age of materials. Botany and zoology could tell us of ancient environments. Geology, of course, was essential; so were statistics and soil analysis. Social anthropology was a canvass of human behavior. To master all of these disciplines would require an intellectual monster. So archeologists must work with scientists of many different fields.

The pan-scientific attack is today almost taken for granted. It has had an incalculable effect on our views of prehistory. I think that this, more than anything else, was the critical discovery that came out of Pecos. There are many different strategies needed for understanding the past.

Built into the walls of the canyons beneath great ledges of bulging rock, they seem to catch fire in the reflected heat of the sun. In the abandoned Southwestern pueblos—hundreds of empty stone and mud-walled rooms— there is little more than the flutter of a bird or the sound of the wind. Who lived there? Where did they go? These are very old questions in the West. Today there is still much about the houses we do not understand. They are the relics of an intricate process—a transformation of Southwestern life—that may have had its beginnings some 4,000 years in the past.

Networks of technological change

It was becoming a rainier country, or at least some archeologists think so. In many places the soil was moist; the water table was high. Cynthia Irwin-Williams has suggested that this gradual change in the weather made it possible for foragers to add new plants to their diet.[4] Corn and beans from the Valley of Mexico could be grown in the moisture-rich soils. This made it possible for hunters and gatherers to settle down for longer periods of time. Populations were probably increasing in the American West.

The new plants traveled north to the highlands—exchanged from one group to another—and made their way to the rivers and streams of the Colorado Plateau. At Clydes Cavern in east-central Utah, archeologist Jo-

---

[4]Cynthia Irwin-Williams, "Picosa: The Elementary Southwestern Culture," *American Antiquity* 32, no. 4, 1967, pp. 441–55.

seph Winter discovered tiny cobs of maize that date from 300 BC[5] Dried fecal samples in the layer did not contain any traces of corn. The grain might have been grown, but it was not an important part of the diet. Not until 700 years later do cobs appear in human fecal material. Corn has improved through favorable genetic mutations. It was probably no simple matter, this modification of foraging life. There were several different processes triggering a cultural change.

Populations might have been increasing in the watercourses of the arid Southwest beginning in the earliest days of the foraging tradition. Perhaps that was one of the reasons why they were receptive to new kinds of plants and began growing them near their crops when the rains began falling more often. Wild grass began crowding their gardens, taking root in the roughened ground. But the grass seeds could be eaten; they were closely related to corn. Perhaps then there was hybridization, and mutated corn appeared in the gardens. Or new strains might have been traded from Mexico into the West. However the process happened, the gardens began providing more food. People settled alongside them and tended them most of the year. In time, where once there were foragers, tiny villages began to emerge. Mud houses were dotting the streams along the foot of the mesas.

The Mogollon people

In the dry country to the west of Texas, changes were at work in society. Squash and tiny cobs of maize brought out of the Mesa Central were grown along the fringes of the hunter-and-gatherer camps. Conceivably as early as 2000 BC foragers began scattering the grain: a casual gesture that had little effect on their everyday life. There were places where a small band of foragers lived among enough maize, wild plant-food, and game so that—perhaps for a few months of the year—there was settled existence. A shallow depression was scooped out of the earth, posts were set around it, and a framework was built. Hunters and gatherers could live there as long as the food was abundant.[6]

But these pit houses—for so they are called—were never clustered into a village. Twenty-three long centuries passed until that occurred. Even then, they were the smallest of settlements—six houses or so on the average—all close to one another but arranged in no particular pattern. Along the northerly deserts of Mexico, southern Arizona, and southern New Mexico, the clusters were appearing where once there had only been hunters.

For centuries the pit-house villages—the remains of the Mogollon cul-

---

[5]Joseph C. Winter, "The Processes of Farming Diffusion in the Southwest and Great Basin," *American Antiquity* 41, no. 4 (1976), pp. 421–29.

[6]The account of Mogollon transformation is taken from Michael E. Whalen, "Cultural-Ecological Aspects of the Pithouse-to-Pueblo Transition in a Portion of the Southwest," *American Antiquity* 46,1 (1981), pp. 75–92.

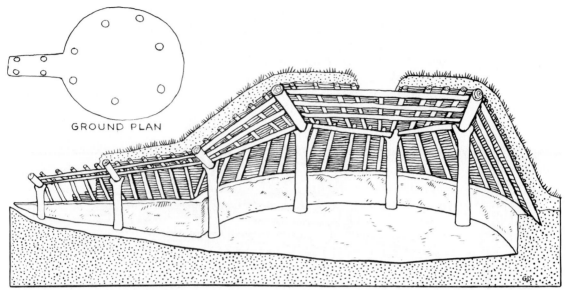

GROUND PLAN

Ground plan and postulated framework of a Mogollon pit-house.

ture—are almost the same as the earliest ones ever built. The houses are all much alike; none are large or unusually furnished. Burials have very few grave goods; the body was flexed and placed into the ground. It seems likely that the Mogollon people lived in egalitarian communities. Political power, whenever it existed, was probably fleeting at best. Extra water or food in emergencies, and knowledge of droughts that had occurred in the past—out of this came community leadership—but never for long.

Even when they abandoned their settlements, it was likely a collective decision—and the villages indeed were abandoned at AD 1,000. By that time the pit-house communities were perhaps too large for the available food. Pit-house clusters in the west part of Texas covered an area that was seven times larger than the village area in the earliest days of the Mogollon people. It became a matter of argument and strategy: where should the new community be? For many villagers, the answer was the hills at the edge of the mountains.

In the hills were the freshwater streams that cut gullies as they flowed from the mountains. Here there was more available water for growing their crops. Archeologist Michael Whalen has found that the new settlements at the edge of the mountains grew much more repidly than they had in earlier days. The houses themselves became different: they were *ground-surface,masonry, multiroomed* dwellings. Pit houses were gone and *pueblos* had taken their place. The new houses could be added on to simply

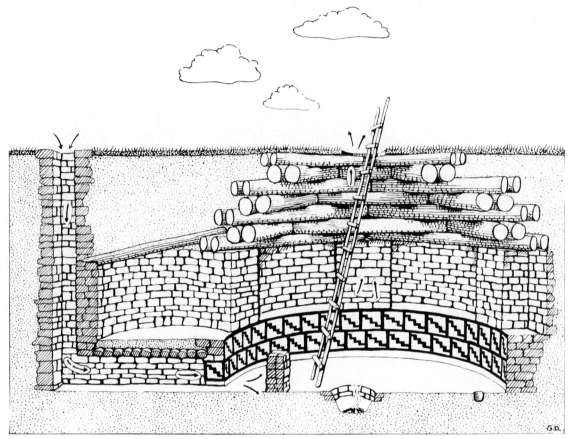

Field Museum of Natural History

The Kiva. Ritual activities within these ceremonial structures may have been the system of Mogollon social control.

by building additional walls; you did not have to dig out a new pit to construct a new room.

And yet, these pueblo communities growing up along the stream-fed hills probably never experienced the rise of a ruling elite. We still do not find lavish houses or rich furnishings in any of the graves. Conceivably, the move to the foothills and the adoption of new crops through exchange avoided the scarcity that can lead to political power. Perhaps too there was an understood ethic of providing for community needs, just as there was among the later Pueblo societies. Drawings on rocks near the villages depict altars and ceremonial dances. Round structures—possibly for rituals—were found in Texas and New Mexico sites. For Michael Whalen the discoveries are evidence of the ceremonial life of the Mogollon people. It may have been that the customs of the village were never enforced by a ruling elite but made sacred in community gatherings through dancing and prayer.

At the time that the Mogollon people were settling in the stream-laced rim of the mountains, other villages were growing in the deserts that lay to the west. In southern Arizona near the Salt and Gila rivers, canals were dug to bring water to the corn. New settlements were built where before had been barren desert.[7] At Snaketown, a village near the Gila, water was channeled for more than a mile. Maize, beans, and cotton were grown near the life-giving ditches. The village had no particular pattern; like the Mogollon settlements, it was a scattering of houses. Vertical posts were set next to a pit, there was a weavework of branches and a cover of mud. Hohokam houses were much like one another and changed very little.

Yet the settlements were more than mud houses. Other structures were built in these villages. They are the evidence of cultural connections with the world to the south. At Snaketown there was an oval depression with earthen embankments piled up on the sides. It is much like the ball courts of the Mexican Mesa Central. At the Gatlin site, not far from Snaketown, there was a ball court 100 feet long. A platform mound was built out of trash and covered over with mud. Archeologist Charles DiPeso has argued that conflicts in Mexican cities were driving ruling groups into refuge in southern Arizona.[8] Once there, these desert émigrés strongly influenced the lives of the villagers. Ball courts and mounds were constructed in the small farming hamlets. Perhaps, as Albert Schroeder once suggested, the uprooted elite had been Mexican merchants who became powerful because of their connections with the Mesa Central. And it is possible that there was no such movement—that there was influence without immigration. Seeds of maize, stone effigy carvings, copper bells, stone palettes, and mirrors—all of these and perhaps information about pyramids, ball courts, and ceremonies may have been passed by word of mouth and exchange into the southwestern desert.

Connections with the Valley of Mexico may have transformed their ceremonial life, but strategies of coping with the desert changed little at all. They dug their deep irrigation canals as far as two miles from a river. They built terraces and "check dams" on hills to trap run-off from storms. But the desert is the most fickle of worlds with its droughts, sudden windstorms, and floods. There were no guarantees that the harvest would provide enough food. So like the Pima of centuries later, they grew crops and they hunted and gathered. It was a "resilient" strategy for coping with unpredictable change.[9]

Irrigation and the Hohokam

---

[7]Details of the Hohokam adaptation are taken largely from Vorsila L. Bohrer, "Ethnobotanical Aspects of Snaketown, a Hohokam Village in Southern Arizona," *American Antiquity* 35, no. 4 (1970), pp. 413–30.

[8]Alternative theories of Hohokam cultural development are discussed in Lipe, "The Southwest," pp. 349–54.

[9]The concept of environmental "resiliency" has been developed by Linda S. Cordell and Fred Plog, "Escaping the Confines of Normative Thought: A Re-Evaluation of Puebloan Prehistory," *American Antiquity* 44, no. 3 (1979), pp. 405–29.

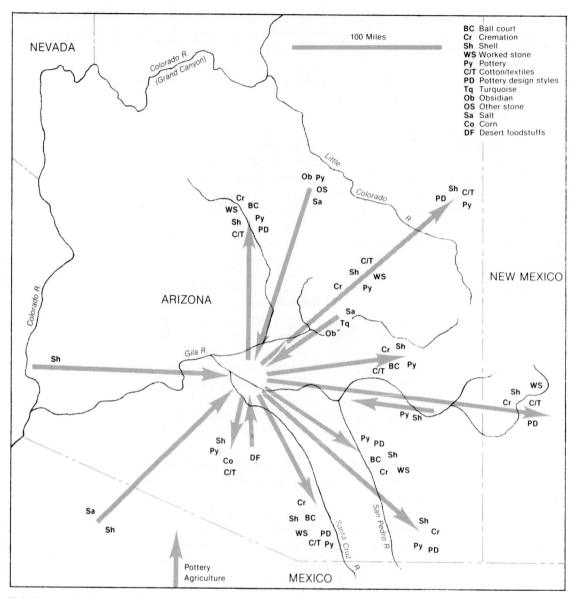

Hohokam exchange connections.

Anasazi of the Colorado Plateau

In the northerly forests and canyons—Kidder's "wild and barren" Colorado Plateau—southwestern society has left its most striking remains. Northern Arizona, northern New Mexico, southern Utah, and southwest Colorado was the domain of the cliff-dwelling Indians who are called Anasazi. Beginning as hunters and gatherers who scattered maize on the

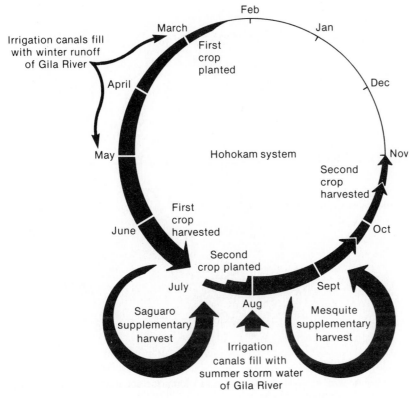

Irrigation canals fill
with winter runoff
of Gila River

March

Feb

Jan

Dec

Nov

First
crop
planted

April

May

Hohokam system

Second
crop
harvested

Oct

First
crop
harvested

June

Second
crop planted

Sept

July

Aug

Saguaro
supplementary
harvest

Mesquite
supplementary
harvest

Irrigation
canals fill with
summer storm water
of Gila River

The seasonal strategies shown here were followed by the Pima Indians. A similar adaptation likely characterized the Hohokam.

ground near their campsites, they developed large communities, ceremonialism, and networks of trade.

Like the Hohokam and the Mogollon people, they survived by a resilient technology. They farmed—but hunting and gathering was always a part of their lives.[10] If a stream was dependable enough, they dug canals for their corn, squash, and beans. But in the spring on the plateau, many streams dried into mud. So for many of the Anasazi, the gardening depended on rain. It was delicate, even risky, strategy—closely cued by the flow of the seasons. In the loftier heights of the mesas, winter brings a mantle of snow. With the beginning of spring, the moisture seeps into the ground. In these wetter soils the crops could be planted and could survive through the dry months of spring—until the canyons would echo with the thunder of summer storms. And yet, often at these higher ele-

[10]Linda S. Cordell, "Lake Anasazi Farming and Hunting Strategies: One Example of a Problem in Consequence," *American Antiquity* 42, no. 3 (1977), pp. 449–61.

Distinctive Anasazi ceramics provide valuable information about that society's cultural boundaries and systems of trade.

vations, the growing season is threateningly short. Warm weather does not last long enough for the crops to mature. Farther down, the valleys are protected, but they are vulnerable to summer floods. And erosion from the slopes can cover up the canals and the crops. For these reasons, it is hardly surprising that the Anasazi still hunted and gathered. Wild foods in the canyons were needed to help them survive.

Their villages were built near the rivers in the level bottomland of the canyons.[11] In Chaco Canyon in northern New Mexico at about AD 1000, over 100 villages flourished below a maze of cliffs. One of these was Pueblo Bonito, a crescent-shaped structure of over 800 rooms. It is a four-story building that looks like an ancient apartment. The crescent encloses a plaza containing sunken circular structures. It is possible that the structures were *kivas*—centers of ritual and Anasazi belief. If so, the larger ones in the plaza were for the community's ceremonial life. Smaller ones in the homes were conceivably for private devotions.

---

[11]Site descriptions are taken from Lipe, "The Southwest."

Field Museum of Natural History

Mesa Verde. The location of Anasazi settlements afforded protection from raids and provided access to a variety of natural resources.

Pueblo Bonito was one of 12 large villages built up on the floor below the cliffs. To the north there were villages built into the cliff walls themselves. One of these was the Cliff Palace village in Mesa Verde in southern Colorado—pueblo dwellings built into a cavity in the face of a cliff. It was a settlement of over 200 rooms and 23 of the kivalike structures—tucked inside a natural cavity in a sheer wall of rock.

It is tempting to say of these villages that they are the architectural evidence of conflict—that their style of construction was dictated by needs of defense. This might explain why they built them in cliffs, only accessible through a difficult climb. It might explain why, at Pueblo Bonito, the villagers sealed off their ground-floor windows and doors so that the settlement could only be entered by climbing a ladder. It is tempting—and yet there are problems. Though the buildings might seem to be evidence of a society beleaguered by raids, archeological evidence does not always suggest this was so. Some of the villages were, in fact, raided, but many communities were simply abandoned: the vacant rooms of the houses inherited by swallows and wind.

It happened in a few short centuries, beginning after AD 1000. By 1200, most of the Anasazi had left the plateau. Elsewhere throughout the

Artist's reconstruction of Pueblo Bonito.

Southwest it was a time of disturbance and change. Mogollon were leaving their villages and crowding into a few large communities. In a few generations, most of these would be abandoned as well. Hohokam were enlarging their settlements; they were extending their irrigation canals. They were building mounds and ceremonial structures—and then they were gone. Archeologists have debated for decades this transformation of the American West. Today, some idea of what happened has begun to emerge.

Natural cycles and the end of complexity

From the days when the first villages were built near the streams and the edges of mesas, settled life in the Southwest had been closely bound up with the seasons. The snows and the wintertime rains provided moisture for the springtime planting. Corn would be green for the arrival of the summer storms. Always there was game and wild-plant food in the canyons, the foothills, and the desert—ways of coping with the hazards of living in an unpredictable world. Probably, too, as the communities flourished, they were stitched together by threads of exchange. Commodities were carried over trade routes for hundreds of miles. Northwest of the village of Snaketown were Hohokam turquoise mines where the mineral was extracted for exchange with the Mesa Central. To the north, in the Anasazi homeland, the mineral was mined and then fashioned by artisans. It was traded to Mexico in exchange for feathers, live parrots, and copper. Although there is little evidence for it, there were conceivably food exchanges as well: a way of minimizing the chanciness of life in the Southwestern villages.

Agriculture, foraging, and exchange meant survival through multiple strategies. Yet, beginning about AD 1000, the system collapsed. Much of the reason might lie in the difference between short-term and long-term survival. Perhaps southwestern societies were not adapted to long cycles of change.[12] Floods and seasonal droughts, quirky rainfall, and a premature winter all were a familiar part of life in the American West. But there is another cycle as well—of drought and then heavier rainfall. It is a cycle that unfolds over centuries and not day-to-day. In the generations when rain came more often, there was an increase in arable land. Soils were moist, and surface vegetation was rich. There were generations of community life in places where, earlier, no one could settle. But the inexorable cycle continued: the rains disappeared. If it was possible, a village survived through exchange or through hunting and gathering. But often they abandoned their homes to crowd close to the rivers. There they lived through the dry generations until, slowly, the wet weather returned. Villages would spring up anew as the land was resettled.

When village life was beginning in the West, the cycle was not a serious problem. Populations were low; there was little pressure on available food. But settled existence over the centuries caused the size of the villages to grow. In time, this created new pressures in the dry years of the southwestern cycle. Greater numbers of people were crowding the land near the streams.

The crisis was reached about 1,000 years ago. An intricate system began falling to pieces. Archeologist William Longacre has found that, on the southern fringe of the Colorado Plateau, village after village was abandoned in the wake of the drought.[13] Between AD 1200 and 1300, settlements declined from a hundred to a dozen as their inhabitants migrated to centers of arable land. One of those centers, Grasshopper Pueblo, grew from 100 to 1,000 people—a burst of growth that happened in less than half a century. Under such pressures it was no longer possible to gain a living through farming and foraging; there were too many people crowded onto limited land. Exchange was not enough to save them because the middlemen were fast disappearing. Deserted villages in eddies of sand were on the pathways of trade. The teeming villages also were abandoned as people moved toward faraway settlements. A chain reaction was happening across the entire Southwest. The Anasazi moved south to the foothills at the edge of the Colorado Plateau—hills that for generations were the home

---

[12]The theory presented here was strongly influenced by Cordell and Plog, "Escaping the Confines."

[13]William A. Longacre, "Population Dynamics at the Grasshopper Pueblo, Arizona." *American Antiquity*, April 1975.

Controversial Salado ceramics are believed by some archeologists to be evidence of Anasazi movements into lands to their south.

of the Mogollon people. Then either—or both—of these societies may have pushed westward into Hohokam country, overcrowding the canals and the scattering of food on the desert.[14]

In the end they all returned to the wilderness, leaving the last of the adobes behind. They foraged in the hills and the desert. They shifted their camps with the flow of the seasons. The balance of life was restored to a changeable world. All around them the play of the winds covered their settlements with lappings of sand. Summer storms still returned to the canyons, but no human voices gave praise to the rain. Lightning flashed on the dark empty houses huddled under the walls.

To the south of the village-dwellers was a country of thorn forests and streams where the human community experienced remarkable change. Much of their story—at least the beginning—is reminiscent of the southwestern peoples. But beginnings are deceptive; the two prehistories are far from the same. This was Mexico's Mesa Central, that broad expanse of semiarid plateau between high ridges of mountains that lie to the west and the east.

Village life in the Mesa Central

Here, as in the American Southwest, there had been hunters for thousands of years—a tradition that extended to the tundra of Europe and Asia. Like the hunters of the southwestern grasslands, they too had watched the game disappear as the country around them turned into thorn forest and sage. In both regions there were scattered groups of foragers gathering wild-plant foods and hunting small game. In time, in Mexico and the Southwest, people grew their own food.

The early crops were the subtlest of changes, hardly crops in our sense of the word. As populations grew in the oases, the humid canyons, and the stream-fed *barrancas*, they collected many species of plants to provide enough food. Many of these grew at the edges of campsites, in trash piles, or in roughened soils; other varieties were collected as the foragers ranged through the valley. A diversity of Mexican plant foods were gathered together within a small space. The probability of genetic mutations dramatically grew. In time there were corn, beans, and squash growing near the fringes of the Mexican campsites, a practice that was slowly transmitted to the American West.

---

[14]Much about these cultural influences is still a subject of considerable debate. Were different ethnic groups within the same villages, or did the territory of a culture contract? Perhaps each of these processes was present in different locations. Even the direction of the cultural influences is itself an unsettled problem. Lipe reports an "Anasazi character" in the villages of the late Mogollon, hastening to add that the connection "has not yet been fully demonstrated." Similarly, for the late Hohokam, there is a mysterious "Salado" intrusion, identified both as Anasazi and Mogollon migrants. A Salado symposium (1976) did not result in any general agreement. Thus, the "fate" of the Hohokam people is an unsettled question. For all these reasons, it is evident enough that the prehistory of the American Southwest will remain a focus of debate for many decades to come.

Mesoamerican agricultural sites.

Here the stories begin to diverge—with the transition to agricultural life. Highland Mexico became very different than the world to the north. In the Mesa were rivers, streams, humid canyons, oases, and springs. Village life was more permanent here than it was in the West. The openness of the Mesa itself made it a region of cultural contact for exchanges of minerals and critical foods over hundreds of miles. Settled life was perhaps not as risky; farming villages dotted the Mesa. They were knit together by far-reaching networks of social exchange.

By as early as 5,000 years ago there were small camps in the Mesa Central where cultivators probably lived every month of the year. Like the early houses in the American Southwest, these were oval-shaped, partly sunken dwellings. To these camps the people of the Mesa brought harvests of corn, beans, chili, and squash. They brought the wild plants and the game they collected as they ranged through the valley. A thousand years later, pottery vessels were being used by the Mexican farmers. Discovered in the Tehuacan Valley, the fragments are remarkably similar to shards that were found in the Pacific-coastal state of Guerrero. Conceivably, by 4,000 years ago, social networks were already emerging among the small agricultural hamlets of the Mesa Central.

In the Oaxaca Valley to the south of Tehuacan, farming groups were settling along the rivers. The small hamlets were waterway communities—tiny houses near the edges of streams.[15] Near their waters the soils were moist enough to nourish plants in the dry months of the year. On the slopes that lifted up to the mountains were prickly pear, mesquite, and acorns; peccary, deer, and rabbit were hunted to provide extra food.

One of these hamlets—San Jose Mogote—was built on a ridge near the Atoyac River. Its cultural connections extended outside of the valley.[16] At about 1600 BC it was a small group of wattle-and-daub houses. Three centuries later it coordinated trade to the west and the east. By that time it had grown into a village of some 15 to 30 households. Some of these homes were on earthen platforms with stairways that led down to patios. Conceivably, these were the houses of the local elite. Inside them, Kent Flannery and Mark Winter discovered "pan-Mesoamerican" pottery—certain types of ceramics found everywhere on the Mesa Central. Neckless jars, flat-based bowls, incising or stamped decorations, hematite coloring, and smudging on the surface all are telltale features found throughout the Valley of Mexico in agricultural sites that are approximately 3,000 years old.

Flannery is quick to point out that there was no mysterious "neckless-jar people" that suddenly emerged in every nook of the Mesa Central. The shards are not exactly alike; each region has its own variations. More than likely, these fragments are evidence of an intricate skein of connections between powerful groups controlling the flow of exchange. Pearl oysters and shells from the Pacific were traded into San Jose Mogote, fashioned into ornaments, and traded to other parts of Oaxaca. Iron-ore mirrors and black-and-white mica were produced and exported as well. Conceivably, foodstuffs were traded through much of the mesa. In Mexico, as in the Old World, exchange was more than the simple flow of commodities. It also contributed to permanent political power. Groups with commercial

---

[15]Oaxacan settlement patterns are discussed by Kent V. Flannery and James Schoenwetter, "Climate and Man in Formative Oaxaca," *Archaeology*, April 1970, pp. 145–52.

[16]Ibid.

The feathered serpent and the jaguar were Mesoamerican motifs that were shared by elites who directed the systems of trade.

connections had an inventory of valuable items that could be traded for food, for alliances, or for help with the harvest. Possibly too, commodities were traded for information about diseases or curing, for sacred knowledge, or for secret "intelligence" about a possible raid.

Such a network was a critical factor in the genesis of political power, and there were particular communities where this was especially true. Archeologist Kenneth Hirth has suggested that certain villages were "gateway communities": they held strategic locations for regulating the movement of trade.[17] Such a community is something of a bottleneck; a very wide area must use it for exchange. Perhaps it is a narrow valley more convenient to go through than around; possibly it has more water or conceivably less-rugged terrain. For the villages in these locations there is constant movement of valuable goods. It is possible to demand services or commodities for the right to pass through. The toll extracted at the gate can accelerate political power. The village of Chalcatzingo to the southeast of Mexico City was probably involved in these strategies of early exchange.[18] Jade, obsidian, hematite, gulf shells, green stone, and kaolin were brought through the village on routes between the Gulf and the sea.

Here as on the Iranian Plateau we discover the workings of a subtle process. Commercial systems and gateway communities were giving rise to a ruling elite—local chiefs who could maintain a storehouse of critical goods. But the system was growing in complexity—and extending well beyond the Mesa Central. Larger inventories meant political security; they could easily be converted to food. Mexican chiefs were probably seeking to discover new clients. Societies outside the Mesa Central needed the trade goods of the Mexican networks. Living in the lowlands of the Gulf and the Pacific, they required salt, obsidian, and metals. In return they offered shells and, conceivably, food from the ocean. It was not long before the shores were connected through villages such as Chalcatzingo. Commodities and information were circulating between the Gulf and the sea. In this way, about 3,000 years ago, trade developed between the highlands and the lowlands. This circuit, as we will see very shortly, would in time play a critical role in the evolution of urban society in Mesoamerica.

Its face was almost vacant of expression, and its arms were rigid at its sides.[19] Its eyes were made of marine shells. They stared forward; its lips did not smile. Its forehead was a red-and-black color. Paint was on the neck and the palms. The curious doll—about five inches long—was discovered on the coast of Peru. Villagers some 3,000 years ago were carving many of these dolls in the Andes. The special meanings the craft may have had perhaps will never be known. Yet there is something that these figurines tell us about early Andean society. The tiny doll had been carved out of *chonta*—a heavy, palm wood of the tropical forest. The jungle and the coast were connected by a network of trade.

Networks and ritual in the Andes

---

[17]Kenneth G. Hirth, "Interregional Trade and the Formation of Prehistoric Gateway Communities," *American Antiquity* 43, no. 1 (1978), pp. 35–45.

[18]David C. Grove, Kenneth G. Hirth, David E. Buge, and Ann M. Cyphers, "Settlement and Cultural Development at Chalcatzingo," *Science*, June 18, 1976, pp. 1203–10.

[19]Donald W. Lathrap, "The Antiquity and Importance of Long-Distance Trade Relationships in the Moist Tropics of Pre-Columbian South American," *World Archeology* 1, no. 5 (1973), pp. 177–78.

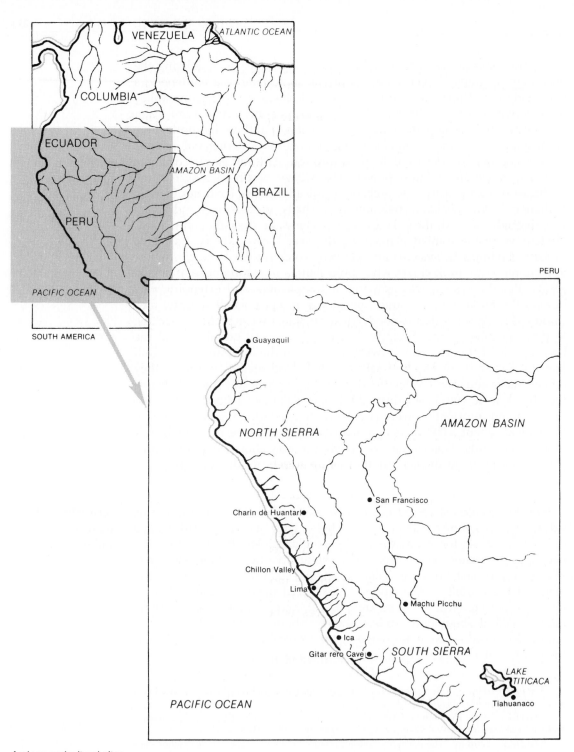

VENEZUELA

ATLANTIC OCEAN

COLUMBIA

ECUADOR

AMAZON BASIN

PERU

BRAZIL

PACIFIC OCEAN

SOUTH AMERICA

PERU

Guayaquil

NORTH SIERRA

AMAZON BASIN

San Francisco

Charin de Huantar

Chillon Valley

Lima

Machu Picchu

Ica

Gitar rero Cave

SOUTH SIERRA

LAKE TITICACA

Tiahuanaco

PACIFIC OCEAN

Andean agricultural sites.

These linkages had their beginnings perhaps 7,000 years before the present, when cultivated crops were being brought across the spine of the mountains. Guitarrero Cave is in the western Andes—the slopes that drop to the desert and sea. But in its soils were species of beans native to the tropical forest—the great jungle expanse that lies on the other side of the peaks. It was a time of tentative beginnings, or travelers finding their way through the valleys. As the centuries passed there was a network of paths in Peru.

Uncertainty and astonishing diversity have always been true of the Andes. The conditions were a prelude to the developing routes of exchange. In the jungles to the east of the mountains there are droughts, and the rivers are low. Heavy rainfall can come to the forest, and then there are floods. Resources are scattered and distant—including varieties of edible plants. From very early times there were forest-dweller systems of trade. There are some stretches of low-lying jungles where these patterns have survived to our time. In the northeast South American tropics, villagers specialize in particular products and trade them by boat and on foot over hundreds of miles. Wrote an early explorer:

> The Otomac were widely recognized for their clay pots; the Arekuna for their cotton and blowpipes; the Makusi for their curare poison; the Maiongkong and Taruma for both cassava graters and hunting dogs; the Warrau for their corials; the Waiwai for their fiber of tucum and kuraua; the Guinau for their hammocks, cassava graters, aprons, girdles of human hair, and feather decorations; the Oyapock River natives for their 'spleen and metate' stones. Nothing came amiss, a market being always forthcoming sooner or later for everything—even for dried turtle with its preserved eggs and extracted oil; slaves, dried fish, hammocks and green stones, smoked and salted fish, sandstone for sharpening knives, even bark shirts.[20]

Connections like these may have had their emergence in the days of the foraging tradition. By 7,000 years before the present they were reaching the Andes.

For people living on the coast or on the mountains, the world was varied and far from secure. There were strategic connections for coping with hazards of life. Not even the sea was as bountiful as archeologists had earlier thought. There were times when the Peruvian Pacific was barren of food. El Niño, the "Christ Child" current—it appears a few days after Christmas—sweeps down from the north and flows along the Peruvian coast.[21] The current raises the water temperature; it reduces the nutrients and the content of salt. Fish that inhabit these waters are not adapted to live in El Niño. They die by the thousands in the months that the current

---

[20]Ibid., p. 172.

[21]David J. Wilson, "Of Maize and Men: A Critique of the Maritime Hypothesis of State Origins on the Coast of Peru," *American Anthropologist* no. 1 (March 1981), pp. 93–120.

Milwaukee Public Museum

The Peruvian Andes. Altitudinal differences made this a region of varied environments. But it also has severe droughts and erratic changes in weather.

is there. Fishers on the Peruvian coastline cannot predict when the current will happen. It has been recorded at intervals of 6 to 34 years.

Nor is life in the highlands much easier; existence there can be chancy at best.[22] There are droughts and sudden freezes in the mountains; there are years of far too much rain. Epidemics can kill the tubers of potatoes. Violent hailstorms batter the crops. Because of such turbulence it was likely that herding animals were first tamed in the Andes—the llama and the alpaca found in the mountains today. That strategy may have had its beginnings some 7,000 years before the present in the Junin Plateau high above the modern city of Lima. Herds could graze on the marsh-dotted pastures along the mile-high slopes of the mountains. If crops did not flourish, the animals could be slaughtered for food. But this strategy, too, has its problems. The lives of the herders were seldom secure: the animals can die from parasitic diseases; their pastures can freeze; they can wither from drought. Everywhere in the mountains was catastrophe, accident, and change.

But it is not simply an endless disaster; the region is more subtle than

---

[22]David L. Browman, ''Pastoral Nomadism in the Andes,'' *Current Anthropology* 15, no. 2 (June 1974), pp. 188–96.

that. Variety is a part of this country—and a part of survival. John Murra has called it "verticality": a vast profusion of natural worlds that a traveler encounters by moving up and down on the slopes.[23] A Q'ero Indian leaves home in the morning when light is just touching the tundra. His breath is a frosty, white cloud as he moves down the ridge. As he travels, the weather grows hotter. Air becomes humid and the slope disappears. Reaching his garden, he gathers the corn that he will carry to his house in the mountains. All around him is the riot of jungle and the chatter of birds.

Movements of Q'ero on the Andean foothpaths are remnants of an earlier strategy that farmers and herders attempted in this part of the world. With their herds on the upland pastures and their gardens lower down on the slopes, their life is a series of journeys in an up-and-down land. Their houses are built near their gardens and also near their cloud-covered pastures. It is not unusual for a house to be abandoned for much of the year.

Conceivably, early Andean farmers followed Q'ero-like patterns of movement. But as populations grew in that region, the strategy changed. Robert Kautz and Peter Jensen have suggested that early settlements slowly grew larger.[24] Kin groups "budded off" and migrated to other locations. It was no longer necessary to constantly travel between your garden and your high-country herds. You could meet with your kinfolk; you could celebrate, gossip, and trade. This strategy made life easier in the unpredictable Andes. If a hailstorm ruined your potatoes, your high-country relative could give you a llama. If disease struck his herd, you could give him some corn from your field.

A permanent net of exchange extending from the jungle to the edge of the sea made possible a sedentary life in the Andes. Because of that settled existence, populations grew faster than ever before. Real Alto on the coast of Ecuador was an encampment of foragers and fishers until farmers arrived there some 5,400 years before the present.[25] A brief 3 centuries later, it was a community of 1,500 people: a center of exchange with an elaborate ceremonial life. Oval-shaped houses with upright-log walls were built on mounds surrounding a courtyard. These earthen embankments were over a thousand feet long. But the pattern of houses-and-courtyard itself surrounded a large central plaza. In that space was a remarkable structure christened the "fiesta house." Whatever went on in that structure was probably fun. Fragments of seafood delicacies such as rock crab were found

---

[23]Murra's "verticality" and the Q'ero adaptation are described by John E. Pfeiffer, *The Emergence of Society: A Prehistory of the Establishment* (New York: McGraw-Hill, 1977), pp. 383–85.

[24]Peter M. Jensen and Robert R. Kautz, "Preceramic Transhumance and Andean Food Production," *Economic Botany*, January-March 1974.

[25]Donald W. Lathrap, Jorge G. Marcos, and James A. Zeidler, "Real Alto: An Ancient Ecuadorian Ceremonial Center," *Archaeology*, April 1977, pp. 3–13.

Field Museum of Natural History

Statue and passageways of the Castillo, Chavin de Huentar. The elaborate ceremonial center was a node of Andean trade.

on the floor. There were lobster claws, scallop and clam shells, and sea turtle bones. A large number of broken drinking bowls were buried within the floor of the house. It was probably a center for feasting and group celebration.

Many centuries after Real Alto, ceremonialism spread through the Andes. The ritual center was a part of community life. By 3,000 years before the present elaborate circuits of belief and exchange extended from valley to valley in the heart of the mountains. At its center was Chavin de Huantar, a massive stone ceremonial center constructed in the fog-covered world of the high, eastern slopes.[26] Five hundred years in the making, built with stones dragged through the mountains, it is both a ceremonial center and an expression of art. An older, U-shaped structure of stone surrounds a circular, sunken court; a later structure was built on the sides of a rectangular plaza. The base of the old ''U''—the Castillo—is partly hollow, with galleries inside: a system of passages connected in an intricate maze. Still standing in this ancient labyrinth was a figure carved out of white granite. Snakes seem to flow from its head. It had the crocodile mouth of a caiman. It had huge canine teeth and lips that curled up at the corners. For more than a few archeologists, the curious figure is their own Mona Lisa. Is the god really smiling—or is the expression a snarl?

More important than the statue's expression is the influence that spread

[26]Site description of Chavin de Huantar is taken from Michael E. Moseley, ''The Evolution of Andean Civilization,'' in Jennings, *Ancient Native Americans*, pp. 517–21.

Gift of Mr. and Mrs. Bruce Graham, The Art Institute of Chicago

This stirrup vessel of the Chavin style is one of a complex of artifacts useful in determining pathways of Chavin exchange.

from this center, reaching villages that were more than 700 miles from Chavin. Distinctive ceramic and textile designs were the special motifs of Chavin de Huantar. But more was involved in this process than commercial exchange. It seems likely that this intricate system was a mix of commerce, religion, and art, touching thousands of villagers living in ancient Peru.

Footpaths and two different rivers were joined together at Chavin de

Huantar. It was a junction for llamas and people bringing goods on their backs. Obsidian, dry-frozen potatoes, meat, and wool from the highland villages were brought to the center by travelers as they moved down the slopes. Dried fish and manioc from the jungles were being carried in the other direction. It is likely that Chavin de Huantar was a hub of exchange. It may have begun as a gateway community, like Chalcatzingo in the Mesa Central, controlling a corridor and living off the fees it charged. Trade that moved over the mountains was responsible for its existence, so trade became a sacred activity: an act of the pious.[27] Ceremonies were performed at the center, ritual items were given to travelers. Exchange became a pilgrimage infused with religious belief.

If commerce is a sacred activity, then it is "performed" on a regular basis. Religious elites were stabilizing the networks of trade. Such a strategy was probably practiced at Chalcatzingo and at San Jose Mogote to strengthen the commercial connections of the Mesa Central. It may have begun in the Andean region with Real Alto's ceremonial life and grown through the centuries until the days of Chavin de Huantar. This melding of belief and exchange, in the Americas and in the Old World, grew more elaborate as the maze of commercial connections evolved. It would be one of the critical processes (one of several we have seen in this story) that would cause villages to turn into cities—and chiefs to be kings.

---

[27]This interpretation has perhaps been most explicitly developed by Thomas C. Patterson, "Chavin: An Interpretation of Its Spread and Influence," in *Dumbarton Oaks Conference on Chavin* (Washington, D.C.: Dumbarton Oaks Research Library and Collections, 1971).

Part Three / The Rise of Urban Elites

16 / The Evolution of the Urbanized State

Rooms, I thought. The world had become
a ball of rooms, a hive, where once it
had been a vast out-of-doors lightly
dented with pockets of shelter.

John Updike

It must have happened thousands of times. A small family, covered with dust, carrying all that they could on their backs, dropped their burdens at the edge of the path and looked ahead down the trail. They could see, far off in the distance above the shimmering heat of the plain, a windowless wall built high on the crest of a hill. They knew—because others had told them—that the world inside the wall would be different. But they had left the old home in the village. They were not going back.

In the last fraction of time before history, there was abandonment; perhaps there was hope. Ways of the village were eclipsed by the whirl of the city. It was a new kind of human community—often larger, but much more than that. The city was a product and an agent of cultural change.

What is the city? Because it is so familiar and so much a part of our everyday lives, it is surprising that for so many years it has been hard to define. Sometimes it was thought that the city was a criterion of "civilization." For many scholars in ancient societies they were one and the same. But this only begs greater difficulties as to the meaning of a "civilized" life. A spring day in the park, the theater, and the faint glow of lights on a river seem, to many people, preferable to life in the New Guinea highlands. But there are values and emotions at work here—those of the society into which we are born—which are impossible to use as a yardstick for civilization. Indeed, such notions of a gentler existence, the civility of civilized life, very poorly describe the society of the earliest cities. There was violence within and between them. There was shortage, overcrowding, and want. Civilization for many was in no way an easier life. Perhaps it is best for us to think of the *city* as a *special form of the human community*

Field Museum of Natural History

The world that was eclipsed by the city. In the last fraction of time before history, immigrants from farming villages flowed into the burgeoning towns and found a new way of life.

with dense populations and multiple social traditions. Unlike the village—the "little tradition"—the city was a mixture of custom and creed. Diversity was always a part of our urban existence.

The costs of urbanization

But it was more than a cultural diversity, as critical as that factor was. I believe it is useful to look closely at the urbanized world. There was much about it, in the past as today, that made the city a harsh world to live in. Perhaps it is valuable to begin on such a negative note. For one thing, there was the fact of sheer numbers—human animals packed closely together. This had an effect on every conceivable aspect of life. It is true that what is thought of as "crowded" varies greatly between human societies, but it is also true that the city was denser than the village had been. This meant that infectious diseases could strike more people than ever before.[1] Epidemics have long been a part of our years in the city. The origin and the spread of infection were probably hastened by ancient hygiene—the difficulty of disposing of garbage and animal waste. Cities

[1] Don Brothwell, "Community Health as a Factor in Urban Cultural Evoluton," in *Man, Settlement, and Urbanism*, ed. P. J. Ucko, R. Tringham, and G. W. Dimbleby (Cambridge, Mass.: Schenkman Publishing, 1972), pp. 353–60.

United Press International Photo

One of the problems of an urban environment is the efficient removal of waste. The consequence is often the problem of infectious disease.

that grew up on the Indus coped with this problem remarkably well. But many cities did not solve the problem. Many have not today.

City-dwellers exchanged more than their microbes: they traded insult, threat, and abuse. Group life was presenting more conflicts than ever before. Vernon Reyonolds has observed that villages of gardeners in the Amazon Basin will "bud off" long before there is a problem of not enough food.[2] There seems to be a critical level, something akin to a "bickering threshhold," when arguments become too much for the village to bear. Robert Carneiro pessimistically reasons that a band of only 25 people has 300 possible combinations of disagreeing pairs.[3] A city of 10,000 inhabitants has 50 million of these possible conflicts! One wonders how it was possible for the city to develop at all.

That question should wait for a moment while we look closer at our urban existence—especially at the conflict that was always at the heart of this world. There is something about urban clashes that sets them apart from the band or the village so that, once it has happened, a crisis is not easily solved. Within forager and village society there was a sharing of belief and behavior, a shared language, and shared expectations in the rhythm of life. Conflicts, of course, were inevitable, but they occurred in

[2]Vernon Reynolds, "Ethology of Urban Life," in ibid., pp. 401–8. David Harris, P. E. L. Smith, and Anthony Forge have all made similar observations concerning this phenomenon.

[3]Carneiro's calculations and related issues of conflict and control among large groups of humans are discussed in John E. Pfeiffer, *The Emergence of Society: A Prehistory of the Establishment* (New York: McGraw-Hill, 1977), pp. 83–104.

an informational system. Bickering is unpleasant but is a channel for the exchange of ideas. In the city, this was often less easy because the languages and the cultures were different. Urban society is, in a very real sense, an information mosaic. Not able to bicker or ritualize, fearful of what they could not understand, conflicting groups in the cities have often resorted to force.

Frustration was only intensified by the anonymity of urban society—of streets overcrowded and filled with the faces of strangers. Alienation is the stuff of our poets, but is—perhaps—neurologically real, catalyzed by the web of the city and the maze of the brain. Every growth of the human community, from hunter and gatherer, to village, to city, was a growth in the spectrum of meetings and of daily acquaintance. Remember Ukwane when he sat at the fire. He knew Tsetchewe, Gai, and the rest—the quirks and personalities of the people in his band. Such intimacy is not at all difficult when one's society is 25 people. But our memories were taxed as our numbers continued to grow. Increasingly in the human condition, we have interacted with *categories of persons*. We do not know what their personalities are; we have learned not to care. The clerk, the priest, and the policeman are the figures of our urbanized lives. Most inclusive of all our social labels is probably "stranger."

Little wonder that for thousands of years the city has been viewed as a menacing world: a warren of disease; a container of conflict and crime.

Shoppers in the city. Villagers use such meetings as opportunities to bargain and gossip. But the transaction here is impersonal; eyes do not meet.

United Press International Photo

Willy Loman shuddered at the skyscrapers that blocked out his view of the sun; Villon wrote of the waste and the diseases of medieval towns. For Saint Augustine there was only one city—the city of God—because the others were damned. The Apostles were grimly aware that their hour would come. But artists have only intensified a common knowledge that was there all along. Barred windows a few feet away from the snow-whipped tracks of elevated trains tell the mood of the city in a language no poet has dreamed.

And yet, though it is all of these things, there is something else to be said of the city: it acts as a center of innovation and cultural change. The remarkable diversity of urban existence includes not only its social traditions but also a vast collection of talents and trades—human specializations. There were specialists, of course, in the village—potters, weavers, metalworkers, and priests—who emerged out of scarcity and became part of a web of exchange. But often, when it was small in numbers a single village might have only one specialty, its knowledge inherited by kinship over hundreds of years. When cities came into existence, there were scores of such specializations—and hundreds of specialists—found within the urban community. **In praise of the city**

This was more than just an increase in numbers; it was a change in information as well. If metalworkers from many different regions emigrated toward the same city, they brought different techniques, different tools, and different-quality ores. They soon discovered that sharing their knowledge was much more practical than working apart. This was not because of lofty ideals concerning the progress of their specialized craft; it was because such collusion was a route to political power. Metallurgists, by working together, could control many different sources of ore and combine a variety of tools and techniques in the making of metals. This simultaneously improved their efficiency and made control of their craft more complete. It placed them in a better position to demand privileges, resources, and service. Cultural differences between them were subdued. They became permanent goups.

The identical political logic applied to relations *between* different specialities: there was more power in working together than in working apart. And the simple physical convenience of residence within the same city allowed more interchange between specialties than ever before. The "coppersmith" as Childe once expressed it,

> is a master of the hammer and of casting, and is probably employing the *cire perdue* process.* And so he can provide his fellow craftsmen

---

Cire perdue is "lost wax." The hard wax is carved into shape and is then covered with clay. All but a small opening is covered, and then the object is baked. Melting wax drains out through the opening; the clay covering is now a mold. It could be filled with heated copper or, eventually, an alloy like bronze.

with a variety of delicate and specialized tools—axes, adzes, chisels, gouges, drills, knives, saws, nails, clamps, needles, and so on. Jewelers can now pierce the hardest stones and engrave them for seals. Sculptors are beginning to carve vases and statuettes out of limestone and even basalt. The carpenter, besides boats, chariots, and couches, fashions harps and lyres. Naturally there are professional musicians to play upon them; these actually take their places in the tomb beside their royal masters.[4]

This flourishing of interdependency amounted to an early information explosion: a sudden burst in the knowledge and decisions of specialist groups. Involved here were (at least) two different processes by which the amount of information increased. One of them, and probably the most

Concert in Central Park. The city is an intricate artifact with multiple specializations. Much of science, technology, and the arts has evolved in this world.

United Press International Photo

---

[4]The passage is taken from V. Gordon Childe, *Man Makes Himself* (New York: New American Library, 1951), p. 150. The book contains valuable discussions of specialist groups in urban society.

obvious, is the pooling of individuals' knowledge. The total knowledge of 10 people is more than the total knowledge of 1. But more than this, when they are working together, the probability of *inventions* increases: there are more *unique combinations of previously existing ideas*. Three different methods of smelting can now be combined into a novel approach. Innovation was dramatically increasing the growth of knowledge.

Because of craftsworkers, artists, priests, shipbuilders, and the relations between them, the city has often been the center of cultural change. Consistently, for the last five millennia, the direction of change has been from city to village. Less often have villages and hamlets transformed a society. A naturalist might have gone to the woods to celebrate the virtues of rural existence; but he did so with literary skills acquired in Boston. Discoveries by Newton and Darwin were formulated in country retreats, but the men drew largely from a body of knowledge in an urbanized world. Science, mathematics, theater, architecture, medicine, law: a great deal of what we know of each one was born in the city.

It is true enough that destructive ideas have also been conceived in an urban environment. On that fact turns the critical point of the city's significance. An urban center is an intricate artifact for transforming our social existence. We can use it to make our lives richer—or to make them much worse. But romantic escape to a village society, to life that is thought to be close to the earth, is mere capitulation; in the end it solves nothing at all. Only out of the elaborate matrix of strategies found in the city is it likely that changes will emerge to make our lives better. The city is troubled and vilified but is our most powerful agent of change. It is more necessary for humanity today than it ever has been.

Urbanization and the problem of power

If it is true that the city is dynamic because of the flow of specialized information, it is also the case that this required some time to evolve. Consider: I have told how the city was a mixture of social traditions—with barriers of language, of custom, and of religious belief. In the same breath, I have also described the interactions between different groups and how this transforms the city into an agent of cultural change. Here, of course, is a clear contradiction, one that requires some time to explain. The story of the city is also a story of power.

How did it happen that different traditions began cooperating more throughout time? How was it possible for so many traditions to share the same city? If Carneiro is even close to correct in his calculations of possible conflicts, what was it that kept the first cities from flying apart? Then too, how was survival in the city managed? In the simpler days of the village, your garbage went out the back door; the food for your family was grown in the field near your house. But now there were thousands of people living more closely than ever before; and often in the city they were miles from where crops could be grown. Cooperation was the critical factor, but how did it ever evolve? As I mentioned, there were groups in the city discovering the value of shared information, there was more power in working together than in working apart. But this was only part of the story; power in the city was more subtle than that. The emergence of the city was also the rise of the *state*.

It is the most intricate form of government that humanity has ever devised. It is powerful. It has spread—and is spreading—in every part of the world. Intuitively, we know what it is; yet perhaps, it is best to define it. I view it as a *hierarchical arrangement of groups with differential access to strategic resources; it makes public decisions and manages territorial affairs*. As you know, there is more to it than that. It wages war and raises taxes and armies. It has its charisma, its rituals, and its creeds. Scientists and philosophers have studied it for hundreds of years.

Yet beneath all the surface complexity, there is a structure, and also a process, found in the earliest states and the ones that exist in our time. Every state is a hierarchical system: it has levels at which decisions are made. And these hierarchies, in a sense, are an outgrowth of decisions themselves. A bit farther on in the chapter, we can look at the particular processes probably involved in the emergence of the earliest states. For the moment it is enough to say that human behavior was more complicated; more decisions were necessary in the conduct of everyday life. Archeologist Henry Wright has suggested that, in a way, we have a "channel capacity": there are only so many decisions that a person can make.[5] Individuals and groups can become overloaded. Thus, a new level comes into existence. A group will make certain decisions and then transmit them to the next higher group. Those decisions will be evaluated; a course of action will be decided upon. The right to decide that general course of action was once done on one level. But the problem of too much information made that impossible for many societies. It was more efficient for two separate levels to come into existence.

As for the groups on the higher level, the original consultants in human society, they soon discover that decisions they make will affect one another. Their decisions are general and powerful; they affect large systems below them. Such decisions can have an effect on the entire society. This means that, in time, it is necessary for a system to exist at the top. The role of this centralized grouping is to examine the general courses of action and, ultimately, to formulate a policy for the entire society. For Henry Wright and many other archeologists, such a system is an "atomistic state": a minimal three levels for managing an information explosion.

But we should not drift into a simple romanticism about the "beauty" of this human creation. There are problems and considerable dangers built

---

[5]Henry T. Wright, "Toward an Explanation of the Origin of the State," in *Origins of The States: The Anthropology of Political Evolution*, ed. Ronald Cohen and Elman R. Service (Philadelphia: Institute for the Study of Human Issues, 1978), pp. 49–68.

into such rule. No state has ever reigned in a vacuum; its connections are remote and complex. Accidents, raiding, famine, and the expansion of other societies are changes petty and large that affect the state. For this reason, any group in the hierarchy, whether at the bottom or close to the top, can suddenly become more important than it ever has been. If there is no warfare, a military agency might virtually slumber with little to do. If there is an invasion, they find their importance has suddenly changed. And so it is with the irrigation agencies during a time when there is need for more water, or with merchant cooperatives in a time when there is need for more trade.

So what happens? Kent Flannery has suggested that one of two processes comes into being to accommodate the changing importance of one part of the state.[6] One of these is called *linearization*. It is a by-pass operation of sorts. If there is, say, a shortage of water then it might happen that the rulers of the state will suddenly take over the management of all the canals. In our time, this has often been justified in terms of a state of emergency. It is also a strategy for rulers to increase their power. If the top reaches down to the bottom, the groups in-between could, in time, disappear. There remains only an unstable society of ruler and ruled.

The alternative political strategy, more flattering perhaps than the first, is the *promotion* of a group to a more powerful role in the state. The problem of not enough water could mean that supervisors of local canals could be elevated to positions of power not far from the throne. This, too, can be an emergency measure—a more direct way of keeping in touch—but in promotion, as in linearization, is an element of risk. The act of promotion communicates clearly that a particular group has increased in importance. The group is aware that it is much more powerful than it was in the past. Conceivably, if they are willing to chance it, there is the possibility of even more power. They can become so influential that, in fact, they are controlling the state.

The dangerous potentials of these two processes, which Roy Rappaport has called their pathologies, have likely been a problem for as long as the state has existed.[7] Certainly within our own century we have seen states become so linearized that their rulers were in control of almost every dimension of life. European fascists controlled their own industries, trade, education, and domestic affairs. They even controlled archeological research. It was the age of Kossina. A bit earlier, near the turn of the century, was an era of promotion in American life. A limited number of entrepreneurs—robber barons, they are usually called—were rapidly becoming an

---

[6]Kent V. Flannery, "The Cultural Evolution of Civilizations," *Annual Review of Ecology and Systematics*, vol. 3, 1972, pp. 399–426.

[7]Roy A. Rappaport, "Sanctity and Adaptation," prepared for the Wenner-Gren Symposium on The Moral and Esthetic Structure of Human Adaptation (New York: Wenner-Gren Foundation, 1971), pp. 24–26.

American ruling elite. Controlling most of the railroads, the wheat, the factories, the mines, and the steel, they were economically powerful and a dominant political force. States exist in a delicate balance between pathological changes in process. It was often said, in the days of the fascists, that at least the railroads were running on time; in the robber-baron days, that the railroads were running the country.

Every generation of archeologists has become increasingly aware of the complexities involved in the evolution of cities and states. In recent years, a better understanding of urban society has begun to emerge. What was it that created the city? How was this related to the rise of the state? These are among the most difficult questions in human prehistory.

City and state: The development of theory

Every archeologist who has dealt with the question of the emergence of the first city-states has been aware of the complexities of this new form of human community. Even the so-called prime-mover theorists, who emphasized one particular factor, were aware that the factor they wrote of was highly complex. There is a sense in which *all* of the theories are managerial approaches of sorts. They recognize systems in human society that were evolving into greater complexity, generating information, and requiring that more decisions be made.

V. Gordon Childe was aware that the villagers who lived in the soon-to-be cities and states were "overloading their channel capacity," as Wright would express it.[8] He suspected that irrigation systems demanded more decisions than ever before. And he was aware of the informational loading in networks of trade. In Egypt, Mesopotamia, and, very likely, in Indus as well, the canals were becoming more intricate as villages grew.

Major features of the irrigation theory of V. Gordon Childe.

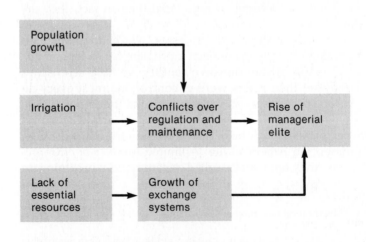

---

[8]Childe, *Man Makes Himself*, pp. 114–15.

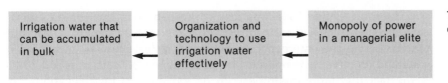

The "hydraulic" theory of Karl Witt Fogel.

Problems of regulation and maintenance and disagreements over the need for more water were increasing in the agricultural villages on the alluvial plains. Then too, the river-valley settlements were often lacking in critical resources. As their populations grew, they demanded a greater volume of trade. These "transactions," as Childe once expressed it, were "growing ever more complex." There had to be merchants to regulate trade, professional armies to accompany convoys, and scribes to keep regular accounts of the movement of goods.

A generation later, the thought of Karl Wittfogel was almost an echo

Date palm irrigation, Iraq. The complexities of hydraulic systems have been proposed as a major factor causing urbanized states to evolve in different parts of the world.

Field Museum of Natural History

of V. Gordon Childe.[9] He was less concerned with the complexities of commerce; he focused more directly on the ancient canals. Hydraulics was the key to the emergence of cities and states. He was impressed by water and its physical properties, by its tendency to "gather in bulk," and by the fact that large quantities can be moved to a low elevation. This means that irrigation societies must organize schedules, construction, and labor. New levels of decision-making groups will come into existence.

The specific weakness in both of these theories has been emphasized so many times that archeologists have occasionally overlooked their more general strengths. City-states had existed for centuries before the beginnings of irrigation in China. Canals were, most likely, a minor factor in the emergence of the Maya. Yet apart from these technical errors is a valuable emphasis on the growing complexity that humanity was encountering in adapting to the natural world. Pressures for correct decisions and for higher levels at which decisions were made were generating a hierarchical structure in human society.

The critical factor of channel capacity can involve human conflicts as well. Organized war involves a great many skills and is often complex. Archeologists of a later generation, heirs to the thinking of Wittfogel and Childe, have long suspected that the scale of violence helped engender the state. There were societies, thought Robert McC. Adams, living in those parts of the world which were a mosaic of resources and strategies of human subsistence.[10] Pastoralists, hunters and gatherers, and farmers on irrigated lands were living in a country where resources were scattered and varied. Survival in such a patchwork environment required a regularized flow of exchange. Even so, there were times when exchange could

The theory of Robert McC. Adams emphasized a close relation between war and exchange. It is similar in its essentials to the discussion in the latter part of this chapter.

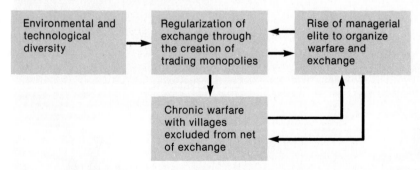

[9]Karl Wittfogel, *Oriental Despotism: A Comparative Study of Total Power* (New York: Vantage Press, 1981), pp. 17–18.

[10]Robert McC. Adams, *The Evolution of Urban Society: Early Mesopotamia and Prehistoric Mexico* (New York: Aldine Publishing, 1966), pp. 102, 125, and 137.

not meet human needs. The alternative could well have been warfare; it too was becoming regularized. It may have been that these developing trends were very closely related.

A cluster of cooperating villages might share enough resources among them that they could exchange only with one another and meet all of their needs. Such a strategy, a de facto monopoly, makes perfect sense to the people involved.[11] If exchange is confined to those villages which share an abundance of all that is needed, the probability of scarcity shrinks; life becomes more secure. But ones who are outside the monopoly have a tendency not to see it that way. Their survival is threatened; the alternative before them is war.

The regularization of conflict changes the process of conflict itself. If your survival is dependent on warfare, then it is no longer a hit-or-miss thing. It requires manpower, schedules and planning, even specialization. Robert Carneiro at one time suggested that chronic warfare between farming villages was one of the major factors involved in the emergence of states.[12] He reasons that if Adams' "patchwork" was overburdened with growing populations, then exchange was not a reliable strategy of human survival. If war was the other road taken, then it demanded greater social complexity. There had to develop new levels of command to channel the information of organized war. There had to be agencies for governing territories and collecting tribute.

They may differ on certain particulars, but in these views is a theme of agreement: the complexity of life giving rise to higher-level controls. The scale of information was growing in Mesopotamia, the Indus, and Egypt. It was growing in Mesoamerica and the Peruvian Andes. In each of these regions, cities evolved and people were governed by the earliest states. Perhaps there were similar processes at work in each one of these centers which generated a new kind of community—and a new form of rule.

I suspect that we will never be satisfied in the development of a city-state theory if we search for the revolutionary changes that brought it about. Urbanization was indeed a revolution in terms of its effects upon human society. The rate of social change ever after was never the same. But these are repercussions, not causes. The causes are likely more subtle

A general theory of the urbanized state

---

[11]Possibilities of entrepreneurship in village and urban exchange systems are discussed by Robert McC. Adams, "Anthropological Perspectives on Ancient Trade," *Current Anthropology* 15 (1974), pp. 239–58.

[12]Robert Carneiro, "A Theory of the Origin of the State," *Science* 169, pp. 733–38. In a later elaboration of his view, Carneiro suggests that increased organizational efficiency, and not significant technological change, was the result of warfare and environmental pressures on the earliest states. The refinement is presented in "A Reappraisal of the Roles of Technology and Organization in the Origin of Civilization," *American Antiquity* 39, no. 2 (1974), pp. 179–86.

in nature. Urbanization, I believe, was the result of slow changes through time.

Certain processes had long been developing, for generations, for thousands of years, until ultimately a threshold was reached and new systems were born. Henry Wright and Gregory Johnson discovered no sudden increase in the flow of exchange in southwestern Iran before the emergence of. cities and states.[13] Populations, they found, were increasing—but not dramatically—in Southwestern Asia. Perhaps this was true for technology and warfare as well. Yet, the slow rate of change in a process does not mean the process is a trivial thing; glaciation, I suppose, is the most obvious example of that. For that reason, it is still very possible that, for example, exhange was a factor—even if it increased very slowly before urbanization. I believe it was the slow-acting process, not the sudden, discontinuous change, that created hierarchical cities in human society.

In the half-dozen centers on the planet where village societies became city-states, there was a cluster of factors likely unique to these regions. In every center the village environment was a mosaic of scattred resources— a condition that profoundly affected the flow of exchange. Here, I think, it is important to realize that we are considering *strategic* resources: those

Market scene in La Paz, Bolivia. Trading played a significant role in the emergence of an urbanized state.

Photo by Dr. Allyn M. Stearman, Department of Anthropology and Sociology, University of Central Florida

[13]Henry T. Wright and Gregory A. Johnson, "Population, Exchange, and Early State Formation in Southwestern Iran," *American Anthropologist* 77, no. 2, 1975, pp. 267–89.

that are needed to efficiently adapt to some part of the world. Metals, asphalt, basalt, obsidian, or surplus food—every one of these resources has been a strategic commodity. Services are also important. Military assistance and information, and protection of commercial convoys are resources too, just as much as a basket of wheat.

In this sense then, the city-state centers were environments of scattered resources. Mesopotamia did not *seem* highly varied, with grassy uplands and southerly marsh. This was deceiving; there was considerable diversity in this part of the world. Pockets of arable land, labor service, military alliance, the water table, outcroppings of copper, asphalt springs, and the rivers themselves made Mesopotamia a more variable world than it seemed. This was so of every one of the regions in which villages became city-states. There were *scattered resources* linked together in a web of *exchange*.[14]

As we have seen earlier in the story, exchange has a way of increasing itself. This is a process that archeologists refer to as *self-amplification*. Remember the Andean Indian climbing down from the clouds to the jungle. Such journeys disappeared long ago in many parts of the world. If you have kinfolk or friends at a distance, you can settle down to live in one place. If you are lacking resources, you can acquire them through long-distance trade. Such a system came into existence during the days of the earliest chiefdoms. For many people in marginal areas, it made possible a settled existence. With a more stable life, populations grew ever more large. That, in turn, created greater demand for different resources acquired through trade. When exchange is efficient, it often continues to grow.

If the security and stable existence of village societies is dependent on trade, then every effort is made to make trade a dependable system. The strategy of ancient monopolies was, perhaps, one way to make trade more secure. Beyond that, it was possible for trade to be a sacred activity.[15] A journey from village to village could be a pilgrimage to a shrine. It is possible that both of these strategies evolved from the growth of early exchange. Increasingly in Mesopotamia, exchange was confined to particular villages with specialized craftworkers or abundant resources for trade. Early shrines in Mesopotamia and ceremonial centers in Oaxaca and the Andes are evidence for use of the sacred in early exchange.

But the paradox of both of these strategies is the uncertainty they brought into existence. *Highly organized raids* and exchange were evolving to-

---

[14]The significance of exchange systems in state formation has been most strongly emphasized by William L. Rathje, "The Origin and Development of Lowland Classic Maya Civilization," *American Antiquity* 36, no. 3 (1971), pp. 275–85, and numerous other writings. My own views on the origins of the urbanized state were most strongly influenced by the contributions of William L. Rathje, David L. Webster, and Henry T. Wright.

[15]This interpretation of the role of the sacred in systems of exchange was derived from Thomas C. Patterson, "Chavin: An Interpretation of Its Spread and Influence," *Dumbarton Oaks Conference on Chavin* (Washington, D.C.: Dumbarton Oaks Research Library and Collections, 1971).

gether. David Webster has recently suggested that "war" in those days was a hit-and-run skirmish, not the large-scale conflict that evolved once the state was created.[16] As exchange became much more predictable, it likely contributed to such organized raids. For the herder in a year of bad weather or the forager who could not find enough game, food on the routes was a way of preventing starvation.

If such organized raiding existed, then it amounted to human predation. People and commodities that moved on the routes were the prey. Like many predator-prey relations, it continually became more complex: "one-upmanship" was a critical strategy of human survival.[17] You are bringing barley from Ur to Hassuna, but it might be the last thing you do. There is an obvious advantage in making a change in your schedule; or you might take an alternative trade route, perhaps one that is traveled less often; or you might travel with an army to safeguard your goods and your life. But then, consider the lot of the "predators." *Their* strategies must become intricate too. They must observe the alternative trade routes and detect new schedules for the movements of goods. Each system was pressuring the other into greater complexity.

For villagers who lived on the trade routes, the world was becoming a bewildering place. There were too many decisions that had to be made by too few. Beyond that, there were crowds of strange faces; new houses appeared in the village. The community was becoming a mixture of social traditions. Archeologist Malcolm Webb suggested that many villages grew into cities because of their ceremonial centers and religious behavior. Transformation of the human community

> was caused not by any environmental advantage but rather the operation of belief systems and social prestige in conjunction with kin ties. It is probable that the leaders of major kin groups were able to gather followers about them who would in turn provide the labor needed for programs of large-scale religions and building activity precisely because of the pleasures which these activities themselves provided.[18]

But I find it doubtful that ancient villagers would abandon the only life that they knew for the "pleasures" of moving stone blocks and constructing

---

[16] David L. Webster, "On Theocracies, " *American Anthropologist* 78 (1976), pp. 812–28. The observation is more forcefully expressed in his "Warfare and the Evolution of Maya Civilization," in *The Origins of Maya Civilization,* ed. Richard E. W. Adams (Albuquerque: University of New Mexico Press, 1977), pp. 335–73.

[17] The value of models of predation in understanding state evolution was discussed by Patricia L. Gall and Arthur A. Saxe, "The Ecological Evolution of Culture: The State as Predator in Succession Theory," in *Exchange Systems in Prehistory,* ed. Timothy K. Earle and Jonathan E. Ericson (New York: Academic Press, 1977), pp. 255–68. Their use of a predation analogy, however, is different from the use made of it here.

[18] Malcolm C. Webb, "The Peten Maya Decline Viewed in the Perspective of State Formation" in *The Classic Maya Collapse,* ed. T. Patrick Culbert (Albuqueque: University of New Mexico Press, 1973), p. 388

a shrine. I suspect that they abandoned their villages because they were remote from major routes of exchange. As trading systems grew increasingly polished, the faraway hamlets could no longer compete. If they wanted services and commodities they had to move closer to the points on the circuit. They had to settle in those villages or in hamlets that were not far away.

Out of this then, came a mixture of cultures: the world's earliest cities were born. It was a process inextricably connected with the rise of the state. As I described once before in the story, when immigrants moved into each village, they created communities with a plurality of political power. One kin group was skillful at smelting, another at weaving, another made pots. One group had extensive connections through much of the region. If a group did not have any specialty, it had sheer manpower, useful in war. As a service, they could go with a convoy and protect it from raids.

For the elites who were old-time villagers controlling the flow of exchange, the arrival of immigrants was remarkably attuned to their needs. The very polishing of regional exchange, which made the immigrants arrive in the first place, was creating more problems than their leaders could handle alone. So for them, a group of weavers or potters not only had a specialized trade, they were useful in removing the stress of an information explosion. Leaders of immigrant kin groups could make decisions regarding exchange; they could also direct the production of specialized goods. The elite, in a kind of consultancy, could make decisions about their decisions: a generalized policy for leaders of kin groups to follow.

Of what value was this to the immigrants? Why did they agree to such a system at all? Conceivably, it was a matter of privilege and of social prestige. If the elite wished to have their assistance, then the elite would have to give them rewards.[19] Luxury goods from the trade routes and their pick of commodities that came to the city were the conditions of service to the urban elite. Simple coercion was likely not possible, not in those embryonic days of the state. The city elite was a small group of people still adapted to the days of the village. Reward was their only possible means of political rule.

The strategy was deeply ironic in its effects upon our social behavior. Since the time of the earliest foragers, our kinship relations had held us together. You hunted and gathered, you farmed, and you prayed with your kin. In the days when villages bustled with immigrant crowds that transformed them into cities, these kinship connections were vital to the local elite. They were a ready-made authority structure: the traditional leader and the obedient group. Rewards and orders were passed down the line. Had it not been for this feature of kinship, it is unlikely that

[19] The reconstruction that follows was strongly influenced by David L. Webster, "On Theocracies."

Field Museum of Natural History

Mayan musicians depicted on Bonampak murals. During the urbanization process, artists and craftworkers offered services and commodities to local elites in exchange for political power.

there would have been states. Thousands of people flocked to the city, but their traditional leaders were a much smaller group. Through those leaders, the elite in the city could remain in control.

Yet the irony in this ancient episode is that the longer the process continued, the more it weakened the kinship alliances in human society.[20] Kin leaders had a great deal in common—including, especially, the rewards they shared. It was far better for a kin leader's children to marry the children of another kin leader. Rewards, in that way, would accumulate. It was preferable to marrying the less-better-off. Through homogamy ("like-marrying-like") rewards were maintained on the kin-leader level. Class was interfering with kinship in ancient society. The process was likely accelerated by the growth of information exchange. Kin leaders who also were specialists were discovering the power in a pool of ideas. Hierarchies were becoming more fixed in the earliest cities.

In time and perhaps inevitably, behavior was justified in terms of belief. Our species has never had any problem concocting and altering its sacred

---

[20] Adams, Evolution, p. 119.

Courtesy of the Oriental Institute, University of Chicago

Early Mesopotamian dynastic statues. The prayerful attitude reflected here suggests a feature of the earliest states. In the absence of large-scale armies, religion was a valuable strategy for intensifying the power of centralized rule.

ideas to accommodate some change we have made in our daily behavior. the shrines and the gods of the household were slowly replaced by elitist religion. Its rituals were shared by the uppermost level of state.

Imitation, most sincere of all flattery, caused this process to repeat through the years. No wisdom was necessary to discover what had to be done. Rewards in the earliest cities were held by the elite and the next higher levels. So to acquire rewards, you were loyal to the level above you. In a way, then, much more than rewards were being transmitted from the top to the bottom. The strategy of creating a level—of sharing luxuries and information within it—was spreading like a ripple from the center of the urban elite.

Since that ironic subversion of kinship, human society was never the same. There were *hierarchical groupings of people differing in resources and social prestige*. Near the end of prehistory, *class* had come into existence. The highest levels of the urban establishment were the individuals who made up the state. But below them were soldiers, metallurgists, farmers, shipbuilders, merchants, and spies. All of them belonged to their levels, shared information, and sought their rewards. Kinship had now become private. It had little to do with the public domain. *The System*, as we cynically call it, was now in existence.

Early states, wherever they emerged, reinforced their power through the use of exchange—those elaborate networks that first brought them into existence. Remember that these early establishments were constructed in regions of scattered resources. State officials, who lived in the cities, were directing the flow of exchange. People in the rural communities depended on this urban control to provide them with goods that they otherwise would never obtain. This power made it possible to demand a higher volume of trade. Bureaucrats, petty officials, artists, craftsworkers, musicians, and priests needed food from the farmers in order to eat—and to survive. To get the food, the state began to demand it. Subjects could do little else but obey. A portion of personal production was sent to the state.

More was involved in this strategy than simply supporting a class of officials. It was not a straightforward technicolor spectacle of mud-spattered agricultural workers supporting a despot surrounded by music and dance. This is not to deny exploitation or the fact of increasingly centralized power. It *is* to say that such early taxation—surrendering a portion of your yield to the state—was probably an adaptive necessity in these early societies. Beyond the fact that there were groups of administrators depending on taxes to meet their own needs, there was also the practice of surpluses placed into *storage*. If extra grain, as well as other resources, was maintained by the ruling elite, this was a strategy of buffering uncertainty in the earliest states. If there were famine somewhere in the territory, a blight of insects, or not enough rain, then the ruler's reserves could be used for community aid. This was not just an act of benevolence; it was a pragmatic political move. A failure of some part of the system could adversely affect the whole net of exchange. Trading and middleman connections could be disrupted because of such breakdowns. Cautious rulers had little alternative except to offer such aid.

For the advantage of the buffering strategy, the state paid a considerable price. Early states expanded their boundaries; they were often at war. As each state increased the cohesiveness of its territorial net of exchange, this generated conflicts for communities that lived near its borders.[21] Suppose you resided in a village where there was a bubbling asphalt spring. You traded your asphalt to a village a few miles away. From them you got barley and copper; that was the way it had always been done. But suddenly—in a few generations—the arrangement changed.

Now that village sent its copper and barley to cities and towns that were remote from your village. You were on the outside looking in, and your trade disappeared. The maturity of urbanized trading was somewhat

---

[21]A probable additional factor was population growth within the state's territory.

similar to its early beginning: it was commercial behavior closely related to war. There were likely many border conflicts as trading systems evolved through the years. You could raid them for their barley and copper, but such a maneuver would seldom succeed. You were not simply raiding a village, but a community now part of a state. Beyond that, what you actually needed was not the booty of a successful attack, but the commercial connections that had sustained you for hundreds of years. In the end then, came capitulation: your village became part of the state. And the resource diversity of its territory again was increased.[22]

A development so novel and intricate will not be thoroughly researched overnight. Archeologists are rapidly discovering the many subtleties of cities and states, but as everyone is aware, there is much that remains to be done. I suspect that the more we learn of these urbanized systems of power, the more we will discover their relation to ancient exchange. I think *scattered resources*, widespread *exchange*, and the *warfare* that went along with it, were the critical factors in the emergence of the earliest states. In that perspective, we should look at those regions where the great transformation occurred: where hierarchies of power appeared at the first light of history.

---

[22]Gall and Saxe, "Ecological Evolution."

17 / Highlands, Lowlands, and Conflict in Mesopotamia

Not long ago in terms of this story, perhaps 6,500 years before the present, tiny mud-and-clay houses were scattered throughout Mesopotamia. A traveler from the Taurus Mountains could journey south on the crooked, old roads through tussocky hills that in time would be known as Assyria. The country would flatten and grow hotter. Hills would dissolve into swamplands and streams. Great rivers would disappear into the Gulf. Beyond that was the sea.

Everywhere on the Euphrates and Tigris—the grassy north and the wet world to the south—were the smallest of settlements, scarcely the beginnings of towns. Yet, almost unseen by the traveler, a process was at work in this world that in centuries to come would cause temples to rise near the rivers. Our traveler might have *felt* isolated—the road ahead stretched empty for miles—but, season after season, more people were afoot on the trails.

Pottery tells part of the story of the emergence of widespread exchange. During the days when the Al Ubaid village was growing up among marshes and reeds, its style of ceramics was scattered throughout Southwestern Asia. Fragments have been found on the Taurus and in the settlements of the Arabian plateau; they have been discovered on the Iranian highlands, the bridge to the east. More than the fragments of pottery, there is the settlement pattern itself and the remains of the goods carried from village to village. Earlier in the story we saw how settlements in the highland country bridged Mesopotamia with people as far east as Indus. From that bridge, from Anatolia, and from boats that sailed into the Gulf, critical commodities were moving to the Tigris-Euphrates. Out of sites such as Tepe Sialk, copper was brought to the alluvial rivers. Pastoralist in the north brought the meat, milk, and hides of the herds. Asphalt was brought to the rivers from northern Iran or the Anatolian Plateau. Basalt, alabaster, and obsidian were imported as well.

But of all the different commodities that circulated throughout Southwestern Asia, one type in particular has suggested the scale of trade. At Tepe Yahya in southwestern Iran, halfway between Mesopotamia and Indus, craftworkers were manufacturing bowls carved out of green chlorite.

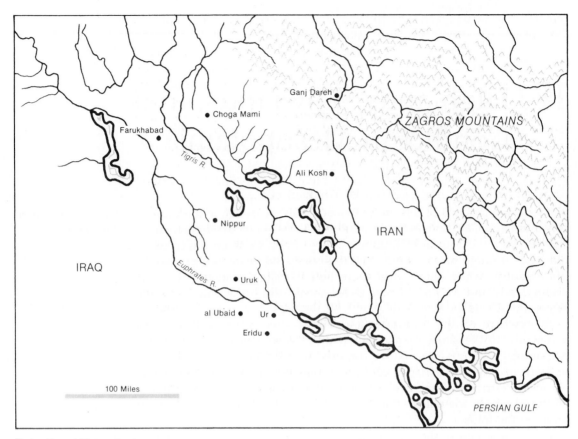

Early cities of Mesopotamia.

* What these bowls originally contained we still do not know. But a great
deal has been learned from the designs carved on their sides. They were
probably pictorial trademarks—the "girl with the umbrella on the package
of salt"—which identified the village, perhaps even the workshop, that
made them.

Swirlings, squares, rosettes, chainlike designs, mythical creatures,
fighting serpents, scorpions, and date palms were carved in the chlorite.
Archeologist Philip Kohl has found evidence that, once the bowls were
manufactured in Yahya, they were traded to villages and towns throughout
the Near East.[1] The delicate designs have been discovered in Syria, Mesopotamia, and the west Persian Gulf. They have been found north of
Afghanistan's mountains and to the east on the Indus. With every gen-

---

[1]Philip L. Kohl, "The Balance of Trade in Southwestern Asia in the Mid-Third Millenium
BC," *Current Anthropology* 19, no. 3 (September 1978), pp. 463–92.

eration that passed, the boat and the caravan were commonplace sights. The world was already growing small as prehistory ended.

As Henry Wright and Gregory Johnson discovered, there was no dramatic increase of trade, at least in the critical centuries of urban emergence.[2] Buried in the Susiana Plain, east of the Tigris in southwestern Iran, is the indirect evidence of a prehistoric volume of trade. Message sealings were carried by travelers—often a hollowed sphere made of clay. These bulla, as today they are called, would be broken by the person receiving the goods. Inside were tiny clay tokens representing certain items of trade. These were matched with what the traveler delivered; a person could see if the total shipment were there. There were also commodity sealings. A rope was tied around a jar or a bale. The knot of the rope was plastered over with a layer of clay. This would be stamped with a special design, perhaps indicating the source of the product. When a person received the commodity, the clay-covered knot was immediately checked. It indicated the source of the item and if the product had been delivered untouched. Untying the knot of the shipment would have broken the clay. These sealings are preserved in the soil, and in this way, they are a measure of trade. At 3500 BC, and then gradually for the next 500 years, they increase in the deposits of sites in southwestern Iran.

So there might not have been a burst of exchange, but that might not be the significant feature. More important, perhaps, is the evidence of social control. Early sealings of whatever type reveal a growing regulation of commerce: source, destination, and quantity were governed by rules. Some of the rules became extremely elaborate—they amounted to a specialized code—which itself was a strategy for controlling the movement of goods. Stamp seals of the earlier villages with their simple designs in relief were replaced by a new kind of seal more elaborately made. They were cylinders of stone or ceramic depicting warriors, battle fields, or lions; when they were rolled on wet clay, they would leave a repeating design. Exquisite detail made forgery difficult and made the life of the trader complex. Tokens and decorative systems had to be known.

But the bulla, the knots, and the cylinders only regulated trade day to day. It was also becoming necessary to remember trade of the past. Record-keeping may have had its beginnings as early as 3500 BC. It very likely grew out of the complexity of early exchange. Human memory was no longer adequate for the intricate hazards of wide-ranging trade. There was no way to remember the bandits, the washed-out roads, and the springs that went dry in decades of trading with hundreds of different communities. Even if much *was* remembered, a faulty recollection might well have proved fatal: it could result in the loss of a traveler or of a

---

[2]Henry T. Wright and Gregory A. Johnson, "Population, Exchange, and Early State Formation in Southwestern Iran," *American Anthropologists* 77, no. 2, pp. 267–89.

Mesopotamian stamp
seals, used for
property identification.

Courtesy of the Oriental Institute, University of Chicago

shipment of goods. So experience was put into "storage" as cuneiform
writing began—the wedge-shaped impressions in clay done with a reed.[3]

---

[3]The empire of the Peruvian Inca is widely cited as an exception to this principle. It is
true that they developed no writing, but their empire lasted only a very short time. Even
so, while it *was* in existence, they developed knotted strings (*quipu*) to record economic
transactions. Evidently the pressure for stored information had already begun among the
Inca. Whether this would have resulted in writing, of course, will never be known.

Courtesy of the Oriental Institute, University of Chicago

Increased volume of trade made cylinder seals a necessity. Used for marking exchange commodities, their elaborate designs made forgery difficult.

The cuneiform tablets of Mesopotamia were likely a resource that regularized trade. They were not stored away and forgotten, but were constantly read. This made possible the discovery of economic trends which facilitated prediction and stabilized trade.

Early tablets discovered at Uruk bore nearly 2,000 pictorial signs which had to be mastered by a communicating merchant elite. The tablets, it is often suggested, were early records of the movement of goods. They are evidence that commercial activity was growing complex. But this is only part of the story; there may have been more to the records than that. I suspect that these cuneiform tablets were not only records but a resource as well. They were not stored away and forgotten; they were constantly read. For the small percentage of people who could read them, they were a connection with an unvarnished past—with events that were not colored by myth or self-glorification. There is power to be gained from such diligence, from reading the details of day-to-day trade. In these monotonous accounts of transactions there was evidence of economic trends: of striking—and subtle—fluctuations in the flow of exchange. Early merchants were early historians and likely dabbled in prediction as well. This afforded them a powerful position in human affairs. Decisions such as when to trade, with whom, and when *not* to could be more carefully made. They could be based on the detailed records of events in the past.

Exchange, then, had likely grown slowly, but a critical threshold was reached. In many villages there may have been a burst of information on trade. There was not only day-to-day information about the caravans that came to the villages, there was also the stored information about trade in the past. This could very well have been the attraction that drew immigrants to towns such as Uruk. More dependable trade in these settlements made life more secure.

A change coming over the landscape reflected the power of trade: Mesopotamian settlements were growing in regular patterns. By as early as 4000 BC many villages of the Tigris-Euphrates were no longer located where obvious resources were found. Instead they were becoming "geometric", if we do not press the idea too far.[4] Larger villages grew at the center of satellite hamlets about six miles away. In these hamlets, there often were buildings decorated with distinctive mosaic: cones of ceramic were placed in the interior walls. Gregory Johnson suspects that these buildings were very likely administrative centers. They coordinated the outlying trade of the centralized towns.

But urban life in Mesopotamia was not simply a matter of trade. Within the fast-growing communities there was variety and excitement as well. If we visit in our mind such a settlement and walk through the gate in its ponderous wall,

> we are soon lost in a maze of narrow streets, thronged with people and traffic. Naked children play near the open doorways, from which comes the clang of hammers on metal, the grunt of saws, the whirring of potters' wheels. This is the artisans' quarter. Sometimes the clatter of a military chariot drowns other sounds, as the heavy, solid-wheeled vehicle with its helmeted driver and spearman, thunders along the street, sending men, women, and children scurrying for safety. Ripe Sumerian curses follow it.
>
> Higher still we enter a rich, somewhat quieter area, where the houses are larger, though the small, narrow windows fronting the streets afford no indication of the beauty and elegance within.
>
> These are the homes of the rich merchants and the higher officials of the Court. Glance through one of the window-grills (there is no glass, only bars of mud-brick) and we see a dinner party in progress. The guests are seated on backless chairs, beside light tables of wood or reed wickerwork. The food includes garlic in sour cream, milk and barley soup, roast Tigris salmon, and roast pig. The dessert comprises various fruit such as dates, pomegranates, and figs, and there is an excellent goat's milk cheese. To accompany the feast there is an abundance of wine, for the vine—the inevitable accompaniment of true civilization—is grown in Sumer as it was in Egypt, Persia, Greece, and Rome. For those who prefer it there is also beer, which is usually drunk through a straw.

---

[4]Gregory A. Johnson, "Locational Analysis and the Investigation of Uruk Local Exchange Systems," *Ancient Civilization and Trade*, ed. J. A. Sabloff and C. C. Lamberg-Karlovsky (Albuquerque: University of New Mexico Press, 1975).

The girls are "lashed-up" to the eyes. Heavy discs of gold dangle on soft brown shoulders, and the lustrous black wigs, framing the dark, deep-shadowed eyes, are adorned with gold beech-leaf pendants overhanging the brow. Crowning the wigs are intertwined strings of blue and red beads, from which spring delicate artificial flowers made from lapis lazuli and gold. The women drink with the men, from fluted goblets of gold and silver, while in the background musicians play for the dance or provide a thrumming accompaniment to the impassioned recital of some old Sumerian poem. It might be, perhaps, the epic of Gilgamesh and of how he fought the storm-god and won the love of the goddess Inanna; it might be the story of the Great Flood, and of Utnapishtim, who built himself an Ark which was borne up on the waters which destroyed the world.[5]

Everywhere on the southerly marshlands was the bustle of the new, crowded towns. Within them lay power, and a rich ceremonial life.

Ideology and the rise of the state

Within those towns that were growing to be cities, there were specialized building as well. The smallest of shrines were becoming elaborate temples. In the early days of the Eridu village, about 4500 BC, the shrine of the community was a building 10 feet on a side. During the next 15 centuries the early shrine became a maze of rooms: small cubicles surrounding a sanctuary with an offering table. A hundred miles to the northwest of Eridu was a community known as Nippur. In this village too there was an emerging religious elite. A mud-brick building about 40 feet long at around 3500 BC became 80 times larger in the course of only 500 years.

Behind the architectural changes lie the strategies of political power. Early shrines were the places of worship, perhaps of a chief and his kin in the village. But the number of religious personnel was increasing through time. A temple position may have been a reward to the leader of a kin group that moved to the village. In exchange for this favor, his group would support the elite. More than that, the elaborate temples were storehouses of regional trade. Surpluses were apportioned to communities all over the area. With easy access to a wealth of commodities, rewards could take material form. Exotic goods could be awarded to leaders who awarded their kin.

The temples in time became precincts at the center of Mesopotamian cities—elaborate districts that loomed over houses and marsh. Generations of quarrying and bricklaying, done to achieve some reward from the king, built the temples and pyramids that celebrated rulers and gods. In Uruk

---

[5]Leonard Cottrell, *The Land of Shinar* (London: Souvenir Press, 1965), pp. 140–41. This discription of a typical Mesopotamian city refers to the period ca. 2700 BC. But towns were probably much like this at the time of early urbanization.

a whitewashed building commemorated Anu, the god of the heavens.[6] A stepped pyramid nearly 40 feet high with a triple stairway approaching the summit, it is typical of the ziggurats built near the Tigris-Euphrates. To the east were courtyards and temples dedicated to the goddess Inanna. Six separate temples and a ziggurat rose in her name.

Here too was the strategy of kingship working in intricate psychological ways. Religious beliefs were enhancing political power. Later writings from the Tigris-Euphrates tell us much about the faith of those times—of how city-state rulers were figures of religious belief. The gods, thought the Mesopotamians, created humans to relieve them from toil—to labor on estates as a servant would work for a lord. But this is more than just simple humility; it has a subtle dimension as well. Because workers need enlightened direction, gods had created overseers of sorts. These, as you might expect, were the kings in control of the cities. Though they were mortal, they were chosen by gods and given the duty of ruling the city. It is probably the earliest example of the divine right of kings.

Historian Thorkild Jacobsen offered a somewhat romantic account of the god-given duties of Mesopotamian rule. If you read his description carefully, you will see that not much is left out. The god-appointed tasks were a recipe for total control:

> We call the *ensi* (king) manager of the god's estate; and his position vis-a-vis the god was actually closely parallel to that of an estate manager, a steward, vis-a-vis the owner. A steward appointed to manage an estate is expected, first of all, to uphold and carry on the established order of that estate; second, he is expected to execute such specific commands as the owner may see fit with respect to changes, innovations, or ways to deal with unexpected situations. Quite similarly, the *ensi* was expected to uphold the established order of the god's temple and city in general, and he was expected to consult the god and carry out any specific orders which the god might wish to give.
>
> To the first part of the ensi's task belonged the administration of the temple and its estate. He was in complete charge of all the agricultural tasks, of temple forests, and temple fisheries, of the spinneries, looms, mills, breweries, bakeries, kitchens, etc., which formed part of the temple manor. Minute accounts were kept of all these activities by a corps of scribes, and these accounts were submitted to and approved by him. As he managed the temple of the city god, so his wife managed the temple and estate of the divine spouse of the city god, and his children managed the temples of the children of the city god.
>
> In addition to these tasks, the *ensi* was responsible for law and order in the state and was to see to it that everybody was justly treated. Thus we hear about one *ensi* that he contracted with the god Ningirsu that he

---

[6]M. E. L. Mallowan, *Early Mesopotamia and Iran* (New York: McGraw-Hill, 1965), pp. 36–58.

would not deliver up the orphan and the widow to the powerful man. The *ensi*, therefore, was the highest judicial authority. But he had other duties also: he was commander in chief of the army of the city-state, he negotiated for his lord the god with *ensis* representing the gods of other city-states, and he made war and peace.[7]

Such matters might strike us as quaint—the curious beliefs of a long-vanished time. For V. Gordon Childe, they were the irrelevant part of the past.[8] But when the beliefs are examined in detail, there is a pattern that seems to emerge: instability gives rise to ideologies of total control. In early states, as David Webster has suggested, the possibility of coercion was low. A powerful kin group at Uruk may have had land or commercial connections but likely did not have enough warriors to police the whole state. This was because that kin group for centuries had been living a village existence, in which redistribution was sufficient for social control.

But the transformation from village to city saw new people and new centers of power. To keep control of an urban community there was usually the device of reward: the gold and the lapis handed out for supporting the crown. But what about a season of crisis—when there was raiding on the routes of exchange? What would happen if—for whatever reason—there were no rewards?

Belief was a possible answer. It was a remarkable method of social control. It required no soldiers or armaments; its policing was done from within. Allegiance to the state became an article of personal faith.[9] This was why, when the king died in Ur, the court followed him into his grave. Dressed in their finest, they drank poison and died in his tomb. In the formative years of a state, ideology is a powerful tool. It can strengthen a ruler in the absence of physical force.

The role of political ideology was never buried in the sands of Iraq. State systems in periods of crisis recycle their past. There was fealty—allegiance to the lord—in the Middle Ages when kingdoms were weak. Early modern times witnessed again the divine right of kings. In the industrialized states of our time, ideology was often intense, especially in those times when a government sought to survive. The early days of the Soviet Union and the years of the fascists that sprang up in Europe were days of upheaval, insecurity, and the state-as-one's-faith. Very clearly,

---

[7]Thorkild Jacobsen, "Mesopotamia," in *The Intellectual Adventure of Ancient Man: An Essay on Speculative Thought in the Ancient Near East*, H. Frankfort, H. A. Frankfort, J. A. Wilson, T. Jacobsen, W. A. Irwin, contributors (Chicago: University of Chicago Press, 1946), pp. 188–9.

[8]P. Gathercole, "'Patterns in Prehistory': An Examination of the Later Thinking of V. Gordon Childe," *World Archeology* 7, no. 4 (1971).

[9]This is perhaps the political equivalent of what Linda Cordell has called a resilient system. Ideology and prestigious rewards coexisted in the earliest states. If either system became weakened, then the other could be emphasized. It is conceivable, of course, that both systems might fail, which would be the immediate (proximate) cause of a state's collapse.

statist loyalty as internal belief is dangerous strategy. If the state is of the highest importance, then human life become trivialized. Atrocities can then become trivial; very often in history, they have. In Hannah Arendt's excellent phrase, it is a frightening "banality of evil."[10] It is as ancient as Mesopotamia and as new as our time.

Like many states and nations that followed them, Mesopotamians believed they were favored. Watched over by gods, supplication would help them survive. But prayer alone did not save their society and has never saved anyone else. A seed of destruction was part of their world from the start.

Mesopotamia at the beginning of history

Philip Kohl has suggested what happened in the years after 3000 BC, as Mesopotamians heightened their volume of trade.[11] Kings in the lowland cities needed the treasure—the lapis and gold—to reward their supporters and make their own lives more secure. They needed the stone and the metals which were impossible to find in their country for constructing their houses, temples, and weapons of war. In return they sent cereals and textiles—the agrarian fruit of the south. They dug more elaborate canals as their commerce increased with the highlands. Mesopotamians were exporting more cereals than ever before.

For the people in the high-country grasslands, growing trade seemed to offer a promise. They would not have to depend on the rainfall or the waters of the drought-troubled wadis. They could manufacture precious commodities and import their food. Tepe Sialk could send out metals; Farukhabad had asphalt to spare. From Lake Van in the east Turkish mountains, obsidian could be dug from the quarries and sent to Ali Kosh where it was made into tools for the south. In the centuries before the first cities, striking changes were at work in the hills: villages became specialized factories for the Tigris-Euphrates.

As archeologist Colin Renfrew has put it, such a system is "action at a distance": through trade we can affect a society we never have seen.[12] Indeed, the repercussions were greater than the development of specialization. Powerful chiefs in the highlands had begun to emerge. After all, if an Iranian village could export some critical item, it could acquire a

---

[10]The deep irony of this pattern of behavior is not only that atrocity is trivial, but that the trivialization is viewed as being morally correct. Thus an individual rebelling against atrocity would feel as though he were doing something wrong. The issue is discussed by Michael Denneny, "The Privilege of Ourselves: Hannah Arendt on Judgment," in *Hannah Arendt: The Recovery of the Public World*, ed. Melvyn A. Hill (New York: St. Martin's Press, 1979); and by Arendt herself, *Eichmann in Jerusalem: A Report on the Banality of Evil* (New York: Viking Press, 1964). One of the most striking prehistoric examples (the Aztec) will be described at some length in a later chapter.

[11]Kohl, "Balance of Trade."

[12]Colin Renfrew, "Trade as Action at a Distance: Questions of Integration and Communication," in Sabloff and Lamberg-Karlovsky, *Ancient Civilization*, pp. 3–59.

surplus of food and then use it for trade. Then too, there was always the strategy of strengthening local alliances and creating a monopoly to pressure the lands to the south.

Mesopotamians, to drive their own bargains, would trade with a variety of clients. If an obsidian-producing community was not pleased with the rules of exchange, then obsidian blades were imported from a competitive village. This meant, too, that the exports of cereals were no longer sent to the earlier client. These may have been the earliest embargos in human prehistory.

Strategy and counter strategy became part of this network of trade, especially as political leaders emerged in the north. In time, there were intricate alliances among villagers who lived in the foothills. Pastoralists who lived in this country made a valuable ally for raids. It seemed clear that the only solution was to storm the Mesopotamian cities. The canals, the cereals, and the textiles would belong to the highlands. From Akkad, near present-day Baghdad, warriors of Sargon invaded the south. City-states fell and the weapons were "cleansed in the sea." But occupation of Mesopotamia was always a fragile arrangement at best. It had never been politically unified; it was always a region of small city-states. Conquerors found themselves drawn into local disputes. And so "Akkadia" collapsed into chaos in 2200 BC. Cities were ravaged by nomads who came from the hills. Warriors in Ur brought stability, but it lasted only 200 years. For centuries the Tigris-Euphrates was shattered by war.

Babylonians, Assyrians, Elamites, Persians, and Macedonian Greeks each abode for an hour and then went their way. By that time, Mediterranean poets were singing of journeys on a wine-dark sea. Audiences were shocked by the incest of *Oedipus Rex*. But in the south, not far from the ocean, there was a land where two rivers still flowed. Fragments of its old broken cities were now covered by mantles of sand. Travelers on the roads plucked pottery from curious mounds. Seasons passed; the timeless mud-houses rose again upon the ancient debris. Goats nibbled the bunches of grass on the wreckage of kingdoms.

18 / Exchange, Reward, and Coercion: Early Urbanization in Indus, Egypt, and China

It flourished for all of six centuries—a mere flash in evolutionary time. It had cities unlike any other; massive buildings with windowless walls. It had aqueducts, drains, sacred buildings, and elaborate pools. Beyond its streets lay a vast, humid forest where there were elephants, date palms, and deer. A turbulent river both endangered and nourished its days. Before vanishing it committed its history into records that no one can read.[1] Travelers on the river found its cities abandoned and still.

Indus Valley urbanization

Prehistorians know it as the Indus Valley. No one knows what it was called in the past. How it began and what became of its culture is largely unknown. In its homeland, the rivers of Pakistan, archeology has only begun. There are hundreds of settlements of which very little is known. Excavations done in one of its cities have left the deepest layers untouched. Evidence of its early beginnings is covered by water.

But Indus is not completely a mystery. We can say something about how it began. The vast arc of buckled uplands that stretched east over northern Iran was a circuit of commerce between Indus and lands to the west. Here there were metallurgists and miners, as well as middlemen regulating exchange. Here there were specialists who traded with Mesopotamia. To the south was another connection: the sea-lanes of maritime trade. Boats sailed out of the Indus Valley to Persian Gulf towns.

What has been learned of those networks of commerce has given rise to more questions than answers. There is very little evidence of prehistoric

---

[1]But I do not mean to suggest that the situation is hopeless. True enough, the Indus script and characters on the stamp-seals as well have been related by scholars to Sumerian, Sanskrit, and Dravidian. Others argue for Hittite linkage, though some believe that the script is Etruscan. One analyst holds out for a connection with Easter Island! I am sympathetic with John E. Mitchiner that the inscriptions are akin to Sumerian, especially in view of exchange with the Tigrus-Euphrates. Suggestive parallels exist between writings discovered in both of these regions. Tentative interpretations of phrases have already been done. The research is discussed by John E. Mitchiner, *Studies in the Indus Valley Inscriptions* (New Delhi, India: Oxford and IBH Publishing, 1978), pp. 1–18, 26–28.

The cities of Indus.

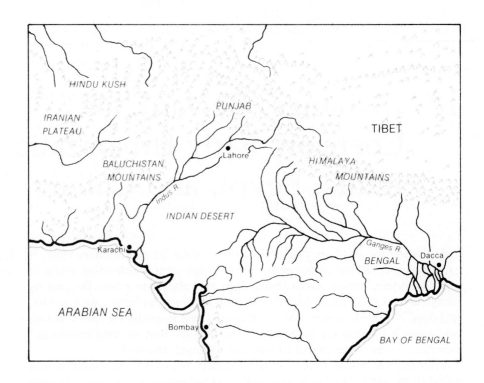

balance of trade.[2] Ceramics like those in the Indus Valley have been discovered at sites in the highlands; Indus trade may have extended as far
as the Caspian Sea. Stamp-seals are perhaps more convincing; there is
little doubt about where they were made. Elephants, bulls, and date
palms—and of course, the writing—carved onto the seals have marked
them distinctively as artifacts out of the east. The seals have been discovered
at Failaka, a Persian Gulf trading community. They have been dug from
the sand of Nippur in Mesopotamia. Yet there is still something missing,
a curious silence in what has been found. There is little evidence of Mesopotamian trade with the valley. Indus seals have been discovered at Nippur
and other cities of the Tigris-Euphrates. But nothing Mesopotamian has
ever been found near the Indus.

   It is a persistent—even nettling—question. Why was it that Indus society
with its widespread channels of trade received little or nothing from merchants of Mesopotamia? Could it have been that the Tigris-Euphrates was
really an ancient colonialist state? Is it possible that, searching for markets
and new producers of goods such as metals, they created a Mesopotamian
colony that grew into Indus? This would seem to be a possible answer; it

---

[2]C. C. Lamberg-Karlovsky and Jeremy A. Sabloff, *Ancient Civilizations: The Near East and
Mesoamerica* (Menlo Park, Calif.: Benjamin-Cummings, 1979), pp. 197–202.

is a view that has time on its side. The cities of Indus Valley society *did* develop after Mesopotamia. But aside from that simple chronology, there is little to support such a view. If Indus really had been an outpost, there would be no archeological silence. Evidence of Mesopotamians would litter the ground. Colonialism has always meant colonists and the baggage they have brought from their homeland. It has meant administrative centers and the writing of the ruling society. The shaky, temporary attempt of the Romans to colonize Britain left forts and administrative centers all over the land.

So if expansion (or diffusion) is doubtful, then perhaps it was the structure of trade that created the one-sided finds in the archeological record. Perhaps the Indus Valley exported commodities which were readily preserved in the soil, while Mesopotamians were sending their perishable goods. Barley, vegetables, and textiles could have been sent from the Tigris-Euphrates, and all of them might have decayed in the Indus deposits. But the weakness I find in this theory is the country of the Indus Valley itself, which very likely would have had little need for these imports at all. The Pakistani and the Punjab foothills had hundreds of pastoral nomads who could easily have delivered their textiles to cities and towns. Cereal grains, cattle, pigs, dates, melons, sesame, and peas could thrive on the mineral-rich plains that were close to the rivers.

I suspect that the cities of Indus were a "product" of Mesopotamia, but only in the sense that a commercial advantage was seized. As we saw earlier in the story, rise and decline are very relative things: the collapse of one society is also another's growth. Mesopotamia had always been fragile, with its agricultural wealth in the south and almost everything else that it needed in the northerly highlands. When the circuits between

Characteristic stamp-seals of Indus have been found on the Persian Gulf. Indus likely profited from the crisis in Mesopotamian trade.

Milwaukee Public Museum

the two regions were broken by plunder and war, a strategy was opened for the merchants of Indus society.

The Indus Valley had always been different: the flat, superheated country that nourished its cereal grains was flanked by a vast chain of foothills that lay to the west.[3] There were textiles and meat in those foothills and dairy products from the herds. Copper, lead, and silver deposits were mined on the slopes. Timber was not far from the rivers and also on the shores of the Arabian Sea. For the most part, whatever you needed was not far away. Villages growing in the Indus Valley were probably closely connected by trade. Many of them were probably centers of commercial exchange.

Of course, immigrants came to such centers just as they did in other parts of the world. Villages about to be cities had problems of power. Kin groups who ruled the old villages were in need of a supply of rewards. This alone was incentive for widening the networks of trade. Conveniently, in Mesopotamia, an opportunity presented itself. Highlanders were no longer trading with the cities of the Tigris-Euphrates, but they were specialized producers in need of agricultural goods. Perhaps, though we know less about it, cities near the Gulf were in need of connections for the stone and the metals that had formerly come from the north. Indus, more self-sufficient, provided easier conditions of trade. Village by village, its influence grew in the west.

This may have been why Indus society emerged in 2400 BC, when Mesopotamian networks were falling to pieces. It would explain why Indus artifacts have been found on the Iranian Plateau and in deposits of trading communities on the shores of the Gulf. It would suggest a spreading web of connections that grew powerful enough through the years so that envoys from Indus could manage Mesopotamian trade. Stamp-seals at Ur and Nippur suggest that such managers may have been present. These cities, badly battered by warfare, needed the networks of Indus society to supply them with the stone and the metals remote from the rivers.

If such a strategy actually happened, it created events "at a distance." Middlemen flourished on the stabilized routes of exchange. Villages east of the Caspian—akin to Djeitun of the "land in-between"—coordinated trade between Indus and highland societies. These villages in time became cities—a fully urban "Namazga" society—as Mesopotamia crumbled into chaos and war.[4] To the south, near the Indian Ocean, sailing vessels were

---

[3]Walter A. Fairservis, Jr., *The Roots of Ancient India* (Chicago: University of Chicago Press, 1977), pp. 1–28, 166–217.

[4]Namazga developments of this period are described by V. M. Masson and V. I. Sarianidi, *Cental Asia: Turkmenia before the Achamenids*, (New York: Praeger Publishers, 1972), pp. 97–111.

Field Museum of Natural History

An Indus-type sailing vessel with triangular sail. Boats very similar to this one sailed between the Persian Gulf and the Arabian sea.

laden with goods as Indus Valley society expanded its maritime trade.[5] Ancient Dilmun, which now is Bahrain, a tiny island off Saudi Arabia, flourished as a middleman city on the seagoing routes.

Branches of this intricate system extended for thousands of miles. Sailboats and oxen brought cargo to cities in Indus.[6] Harappa on the Ravi

---

[5]The exact nature of the relationships between Persian Gulf communities of Saudi Arabia and urbanized societies of Mesopotamia and Indus remains uncertain. Geoffrey Bibby speculates that Indus brought timber, cotton, ivory, and lapis in exchange for supplies of fresh water. Earlier, in the days of Al Ubaid, Mesopotmians may have settled in the area for fishing, pearl diving, trade, or control of the Gulf. See Geoffrey Bibby, *Looking for Dilmun* (New York: Alfred A. Knopf, 1969), pp. 192–94; and J. Oates, T. E. Davidson, D. Kamilli, and H. McKerrell, "Seafaring Merchants of Ur?" *Antiquity* 51, 1977, pp. 221–34.

[6]Harappa and Mohenjo-Daro are described by Fairservis, *Roots,* pp. 252–53, 246–47.

River, a stream that flows into the Indus, was a city with granaries and, possibly, a centralized temple."Possibly," because it is ruined now; it was plundered within our own time. Millions of bricks for a railroad were looted from the heart of the city. This century has ravaged Harappa much more than the past. There were granaries, large earthen platforms, and a row of furnaces, perhaps used for smelting. Two rows of barracklike houses were enclosed by a wall. Mortimer Wheeler suspects that such housing was "a piece of government planning." But there is much about Harappa that we probably never will know.

Archeologists have learned more of the Indus Valley from its cities that lay to the south, especially from the ruins that are known as Mohenjo-Daro. Over 300 miles from Harappa on the flood-drowned Indus plain, it is the largest of the Indus cities ever found. Its deepest layers are covered by water because the river has shifted through time. Mortimer Wheeler pumped out enough water to discover 26 feet of debris. When he returned to the site the next day it was flooded again. But he has excavated much of the city—about 36 percent of the site. It was a very different settlement than those of the Tigris-Euphrates.

Communities in Mesopotamia were a madness of courtyards and streets, a maze of alleys that wandered in every which way. But in the city of Mohenjo-Daro, like others of the Indus plain, there is an eerie precision: you know that this city was planned. Broad thoroughfares 30 feet wide run east-west and north-south through the city. They intersect with other streets and create a rectangular grid. There were sewers and, for that matter, manholes, and drainage ditches that followed the streets.[7] There were districts with shops and neighborhoods where townspeople lived.

For Wheeler the brick streets and the windowless walls were "miles of monotony." Buildings that bordered the thoroughfares were closed off on the side near the street. To enter them, you walked down an alley and went in from the side. More than that, there was a curious sameness in the appearance of the townspeoples' houses. Does this mean there was regimentation? Were the lives of the citizens planned? It is difficult to say until we learn more about their society. Planned cities have been built by democracies and built by absolutist systems as well. We know little of the structure of power in Indus society.

Yet power played a role in these cities; there can be little doubt about that. Northwest of the residential quarter was the citadel of Mohenjo-Daro: a structure that had likely been built for the ruling elite. A large hall about 90 feet square was divided into aisles by rectangular pillars. It was possibly for government meetings, but no one is sure. Close by was the municipal "swimming pool," or so it has sometimes been called. A rectangular basin of brick, lined with asphalt, and equipped with a drain,

---

[7]The drainage system was perhaps an adaptation to the occasional storms of the region. They removed water with a high level of efficiency—essential in a city built of clay.

Photos courtesy of Dr. Richard B. Woodbury

Mohenjo-Daro: A fired-brick city with windowless walls. Note drain in the right-hand photo.

it was possibly for the ritual baths of a religious elite. Towering over both of these structures was a granary of brickwork and timber: the storehouse of food critical to the affairs of the state. From its coffers came food for the specialists and perhaps rewards for supporting the throne. It could have served as a buffer for shortage in Indus society.

Harappa and Mohenjo-Daro might have coordinated riverine trade, for the stream was a gateway that led from the sea to the mountains. But there may have been sailing vessels that never traded on the Indus at all. Instead, they may have followed the winds of the Arabian Sea. Southeast of the mouth of the Indus, directly north of what now is Bombay, the port city of Lothal looked out to the Indian Ocean.[8] Here too were the gridded, brick avenues, the granaries, the baths, and the drains. A raised platform was similar to the citadel of Mohenjo-Daro.

But there was also a rectangular enclosure twice as long as a football field. It was made of bricks set in asphalt; a sluice gate was built in one end. S. R. Rao suspects that this structure was a harbor for ships at low tide.[9] There has been disagreement over this, but as of yet, no alternative

---

[8]Ibid., pp. 270–71.

[9]S. R. Rao, *Lothal and the Indus Civilization* (London: Asia Publishing House, 1973).

view. Even so, it seems more than likely that Lothal was an axis for trade. Gregory Possehl has said that this city was "sitting at the hub" of commerical exchange.[10] It touched the ocean and was nearly encircled by forest societies. This made possible exchange adaptations with foragers on the edge of the city—a system in existence today in this part of the world.

The Indus collapse

Its flame burned for all of six centuries, and then suddenly it guttered and died. Upper layers in the wreck of its cities have the stubs of irregular buildings. Walls are every which way; the old regimentation is gone. In the city of Mohenjo-Daro, skeletons were found in the houses and streets. Their bones bore slash marks. Victims had been left where they fell. In the years since this first was discovered, archeologists have wondered what happened. What extinguished the flame that was burning for so little time?

> Fed by wood, with blazing tawny mane,
> He sends up his smoke like a pillar to the sky,
> or like a wavering banner.
> Though headless and footless, he rushes through the woods
> like a bull lording it over a herd of cows,
> roaring like a lion or like mighty waters.
> He envelops the woods, consumes and blackens them with
> his tongue; with his burning iron grinders, his sharp,
> all-devouring jaws,
> he shears the hairs of the earth like a barber
> shaving a beard.[11]

These wild and whirling words were sung in praise of the fire-god Agni. They are from the *Rig Veda*, a Sanskrit hymn to the gods. Composed perhaps 3,000 years ago, they are reverent—often violent—hymns. They sing praise to storms and lightning, to fire and war. Many scholars, including V. Gordon Childe, have suspected that some of the stanzas were the creation of a warrior group that came out of the north. But "north" has meant east of the Caspian, Western Europe, and even the Pole! There still is no certainty about when, and by whom, it was written.

But it is possible, though far from established, that in the *Vedas* is an actual event: a warrior invasion that happened in the cities of Indus. The only good evidence of this has been discovered in Mohenjo-Daro. But there are many communities in Indus that have never been dug. Yet, even if there was an invasion, there is more to the story than that. There were troubles in Indus many years before warriors came.

---

[10]Gregory L. Possehl, "Lothal: A Gateway Settlement of the Harappan Civilization," *Studies in the Paleoecology of South Asia* (Ithaca, N.Y.: Cornell University Press, 1976).

[11]Herbert H. Gowen, *A History of Indian Literature from Vedic Times to the Present Day* (New York: Appleton-Century-Crofts, 1931), p. 56.

Nature might have been part of the problem, although this question has never been solved. Hydrologist Robert Raikes has argued that the unstable earth of the region once triggered a process that caused the mighty river to flood.[12] Floods, of course, were hardly novel in Indus; they had been a danger for thousands of years. But here was a disturbance greater than ever before. The subcontinent of India and Pakistan is a shelf of the earth's crust 40 miles thick. Near the end of the Age of Reptiles, the shelf had floated for thousands of miles. Eventually the "island" collided with the belly of Asia.

The collision is still going on, causing buckles and shifts in the earth. It may have been that nearly 4,000 years ago, land was lifted near the mouth of the Indus, backing up the river and drowning its cities and towns. Ancient traces of beaches are island; they are found many miles from the sea. Could it be that the floods were the greatest invader of all?

It is possible that such a thing happened, but it was also a local event. There is no evidence of floods in the cities that lie to the north. Then too, the event was not sudden, in the sense that it occurred overnight. For many years, the dwellers of Indus were building walls to hold back the river. The flooding was gradual. There was probably time to prepare.

I suspect that what happened in Indus was less dramatic than raiding or floods. But raiding and floods *were* related to an earlier change. Fragments of pottery dug out of Lothal had curious flecks dotting their surfaces. Viewed closely, the marks were discovered to be imprints of rice.[13] Plaster that covered the granaries and bricks of the buildings bore marks of the grain. People in Lothal were caught up in an economic change.

It may have been that the people of Indus were simply doing what they always had done: seeking new clients and expanding their systems of trade. To the east of Lothal is a forest washed by summer and winter monsoons. It extends into what is now Burma and the jungles of Southeastern Asia. Lothal was conceivably in touch with a rice-growing world. If rice was traded into Lothal and other communities to the north of Bombay, it created a new set of choices for Indus society. Families knew it was no longer necessary to grow barley at the edge of the river, labor in canals, and be exposed to the danger of floods. The country to the east of Lothal was humid, with heavier rainfall. Yields would be great and the dangers conceivably small.

In the final centuries of Indus Valley society, the great cities were slowly abandoned. A farming population was taking a chance in the east. Old cities were robbed of their labor force, the most critical resource of all.

---

[12]Robert Raikes, "The Mohenjo-Daro Floods," *Antiquity* 39, pp. 196–203.

[13]The view of Indus decline presented here is derived from John E. Pfeiffer, *The Emergence of Society: A Prehistory of the Establishment* (New York: McGraw-Hill, 1977), p. 208, and an exchange of ideas with Julian M. Granberry of St. John Fisher College concerning cultural connections between Southeast Asia and the Indian subcontinent. Evidence of rice at Lothal is discussed by Fairservis, *Roots*, pp. 310–11.

Crop yields declined on the Indus; fewer people were at work in the fields. That alone might have upset the balance between farmers and pastoral peoples. Their trading relations dissolved in the violence of raids. Fewer people could be found in the cities for the work that always had to be done: construction and repairs of the dikes at the edge of the river. Cities became more vulnerable to the floods of the changeable Indus. The river and the raids took their toll. The old cities were gone.

But out of the ashes of Indus came the phoenixlike cities of India, as rice-growing farmers settled on the rain-watered plains. In the space of perhaps seven centuries, there were sailboats again on the seas, as merchants from India traded with Southeastern Asia. They would establish commercial connections and would be carriers of cultural change. The presence of India would always be a part of the East.

Egypt: The desert and the river

There are places in the Nile River Valley where you can straddle two different environments—one foot on the grass, the other on the sand of the desert. More often in the natural world, transitions are fuzzier than this. Evergreens will fade away into tundra, and the change will be a gradual one. There are patches of trees that make ragged the edge of the woods. The Nile is not as subtle as this; it is a sharper division of life. On its floodplain are reeds, date palms, hippopotami, and marsh-loving birds. Beyond that plain, to the west and to the east, there are gravel and dunes.

In a sense, this natural world has misled us; or perhaps it was our fault, after all. Archeologists have written for decades of how the Nile was a green "slash of life" bordered on its plain by a desert nearly empty of people. This meant that Egyptian societies, in a way, were a "gift of the Nile": they could only survive on the flood-freshened plain of the river. But the region is constantly changing; it was a very different world in the past. The river has broadened and narrowed, rains have fallen, and the desert has bloomed. The valley of the Nile was not always as we find it today.

In some ways, the workings of nature changed the lives of the Nile-valley people. But exactly what happened is shadowy, not well understood. As recently as 8,000 years ago hunters and gatherers still lived in the delta. There were foragers in the south as late as 4000 BC.[14] Yet, only a millennium later, which is suddenly in terms of this story, there were cities, monuments, chronicles of battles, and kings.

How did this happen so quickly? It is far from being well understood, but the answer may lie in a world long overlooked. Archeologists are beginning to realize the significance of the African desert: the great gravelly waste that extends to the edge of the sky. There was a time, perhaps

---

[14]Philip E. L. Smith, "Stone Age Man on the Nile," *Scientific American* 235, no. 2 (1976), pp. 30–5.

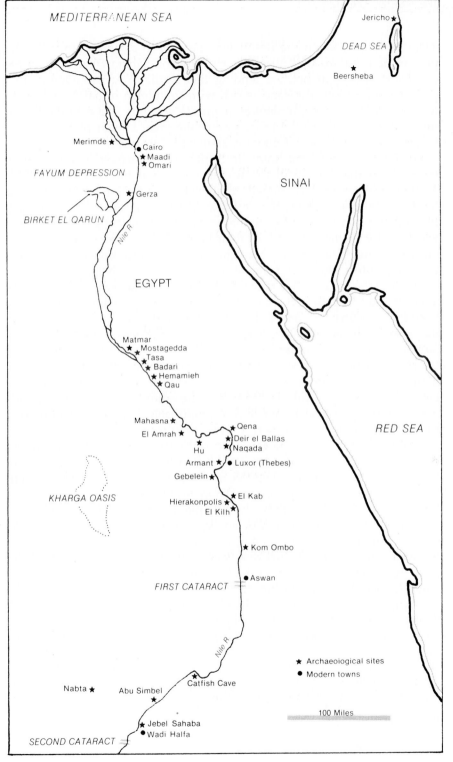

The cities of Egypt.

MEDITERRANEAN SEA

Jericho ★

DEAD SEA

Beersheba ★

SINAI

Merimde ★

● Cairo
★ Maadi
★ Omari

FAYUM DEPRESSION

★ Gerza

BIRKET EL QARUN

Nile R.

EGYPT

Matmar
★ Mostagedda
★ Tasa
★ Badari
★ Hemamieh
★ Qau

RED SEA

Mahasna ★
El Amrah ★

Qena ★
★ Deir el Ballas
★ Naqada

Hu ★

Armant ★ ● Luxor (Thebes)

Gebelein ★

KHARGA OASIS

Hierakonpolis ★ ★ El Kab
El Kilh ★

★ Kom Ombo

FIRST CATARACT

● Aswan

Nile R.

★ Archaeological sites
● Modern towns

Nabta ★   Abu Simbel   ★ Catfish Cave
              ★

100 Miles

★ Jebel Sahaba
● Wadi Halfa

SECOND CATARACT

8,000 years ago, when the desert may have been a rainier land. On the plateau of Tassili-n-Ajjer near the center of the Sahara Desert, there are curious drawings of herders tending their cattle.[15] At the edge of that plateau, in Amekni, the sand is rich with the pollen of oak trees. There was pollen from typha, a plant abundant in swamps. Wa-n-Muhujjiaj, to the east of Amekni on the other side of the great Libyan plateau, was a rock shelter with bones of domesticated cattle and sheep.

For Fred Wendorf and Romuald Schild, such discoveries are traces of times when the African desert was a wetter and more gentle world.[16] Cattle nomads may have moved through these grasslands, watering their herds at the edges of wadis. Perhaps, like the Egyptian Bedouin, they planted crops in the mud near the water. If the season grew dry, there was food for themselves and for their herds. It seems possible that plant-growing nomads might have brought their crops into the valley. Foragers became planters; there were cereals at the edge of the Nile.

But was the countryside really that rainy? Was the Sahara a more hab-itable world? Not all archeologists are in agreement with Wendorf and Schild. Brent Shaw is unconvinced by the findings—by the pollen and the bones in the desert. He is skeptical of the drawings on the time-scoured faces of rock.[17] The problem with these desert discoveries is that they are often very close to plateaus. Temperatures on these uplifts are lower; the high country is a rainier world. Water flows down the edge of these high-lands; pools and marshes are formed at the bottom. These fragile islands of swampgrass and water nourish cattle, hippopotami, and fish. But beyond the edge of the uplifts, the desert grows ever more dry.

If Shaw is right, then we can look to the desert for an understanding of Egyptian society—of how agriculture first found its way to the edge of the Nile. By as early as 12,000 years ago, in the wadis of the eastern Sahara, wheat and barley were probably grown and cattle were raised.[18] But rain became rare in that country; plants clustered near wadis and highlands. Pastoralists survived by an elaborate net of exchange. Navigators in an ocean of desert, they memorized the world of the sands: the oases, the wadis, the highlands, the dust storms, and the stars. Tiny pockets of plant foods and cattle, if they were connected in a webwork of trade, made it possible to live in this almost impossible land.

Foragers who lived on the river were influenced by changes in the desert. Their hunting-and-gathering existence was nearing an end. Ar-cheologist Michael Hoffman has found—at Hierakonpolis in the upper

---

[15]Site descriptions are from Brent D. Shaw, "Climate, Environment, and Prehistory in the Sahara," *World Archaeology* 8, no. 2 (1975), pp. 133–49.

[16]Fred Wendorf and Romuald Schild, *Pehistory of the Eastern Sahara* (New York: Academic Press, 1980), pp. 271 and 277.

[17]Shaw, "Climate," pp. 133–49.

[18]Wendorf and Schild, *Prehistory*, p. 274.

Nile valley—pollen evidence that rainfall was rare on the river-drenched plain.[19] By 3300 BC the river was no longer reaching the wadis. The Nile itself was becoming more shallow; its floods covered less of the pain. Plants shriveled and died as old sediments were covered by sand.

Perhaps in these bad-weather centuries, the Nile people became linked in exchange to desert societies that provided them with cattle and crops. The river might have become a corridor but not in the way often supposed. There is little evidence of towns or cities throughout much of the Nile River valley, even as recently as 2600 BC.[20] Conceivably, this is because the trade routes did not follow the course of the river; they *crossed over* the Nile as they linked up the desert societies. Indeed, there is one place on the river—the lower Nile to the south of the delta—which may have been the hub of a far-reaching system of trade. The Libyan Desert, the Arabian Desert, the Sinai Peninsula, and the routes of the sea were easily reached from the south of the delta. For the foragers of the Nile River valley, the region provided the crucial connections that could help them survive in a drier and difficult time. Egypt's villages grew in that region; merchant communities were managing trade. The process, in time, may have led to its earliest cities.

At the apex of the Nile River delta, where the river fans out to the sea, caravans were bringing their goods from the paths of the desert. The village of Maadi emerged there at about 3600 BC and was probably a center of trade in its earliest days.[21] There were cellars to the south of the village: stone-walled pits six feet in the ground. Roofed over with timbers, they stored the early items of trade. Carnelian beads, stone jars, limestone dishes, lamps, and Palestinian-type pottery were discovered in the cellars of Maadi. Some cellars were linked together and contained a greater number of goods. There may have been merchants in Maadi who controlled a higher volume of trade. Goods could be used as a route to political power.

There was another center that lay to the south, about 300 miles up the river, where desert traders could meet with the merchants of the African grasslands. *Gerzean towns,* as archeologists call them, were built near the banks of the river in the years when the Nile was receding and the weather was dry. Canals were dug to the edge of the desert; there was water for the growing of crops. There was a surplus for emergency times and for use in exchange. Hierakonpolis, a walled town with houses of mud, grew in this country. It was a town of craftworkers connected with African trade. Copper and malachite came from the Sinai; ivory came from the lands to the south; flint was brought from the Red Sea desert; and basalt

---

[19]Michael A. Hoffman, *Egypt before the Pharaohs: The Prehistoric Foundations of Egyptian Civilization* (New York: Alfred A. Knopf, 1977), p. 311.

[20]Elman Service, *Origins of the State and Civilization* (New York: W. W. Norton, 1975), p. 228.

[21]Site description of Maadi and Hierakonpolis are taken from Hoffman, *Egypt.*

came from as far as Fayum. Silver and lapis lazuli were discovered in Hierakonpolis' tombs. These exotics must have come from the highlands north and east of Mesopotamia's towns. But exactly how they came into Egypt we still do not know. Craftworkers in Hierakonpolis fashioned vases from imported basalt. Knives were made of flint, and the lapis was carved into jewels.

Trading settlements flourished for centuries in the south and at the base of the delta. Archeologists have debated for decades about the long stretch of river in-between: was it dotted with towns or, perhaps, nearly empty of people? John Wilson once described early Egypt as a civilization of agricultural villages. There was no chain of cities lining the banks of the Nile.[22] Barry Kemp suspects it might have been different—that there were patterns of settlement size.[23] Perhaps, as in Mesopotamia, cities were surrounded by villages; villages were ringed by the hamlets that were smaller in size. Perhaps—but the picture is cloudy, more so than in other parts of the world. Kemp only examined the settlements in the southerly part of the river; we still do not know about the country that lay to the north.[24] For the moment, it seems that the settlements were most abundant at the base of the delta and near Hierakonpolis, growing up far to the south. If this pattern is not an illusion, it suggests that these gateways of trade controlled overland routes and not commerce that flowed down the Nile.

Power in Egyptian society

But urban growth is apt to be dangerous, and in early Egypt it probably was. As people flowed into the villages near Hierakonpolis and the south of the delta, there were many new groups competing for political power. This may have meant, as David Webster has argued, that there was a need for prestigious rewards—exotic goods to kin leaders in exchange for their kin group's support. That, in turn, implied competition—attracting new connections of trade. Relations between the north and the south were becoming more strained. Competition became open warfare at about 3100 BC. A man named Menes, a minor official, rose in the warrior ranks of the south and captured the villages that lay at the base of the delta. The "Scorpion King," as they called him, built Memphis near the old town of Maadi. The north and the south were united in the rule of one king—a pattern that time and again would be a part of Egyptian existence. Competition between the two regions continued under unification. Their set-

---

[22]John A. Wilson, "Three Comments on Orthogenetic and Heterogenetic Urban Environments: Cities in Ancient Egypt," in *Economic Development and Cultural Change III,1954–55*, p. 74.

[23]Barry J. Kemp, "The Early Development of Towns in Egypt," *Antiquity* 51 (1977), pp. 185–200.

[24]Ibid., p. 186.

tlements grew; there was need for exchange and rewards. Over and over, this brought them to conflict. Flannery's "promotion" would come into play. An unimportant person, like Menes, would soon become a military leader: a ruler created from the alchemy of organized war.

Regional conflicts of Egypt were a threat to its stable existence. But perhaps, paradoxically, they also helped Egypt survive. When Asian nomads conquered the delta at around 1800 BC, the southerly settlements rallied and drove them away. These Hyksos discovered, like Sargon, the dangers of conquering a rivalrous country. Southern Egypt drove out the invaders, probably not for any love of the north, but to strengthen their political power throughout the length of the Nile. It may have been precisely this paradox—internal divisiveness turned to advantage—that let Egypt endure when other kingdoms were grass-covered ruins.

For generations the people of Egypt lived their lives under powerful kings. The ruler was a *pharaoh* who presented himself as divine. In the early years after Menes built Memphis, the pharaoh's power was not yet secure. There were no large-scale armies that could come to the aid of the throne. Because of this, he rewarded his followers; raw coercion was a dangerous thing. In exchange for rewards they provided him with symbols of power. The first of the celebrated pyramids arose near the Nile River plain. Never has architecture produced a more enduring debate.

Directors at Metro-Goldwyn-Mayer have had their theory of pyramid building. To be fair to those moguls, archeologists once agreed with their view. Prehistorians have often suggested that earthen ramps were constructed in Egypt.[25] Thousands of slaves pulled stones along rollers to the top of the ramp. The stones were at last set in place, and the ramp was built up with more earth. When the pyramid was finished, the ramp was shoveled away.

But engineers, notoriously unromantic, have insisted this could not have been done.[26] The size and the weight of the pyramid's stones and the restricted working space near the top would have made it impossible to build the highest part of the structure. Perhaps they were raised by the methods used by Egyptians today when they remove large blocks from ruins at the edge of the Nile. Stone weights are piled in a sling at one end of a long wooden lever. The block in the opposite sling can be lifted and moved. Quarried stones may have been hauled on greased skids up the angular walls of the structure. Lever devices would lift them and set them in place.

The physics of pyramid building is more than a debate about pulleys and levers. It affects our understanding of the structure of Egyptian society. If recent calculations are accurate, the Great Pyramid constructed at Giza would have required a laboring force of some 3,000 men. Such a figure is

---

[25]L. Sprague de Camp, *The Ancient Engineers,* (New York: Ballantine Books, 1974), p. 34.

[26]Olaf Tellefsen, "A New Theory of Pyramid Building," *Natural History,* November 1970.

drastically lower than the estimate of 100,000 which would have been needed to build and demolish the ramps. More than that, those 3,000 workers were primarily in specialized crafts. It was not the simple, drudgery labor demanded of slaves. There were pulling teams, gangs on the skidways, masons, repairmen, and riggers. Supervisory personnel were required for all of these tasks. Of course there were mathematicians, engineers, and a collection of scribes—the literate few who recorded what had to be done. Participation in pyramid building was the display of one's specialized talents—the skills that were increasingly needed in an urbanized state. Because the specialists were probably not slaves, there was the possibility of promotion as well: from worker to foreman to mason's assistant to mason. And that, in turn, meant rewards from the ruler—the real incentive for building the structure. As for the pharaoh himself, the somber construction would serve as his tomb. But more important was the role it played while he was still alive. A ruler in a rivalrous region without a large permanent army, he needed to establish a system of tasks and rewards. In a sense then, the building of pyramids was political socialization. Citizens were "schooled" to obey and to seek favor from the ruler of Egypt. The pyramids were built, and the pharaoh became more secure.

He reigned as an absolute monarch over a world that seemed never to die. He was first among a clutter of bureaucrats who passed on their offices to their heir and watched over the tiniest matters of life in the

An early theory of pyramid building proposed that earthen ramps corkscrewed up the sides. But the use of a counterweight system would have required far fewer workers. The building of pyramids was likely a specialist endeavor.

Field Museum of Natural History

An Egyptian scribe. A significant number of bureaucrats "put writing into their hearts." Their offices were often a form of political reward.

state. Palaces and government buildings teemed with a crowd of educated officials, many of whom were aware of the fact that they had little to do. "Put writing in they heart," wrote a bureaucrat giving advice to the young and the favored, "so that thou mayest protect thine own person from . . . labor and be a respected official."[27] Very likely this top-heavy system was the outgrowth of earlier days when offices were given to kin leaders as a form of reward. Offices would splinter and multiply as they were transmitted to an official's descendants. If you had the right kin, there was always some room near the top.

But not everyone was totally useless. The business of state was accomplished as well. The economy of Egypt was often under careful control. A portion of harvests was routinely collected for local emergencies and to feed the officials. Irrigation agriculture was closely supervised by the state. Craftworkers were watched over by foremen as they made specialized products for trade. Commandeered labor was used on the large public works.

The figure at the heart of this system was the pharaoh—the god-king himself. His power was reinforced by an ideology of total control.[28] The notion of divine right of kings became, in Egypt, the divine right of gods. The king was a god in human form ruling over the land. Divinity could only marry divinity, so the ruler thus married his sister. The lineage became officially closed to an outside connection. All-powerful and also all-knowing, his rule was not open to question. He was the protector—benefactor-at-large—watching over the state. But the ideology carefully included an element of unpredictable danger: the benefactor could also be harsh or capriciously cruel. This was because the Egyptian divinities were believed to take many different forms. A god could change into an object—or into a different god. So the attributes of any divinity could become the attributes of the king. He could be generous like Osiris or Horus; he could be as dangerous and deceitful as Seth. The Egyptians could never be sure, so they prayed for the best.

This awkward, divisive theocracy survived for over 3,000 years—until the Mediterranean was ruled by the legions of Rome. By that time the Assyrians, the Persians, and the Macedonians of Alexander the Great had conquered the cities believed to be favored of god. Its old towns had been covered by sandstorms, and its pharaohs were buried and gone. Tomb robbers discovered its treasures and found a writing they could not understand. They found granaries, fragments of palaces, and the graves of a royal elite. They saw strange pointed structures in the sand at the edge of the Nile.

---

[27]John A. Wilson, "Egypt" in *The Intellectual Adventure of Ancient Man: An Essay on Speculative Thought in the Ancient Near East*, ed. H. Frankfort et al. (Chicago: University of Chicago Press, 1946), p. 87.

[28]Ibid., pp. 66–67.

She sat with friends in the warmth of the sunshine, watching a bird in the afternoon sky.[29] It was black and held an egg in its beak. The bird flew over her; she saw the egg fall. Playfully, she opened her mouth, caught the egg, and then swallowed it whole. But the bird—who was really a god—had tricked the woman into swallowing the egg. She was pregnant. The descendants of god were now part of the earth.

The story of the blackbird miracle is as ancient as the cities of China. It echoes the magic believed to be part of their birth. Here, as in Mesopotamia, in Egypt, and perhaps in Indus as well, was a lineage of kings thought to have the powers of god. The timber palace where the ruler resided received the blessings and the threats of the heavens. Divinity flowed from its gates to the edge of the world.[30] In time, there was a mound near the palace colored with symbols of the earth and the seasons. There was green for the spring, for ripening, and for the Dragon that lived in the east. There was red for the south and the phoenix that rose from the flames. On the north was the black earth of dampness for the bleakness of nomads and war. On the west was a cover of white for the land of the tiger. This was the gunmetal shading of autumn—the color of war, of executions, and of regrets. It was the color of harvest, of twilight, and of mistakes in our lives.

Beneath these imaginative symbols of the cities and the rulers of China was a set of beliefs that was part of political rule. Ideology and centralized power grew together in urbanized China, in a turbulent country that often exploded in war. From the days of its earliest cities, China had been threatened—without and within. Uncertainty itself played a role in the rise of the state.

As early as 4,000 years ago China was becoming a volatile world. Farmers—and the idea of farming—had spread from the loess-richened streams of the north along the rivers that veined the wet world of the tropical lowlands.[31] Rain falls in this southerly country over 300 days of the year. It was a region remarkably suited for the growing of rice. Yet, curiously, it rarely was peaceful. Riverine villagers were often at war. They built walls of pounded earth for protection and buried their warriors with daggers and clubs. Bones in the graves show the evidence of violent death.

Perhaps a critical resource was lacking on the rain-swept rivers. For lack of it, rice-growing farmers resorted to war. There may have been no suitable animal for clearing out trees and heavy roots from the soil. Bones of cattle, Charles Higham has noted, are not structured for a task such as

The earliest cities of China

---

[29]Kwang-chih Chang, *The Archaeology of Ancient China* (New Haven: Yale University Press, 1977), p. 283.

[30]Chinese urban symbolism, including multicolored mounds, is discussed by Paul Wheatley, *The Pivot of the Four Quarters: A Preliminary Enquiry into the Origins of the Ancient Chinese City* (Hawthorne, N.Y.: Aldine Publishing, 1971), pp. 434–35.

[31]The expansion of agricultural technology in China is described by Chang, *Archeoloy,* pp. 144–84.

Shang archeological sites.

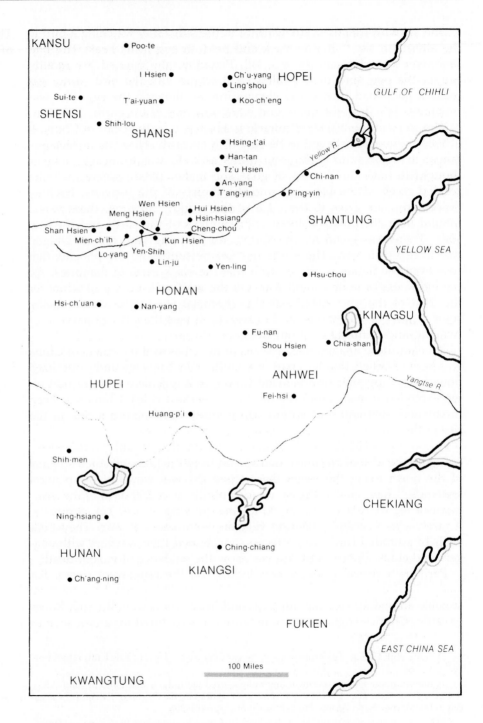

this.[32] Water buffalo are much better suited for the growing of rice. But that beast was not found in the lowlands. It first appeared on the Huang Ho in the north.[33] Growing villages confined to the rivers could well have been pressured for space. Raiding and warriors became part of the forested south.

Less is known about the cold, windy steppe that lies north of the Huang Ho River, that tussocky country where herders watched over their sheep. Winters are long on the grasslands. There is little rain for the planting of crops. For centuries, nomads have followed their sheep on the steppe. Somewhere on those vast, chilly pastures nearly 4,000 years before Christ, a herder was able to stay on the back of a horse. It might have been on the Ukranian grasslands—no one is sure where it first happened. But after it happened, prehistory was never the same. It was not only that pastoral peoples could move more rapidly from pasture to pasture; it meant they could move very quickly in organized raids.[34]

At Nan-shan-ken in eastern Mongolia, warriors were buried with helmets and daggers.[35] Fittings of horses had also been placed in the tomb. The burials are 2,500 years later than the horse bones found in Ukrania. But mounted nomads may have come even earlier to the grasslands of China. In the early cities of the Huang Ho River, horses and chariots were buried in tombs. Mounted warfare could well have been learned from the pastoral steppes. Relations between herders and farmers were traditionally unstable at best. The land to the north was most likely an unstable world.

Villagers who lived in the loesslands were bordered by dangerous regions. Raids—or the threat of them—were very much a part of their lives. But perhaps their land had another significance: it may have been a center for Eastern exchange, a riverine border dividing two natural worlds. To the north were the products of herders and trading connections for thousands of miles. To the south were the lowlands, the forested rivers and the rice. That region could have become more productive with water buffalo brought from the north. Possibly the animal was an item of early exchange. Beyond that, the rich, murky river was a corridor that led to the sea, where farmers and fishers had settled for hundreds of years. Fish

---

[32] Charles Higham, "The Economic Basis of Prehistoric Thailand," *American Scientist*, November–December 1979, pp. 676–77.

[33] Chang, *Archeology*, pp. 289–90.

[34] The significance of mounted animals for specialized pastoral societies is discussed by Susan H. Lees and Daniel G. Bates, "The Origins of Specialized Nomadic Pastoralism: A Systemic Model," *American Antiquity* 39,no, 2 (1974), p. 191. Instability of pastoralist-farmer relations is discussed by A. M. Khazanov, "Characteristic Features of Nomadic Communities in the Eurasian Steppes," *The Nomadic Alternative: Modes and Models of Interaction in the African-Asian Deserts and Steppes,*ed. Wolfgang Weissleder (The Hague: Mouton, 1978), pp. 124–25.

[35] Chang, *Archeology*, p. 393

Shang Dynasty bird-shaped wine vessel.

The Buckingham Collection, The Art Institute of Chicago

and agricultural products may have been brought from these shoreline societies to the villages growing to cities along the Huang Ho.

At Erh-li-t'ou on the Lo, a tributary of the Huang Ho River, archeologists have discovered the evidence of conflict and trade.[36] Remains of

---

[36] Site descriptions of Chinese cities are taken from ibid., pp. 209–95.

pounded-earth walls were uncovered near the edges of settlements. Mutilated skeletons were encountered in some of the graves. Anthropologists examined the bones and also found the markings of malnutrition. Prisoners taken in warfare may have been worked in the city until they starved. Then, unceremoniously, they were killed and tossed into a grave.

But commerce as well as conflict left its traces at the Erh-li-t'ou site. There were arrow heads and spear heads of stone, vessels and fishhooks fashioned from bronze, and luxury ornaments carved out of torquoise and jade. Clay molds for bronze manufacture and clay crucibles were found at the site. Very likely there were bronze-working specialists alloying imported copper and tin to produce luxury items and, possibly, products for trade.

Eastward along the Huang Ho was another center of war and exchange: the walled city of Chengchou that was built near the edge of the river. A rammed-earth barrier some 30 feet high and over 100 feet wide at the base surrounded a district that was home to a ruling elite. Archeologist An Chin-huai has calculated that 3 million cubic meters of earth were quarried and brought to the city while the wall was built. This would have required some 10,000 workers laboring over 300 days of the year for nearly 20 years until the wall was eventually done. Whether citizens or captives constructed it we still do not know. But there is little doubt that Chengchou was a city in need of defense.

Within that wall were grisly reminders of the possibility of prisoners of war. In the northeastern part of the city was a pounded-earth cluster of floors with a section of ditch littered with human remains. About a hundred human skulls had been dumped there—sawed-off near the eyebrows and ears. These may have been "scrap" from the "industrial" part of the city. Nearby were the remains of a workshop where human skeletons were carved into hairpins. Along with the humans, the workers used cattle and pigs. It is one of our most vivid examples, in the prehistory of the earliest states, of the banality of death in a system of centralized rule.

Outside the wall the bronze-making workshops, were turning out vessels and weapons of war. There were 14 pottery kilns to the west of the site. Near the bronze-shops were earthen foundations of four different structures that may have been dwellings. Craftworker kin groups conceivably lived in the homes. Ordinarily a Chengchou citizen lived in a tinier, half-sunken house. Manufacture of specialized products might well have meant greater prestige, especially if the city was expanding its networks of trade.

In the forests to the north of Chengchou where the Huan River flows to the sea was another community of rituals, commerce, and war. Anyang, like other cities in China, did not have massive citadel structures. No soaring, royal residence was visible miles from the river. Yet it did have the trappings of power and of despotic ceremonial rule. Belief at An-yang was a powerful tool of the state. Earlier, in the days of the vil-

The Art Institute of Chicago

Bronze wine vessel. Metallurgists in Shang manufactured bronze items for trade.

lage, there was a tradition of ancestor worship.[37] It was private behavior, a linkage, a remembrance of kin. A lighted wick or, perhaps, heated bronze was touched to the shoulder blade of an animal. Cracks in the surface were messages from a supernatural world. In later times, there were marks on the surface: an elaborate pictorial script. Of some 3,000 characters, perhaps about a third can be read. They are the intimate questions of people talking to kin who are no longer alive. They ask advice about marriages, children, their dreams, and the seasons.

Thirty thousand of the oracle bones were discovered in the heart of

[37] Divination is discussed in ibid., pp. 210–11, and Pfeiffer, *Emergence of Society*, pp. 225–26.

Shang oracular turtle-shell. The practice of divination was orginally a household rite. But in Shang communities, it reinforced centralized rule.

An-yang. They were not found in the half-sunken houses where farmers and laborers lived. They were stored near the elevated homes of a religious elite. Fifteen houses of wattle-and-daub were built on a platform of pounded earth. Oracle bones were uncovered very close to their walls. What once had been a household religion was now a practice that belonged to the state. Ancestor worship was part of political rule.

Taken over by the royal lineage, the old beliefs had a menacing touch. Rulers spoke to their own distant ancestors through the medium of the curious bones. They spoke to people that no one remembered, vanished figures of centuries past. They spoke to mythical spirits who demanded satisfaction in blood. Human sacrifice was growing in scale and becoming part of ceremonial life. In the royal cemetery north of the palace and on the opposite bank of the Huan, sacrificial victims were placed in the tombs of the kings. Royal tomb 1,001, shaped like a cross and over 30 feet deep, held the dismembered skeletons of 164 men.[38] But burial was not the only occasion for the ritualized taking of life. Sacrifice accompanied the daily affairs of the state. Completion of a single "house" (a temple?) caused the deaths of over 600 people.[39] Captives taken in warfare were regularly brought to the city. They were used as slave labor and killed for the ancestral world.

---

[38] K. C. Chang, "Urbanism and the King in Ancient China," *World Archeology*, June 1974, p. 6.

[39] K. C. Chang, *Shang Civilization* (New Haven: Yale University Press, 1980), p. 194.

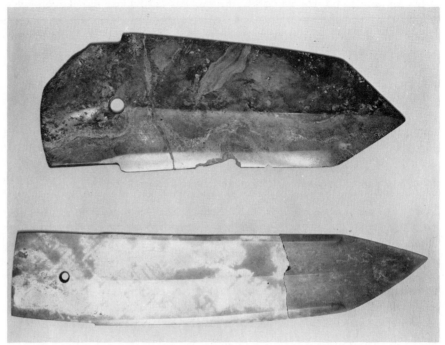

The Art Institute of Chicago

Shang dagger-axe pendant. Motifs of conflicts were not unusual in society that was often at war.

In this piously violent city, commercial transactions continued to grow. The community was a focus of early manufacture and trade. Bronze foundries, pottery kilns, and stone workshops were found near the palace. Exotic commodities were discovered in some of the graves. Bronze weapons and chariot fittings were manufactured in the city itself. No one knows where the copper came from; the nearest deposits of tin were Malayan. Possibly there were commercial connections with Southeastern Asia. Whalebone found at An-yang is evidence of trade with the coast.[40] Cowrie shells were also discovered in parts of the site. The shell is from a warm-water snail which might have been traded from the south coast of China; or it might have come from the Indian Ocean through the Straits of Malacca.

How was it that religion, sacrifice, chronic war, manufacture, and trade were melded together in the earliest cities of China? I think that a great deal of the answer will be found in the outlying regions, in the country that for so many years was an unstable world. Horsemen on the north-

---

[40] Evidence of Chinese maritime trade is discussed by Carleton S. Coon, *The Story of Man* (Alfred A. Knopf, 1974), p. 331.

erly grasslands and rice farmers in the rain-watered south may have played a critical role in the emergence of China. Here, as in the westerly cities, were complexities of trading and raids. In that powerful mix is the chemistry of rising elites.

For villagers on the Yellow River, like others we have seen in this story, the quickening of life was related to the flow of exchange. Stone, metals, and precious minerals were lacking in the countryside near the Huang Ho. To acquire them, villagers depended on their systems of trade. It seems likely that they exported cereals and, perhaps, traction animals as well. Their connections extended to the steppes and to the south and the sea. Distant linkages are usually vulnerable to the danger of organized raids. Predation, as we saw a bit earlier, was evolving along with exchange. But in China, more than in Indus or in Egypt—or in Mesopotamia, at least at the start—the threat of predation was intensive on pathways of trade. A difference in degree was at work here: a greater risk than in other parts of the world. The difference played a critical role in the shaping of China.

China in the presence of enemies

Lowland rice-farming regions were at war before the cities began. Pastoral steppes very likely exploded in raids. Life along the Huang Ho River in a sense was a very mixed blessing. True enough, it was an ecotonal setting between the steppes and the rain-watered south—a location favorable for the emergence of middleman trade. But the river was also a boundary between two socially unstable regions. Exchange on the stream was a strategy to protect it from raids. Exchanges of grain for the nomadic steppelands, draught animals, and grain for the south were a means of insuring more peaceful relations.

But any farmer or specialized craftworker who lived along the Huang Ho River could see a flaw in this scheme of security as a result of exchange. Defenseless villagers had no real assurance that stable relations could ever endure. Erosion, a year with no rainfall, flooding on the river, or a sudden seasonal change could break the connection and lead to new raids. A year of low yields on the river would mean that farmers kept grain for themselves. For their clients, there was little choice other than the resumption of war. The wisest strategy was to not be defenseless but keep warriors on call at all times. More than that, because village security depended on the delivery of agricultural goods, warriors were probably needed to travel the roads.

This, of course, did not solve the problem of the uncertainty of agricultural life. It simply meant that a raid could be countered by local defense. Kin groups successful in commerce, very likely, were heavily armed. This helped stabilize their trading connections and afforded them local prestige. People in outlying hamlets, lacking the connections and smaller in size, would be drawn to the towns of the warriors with stabilized routes.

The urbanized state that grew out of this process was different than the ones to the west. The traditional elite in its cities was supported by a warrior force. There was less need to reward new immigrants. Coercive power was already in place.[41] Rewards were more necessary to stabilize outer frontiers. This is why there is very little evidence of a massive bureaucracy receiving rewards or of extensive housing areas for the better-off groups in society. Instead, there was a tiny minority practicing trade, manufacture, and war—and the remainder of people continuing to farm near the river. Said Cheng Te-k'un,

> In the upper stratum was the ruling class who enjoyed a highly developed luxurious bronze age culture, and lived inside a walled city. In the lower stratum was the rural population, who kept to their Neolithic way of life and survived in villages in the countryside. In a way the upper class exploited the rural population who contributed much to the maintenance of the luxurious life inside the city, but on the other hand, the people were always free to follow their own course and were no less adventurous and enterprising for their humbler status.[42]

How free they were to take their own chances is a matter for serious doubt. But the polarity of urbanized China is indeed reflected in the cities themselves—the garrisoned elites surrounded by farming societies.

The Shang Dynasty evolved from this process at about 1700 BC. It ruled over China for over six centuries. It was defended by bronze and belief but was never secure. A decline in the farmers' yield could trigger a new spasm of raids. There were times when the enemy surrounded the capital city. High danger was the seed of reprisal as the paranoid dynasty fought to survive. Thousands of captives were marched through its cities, killed to make hairpins, and massed into graves. Still the raiding went on and the dynasty was never secure. Documents of later historians record that the capital was moved seven times.[43] No matter where they built it, it was always endangered by war.[44]

The desperate shifts of location created a challenge for religious belief. Shang rulers held court in a district believed to be directly in touch with the heavens: sacred power flowed through it and out to the inhabited world. So *geomancy* was quickly invented to modify the blasphemy of pulling up stakes.[45] Geomancers were the rulers' own specialists who could

---

[41] The highly coercive nature of Shang China is discussed by Chang, "Urbanism," p. 11; and Chang, *Shang*, pp. 194–200.

[42] Cheng Te-K'un, *Prehistoric China*, vol. 1, Cambridge: W. Heffer and Sons, 1966, p. 103.

[43] K. C. Chang, "Urbanism," p. 4.

[44] An alternative possibility is the movement of the capital as an offensive tactic to stabilize an area in which raiding is especially severe. Whether shifts were offensive or defensive would have depended upon human resources, organization, and other military factors.

[45] Geomancers assured the ruler that the new location of the capital was a place well adapted to currents of "cosmic breath." They were, however, not reluctant to remove boulders or even small hills to reconstruct the landscape and make it appear more divine. Their specialty is discussed by Wheatley, *Pivot of Four Quarters*, p. 419.

"discover" new, sacred locations. Belief, once again, was adjusted to political rule.

Generations of later historians painted their writings on slivered bamboo. They spun a tale of the turbulent centuries that followed the Shang. Horsemen were still raiding the river in the days of Imperial Rome. They were raiding it when cities and cathedrals were rising in Europe.[46] Until the time of the 20th century, Chinese society was a polarized world with a powerful elite and the thousands that worked on the land. In its own way this serves to remind us of how minor are the distinctions we make between recent societies and the people who live in prehistory. "The past is not dead," said Faulkner. Very often, "it is not even past." Ancient patterns outlive their creators. They endure and affect our own time. At every moment a living society recaptures its past.

---

[46] William H. McNeill, *The Rise of the West: A History of the Human Community* (New York: Mentor, 1963), pp. 332–42 and 577–87.

19 / Elites in Mesoamerica: From Olmec to the Mayan Decline

Children race down the cobblestone streets past markets crowded with flowers. They press and jostle in front of the sweetshops and grab for their candy. One buys a skull made out of sugar with his name written on it in icing. Another buys a coffin of chocolate with miniature bones. They join the crowds that are filling the streets now and walk with them to the graves of their kin. The ground of the graveyard is covered with candles and blooms.

Early November in the town of Mixquic is the season for the Day of the Dead. It is an autumn of memories and for thinking of death without fear. No one is certain of when it began, but it is probably centuries old. It is a linkage with the turbulent days of the Mexican past. It might have begun as an Aztec holiday to make contact with underworld gods. Mixquic was believed to be built upon sacred ground. Today—the old empire shattered—there is still a memory in flowers and candles: an intricate ceremonial mixing of present and past.[1]

Ancient Americans are remembered everywhere in artifact, language, and prayer. The clack of a loom is the echo of an earlier kingdom. In Mexico, Guatemala, and Yucatan—and on the spires of the Peruvian Andes—there were farmers, nobles, astronomers, merchants, and kings. Archeologists for over a century have explored the wrecked cities and temples. They are discovering the patterns of American urban societies. Separated for thousands of years from the evolution of the Old World peoples, kingdoms of the ancient Americas developed apart. Yet there is much in their story reminiscent of the earliest urbanized states. Here too were emerging elites and a matrix of trade.

Those beginnings have long appeared curious. It seems odd that they occurred where they did. The mountain-rimmed Mesa Central tapers down

Olmec beginnings

---

[1]The holiday is described by Gene S. Stuart, *The Mighty Aztecs* (Washington, D.C.: National Geographic Society, 1981), p. 189. The "Day of the Dead" may be the synthesis of the Christian All Saints Day with Aztec (or earlier) ceremonialism and belief.

Mesoamerican cities.

to a bottleneck region that spreads out into the flat, lowland shelf of the Yucatan jungles.[2] The bottleneck is a world of forest, winding rivers, estuaries, and lagoons. It is a hot—even sweltering—country for those not adapted to tropical sun. Air is humid; throughout much of the year there are torrents of rain. A hundred inches or more drench the forest in the months between June and November. Rivers become swollen, and the jungle is covered by floods.

---

[2]Richard E. W. Adams, *Prehistoric Mesoamerica* (Boston: Little, Brown, 1977), pp. 82–83.

The dusty idea that complex society could never develop in tropical lands was shaken by discoveries made in this part of the world. Platforms of clay and adobe were untangled from the deep jungle thickets. Basalt sculptures up to 9 feet tall and weighing about 18 tons were unearthed from the soils of the old ceremonial ruins. In time it was obvious enough that these rain-flooded gulf coastal lowlands had been the setting for conflicts and rituals, for power and trade.

What these people were called in the past we still do not know. *Olmec* is the name archeologists give them today. Their beginnings might date to a time nearly 4,000 years in the past when slash-and-burn farmers may have settled the land near the rivers. Or it might not have been that simple, though no one at the moment is sure. Gareth Lowe has chopped through the thickets on the other side of the bottleneck country, through the marshes and the mangrove swamps that overlook the Pacific.[3] There he found platform structures similar to those near the Gulf. He turned up fragments of burnished pottery decorated with speckles of red. Very similar shards have been found near the opposite shore. Perhaps in the days before Olmec there were settlers on both sides of the isthmus, connected by rivers in a waterway system of trade.

Their emergence is warmly debated, but much more is known about what they became. It might be wisest to begin by explaining what Olmec were not. They never were an urban society; villages were always a part of their lives. Almost all the Olmec people cleared and planted in the tropical forest.[4] Deer and fish could be taken along the coastal rivers and forests, but slash-and-burn farming provided them with most of their food. Populations were usually small and were scattered over the arable jungle. Less than 200 people could live on a square mile of land. Their imposing ceremonial centers were nearly deserted throughout most of the year. Perhaps when the maize had been harvested, or conceivably on the first day of spring, crowds gathered at the centers and rekindled their ritual life.

Slash-and-burn farming in the gulf coastal jungles likely never produced high enough yields to support a menagerie of small bureaucratic officials. Pyramids and ceremonial platforms were the home of a tiny elite, presiding in pomp over a world made up of farmers. From that tiny percentage of people came the decisions that changed the society—its economic and political behavior, religion, and art.

The elite was very likely created out of the conditions of nature and trade. In this sense, their society was kin to other parts of the world. Green thickets of the Veracruz jungles are, surprisingly, a varied environment. It is not simply an endless monotony of rainfall and trees. Trails that lead out of the jungles thread their way into a low line of hills. Rivers

---

[3]John E. Pfeiffer, *The Emergence of Society: A Prehistory of the Establishment* (New York: McGraw-Hill, 1977), pp. 345–46.

[4]Adams, *Prehistoric*, pp. 82–83.

from these highlands flow down and empty into the Gulf. Along the rivers—the Papaloapan Drainage—soil is rich, and the water table is high. Flooding of the streams brings a mantle of mineralized silt. Beneath the ground is a thick shelf of limestone that keeps minerals from being drained from the soil. Lime is mixed with the earth; it is rich for the growing of crops. Not only that, but these wilderness rivers become shallow near the shores of the Gulf. They drop their silt and create giant levees at the edge of the sea.

Back-country woodlands away from the rivers were probably a more difficult world. Farmers in this marginal country were likely more dependent on rainfall. Soils were poorer; the surplus was probably small. Like cultivators in Southeastern Asia, Olmec designed a wide net of exchange. Maize, beans, and squash were carried on moist jungle trails. It was a way of equalizing resources and binding together distant social relations. The bindings—the links—were a buffer against the uncertainties of Olmec existence. Droughts, sudden storms on the coastline, diseases, pests, fires, and floods were likely the pressures that led to interacting societies.

Networks in Veracruz

Evidence of cultural connections has been discovered in a roundabout way but nonetheless hints at a developing lattice of trade. Robert Heizer once calculated the labor force required to construct the pyramid at La Venta, a clay monument over 100 feet high on a swamp-bordered island.[5] Allowing for farming requirements, seasonal changes, and the dates for the site, he arrived at a final calculation of nearly 2,000 men. More recently, Timothy K. Earle analyzed the density of sites in the jungles.[6] A square kilometer of tropical forest—or so his calculations suggest—would likely have been home for an average of three to nine people. He figured that an Olmec family might have numbered no more than five persons and that one of the five would have been chosen to work on the pyramid. The 2,000 men in the workforce, then, suggests a territory with 10,000 people. They were dispersed over an area of, perhaps, a few hundred square miles. When the computing at last was completed, Earle had arrived at the probable distance between each of the ceremonial centers of the ruling elite. That result, about 28 miles, is almost exactly the distance between Laguna de los Cerros and the center called Tres Zapotes.

The mathematics falls into a pattern reminiscent of Old World communities—the spacing of settlements on the plain of the Tigris-Euphrates. Major centers surrounded by villages that interact with the outlying hamlets—perhaps something like this was emerging in Olmec society. The

---

[5]Robert F. Heizer, "Agriculture and the Theocractic State in Lowland Southeastern Mexico," *American Antiquity* 26, no. 2 (1960), pp. 219–20.

[6]Timothy K. Earle, "A Nearest-Neighbor Analysis of Two Formative Settlement Systems," in *The Early Mesoamerican Village*, ed. Kent Flannery (New York: Academic Press, 1976), pp. 220–22.

spacing seems deliberate and regular; it is not aligned with the local resources. The pattern seems to reflect regulated exchange. If this is true,
then a vast arc of jungle was becoming part of an intricate system. It
reached its height of complexity some 3,000 years in the past. Tres Zapotes,
Laguna de los Cerros, San Lorenzo, and the site of La Venta were each
likely a focus of ritual and a hub of exchange.

Some feeling for their ritual complexity was captured by Michael D.
Coe on a 150-foot mesa in east Veracruz.[7] San Lorenzo could only be
reached by weatherbeaten boats that churned along the Chiquito. A camp
was hacked out with machetes, and the clearing was burned. Clouds of
mosquitos, poisonous snakes, "ticks by the millions," and drizzling rain
were the penalties of attempting research in this part of the world. There
were not any grandiose pyramids; there were 200 small mounds on the
site—heapings of trash from the houses of wattle-and-daub. But on the
western side of the site, Coe discovered a slab of basalt. He began digging
to the north so he could excavate the slab from the side. It was then that
his excavation discovered a statue that was headless and armless—a muscular figure with insignia and clothed by a belt. By digging on the north-
south line created by the slab and the remains of the statue, a chain of
buried monuments were encountered one after the other. There was a
jaguar statue with walruslike tusks, a loose drainstone, a four-sided column,
and a curious eight-legged statue that was likely a spider. Not only were
all of these sculptures uncovered on a north-south line, several were broken—and they all had been covered with fill. Coe believes that a revolt
might have happened, perhaps about 900 BC. Like the Hungarian revolutionaries that tipped over the statue of Stalin, San Lorenzo society was
destroying its symbols of rule.

Was there really a San Lorenzo rebellion? At the moment, it is not easy
to say. But there remains little doubt about the existence of a ruling elite.
Not only along the Chiquito, but at the site of La Venta as well, there is
evidence of centralized power and rising prestige. On an island surrounded
by swampland and the bends of the Tonala River, its pyramid and its two
earthen mounds are aligned to the north. Within the ceremonial area were
four heads carved from basalt. Quarries for the stone were probably 80
miles to the west. Nine feet tall on the average and weighing about 18
tons, they probably were brought from the quarries by rafts on the river.
They have stern—perhaps sneering—expressions; protective helmets are
carved on their heads. Were they gods or a warrior cadre in Olmec society?

Before we can be sure of the answers, work remains to be done. Much
of the gulf coastal lowland is still unexplored. And yet, our understanding
of Olmec may be strengthened by other discoveries in the cooler, more
temperate country of the Mexican highlands. Olmec, as we might have

---

[7]Michael D. Coe, *America's First Civilization: Discovering the Olmec* (New York: American
Heritage Publishing, 1968), pp. 76–86.

Olmec basalt head. The labor involved in such works symbolically intensified the power of chiefs.

suspected, was not a hermetically sealed world. It was embedded in a system of Mexican complex societies.

As we saw earlier in the story, many villages like Chalcatzingo were gateway communities—corridors for the movement of trade. At that site was a "rain god" carving done in relief on a surface of rock.[8] The god

---

[8]David C. Grove, "Chalcatzingo, Morelos, Mexico: A Reappraisal of the Olmec Rock Carvings," *American Antiquity*, October 1968.

Field Museum of Natural History

The motifs of Olmec society spread throughout the Mesa Central.

was seated in a cavern under storm clouds and droplets of rain. It is similar to Olmec sculptures found in the centers near the shores of the Gulf. But the sculpture is probably as much as 3,000 years old. This was the time when ritual centers were only beginning in Olmec society. Why was a similar sculpture found so far away?

Such discoveries are nettling problems for the theory of the colonial Olmec. This is the view that these jungle societies sent out traders, missionaries, and soldiers; highlanders were converted to the faith of the Olmec elite. From that conversion came many of the features of later societies in the Mesa Central. Much of Mexican civilization derives from that time.

But it probably was never that simple, as the discovery at Chalcatzingo implies. More than likely, the highlander networks were developing at about the same time as the ritual centers in the heartland of Olmec society. Kin leaders in both of these regions were aware of one another's existence. A matrix of subtle relations was slowly designed.

Like the gulf coastal lowland peoples, highlanders inhabited an uncertain world. If rains come too late to these uplands, plants will not germinate until the last days of June. Before they mature, they are apt to be killed by the frost. Exchange between highlands and lowlands would have minimized some of the risk by broadening the available food of these early societies.

Elites, by reducing uncertainty, were increasing their political power. They were surrounding themselves with the trappings of rising prestige. In return for controlling a food web that made life in those times more secure, they were given the material symbols of centralized rule. Stones

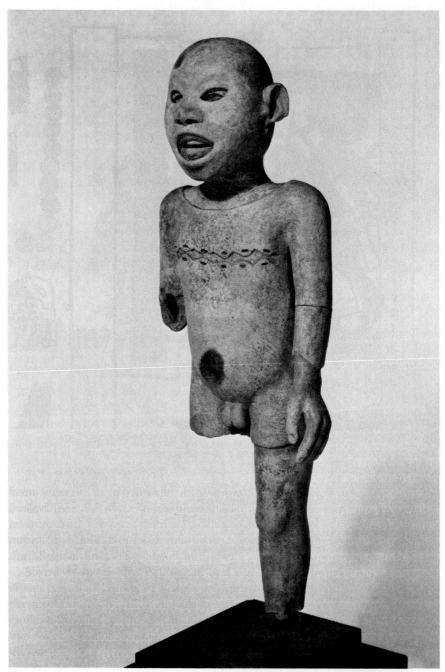

Olmec jadeite figure. Artifacts of exotic materials possibly symbolized the distant connections controlled by a chief.

were quarried, carved as ordered, and erected in the ceremonial centers. Jade figurines, magnetite mirrors, obsidian, and stingray spines were placed in the burials of highland and lowland elites. In death, as in life, these were symbols of permanent—and distant—commercial connections that buffered the uncertainties of life in a changeable land.

But if power was directly related to the stability of commercial connections, it could fade very quickly with a change in the volume of trade. In such systems there is always a danger of the individual entrepreneur: the rival that quietly creates his own net of exchange. Records of the Mesopotamians tell a story of local ambition: of advantages gained from transactions with partners and kin. Such a process could easily happen in virtually any part of the world where control of connections was a path to political power. Perhaps this was one of the reasons for the infusion of religious belief into the commerce of the earliest rulers in Mesoamerica.

Elites in the jungles and highlands did not have a developed system of writing. What we know of their religion is largely an intelligent guess. At Laguna de los Cerros and Rio Chiquito—near San Lorenzo and the broken statues—two sculptures were found that are remnants of Olmec belief. A woman copulating with a jaguar was represented in both of these works. Fragments of an origin myth were preserved in the stone. From that union, Michael Coe has suggested, came beings half-human, half-cat: the "werejaguars" widely depicted in Mexican art.[9] Very often, these figures are shown rendering assistance to the god that gave rain—a deity often represented by the head of a cat.[10] This art has an intriguing resemblance to the Old World divine right of kings: the notion that elites were specifically chosen by god. Conceivably, dominant kin groups were believed to be the "jaguar's children"—descendants of humanlike cats that emerged in the past.

Traces of this Mexican genesis have been discovered in sculptures and masks and on broken pottery that litters the floors of the homes. Nanette Pyne found that jaguar designs on shards in San Jose Mogote were on the floors of particular homes and were absent in others.[11] In the other homes, the fragments of pottery were decorated with fire serpent designs. The snake with its eyebrows aflame was a god of the Olmec. It seems likely that the Veracruz jungles and the growing villages of the highlands

---

[9]Michael D. Coe, *The Jaguar's Children: Pre-Classic Central Mexico* (New York: Museum of Primitive Art, 1965).

[10]Y. V. Knorozov and R. V. Kinzhalov have offered an intriguing speculation about the jaguar deity and its close relation to farming. Forest herbivores such as deer, "were the greatest source of damage to the crops raised by the people who had taken up farming, and so the jaguar, the lord of the forest who scared away the animals and never touched the maize himself, was regarded as the protector of fields and farmers." R. V. Kinzhalov, "Toward the Reconstruction of the Olmec Mythological System," in *Cultural Continuity in Mesoamerica*, ed. David L. Browman (The Hague: Mouton: 1978), p. 282.

[11]Nanette M. Pyne, "The Fire-Serpent and Were-Jaguar in Formative Oaxaca: A Contingency Table Analysis," in Flannery, *Early Mesoamerican*, pp. 272–82.

as well were sharing in the symbols and rites of religious belief. Perhaps the kin groups within these communities that were directing the flow of exchange were presenting themselves as being closely related to gods.

Such a myth likely had its advantages. It would have reduced the local rebellions—the revolutions suggested by Coe. Entrepreneurs were less likely to challenge the ruling elite. Exchange with dominant kin groups was becoming a matter of faith. This added stability to systems of regional trade. For Ronald Grennes-Ravits and G. H. Coleman, the commercial journey was a rite of belief: a pilgrimage made to a center of commercial life.[12]

Olmec decline

This quickening pulse of commercialism might have transformed Olmec society into the earliest state that developed in Mesoamerica. As it happened, though the point is debatable, there seems to be nothing dug out of those jungles which hints that the Olmec were anything more than a chiefdom.[13] Not in the art or the settlement pattern, nor in the furnishings found in the graves, is there a glimpse of hierarchial groups that make public decisions.

Instead, 2,400 years ago, there is the evidence of Olmec decline—territorial restriction and contracting of networks of trade. Marcus Winter and Jane Pires-Ferreira see a web drawing into itself as exotic commodities fade from the gulf coastal societies.[14] Magnetite mirrors and jade figurines, once discovered in highland communities, are found even closer to centers

[12]Ronald Grennes-Ravits and G. H. Coleman, "The Quintessential Role of Olmec in the Central Highlands of Mexico," *American Antiquity* 41, 1976, pp. 196–205. Their theory of ritually sanctioned exchange systems is applied only to the gulf coastal lowlands, but it was possibly true for the highland regions as well. The participation of highland communities in the Olmec net of exchange is suggested by David C. Grove, "The Highland Olmec Manifestation: A Consideration of What It Is and Isn't," in *Mesoamerican Archeology: New Approaches,* ed. Norman Hammond (Austin: University of Texas Press, 1974), pp. 124–25.

[13]The classification of the Olmec as a chiefdom was suggested by William T. Sanders and Barbara Price in *Mesoamerica: The Evolution of a Civilization,* (New York: Random House, 1968), p. 127. But the idea has been vigorously challenged in the writing of Michael D. Coe. The Olmec of San Lorenzo, he feels were "the center of a coercive state of grandiose proportions." Large-scale public works, in particular, have influence his view of the matter. "We are dealing with a people who could drag multiton stones incredible distances. And we are dealing with a highly sophisticated population which included artists working in a sculptural style that can only be called 'great'." Leaving aside the slippery problem of evaluating the "greatness" of art, the appeal to grandiose public works is not entirely convincing. Such constructions were possible in Europe, where evidence of bureaucratic classes is lacking. This would also appear to be true for Pacific societies. His other criteria include widespread exchange, organized warfare, a "national" law, and (frequently) required participation in a "state" religion. Using labels such as "national" and "state," he is assuming what he wishes to prove. But all these behaviors are possible in a chiefdom society. Michael D. Coe, "San Lorenzo and the Olmec Civilization," *Dumbarton Oaks Conference on the Olmec,* ed. Elizabeth P. Benson (Washington, D.C.: Dumbarton Oaks Research Library and Collection, 1968), p. 60.

[14]Marcus A. Winter and Jane W. Pires-Ferreira, "Distribution of Obsidian among Households in Two Oaxacan Villages," in Flannery, *Early Mesoamerican,* p. 325.

in the tropical forest. Like Mississippian and Hopewell societies, or the peoples of the ancient Pacific, the Olmec are a reminder of the openness of cultural change. A society is not committed to follow any fatal trajectory. A chiefdom will not necessarily turn into a state.

At the moment, very little is known about why their society changed. It might even be wrong to refer to the change as "decline." Indeed, the old ceremonial buildings became covered by jungle in time, but intricate political systems might still have survived. Evon Vogt, not long ago, studied the Mayan people of Zinacantan, in central Chiapas southeast of the bottleneck world.[15] He found elaborate networks of leaders who make decisions in everyday life. It is a process that likely would leave little trace in the ground. *Caciques*—the leaders of hamlets—are supported by lineage heads. But in all of the villages, shamans have power as well. Successful farmers are listened to; so are those involved with ritual life. Such systems might well have existed a very long time.

Something like them may have lasted for centuries as the monuments crumbled away. The decline might have been little more than a shift in exchange. To the south in the Oaxaca highlands, a new gateway was coming to be. Zapotec Indians were creating a lattice of trade. They might have attracted the clients that traded their wares to the Gulf; and the Olmec returned to their systems of local exchange.

Monuments built in the forest became relics of a world that was gone, But its patterns of art, calendrics, architecture, and religious belief were now part of the developing cultures of Mesoamerica. When their centers had sunk into forest, they could be remembered in ritual and art—heirlooms of the early beginnings of ceremonial life.

Travelers were gone from the footpaths that led down to the Veracuz jungles. But they were crowding the trails that wound through the Mexican hills. On a ridge in the Valley of Oaxaca, just to the north of San Jose Mogote, a new kind of community was changing the life of the highlands. About 2,400 years ago, when Olmec power was fading, Zapotec Indians were building the town that would become Monte Alban. Richard Blanton, surveying its ruins, discovered three separate clusters of houses.[16] Possibly the earliest settlers had arrived from the "gates" of the valley: three natural corridors that long had been pathways of trade. This might have been a simple alliance of kin groups controlling the valley—the most casual of changes with cascading social effects. Perhaps it began as convenience, this gathering on a Mexican ridge. From the hill it was possible to coordinate

Monte Alban and Teotihuacan

---

[15]Evon Z. Vogt, *Zinacantan: A Maya Community in the Highlands of Chiapas* (Cambridge, Mass.: The Belknap Press of Harvard University Press, 1969), pp. 246–95.

[16]Richard E. Blanton, "The Origins of Monte Alban," in *Cultural Change and Continuity,* ed. C. E. Cleland (New York: Academic Press, 1976).

The Arizona State Museum, The Arizona State University, E.B. Sayles, Photographer

Monte Alban, Oaxaca, Mexico—Zapotec ruins, 1951.

trade in Oaxaca. Villagers could live in the gateways and bring products to the chiefs on the ridge. They could bring news about weather and raiding on the rim of the valley.[17]

Here, as in Old World villages that in time became the earliest cities, was a strategy for urbanization and social control. Commodities and information found their way to the ridge-top community: the critical ingredients for creating the strata of power. Goods could be used as rewards or as buffers for the outlying hamlets. They could also be hoarded from rivals who threatened the state. Information brought to the hilltop meant efficient regulation of trade. Outlying villages were losing their control of exchange. The community turned into a city as villagers moved to the ridge. The three original separate neighborhoods were architecturally merged into one. Kin leaders were conceivably creating a stratum of power.

---

[17]The centralized hilltop position, remote from water and prime farming land, was likely chosen to coordinate commercial and military activity. This theory has been recently challenged by archeologist Robert S. Santley, who views population pressure as critical in Monte Alban's emergence. His reconstruction, however, is flawed by inaccurate site description and insufficient attention to environmental reconstructions of Oaxaca. See Robert S. Santley, "Disembedded Capitals Reconsidered," *American Antiquity* 45, no. 1 (1980), pp. 132–45; Richard E. Blanton, "Cultural Ecology Reconsidered," *American Antiquity* 45, no. 1 (1980), pp. 145–51, and Stephen A. Kowalewski, "Population-Resource Balances in Period 1 of Oaxaca, Mexico," *American Antiquity* 45, no. 1 (1980), pp. 151–65.

Hundreds of acres of hillside were terraced for construction of houses. More than 2,000 steps were cut into the side of the hill.

Temples and pyramidal monuments emerged in the heart of the city, constructed by rulers and likely in exchange for rewards.[18] A central plaza surrounded by pyramids was oriented along a north-south line, a practice that probably began in the days of the Olmec. Burials found in the city are the relics of social stratification; there are tombs decorated with murals and furnished with urns. One of the tombs, numbered 104, depicts the rain god surrounded by priests. Monte Alban was possibly the home of a religious elite.

To the north in the Valley of Mexico there were similar stirrings of change. A village was becoming a city on the shores of a lake. Only two centuries after the ridge at Oaxaca was settled, a small group of craftworkers and farmers had come to the valley. They quarried out local obsidian, which they fashioned into ornaments and blades. The products found

Teotihuacan. Pressure on local resources may have led to the city's decline.

Milwaukee Public Museum

---

[18]Site description is taken from Muriel Porter Weaver, *The Aztecs, Maya, and their Predecessors: Archeology of Mesoamerica,* (New York: Seminar Press, 1972), p. 147.

their way to Oaxaca and the shores of the Gulf. At about 150 AD Teotihuacan emerged from that village. It became one of the largest cities in existence anywhere in the world.

In the time when the Roman Empire was falling and St. Augustine feared the end of the world, over 100,000 people were at home in this remarkable city.[19] They lived in over 2,000 dwellings along with stoneworkers, weavers, and potters. Local craftworkers turned out their products for Mexican trade. Obsidian tools, clay vessels, slate, basalt, feathers, textiles, and beliefs were traded through a network that extended for hundreds of miles. Like Harrappa and Mohenjo-Daro, much of this city was deliberately planned. Dwellings were strikingly similar. Streets were constructed on a right-angled grid. Monumental structures were built on the "Street of the Dead." The "Pyramid of the Sun," built of earth and adobe, was over 200 feet high. A short distance away was the smaller "Pyramid of the Moon."[20]

Rene Millon, when he surveyed the city, encountered the remains of irrigation canals. Crops of corn could be traded and stored and could support the elite. That, perhaps, was a bit more expected than another feature found at the site: a neighborhood especially reserved for an immigrant group. Houses built in this district looked like the ones in other parts of the city. Differences only were evident inside their walls. There were fragments of Oaxacan-type pottery and Oaxacan-style ritual urns. A stone-lined tomb in the district resembled the Monte Alban burials. No other such tombs were found anywhere in the city.

This district has been called a *barrio* —a tiny enclave for an immigrant group. And almost certainly the people who lived there had come from Oaxaca. What were they doing there? Millon is not certain—nor, at the moment, is anyone else. Had these people abandoned Oaxaca seeking better conditions of life? Or were there specialized groups that commuted between the two regions? Perhaps they were actually prisoners, compelled to live there year after year. If there was trouble with Oaxaca, they were insurance against possible raids.

Most persuasive, I think, is the theory that a community of merchants was there. They produced special wares and, perhaps, had political power. Settlement within the city avoided the problems of long-distance trade. There might always be theft or bad weather, but there was another difficulty as well. Without any beasts of burden, commodities were carried by people themselves. Certainly this placed limitations on the volume of trade. By manufacturing wares in the city the limitations of transport were gone. Production was more closely related to demand for the goods. Beyond

---

[19]Rene Millon, "The Study of Urbanism at Teotihuacan in Mexico," in Hammond, *Mesoamerican Archeology.*

[20]These are modern names for these architectural features, not the names used in the past.

that, since they lived in the city, merchants were closely in touch with its people; their presence may have a political dimension as well. It was easier to bargain for favors, alliances, and better conditions of trade. Like the guilds of medieval Europe, such strategies were part of the barrio's life. Merchant-craftworkers were likely a rising elite.

The discovery is a striking reminder of the subtlety of social relations between the great city and the valley that lay to the south. Discoveries unearthed in the barrio suggest connections with ancient Oaxaca. Discoveries in Monte Alban reflect Teotihuacan's life. Vessels and urns on the ridgetop suggest influence of the north.[21] The two cities were intimately aware of one another's existence.

In fact, that awareness might have played a role in the cities' decline. Refugees from one fading metropolis crowded another. George Cowgill has viewed Teotihuacan as a city in a race against time as its growing populations put pressure on arable land.[22] There was limited space near the city suited for irrigation canals. After centuries of growth, there was a shortage of available food. This meant that Teotihuacan dwellers increasingly depended on routes of exchange. But if trade was the primary source of their food supply, they could be forced into buying it dear. Uncertainty was becoming a part of Teotihuacan's life.

At some time near the year 650, the entire city was deliberately burned. An elaborate metropolis was gone from the world overnight. Whether the fire was set by its citizens in a protest against the elite, or whether it was raided we still do not know. We *do* know that out of its burning came an exodus of nobles, artists, craftworkers, politicians, and farmers to the forests and hills. They may have pushed into the Yucatan lowlands and built a temple to the god of rain. Their beliefs may have slowly been woven into Mayan tradition. As well, they might have moved to Oaxaca and joined their rivals of 800 years: Monte Alban still ruled in the valley from its perch on the hill.

Intriguingly, that ridge-top city burst into a spasm of growth at the time when the migrants were spreading through Mesoamerica.[23] Craftworkers and uprooted nobles might have fled from Teotihuacan's ashes and settled on the hill in the hope of rebuilding their lives. It is possible, but yet far from certain; much of the city is still unexplored. All the digging ever done on the hilldop, Marcus Winter once said of the problem, has never even touched over 90 percent of its homes.[24]

---

[21]John Paddock, "Oaxaca in Ancient Mesoamerica," in *Ancient Oaxaca: Discoveries in Mexican Archeology and History* (Stanford: Stanford University Press, 1966), p. 127.

[22]George Cowgill, public lecture, Seattle, 1976, cited in Robert J. Wenke, *Patterns in Prehistory: Mankind's First Three Million Years* (New York: Oxford University Press, 1980), p. 591.

[23]T. Patrick Culbert, "Mesoamerica," in *Ancient Native Americans,* ed. Jesse D. Jennings (San Francisco: W. H. Freeman, 1978), p. 432.

[24]Marcus C. Winter, "Residential Patterns at Monte Alban, Oaxaca, Mexico," *Science,* December 13, 1974, p. 981.

Whatever might have been the real reason, the city seems to have exploded in growth. But the change was deceiving; Monte Alban was at the end of its days. John Paddock has told how the region was cleared of its forests and planted.[25] Terraces were not cut into slopes for the newly cleared fields. Perhaps the city was growing so quickly that there was not time to cut steps in the hillsides. That time could be spent in planting and harvesting crops. But the shortcut proved futile as the soils eroded away. The destructive technique was pushed farther away from the city. Water too was becoming a problem because it had to be hauled up the hill. There were not animlas to help with the labor; it was brought up in jars and on foot. Thirty thousand people were living on trips to the streams.

Monte Alban was slowly abandoned, beginning about AD 700. There was not any "vengeful destruction," wrote John Paddock of that difficult time.[26] Over decades it fell "stone by stone" for lack of repairs. Like other cities that had fallen to ruin, it was remembered by the Mexican people in years when the last of their empires were broken and gone, But in that time when the astonishing hilltop was being covered by cacti and dust, new centers of powers were developing to the east. Past the arc of the gulf coastal lowlands, in the highlands and tropical forests, new inheritors of ancient traditions were shaping a world.

Peten networks

When pilgrims were following footpaths to the platforms at San Lorenzo, houses were rising on the floor of the tropical forest.[27]Settlers on the Pasion River, perhaps as early as 1000 BC, left pottery fragments and shells on the banks of the stream. These shadowy people, known as the *Xe,* may have been the earliest human society to adapt to the jungles that in time would be the land of the Maya.

The forested south of the Yucatan peninsula is the region called the *Peten.* Lakes of its interior are fed by meandering streams. Just to its north are the rain-washed woodlands where water disappears from the earth: it drains down to a deep shelf of stone far out of reach. Only in the far northern lowlands is the limestone close to the top. Underground streams have scoured out wells there which are natural basins of water. Near *cenotes,* as they are called, it was possible to live through the year.

For the Xe and the groups that followed them, the Peten was a pioneer's world. Like the farmers of old Karanovo who chopped their way through the thickets of Europe, these discoverers were making their home in an unsettled land. Little is know about their technology, but they might well had been slash-and-burn planters. Cultivation had been practiced in Mexico

---

[25]Paddock, *Ancient Oaxaca*, pp. 151–52.

[26]Ibid., p. 152.

[27]Ecology of Mayan territory and archeological evidence of Mayan emergence are taken from Adams, *Prehistoric Mesoamerica*, pp. 116–21.

for thousands of years. They had their pick of wide stretches of forest, caches of water, and permanent streams. They could live far apart from their neighbors, their settlements dispersed on the land, so that slashed-out clearings, in time, would be jungle again. More than that, the riverside thickets were rich with wild pigs, rodents, and deer. The Pasion's currents were teeming with turtles and fish. This meant a buffer—a backup system—in the form of a foraging life. For these first generations, their world was remote and secure.

So it was for the next five centuries: a great eddy protected from change. Currents of political strategy, exchanges, and ritual life swirled around it in the Veracruz lowlands and the Mexican hills. Not until 2,500 years ago did the Yucatan suddenly change: forest people were beginning to share a ceremonial life. At Dzibilchaltun, far to the north, villagers constructed ceremonial mounds. This may have been a center for ocean-and-forest exchange. At Altar de Sacrificios, near the banks of the Pasion River, platforms of lime, shells, and mud mortar were foundations for temples of thatch.

Very likely these ritual centers were the nodes of a cultural webwork that extended from the swamps of Peten to the edge of the sea. Ceramics are the hint of a process of communities meeting together—a sameness emerging from gatherings for ritual and trade. Twenty-five hundred years before the present, their pottery was painted in red, black, and cream. From the swamps to the Gulf, every fragment is almost the same. *Mamom* is the name of the pottery and of the time in which the shards first appear. It remains almost exactly the same over hundreds of years. A later style, which is called *chicanel*, was in use until AD 150, but the colors remain almost unchanged for six centuries.

Ceramics, then, were almost identical over 97,000 square miles. Plazas and pyramids were constructed in clearings in the midst of the trees. Together with the striking diversity which is part of the Yucatan world, this is evidence of a far-reaching system of forest exchange. The earliest Xe pioneers could ignore the other folk of the woodlands. They had their own water, large forests, and woods filled with game. But later generations of farmers, budding off into marginal lands, inherited country removed from the wells and the streams. Not only that, but the pioneer settlements were likely affected by the people who left. Budding off from traditional villages likely filled up the space in-between. For slash-and-burn farmers the land was becoming too small.

An elaborate, ritualized network most probably came into being to minimize the growing uncertainty of Yucatan life. Left to itself, there is a good possibility that local chiefs would have managed the trade; that powerful groups would have ruled in this intricate land. But isolation was, in fact, an illusion. Hierarchies of power were at the edge of their world. Lowlands were prey for the strategies of immigrant kings.

That may have been exactly what happened at about AD 150, when society was shaken and forests were never to be the same. Strangers came to Belize in the Yucatan, very likely from lands to the south. They discovered that circuits of power were already there. A curious, multilined pottery appears suddenly in sites of this region. It is suggestively similar to fragments in Central America. Stone monuments, fresco paintings, an art style, and a system of writing appear in a flash through the jungles of the southeastern coast.

Elites practiced at statecraft, finding a web of connections in place would happen again in the jungles of Southeastern Asia. In Belize it quickened the pace of a process already occurring—of centralized power emerging on routes of exchange. In time, near the springs and the rivers, there would be cities where jungle had grown. New cadres of power were coming to a wilderness world.

New people coming into the lowlands and triggering a political change—such disturbance might well have occurred in what now is Belize. But this is not all of the answer, not even the most critical part. The problem of Maya beginnings is concerned with much more than Belize. It involves all of the peninsula and the neighboring highlands as well. In other regions there is not any evidence of intruders from Central America. Traditional cultures themselves were beginning to change.

The Maya: Commerce and conflict

That difference is itself a reminder of the complexity of Mayan emergence. Different parts of their country were changing in different ways. We might look at their historical records to see what they said of themselves; that might help us unravel the story of their early beginnings. But the search would be a disappointment; they had little to say of such things. Like the Chinese, the Sumerians, and the Cretans, their records were for them and not for us. Their view may have been that of Thucydides, a historian of classical Greece: he felt that nothing of importance had happened before his own time.

Yet even in the absence of history, we can say something of how the Mayans began. The Peten region itself tells a part of the story. All along, it was a variable country, with subtle changes in landscapes and life. Soils alone in the Peten were a bewildering mixture of types. The differences could directly affect agricultural yields. William Sanders has told how they varied in their moisture and mineral content, how some were friable—easily crumbled—and others were not. They differed in their distance from rivers, where the water table was apt to be high. They differed in contour and in the tendency they had to erode. If we recall that vegetation is varied and that water is often not easy to find, we can better understand how societies lived in this land.

The Mamom and the Chicanel pottery are hints of a cultural strategy that had its beginnings as early as 500 BC. After early agricultural peoples had settled in the best of the lands, later generations moved into a riskier

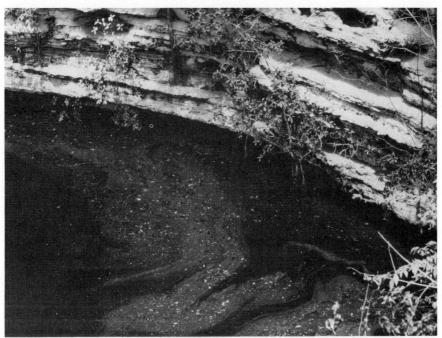

Photo by Dr. Allyn M. Stearman, Department of Anthropology and Sociology, University of Central Florida

Yucatan *cenote*. Settlements in the region were close to these natural waterholes or near the artifical wells that were called *chultuns*.

world. Very likely, old kinship connections were critical in their earliest days. Your ancestral village could help you in difficult times. But reliance on kinship connections can be a precarious thing. Your new home and your ancestral village are probably not far apart. What if both of them are stricken by drought at the very same time?

I suspect this is likely the reason why original trading connections were soon widened to include many villagers who lived far away. If more villages came into the system, then the uncertainty of life was reduced. Perhaps villages in the Peten were manufacturing specialized products in a strategy for becoming part of a network of trade. Moist tropics. Donald Lathrap has argued, are most often mosaic environments with routes of exchange that extend over hundred of miles.[28]

But exchange, as we noticed much earlier, involves complicated human behaviors. It is more than commodities carried along forest trails. Salt, pottery, stone for corn-grinders, fish, and maize from the fields could well have been traded from village to village. Such a system would have

[28]Donald Lathrap, "The Antiquity and Importance of Long-Distance Trade Relationships in the Moist Tropics," *World Archeology* 1, no. 5 (1973).

been more reliable if it was strengthened by human belief. The journey to the village downstream was becoming a rite.

Archeologist William L. Rathje, at the Peten site of Tikal, discovered possible evidence of ritual related to trade.[29] Elites in this southerly center may have shrewdly directed their artists to sculpt and carve out a collection of sacred commodities. From Tikal this ritual complex would be traded to distant communities. Each object was woven into lowland ceremonial life.

Consider encyclopedias: they were all you really wanted to buy. But the merchant who arrived at your door will not have it that way. You *must* own the 500-page atlas, the brand-new index, and the updated books. You can't be without their abridgement and color brochure. You discover— unless you say no—that you are buying into part of a complex. If you purchase one part, you are pressured to purchase the whole.

The comparison is not quite perfect, because the books are not infused with belief. They are not thought to be related to a powerful supernatural world. But the polychrome pottery, temples, altars, feathers, and knowl-

Tikal. A complex of ritual artifacts circulated out of this center.

Photo by Dr. Allyn M. Stearman, Department of Anthropology and Sociology, University of Central Florida

<hr />

[29]His model has been developed in numerous publications. I relied most extensively upon "The Origin and Development of Lowland Classic Maya Civilization," *American Antiquity* 36 (1971), pp. 275–85; "Classic Maya Development and Denouement: A Research Design" in *The Classic Maya Collapse,* ed. T. P. Culbert (Albuquerque: University of New Mexico Press, 1973), pp. 405–54; and "The Tikal Connection" in *The Origins of Maya Civilization,* ed. R. E. W. Adams (Albuquerque: University of New Mexico Press, 1977), pp. 373–82.

Mayan ceramic.

Field Museum of Natural History

edge that came out of Tikal were a collection that Yucatan villagers held to be sacred. By circulating ceremonial items along trails that wound through the lowlands, religious elites were stabilizing the networks of trade. Such efficiency caught the attention of distant Teotihuacan merchants. Highlands and lowlands were knitted by threads of exchange.

Success did not arrive without penalty, here as in other parts of the world. Beyond the belt of southerly forests were communities that once were connected with neighboring peoples in traditional systems of trade. Those neighbors perhaps had sent maize in canoes paddled upstream. Obsidian was possibly traded to them in return. But imagine that one of these villages was now brought into the web of Tikal, conceivably attracted

Mesoamerican elite:
Litter bearers depicted
on Mayan ceramic.

by a much greater volume of trade. The old neighbor would have more than hurt feelings; a valuable resource connection was gone. A peaceful relation was suddenly endangered by raids.

Such friction at the edge of the system served the needs of the central elite. It provided a rationalization for going to war. If the outsider group were defeated, it could be forced to be part of the web. The new connection in time could be strengthened by religious belief. The net could grow wider and wider by attracting new clients or launching a raid. As it widened, the lives of its members became more secure.

Something very much like this may have happened at the site of Becan, a fortified town in the forests to the north of Tikal.[30] Limestone platforms covered with plaster, pyramidal structures, stairways, and walls are the remains of a center of Mayan ceremonial life. It sprawled across 46 acres, but there was more to the site than its size. At the settlement's edge was the massive architecture of war. Archeologist David L. Webster mapped and surveyed remains of a moat. The defensive structure extended for nearly a mile. Above it was an earthen embankment and, possibly, a log palisade. The total effect was a barrier 40 feet high.

At the time the moat was constructed, perhaps around AD 100, political tension was growing in the town of Becan. Tikal had only started its scheme of trading a complex of objects to create a commercialized web in the Yucatan forests. Becan, with its store of obsidian, fertile soils, and trading connections, stayed aloof from the curious system at work in the south. That strategy ended in failure as the forest exploded in raids. Becan might have been losing clients to the competitive web of Tikal. Tikal might have needed Becan for additional goods. Either way, they were volatile rivals— and Becan was taken up in the web. Artifacts of their ancient religion disappeared from the town in a flash. They were replaced by trappings that emanated out of Tikal.

Friction at the edge of the system was the price of commercial success. It was also a pressure for the rise of hierarchical rule. Complexities of trading connections were exquisite and constantly growing. Added to these were the problems of raids in the outlying lands. Violence is not very simple, as David Webster is quick to suggest.[31] The spoils of victory can be a danger as great as the fight. Mayan rulers, like other elites, were not supported by organized armies. They rewarded their followers with presents of prestigious goods. Such a system of buying loyalty has an ironic and dangerous flaw. The prestigious items must always be locally scarce. Suppose you were a victorious Mayan, rewarding your followers with parcels of land. One morning when you capture a village, you soon discover that a vast tract of forest, abundant fresh water and fertile soils, were captured as well. Your followers can be richly rewarded, and that is precisely when the problems begin. They now have their own cache of resources; they have land and the promise of crops. Surpluses of food can be a basis for trading connections. They can buy military alliance, and if they wish, they can launch their own raids. With those possibilities, why do they need you at all?

---

[30]Site description is taken from "Rio Bec Archeology an the Rise of Maya Civilization," in Adams, *Origins of Maya* pp. 82–85.

[31]David L. Webster, "Warfare and the Evolution of Maya Civilization," in ibid., pp. 335–72.

Maya warrior with
jaguar mask.

In this, David Webster has argued, lies the subtlety of staging a war.
You must always be successful enough so that warriors are paid for their
pains, but never so successful that they no longer need your rewards.
This calculus of ambush and conflict—*boundary maintenance*, as it sometimes
is called—was a critical feature of a stabilized system of power. Raids on

the web's outer fringes could create a usurping elite or they could generate rewards for enhancing traditional rule.

Inside the Peten region, trading and conflict continued to grow. In that *core*, as William Rathje has called it, strategic resources were lacking. People near Tikal were depending on systems of trade. They had corn from their slashed-out farmlands; they had fertile orchards of breadnut trees. But they were lacking mortars to pulverize the crops into meal. And supplies of obsidian, which formed razor-sharp blades used in making other tools, were needed as populations increased in the region.

Brian Hayden and Margaret Nelson, in an experiment in "living pre-history," observed the uses of glass in the Guatemalan highlands today.[32] It is likely that a cultural substitution happened in more recent times: the replacement of obsidian by modern industrial glass. If so, then the glass-using farmer gives us insights into earlier times—into the importance of obsidian for ancient Mayan society. Modern bottles are broken and used for the finishing work on a shaft—the final shaving done on the handle of an axe or a hoe. Glass is used to make ritual implements: deer-rattles and blood-letting balls. If a complex of sacred materials was crucial to the trade of the past, then obsidian was needed to fashion these items as well. Beyond that, they also discovered the importance of quarried basalt. The stone today plays a critical role in agricultural life. Vesicular basalt, softer and pitted, is raw material for making *metates*—the corn-grinding mortars used in this part of the world. Volcanic basalt, which is harder, is used for the tools that carve out the mortars. Both stones are valuable resources—and they are items of regional trade. It seems very likely that this also was true in the past.

Salt from the northerly coastlands and, perhaps, fish from that region as well may have been traded to villages that grew in the core. In return for strategic commodities went the ritual goods from Tikal—the complex infused with elaborate religious beliefs. Manufacturing ritual paraphernalia and importing stone, salt, and blades was the system directed by Mayan elites. As it widened, it triggered more conflicts—and decisions of how much to gain. Life in this forested country was growing complex.

At Tikal, and other centers as well, the flow of information increased. Ruling kin groups coordinated rituals, conflict, and trade. Something like this had happened much earlier to the chiefs in the Veracruz jungles. But Olmec had never created hierarchical rule. Yet, in the Peten, it somehow was different; the decision-making levels emerged. The reason perhaps can be found in the natural world. Out of rich soils in southerly Yucatan, the lakes, the streams, and the rain came a surplus of corn in the outlying farms. Beyond that were the Peten *bajos*—the swamps that fill up with

---

[32]Brain Hayden and Margaret Nelson, "The Use of Chipped Lithic Material in the Contemporary Maya Highlands," *American Antiquity* 46, no. 4 (1981), pp. 885–98. The article is a good example of the developing science of ethnoarcheology: the reconstruction of the past through the study of living societies.

the rains. These marshes cover nearly one-half of the forested core. Swamps might have been drained and planted; it was a source of additional food. Terraces may have been cut into some of the slopes. Most important of all was the breadnut (ramon) which flourished in the woods of Peten. The crop from its trees was a food richer than maize. One acre planted in orchard will produce half a ton of these nuts. It might have been possible to keep them in storage for over a year.[33]

Such strategies were likely created out of pressures on arable land, but they could also be used for supporting a rising elite. Chiefs in the ritual centers became rulers of Yucatan states. Classes of managers watched over warfare and trade. An industry of ritual paraphernalia kept specialists at work through the year, routinely manufacturing relics believed to be sacred. Such products as feathers, carved wooden objects, polychrome pottery, textiles, and stones came out of their shops and moved on the trails. Scribes kept detailed records of the circuits of Mayan exchange. Warriors routed their rivals—but never too far.

The elaborate circuits of trading extended well beyond the Peten. Powerful rulers emerged in the highlands as well. In the uplifts of Guatemala, Kaminaljuyu was built.[34] South of that city were the lowlands along the Pacific. From that region, Kaminaljuyu imported cotton and also *cacao:* an evergreen tree used for manufacturing chocolate. In the uplands were

Talud-tablero architecture.

Field Museum of Natural History

---

[33]The specific details of Mayan technology are still extremely controversial. A good introduction to recent debate is provided by Adams in *Prehistoric Mesoamerica;* and by the "Comments" of David Webster, D. Bruce Dickson, Kathryn J. Elsesser and others in the October 1981 issue of *American Antiquity* and by writings cited in the articles' bibliographies.

[34]A good summary of the site is provided by Muriel Porter Weaver in *The Aztec, Maya, and their Predecessors: Archaeology of Mesoamerica* (New York: Seminar Press, 1972), pp. 148–52.

obsidian quarries—sources of cutting-tools for the Peten. The highland community controlled a wide system of trade. At about AD 400, laborers in the north part of the city were constructing a center of ritual and political life. High buildings, with facings of pumice, covered with clay, and plastered in white, looked over a plaza—the ball court of Kaminaljuyu.

It is *talud-tablero* construction—a terracing of plaster and slabs. It is reminiscent of buildings that line the "Avenue of the Dead." More than that, there is something peculiar about the tombs of this city as well. Traditionally, the Maya who lived there buried their dead within mounds, in rectangular chambers roofed with a cover of logs. But 1,600 years ago, this burial practice was changed. The chamber and logs still existed, but the tombs were in front of the mounds. What is more, the artifacts with the dead were no longer the same. There were lidded, cylindrical pots, incense burners, and slender-necked jars. There was pottery with the face of Tlaloc—the god who brought rain.

What is unusual about these discoveries is that they probably are not Mayan at all. They resemble Teotihuacan finds more than anything else. What was happening at Kaminaljuyu when it grew to the height of its power? Was the city controlled in those days by a foreign elite?

Just before the remarkable changes in Kaminaljuyu's style, the growing community had fallen on difficult times. Fewer buildings had emerged in the city; the populations might well have declined. Pottery of that time, for the most part, was carelessly done. Perhaps the rulers who lived in the city had pressed their advantage too far—like the kings of Mesopotamian lowlands in earlier times. Surrounded by volcanic soils and nourished by convectional rains, the highlands could usually generate two crops a year. Control over food—and minerals—gave them a decided advantage in trade, especially with regard to the lowlands that lay to the south. If they demanded too much from that region, it may have led to a breakdown in trade. Teotihuacan merchants might well have arrived at that time. Their elaborate Mexican networks provided favorable conditions of trade. The intruders remained in the city for 200 years.

For Joseph Michels and William T. Sanders, it was likely not a conquest at all—not, at least, in the usual military sense of the word.[35] New merchants with widespread connections provided goods for the local elite. For the Mayan rulers, exotic trade items were a means of increasing their power. Weak as they were, they could never have needed it more. Foreign merchants in Kaminaljuyu were expanding their connections of trade. Both groups benefited; their power increased through the years.

The maneuver was remarkably clever but it collapsed in two centuries'

---

[35]Teotihuacanos at Kaminaljuyu have been the subject of considerable debate. The reconstruction here is adapted from *Teotihucan and Kaminaljuyu*, ed. William T. Sanders and Joseph W. Michels (University Park: Pennsylvania State University Press, 1977). I was especially influenced by Kenneth L. Brown, "The Valley of Guatemala: A Highland Port of Trade," pp. 205–396 in that volume.

time. Mayan peoples north of the city were observers of cultural change. They watched as Teotihuacan peoples, through marriage and religious belief, brought Kaminaljuyu much closer to its web of exchange. It seemed less and less "their" city, so they began to byass it in trade. They sought out Guatemalan connections took them out of Teotihuacan's realm. Foreign merchants lost power. They left—and returned to their homes.

The events are a striking reminder of competitive systems of power that existed in highlands and valleys beyond the Peten. Everywhere in the Mayan communities, the scale of decisions increased. New levels were added to a growing bureaucratic elite.

That pinnacle of Mayan society was defended by religious belief—by the myth of a permanent link with the spiritual world. Elite were elaborately buried in tombs under the temples. But the graves very possibly had a political "life." A small tube led up through the flooring from the tomb to the living elite. Conceivably, a ruler's decisions involved "consulting"—through the tube in the floor—the spirits of the departed elite buried below. In Maya, like other societies, religion was enhancement of power. The supernatural was always a part of the political realm.

The classic Maya collapse

It probably seemed to the Maya that their world had been favored by gods. For nearly 600 years their cities and influence grew. The symptoms of slash-and-burn, bajo and orchard, and terraces cut in the slopes supported a specialist class. Astronomers, mathematicians, architects, artists,

Mayan mathematics facilitated prediction of astronomical events. Such prediction was a valuable element of political rule.

MAYA NUMERALS

| ZERO | ONE | TWO | FIVE | EIGHT | TEN | NINETEEN |

COMPARISON OF SYSTEMS OF WRITING NUMBERS

OUR SYSTEM (DECIMAL)	Number to be Written	3rd position Units of 100	2nd position Units of 10	1st position Units of 1	Result
	405	4 $4 \times 100 +$	0 $0 \times 10 +$	5 $5 \times 1 =$	405

MAYA SYSTEM (VIGESIMAL)	Number to be Written	3rd position Units of 400	2nd position Units of 20	1st position Units of 1	Result
	405	• $1 \times 400 +$	$0 \times 20 +$	$5 \times 1 =$	405

Field Museum of Natural History

and scribes shared their knowledge, and the pace of discovery increased. They recorded the locations of the planets, the constellations, the moon, and the sun. The Maya predicted eclipses; they made observations of Venus as well. They designed a mathematical system including a zero. Their calendrics included a year made up of 365 days. Their elaborate mythological figures were carved out of jade.

And yet, near the year 900, it all began falling to pieces. Cities were abandoned; pyramids crumbled to ruin. A "wondrous mystery," said one archeologist.[36] That, in fact, is what it always has been. Like Indus society, their power was gone overnight.

Collapse, so swift when it *did* come, very likely had been building for years. From the very beginning, there were dangers in the Mayan design. The core where the cities developed was a pocket of arable land. It had water, good soils, and bajos; there were orchards and rain. All around was marginal country—the *buffer area,* it sometimes is called—where resources never were as rich as they were in the core.

Yet the margins had critical resources: obsidian and deposits of stone. Both of these were needed for the farming done in the core. Food grown in the pocket was needed by the farmers themselves; the surplus was kept and consumed by the specialist class. So the core traded out to the margins the only resource it had for exchange: the elaborate paraphernalia of sacred beliefs.

In the days when populations were smaller, the danger in the system had never been seen. It was obvious enough when the stresses began to emerge. The core was filling with people; there was pressure on available food. A whole set of technological strategies—including terrace, bajo, and orchard—were used to their limits; there was very little left to be tried.

Farmers in southerly Yucatan were trapped in an impossible game. They needed all of the food from their croplands, and they might have kept every bit for themselves. They might have held the contribution that went to the specialist class. But consider: if there were no specialists, then there was nothing that the pocket could trade. This would mean that hardstone grinders and supplies of obsidian blades would no longer be brought from the margins outside the Peten. Without the labor of the specialist class, the connection for tools would be gone. Yet, if the contributions continued, the danger of malnutrition increased; and a hungry population is vulnerable to the spread of disease.

The final blow might have come from a distance, when the city of Teotihuacan fell. Mayan rulers, alert to their problem, saw a vacuum in the networks of trade. New clients and new connections could come to the

---

[36]William L. Rathje, "Classic Maya Development and Denouement: A Research Design," in Culbert, *Classic Maya Collapse,* p. 405. This article and William T. Sanders, "The Cultural Ecology of the Lowland Maya: A Reevaluation" in Culbert, *Classic Maya Collapse,* pp. 325–65, are the basis of my discussion of Maya decline.

aid of Peten. They might have thought the highland societies could provide them with additional food. It was urgent to increase the supply of specialized goods. Craftworkers, now more than ever, were fashioning their carvings, stones, feathers, and polychrome pots for the outlying lands. There was no reduction in the number of specialists; possibly they increased. Hunger spread through the hamlets and was more than the farmers could bear.

The strategy of attracting new clients happened too late. Farmers were weakened by hunger; their patience was gone. They left their hamlets and took to the trails. Their fields were abandoned to weeds. Huts fell apart in the drench of the tropical storms. Warriors from the gulf coastal lowlands—a people who were called the *Putun*—ravaged what little was left of the Yucatan core.

The centuries after the Mayan catastrophe were a time of reemergence and growth. New structures of power developed beyond the Peten. The Putun avoided the dangerous pocket where the cities of Maya had been. They traded their wares on the rivers and on the Yucatan coast. Cotton, pottery, salt, and obsidian were floated by canoe on the streams. Towns of the margins were knit in a network of trade. Yet, a short two centuries later, the Putun were defeated in war. A people called *Toltec* captured their routes of exchange. They ruled out of Chichen Itza, a city built far to the north. Commercial connections extended for hundreds of miles. Even so, in the 13th century, they too would fall victim to raids. A small group in the Mesa Central would become astonishingly skillful at war. Ancient America would come to its violent end.

20/Kingdoms at the End of Prehistory: Aztec and Inca

They seem to have come out of nowhere. No one is sure how they really began. Legends of the earliest Aztec were created by the Aztec themselves. Like many people before and after them, they played with their past. Works of the Aztec historians were burned by the Aztec and written again. New chroniclers wrote a flattering tale of the rise of the state.

But their writings, legends, and language all tell us something of their early beginnings. And much has been learned from what seems an improbable source. When the Spanish encountered the Aztec, they saw Satan in the Mexican hills. Devils were hanged, and their writings were put to the torch. But the conquerors were incurably curious about the people who fought them for years. Where did they come from? What was their manner of life? And so the soldier now was the historian, recording what he had almost destroyed. From this and from their legends we learn of their remarkable past.

They were living in the Basin of Mexico, south of the Mesa Central, when Chaucer was alive and when England and France were at war.[1] They had settled on Lake Texcoco's shallow waters bordered by swamps. All around them were the towns and the trading of powerful kings. One of these, perhaps a Tepanec ruler, was at war with other kings near the lake. He called on the Aztec for help and they quickly agreed. In the ambush and raiding that followed, a new strategy began to unfold. Aztec were making alliances in the days when they were fighting their wars. They were polishing tactics and learning the basin's terrain. The Tepanec discovered their blunder when they themselves became victims of raids. They were defeated—usurped by the Aztec. A new kingdom was born on the lake. The Aztec had suddenly emerged as a warrior state.

From that time until their very last moments, they were a people always at war. Violence spread through the towns of the Mesa Central. It never seemed to have a real purpose—as though the wars were an end in them-

The Aztec

---

[1]The presentation of Aztec ecology, social organization, and probable political development is taken largely from Richard E. W. Adams, *Prehistoric Mesoamerica* (Boston: Little, Brown, 1977), pp. 25–44.

The Valley of Mexico.

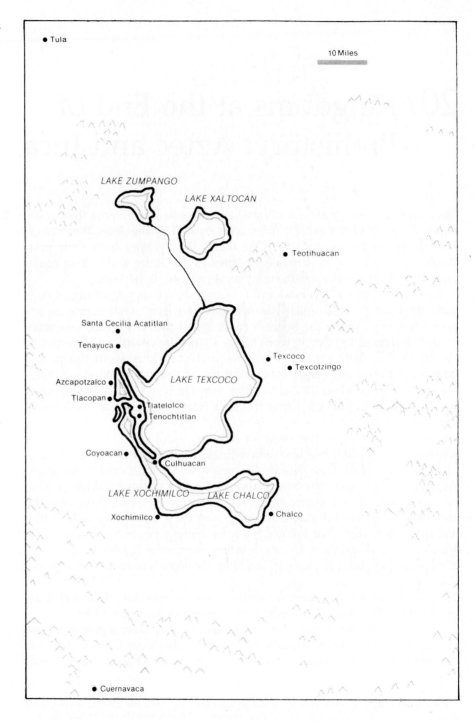

Aztec warrior.

Gift of Mr. and Mrs. James Alsdorf, The Art Institute of Chicago

selves. A territory, once it was conquered, was then abandoned—and conquered again. There was seldom an attempt to control it as part of the state. Is it possible that Aztec society had a strange infatuation with war? Were they fighting their enemies simply to fight them again?

We cannot really answer such questions unless we know more of the Aztec themselves: of their cities, their trading, their politics, and their ritual life. Much more than a fortress of warriors, they were an intricate, urbanized state, with cultural connections extending for hundreds of miles. A multiple set of technologies and a widespread net of exchange provided support for a centralized system of rule. And here, as in other societies, was the power of official belief—religion and ritual shaped to the needs of the state.

Much of what we know of these people has been learned from their capital city—Tenochtitlan—built in the midst of a lake. A cribbing of posts in the bottom was piled over with mattings of wicker. Mud and vegetation were added; an island in the lake was enlarged. Water plants surrounded by frames were pulled and attached to the site. Mud from the bottom was piled on top of the plants. The island was mostly artificial, and it grew to over four square miles. Three major causeways connected the site to the shore. Temples, administrative buildings, arsenals, ball courts, and shops were built on the mud from a Mexican lake.

The lake had been the source of the city and had provided much of its food. The water-plant fields—the *chinampas*—were planted in tomatoes and corn. Canals were excavated around them; water seeped into the soil. A single garden might generate seven different harvests a year. Then too, there were trading connections and the tribute resulting from war. Tons of cereals and grains were delivered to the heart of the city.

Commerce, ongoing warfare, and scheduling of ritual life involved thousands of decisions that had to be made every day. More than that, there were hydraulic problems when the lake would periodically flood. Salt water would spread through the lake and seep into the rafts. Engineers built dikes near chinampas and ran channels to the freshwater springs. It was an intricate system that had to be carefully watched. Management of the Aztec society demanded hierarchies of power supported by chinampas, tribute, and systems of trade.

Information was growing in Aztec, and the structure of society changed. "Promotion," as Flannery calls it, very likely played a critical role. If you were known as a threatening warrior, good at your strategy, and skillful at raids, then you might find yourself suddenly placed very close to the throne. Or perhaps, in a saltwater crisis, you knew all about channels and dikes. Almost overnight you became an elite engineer. The dizzying social transitions were transforming political life. The power of kin was eclipsed by the power of class.

In the cities there still were *calpulli,* the ranked lineages from earlier days. They farmed their chinampas together; they had their own leaders and ritual life. But change had come into the system. The calpulli were never the same. You might be in a low-ranking lineage, taking orders from everyone else. One word from the ruler and your kin would take orders from you. Warfare, technical knowledge, or talent at performing a ritual act could suddenly change the political life of your kin.

And so the nobles surrounding the emperor were seeing new faces in court—the bourgeois gentlemen now a part of their class. *Gray knights,* Robert McC. Adams called them, remembering an old system in Spain. Their lands and their powerful status would continue until the end of their days. When any one of them died, his land would revert to the throne. What became of that land in the future? Of course, the emperior would use it again. It would reward someone else who deserved to be placed near the crown.

It was clearly a turbulent system of hierarchies coming to be. The politics of kinship was shaken, but gray knights could not pass on their power. There was a hereditary elite and, below them, a system in flux. Robert McC. Adams has seen such disturbance as a stage in the growth of the state. If that growth had been allowed to continue, then the knights would have ceased to be gray. Information alone would have done this, as the need for decisions increased. Promotions would have fattened the knighthood; there would have been more of them than ever before. They would have been in a position to argue that they would never surrender their lands. Their descendants could have it, and some could be used for rewards. The process would have likely repeated, as it did in other parts of the world. A ripple of rewards would have generated class after class.

But that pattern was never to happen. Their society was too quickly destroyed. The Spanish invaded but should not be given all of the blame. For many years, the Aztec societies had been destroying themselves in their wars. Destruction itself was built into their ritual life. Temples that rose from their cities were used to sacrifice prisoners of war. This was done on a scale unknown in any part of the world. In the most typical form of sacrifice, according to Jacques Soustelle,

The problem of Aztec sacrifice

> the victim was stretched out on his back on a slightly convex stone with his arms and legs held by four priests, while a fifth ripped him open with a flint knife and tore out his heart. The sacrifice also often took place in the manner which the Spaniards described as *gladiatorio:* the captive was tied to a huge disc of stone, the *temalacatl,* by a rope that left him free to move; he was armed with wooden weapons, and he had to fight several normally armed Aztec warriors in turn. If, by an extraordinary chance, he did not succumb to their attacks, he was spared; but nearly always the "gladiator" fell, gravely wounded, and a few moments later he died on the stone, with his body opened by the black-robed, long-haired priests. The warriors who were set apart for

Xipe figure.

Gift of Florene May Schoenborn, The Art Institute of Chicago

this kind of death wore ornaments and clothes of a special nature, and they were crowned with white down, as a symbol of the first light of the dawn, of the still uncertain hour when the soul of the resuscitated warrior takes its flight in the grayness toward our father the sun.

But these were not the only forms of sacrifice. Women were dedicated to the goddesses of the earth, and while they danced, pretending to be unaware of their fate, their heads were struck off; children were drowned as an offering to the rain-god Tlaloc; the fire-god's victims, anaesthetized by *yauhtli* [a hallucinogen?] were thrown into the blaze; and those who personified the god Xipe Totec were fastened to a kind of frame, shot with arrows, and then flayed: the priests dressed themselves in the skin.[2]

Although at times the home population might furnish sacrificial victims, this practice was usually reserved for the prisoners of war. According to Aztec descriptions given to the Spanish at the time of the conquest, many thousands of the enemy were killed on a single occasion. When the pyramid at Tenochtitlan was completed in the name of the gods, four lines of victims stretched as far as two miles. Executioners at the top of the pyramid worked continually for four days and nights. Fourteen thousand prisoners were probably killed at that time. The ritual happened over and over. The death toll was frighteningly high. A skull rack in the capital city had 136,000 heads. Jawbones of victims were used in the construction of towers.

Why was a literate, urban society of engineers, poets, and priests trapped in a suicidal frenzy of ritual death? For more than a few archeologists, the answer can be found in belief, in an Aztec religion quickly destroying the faithful. Wrote Jacques Soustelle,

> It was their response and the only response that they could conceive, to the instability of a continually threatened world. Blood was necessary to save this world and the men in it: the victim was no longer an enemy who was to be killed but a messenger, arrayed in dignity that was almost divine, who was sent to the gods. All the relevant descriptions, such as those that Sahagun took down from his Aztec informants, for example, convey the impression not of a dislike between the sacrificer and the victim nor of anything resembling a lust for blood, but of a strange fellow-feeling or rather—and this is vouched for by the texts— of a kind of mystical kinship . . . . It is only these foregoing considerations that allow one to understand the meaning of war for the ancient Mexicans, the meaning of the continual war towards which all the energies of the city were directed . . . . As the Mexican dominion spread, so their very victories created a pacified zone all around them, a zone which grew wider and wider until it reached the edges of their known world. Where then were the victims to come from? For they were essential to provide the gods with their nourishment, *tlaxcaltiliztli*. Where could one find the precious blood without which the sun and the whole frame of the universe was condemned to annihilation?[3]

This view has been so widely criticized that its value has been overlooked. Like Hopewellian funerary behavior and concern with burial and

---

[2]Jacques Soustelle, *Daily Life of the Aztecs on the Eve of the Spanish Conquest* (New York: Penguin Books, 1968), pp. 110–11.

[3]Ibid., pp. 112–14.

death, it is a theory of the past that does not really tell us enough. We need to know *why* they believed this; what caused such a religion to be? What created an ethos that condemned them to cycles of death? Yet Soustelle has not avoided the comparison of Aztec with more recent times. He has shown us the traditional danger of statist belief. The experience of ritualization can be a powerful political tool. It reduces the need for coercion in urbanized states. When violence, including, atrocity, is routinely presented as sacred, it can generate a society of citizens programmed to kill. Soustelle reminds us that in our own century there was a civilized nation in Europe that systematically sacrificed millions in the name of belief.[4]

What created the Mexican carnage? What was behind such a view of the world? Perhaps Aztec society had grown past a critical point. For Sherburne Cook, sacrifices and warfare were a form of population control.[5] Large cities put stresses on water and arable land. He calculates that cycles of warfare raised the death rate by 25 percent. It was a means of relieving the pressure on limited food.

But even if the rise in mortality was as great as his figures suggest, the population problem could not have been solved in this way. Wars took a toll of the males; the female population was spared. As long as this was true, the numbers would always stay high. Then too, if the object of warfare was nothing other than population control, there was not any purpose in sacrificing prisoners of war. It was far simpler to kill them in battle rather than to bring them all back through the towns. Sacrificial killing is left unexplained.

That same problem, the business of sacrifice, is not solved in an alternative view that the morbid behavior was a form of political terror. Archeologist R. C. Padden, reading the records that tell of that time, found the tale of a frightening ruler who came to the crown.[6] Tlacaelel had once been a general, then a counselor, then a maker of kings. A psychopathic strategist was now very close to the throne. Tlacaelel discovered that sacrifice was a terroristic style of control. It was a way of discouraging enemies from threatening the state. At the dedication of one of the temples, some 80,000 prisoners were slain. Rulers from enemy cities were invited to sit at a feast. Bodies of many of the victims were eaten by Tlacaelel's men. Horrified guests were released to tell others the story.

But if terrorism alone was the motive, it was done in a dangerous way. This strategy is used to advantage when it happens in the enemy's midst. Terrorism-by-tales has distance and loses effect. This is why generations of terrorists have wreaked their havoc in the enemy's towns. The event

---

[4]Ibid., p. 112.

[5]Sherburne Cook, "Human Sacrifice and Warfare as Factors in the Demography of Pre-Colonial Mexico," *Human Biology* 18 (1946), pp. 81–102.

[6]R. C. Padden, *The Hummingbird and the Hawk: Conquest and Sovereignty in the Valley of Mexico* (Columbus: Ohio State University Press, 1967), pp. 1503–41.

is immediate, not a story someone has told. Then too, this curious terrorism brought the enemy to the heart of the city. Why would any political strategist take such a chance?

Perhaps something else was involved here in the capture of prisoners of war. If they *had* to be brought to the city, if their captors had no other choice, then their presence would be exploited for all its political value. A hint of the possible reason is suggested by Padden's account: Tlacaelel and many others could well have been "cannibal kings." Anthropologist Michael Harner discovered in the writings of Bernal Diaz a description of events that occurred when a person was killed. He recorded,

Nutrition, sacrifice, and conquest

> They kicked the bodies down the steps, and the Indian butchers who were waiting below cut off their arms and legs and flayed their faces, which they afterwards prepared like glove leather, with their beards on, and kept for their drunken festivals. Then they ate their flesh with a sauce of peppers and tomatoes.[7]

Underlying the industrial slaughter was an Aztec nutritional crisis.[8] Populations were exhausting the supply of available meat. Since the days when Mexico was discovered, hunters had taken their toll of its game. Animal species were becoming increasingly scarce. The horse was hunted out of existence; deer and antelope were harder to find. Lakes were too shallow and salty to provide many fish. The crisis of protein deficiency led to wars to provide enought meat. The elite of Aztec society was fed by the prisoners of war. Combatants were captured because they were needed for food.

This explains the sacrificial behavior and the religion that made it seem right. It explains why the Aztec societies were always at war. More than that, it explains why the defeated almost never became part of the state— why the victors withdrew so that later they could fight them again. Adding them into the territory would only increase the nutritional stress. It was better to keep them close by, like a private preserve.

In the Aztec year *4 Calli* or—for Europeans—1509, a glowing streamer of light was sighted in the Mexican sky.[9] Night after night it appeared as darkness came over the east. Montezuma was watching, and he feared for the city he ruled. A bird caught in the swamplands was said to have

---

[7]Michael Harner, "The Enigma of Aztec Sacrifice," *Natural History,* 1977.

[8]The cannibalistic interpretation of Aztec sacrifice is highly controversial and involves more points of view than can adequately be surveyed in a text of this nature. The interested reader should consult the discussion by Michael Harner, *American Ethnologist,* 1977, pp. 117–35; critiques by Bernard R. Ortiz de Montellano, *Science,* 1978, pp. 611–17; and Stanley M. Garn, *American Anthropologist,* 82, 1980, pp. 389–91 for an introduction to one of the liveliest debates in all of prehistory.

[9]Soustelle, *Daily Life,* pp. 125–26.

Aztec sacrifice. The ruling elite were conceivably "cannibal kings."

Field Museum of Natural History

been brought to his throne. In the middle of its head was a mirror that looked like the sky. Montezuma, looking into the mirror, saw soldiers mounted on horses. When he called for his prophets, the bird vanished out of his hand. There seemed to be a strange apprehension settling over the Mexican hills. The cry of an invisible woman was heard in the wind.

Much of this record is fantasy and, perhaps, a zodiacal light. Much of it was paranoid visions of people at war. For the Spanish sailing to Mexico, the forebodings would help them survive. The Aztec would see them as gods at the end of the world. Cortes himself was probably thought of as the Aztec Quetzalcoatl: the exiled god who would someday return from the east.

And so the Spanish were favored by omens and by military tactics as well. Horses were brought into Mexico, which made it possible to carry supplies. Warriors in Aztec society had been masters of hit-and-run raids. But never in their lives had any of them witnessed a siege. Then too,

Cortes had made allies as he moved across the Mexican basin, something the Aztec had seldom been able to do.

In the end, their cities were ravaged, and churches were built on the ruins. Their writings were burned, and their warrior-leaders were hanged. Out of this came an intricate mixture of Christianity and Aztec belief. It lives today in the smallest of villages—and it lives in the industrial towns. It is living on graves covered over by candles and blooms.

The Andean kingdoms

A great web was encircling the globe now, connecting the Old World with the New. A mostly illiterate and feudal society, living in villages ruled by a king, was sending out ships to discover other parts of the world. And they found mostly illiterate peoples living in villages governed by kings: peoples as violent and deeply religious as they. The deep irony of feeling superior to the cultures of the ancient Americas was seldom perceived by the nations that set out to sea. Occasionally a Michel de Montaigne, a modern anthropologist out of his time, was aware that explorers, in a sense, had discovered themselves.[10] But for the most part, discovery was conquest: nationalistic expansion and war. Old patterns of life were disappearing at the point of a sword.

Even the mountainous, foggy kingdoms far to the south of the Mesa Central were not safe from the boats that in time would discover their land. But they knew nothing of what was ahead of them; they went on with the rhythm of life. Society continued to change in this cloud-covered world. On the desert that bordered the coastline, laced by rivers that flowed to the sea, villagers were growing their maize at the edges of streams. They grew squash, potatoes, and manioc; fields of cotton were picked for the loom. Llama and alpaca were raised for their meat and their wool. In the highlands were fields of quinoa, a starchy, high-altitude herb. Potatoes were grown and chilled by the mountainous air. On the east was a green roll of jungle stretching out to the edge of the sky. From people who lived in that forest came manioc and fish from the streams. The Andes mountains were threaded by systems of trade.

Merchants leading their llamas along the zigzagging roads of the peaks had slowly become part of a ritual net of exchange. *Chavin,* as archeologists call it—a tapestry of art and belief—had stabilized trade in the mountains for hundreds of miles. At about 900 BC there were shrines tucked away in the valleys. Villages nested around them where travelers would meet. Here, as in other societies, trading was fused wth religious belief. The trek through the peaks was a pilgrimage made for the gods.

---

[10] In "The Cannibals," Michel de Montaigne said of American Indian warfare; "I do not regret that we have perceived the barbarous horror in such an activity; but I deeply regret that when we judge them so severely for their faults, we nevertheless seem blinded to faults of our own" [my translation]. This comparative observation was written over 300 years ago, but it is as fresh as the anthropology of the present time.

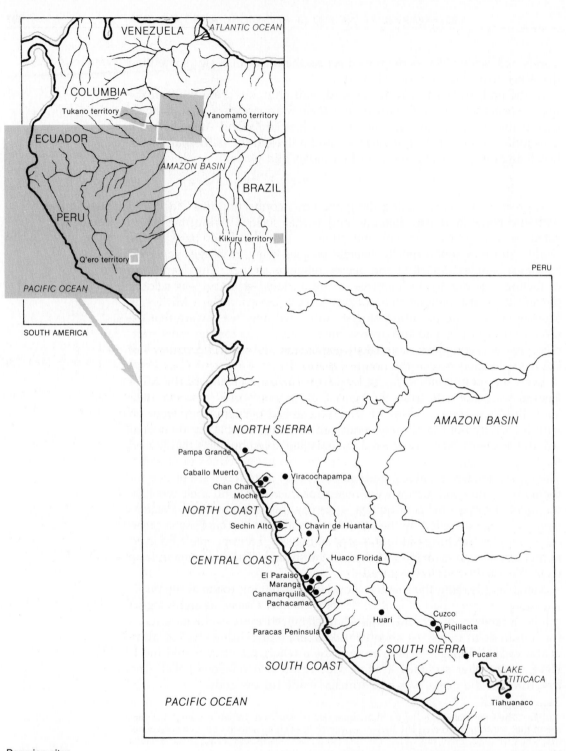

Peruvian sites.

Vessel of distinctive
Chavin style.

Gift of Mr. and Mrs. Bruce Graham, The Art
Institute of Chicago

Trade had a thousand uncertainties, born of the turbulence of nature itself. The mercurial shifting of currents meant that boats could be empty of fish. Droughts and hail could ravage the highlanders' crops. A sudden blizzard could strike in the mountains where there was not any shelter from storms. John Murra, on an Andean trail, pitched a tent under threatening skies. It collapsed with the blizzard; he was covered by the weight of the snow.[11] Even today, piles of rocks on the trails help travelers in finding their way. Exchange in the Andes always had a measure of risk.

The nodes of this elaborate system, perhaps the natural gateways of trade, demanded decisions as well as a ritual life. In the centuries that followed Chavin, cheifs were enlarging their staff of assistants; on the coast and in the highlands were beginnings of Andean states.[12] At the site of Huaca de la Luna, on a hill near the coast of Peru, a terraced platform was constructed with homes for a ruling elite. To the south, on the same desert coastline, adobe temples were built in a valley. Cahuaki was probably a focus of regional trade. Complexity brought competition; raids are the price of exchange. Centers required connections to support their emerging elites. Conceivably, centralized rulers attracted clients from neighboring states. Such changes in the volume of trade could have led to a war. Fortifications appeared in the valleys. Battle scenes were painted

[11] Murra's adventure, and the frequent difficulty of travel on the Andean slopes are discussed by John E. Pfeiffer in *The Emergence of Society: A Prehistory of the Establishment* (New York: McGraw-Hill, 1977), pp. 394–95.

[12] The discussion of Andean social evolution is taken from Thomas C. Patterson, *America's Past: A New World Archaeology* (Glenview, Ill.: Scott, Foresman, 1973), pp. 98–105; and Michael E. Moseley, "The Evolution of Andean Civilization," in *Ancient Native Americans*, ed. Jesse D. Jennings (San Francisco: W. H. Freeman, 1978), pp. 521–38.

on the surface of pots. Spears, axes, and helmets were discovered in some of the graves.

There might have followed a quieter century, beginning at AD 450 when clouds gathered on the mountains and the rivers were richened with rain. For Thomas Patterson, this meant that the people living downstream in the desert had more water for their crops; they could move into unsettled land. [13] Canals were dug away from the rivers into regions where no one had lived. For several generations the face of the desert was green. It lasted for all of a century, and then suddenly the rainfall was gone. Like the crash of the Anasazi when vegetation dried out into sand, large populations now crowded the edge of the streams.

The event accelerated a crisis that had been building for hundreds of years. Populations in coastal Peru had settled near the banks of the rivers. No one could live on the deserts that lay in-between. This was perhaps their most critical reason for designing a web of exchange. It was the reason why loss of a client could trigger a raid. Pressures on riverine villages were heightened by the vanishing rain. For centuries after, the settlements were often at war.

Villages to the east in the highlands were facing new pressures as well. The last of the rains had been followed by a withering drought. At Lake Titicaca in the Bolivian Andes and Ayacucho in southern Peru, villagers were forced to abandon the marginal lands. Like the people on the streams in the desert, they faced a crisis of not enough food. The highlands and the coast became a theater of ongoing raids. These drought cycles, pressures, and conquests may have helped generate the Andean kingdoms. The pattern would continue until the very last of their days.

One of the kingdoms was Tiahuanaco, ruled from a valley in the Bolivian peaks. The city itself, near Lake Titicaca, was nearly three miles in the air. In the permanent chill of that country, corn and beans were unable to grow. Quinoa, potatoes, and llamas provided their food. A platform of banked earth was surrounded by facings of stone. There were monumental gateways constructed out of gigantic slabs. As many as 20,000 people may have lived in this Andean city. Its power extended across the southern coast of Peru.

But we know more about the rulers of Huari who governed the mountains and the coast to the north. Like the Tiahuanacans, they ruled for only 200 years. To bring resources into their kingdom, Huari leaders resorted to raids. But it is possible that subtler strategies existed as well. Many of the elaborate burials—tombs of the Huari elite—are furnished with ceramics painted with portraits of gods. The old feline god of Chavin days—the cat with a headdress of snakes—had now become a symbol of Huari religious belief. Perhaps here, as in the jungles of Yucatan, political centers had little to trade. They concocted a ritual complex for use in

---

[13] Ibid., pp. 99–100.

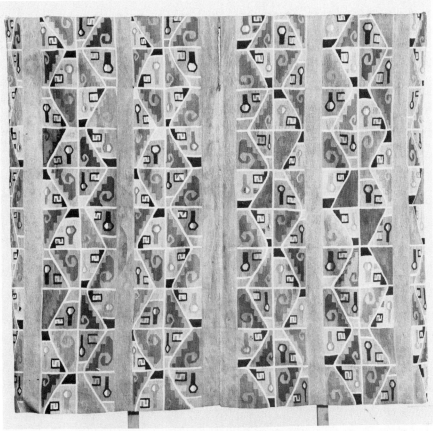

Tiahuanaco textile, an item of trade on the southern coast of Peru.

exchange. People in the outlying villages would give commodities in payment for faith. This was subtler and safer than gaining resources through raids.

Yet their power was remarkably fleeting; Huari collapsed in AD750. If religion, in fact, was their strategy, it probably failed. The need for additional imports would have required more specialized workers to mechanically fashion the critical items for trade. This would have reduced the available workforce for herding and working in the fields. It would have increased the bureaucracy that needed the farmers' support. Then too, the alternative strategy—expanding the borders by war—would have demanded allotments of food for a permanent army. For farmers already pressured by too many people and not enough food, frustration led into rebellion—and the fall of the state.

One kingdom after another probably plotted a similar scheme. A hodge-

Chimu vessel. A suspicious decline in their quality may possibly have been the result of overly rapid manufacture for use in exchange.

podge of power developed when Huari was gone. We know next to nothing about the political life of the Cuismanu, the Chuquismancu, and the Chincha of southern Peru. From Chimu sites of the Moche Valley near the northerly coast of Peru, we have learned almost all that we know of this turbulent time.

Their capital city was Chan Chan. Built less than a mile from the sea, it had 10 residential districts protected by walls of adobe. The neighbor-hoods had houses, courtyards, sunken gardens, terraces, and tombs. Be-tween the districts were stretches of marshlands and the irrigated fields of the city. The metropolis may have covered as much as 11 square miles.

But there was something not right with this city. A curious urgency had come into life. The buried debris is the evidence of things in a hurry. Ceramics tell much of the story of changes in Andean life. Carelessness was finding its way into the world of the arts. Stirrup-spout and figure-bridge vessels, models of animals, houses, and men are of striking quantity, but few of them are very well done. I doubt that this change in ceramics was due solely to artistic decline. I think it is a symptom of pressures in Chimu exchange. Drought was coming back to the Andes and populations were threatened again. The strategy of a ritual complex, that failure of earlier times, was again being attempted by a desperate Chimu elite. Pressures now were keener than ever; the need for connections was strong. Cookie-cutter artists were scribbling out portraits of gods. Exchange and the Chimu army—traveling on roads that were paved—had held the kingdom together for well over 400 years. Now their power at last had been shattered, and not only from pressures within. They were defeated by soldiers from the mountainous south.

The Inca

The usurpers were known as Inca. They came from a valley covered by clouds. Their empire was built and destroyed in a hundred years, time. Like lightning they had raced through the mountains. They fought through Colombia, Chile, and Peru. Their political power extended from jungle to sea.

They were remarkably skillful at raiding, but they did not have a genius for war. Like the sword and the sling, they grew out of a violent time. They had been one of a collection of kingdoms constantly threatened by the danger of raids. Predation put a premium on learning new methods of war. Long before Napoleon tried it, they held some of their force in reserve. If used at a critical moment, it could throw the enemy into retreat. Warriors who battled the Inca were now dealing with unknown factors: the tactics and the numbers of men who were kept in the rear. Intelligence now became critical. How many men had been captured in raids? What was the countryside like? Rulers needed to know. Head counts of all the enemy still alive were made after battles. Clay models were made of the features of conquered terrain.

Overnight, in terms of this story, an Andean empire was born. Stretches of Colombia and Chile, and the entirety of what now is Peru were controlled by a king who presented himself as divine.[14] But the achievement of uni-

---

[14]The organization of the Inca state has been described by Elman R. Service, "The Inca of Peru," *Profiles in Ethnology* (New York: Harper & Row, 1963), pp. 335–65.

Milwaukee Public Museum

Ruins of Macchu Picchu, an Inca city in the Peruvian Andes.

fication at its best was a volatile peace. Populations brought into the empire not only were supporting themselves, they also were laboring to support the established elite. The army and the ruling officials who decided the matters of state were fed from a percentage of produce collected from farms. The state demanded not only commodities but a share of labor service as well. Citizens in subject communities worked on farms owned by the state. They labored on public constructions, built bridges, granaries, and walls. Commandeered labor in Inca constructed much that is standing today. Cities were knit together by a thousand miles of paved roads. Highways cut through the hillsides; they crossed swamps and hugged the edges of peaks. Barriers were constructed to shelter the roads from the wind.

The Spanish would come from a country of stone-walled castles and mountain retreats. But nothing would compare in their eyes with this part of the world. Cieza de Leon would walk through Cuzco and experience an Andean city unlike any city he had ever encountered in Spain. He would later report,

> There were large streets except that they were narrow, and the houses made all of stone. . . . The other houses were all of wood, thatch or adobe. . . . In many parts of this city there were splendid buildings of the Lord-Incas where the heir to the throne held his festivities. There, too, was the imposing temple to the sun. . .which was among the richest in gold and silver to be found anywhere in the world. . , . This temple had a circumference of over 400 feet, and was surrounded by a strong wall. The whole building was of fine quarried stone, all matched and joined, and some of the stones were very large and beautiful. No mortar of earth or lime was employed in it, only the pitch which they used in their buildings, and the stones are so well cut that there is no sign of cement or joinings in. In all Spain I have seen nothing that can compare with these walls. . . . It had many gates, and the gateways finely carved; halfway up the wall ran a stripe of gold two handspans wide and four fingers thick. The gateway and doors were covered with sheets of this metal. . . . There was a garden in which the earth was lumps of fine gold, and it was cunningly planted with stalks of corn that were of gold. . . . Aside from this, there were more than 20 sheep (llamas) of gold with their lambs, and the shepherd who guarded them, and with their slings, and staffs, all of this metal. There were many tubs of gold and silver and emeralds, and goblets, pots, and every kind of vessel all of fine gold. . . . In a word, it was one of the richest temples in the whole world.
>
> As this was the main and most important city of this kingdom, at certain times of the year the Indians of the provinces came there, some to construct buildings, others to clean the streets and districts, and anything else they were ordered. . . . And as this city was full of strange and foreign peoples, for there were Indians from Chile, Pasto, and Canari, Chachapoyas, Huancas, Collas and all the other tribes to be found in the provinces. . .each of them was established in the place and district set aside for them by the governors of the city. They observed the customs of their own people and dressed after the fashion of their own land, so that if there were a hundred thousand men, they could be easily recognized by the insignia they wore about their heads.[15]

Behind these trappings of power, were problems that had never been solved. Villages everywhere in the Andes were putting pressure on the drought-stricken land. The cirsis was heightened by the limits of technological change. There were no traction animals to be found anywhere in the Andes. Water buffalo, cattle, oxen, and elephants in other parts of the world had made a critical difference in changing the human environment. They were useful for clearing, plowing, and expanding the boundaries of arable land. They pulled wagons loaded with foodstuffs and

---

[15]From *The Incas of Pedro de Cieza de Leon,* translated by Harriet de Onis. Copyright 1959 by the University of Oklahoma Press.

products for trade. With these beasts, a technological system could generate much higher yields. And it could do so without any change in the labor supply.

Llama and alpaca were valuable for both their meat and their shearings of wool. But their bodies—and also their temperaments—were not suited for strenuous work. This meant few technological changes for hundreds of years. Inca techniques varied little from ones used in the past. They cut steps into the slopes of the mountains; here was a strategy that had never been tried. By terracing their fields, they were reducing the runoff from rains. Excrement was useful as fertilizer, a technique that was possibly new.[16] But beyond that, they pursued the traditions of earlier times. Canals were dug in the mountains and finished with linings of stone. Desert irrigation increased near the edge of the sea. But both of these were earlier strategies; indeed, the desert was being reclaimed. For the Inca, what little was changing had happened too late.

Not only that, but their desperate gamble of expanding what they already had was increasing the size and the demands of the ruling elite. Decisions about irrigation and the reclamation of desert canals required more officials than ever before. They siphoned off more of the crop yield that farmers might have kept for themselves. Demands of their imperial projects took villagers away from their fields. Frustration was increasing as the costs of the empire grew.

Greater conquest had now become dangerous. The empire stalled in its tracks. In its final four decades, it scarcely expanded at all. Inside its territorial boundaries, its citizens were restless enough. Why add new dangers to an empire about to explode? Instead of that, the massive projects continued, and the danger of rebellion increased. Rulers became more coercive than ever before. Children—especially females—were removed from their village and kin. They were taken to Cuzco to marry the Incan elite.[17] This meant that many Andean villagers had daughters in the capital city. Hostages were captured by marriage rather than war. Requirements of commandeered labor kept citizens away from their homes. They were sent to new regions where language and custom were strange. Conspiracy was all but impossible in this Babel of speech and belief. Uprooted people were less of a threat to the king. Lewis Mumford has called such societies

---

[16]It is widely maintained that crop fertilizers were an Andean Incan invention. It is a claim that, to me, seems very unlikely at best. Herding-and-farming traditions, as the comments of Bridget Allchin suggest, have probably long been aware that excrement is useful for crops. See Bridget Allchin, "Hunters or Pastoral Nomads? Late Stone Age Settlements in Western and Central India," in *Man, Settlement, and Urbanism,* ed. Peter J. Ucko et al. (London: Duckworth, 1972), p. 118.

[17]A somewhat romanticized account of this practice, which ignores its possible political function, is presented by Alfred Metraux, *The History of the Incas* (New York: Schocken Books, 1969), p. 100.

early versions of a "megamachine."[18] People are "components" tuned to the needs of the state. Inca seems to have been something like this, especially in the last of its days. "Interchangeable parts" were controlled by a ruling elite.

In the end, this mechanical strategy only delayed the rebellious wars. People lacked organizing authority to coordinate their threat to the king. But ironically, that was provided by the heads of the realm.[19] The Inca ruler in his palace at Cuzco was regarded as if he were god. Common people could not see him or touch him. His face was concealed by a screen. Near his throne was a handcrafted forest fashioned from gold. Even so, he was a self-made monarch. He only inherited the right to the throne. No treasure or retainers were ever passed down to a king. Suppose you were one of two brothers; suppose your father had sat on the throne. Suppose at his death you were picked to continue his rule. Then you would inherit the throne and the army. Treasury and servants would not go to you; they would go to your brother. You would be ruling the state. But in that position, you could acquire new lands for the crown. Warfare and taxes could capture your share of rewards.

That was probably the critical feature of the Incan political system—the feature born of a culture of ambush and raids. In the time when they were only a kingdom, when they were surrounded by threatening groups, this curious split-inheritance strategy had likely begun. Like lances or models of landscapes and like soldiers held in reserve, the political system itself was adapted to war. It insured that every new ruler would try to conquer new lands for the realm. Rewards that came out of those conquests would make him richer—more powerful, too. They would be useful as payment for the ones who supported his rule.

But now there were rising populations, drought, and limited technical

Inheritance, civil war, and the end

---

[18]The concept is developed in his *The Myth of the Machine,* vol. 1, (New York: Harcourt Brace Jovanovich, 1967), pp. 248–74, but it is implicit in his earlier *Technics and Civilization,* (New York: Harcourt Brace Jovanovich, 1963.)

[19]The discussion of the Inca collapse is an attempt to synthesize the view of Geoffrey W. Conrad (that "split inheritance" played a critical role) with the climatic interpretation of Allison C. Paulsen. Conrad's view is presented in "Cultural Materialism, Split Inheritance, and the Expansion of Ancient Peruvian Empires," and in "Reply to Paulsen and Isbell," *American Antiquity* 46, no. 1 (1981), pp. 3–26 and 38–42. Paulsen's climatic theory is presented in "Environment and Empire: Climatic Factors in Prehistoric Andean Culture Change," *World Archeology* 8, no. 2 (1976), pp. 121–32, and in "The Archaeology of the Absurd: Comments on 'Cultural Materialism, Split Inheritance, and the Expansion of Ancient Peruvian Empires,'" *American Antiquity* 46, no. 1 (1981), pp. 31–37. I am strongly sympathetic with William H. Isbell's "Comment on Conrad," *American Antiquity* 46, no. 1 (1981), pp. 27–30, in which he observes that Conrad and Paulsen are focusing on separate aspects of a valuable model. Of significance, too, is Conrad's suggestion that more detailed environmental studies are required for a better understanding of the Incan decline.

change. Everywhere was the threat of rebellion. Expansion had stalled. A new ruler, unable to conquer, had to collect his rewards from within. But this would be a dangerous strategy; his subjects would likely rebel. He could gather no treasure from conquest. Neither could he gather it from inside the realm. This meant that inheriting position was no longer enough for a king. Along with his status, he required the treasury too.

The inevitable spark was ignited seven years before the Spanish arrived. Huayna Capac, the Andean ruler, was survived at his death by two sons. The official quarrel that developed between them was over the question of who would be king. But it was probably fueled by the problem of the royal estate. The regal argument soon left the palace and developed into full-scale war. It was not that the Andean farmers, especially those new to the realm, cared in the least about which of these brothers was king. They sought escape from their own exploitation in the possibility of gaining rewards. Armies formed—and the fog-covered mountains were ravaged by raids. For the Spanish led by Pizarro, the work of conquest was already done. Arriving in the war-torn mountains, he moved unmolested to the heart of the realm. Reinforcements followed soon after—and so did European disease. In the space of a decade, over 4 million Inca died.

In tragedy the worlds were united, and the linkage has lived to our time. No longer would the human community be divided by mountain and sea. Other divisions would linger to confront us today. A globe of interacting societies would face the old problems of hamlets and states. The rewards and the dangers would be greater than they were in the past.

21 / The Modern World and the Role of Prehistory

In the summer of 1837, *Oliver Twist* was published in London. It appeared in regular installments as the author completed a chapter. It was rushed to the press and found its way to the shops and the streets. Everywhere, when the day's work was over, people gathered in groups in the city. They listened quietly as one who could read spoke the pages aloud.

One who could read: the rare individual who could translate the letters to sound. It was a skill slowly increasing in the Westernized world. Archeology traditionally used it as a criterion for the end of prehistory. Antiquity ended when people could write of themselves. But archeologists were only half-serious when they established this view of the world. Certainly they have never really followed the rule they made.

They excavated Roman hill-forts and the grounds of medieval cathedrals. They excavated cabins of slaves in the American South. The field of Historical Archeology explicitly studies our recent existence—the people who wrote of themselves and were close to our time. It was inevitable that sooner or later the human past would extend to ourselves. Archeologists now study people living today.

These developments in archeology are not simply the growth of a science. They are the result of a better understanding of cultural change. Prehistorians exploring the Tigris, the Huang Ho, or the banks of the Nile discovered the ruins of an era when writing began. But there were curious continuities in the relics dug out of the ground. People with history seemed much like the people before.

Of course—why should this not be? The answer was there all along. Letters inscribed on a tablet or delicately painted on papyrus or silk could only be deciphered by a handful of ruling elite. For everyone else in society, life went on as it had in the past. The invention had little effect on their everyday lives. Elites could become more organized; they could keep records of raiding and trade. But farmers and herders preserved their traditional ways.

The monopoly over reading and writing reaches almost down to our time. Only in our century is the pattern beginning to change. The effects are perhaps most visible in African and Asian societies where literacy is a difference that separates parent and child. An Egyptian archeologist told me that his parents could not read or write. His household, he laughed, was most likely a "prehistoric" society.

But a shift is there—and remarkable. There has been nothing like this before. Margaret Mead, returning to Peri, an island to the north of New Guinea, found that many of the fishers and gardeners had now learned to read. As she remembered it later,

> I had thought I knew what the word *literacy* meant. I had helped pre-pare the material for the UNESCO report on fundamental education. I had listened to impassioned accounts of teaching ordinary Chinese troops to read and write in a simple phonetic script; and I had lived with and spoken the languages of peoples without writing, and had lived with one people, the Balinese, among whom only a few priests and scribes could write. But this was different. The experience of open-ing this letter, of reading the notes written by people whom one had never visualized as becoming part of the modern world, with whom, in truth, there had been no hope of real two-way communication, had a quality that I had never imagined. I felt almost as if someone—and I was not quite sure who it was, they or I—had been raised from the dead. Someone who, not knowing it, had been dead, and lived again.[1]

The "quality that was never imagined" captures the attention of re-searchers today. As literacy becomes more commonplace, what effect does it have on society? How does it restructure old patterns of act and belief? Jack Goody, a sociologist in England, has lived with the LoDagaa of Ghana—a people who have only become literate in the last 30 years. He speculates that systems of logic and even the creative process as well are being changed by the adoption of print in that part of the world. He has argued,

> Logic in our modern sense seemed to be a function of writing, since it was the setting down of speech that enabled man clearly to separate words, to manipulate their order and to develop syllogistic forms of rea-soning; these latter were seen as specifically literate rather than oral, even making use of another purely graphic isolate, the letter, in its orig-inal formulation. . . . It is certainly easier to perceive contradictions in writing than it is in speech, partly because one can formalize the state-ments in a syllogistic manner and partly because writing arrests the flow of oral converse so that one can compare side by side utterances which have been made at different times and at different places.
>
> This is no trivial consideration; what happens here is part and parcel of the tendency of oral cultures towards cultural homeostasis (stability); those innumerable mutations of culture that emerge in the ordinary course of verbal interaction are either adopted by the group or get elim-inated in the process of transmission from one generation to the next. If

---

[1]Margaret Mead, *New Lives for Old: Cultural Transformations—Manus, 1928-1953* (New York: Mentor, 1961), p.33.

one is adopted, the individual signature. . .tends to get forgotten, whereas in written cultures the very knowledge that a work will endure in time, in spite of commercial or political pressures, stimulates the creative process and encourages the recognition of individuality.[2]

It is not necessary to agree with Jack Goody to see that mass literacy *might* have the power of changing not only our knowledge but ways that we think. More than that, our social relations, within societies and between them as well, are undoubtedly affected by thoughts that appear on a page. Books, Lewis Mumford has written, are a release from the immediate world. To exist in a world that was literate, in a way was

> to exist in print: the rest of the world tended gradually to become more shadowy. Learning became book-learning and the authority of books was more widely diffused by printing, so that if knowledge had an ampler province so, too, did error. The divorce between print and firsthand experience was so extreme that one of the first great modern educators. . .advocated the picture book for children as a means of restoring the balance and providing the necessary visual associations.[3]

More recently—more pessimistically—other critics have written of writing—it is only a small part of the story; much more is involved. Television, radio, and computers, the very stuff of "technetronic" society, put more people in touch with more knowledge than ever before.[4] In naivete, Marshall McCluhan once remarked that our world was a "village": that nations and cultures connected and were brought face-to-face. But our planet is anything but that; it is more of a "city" than anything else. There are not the shared understandings, shared expectations or shared religious beliefs that made the village such a durable part of the earlier world. Information that flows from Manhattan to a transistor radio on the Afghani hills is only a reminder of how strikingly different we are.

It might seem that the science of archeology, which normally travels in antique lands, has very little place in a world of such turbulent change. Perhaps, in fact, we are "post-historic": discontinuous with all that has been. Because we are so different, there is no need to study the past. The old homily of George Santayana—that we must study the past or be condemned to repeat it—is far less convincing when we think of ourselves as unique.

But our uniqueness, at least as I see it, is in the *rate* of our cultural change. The fundamental process is still what it was in the past. Humanity must alter its habitat and channel its energy to meet its own needs. It

---

[2]Jack Goody, "Evolution and Communication: the Domestication of the Savage Mind," *British Journal of Sociology*, March 1973, pp. 7 and 9.

[3]Lewis Mumford, *Technics and Civilization* (New York: Harcourt Brace, Jovanovich, 1963), p. 136.

[4]The argument here is adapted from Zbigniew Brzezinski's *Between Two Ages: America's Role in the Technetronic Era* (New York: Viking Press, 1971), pp. 9–23.

United Press International Photo

Contemporary peoples differ from past ones in the rate of their cultural change. Transformations that required millenia can now occur in a few decades' time. Because archeology studies the causes of such large-scale social change, it is perhaps more relevant today than it ever has been.

must coordinate technical strategies through information about behavior and tools, including the information involved in a network of trade. It must adapt to these intricate systems through its customs and social beliefs. This much will probably always be true of our lives.

The feature that *does* make us different—the rapid pace of our cultural change—makes archeology more relevant today than it ever has been. A refinery appears in the desert, built with parts manufactured in Europe. It is managed by specialists trained in American schools. Its products and the parts that repair it flow through an elaborate net of exchange involving millions of people in many different parts of the world. Little wonder that human societies seem to race through their patterns of change. What transpired over thousands of years now occurs overnight.

Transformations happening around us are akin to what has happened before. The difference today is that they happen in a much shorter time.

An understanding of the intricate problems involved in the emergence of present-day states is enriched by a knowledge of how they evolved in the past. The same is true of hierarchies of classes, developing now in many parts of the world. It is true of our beliefs in relation to political life. Archeologists, aware of this linkage, touch the present in the fragmented past. Over and over they discover themselves among those who have vanished.

The literature of archeology is enormous. There is no way of comprehending it all. Those books I found especially valuable have been specifically mentioned in the text. There are technical and popular journals that are useful as well. *American Antiquity* is the leading journal treating New World archeology. Its articles are often highly technical, but the range of its topics is wide. A global perspective is offered by contributors to *World Archaeology*. They often examine theoretical questions of major significance in world prehistory. The style of the articles is more accessible than that of most technical journals. Very readable and accurate articles are provided by *Archaeology*, published bimonthly by the Archaeological Institute of America. A more direct understanding of ancient society is made possible through the museum. The American Museum of Natural History and the Smithsonian Institution—as well as local and state museums—are well worth the visit. Acutal excavation is frequently possible through professional organizations. Information about these is usually available in *Archaeology*, mentioned above. One organization, Earthwatch, provides excellent field opportunities. Their address is 10 Juniper Road, Box 127R, Belmont, Massachusetts, 02178. Each of these forms of involvement has its own special rewards. Every one of them offers the pleasure of exploring the past.

For further exploration

Glossary

Adze a woodworking tool with a blade at right angles to the shaft.

Archeology the study of ancient societies.

Band a human structure numbering about 25 people who believe themselves to be kin.

Boreal forest a subarctic woodland that is dominated by coniferous trees.

Brachiation a hand-over-hand pattern of movement.

Burin a chisel-shaped blade.

Chiefdom a ranked society in which the chief, in an inherited office, managed everyday public affairs. His power was based on reward and religious belief.

City a special form of the human community with dense populations and multiple social traditions.

Class hierarchical groupings of people differing in resources and social prestige.

Cognatic traced along either male or female lines.

Composite tool a useful implement that is made of different kinds of raw materials.

Cranial vault a part of the skull that encases the brain.

Cultural systems patterns of technological behavior, social relations, and religious beliefs that are humanity's means of adapting to the natural world.

Double canoe two parallel canoes with a platform of logs on the top.

Ecotone a borderline that separates two very different environments.

Ethos a widely shared cultural value.

Exchange the trade of services, goods, and information between human societies.

Foraging tradition a mobile, unspecialized collecting of animals and plants.

Foramen magnum the opening through which the spinal cord passes to connect with the brain.

Henges great standing stones.

Intensification concentrating on particular reponses.

Kinship a concept of organic relatedness; recognition of a biological link.

Mesopotamia the Tigris-Euphrates region of Southwest Asia.

Monsoons moisture-bearing winds.

Neoteny preservation into adulthood of infantile characteristics.

Paleo-Indians the hunting societies that migrated across Beringia into the Americas.

Parsimonious explaining a large number of facts.

Pastoralism a form of technology that almost totally involves the herding of animals. It usually does not emphasize plant collecting or cultivation.

Pebble tool a large, rounded rock that has been smashed against another, resulting in flakes and an irregular cutting edge.

Pueblos ground-surface, masonry, multiroomed dwellings.

Sagittal crest a vertical ridge of bone to which a set of jaw muscles attaches.

Scarcity a critical resource not present in sufficient supply. Because of this, the culture begins to experience stress.

Sexual dimorphism the occurence of male and female differences apart from their primary sexual characteristics.

Shaman a religious practicioner in a hunter-and-gatherer society. A religious specialist who uses charisma and sleight-of-hand to create the appearance of a link with the supernatural world.

Slash-and-burn farming on temporary clearings in the forest.

Species a reproductively isolated population.

State the hierarchical arrangement of groups with different access to strategic resources; it makes public decisions and manages territorial affairs.

Symbol a thing which represents something else.

Technology material culture, behavioral strategies, and adaptive information that exist as a system and modify the natural world.

Theory a causal statement which is susceptible to falsification.

Totemism recognition of a kinship link with the natural world.

Tribe a group that is usually lacking in permanent political authority. It is made up of neighboring bands that maintain contact with one another and share a common language and cultural tradition.

Tundra a plant and animal community of the northern subarctic regions in which the soil is frozen a few feet beneath the ground.

Index

This book has been set Linotron 202, in 10 and 9 point Palatino, leaded 2 points. Part numbers and titles are 24 point Palatino. Chapter numbers are 30 point Palatino and chapter titles are 24 point Palatino. The size of the type page is 36 by 46½ picas.